# THE NEW ILLUSTRATED
# ENCYCLOPEDIA OF
# RAILWAYS

# THE NEW ILLUSTRATED
# ENCYCLOPEDIA OF
# RAILWAYS

## EDITED BY ROBERT TUFNELL

Revised and updated by John Westwood

CHARTWELL
BOOKS, INC.

Published by Chartwell Books
A Division of Book Sales Inc.
114 Northfield Avenue
Edison, New Jersey 08837
USA

ISBN  0-7858-1105-2

QUMEORL

This book is produced by

Quantum Publishing
A division of Quarto Publishing PLC
The Old Brewery
6 Blundell Street
London N7 9BH

Project Manager : Joyce Bentley
Designer : Mike Head / Malcolm Couch
Editor : Alex Revell
Author : John Westwood

Printed in Indonesia by APP Printing Pte Ltd
Manufactured in Singapore by United Graphics Pte Ltd

# CONTENTS

# THE
# STORY OF
# RAILWAY
# MOTIVE
# POWER

# THE STORY OF RAILWAY MOTIVE POWER

The story of railway motive power began with a Cornishman, Richard Trevithick. Born in 1771 into a Britain ruled by King George III, a king with fading oligarchical power in Parliament, Trevithick became a mining engineer, looking into ways of improving the Newcomen steam pumping engines that cleared the mines of water. As such he was a true son of the first Industrial Revolution, ever seeking better ways of doing things. He promoted better steam engines with higher boiler pressures. The higher pressure, although only about 30psi ($2kg/cm^2$), made the whole machine much more compact - so much so that Trevithick had the idea of steam traction on rails.

Trevithick was familiar with tramways, most of which at that time were used to take ore and coal from the pithead of the mines to furnaces or the nearest canal or river. The first record of a tramway in England dates from 1597: it ran down to the River Trent, at Attenborough, near Nottingham. Over 100 years before that, however, central European mines are known to have been served by tramways. These were crude affairs at first, with wagons pushed or pulled by hand. Soon horses became common as motive power. Trevithick's idea was that steam could replace horses, and in 1803 he was

to be found at Abraham Darby's ironworks in Coalbrookdale, designing a steam locomotive. Nothing came of this venture, save perhaps the making of some locomotive bits and pieces, but then Samuel Homfray, the owner of furnaces at Penydarran in South Wales and of a tramway to a canal at Abercynon, stimulated the enterprise by ordering a Trevithick steam locomotive.

The first railway journey behind steam was made over the Penydarran tramway on 13 February 1804. The crude steam locomotive was up to its task, but there were two points of note. Firstly, the locomotive was too heavy (about 5 tonnes, or 11,250lb) and damaged its track. Locomotives have tended to do this right up to the present day - or, rather, as track engineers now know a thing or two, a lot of preventive track maintenance must be done to avoid it. Secondly, as the idea was new, many people condemned it outright.

In 1808 Trevithick built a second locomotive, which was displayed running around a circular track sited on land that is now occupied by the west side of Euston station in London. However, nothing came of the matter and Trevithick turned to mining rather than railways, spending some years in Peru. Years later, back in England, he

petitioned Parliament for a pension, on the grounds that he was the inventor of the steam locomotive. Parliament turned him down: such ad hoc pensions were going out of fashion.

The next to try his hand at a steam locomotive was John Blenkinsop, superintendent of the Middleton Railway, a colliery railway near Leeds. The locomotives for his venture were built by the engineer Matthew Murray. Blenkinsop held that the ability of a wheel to push itself along a

*A 16th century mine tramway truck from central Europe.*

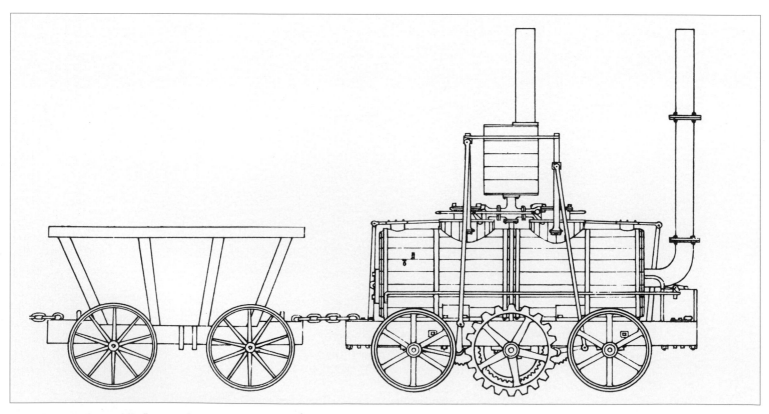

**Prince Regent,** *the world's first rack locomotive, built for the Middleton Colliery Railway, 1812.*

smooth rail was insufficient, so installed a line of rack teeth along the left side of his track. The locomotive cylinders drove a pinion or cogwheel which engaged with the rack. In 1812 Murray's first locomotive, *Prince Regent*, was a success, and three more were ordered for the Middleton Railway at once.

Trevithick's Penydarran locomotive had had a single cylinder, a system which had the disadvantage that, should the piston inside it be in certain positions, steam could not reach it to make a start. The *Prince Regent*, however, had two cylinders, with the cranks on the pinion shaft at 90° to each other. This meant that one piston or the other was always ready to make a start, and has been the usual arrangement on steam locomotives ever since.

William Hedley, the manager at Wylam Colliery near Newcastle, disagreed with Blenkinsop's view that the adhesion of driving wheels on smooth rails was insufficient to move trains. After much demonstration of the matter on paper, in 1813 Hedley had two locomotives built, *Puffing*

*Richard Trevithick's pioneer steam locomotive design for Pen-y-darran, 1804.*

*William Hedley's colliery locomotive Puffing Billy, 1813. It is preserved now in the Science Museum, London.*

*A replica of an early (1830) American-built locomotive, the vertical-boiler Tom Thumb of the Baltimore & Ohio RR.*

*Billy* and *Wylam Dilly*. These had their cranks on a jack-shaft, which in turn was geared to two pairs of driving wheels. Hedley was proved right; rail adhesion was sufficient, and this principle has been used until this day. True, in poor conditions adhesion can be lost and the wheels can spin, but precautions, usually involving the cutting off of power for a short time, can be taken against that.

George Stephenson saw Hedley's locomotives for himself, and at Killingworth Colliery near Wylam he built improved models over a period of years from 1814. The steam regulator was introduced to control the amount of steam reaching the cylinders from the boiler.

The engine's cranks were put on the driving-wheel axles, and the machinery that had hitherto been considered necessary between them and the pistons in the cylinders was greatly simplified.

In a Stephenson locomotive of 1816, two driving axles were coupled together by a chain. It was one of Stephenson's men, Timothy Hackworth, who suggested that driving axles might be coupled instead by a rod connected to cranks on each axle. Such coupling-rods were adopted, and they can be seen on Stephenson's well-known *Locomotion*, built for the Stockton and Darlington Railway in 1825. The Stockton and

Darlington was the world's first public railway; Timothy Hackworth took charge of its workshops at Shildon.

At Shildon in 1827, Hackworth built the locomotive *Royal George*, in which for the first time the exhaust from the cylinders was directed as a blast up the chimney to create a strong draught for the fire. True, both Trevithick and Hedley had passed the exhaust up the chimney (hence the name *Puffing Billy* for one of Hedley's locomotives), but beyond observing that the fire burned well they appear to have failed to realize the significance of forced combustion. After the *Royal George* the blastpipe became a standard steam-locomotive feature.

George Stephenson's son Robert had already come upon the scene. The world's first locomotive building firm, Robert Stephenson & Co., was founded in 1824: this firm built the first steam locomotives for France (1828), Germany (1835), Belgium (1835) and Austria (1838). From the later 1820s, while George Stephenson was preoccupied with building railways rather than with steam-locomotive design, Robert and the company increasingly took over the latter work.

An important design leap occurred with *Lancashire Witch*, built by the Stephensons for the Bolton and Leigh Railway in 1828. Instead of having its cylinders vertical, this four-wheel locomotive had them sloped at an angle of 39°, a feature which permitted the fitting of metal locomotive springs, ruled out by previous vertical cylinders. As far as heavy motive power is concerned, the purpose of springs is not to enhance the comfort of riders in the vehicle, but to protect the track by moderating the stresses caused by a unit moving along it.

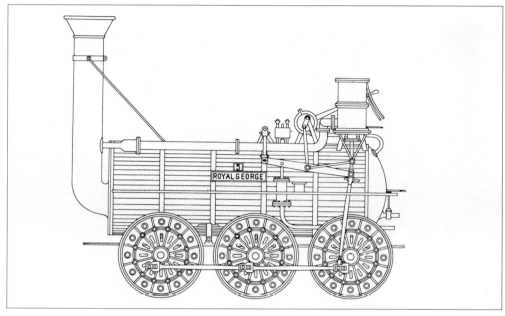

*Stockton & Darlington Railway, 1827. Timothy Hackworth's Royal George, with three-coupled axles.*

*Stephenson's Patent Engine, 1841.*

# MULTITUBULAR BOILERS

ost locomotives built up to 1828 had a boiler containing a large-diameter U-tube in the barrel. The grate occupied one end of the U-tube, and hot gases flowing through the remainder towards the chimney transferred more heat to the surrounding boiler water, the chimney and grate being at the same end of the boiler. Henry Booth, secretary of the infant Liverpool and Manchester Railway Co., suggested that greater heat transfer would take place if the hot gases flowed instead through nests of small-diameter tubes in the boiler barrel, and this proposal was picked up by George Stephenson.

It may be wondered why a company secretary was making engineering suggestions. At the time a handful of able men in the Liverpool and Manchester service were inventing virtually all the features of future railways. Good ideas to solve the numerous problems that arose were welcome, whatever the source. That everyone knows all about the business of everyone else is one of the attractions of small management units, although as a management technique it is unsuitable for a railway longer than a few miles.

The Stephenson locomotives that went to France were run by Marc Seguin. He too had had the multitubular boiler idea, and in 1829

*William Calloway a replica of William Norris's 1837 4-2-0 for the Baltimore and Ohio R.R.*

he built a locomotive incorporating it. Unfortunately, the Hackworth blastpipe was not a feature, and in its place a complicated system of fans was used to provide draught. The Stephensons' first multitubular boilers were also built in 1829, and Seguin later gracefully acknowledged their priority.

George Stephenson's locomotive of 1829, in the design of which his son Robert had a hand also, was the famous *Rocket*. In this locomotive for the first time the multitubular boiler was used in conjunction with the blastpipe up the chimney, and the success of the *Rocket* made these two features a standard. In one particular, however, the *Rocket* was at fault. The firebox was outside the boiler-barrel, and wasted its heat on the ambient air. This error was soon corrected in subsequent locomotives of the same type.

Robert Stephenson had noted that water was apt to shower from the *Rocket's* chimney. He concluded that steam was condensing in the outside cylinders. In his next design, therefore, he protected the cylinders by placing them horizontally inside the frames and under the smokebox. This locomotive was the *Planet* of 1830, a four-wheeler but still with a single pair of driving wheels. A timber frame plated with iron was used outside the wheels, together with no fewer than four frames inside to help support the crank axle and restrain the thrust of the pistons upon it. Freight versions had two coupled axles.

The *Planet* type was popular, and Robert Stephenson & Co. had more orders for it than the firm could handle. Among their deliveries was a four-coupled locomotive for the Camden & Amboy Railroad in the United States: the two named towns are across the river from New York and Philadelphia respectively.

Isaac Dripps was the master mechanic of the Camden & Amboy, and, on taking a look at his new locomotive from England (not the first delivery in the United States), he saw that it would not do for US conditions. Among these at that time was strap-rail. This had been

*Liverpool & Manchester Railway, 1829. Robert Stephenson & Co's Rocket with a multitubular boiler (left), Inside a smokebox (opposite).*

introduced to reduce the wear of the wooden rails and was created by laying a strip of iron along the top surface of the rail. This strap-rail did not take kindly to the weight of a locomotive.

Dripps uncoupled the two axles of his Stephenson locomotive, giving the front, non-driven axle some lateral play. Next, on th outside ends of this leading axle he suppor a timber frame which led the locomotive was supplied with two more leading wh these wheels were also given lateral play. very front of the frame was a wooden gril world's first pilot or cow-catcher. Thus a the locomotive was named *John Bull.*

Dripps was faced also with the pro created by the use of wood as a locomotive He devised the first spark-arresting chimr 1833. The immense inverted cones to s sparks around the chimneys of locomotives wood-burning railways became a familiar sight.

e Bury 'haystack' firebox of an 1846 0-4-0 belonging to Britain's Furness Railway.

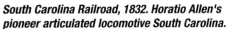

*South Carolina Railroad, 1832. Horatio Allen's pioneer articulated locomotive South Carolina.*

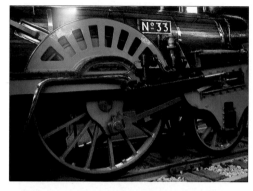

*Buddicom's outside-cylinder alternative to the Stephenson" vulnerable inside cylinder layout.*

Dripps is credited also with the use of the first oil-burning locomotive headlight.

US locomotive-building started in earnest in 1830, the West Point Foundry, New York State, being a well known manufacturer. During the 1830s there was a fashion for vertical-boiler locomotives, the Baltimore and Ohio Railroad in particular favouring this type. Normal-boilered locomotives were built as well including, in 1832, the world's first with a leading truck or bogie. John Jervis was the designer of the bogie locomotive, which had a single pair of driving wheels at the rear and was called *Experiment*. It is said that it was Robert Stephenson who

*Liverpool, Edward Bury's freight engine for the Liverpool & Manchester Railway. Its haystack firebox and bar frames were widely used in American designs.*

actually suggested the bogie during a discussion with a group of visiting US engineers about the problem of getting locomotives to go around curves.

Incidentally, the ordinary four-wheeled truck is still called a bogie (or bogey) in northeast England and as far north as central Scotland. In North America the term 'truck' replaced bogie.

The leading truck was a way of getting around curves, but it was beginning to be appreciated in the United States that more powerful locomotives were needed, and that such locomotives must have more driving axles. In any case, more axles were needed to support the larger boilers that were the source of power. Horatio Allen (a noted US railway pioneer) designed the world's first jointed, or articulated, locomotive -- indeed, the world's first four-cylinder locomotive -- in 1832. This was the *South Carolina*, built by the West Point Foundry.

The *South Carolina,* had a large central firebox, with the fire-door to one side. Two boiler barrels, fore and aft, led off this central firebox. A four-wheel truck was pivoted to each boiler barrel. Each truck had a pair of inside cylinders, a single pair of driving wheels, and a carrying axle at the outside end (that is, at front and rear of the locomotive). The arrangement meant that exhaust steam-pipes, and more importantly live-steam pipes, had to be articulated. The articulation of live-steam pipes, carrying steam at high pressure to the cylinders, would continue to be a source of trouble in articulated locomotives.

Horatio Allen's articulated type would be later repeated by Robert Fairlie in Britain, with outside

*London & Birmingham Railway, 1835. Edward Bury's variant of the Planet type.*

*A full-size working replica, once named William Galloway, of William Norris's Lafayette, built for the Baltimore & Ohio Railway in 1837. Norris locomotives became very popular in Europe as well as in the USA.*

cylinders. Fairlie took out a patent in 1863, and his locomotives performed a great deal of work in many parts of the world. The type was preceded by the Meyer articulated locomotive type, another which has been used quite widely. Jean-Jacques Meyer and his son Adolphe took out a French patent in 1861. The Meyer locomotive had a single normal boiler, and the cylinders of the powered trucks were outside but in the centre of the locomotive. These and other articulated locomotive types are mentioned in succeeding pages.

Meanwhile, returning to Great Britain, a little before the Planet type, Edward Bury had built a similar inside-cylinder four-wheeler for the Liverpool and Manchester Railway in 1830. This, Liverpool, had the two axles coupled together. For a firebox Bury used an upright cylinder, with the grate at the bottom and closed at the top by a domed cover. The boiler-barrel projected out of a flattened face of this upright cylinder, the latter being known as a haystack firebox.

Instead of plate frames, Bury used iron bars, a feature which, together with, for a time, the haystack firebox, crossed the Atlantic and became established in the United States. Bar frames were standard for US locomotives throughout the years. Towards the end of the steam age the whole of a bar frame for a large locomotive might be poured as a single steel casting, which was known as the locomotive bed.

The Planet type locomotive and Bury's variant represented a great advance on what had gone before, but they had their drawbacks. Firstly, as short-wheelbase four-wheelers they tended to pitch from back to front as they ran along, a motion probably combined with hunting from side to side. Secondly, a satisfactory inside crank axle was almost beyond the technology of the time. Should a crank axle break, the locomotive was in dire trouble, and might overturn. In Austria, this sort of accident had led to the use of Planet-type locomotives being forbidden by law.

# STEAM LOCOS COME OF AGE

Robert Stephenson set about ameliorating the defects of the Planet-type locomotives. His principal measure was to add a third axle behind the firebox to check the pitching motion. With an axle both before and behind, should the crank axle break the locomotive had a better chance of staying on the track. Using the wheel-notation system devised in America by Frederick Whyte in about 1900, this locomotive would be described as a 2-2-2, in contrast with its Planet predecessor, which was a 2-2-0. The first locomotive of the new type was named *Patentee*, for various of its details were protected by patents.

The passenger Patentee-type 2-2-2 was built first in 1833, and in the same year a freight version appeared, with the two leading axles coupled together and with one trailing axle - that is, it was an 0-4-2. In 1834 came an 0-6-0, with all axles coupled, a scheme which was very popular from then on for freight locomotives. The 2-4-0 came out as a passenger locomotive some years later, and shared equal popularity

*Great Western Railway, 1837. A giant Patentee-type locomotive.*

*One of the last American-type 4-4-0's to remain in service. This Canadian Pacific locomotive worked in New Brunswick up to the late 1950s.*

*(opposite)* The 'Single' locomotive with just one pair of driving wheels made a come-back in Britain at the end of the 19th century. This is a 'Stirling Single' of the Great Northern Railway.

locomotive, and the trapped steam in the cylinders acted as a cushion to slow the train. It was left to Louis le Chatelier, a Frenchman, to perfect the counter-pressure brake and to conduct a successful test on the Northern Railway of Spain in 1865. The brake was used extensively in continental Europe, until the general equipment of rolling stock with the air-brake from about 1905.

*The Lion, an 0-4-2 built by Todd Kitson & Laird, 1838*

with the 0-6-0 version. Indeed, some 0-6-0s and 2-4-0s of Patentee-type in all but actual age and length of service survived in British Railways' service after 1948.

In the shape of Patentee the basic steam locomotive was in existence in 1833, and in essentials it has not changed. Indeed, the fact that the type was so long-lived is an indication that what amounted to a modern locomotive had been evolved. Only the superheater (see below) was missing. However, while the design of Patentees might have been on the right lines, the construction was still that of the Planets. In many respects - construction materials, building methods, and the addition of various details to make for easier operation -. there was still a great deal of room for improvement.

A fresh feature of *Patentee* was the counter-pressure brake; this was ahead of its time, and did not then catch on. Steam was admitted to the `wrong' side of the pistons of a moving

*The Austro-Hungarian version of the long-boiler type, with outside cylinders and valve gear.*

*Descendents of the Stephensons' long-boiler six-wheelers survived into the 1950s. This is a Spanish example, working in Barcelona Docks.*

Another new locomotive fitting of 1833 was a device for giving a warning of a train's approach. In that year a carter using a level crossing on the infant Leicester and Swannington Railway lost his cartload of eggs when it was hit fair and square by an oncoming train. When news of the incident reached Robert Stephenson and Co., the 'steam trumpet' was promptly invented. This was the familiar railway whistle, whose sound is known all over the world.

In the United States, Garrett and Eastwick built the first outside-cylinder, four-coupled locomotive with a leading truck (that is, a 4-4-0) in 1837. This was *Hercules*, made for the Beaver Meadow Railroad in Carbon County, Pennsylvania. The important feature introduced on this locomotive was spring-compensation by levers on either side, designed by Joseph Harrison Junior. A massive cast-iron lever was pivoted on the frames between the driving axles, and rods from each end rested on the adjacent ends of the driving-wheel leaf-springs. Thus any movement of one spring was compensated by the other spring.

Spring-compensation was just what was needed for the rough railway track of the time. Moreover, the locomotive frame was suspended from two points at the rear (the compensating-lever pivot pins) and the single rotation point of

*Not all that far removed from the* Patentee design was this 4-4-0 used by the Great Western Railway in the late 1940s.

the bogie pin at the front. Three-point suspension such as this promotes good riding over the track, and compensation levers became standard in the United States.

As the pioneer outside-cylinder 4-4-0 locomotive, Hercules was the ancestor of the famous American-type 4-4-0. During the second half of the nineteenth century over 25,000 American-type 4-4-0s were built in North America. They differed from each other in minor detail only, and locomotives of this type could be ordered from the makers almost as off-the-shelf items.

*In continental Europe Stephenson's long-boiler six-wheeler developed into the eight-wheeler. This Russian 0-8-0 of the late 19th century is a descendant of those early freight locomotives.*

# THE TIDE OF INVENTION

Steam in a locomotive cylinder cools as it does its work, so much so that water-vapor droplets condense out. Vapor-bearing steam has a greater unit volume, and so the pressure in a cylinder does not fall as fast as it might. That is, the steam expands as it cools. Until 1839 there was no thought of taking advantage of this effective expansion of cooling steam: the gab valve gear used to reverse the locomotive could not vary the quantity of steam admitted to the cylinders by the valves when in motion, which meant that more steam was admitted to the cylinders than was needed. Once a train was in motion, only a little steam was really required to keep it going.

In 1839, however, John Gray made some experiments on the Liverpool and Manchester Railway. He devised a not very satisfactory 'horse-leg' valve gear which, while admitting steam for the full stroke of the piston at starting, could be adjusted when in motion to cut off the

*Contemporary textbook cross-section of a locomotive boiler, sgowing three types of fusebox. The vital brick arch is also shown (left), An inside version of Walschaert's Valve Gear was used on GWR four cylinder locomotives (below).*

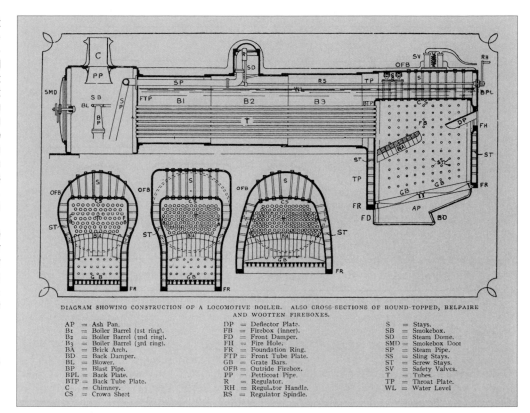

DIAGRAM SHOWING CONSTRUCTION OF A LOCOMOTIVE BOILER. ALSO CROSS-SECTIONS OF ROUND-TOPPED, BELPAIRE AND WOOTTEN FIREBOXES.

| | | | | | | |
|---|---|---|---|---|---|---|
| AP | = Ash Pan. | DP | = Deflector Plate. | S | = Stays. |
| B1 | = Boiler Barrel (1st ring). | FB | = Firebox (inner). | SB | = Smokebox. |
| B2 | = Boiler Barrel (2nd ring). | FD | = Front Damper. | SD | = Steam Dome. |
| B3 | = Boiler Barrel (3rd ring). | FH | = Fire Hole. | SMD | = Smokebox Door. |
| BA | = Brick Arch. | FR | = Foundation Ring. | SP | = Steam Pipe. |
| BD | = Back Damper. | FTP | = Front Tube Plate. | SS | = Sling Stays. |
| BL | = Blower. | GB | = Grate Bars. | ST | = Screw Stays. |
| BP | = Blast Pipe. | OFB | = Outside Firebox. | SV | = Safety Valves. |
| BPL | = Back Plate. | PP | = Petticoat Pipe. | T | = Tubes. |
| BTP | = Back Tube Plate. | R | = Regulator. | TP | = Throat Plate. |
| C | = Chimney. | RH | = Regulator Handle. | WL | = Water Level. |
| CS | = Crown Sheet | RS | = Regulator Spindle. | | |

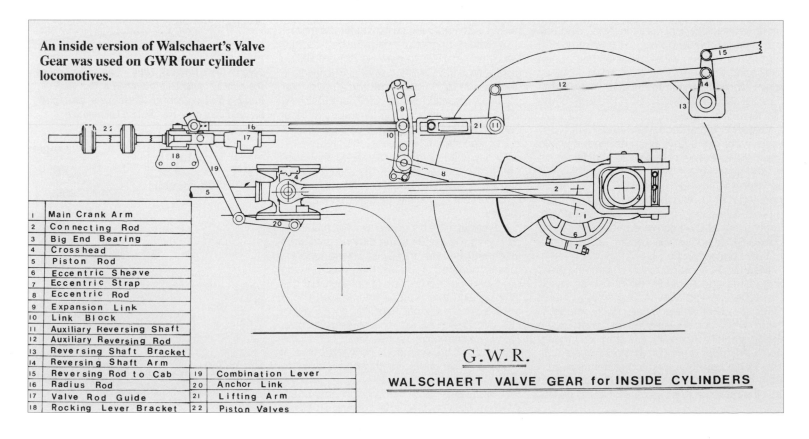

**An inside version of Walschaert's Valve Gear was used on GWR four cylinder locomotives.**

| | |
|---|---|
| 1 | Main Crank Arm |
| 2 | Connecting Rod |
| 3 | Big End Bearing |
| 4 | Crosshead |
| 5 | Piston Rod |
| 6 | Eccentric Sheave |
| 7 | Eccentric Strap |
| 8 | Eccentric Rod |
| 9 | Expansion Link |
| 10 | Link Block |
| 11 | Auxiliary Reversing Shaft |
| 12 | Auxiliary Reversing Rod |
| 13 | Reversing Shaft Bracket |
| 14 | Reversing Shaft Arm |
| 15 | Reversing Rod to Cab |
| 16 | Radius Rod |
| 17 | Valve Rod Guide |
| 18 | Rocking Lever Bracket |

| | |
|---|---|
| 19 | Combination Lever |
| 20 | Anchor Link |
| 21 | Lifting Arm |
| 22 | Piston Valves |

## G.W.R.

### WALSCHAERT VALVE GEAR for INSIDE CYLINDERS

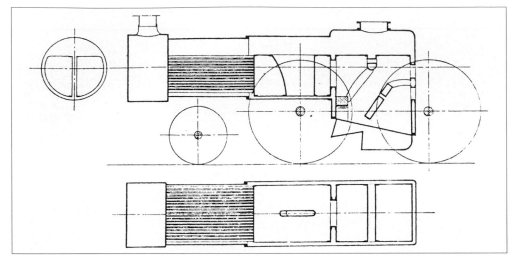

*Saxon Class, one of the designs of firebox intended for the burning of coal before the advent of the brick arch.*

*Belgian State Railway, 1864 . Type 1, the first on the railway in series production with a coal-burning firebox (above), Walschauts' valve gear as used on a post-war British Locomotive (below).*

flow at an earlier point. His experiments were followed up by those of a Frenchman, Benoit Paul Emile Clapeyron, on the Paris-Versailles (Rive Droite) Railway in 1840: Clapeyron adjusted the valves for a short cut-off at all times.

Both Gray and Clapeyron successfully showed that a shorter cut-off allowed less steam, and thus less fuel, to be used for a given output. Robert Stephenson and Co. devised a more satisfactory valve gear in 1842, and this has been used widely to vary valve events during motion. Equally widely used has been Walschaert's valve gear, devised in 1844 by Egide Walschaert, locomotive foreman at the running shed at Schaerbeek in Brussels of the Belgian State Railway.

Over the years since 1842 and 1844 many other valve gears have been devised: it would seem that scheming out how to transfer forces in the gear from one point to another is a satisfying intellectual exercise. Gooch's valve gear, Allan's, Joy's, Baker's - all have been used more or less widely, and there are many others. The advent of the internal-combustion engine gave a fillip to poppet valve gears, such as those of Lentz and Caprotti.

Meanwhile, sporadic research over the years suggested that electricity might be harnessed to propel locomotives. A Scotsman, Robert Davidson, built an electrically driven model in 1838 which was displayed at work in the Egyptian Hall, Piccadilly, London, in January 1839. A timber drum carrying bars of soft iron surrounded an axle. Electromagnets powered from a voltaic cell were switched on and off so that they attracted the iron bars for a brief period,

one after another, with the result that the axle and wheels turned.

Davidson tried out a full-sized trolley on the Edinburgh and Glasgow Railway in 1842. It moved, but at not much more than walking pace, and the experiment ended abruptly when the trolley was broken up by vandals. In the United States in 1847 and 1850 Professor Moses Farmer and Thomas Hall ran similar trolleys with improved switching for the motor.

In Britain, concerned citizens had caused Parliament in 1829 to pass an Act prohibiting locomotives from emitting smoke. But its terms were vague, and colliery railways in particular paid no attention when their coal-burning locomotives blackened the atmosphere. Most railways, however, conformed and burnt coke in the fireboxes. In any case, the fireboxes in early days had no great volume, so that coke had to be burned to gain the steam output needed. For this latter reason, coke was used on a number of continental European railways as well.

Coke was more expensive as a fuel than coal, so during the 1840s some experiments were made with the latter; these met with no success. It was grasped correctly that coal-burning produced large quantities of combustible gas (smoke), and that extra air was needed above the fire to burn this gas. One designer, Samuel Hall, did achieve this aim, on a Midland Counties Railway locomotive named *Bee*, but in the wrong place: the smokebox door at the front of the locomotive under the chimney was apt to glow red-hot.

Joseph Beattie of the London and South Western Railway tried coal-burning fireboxes

from 1853. At the cost of complications, he was successful ultimately with his Saxon class outside-cylinder 2-4-0 freight locomotives of 1855.

Beattie's patented firebox had a rear grate that was fired with coal in the normal way. Gases rising from this fire had to climb over a water bridge - that is, a barrier containing boiler-water that connected the two sides of the firebox. Above the barrier the gases were deflected downwards towards a front grate by another water bridge. The front grate was fired with just sufficient coal to keep its fire incandescent. To finish off, the firebox was extended a little way into the boiler-barrel to act as a combustion chamber. All gas was burnt by this arrangement.

From 1856 Matthew Kirtley, locomotive superintendent of the Midland Railway, likewise interested himself in coal-burning. Kirtley had started under the Stephensons, and, as he then ran the Derby locomotive works, the largest employer in Derby, he was regarded locally as a very important man. Several times mayor of

the city, he was called the 'Father of Derby'; unkind gossips, in view of his fondness for female society, suggested that he was the father of far too much of Derby.

Kirtley's assistant, Charles Markham, was in charge of the coal-burning trials, and by 1859 he had got it right. It has been pointed out that the 0-6-0 locomotives used for the trials had high-volume fireboxes in any case, and that this contributed to the success of the experiments. Markham's solution to the problem was to build a brick arch over the grate from the boiler tubeplate backwards nearly to the firedoor. To get round the brick arch, gases had to flow back over the fire, burning all the way. Secondary air was admitted through the firedoor.

About the time that the Midland Railway adopted brick arches, they were picked up also in the United States. From 1862 Alfred Belpaire, in charge of the locomotives of the Belgian State Railway, made experiments too. Belpaire's first 2-4-0 design for coal-burning after his trials had a firebox with, externally, a flat roof and flat sides.

This locomotive of 1864, with its square appearance to the firebox, was promptly held to herald a new type of boiler, christened the Belpaire boiler. The coal-burning innovation was missed completely, as was the fact that Belgian locomotive-builders had been putting Belpaire boilers on to their locomotives for a year or two before 1864.

# THE SUPERHEATER

At the end of the 19th century, when much interest was focused on alternative forms of prime mover, the steam locomotive was nevertheless still being developed. Indeed, due to changing operating conditions it was becoming larger and faster. In Europe, both passengers and freight called for speed, and in the former case trains were becoming heavier, too, as luxuries such as dining-cars were added.

In the United States the same conditions applied to passenger trains, but the rise of the 'brotherhoods' (trade unions) meant larger locomotives on freight trains as well. The unions negotiated industrial agreements that called for at least six men to work each train. This was just before the general adoption of the Westinghouse air-brake and the automatic coupler, which should have enabled fewer men to work a train. So US freight trains tended to be overmanned, and one way of holding down the consequent high labour costs was to operate fewer but longer trains.

Longer trains needed correspondingly large and powerful locomotives to haul them. Hence the North American 'big-engine' policy adopted in the late 1890s.

It was Archibald Sturrock, locomotive superintendent of an English railway, who laid down the dictum that 'the power of a locomotive is measured by its capacity to boil water.' Accordingly, designers of the late 19th century elected to increase boiler heating-surface. They used larger boilers, mounted on locomotives which were larger all round. Unfortunately, too often the results were disappointing; there were even cases of large locomotives turning in a worse performance than the smaller locomotives they had supplanted.

Later investigations have shown that increased heating-surface is insufficient in itself. When burning good-quality coal the firebox volume should be as large as possible. The free-gas area - that is, the sum of the cross-sectional areas of all the tubes and superheater flues (see below) - must be at least 16 per cent of the grate area, and preferably more. The two requirements have an effect on boiler diameter or on the shape of boiler to be adopted.

Considering a single tube through a boiler, its length must be 100 times its internal diameter. Too small a diameter for the length, and gas-flow is impeded by friction against the walls. To overcome the friction the blast up the chimney has to work harder, which in turn increases back-pressure on the pistons so that less power is available for traction. Too great a tube diameter, on the other hand, and a 'skin' of relatively cool gas forms against the tube walls, so that hotter gas shoots straight down the centre of the tube and up the chimney.

A more sophisticated form of this tube length/diameter ratio is used to take superheater flues into account: it is known as the A/S ratio. The free-gas area through the boiler related to the total tube and flue heating-surface should be 1:400. All the same, should a boiler be designed to these precepts it is likely to be too heavy and almost certainly too long. Designers must therefore seek compensations of one sort or another, which is one of the reasons why locomotive design remained an art rather than a science.

A major advance towards greater locomotive power was Wilhelm Schmidt's superheater. Since early days it had been realized that useful heat was going up the chimney. The idea of

tapping this heat by taking the pipes carrying steam from the boiler to the cylinders through the hot gas, so that the steam would be superheated above the temperature ruling in the boiler, had been suggested a number of times. Schmidt produced a practical scheme, and applied it to a Royal Prussian State Railways locomotive in 1897.

Schmidt's original superheater provided for a large-diameter flue at the bottom of the boiler tubes. This took gases into a smokebox of enlarged diameter. The main steam-pipe from the boiler was divided in the smokebox into small-diameter return tubes which were arranged around the smokebox walls. Steam flowing through the small tubes picked up heat from the hot gases in the smokebox before going on its way to the cylinders.

It was shown that superheating steam in this manner saved fuel, or made the locomotive more powerful for the same quantity of fuel. Schmidt then had second thoughts, and designed an improved superheater. The Royal Prussian State Railways was pleased with his original design, and had a large number of locomotives either fitted, or built with it, and therefore declined the second design, so Schmidt had to take it elsewhere for trial. Eventually the second design was fitted for the first time to a 4-4-0 of Caledonian Railway type, a Class 33 built in 1903, belonging to the Belgian State Railway.

This improved type of superheater was an immediate success, and became the standard in general use. In it, six to a dozen large-diameter flues took the place of the upper rows of the small tubes in the boiler barrel. Usually the flues were 5⅛in (130mm) diameter. The small-

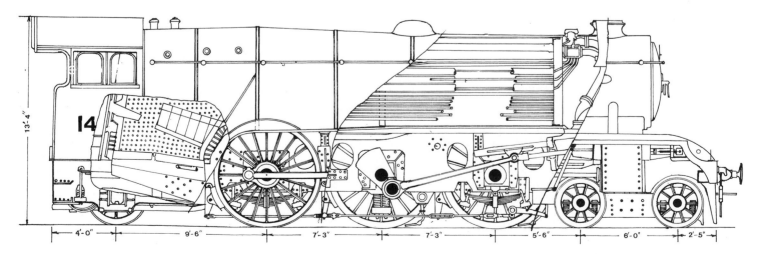

*Diagram of LNER A-1 Class 4-6-2 three cylinder express, cut away to show how superheater elements were place in large locomotive boiler tanks.*

*Superheater elements, in pairs (out and back), bent to fit into the boiler flues.*

diameter boiler-steam tubes ran down these flues and back, among the hot fire gases that the flues contained. Normally, the steam makes a double pass; that is, there are four small steam tubes, known as elements, for each flue. The superheater can be designed to give a preferred maximum steam temperature in the cylinders.

Many names have been attached to superheater designs, but on examination most of them will be found to be variants of Schmidt's ideas. Usually the designers were trying to escape from Schmidt's patents, or they simply wished to parade their own names. Some of the more inefficient devices for raising the steam temperature were those which became known as steam driers. These had a brief period of popularity in some quarters, as the lower temperatures that they reached avoided the need for a higher-grade, heat-resistant cylinder lubrication oil.

# FEEDING THE BOILER

Joseph Beattie's Saxon-class 2-4-0 locomotives of 1855 had another innovation incorporated in addition to their coal-burning firebox. This was Beattie's feed-water heater. Steam exhausted from the cylinders is still hot as it goes up the chimney. Fuel savings can be made by extracting heat from the exhaust and using it to heat the cold water that enters the boiler from the tender: the question was, how? Beattie succeeded in the attempt and, not without some improvements, feed-water heaters were carried by South Western locomotives from 1855 to 1877.

Until 1860 or so, a pump had been used to put water into boilers. The pumps used could be worked by boiler steam or they could be driven by the motion of the locomotive as it ran along the track. As a result of the latter technique, it was not unusual to see a locomotive running up and down a suitable siding by itself: its apparently aimless manoeuvres were in fact directed towards filling its boiler.

Frenchman Henri Giffard introduced his boiler-feed injector in 1859. A jet of steam is directed down a pipe leading to the boiler. At the end of the pipe is a clack valve, normally held shut by boiler pressure. Cold water from the tender is fed into the jet of steam, which entrains it but in doing so tends to cool and condense. Thus the

**North American-style feedwater heater, as fitted to a 4-8-4. Feedwater heaters were fairly common in America.**

steam's latent heat of condensation is given up, which raises the pressure of the jet sufficiently for it to open the clack valve and pass into the boiler.

Giffard's injector was adopted with enthusiasm everywhere, for it was a vast improvement on the pumps that had gone before. He suggested also an exhaust-steam injector, which would function by tapping steam from the blast up the chimney. In the event, it was to be 40 years before the exhaust-steam injector was taken up at all widely.

Injectors cannot handle hot boiler feed-water, so Beattie's feed-water heater still had to rely on a pump and therefore, outside Beattie's own railway, did not have widespread use. Interest was to revive after 1900, when a number of methods for dealing with the problem were devised. Those feed-water systems that have been successful have usually incorporated the feature of purifying the feed-water too. The heat applied causes the feed-water to boil in special chambers, with the result that any scale in the water is deposited in the chambers on surfaces that can be withdrawn easily for cleaning, rather than in the boiler, from where it is more difficult to dislodge. Boiler washouts need therefore be done less frequently. However, only a minority of steam locomotives were fitted with feed-water heaters.

**Although not greatly used in Britain, the feed water heater found widespread use in Europe and the USA, fitted on the front of the boiler, as on the 4-6-4 hauling the Blue Comet.**

# BROAD GAUGES

The Great Western Railway opened in 1838 in England with a track gauge of 7ft 0¼in (2140mm). The United States used broad gauges too: 5ft (1524mm) was popular there, and the 5ft 6in (1676mm) and 6ft (1829mm) gauges were also prominent. That was in the 1870s, just before the inevitable conversion to standard gauge, 4ft 8½ in (1435mm), in the interest of rolling stock interchange.

The American engineer George Washington Whistler, father of the painter, took the 5ft (1524mm) gauge to Russia from a New England railway on which he had been working, and this remains the gauge of railways in the former Russian Empire. A broader gauge, 5ft 6in (1676mm) is used in Spain, Portugal, India and parts of Argentine and Chile, while Brazil, Ireland, and, in Australia, South Australia and Victoria, use the 5ft 3in (1600mm) gauge.

Locomotives for broad gauges were often not very much larger than those for standard gauge. Oceans of ink have been spilled on the advantages and disadvantages of a broader gauge. For steam locomotives with inside cylinders there was one positive benefit which must be acknowledged: the locomotive machinery had more space to occupy between the wheels so that, for example, all the bearings could be made wider and thus more effective. Expressed differently, there are problems in designing narrow-gauge locomotives, as will be shown in a later section of this book.

Perhaps the last word on this gauge question was set out in a vast German report of 1969 which plumped for standard gauge, 4ft 8½ in (1435mm). During the 1960s the German Federal Republic had been considering a high-speed, high-capacity railway running from the north to the south of the country and carrying passengers, road vehicles and containers. As the railway was to be an entirely separate entity from the existing railway network, the question of optimum gauge came up.

The subject of gauge was studied in detail, and it was found that any gauge from 3ft 6in (1067mm) to 7ft 0½in (2140mm) would do. The former was on the borderline where lateral forces become too great; meter gauge (3ft 3⅜in) gauge was ruled out for this reason, while the broader gauge was on the verge of unviable construction costs. The final choice was made merely because it would be slightly cheaper to run rolling stock for repair over existing railways. In fact, the oil crisis of 1974 killed the idea of a German high-speed line, but it had provided a useful demonstration that the 19th century fixation with railway gauge had concealed the fact that the gauge is not all that important, within limits.

*The Indian broad gauge. The turntable has track for both broad gauge (5ft 6in or 1676mm) and meter gauge.*

# FROM IRON TO STEEL

Until 1860 or so, the usual material for locomotive building was iron in the form of either castings or suitably shaped wrought iron. When iron ore is smelted in a blast furnace, the product which runs off is cast iron, having a carbon content of about 1.5 per cent (it is called cast iron because it is too hard to be wrought, and hence must be cast). Prolonged smelting - or, more usually, remelting - of cast iron and stirring this melt produces wrought iron, which has a much lower carbon content, about 0.03 per cent. What has happened is that the stirring of the melt (a process known as puddling) has brought the iron in the melt into contact with ambient air; the carbon present has reacted with oxygen in the air and been drawn off in the form of carbon dioxide gas.

It had been known since ancient times that steel could be produced by puddling cast iron just so far and no further. It was a chancy business, dependent on the skill and judgement of the oldest puddler; he had to catch the melted iron when the carbon content was somewhere between 1.5 per cent and 0.03 per cent, and then give the signal for pouring off. Steel was consequently expensive, and its quality variable.

In the 1850s, wrought and cast iron were beginning to reach the limits of their capabilities for locomotive construction. Designers hesitated to make their locomotives larger and more powerful, not only because of doubts about the

materials but also because it was evident that wrought-iron rails were wearing out much too quickly. Experiments were therefore made with steel, despite the material's expense. It was tried for making inside crank axles (with indifferent success, owing to the quality of the steel) and as a facing to the wheel tyres. In the latter case the softer wrought-iron rails had even less chance of a long life.

It occurred to a young man, Henry Bessemer, that if oxygen were to be blown through a cast-iron melt it should be possible to control the making of steel much more accurately. He set up a furnace - in the almost traditional garden shed - in the parish of St Pancras in London. In 1856 he achieved success despite, on one occasion, the attendance of the fire brigade. Cheap high-quality steel was on its way.

The advent of cheap steel was an event of world importance. Except for the arrival of the steam locomotive itself, it was the most revolutionary event in the history of railways. Heavier and faster locomotives, running on longer-lasting rails, were made possible, and so the whole idea of a railway took a leap forward.

*High-grade steel wheels as fitted to a late 20th century Chinese locomotive.*

*19th century cast-iron wheels.*

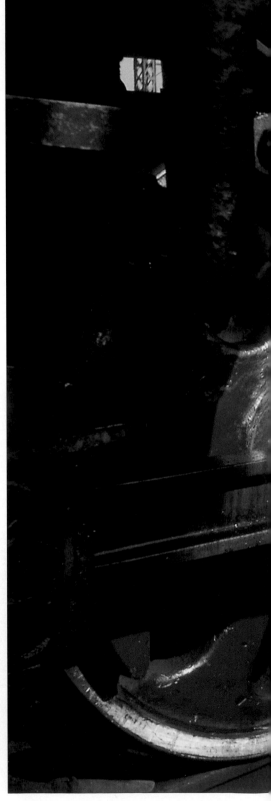

# Narrow-Gauge Locomotives

In 19th-century England the management of the Great Western Railway, which had a broad gauge of 7ft 0¼in (2140mm), used to refer to the other British railways as 'narrow-gauge.' Proponents of this latter gauge, Stephenson's 4ft 8½in (1435mm), scored a great public relations victory by referring to their gauge as 'standard', on the grounds that it was by far the predominant gauge in Britain. Eventually the GWR had to change its gauge to secure conformity, and Stephenson's gauge became known worldwide as the standard gauge, even though many countries have 'standardized' other gauges, narrower in most but broader in Russia (with Finland), Spain (with Portugal), the Indian Peninsula, and parts of Latin America and Australia. In a country like India, where gauges of 5ft 6in (1676mm), one meter (3ft 3⅜in), and 2ft 6in (760mm) coexisted, 'narrow gauge' and 'standard gauge' may be ambiguous. However, for most purposes narrow gauge is taken to refer to gauges narrower than meter gauge.

In terms of locomotive design the difference between standard-gauge and broad-gauge locomotives was not significant. The Great Western demonstrated some remarkably fast runs, unmatched by the standard-gauge interest, but it actually achieved these through superb locomotive design rather than the virtues of the broad gauge. In the 20th century, had the broad gauge survived, it might have been different because bigger locomotives would

*On the 3ft (914mm) gauge Yucatan system in Mexico: a US-built 2-6-0 leaves Merida.*

have been simpler to construct, thanks to the wider space for machinery between the side frames. More space there would have allowed bigger bearing surfaces and room for fitters to do their work without performing a Houdini act. But for most of the steam age, standard gauge was quite sufficient for ever-growing locomotive designs. As with rolling stock, the limiting factor was the external clearances.

With narrow gauge, however, the width between the rails was important for designers, again as with rolling stock. With the latter it was simply not possible to build freight and passenger vehicles of a width approaching those of the larger gauges; they would simply have toppled over if, for example, all the passengers sat on one side of the train.

Narrow-gauge lines became popular only when the Railway Age was well on its way. Major main lines needed the cubic capacities to handle bulk freight and passenger traffic. The narrow gauge began to attract attention when routes of small potential traffic began to be considered. In the pre-automobile age, settlements and areas that still depended on the horse, bullock, mule or camel were likely to fall well behind those communities blessed with rail transport, and knew it. A narrow-gauge railway, though it might be small and cramped, was certainly better than no railway at all.

The attraction of the narrow gauge was the low cost of building it. This was particularly true in hilly areas, because it could tolerate sharp curves and could therefore hug the terrain, rather than demand expensive earthworks and tunnels. Because rolling stock was smaller it was cheaper, and because it weighed less the rails could be lighter and therefore cheaper also. So there was an enormous saving in capital cost, by as much as a third in flat country and two-thirds in hilly terrain. The difference in running costs was not so great, because almost the same number of workers was

*A narrow-gauge locomotive rebuilt to standard gauge. This is a US-built 2-8-0 in Mexico.*

*This picture shows how the narrow-gauge lines could hug the landscape. The line is the 3ft gauge Cuzco & Santa Ana Railroad in the Peruvian Andes.*

*A US-built 2-8-2 at work on the Cuzco & Santa Ana RR.*

*A British-built 4-6-0 on the 2ft 6in (760mm) gauge system of India's Western Railway.*

required, but the fuel consumption was less. The big problem of narrow gauge was that it fitted uncomfortably into a railway system. Where it made a junction with main lines, passengers had to change trains and freight had to be expensively transhipped into mainline freightcars. But for routes that were self-contained, from a port into the hinterland, for example, the narrow gauge was a good bet.

In course of time those narrow-gauge lines which prospered were converted to the broader gauge to bring capacity up to demand. Many of the others were driven out of business by the highways in the first decades of the 20th century; the highway vehicle, which did not have to pay for its track and was best at handling small loads over short distances, was usually cheaper and more convenient than the narrow-gauge train.

In the British Isles it was in Ireland and sparsely populated and mountainous Wales that narrow-gauge railways appeared in numbers. In Ireland they tended to serve market towns and rural communites, while in Wales they found very suitable employment in quarrying. Both the Festiniog and the Talyllyn railways, which still

*The narrow gauge passes under the broad gauge near Baroda, in India. The 4-6-0 locomotive was built in Britain in 1949.*

*A 2-8-2 tank locomotive on one of the 750mm gauge lines radiating from Dresden in Germany.*

*One of three 2ft 6in (760mm) gauge Pacific locomotives built for passenger services out of Bangalore in India. The continental 750mm and the Anglo-Saxon 2ft 6in (760mm) gauges are regarded as identical.*

exist as tourist lines, had the movement of slate to dockside as their main purpose. The British built another narrow-gauge stronghold in India. They had already decided, after laying the main lines there with broad gauge, to build secondary lines with the meter gauge to save costs. Then, the meter-gauge system being more or less completed yet the need for new lines still apparent, they began to build narrow-gauge lines, or approve their building by native princes. The military had some influence in this process, the need to provide transport in case of war on the frontiers being regarded as very important, and the choice between 2ft (610mm) and 2ft 6in (760mm) gauges was partly a military decision. In the end the wider gauge was chosen but the 2ft gauge was also permitted, which was a bad decision from the military point of view, because the existence of the narrower gauge brought only marginal financial benefit and hindered the transfer of rolling stock to a line that might be hard pressed in an emergency.

In North America the narrow gauge was less popular, partly because the possibility of exchanging rolling stock with the railway system in general was highly prized. In Maine, where population was thin and the countryside undulating, a system of 2ft-gauge lines appeared, the so-called 'Maine Two-Footers.' The Rockies was another region suited to these lines, and some long lines were built to carry quarry and mine traffic. Some of these still exist as tourist lines, notably the Silverton Railroad centred on Durango in Colorado, and the

*The standard 0-8-0 750mm gauge locomotive design used by several countries of the post-war communist bloc. This one is operating in northern China.*

*On the Austrian narrow gauge near Garsten. This line, part of which still operates, uses 0-6-2 tank locomotives.*

Cumbres Pass and Toltec Railroad, also in Colorado.

These latter two American lines were of the 3ft (914mm) gauge, which was favoured by American engineers and came very close to the mainline standard of meter gauge. When American companies began to construct railways in South America, they often chose this gauge for the lines they built in the Andes.

France was unusual in that its so-called narrow-gauge lines were actually meter-gauge.

Most of these lines were built in the last quarter of the 19th century and were initiated not by the state but by local governments, or départements. Hence they were termed 'departmental railways.' The last, electrified, was built as late as 1928, but they did not long survive the age of the automobile, although one, starting at Nice and penetrating northwards into the mountains, still survives. In Germany, too, the highway put an end to most of these lines, but politics intervened to save some of them.

When eastern Germany became a communist state after 1945 the new government was reluctant to spend money on converting narrow to broad gauge or on improving local highways, so the narrow-gauge railways survived long enough for most of them to rejoin a united Germany, and many of them are destined to continue, with a strong emphasis on tourist traffic.

The Russian tsarist government also became interested in the narrow gauge when it was

*The standard post-war Russian diesel locomotive for 750mm gauge lines, several hundred of which have been built.*

*One of a class of diesel locomotives built for the Austrian narrow-gauge lines. The outside coupling rods are unusual, but space between the frames is limited.*

persuaded that it could develop its railway network very cheaply by this means. Officials, however, were worried that such lines would not be able to handle the traffic on offer. Some of them came as a delegation to view the Festiniog Railway, which claimed to have solved the problem of raising capacity, largely by means of the revolutionary 'Fairlie' locomotive. Later, the British-owned Barsi Light Railway in India, whose engineer, E. R. Calthrop, was a devoted and clever narrow-gauge enthusiast, set new standards. Calthrop favoured the 2ft 6in gauge and felt that locomotives should have an axle weight of only five tonnes maximum. Light rails of 30lb/yd (15kg/m) could then be used, which, if a maximum speed of 15mph (24km/h) were imposed, would last well and require little maintenance. Unlike the British home railways, the Barsi line used stressed-steel freightcars riding on four-wheel trucks. The locomotives included some 4-8-4 tank units which combined an adhesion weight of 20 tonnes with an axle weight of only five.

But it was the Fairlie locomotive and, later, the Garratt and Mallet, which promised to provide really powerful traction power for these small lines. All three of these patented concepts used a flexible wheelbase so that a long, big, locomotive could tackle sharp curves. The Garratt and Mallet, which became primarily mainline machines, will be described in a later section. The Fairlie was built occasionally for some of the larger-gauge railways (including the

*On the French Vivarais Railway, once a meter gauge departmental line but now a tourist attraction.*

broad-gauge Russian Transcaucasus line), but was essentially narrow-gauge equipment.

Designed by a Scotsman, used in Wales, the Fairlie attracted worldwide attention in the 1870s. The first was built in 1865 for the Neath & Brecon Railway. It had two boilers, back-to-back, and therefore a chimney and smokebox

at each end. There was a single firebox in the centre, where the cab was situated. This arrangement, especially on the narrow gauge, made life somewhat difficult for the driver and, especially, the fireman, but at that period this was not considered to be of overriding importance. The two boilers supplied two

*The Pithiviers Railway in France. Once a centre of agriculture narrow-gauge lines, Pithiviers now has just a tourist railway.*

cylinders at each end; this being the narrow gauge, there was no space for that British favourite, the inside-cylinder arrangement. The cylinders were part of, and drove, pivoting power trucks, or bogies. *Little Wonder* of this type made a great impression working on the Festiniog Railway in 1870 and halfway through that decade 43 of the world's railways used the type. Single-boiler versions were also produced, and in the USA the Mason Machine Works built its own variant of the single-enders. The weakness of the concept was the need to have flexible steam-pipes, because the cylinders moved as the power unit pivoted over curves. Steam leakage at the flexible joints was hard to avoid. Also, because of the big overhang, these locomotives could usually only be safely operated at low speeds. Fairlie locomotives can

*An electrified narrow-gauge railway, the prosperous Zugspitzbahn in the Barvarian Alps.*

*A 1950s scene on the Bosnia-Herzegovinian 750mm gauge system at Gruz. The train on the right is an 'intercity' from Dubrovnik to Sarajevo. The line has since been converted to standard gauge and is no longer part of Yugoslav Railways.*

still be seen hauling passenger trains on the Festiniog Railway; one of them was built recently, using the old drawings.

On the 3ft gauge, locomotive design problems were not so great, and there were cases of locomotives being changed from narrow-gauge to standard gauge when a line was reconstructed to join the mainline system. There were also cases where a mainline engine was converted to narrow gauge. This was rather more difficult, but the Denver & Rio Grande Railroad claimed to have done this when its Silverton line became short of traction power ('claimed' because some critics believed that these were 'accounting' rebuilds, using very few parts from the original locomotives).

*On the Vivarais Railway in France. A Mallet locomotive is in charge of the daily summer passenger service.*

# Vertical Boiler and Tram Locomotives

*An Indonesian State Railway Beyer, Peacock tram locomotive of 1884 at work in Surabaya local service in the 1970s.*

Two of the unsuccessful competitors at the Rainhill locomotive trials in 1829 had vertical boilers. Such boilers took up less space, their ash was more easily removed, and they could raise steam quickly. Vertical-boiler locomotives could be short, and were therefore suited to sharp curves, which is why so many were used on quarry lines. However, there was an ultimate limit to their size, because height restrictions prevented the use of big boilers. The Stephensons tried to beat this restriction by building a locomotive with two vertical boilers, one behind the other, but this arrangement was awkward for the fireman.

Nevertheless, such locomotives, being cheap and easy to build, had their uses. In the United States the earliest home-built locomotives were of this type, including John Stevens's 1825 locomotive, and the celebrated *Tom Thumb*, *York*, and *Best Friend of Charleston*. These were

so simple that ordinary engineering companies often built them, either for doing their own yard work or for sale. In England, mowing-machine companies were among those building them. These rough-and-ready machines were usually all that was needed for yard work although, because plain (tubeless) boilers were typically used, they had a quite high fuel consumption. But some survived many decades. One of the most successful types was the de Winton, of which several examples have been preserved, including one that has been occasionally operated by the Leighton Buzzard Narrow Gauge Railway in Britain.

A more sophisticated but essentially similar vertical-boiler machine was used for passenger service, either by incorporating it in one end of a passenger vehicle to form a steam railcar, or by designing it for tram use. In the latter case it would haul one or more passenger vehicles,

typically over rough track laid along highways. For the safety of the crew and of other road-users it was boxed in, with the metal sheeting extended downwards to cover the potentially dangerous wheels and rods. Although most vertical-boiler machines had two small vertical cylinders using gears to drive the wheels, some had conventional horizontal cylinders driving cranked axles by means of rods. The Plynlimon & Hafan line in Wales even had a locomotive that had both vertical and horizontal cylinders.

In the pre-automobile age, passenger tramways were profitable and popular. Some survived into the second half of the 20th century. By that time the vertical-boiler tram engine had been supplemented by larger units, using a small horizontal boiler. The British locomotive builder Beyer, Peacock sold many of these, and some others were built under its licence. The Dutch East Indies was a rewarding market, and

*A Sentinel locomotive once used by British Railways but now employed by the resurrected Middleton Railway, near Leeds.*

Beyer, Peacock tram engines survived there for many decades. The flat lands of Belgium and the Netherlands were another field of activity for steam trams, linking villages that were too small to justify a full-scale railway. Steam trams used on city streets often passed their exhaust steam into the cold water tank to condense it, and thereby avoid complaints by citizens enveloped in wet fog. This did not work very well, but was not completely ineffective. The other solution that was adopted, fitting superheaters to raise the temperature of the steam after it left the cylinders, was economically absurd and not very effective either.

A high-technology vertical-boiler locomotive design appeared in the 1920s. This was the 'Sentinel', built by the Sentinel Waggon Works at Shrewsbury in England, which previously had specialized in steam highway trucks. Like its ancestor, it was suited to bad track, sharp curves, and small clearances. It had been designed with some ingenuity. The boiler, though vertical, was highly sophisticated and had a superheater. It was square, situated at the cab end, and was fired from the side. Its pressure

*Tiny, a broad-gauge vertical boiler locomotive acquired by the South Devon Railway in 1868 to work a dockside branch.*

39

*The steam railcar, the sequel to the steam tram. This one worked in Australia's outback.*

was actually higher than that of conventional steam locomotives, being 280psi (1,930kPa) The point of this high pressure was that it allowed the small boiler to have a big reserve of steam, which suited locomotives that stood around for much of the time and were then required to carry out a frenzy of switching and shunting. Another unusual feature was that the cylinders (in the middle, because the front end was used for water storage) did not act on the wheels through rods, but by chains and sprockets. Chain drive and, where fitted, chain coupling of the wheels, gave a much more flexible wheelbase and was ideal for bumpy track. It also made wheel-slip less likely, so that greater loads could be started for a given weight of locomotive. Controls were on both sides of the boiler, in the cab, so the locomotive could be operated by one man if required.

In England, the Somerset and Dorset Joint Railway was a satisfied user of Sentinels. It preferred 200hp (149kW) units for serving primitive colliery sidings. These units consumed only one third of the coal used by saddletank locomotives of equivalent power, largely because consumption at rest was so low. Moreover, the Sentinels were only about 10ft (3m) high, compared with the 11ft (3.3m) of the saddletanks, and weighed only 27 tonnes rather than the saddletanks' 33 tonnes.

Outside Britain, but under British influence, Egypt was also a heavy user of the Sentinel. The 2ft (610mm) gauge Egyptian Delta Light Railway ordered 50 tram-style units for use in its cotton-growing territory. The Egyptian mainline railway also used four big passenger-service Sentinels. These had horizontal boilers and rather resembled orthodox locomotives, except for the chain drive and apparent absence of cylinders. Sentinels that were intended for 'railway' rather than mere yard service were often double-geared, although the gear could be changed only when the locomotive was stationary. With the single-geared locomotives, sprocket ratios could be varied, giving a choice of higher speed and light load, or slower speed and heavier load. A 100hp (74.5kW) Sentinel on level track could move 400 tonnes at the lower ratio, and reach 37mph (59kp/h) at the higher.

*One of several steam tram locomotives preserved in the Low Countries. This unit was built in Belgium.*

# INDUSTRIAL LOCOMOTIVES

The first steam locomotives were built for use in industry. Trevithick's locomotive of 1804, credited with being the world's first, ran on an industrial railway in South Wales. George Stephenson gained his first experience with the steam locomotives that were beginning to displace horse traction in the mining region of northeast England. Industrial railways are defined as those built to serve a particular industry exclusively. Sometimes they are simply part of a production process, like ironworks railways that move ore and partly-processed metal from one part of a plant to another. More usually, they connect an industrial site with the mainline railway but are owned and operated by the particular industry or enterprise. Many are therefore little more than an elongated factory siding. Railways that are owned by an industry mainly to serve that industry, but earn money by carrying other traffic are not, strictly speaking, industrial railways; such lines include the Missabe and Iron Range RR and the Bessemer & Lake Erie RR in the USA which, though primarily built as ore haulers, acted as public carriers and were major railroads.

In the early railway age industrial railways often had the right to move their trains over the rails

*On the Seaham Harbour and Docks Railway in north-east England. The nearer locomotive was built by a long defunct Dorsetshire builder, Stephen Lewin, in 1877, and survived until 1970.*

*On a Chinese timber-hauling railway linking forest with sawmill.*

0-4-0 and 0-6-0 wheel arrangements were usual, with the locomotives carrying their water in saddle tanks resting over the boiler. Cylinders might be outside or inside, but in Britain the valve gear was typically inside. There were some side-tank locomotives, too. In America, side-tank six-wheelers were favoured, with outside valve gear and the wheelbase so short that the wheels almost seemed to touch each other. Simplicity, a light axle load, and a short wheelbase to negotiate curves were the usual requirements in all countries. A number of manufacturers specialized in building industrial tank locomotives: Porter, Davenport and Vulcan in the USA and Peckett and Avonside in Britain, to mention a few. The Peckett designs were notable for a high degree of component standardization, enabling prompt supply of spare parts.

Some industries had very large locomotive stocks. In Britain the National Coal Board of the 1950s had a total track mileage greater than the mileages of the state railways of some countries, and it had a variegated stock of locomotives, some purpose-built and some bought secondhand from mainline railways. The timber industry also was a big railway builder, and forestry lines are still important, especially in Russia, China and to a smaller extent Roumania. Building contractors used industrial locomotives over temporary trackage laid at construction

*A scene on the Kettering Iron & Coal Company's system in the English Midlands, showing locomotives by Manning Wardale, one of the specialist builders of industrial locomotives.*

of adjoining mainline companies, and in some cases this right continued into the 20th century. This meant that such railways needed to equip themselves not simply with small yard locomotives, but with designs that could run safely and smoothly over 'real' railways. Some industrial railways themselves have long, well-engineered, main lines, and these were often built to link raw material deposits with a seaport or with an existing railway. A modern example is the Hamersley Ore Railway in Australia. This ore-carrier was opened in 1966 and has since grown to a 237-mile (382km) main line, with branches in addition. It passes trains as heavy as 28,000 gross tonnes, carrying iron ore from a remote region of Western Australia to dockside at Dampier. To handle this traffic it employs over 30 modern US-made diesels, notable for providing microwave ovens and CD-Roms in their cabs for the benefit of the one-man crews. There are other big ore carriers elsewhere, notably in Australia and North America.

However, the typical industrial railway of the steam age was fairly short, and operated what were essentially yard locomotives. In Britain the

*Bass Breweries at Burton on Trent had twelve of this class, painted turkey-red and always with shining brasswork.*

*In the Queensland sugarcane fields near Bundaberg. The locomotives were built locally, although based on earlier British designs.*

sites; the builders of the Manchester Ship Canal used about 170 locomotives. Such locomotives travelled around a country, from one site to another.

Many well-known companies built their own railways. They included Kodak at Rochester in New York, the Ford Motor Company at Dagenham (a pioneer in the use of diesel locomotives), Cadbury's (which operated a fleet of chocolate-coloured tank locomotives at Bournville), and big breweries such as Bass and Guinness. The Anheuser-Busch brewery still operates 42 miles (68km) of line in St Louis, Missouri, and uses 11 diesel locomotives in the service. Its railroad is titled, very appropriately for an industrial line, the Manufacturers Railway Co. Another industry requiring heavy inputs was, and is, the cement industry. Southwestern Portland Cement in California, for example, uses modern mainline-style diesel locomotives on its 15-mile (24km) line. A more typical example, so far as Britain is concerned, is the Portland cement works at Foxton in Cambridgeshire, where there is a glorified works siding of about a mile and a few storage tracks. In steam days, a solitary saddletank would trundle up and down once or twice daily, but spend most of its life positioning cars for loading and unloading.

American industries, with their somewhat greater mileages and heavier trains, often acquire diesel locomotives from the mainline railways. But they have also relied heavily on the

range of switchers, 44 and 70-tonne, produced by General Electric. Some still operate Whitcomb diesels. The two world wars had their effect on industrial lines everywhere. After the First World War there was a surplus of 'trench locomotives', both steam and internal combustion. Those industrial railways that were

narrow gauge bought these cheaply, to modernize their stock and, in some cases, to eliminate steam traction. A similar pattern emerged after the Second World War. Many British lines acquired the standard 'Austerity' six-wheel saddletank that had been built for the army, while in the USA, apart from diesels, there

*One of the last European coal-mining steam operations, that of the collieries at Aachen in Germany.*

*On the Richmond Vale Railway, serving the New South Wales coalfield. The locomotives are of a class supplied by Beyer, Peacock of Manchester.*

in the copper railways of Arizona. Its pantograph picked up power on the 'mainline' stretches of its line, and a diesel engine was switched on for work nearer the pits, where lines tended to be temporary and therefore not electrified. Arizona had numerous copper-mining railroads, and some still exist. The Magma Arizona Railroad, narrow-gauge until the 1920s, once used steam tender locomotives on its 15-mile (24km) 'main line'. These railroads had very steep gradients, especially in the workings, and needed powerful traction. Some were not strictly industrial, in that they also carried mail and non-industrial freight.

Also in Arizona was built one of the most impressive modern industrial railways. This was the Black Mesa & Lake Powell RR, an isolated 78-mile (125km) single-track, heavy-duty line linking coal mines at Black Mesa with generating stations at Page. Using an exceptionally high voltage system (50,000V), this railroad was equipped with three C-C electric locomotives designed to triple-head the railroad's single train of nearly 80 coal hoppers. Making a return trip three times daily, with loading and unloading done while the train proceeded, and with reversing circles at each end, the one train could move 23,000 tonnes of coal daily. The locomotives were designed to be driverless, but some opposition to this idea meant that fully

was an influx of the US Army's 0-6-0 side-tank locomotives.

The purpose-built industrial steam locomotive was a specific type, and other concepts were developed especially for industrial requirements. One of these was the fireless steam locomotive, used on industrial sites where a stray spark might cause a serious fire. For years a big British biscuit manufacturer used one of these at its Reading factory. Others were favoured by a number of US power companies. Paper companies and furniture companies were also users. The fireless locomotive resembled a conventional locomotive externally, save for the absence of a chimney. Closer scrutiny would reveal the absence of a firebox, so what resembled its boiler was merely a pressurised tank. At intervals it would refill this cylinder with high-pressure steam from a ground installation and proceed about its work until it needed further replenishment. Some of these locomotives still exist, usually on standby duty. One which sees regular use is at the Manchester Museum of Science and Industry, where it hauls a passenger car for the benefit of visitors.

The other slightly unorthodox type is the electro-diesel. This was to be found especially

*On a Chinese colliery line. The miners at left are about to catch the passenger service provided between suburb and pit.*

An SY 2-8-2 locomotive, still being built for Chinese industrial railways in the 1990s.

*In the diesel age, some industrial steam locomotives were kept for stand-by use. here is one British survivor at work.*

*A fireless locomotive as used by a US power company and styled to match the streamline age.*

automatic operation was postponed. Automation, however, is not unknown elsewhere.

Another railway that is really a single-commodity mover is the Quebec North Shore & Labrador Railway. This uses standard General Motors diesels to haul its ore trains, which are typically of 14,000 short tons but sometimes extend 1.8 miles (3km) behind the locomotives to total 33,000 gross short tons. Because there is little alternative transport in its inhospitable

hinterland, it operates other services, including passenger trains. It has dabbled in driverless operations, but its mainline trains have a crew in the lead locomotive, with the mid-train locomotives controlled by Locotrol equipment.

One of many medium-size ore railroads is the Lake Superior & Ishpeming RR, with an 18-mile (31km) main line passing 11,000-tonne trains of iron ore pellets and bentonite. It currently uses about a dozen General Electric diesel locomotives. Some of the locomotives that it

used in its steam days have been passed on to tourist railroads. Also in the USA, the Bethlehem Steel Corporation, like several other major metallurgical giants, administers a number of separate railroads, modest in length, which serve its various constituent companies. It has a railway department at its head office and this, among other things, supervises a locomotive pool to ensure that locomotives are moved between plants according to need.

Some railways, while technically industrial, are in fact agricultural. Among these are the sugarcane lines, usually but not always narrow

*Although now elevated to passenger service on the Grand Canyon Railroad, this locomotive once worked for the iron ore-hauling Lake Erie and Ishpeming RR.*

gauge. These work only in the cutting season and use primitive track to transport the cut cane to the refining works. In steam days the locomotives burned canefield waste; apart from this ability the main requirement was for locomotives that would have very light axle loads and short wheelbases, because the track was so rickety. Cane railways were and remain particularly important in Queensland, Indonesia, the Philippines, India and Cuba. Those of Cuba still use much steam traction, of US origin. In countries of a different climate sugarbeet railways are not unknown; Lincolnshire in Britain

had one which survived until after the Second World War, using an ordinary saddletank locomotive.

Not dissimilar are peat, or turf, railways. These, too, have movable tracks that follow the cutting. They convey the cut turf to power stations. As with other lines, they were once steam-powered but are now dieselized. Ireland has an extensive 3ft (914mm)-gauge system managed by the Bord na Mona, which recently has also organised a tourist train operation. Peat railways were built in other parts of Europe; the USSR at one time showed some enthusiasm for them.

Industrial railways, though reduced in number, still exist and are important. In China they still use steam power to a large extent. However, the steam lines of the New South Wales coalfield near Newcastle, for long a railway enthusiast's Mecca, have disappeared except where local organizations have converted them to tourist or museum use.

*A metallurgical works diesel locomotive exchanges freightcars with an electrified Russian main line near St. Petersburg.*

# FLEXIBLE-WHEELBASE LOCOMOTIVES

Diesel and electric locomotives run on powered, swivelling, trucks (bogies), but with steam traction there was a real problem with designing powerful locomotives that could negotiate curves at speed. As traffic built up, heavier trains became necessary, both to reduce operating costs and to enable existing lines (which, after all, could pass only a certain number of trains per hour) to cope with demand. If more powerful locomotives were not available there had to be double-heading, two locomotives per train, which was not economical. Various railways at various times were obliged to practise double-heading as a matter of regular policy. The American coal-haulers crossing the Alleghenies had to adopt this method. In Britain the Midland Railway had a 'small-engine policy' which meant that double-heading was normal, while the proud London & North Western at one time provided its crack passenger trains with two locomotives because its locomotives were so unpredictable. Stalinist Russia was also a double-heading territory, because the government did not provide the means to lay track capable of bearing heavy tractive power. A similar situation exists in China, where traffic in the final decades of the 20th century was growing faster than railway investment.

To produce a more powerful locomotive, designers had to find a way of combining greater boiler power, bigger cylinders and more

*The big post-war Garratt locomotives of the New South Wales Government Railways in Australia. They had 16 coupled wheels and were used usually mainly around Newcastle.*

adhesion between wheel and rail. Boilers could be enhanced by using a higher boiler pressure, at the expense of heavier maintenance costs, and by providing a greater heating surface. The latter needed a bigger boiler, but because of height restrictions there was a limit to increases of boiler diameter, while a longer boiler meant a longer wheelbase, and therefore difficulty in negotiating curved track. Increasing cylinder volumes also had its limits because there was a width restriction. For example, the 'King' class of Britain's Great Western Railway, with four cylinders side-by-side, was the largest and most powerful steam locomotive that could be accommodated within that railway's width restrictions. Even if it was possible to increase tractive effort, lack of adhesion could mean that the extra power was simply dissipated by slipping wheels. But to increase adhesion required either more weight on the coupled wheels, or a greater number of coupled wheels. The first solution was limited by the strength of the track, and the second, again, by the need for a short wheelbase.

Locomotive designers thought up several ways to overcome this dilemma. The Fairlie locomotive, basically two locomotives back-to-back running on powered trucks, has already been mentioned, and had some success on narrow-gauge railways. Fairlie had the right approach, seeing that the key to the problem lay in somehow providing a flexible wheelbase.

*The expensive alternative to flexible-wheelbase locomotives, double-heading with conventional units. These are paired 2-10-2 locomotives of Chinese Railways.*

*The first Garratt design, a narrow-gauge machine built for Tasmania and now preserved in the National Railway Museum at York.*

This would allow more coupled wheels and hence higher adhesion, and a longer total wheelbase that would permit a longer boiler and firebox.

Another solution to the problem for narrow-gauge railways was the Saxon-Meyer type. Like the Fairlie, this was a machine with two power trucks. However, there was a single boiler, so above the frames this locomotive resembled a conventional tank locomotive. The power bogies were at the two ends, and their cylinders, back-to-back, were in the middle. Invented by an Alsatian in the 1860s, the type was not popular until improved in the 1890s and used for narrow-gauge lines in eastern Germany. A few are still operating there.

A much more important solution, ultimately, was the Mallet articulated locomotive. Mallet was a Genevan engineer who was interested in compound locomotives, in which steam passes first into one, or two, high-pressure cylinders and then into one, or two, larger low-pressure ones, thereby gaining a considerable economy. Compounding brought several unwanted side effects, and so did the power-truck concept, but Mallet, in devising his articulated locomotive, believed that he had killed two birds with one stone, making both the flexible-wheelbase and compounding concepts totally viable. In this he was proved right. His first machines were designed for narrow-gauge lines, but over the years the Mallet type became very popular for bigger gauges, especially in the USA.

The weakness of the Fairlie and Meyer types lay in the flexible steampipe joints, which tended to leak. Mallet saw that if he combined compounding with a flexible wheelbase he could pass steam straight from the boiler into the high-pressure cylinders and only then, after it had lost some of its pressure, would it proceed via a flexible joint to the low-pressure cylinders. Thus the weak part of the steam passage would be passed only by low-pressure steam, making it easier to prevent leakage. So that the high-pressure steam passing from the boiler would not need to pass through flexible joints, Mallet

*A Beyer-Garratt locomotive of East African Railway approaches Mombasa.*

A Saxon-Meyer *locomotive at work in what was at the time the German Democratic Republic.
Several such machines still survive on German narrow-gauge lines.*

*A Garratt locomotive in South Africa, one of several variations used there through most of the 20th century.*

had only the forward, low-pressure, power unit attached by pivot. The boiler and the high-pressure cylinders were on the same, rigid, frame. With only the forward unit pivoted there was still a flexible wheelbase, because each part could swing in relation to the other.

After a small Mallet prototype was exhibited in action at the Paris Exhibition of 1889, several narrow-gauge railways ordered similar units, of the 0-4-4-0 wheel arrangement (that is, running

on two 4-wheel powered trucks). They were a great success, and builders in Switzerland and Germany built larger, tender, versions of the concept.

Then, in 1904, the Baltimore & Ohio RR ordered a Mallet 0-6-6-0 from the American Locomotive Company for use on a standard-gauge incline in the Alleghenies. After this the Mallet type was widely adopted in the USA for mainline use, where great power was required.

It was not long before the Virginian Railway bought enormous 2-10-10-2 units with low-pressure cylinders no less than 4ft (1220mm) in diameter. This was about as large as was possible; any further increase in power had to come from reversing Mallet's original concept by abandoning the compound principle. That is, extra power was obtained by having all four cylinders working on high-pressure steam. By this time greater finesse had been achieved in designing, manufacturing and maintaining flexible steampipe joints.

Americans also modified the original Mallet concept by improving the suspension of the forward, pivoting, power truck. Hitherto this had been loosely fixed, which meant that Mallet locomotives were roughriding except at slow speeds. The Union Pacific RR succeeded in designing a firmer form of articulation and this, when combined with unpowered four-wheel leading and rear supporting trucks, enabled higher speeds to be reached safely. The UP's Challenger 4-6-6-4 could run at 80mph (129kph), and its successor the Big Boy 4-8-8-4 was also speedy.

Apart from European narrow-gauge railways, not many lines outside the USA used the Mallet type. They did not have a need for such powerful machines. There was a need, however, for designs more powerful than conventional locomotives yet capable of operating on light and curving track. This need was especially evident in developing colonial territories, and it was therefore apt, and perhaps to be expected, that the British Empire produced such a machine, the Garratt.

*Mallet's original concept, a compound articulated tank locomotive for narrow-gauge lines in difficult terrain.*

*A Heisler locomotive on exhibition in the Pennsylvania State Railroad Museum.*

*One of the latest Shay locomotives to operate regularly was this unit used in Bolivia for a heavily-graded line in La Paz.*

Herbert Garratt's patented idea was for a locomotive with two powered, pivoted, units placed well apart, with a single boiler slung between them rather than over them. Essentially, a Garratt locomotive could be produced using the frames, wheels and cylinders of two conventional locomotives and the boiler of one. Because there was nothing beneath the boiler it could be low slung and therefore of wide diameter, and there was very good air access to the fire. The leading engine unit carried the water tank and the rear unit the coal; until these were depleted, they provided extra adhesion weight. The large number of coupled axles meant that adhesive weight was high but axle weight was low. Moreover, this weight was distributed over a very great length of track; in colonial territories where there were no great bridges the weight of a locomotive would never be concentrated on one span. There was no serious overhang problem on curves, as there was with the Mallet.

Offering the tractive effort of two locomotives on a normal axle load was the merit of the Garratt. It still had the problem of flexible steam joints, and good maintenance was therefore essential. The type was launched when Beyer, Peacock adopted the concept to fulfil a difficult Tasmanian narrow-gauge contract. The two locomotives that resulted performed so well that in the decade before 1914 orders poured in, at first from narrow-gauge lines and then from others. Beyer, Peacock became the sole producer, except when other companies were licensed to build the type. South and East Africa were the largest markets, but some were sold to Australia, India and elsewhere. The Algerian Railways had some fine specimens, and Spanish National Railways bought some with large wheels for passenger service over curved, hilly, main lines. The biggest Garratts were a class of 4-8-4 + 4-8-4 units sold to the New South Wales Government Railways in the 1950s, and a 5ft (1524mm) gauge 4-8-2 + 2-8-4 sold to the USSR in 1932. In the late 1990s the type was still operated in Zimbabwe and by a number of industrial lines in southern Africa.

The Garratt was never sold in the USA, however, because the Mallet type seemed good enough for heavy haulage, and Americans had developed their own patents for lighter flexible-wheelbase locomotives.

The most widespread of these was the Shay locomotive. The first Shay was put together in the backyard of its inventor in the 1870s, but later units were built under licence by the nearby Lima Machine Works in Ohio. What Shay had been trying to create was a steam locomotive

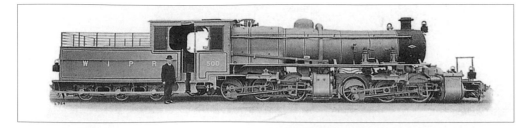

*A builder's picture showing a Scottish-built Mallet delivered to an Indian railway.*

*A one-off Garratt locomotive built for pusher service on the London & North Eastern Railway.*

*A Norfolk & Western RR compound Mallet locomotive at work in the 1950s.*

*The Chesapeake & Ohio RR's final Mallet type. This had a massive 6-wheel rear carrying truck to support the large firebox.*

that could work on forestry lines whose tracks were wooden, sharply-curved and usually portable. Hauling logs down these primitive railways with horse traction was inefficient, not least because horses were constantly being killed in runaway accidents. Shay noted that the flatcars he used did no damage to the track, and sought ways of designing a steam machine that would have suspension resembling that of a flatcar. In essence, he mounted his boiler on what was virtually a flatcar running on two four-wheel trucks. At one side of the boiler he put vertical cylinders whose pistons turned a crankshaft which was coupled by universal joints to horizontal rotating shafts (line shafts) that ran parallel to the wheels on one side (the right, as it happened). These rotating shafts turned bevel gears that worked on the wheels. The supporting trucks were thereby powered, and were relatively free to turn in conformity with the track's curves. The two trucks were some way apart, thereby spreading the locomotive's weight. Because all the mechanism was on the right-hand side, the boiler was fitted off-centre to balance the unit.

Production of Shay units reached a peak of 217 in 1907. The last was built in 1945. Three

*Mallets with 6-wheel power trucks were most favoured up to about 1930. This 2-6-6-2 class was built for Mexican National Railways by Baldwin in 1911.*

cylinders had by then become the norm, and big models had been designed; the days of wooden rails were long past. The 1945 unit weighed as much as 150 short tons, whereas the popular type in the 1880s had been a mere six tons. Some were built with three power trucks, the additional truck being placed beneath the tender. Some of the larger models were bought by mainline railroads. The Chesapeake & Ohio and the Canadian Pacific were among those companies that bought them to operate difficult colliery branch lines. Some Shay locomotives are still in use in the Philippines, while others operate as tourist attractions in Colorado and elsewhere.

The great success of the Shay locomotive prompted other Americans to produce machines of similar capability. In general these competitors used Shay's basic idea with enough variations to avoid infringing the Shay patents. The Climax locomotive used skew gears, hitherto used mainly for small mechanisms such as watches. Skew gears allowed the rotating line shafts to be off-centre and still permit the gears to mesh. In the Climax, this meant that

*One of the Union Pacific RR's 'Big Boys,' regarded as the biggest steam locomotives ever built.*

*Mallet locomotives at work hauling Virginian coal to tidewater. The Norfolk & Western RR's train has two Mallet locomotives pulling and another, out of the picture, pushing.*

the shafts could cross one another. The Climax locomotive, as it finally developed, had two cylinders, one on each side and inclined, driving a set of spur gears which by means of universal joints and sliding shafts connected with the line shafts of the trucks. Gears could be shifted from high to low.

Another competitor was the Heisler. This had the extreme rear and front axles geared, with coupling rods joining the geared and non-geared wheels of each truck. With the Shay, it was the

wheels, not the axles, that were geared, so this was probably the most distinctive feature of the Heisler. Both the Heisler and the Climax were substantial competitors of the Shay, but never approached the latter's sales. One problem was that they were not obviously superior to the Shay; another was that their designers did not have good relationships with the manufacturers.

Shay locomotives were sold mainly in the Americas, but odd units appeared elsewhere in the world. It is not true that they were not seen

in Britain; there was at least one, working for a company at Bilston in the Black Country. Sales in Australia were hampered by the competition of a local creation, the Price locomotive, which apparently combined features of the Shay, Heisler and Climax.

# WAR LOCOMOTIVES

Although some of the world's armies still maintain railway operating battalions, the heyday of the war locomotive was the first half of the 20th century, when both world wars gave birth to locomotives expressly built for war conditions. These locomotives could be divided into those designed to keep supplies moving and those used by an army at the front. The latter were sometimes known as trench engines, and were a feature of the static tactics of the First World War. There was also a sub-category, locomotives designed for use at home and intended to be used by all railways, thereby achieving the economies of standardization.

Locomotives for trench railways were narrow-gauge, usually 2ft (610mm), and ran on portable track that was moved as the front shifted. They pulled trains of munitions and supplies right up to the front line, and also conveyed troops to and from the resting and assembly areas. The Germans began the First World War with specially designed *feldbahn* locomotives, and the French were also well-placed because the trench railway technology was derived from the French Décauville railways, portable narrow-gauge lines originally intended for use on big farms. A French officer developed the 'Pechot' locomotive for these lines. This was essentially

*A surviving US Transportation Corps 2-8-0 shown working on the tourist Keighley & Worth Valley Railway in Yorkshire.*

of traction for an obsolete military concept, fixed fortresses.

The British were caught unprepared in 1914. Their War Office had not really believed that trench railways would have much use, and indeed the War Office would have been right if the war had turned out to be a war of movement and manoeuvre, as expected. But it did not, and the British Army had only a few narrow-gauge tank locomotives (of the 4-6-0 type, built in Leeds), so recourse to the Americans seemed the only solution. Baldwin produced almost 500 4-6-0 saddletanks which had good pulling power but were not ideal for light, rough, track; the wheel arrangement made it clumsy in reverse movement. The rival US builder, Alco, did better with a range of 2-6-2 tank locomotives with side tanks. The British liked these, and Baldwin redesigned its 4-6-0 into a 2-6-2, just in time to supply the US Army's needs when it entered the war in 1917. Perhaps the most impressive achievement was that of the Austrians. Anticipating trouble on the frontier in the Dolomites, and realizing that the terrain was unsuited for standard-gauge lines, the Austrians had preferred to build 2ft 6in (760mm) gauge lines for commercial use in this region, knowing that this would simplify integration with military narrow-gauge lines that would be built in wartime. For these lines they introduced big Mallet articulated tank locomotives, providing haulage power unmatched by any other of the belligerent armies.

*An 'Austerity' saddle tank locomotive serving on the Longmoor Military Railway in Britain. This line, now closed, trained railway troops.*

*A German Kriegslok on Polish Railways, which operated the type into the 1990s.*

Keeping a whole army supplied in war conditions was considered to be beyond the means of normal commercial railways, so on both the Eastern and Western fronts in the First World War army staff took over the railway lines between the main supply depots (or ports, in the case of the Americans and British in France) and the military concentration areas behind the front lines. Foreseeing a locomotive shortage, the French placed orders with British builders for an existing French 2-8-0 design. To provide traction for supply trains between Channel ports and the front, the British railway companies contributed some of their own locomotives. Most successful of these were the 'Dean' 0-6-0 engines loaned by the Great Western Railway, and that company also sent some brand-new 2-6-0 units. However, the home railways were busy with war traffic, and could hardly spare locomotives, so the War Office chose what it considered to be the best existing British freight locomotive design, and ordered hundreds of units for use by its Railway Operating Division (ROD). The choice for the ROD fell on a 2-8-0 designed and used by the Great Central Railway, an outside-cylinder type, fairly rugged, and with a free-steaming boiler. These machines put in good service. After the war they were sold off cheaply, some to the British railway companies, with whom they were known as 'RODs', while others went as far afield as China. In New South Wales they operated on colliery lines until the 1970s.

For its long supply route across France, from the Atlantic ports to the Western Front, the US Army relied heavily on a standard 2-8-0 that became known as the 'Pershing' type. This performed well, the design being a blend of best US practice, and examples continued to work for French railways over several decades.

The US government took the American railroads under its control during the First World War, on the grounds that the different companies would not, or could not, work together for the common cause. It prescribed standard locomotive designs that were to be supplied to all companies, thereby easing production and spare-parts provision. Known as United States Railroad Administration (USRA) designs, they consisted of 12 different types. In retrospect, and as some argued at the time, it would have been better to have concentrated on one type, a general-purpose 2-8-2. In any case, by the time the first USRA locomotives were coming

*Many of the US Army's 2-8-2 locomotives found peacetime use after World War 2. This is one of the class at work in India.*

*After World War 2 redundant 'Austerity' 2-8-0s await disposal at a dump in Britain, together with a requisitioned tank locomotive.*

off the production lines the war was over. Most were built after the war, and some, the most successful, formed the basis of commercial designs built between the wars.

The most popular was the light 2-8-2, of which over 600 were built under the programme.

Next came the six-wheel switcher (255) and the heavy 2-8-2 (233). The heavy switcher (175), an eight-wheeler, was perhaps the most successful in design terms, because it formed the basis for many subsequent variations built in peacetime. The light 4-6-2 was also copied between the

wars, even though only about 80 were built under the USRA programme. The Mallet 2-6-6-2 was a capable design, but few railroads needed it, while the heavy and light 2-10-2 designs, while liked by those railroads that ordered them, were really of an obsolete concept (the ten coupled wheels needed long and heavy coupling rods whose pounding up-and-down loosened the rivets and hammered the track). The 2-8-8-2 Mallet was a good design, and influenced the design of Mallets ordered later; The Norfolk & Western RR's large Mallets owed much to this wartime design.

A smaller-scale repetition of the USRA occurred in the Second World War, although not in the USA. In Britain the four railway companies and their workshops were required to build one 2-8-0 type, that of the LMS Railway, which was judged to be the best design available. Hundreds of these 'Stanier 2-8-0s' were built, some being sent for service in the Middle East.

However, what was a good design in peacetime was not necessarily the best in wartime. War conditions required a locomotive that was reliable, could be kept in service by inexperienced fitters, could be built with the participation of unskilled workers, and economised in metal, both steel and rarer metals like copper and brass (Reichsmarshal Hermann Goering once suggested that locomotives might be made of concrete; a good way of easing Nazi Germany's metal shortage but unlikely to improve the transport situation).

*One of the World War 1 British ROD 2-8-0 locomotives. This unit survived into British Railways ownership.*

It was the Germans who built the ultimate war-service locomotive, which was, and is, known as the *Kriegslok* ('war locomotive'). This design began as a peacetime standard light 2-10-0, the Class 50. As the war progressed, and in particular as the Nazi domain expanded so that supply routes became longer and occupied territories needed better rail transport, more and more of these locomotives were built by the various German locomotive companies. In the course of time the design was modified and became Class 52. Construction was made simpler so that it could be built by foreign prisoners (including the unfortunates used as slave labour). Whereas the 50 Class design consisted of about 6,000 separate components, with the 52 Class 1,000 components were eliminated and another 3,000 simplified. Stamping and welding was preferred to casting and rivetting. Lower-grade metals were employed wherever possible; Class 50 needed seven tonnes of copper, but Class 52 made do with just 128lb (58kg). Because, in occupied territories like Russia, German freight trains could be delayed for days, some of these engines had large totally-enclosed cabs with bunks. Others had tenders with backward-facing lookout cupolas. More than 6,000 units of Class 52 were built during 1942-45, and 3,000 of the preceding Class 50. A larger version of the Class 52, Class 42, also appeared in smaller numbers. In the immediate post-war years these locomotives were working for most railways in central and eastern Europe, and lasted to the end of steam itself in the 1980s. Dozens survive as museum pieces or as operating traction for tourist trains.

In Britain it was decided to supplement the Stanier 2-8-0 with a design more suited to war conditions. In many ways the 'Austerity' 2-8-0 resembled its predecessor, at least in dimensions, but it looked very different. To save asbestos the boiler lagging was eliminated, the outer boiler casing merely enclosing an air jacket. This jacket was of greater diameter than the smokebox, which made the latter look narrower than the boiler behind it, which was aesthetically unfortunate. The chimney, too, was not beautiful, being neither a simple stovepipe nor a shaped flowerpot, but something in between. But, aesthetics apart, these were good and reliable locomotives. Never quite as popular as the *kriegsloks*, they nevertheless performed well on continental European railways. In addition, 150 units of a 2-10-0 version were built, and these, together with many of the 935 2-8-0 units, served on British railways during and after the war. The purpose

*This design was selected as the standard German war-service yard locomotive, but very few were built.*

of the extra driving axle was not so much to improve adhesion as to reduce the axleload, from 15.6 tonnes in the case of the 2-8-0 to 13.5 tonnes for the 2-10-0. The success of this 2-10-0 encouraged its designer, Riddles, to choose the same wheel arrangement for British Railways after the war.

As with trench locomotives in the First World War, the US war designs benefited from experience with British orders in the years before

*One of the US-built World War 1 so-called trench locomotives, now refurbished and working on the Festiniog Railway in Wales.*

*Dean 0-6-0 locomotives of the Great Western Railway, still in their War Department markings, await disposal after World War 2.*

the USA entered the war. Soon after the fall of France the British authorities were seeking war-service locomotives from the USA, to be supplied under the Lend-Lease agreement. The British, perhaps mindful of the previous war, initially requested 2-8-0 locomotives, but were persuaded to opt for a 2-8-2. The American Army engineers found an ideal prototype in a light 2-8-2 that had been supplied by Baldwin in 1924 to a small coal-hauling line, the

Montana, Wyoming & Southern RR. This design was modified slightly; in particular the wheel diameter was increased from 56in (1420mm) to 60in (1520mm) so that the coupling rods would be clear of certain track fittings in the Middle East. When production started, some of the first batches were sent to Allied-occupied Iran to help keep Russia supplied. One shipload was lost at sea. This design was one of the most successful ever built. About 800 units were built,

by eight US and Canadian builders. Long after the war was over a further batch was ordered by the New South Wales Government Railways. Many war-built units operated for several decades in the Indian sub-continent. There, a meter-gauge variant, known as 'MacArthurs', was also at work.

The US Army Corps of Engineers did also design a war-service 2-8-0, which saw service in Britain before being sent across the Channel to support US forces advancing through western Europe. This design was, perhaps, less successful than the 'MacArthur'. Using grease lubrication in place of oil, it tended to run hot. Moreover, because the grease had to be worked up to a warm temperature before it could flow, the British crews of these locomotives often reported warm bearings even when there was nothing wrong. In Britain, a number of these engines suffered boiler fractures or explosions when the top of the firebox became uncovered by the water. Some believed this was because the water-gauge was unfamiliar to British crews, while others believed that the type had a design fault leading to this potentially catastrophic outcome. But the type worked on regardless, many units being operated by post-war railways. Some went to India, some to Russia, and others elsewhere.

The US Army also operated diesel locomotives. Some of these were diesel-electric road-switchers, and many railwaymen, both American and otherwise, had their first experience of what diesels could do while working with these units. There were also diesel switchers, and the military's Whitcomb switcher became something of a classic locomotive design. Another classic diesel design, the

*Introduced in 1940 for domestic service by Britain's Southern Railway, the stark Q1 class was designed with metal economy in mind.*

English Electric 0-6-0, also went to war when units that had been ordered earlier by the London Midland & Scottish Railway were taken over by the War Department. They did very well overseas, and few of them returned to Britain.

For yard work, Britain, Germany and the USA all had their war designs. The British contribution was the 'Austerity' 0-6-0 saddletank with inside cylinders, which represented the best of British practice. Hundreds were built for the War Department and many were later sold off to industry, including notably the National Coal Board. Later, their simplicity and reliabiity found them employment on tourist railways.

The German army ordered units of an existing six-wheel tank engine from French builders, but these do not appear to have been delivered before the war ended, and they were commandeered by French railways. In the USA three builders supplied the US Army Transportation Corps with a six-wheel side-tank locomotive. Here again, the best of existing practice was blended into one locomotive design. They were successful enough to find buyers after the war. In Britain, the Southern Railway acquired some for dock shunting, and

it is not hard to find features of this class in the last steam locomotive designed by the Great Western Railway, the 1500 class. A handful of these engines still existed in former Yugoslavia in the late 1990s, and others were preserved.

*An 'Austerity' tank locomotive finds post-war employment on a tourist railway in the Lake District.*

*One of the relatively few British War Department 'Austerity' 2-10-0 locomotives. This example has been preserved.*

# RACK RAILWAYS

During the 1860s, railway engineers cast their eyes towards the mountain-tops. Sylvester Marsh, in the United States, and a Swiss, Niklaus Riggenbach, both designed in the course of this decade very similar rack railways to overcome steep gradients. Marsh opened the initial part of a rack line up Mount Washington, New Hampshire, in 1868; Riggenbach's line up Mount Rigi suffered delays, but came into operation in 1871. The locomotives for these rack railways had pistons driving a pinion-wheel. The teeth of the pinion-wheel engaged with a steel-runged ladder laid flat between the track rails. Riggenbach's system differed from Marsh's principally in the closer fit between the rungs and the locomotive's cogs. These rungs, however, were apt to break, and other Swiss engineers sought improvements. The Pilatus Railway used the Locher rack, where the rack rail is laid flat and has teeth along each edge. In the Abt system, probably the most successful, there is an upright blade with teeth machined into it. There are often two blades side by side, with their rack teeth staggered so that there is a tooth every 60cm (26in). This is the system used by the Snowdon Mountain Railway in North Wales. With the Abt system, too, came a more careful machining of the cog wheels to secure a closer fit with the rack teeth, thereby reducing vibration, noise, and wear. Emil Strub decided that this system was too complicated. His rack rail was broader, with pinion and rail teeth still machined to fit together, and it was easier to lay because it was bolted directly on to the cross-ties.

Some railway lines in mountainous areas have rack only on the most difficult sections. This is not only to save expense but also recognizes that speeds on rack railways are limited. For such lines locomotives with four cylinders were sometimes built, with one pair of cylinders driving the normal wheels and the other cylinders driving the cog wheels.

*Austria's Puchberg mountain railway. The rack can be discerned between the rails.*

*The rack section of a Roumanian railway. The locomotive is rather large, being intended for operating on flat sections as well.*

*On Wales's rack railway: the Snowdon Mountain Railway in action.*

*On the Manitou & Pike's Peak Railway in Colorado, opened in 1891 and using the Abt cog system.*

*A Swiss-built rack locomotove of the Nilagiri Railway in India. The upper (low-pressure) cylinders drive the rack wheels, which lie between the second and third axles.*

# COMPOUND LOCOMOTIVES

As we have already seen, steam expands as it cools in locomotive cylinders. It can be expanded to give up energy beyond the point possible in a single cylinder.

In 1851 John Nicholson of the Eastern Counties Railway altered a two-cylinder locomotive to his 'continuous expansion' system. Part of the steam exhausted from one cylinder was introduced together with live steam into the second cylinder. The proportions were all wrong and the experiment was abandoned, but not before some fuel saving had been noted.

After Nicholson's attempt, various other inventors took out patents for compound locomotives proper, in which one or two cylinders took live steam from the boiler, their exhausts providing the only supply to one or two other cylinders. The cylinders involved are differentiated by being described as either high- or low-pressure.

In 1867 an American, John Lay, took out a patent for a compound locomotive, and in the following year Erie Railroad No. 122 was altered to compound working. No. 122 was an ordinary American-type 4-4-0 that had originally been built in 1851. It was converted to a tandem compound; that is, the cylinders on each side

were taken off and each replaced by two cylinders, one ahead of the other, both served by the same piston rod and valve spindle. On each side, the high-pressure cylinder was in front with the low-pressure cylinder behind. Later experience showed that cylinder volumes should be in a ratio of a little over one to two. In

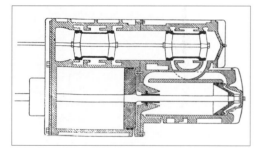

*The Erie No 122, altered to tandem compound in 1868. Tandem cylinders for high and low pressure using a common piston rod are shown.*

*One of the last British 3-cylinder compound locomotives: Merlin of the Great Northern Railway (Ireland), built in 1932.*

*London & North Western Railway, 1882. Webb three-cylinder compound locomotive, Compound. A 2-2-2-0 with uncoupled driving axles.*

*Baltimore & Ohio Railroad, 1904. The first Mallet compound in service in North America.*

*Austrian State Railway, 1906. Two-cylinder Golsdorf compound of a design dating from 1901. Transferred to the Italian State Railways, it later changed its number.*

the case of No. 122, the low-pressure volume was too great, with the result that the steam was expanded to too low a pressure and there was little or no blast up the chimney. Theodore Williamson, the fireman, attested that he could not get the locomotive to steam: a locomotive that cannot produce steam is by any standard a failure.

Anatole Mallet, a Swiss working in France, finally got the compound locomotive right in 1876 with a little 2-4-0 tank locomotive which started work on the Bayonne-Biarritz Railway. It was arranged as a two-cylinder compound, with the high-pressure cylinder on one side and the

low-pressure cylinder on the other. This locomotive worked and showed good fuel saving. The compound was on its way.

As a two-cylinder compound, the Bayonne-Biarritz engine had a starting valve which admitted boiler steam into the low-pressure cylinder should the high-pressure piston be in the wrong position in the cylinder to make a start. Later on, the design of the starting valve (as well as the number of cylinders, of course) usually distinguished the various types of compound locomotive that were built.

Two others took up Mallet's work. August von Borries started to build two-cylinder compound

locomotives for the Royal Prussian State Railway in 1880, and his compound system was used widely by many railways. Francis Webb of the London and North Western Railway in England in 1882 favored three-cylinder compounds. Two small outside high-pressure cylinders both exhausted into a single low-pressure cylinder inside the frames.

Webb's ideas were picked up for France by Alfred de Glehn, an Englishman working for the French engineering company Société Alsacienne and Gaston du Bousquet of the French Northern Railway. The first de Glehn/du Bousquet compound was built for the Northern Railway in 1885. This was a 2-4-0 (or, strictly speaking, a 2-2-2-0, as the driving wheels were uncoupled at first), later rebuilt as a 4-4-0. De Glehn reversed Webb's cylinder arrangements so that he had two high-pressure cylinders inside and two low-pressure cylinders outside.

The names of other engineers became attached to compound locomotive types. Among them were Gölsdorf (two-cylinder), Smith (three-cylinder), and Gölsdorf again and Vauclain (four-cylinder). Samuel Vauclain was chief engineer of The Baldwin Locomotive Works, and his type was used chiefly in the United States. Vauclain compounds had high-pressure and low-pressure cylinders mounted one above the other on each side of the

*(opposite) A German narrow-gauge compound Mallet tank locomotive design introduced in 1897.*

*This 2-6-6-2 compound of the Chesapeake & Ohio RR was built in 1949, to be replaced by diesels just eight years later.*

locomotive. Each pair of cylinders was associated with a common crosshead and coupling-rod to the driving wheels.

Anatole Mallet's name became attached to an articulated locomotive type that was a compound only incidentally. Mallet locomotives have high-pressure cylinders for a set of mainframe driving wheels at the rear. The low-pressure cylinders are at the front, and their driving wheels are carried in a truck swivelling from a point between the high-pressure cylinders. Low-pressure steam had only to flow through an articulated joint to reach the front cylinders.

The first compound Mallet built, dated 1887, was a little 0-4-4-0 narrow-gauge tank locomotive intended for use on industrial railways. The idea was an immediate success. The first standard-gauge Mallet, an 0-6-6-0 tank, was supplied to the Gotthard Railway in Switzerland in 1890. During the 1890s and after, Mallet locomotives, particularly for narrow gauges, poured out of factories in France, Belgium and other countries.

The Mallet compound reached the United States in 1904. In that year the Baltimore and Ohio Railroad put into service an 0-6-6-0 Mallet that was the largest and most powerful

*One of the Norfolk & Western RR's Y6 compound 2-8-8-2 locomotives, introduced in 1936. They had one-piece cast steel frames and roller bearings on all axles. Built for coal haulage, they lasted until 1960.*

*An Austrian Golsdorf 2-8-0 2-cylinder compound of the late 19th century. This particular unit lasted into the 1970s, being employed on a private railway at Graz.*

locomotive in the world. Until the disappearance of the steam locomotive, successive designs of US Mallets could claim this title, culminating in the Union Pacific's 'Big Boy' class, a 345.6 tonne monster built from 1941, and the Chesapeake & Ohio RR's 2-6-6-6, which might have been proved even bigger if it had been properly weighed.

Not all Mallets in the United States were compounds. The four-cylinder simple type was taken up and compounding was dropped. This started in 1912 after not very successful locomotives of the type for Russia in 1902 and became the norm (the 'Big Boy' class mentioned above was a four-cylinder simple). Anatole Mallet himself protested at the omission of compounding, but he was not supported by US railroad men.

# STEAM TURBINE LOCOMOTIVES

Charles Parsons perfected his steam turbine in the 1890s; its first locomotive application was to an Italian industrial shunting 0-4-0 engine in 1907. Two small turbines were mounted outside the front axle and these drove the axle for forward motion. Two similar turbines outside the rear axle served for backward motion. The locomotive can be counted as a success, for it worked for its owners for over 30 years. Large main-line units differently arranged followed, particularly between the wars; some used condensation of steam exhaust for greater turbine efficiency. Other steam-turbine locomotives were turbo-electrics; that is, current was generated on board for direct-current traction motors.

Whatever the type, the steam-turbine locomotive did not catch on, although a few individual designs did run for a number of years, notably in Sweden. A British turbine 4-6-2 that ran for some years was the LMS Railway's No. 6202, which was eventually converted to an orthodox locomotive because its average annual mileage was rather low, thanks to time out of

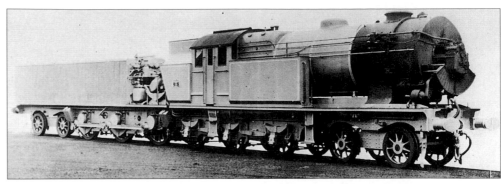

*The Ljungstrom condensing turbine locomotive, which was tried in Britain, but was found wanting*

service for adjustment. The drawback of a simple design like No 6202 was that a separate turbine was required for rearward motion.

Nevertheless, the steam turbine featured among proposals of the 1980s to revive the steam locomotive, in suitable circumstances. One interesting design was for a condensing turbo-electric. Another proposal at that time, not necessarily for a turbine locomotive, was a fluid-

bed firebox, in which powdered coal blown into the firebox was to be held suspended, while burning above the grate, by air-jets from below.

*Decades after steam turbine locomotives came gas turbine propulsion. However, the United Aircraft turbotrain, of which 14 were built in the late 1960s for US and Canadian railroads, was unreliable and short-lived.*

# CONDENSER LOCOMOTIVES

Locomotives that consume their own smoke were sometimes optimistically demanded by local authorities faced with entrepreneurs wishing to build urban, underground, railways. The entrepreneurs themselves realized that the crews of locomotives working underground would require some protection from asphyxiation. In the end, locomotives that condensed their steam appeared, and there was some kind of pretence that such locomotives would be smokeless. The idea was that the steam exhausted from the cylinders, instead of passing out through the chimney, would be piped to the water tanks where, in contact with the cold water, it would condense. This had the added advantage that waste heat would be transferred to the feed water, which would therefore enter the boiler already warmed. This advantage, though, was self-defeating, because the warmer the water became the less steam it could condense.

In London, the partly underground Metropolitan Railway employed these condensing engines, and so did the Great Western, Midland, and Great Northern Railways, whose locomotives regularly worked over the Metropolitan lines. Such locomotives could be recognized by the steam pipes that emerged from both sides of the smokebox and disappeared into the top of the water tanks. They were partly successful in that they did largely avoid excessive steam inside the tunnels, and may have reduced the smoke, but they were not true condensing locomotives.

True condensing locomotives were developed by the German Henschel company. Their purpose was water economy, which was important in some arid countries. Such locomotives were used, therefore, in South Africa and the Soviet Union, and to a lesser extent in South America.

The Henschel system provided a wide steampipe along the side of the locomotive to take exhaust steam back to the tender. The latter was completely transformed, and enlarged so that it could accommodate cooling elements and a pump for the cooling air. Since the steam no longer exhausted through the chimney, a fan had to be provided inside the smokebox to provide draught. This was why condenser locomotives did not puff, but instead emitted a whine that sounded like a jet engine.

These condenser locomotives carried two steam turbines, one for the fan and one for the cooling air, and these added weight and consumed horsepower. One problem was that the returning steam carried oil droplets from the cylinders which eventually found their way into the boiler, which affected the steaming. Another was that it was sometimes difficult to regulate the smokebox fan so that it would provide the correct amount of draught at a given time. Maintenance costs were also high. One bad habit of condenser engines was a tendency to eject fan blades out through the chimney.

In the Soviet Union the condenser locomotive was adopted as a truly revolutionary solution worthy of a revolutionary state. The Communist Party specified that in the late 1930s five-year plan condenser locomotives should be the basic product of the locomotive-building industry. A promising development of diesel-electric traction in Soviet Central Asia was brought to a halt; since the diesel locomotive had been adopted because it did not need water, said the politicians, it was redundant in the Soviet Union, where steam locomotives were being built that could re-use their water supplies. In the end, despite the occasional admonitory imprisonment or execution, Soviet locomotive men did not take kindly to the new locomotives. Sometimes, if the fans were operated too fast in winter, the cooling elements froze up. At other times maintenance problems were so acute that the locomotives were operated as non-condensers. But it was not until after the Second World War, and the advent of renewed dieselization, that this massive campaign was abandoned. However, during the Second World War the Germans used condenser versions of their kriegslok 2-10-0 in Russia. The reason for this was that sabotage and the freezing winter meant that water supplies for locomotives in occupied Russia could not be relied upon.

The South African Railways had rather more success with their Class 24 condenser 4-8-4s, which confidently whined their way across the arid Karroo. But even here the condenser engines were eventually converted to non-condenser function in the 1970s.

*Class 24 locomotives of South African railways, showing their massive condenser tenders.*

# Brakes

George Westinghouse is one of the more familiar railway names. Indeed, the electrical firms that he founded are today making the name familiar in other fields of transport as well as in the world at large. Before Westinghouse, train brakes were for the most part applied by hand. Because their effectiveness was limited, caution had to be exercised in the matter of train speeds, and there was consequently little incentive to design faster or more powerful locomotives.

Westinghouse produced his first straight air-brake in 1869. This was a railway brake that applied a brake-block to the wheel tyre by use of compressed air from a previously filled reservoir. Releasing air from the application cylinder reduced its internal pressure and thereby took off the brake. By 1872 Westinghouse had developed this into an automatic continuous brake that could be applied to wheels down the whole length of a train. 'Automatic', in this instance, refers to the fact that the brake is applied should there be any failure in the equipment or, importantly, any rupture in the train's compressed-air pipe.

In the automatic air-brake, a main air reservoir on the locomotive, replenished as necessary, keeps the train's pipe as well as auxiliary reservoirs on each vehicle charged with compressed air. The driver's brake-valve, when operated, releases air from the brake-pipe, and this drop in pressure causes air from the auxiliary reservoirs to flow into the brake cylinders to apply the brake.

The braking pressure thus exerted is proportional to the drop in pressure in the train's brake-pipe, and this in turn is governed by the length of time the driver keeps his brake-valve open. To release the brake, the driver places his control into the 'normal' position, thereby replenishing the train pipe with compressed air, the rise in pressure releasing air from the brake cylinders and recharging the auxiliary reservoirs. All the operations described are accomplished thanks to a device called a triple valve, placed next to the auxiliary reservoirs and brake cylinders on each vehicle.

In course of time it was found that the drop in air pressure in a train pipe does not occur instantaneously along the full length of a train. Thus it might be that the front of a long train would have its brakes hard on while the rear had no brakes on at all, and the reverse could apply when the brakes were being released. Many devices have been devised to help in these situations, the latest being a cable which carries an electronic signal the length of the train. Variation in the signal will apply the brakes simultaneously on every vehicle, the drop in pressure in the train pipe following up at its leisure.

In Britain until very recently the vacuum brake was preferred. This works like the air-brake, except that atmospheric pressure is set against a vacuum to operate the brake cylinders. In some ways this system is simpler, but it has the ultimate disadvantage that atmospheric pressure is a fixed quantity, and therefore the pressure that can be applied is limited. This became important when heavier and faster trains required more powerful brakes.

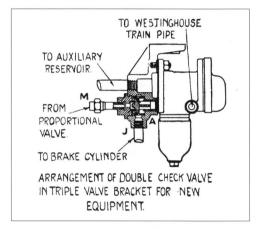

*(above) Triple Valve used on Westinghouse Automatic Brake Gear (below).*

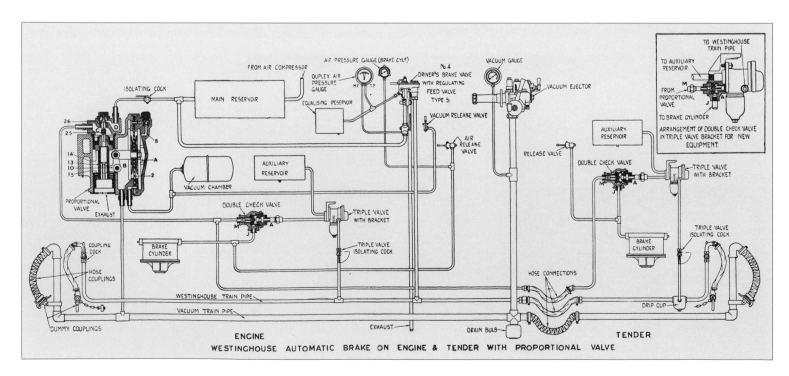

# BOGIES (TRUCKS)

In the United States much attention was given to the guidance of locomotives along the track. The truck, or bogie, was in widespread use, and from 1850 or so was improved, with an increased wheelbase and with better frames. For freight locomotives, Levi Bissell invented his single-axle leading truck in 1857. Guidance was given by an arm pivoted on the locomotive frames and running from there to the truck's rear. Should the truck swing to one side on this arm, it had to mount up a sloped slide. It tended therefore to slide back down again as soon as it could, thereby centring itself.

In Great Britain, W. Bridges Adams, who had a works for building small locomotives in the London suburb of Bow, designed leading or trailing radial axleboxes in 1863. The axleboxes were placed in vertical slides on each side, the slides angled forward in the frames. The angles were judged nicely to correspond with the radius of an arm pivoted on the locomotive's frame and carrying the axle. On rounding a curve, the axleboxes slid out on one side and slid in on the other, thus turning the axle into the curve.

After some improvements were made by Francis Webb of the London and North Western Railway, these radial axleboxes became known as the Adams-Webb type, and were used on many railways. The Hungarian State Railways,

*William Adams' design for the long wheelbase bogie ensured stability and room for the fitting of brake gear.*

for example, had about 2,350 locomotives fitted with Adams-Webb radial axleboxes built between 1905 and 1959.

Close to W. Bridges Adams' locomotive works at Bow was the Bow locomotive works of the North London Railway. The locomotive superintendent there, William Adams, improved the four-wheel truck. On a 4-4-0 tank locomotive of 1865 the truck not only had a long wheelbase but was also given some lateral movement at the bogie-pin. The truck revolved on its pin as before, but it could also follow a curve by moving sideways on the pin.

Within a year Adams had added centring springs for the truck's lateral movement, and the modern steam-locomotive truck for smooth running through curves had been evolved. This truck was widely adopted, contributing greatly, for example, to the American-type 4-4-0 design in the United States.

*The long pivoted arm of the leading truck can be discerned in this picture of an Isle of Man Railway locomotive.*

# LOCOMOTIVE WHEELS

As in much else, early locomotive wheels followed horse-carriage practice. The wheel centres were spoked, and a replaceable metal tyre endured the wear and stress at the contact area of wheel and running surface. When metal (first iron, and later steel) began to be used for the wheel centres, the principle of removable tyres was retained. Tyres were attached by shrinkage; the tyre was heated, placed around the centre, and shrank tight as it cooled. Various retaining pins or notches were patented from time to time. This process, however, created stresses that could lead to cracking and other weaknesses, and this became a problem with increasing speeds and weights. Because the coupled wheels also carried the balance weights needed to counter the thrusts of the mechanism, considerable strength was required to contain the momentum of those weights.

The area of the wheel actually in contact with the rail was exceedingly small, about the size of a present-day penny, so an enormous weight was concentrated on it. Those segments of the rim that were between the spokes were points of potential weakness, as they were unsupported against blows produced by track irregularities and inadequate springing. Usually a failure was merely a case of the rim becoming distorted, but there were some more serious occurrences, too. The number of spokes in the wheel had to be calculated, balancing the weight of the extra spokes against the additional strength gained. There were some cases of locomotive classes being re-wheeled when experience, or changing conditions, rendered the initial decision invalid.

As locomotives became heavier and speeds higher, wheel stresses naturally increased. Moreover, wheels rotated faster because they tended to become smaller over the decades. Steam locomotive designers had always had to compromise on wheel diameter. A small diameter gave greater pulling power, but a large wheel rotated more slowly at a given speed. A fast locomotive tended to have large wheels so that the whole mechanism, including its reciprocating parts, would move slower; this was necessary because lubricants of that time could not cope with very fast-moving sliding surfaces. In time, however, coupled wheels could be reduced in size, giving extra tractive effort. In the mid-19th century an 8ft (2309mm) driving wheel was needed for say, 60mph (96km/h), whereas by the end of the steam age a 6ft (1800mm) or smaller wheel was adequate. The Norfolk and Western RR's fast Northern locomotives, reputed to exceed 100mph

*The wood-cenre wheel, as used on Stephenson's Rocket.*

*A British (Southern Railway) Pacific's BFB wheels.*

(160kph) on occasion, needed only 5ft 6in (1676mm) wheels, and in Britain 6ft 2in (1204mm) wheels were adequate for fast trains, provided the balancing and lubrication arrangements were satisfactory.

It began to be felt that the spoked wheel was becoming obsolete for fast locomotives, and various types of spokeless wheel began to appear. These were generally called disc or box-form wheels, and there were three major types:

*Boxpok coupled wheels as fitted to a 2-10-2 freight locomotive.*

the Boxpok, Scullin, and BFB. They consisted of two cast-steel discs fitted back-to-back, secured to each other by the central boss and the rim. Thus the wheel centre itself was hollow, and therefore light. Extra lightness could be gained by providing holes in the discs at the time of casting. These apertures, apart from reducing weight, also provided points at which balancing weights could be fitted by the locomotive builder. Of these three, the Boxpok gained most favor, at first in the United States and subsequently in some other countries. The BFB (so-called because it was devised by O. V. Bulleid of the Southern Railway and the British steel company Firth-Brown) was similar to the Boxpok but perhaps more complex. It was fitted to the Pacific locomotives of the Southern Railway. The Scullin, an American inter-war design, was recognisible because its apertures consisted of just four or five large holes, whereas the Boxpok had a large number of pear-shaped apertures that preserved a resemblance to conventional spoked wheels. When the New York Central Railroad introduced its new Hudsons on the eve of the Second World War, it specified 25 of them with Boxpok and 25 with Scullin wheels, and did not find much difference between them.

The 'Merchant Navy' and 'West Country' Pacifics of Britain's Southern Railway were unusual in that they used the new box-form wheels not only for the coupled wheels but for the small supporting wheels as well. For most of the steam age the smaller wheels were spoked or, later, of monobloc design (that is, disc-but not box-form).

With the coming of diesel and electric traction, which did not use large driving wheels, new problems arose. One concerned braking. Large locomotive wheels could easily dissipate the heat caused by friction between tyre and brake block, but the smaller wheels of power trucks could not. The wheels would become very hot when the brake was applied, and when it was released the tyre would be rapidly cooled by the airflow, causing thermal stresses that eventually could lead to tyre failure. A first attempt to solve this problem was the combination of improved steels with the use of monobloc wheels. The latter were one-piece; there was no tyre to fail, the flange and tread being forged and machined on the rim of the disc. This solution was not as good as was initially believed, but the tyreless wheel became accepted, although in Britain the very numerous Class 47 diesel locomotive does have tyred wheels, of the so-called 'resilient' type. In the meantime, very-high-speed trains used disc brakes, in which the heat produced by braking is dissipated independently of the wheels.

The resilient wheel has a metal centre encircled by a hard rubber layer which itself is encircled by the steel tyre. Its advantage is that it smooths out some of the impacts imparted at the wheel/rail interface. In other words, it acts as a shock-absorber to supplement the vehicle's spring suspension. As such it can improve the riding qualities of passenger vehicles in high-speed trains. In Britain and elsewhere, where track is good and high-speed trains have good suspension anyway, it was not used for this purpose. When it was applied in Britain to a class of electric locomotives (class 86/2) whose suspension was not good, it was to limit the damage done by the locomotives to the track, rather than the other way round.

The German DB fitted its ICE high-speed trains with resilient wheels, but then suffered the lethal Enschede accident in 1998, which appeared to have been caused by tyre failure. The theory that when high-speed trains brake there can be momentary wheel-slide, generating enormous heat at the rail/wheel interface and thereby changing the physical properties of the steel, may or may not be correct, but after this accident the DB immediately reverted to monobloc wheels for its high-speed trains.

The powered trucks beneath electric and diesel locomotives have faced new design requirements as train speeds have increased. A six-wheel powered truck, or bogie, can create considerable friction, and wear, when traversing curves at speed. The leading pair of wheels, trying to move in a straight line, force the leading outside wheel to bear uncomfortably on the outside curved rail. In steam days some alleviation of this problem was obtained by having a pair or more of flangeless wheels in the coupled wheelbase. With power trucks, an analogous effect can be obtained by allowing the leading and trailing axles to rotate. This is a very complex design problem, but it creates what in effect is a steered truck which not only reduces rail wear but also reduces the power needed to move the locomotive around curves. General Motors introduced such a truck for its SD60 and subsequent locomotive types. The Swedish tilting train has soft suspension between the truck frames and the axleboxes, which allows an axle, under pressure on a curve, to adopt a more comfortable angle of attack.

*An unusual wheel with I-section spokes, as used in Australia on the J class 2-8-0s of Victorian Railways.*

*(Opposite) A fine example of 19th century spoked wheels. the locomotive is a 2-4-2 of the Paris-Orleans Railway.*

*A US-style 2-8-4 of Soviet Railways: because of spare parts problems this particular unit has mixed spoked and Boxpok wheels.*

# CHIMNEYS AND BLASTPIPES

The steam locomotive chimney has two functions, exhaust and draught. In the very first locomotives exhaust was the only function, but it was soon realized that the exhaust steam from the cylinders could be passed up through the chimney in the form of a jet. This entrained the exhaust gases from the firebox, hurrying them along and thereby creating a draught for the fire. This was the purpose of the blastpipe, and was a fundamental component of the steaming process. It had the substantial virtue that it was self-regulating: the harder the locomotive worked, the more steam was used, and the more steam was used the stronger was the draught.

But it was not quite that simple. Too strong a draught could pull unburned particles of fuel out of the fire, creating hot sparks and lowering efficiency. So engineers usually erred on the side of caution, and designed the exhaust

*A late design of smoke deflector, as fitted to post-war Polish locomotives.*

*The long and short of it on French Railways. the chimney on the right has a triple exhaust and belongs to the one-off 4-8-4 No. 242A-1.*

The double chimney of the Chesapeake & Ohio RR's 'Allegheny' 2-6-6-6 class.

A Prussian 4-6-0 with the 2-part chimney common on German railways.

bolted on, making the chimney taller. Should a locomotive be required to work on lines with reduced clearances, the height could be reduced by removing this extension. Many German locomotives had this feature, and it was believed that its origin was the desire to have locomotives that could work on French railways, with their lower height clearance, in wartime.

Whereas, on the mechanical side, the relationships between wheels, cylinders and valves were fairly clear-cut, the steam-raising side of locomotive design was more speculative and unpredictable. Whether a boiler would steam well was uncertain until it was actually

arrangements to produce somewhat less than the theoretical maximum draught.

The height of the chimney was also a factor in draughting, especially when a locomotive was at rest or under easy steam. The tall chimneys of the early locomotives had a definite purpose, and when boilers became bigger, so that there was space only for a short chimney, draught was affected. In the popular mind tall chimneys were old-fashioned, and there were cases of locomotives being designed with chimneys shorter than the optimum possible, simply because of this public image consideration. There were also cases when a two-piece chimney was specified. This had an upper part

A Lemaitre chimney of a Southern Railway 'King Arthur' type 4-6-0.

*(Opposite) The Kylchap double chimney of a French Pacific locomotive.*

*The Giesl exhaust fitted to an Austrian rack locomotive.*

tried in daily service. It was soon realized that draughting was one of the most important factors, and dozens of patents were granted for devices optimistically claiming to improve boiler performance. A handful of these ideas did bring results, though not always sufficiently marked to justify their expense.

The conventional blastpipe provides a vertically-facing nozzle beneath the chimney and sends a jet of used steam up and out of the chimney, dragging along the exhaust gases emerging from the boiler tubes. The faster the jet, the greater the draught, and the narrower the nozzle, the faster the jet. On some occasions enginemen, coping with badly-steaming designs, would find ways of narrowing the nozzle. Although this practice was strictly against regulations, it sometimes made all the difference.

Unfortunately, the faster the jet, the more likely it was to draw unburned pieces of coal from the firebox and eject them through the chimney. Also, with a narrow nozzle, steam escaping from

*One of the celebrated Great Western 'Castle' class locomotives, as retro-fitted with double chimney.*

*A variety of inter-war chimney styles, from back to front, French, Kylchap, British Kylchap and British conventional single exhaust.*

*Aesthetics versus function. The exhaust reveals that this Canadian Pacific locomotive has in fact only a single chimney.*

the cylinders was constricted, causing back-pressure.

The ideal blast is strong, slow and steady, and by the 1930s it was realized that this might be achieved by increasing the size rather than the speed of the steam jet. That is, increasing the area of the jet would produce a stronger, but not fiercer, draught. The simplest way of doing this was to have two steam jets in place of the one. So two blastpipes were provided, one behind the other, and each exhausted up a separate chimney, also one behind the other. Usually the two chimneys were enclosed in a single casing, producing the familiar elongated form. This elementary double chimney increased the jet area in contact with the gases by about 50 per cent. A step further was the Lemaitre exhaust, in which the blastpipe had five nozzles, doubling the contact area of the steam. This exhaust was popular on Britain's Southern Railway, and could be recognized by the very large diameter of the chimney.

An even more sophisticated exhaust was the Kylchap. This had two blastpipes, but each nozzle was divided into four circular apertures, so four jets emerged, touching in the middle. Beneath each chimney aperture there was a vertical petticoat arrangement which first split

each group of four jets and then recombined them into a single jet for ejection through the chimney. This device worked exceptionally well, providing a good steady draught with the exhaust steam drifting lazily out of the chimney, its energy used up. This laziness caused difficulties for the enginemen, whose vision was hampered by the drifting steam. That is why most Kylchap-fitted locomotives (indeed most multi-blastpipe locomotives) had wind-deflector plates fitted alongside their smokeboxes if they were not already streamlined. The final development of the Kylchap exhaust was the triple chimney fitted to the French 4-8-4 prototype 242A-1.

However, the Kylchap was not the last word. At the very end of the steam age the Giesl exhaust was invented, or rather reached its final stage of research and development. In this, the conventional chimney-and-blastpipe combination is replaced by a prefabricated one-piece device. This has an oblong nozzle casting, providing seven steam jets that emerge in a fan shape which, at the top of the smokebox, exactly fills the long outlet that externally takes the form of an elongated straight-sided chimney. Care has to be taken with the proportions, but efficiencies as much as double those of the Kylchap were obtained. In practice this meant that inferior coal was no problem, in contrast to conventionally draughted locomotives. The inventor was appreciated in his own country,

Austria, where by the end of the steam era most of the large locomotives were fitted with his device. East Germany and Czechoslovakia were also big users. British Railways dabbled with the idea but then dropped it, although some locomotives of the East African Railways were fitted with the device. Attempts to sell the device in the United States had bad luck. The first effort was made just as the Great Depression arrived, and the second, which did succeed in persuading the Chesapeake & Ohio RR to fit the device to a yard locomotive, was made just as American railroads were surrendering to the diesel.

*Life after death for a Malayan Railways chimney, serving as a waiting room ashtray.*

# LOCOMOTIVE CABS

Having the locomotive crew standing immediately behind the firebox seemed logical to the Stephensons. The fireman clearly had to be close to the fire-door, and it was easy to bring the simple controls to the back of the engine. This was how the Rocket was laid out, and it set the fashion for the entire steam age, even though there were occasional attempts to place the engine crew elsewhere. One of the disadvantages of the traditional position was that it was the worst possible in terms of forward vision, and subsequent cab design always had to take account of this.

At first there was not the slightest semblance of a cab, just a patch of floor and perhaps a railing. But as train speeds increased, rain, hail and sparks striking the crews' faces became a safety hazard, so in Britain the spectacle plate was introduced in the 1850s. This was merely a vertical forward-facing facade with glass windows.

United States railroads showed more consideration for their crews, and quite well-protected cabs were provided at an early date. Such cabs were more than luxuries, because cold winter winds could stupefy, if not disable, the men on the footplate. In Britain the Stockton & Darlington Railway decided that American-style cabs were a good idea for working over the cold, windswept Pennines. But this was a macho age; other British railway companies did not imitate the idea because they felt that their workers might fall asleep if pampered, and even on the S & D there were enginemen who thought that these better cabs were only for softies.

However, the Midland Railway, afflicted by youths who amused themselves by hurling stones from overbridges at passing locomotive crews, decided there were limits to what its men should endure. It bent back the spectacle plates of its locomotives to provide a degree of overhead protection. The simple roof thus formed was supported by pillars which rattled so loudly that the crews complained. In the end, most British locomotives of the 19th century had the cab that developed from this phase, which was a short bent-over roof without support at the back, and with rudimentary sides.

Later in the century the North Eastern Railway, successor to the S & D, decided to replace these short cabs with capacious American-style ones, but only a handful of British companies followed suit.

Other European railways were less spartan than the British. In mid-century Germany the engineer von Weber (son of the musician) was much concerned with the welfare of locomotive

*Exterior view of the 'comfort cab,' the US development of the Canadian 'safety cab.'*

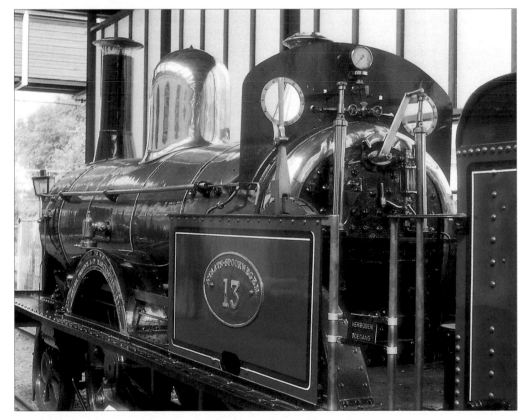

*A Dutch locomotive, built in Britain, and provided with a spectacle plate.*

*A cab-in-front locomotive of the Southern Pacific RR.*

conventional locomotive, would have been badly affected by the dense smoke enveloping the cab. Other novel engines were less kind to their crews. The Fairlie double-ender engines had cabs divided by the firebox and were distinctly inconvenient for their crews. The 'Mother Hubbards' favored by some United States railroads, in which the engineer was perched in a central cab, were also uncomfortable, although in some of them the driver's vision was very good.

Crews of tank locomotives were well protected when it became the practice to provide cabs suitable for running in either direction. Tender locomotives when running rearwards against wind or rain provided little protection. However, a totally enclosed cab was sometimes provided on tender locomotives destined for arduous conditions; this was

crews and tried to give them good protection from the wind, and also designed a locomotve speedometer. In Russia, despite the harsh climate, the locomotives of the early Moscow-St Petersburg Railway had no cabs, but by the 1860s locomotives imported from France and Germany were offering cabs big enough to need side windows.

Except on a handful of railways, it was not until after the First World War that long-roofed cabs with side-doors became accepted practice in Britain, but British locomotive works exported designs with quite cosy accommodation for their crews. In the British Empire there were railways that required large airy cabs to keep their men cool and dry.

Side doors stretching between cab and tender cut out draughts and reduced the risks of men being thrown out of the cab. Such mishaps were far from unknown, because the cab was a tumultuous workplace: swinging, rocking and bucking in all directions. Life was not made easier by the proximity of the fire doors, which, when open, scorched the legs of the men. Control levers, wheels and gauges were often inconveniently placed. It was not until the very end of the steam age that crew convenience became a priority. On the Great Western Railway many locomotives had a huge reversing lever so placed that the driver had to contort his body if he wanted to look ahead through his window. Many British drivers had to operate the heavy regulator lever with their left hand, and there were occasions when they had to ask their fireman for help. It was not until the 1940s that one British company, the Southern Railway, introduced locomotives in which the

*A Fairlie locomotive cab. All except the first locomotive of this type had two fireboxes side-by-side in the cab, making life difficult for the enginemen.*

driver's controls were grouped close to his right hand.

One concession to the locomotive crew was the cab-in-front locomotive, used in Italy and by the Southern Pacific RR. Essentially, this was a locomotive running in reverse, with its cab enclosed and windowed to form a driving cab not unlike that of a diesel locomotive. This arrangement was for engines working uphill through long tunnels, whose crews, on a

achieved by designing the tender with its own cab, which formed a rear annexe of the engine cab.

The replacement of steam locomotives by modern forms of traction promised a revolution in driver comfort, but new problems soon became evident. No longer engaged in a struggle against nature, but settled behind the control stand, locomotive men were more prone to irritations such as cold draughts and engine

*The 'Mother Hubbard' cab arrangement, as used on the Baltimore & Ohio RR.*

noise. Some Russian diesel locomotives were notorious for poor temperature and noise conditions, which wearied their crews and might therefore offer a partial explanation of why those crews so often ran past signals at danger.

Visibility was much improved with the new forms of traction. The General Motors streamlined diesel locomotives, with their gently sloped and wide windscreens, were seen to be a great advance. Nevertheless, it was not until the 1990s that real progress was made in cab comfort. The initiative came largely from

*The snug (wood-lined) cab provided on a Canadian National passenger locomotive of the 1930s.*

*Amtrak 'Genesis' locomotives, with the small windows dictated by monocoque construction.*

Canada, and in particular from the Canadian National Railways. The 'safety cab' was a first step, offering better protection and convenience for crews. In the United States there was a tendency for crew changes to be more widely spaced. This was linked to higher average speeds, and both factors placed greater strain

on crews, so a restful working environment became very desirable. The Santa Fe RR borrowed a Canadian National diesel locomotive (not without some prior skirmishing with US Customs) and from the experience gained cooperated with US locomotive builders to produce a better cab arrangement. The control stand was replaced by a control desk, the outer body was tapered to produce a better rearward lookout, there was a speedometer each side of

the cab instead of just one in the center, and two extra front lights, placed low, enhanced night vision. In general, the driving console was airliner-style, with the main controls close together in the middle and the gauges in a panel in front of the driver. The horn, so necessary in American conditions, was operated by a foot pedal. Some of these innovations soon became standard practice for new locomotives in North America.

*An Indian locomotive, fitted with tender-cab for comfortable rearward running.*

*Hitching a lift in the commodous cab of an Indonesian 2-8-2.*

*A Russian locomotive, with its characteristic skylight.*

The 'Genesis' passenger locomotive built by General Electric for Amtrak was a step further, with the control desk arranged wall-to-wall. Its padded ceiling and insulated floor gave good noise absorption, and it incorporated three visual display units providing information about the serviceability of various components and how various parts were performing, among other things. It was air-conditioned, and a refrigerator was provided for the crew. In anticipation of mixed-gender crews the toilet, hitherto in United States diesels located in the locomotive's nose, was moved to a more modest situation in the equipment compartment. Locomotive men described this cab as the best ever; part of this success was owed to the fact that the manufacturers had consulted appropriate trade union members at the mock-up stage.

Paradoxically, however, the old steam-age problem of enginemens' vision cropped up again in these locomotives. To save weight they had monocoque framing (the body was itself part of the load-bearing structure). This meant that apertures for the windows could not be large, so rather small front windows characterize this design, and vision in the forward-right direction is said to be inferior to that in previous designs. That apart, the 'Genesis' cab was very much a trendsetter.

*The well-protected cab of a German 2-10-0. The tender, of wartime vintage, could accommodate a rearward look-out.*

# STREAMLINING

The 'Windsplitter' of the Baltimore & Ohio RR seems to have been the world's first streamlined train, although today it would be described as semi-streamlined because the treatment consisted essentially of fitting valances along the locomotive tender and the lower part of the train. It was shortlived, because it did not bring the high speeds that had been anticipated.

In fact, streamlining appreciably reduces frontal air resistance only at speeds faster than about 70mph (112kph), a fact that railway managers, and some railway engineers, did not appreciate. The streamlining that became fashionable in the 1930s had two different purposes, to reduce wind resistance and to reduce sales resistance, but publicity of that time rarely recognized this.

Bugatti, the racing car designer, produced a streamlined railcar in France, and in 1934 two United States railroads were operating high-

*One of the Manchurian Railway Pacifics, streamlined during the Japanese occupation.*

*The 'Shovel-nose' style of frontal streamlining used for the celebrated A4 class of the London & North Eastern Railway.*

*Britain's Southern Railway used the term 'air-smoothed' for its Pacifics, like this 'Battle of Britain' class unit.*

*This post-war Chesapeake & Ohio RR streamliner never went into service, being overtaken by dieselization.*

speed streamlined internal-combustion trains, the Union Pacific M-10000 and the Burlington's 'Zephyr'. In Europe, earlier, semi-streamlining in the form of bullet fronts and V-shaped cabs had been tried on a few steam locomotives.

Otto Kuhler, a German immigrant, was the artistic force behind the earlier years of American streamlining. He did not pretend that streamlining would produce great benefits in terms of speed and fuel consumption. The need to make trains look exciting rather than drab was reason enough, he argued. He and other industrial artists devised a series of streamlining initiatives as the United States railroads, aware of contemporary fashion, ordered new streamlined locomotives or decided to enshroud

*The semi-streamline concept, as applied to a Spanish 4-8-2.*

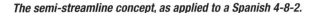

existing machines in streamlined casings. In late 1934 the New York Central put a streamlined shroud over its fast 4-6-4 locomotive *Commodore Vanderbilt*, and the following year the first United States locomotive to be built as a streamliner emerged. This was a brightly-painted 4-4-2 for the Milwaukee RR's new 'Hiawatha' streamlined train.

Some critics referred darkly to 'upturned bathtubs on wheels', and indeed there were some ludicrous creations, but in terms of retaining customers for rail travel, and for countering the impression that railways were somehow old-fashioned, streamlining was successful. It was outside the United States that some of the more astonishing efforts appeared. In Hungary some small tank engines were streamlined, even though they were not scheduled for any great speed. In Manchuria the newly-installed Japanese administration introduced some streamlined Pacifics. In post-war Soviet Russia a narrow-gage forestry line was the scene of a triumphalist endeavour, with a tiny steam locomotive enveloped in streamlining from which emerged a tall chimney complete with spark-arrester.

*Styled in the USA: a post-war WP Pacific of Indian Railways.*

*The familiar General Motors look, with its streamline style of the 1930s that was carried forward into the post-war decades. This is the inter-war stainless-steel 'Nebraska Zephyr.'*

Some locomotive engineers took wind resistance seriously. The Canadian National streamlined 4-8-4 design was tried in a windtunnel before construction. In Britain, the streamlined 'Coronation' class locomotives were also influenced by windtunnel testing. It was a British streamlined locomotive, *Mallard*, which took the world speed record, and this would probably not have been achieved without the streamlining, which would certainly have been influential at that top speed of 126mph (203km/h).

Streamlining was probably least effective in the very place where it was most obvious, the front. Locomotives have a narrow frontage anyway, so pointing it does not have a great effect. But smoothing the airflow along the boiler

*The streamlined front of the Eurostar Channel Tunnel high-speed trains of the 1990s. The nose is longer and lower than those of the earlier HST designs.*

*The streamline style of a Belgiun electric locomotive of 1960s vintage contrasts with the low profile of the 1990s 'Thalys' high speed train.*

by covering up projecting items, and shielding the wheels of both locomotive and train to reduce the resistance caused by wind eddies, did have an appreciable effect at the higher speeds. What would have been most valuable, although dificult to achieve, would have been streamlining against strong sidewinds. Such winds, forcing a train's wheel flanges against the running rail, have a marked effect on rolling resistance.

Streamlining was removed from many locomotives in the Second World War because it made access, and hence maintenance, more labor-consuming. After the war it was not revived for steam locomotives, with some notable exceptions. Hundreds of new WP Pacifics for Indian Railways, styled in the United States, had conical smokebox fronts and smoothed boilers, and Britain's Southern Railway continued to build Pacifics that were described as 'air-smoothed'.

However, it was precisely as the streamlined steam locomotive became unfashionable that streamlining became a serious and relevant issue. New electric and diesel trains began to run at speeds where streamlining could make a real difference to energy consumption and speed. Windtunnel testing no longer sought justification for streamlining, but helped to evolve the most effective profiles. A look at the several types of high-speed train that emerged after the 1960s shows that there is still scope for variety. However, the HSTs of all countries demonstrate that the low frontal slope is an essential ingredient, and that care is taken to ensure that streamlining does not result in a bigger area being presented to sidewinds.

With the current generation of high-speed trains, designed to reach 185mph (300km/h) or more, the fact that air resistance increases as the square of the speed means that it becomes

a vital factor in power requirement, and hence in fuel consumption. Reducing the frontal cross-section of the train, so that less area is presented to the air in front, is one approach, and new-generation high-speed trains do tend to have lower roof lines. Research has also shown the advantage of the long, low nose, and the application of this can be seen in the profile of the 'Thalys' trains as compared with the original French TGV trains; the train driver now sits about five metres behind the front of the train. The new noses reduce air pressure at the front, not only to save horsepower but also to minimize the shock when two trains pass each other.

# LOCOMOTIVE INSCRIPTIONS

The amount of information displayed on the outside of a locomotive has varied from country to country and from period to period. In general, European railways, and especially British, have tended towards wide-ranging information, while in North America little more than the locomotives' numbers and ownership is indicated. Nowadays, when locomotives are often leased rather than bought outright, the operating company's name may still be prominently displayed, but with the name of the bank or consortium that actually owns the unit being displayed on a modest brass plate.

Both in America and elsewhere this permanent information about the locomotive was supplemented by temporary information about its duties at a particular time. In steam-age Britain the position of the oil headlamps indicated what class of train the locomotive was pulling, and a handful of companies supplemented the lamps by white disks in daytime. In America two white flags were carried at the top of the smokebox to indicate an extra

*A builder's plate on a Scotland-built locomotive.*

*Secretive Soviet builder's plate; the works name is not given, just its code number 75.*

*Great Western Railway combined builder's, name and number plate.*

*The brass Great Western nameplate in all its glory.*

train, and green flags to indicate that a locomotive was hauling a part of a scheduled train running in several sections. Identification numbers were also used to mark the train. In Britain these were large, white on black, and persisted into the diesel age but fell into disuse

with modern signalling technology; they continue to be used for former Southern Electric services, where the traditional signalman is still widely employed. In North America, with its train-order system of train control, it was important to identify trains correctly, and for this

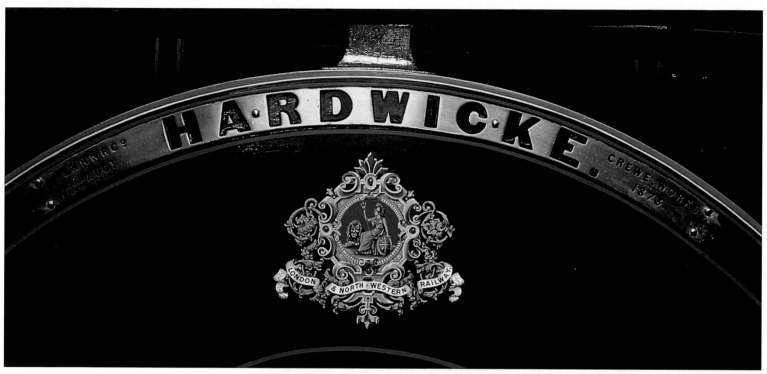

*The brass nameplate of a celebrated London & North Western Railway passenger locomotive.*

purpose many railroads used the locomotive number, which was why it was illuminated at night.

The locomotive number, known as its running number as distinct from its builder's number, could also convey a message. To simplify operations and communication, blocks of numbers in sequence were allocated to given classes or sub-classes, so that the number indicated the locomotive class. On some railways this was carried further. On Britain's Great Western, numbers were of four digits, and the second digit indicated the category; four-cylinder 4-6-0s, for example, had a zero for the second digit, 2-6-0s a '3', and so on. But with this kind of system there was always a tendency for exceptions to be made, so the scheme was rarely foolproof. Modern British locomotives are numbered in five-digit blocks, the first two digits being the type designation. In continental Europe multi-digit numbers were often used, the first digits indicating the class and wheel arrangement. In France and French-influenced countries the axle arrangement came first (for example, a 4-6-2's number would begin with 231), then a letter to indicate the class, and finally the locomotive's individual running number (for example, 231E41, a 4-6-2 once used in the 'Golden Arrow' service). In North America the

*Train identification numbers displayed by British diesel locomotives, an idea outmoded by advance train control techniques.*

railroad companies do not go to these lengths, although they do tend to number classes in blocks. Most big US railroads avoid the use of numbers shorter than three digits.

In Germany the first two digits indicated the class, while in Russia it was usually a letter prefix that performed this function. With modern traction, the Russians prefixed electric locomotives with Lenin's initials (VL), continued with two digits for the class, and then finished with the running number. With diesels the prefix indicated the type of transmission (TE meant diesel-electric, TG diesel hydraulic). With computerization came changes. An extra final number, the check number, had to be added, and in some cases an 0 was added at the front. In Russia, where life is never simple, computerization brought complication, and locomotives continued to carry their old number but a completely different computer number was also allocated, so the locomotives now carry two numbers.

The running number is not the most vital for the identification of a locomotive. Often it is changed to accommodate a new numbering system, or when the locomotive changes ownership. The basic identifying number is the

*The cabside display of a French locomotive. Just above the numberplate can be seen the name of the unit's home depot.*

builder's number, normally indicating the locomotive's position in the manufacturer's orderbook. Builders affixed a builder's plate (known as the works plate) to each locomotive, and each manufacturer had a distinctive shape and design of plate. The plate carried the builder's name, the builder's number for the locomotive and, often, the year of manufacture. This practice has continued into the electric and diesel age.

Russia, again, presents an odd case. With the cult of secrecy rampant in Stalin's time, any piece of information was regarded as a potential state secret, and it was decided that the builder's plate should not indicate to all and sundry the name of the builder! So a code was substituted. The plate would read 'Factory No. 12,' for example. Only those who could be trusted, and had a verified need to know, were intended to know the code.

Confusion is not unknown in other countries. A builder's plate might be transferred to another locomotive during capital repair. This might have happened through negligence if plates were fitted to the smokebox, because locomotives often exchanged boilers. So the ultimate authority for a locomotive's identity is not in fact the builder's plate, but the builder's number (the same number) that was stamped on several of the components. In the final analysis, with a locomotive that has been rebuilt several times in the course of a long life, the number stamped on the frames is taken to be the 'real' number.

*The Coat-of-arms of the Lancashire & Yorkshire Railway, as displayed on its locomotives.*

*In North America, white flags distinguished an extra train.*

A few railways indicate on the cabside the capacity of a locomotive. On Britain's LMS Railway a number from 1 to 8 indicated the haulage capacity of a locomotive, and the letters P or F indicated whether that capacity related to passenger or freight service. Thus the celebrated mixed traffic 4-6-0 was labelled 5P5F, and soon became known as the 'Class 5'. On the Great Western, power was indicated by letters, E being the most powerful, and as the lines were colour-coded according to weight restrictions, so the locomotive cabside also carried a coloured disc to indicate its route-availability. The Canadian National had its own system of calculating a locomotive's capacity, expressed on the cabside as a number followed by the % sign. British Rail's diesel and electric locomotives had a data panel on the cabside

*Russian diesel locomotives with new computer numbers on the cabside and original numbers on the front.*

indicating weight, brake power, train heating capacity, route availability and maximum speed. Many United States railroads indicate the class designation of the locomotive in modest script on the cabside. Usually this designation is that of the builder, but sometimes railroads have their own classification system.

The practice of naming locomotives was most common in Britain. Some companies favoured a painted-on name, but most preferred a metal nameplate. Grandest of all were those of the Great Western, in polished brass. In North America naming was rare, but some companies painted a name on the cabside. In the very early days of railroads the practice was more common, the names sometimes being highly unofficial. A well-known example of a named locomotive class were the 'Presidents' of the Baltimore & Ohio RR, built for the best passenger trains. Other railways from time to time indulged in this practice, notably those under British influence.

With modern traction, names somehow seem less grand, but electric and diesel locomotives in some countries stil carry them. In France many electric locomotives, and also gas-turbine trains, received names, generally commemorating places served by the railway. In Britain various institutions and people have been honoured in this way, but there is a tendency for the nameplates to be removed after a few years.

*The 'hungry lion' logo of British Railways.*

# TANKS AND TENDERS

The tender was designed to carry enough fuel and water to enable the locomotive to pull its train between servicing points. In America the rule-of-thumb for designers was to provide for two refills of water for every one refill of coal, because watering points were closer together than coaling points. In 19th century Britain five tons of coal was considered enough for a day's work and 3,500 gallons (16,000 litres) of water was enough to last between successive watering points. Even so, cases did occur when a locomotive was desperately short of water or coal on arrival; exceptionally bad weather or exceptionally long and frequent delays could be the cause of these crises. In North America, where distances were longer, fuel less calorific and locomotives bigger, tenders had to be much larger. By the end of the steam age, both in America and elsewhere, tenders had grown in line with the growth of locomotives; bigger boilers almost automatically meant faster use of fuel and water. The biggest

*Water scoop of a Pennsylvania RR tender.*

*A post-war South African locomotive with its high-capacity Vanderbilt tender.*

United States articulated locomotives had 14-wheel tenders carrying 28 tons of coal and 25,000 gallons (113,600 litres) of water. The biggest British passenger locomotives had six-wheel tenders carrying 10 tons of coal and 4,000 gallons (18,200 litres) of water. That coal was enough for the London-Scotland services, but water was replenished several times en route. Often the size of the tender was limited by the size of the turntables installed at locomotive depots, and this consideration meant that sometimes a long locomotive was married to an absurdly small tender.

Most of a tender is occupied by the water tank, on top of which, towards the front, is the fuel space. Sometimes railings are provided so that coal can be loaded high, and this is really a requirement for wood-burners, since wood fuel is much more bulky. Inside the tank there are vertical baffles to prevent dangerous surges of water. These baffles serve also as support for the coal space above them. At the upper rear there are air vents and filler holes for the water tank.

In Britain, and on a few lines in the United States and France, water troughs (track pans)

*A British saddletank locomotive (above), With neither tank nor tender. A German-built fireless locomotive (below).*

*London, Brighton & South Coast Railway No 72 Fenchurch, as preserved. Built 1872, shown wearing the later Brighton brown livery.*

were provided between the rails, from which locomotives could scoop up water without stopping. For this purpose a movable pick up scoop was provided beneath the tender, operated by the fireman. Tenders with such gear also had a dome in the ceiling of the water tank, which caught and deflected downwards the water rushing up from the scoop.

Locomotives whose fuel consumption was beyond the strength of one man were fitted with mechanical stokers. The principle element of these was a rotating screw that picked up and moved coal from tender to firebox. A small steam engine driving the screw had its own compartment at the front of the tender. Such stokers were found on a large scale only in North America and Russia. Oil burners, of course, did not need them.

An interesting variety of tender was used by the London & North Eastern Railway for its London-Scotland trains. This had a side corridor leading to the first coach of the train, enabling crews to be exchanged en route on a non-stop-schedule locomotive.

The main technical problem in tender design was the suspension, because the weight was

*Big by British standards: a 4-axle tender used by the former London & South Western Railway, a line without water troughs.*

much less at the end of a trip than at the beginning. A distinctive type was the Vanderbilt tender, which originated in the United States. In this, the water tank is cylindrical, which offers some advantage in strength and capacity.

Hauling a heavy tender required energy, and moreover tender-first running was not advisable at the higher speeds. The tank engine, carrying its fuel and water on the locomotive itself, was one answer to this. Locomotives whose trips were only short, such as those in suburban and yard service, did not require large water stocks. Thus the tank locomotive became very popular, and took several forms. The most common was the side-tank, which carried water in tanks flanking the boiler and in a small tank beneath the coal bunker at the rear. Smaller designs often had a saddle-tank instead, which was draped over the boiler and, among other advantages, gave enginemen better access to the machinery between the frames. The pannier tank, favoured by the Great Western Railway, had rectangular tanks suspended on either side of the boiler, again providing access to the working parts, which needed to be oiled quite frequently, without unduly obstructing the enginemen's vision. There was also the well tank, in which the water was carried between the frames. A

*A Pannier tank of the Great Western Railway, which operated several hundred of these six-wheelers (top), The well-tank locomotive of a Dutch tourist line takes water (above).*

*The Vanderbilt tender of a North American locomotive.*

much rarer type was the tender-tank, which carried water on the locomotive but pulled a small tender of fuel as well. A sub-type was the Forney tank, a United States variation that carried the water in a large rectangular tank behind the cab. The Forney was the only tank engine at all popular with US mainline companies, small tender engines usually being preferred for commuter and yard work. However, US industrial lines used tank locomotives for their yard operations. On the other hand the British railways, with their more intensive and shorter distance services, were big users of such locomotives, which made up more than half of their locomotive stock. Some British railways built tank engines for quite long hauls. The British Railways 2-6-4 tank design, derived from an LMS original, could carry 2,000 gallons (9,000 litres) and more than three tons of coal, making it suitable for fast outer-suburban

*All neat and tidy: the tender of a German 2-10-0.*

# LOCOMOTIVE FUEL

Hand coaling at Ahmedabad in India, a method only viable where wages are low.

At the beginning of the steam age it was by no means certain that coal would be the preferred fuel. Coke seemed to have better prospects, especially as it was virtually smokeless. However, coal soon triumphed, but both the designers and the users of locomotives had to take into account the widely different qualities of its several varieties. The heat-producing elements of coal are carbon and hydrogen, and a high proportion of these produces coals that are described as high-calorific. Coals that are high in ash and sulphur present problems, including the formation of clinker on the firebars, which chokes the air supply needed for combustion. Railways had the 'acid rain' problem long before that term was invented; sulphur in the coal could combine with the moisture content to form an acid that slowly attacked the metal surfaces of the firebox and smokebox.

Coal could come in various sizes, and in post-war Britain firemen had to cope with slack and coal dust mixed in with the lumps. The coal dust, and often the slack, was simply swept up the chimney, largely unburned. Other sizes were all acceptable. Small coal was advantageous when a high steaming rate was required from a small grate, while larger lumps were more convenient

A combined watering and coaling facility of the Canadian Pacific Railway at Winnipeg.

*An overhead, car-hoisting, coaling plant of the London Midland & Scottish Railway.*

*A wooden-built overhead coaling plant at Newcastle, New South Wales.*

for the fireman and probably more efficient at most steaming rates.

Some American railroads tried to make use of the plentiful anthracites of Pennsylvania. Eventually the Wootten firebox was developed to burn this fuel; it was very wide and shallow and because of its size popularized the 'camelback' layout, in which the driving controls were placed in a cab on top of the boiler. The Lackawanna RR made its use of anthracite a selling point, its publicity stressing the absence of the smuts which passengers on competing railroads allegedly had to endure. A mythical 'Phoebe Snow', clad in unsmutted white, was a feature of its posters.

Railway companies tended to obtain their supplies from just one or two collieries so that the quality would be predictable. Some coals were especially prized, including Welsh steam coal and the similar Donetsk coal in Russia. The Great Western Railway designed its locomotives on the assumption that Welsh coal would be used, and they were celebrated for their high steam output per square foot of firegrate area, and also for their virtual smokelessness.

*A US-built Paraguayan 2-8-0 halts while logs are pitched forward from the fuel car.*

Black smoke billowing from a locomotive's chimney was a sign of inefficient combustion, but it was not always due to poor-quality coal. Bad firing practice could produce the same result. Lazy firing, the heaping up of coal in the firebox so that firing needed to be only at long intervals, was a sure way to make smoke.

Keeping locomotives stocked with coal was a laborious and dirty business. Hand-coaling was used where labour was cheap, but to speed the process and to save labour many railways built mechanical coaling plants, ranging from simple installations in which coal was unloaded into tubs that were then hoisted up and tipped

into the tender, to huge concrete plants, with which freightcars of coal were lifted up about 60ft (18m) and their contents tipped into a bunker, from where the coal was eventually released via a chute into the tender below. These mechanical plants did, however, break up the coal, producing some dust and slack. This was the reason, or at least the claimed reason, why the GWR stayed with hand-tub coaling.

Some countries did not have plentiful suppplies of home coal. Italy was a notorious example, its locomotives having to use imported coal. Germany and Austria, among others, often burned soft coal (lignite or 'brown coal'), which

was very smoky and of low calorific value. A number of designers experimented with the use of pulverized coal (in essence, man-made coal dust) because it was cheaper. But the elaborate smokebox arrangements, including a fan to make artificial draught, made this an expensive process.

Firewood was a significant competitor of coal in some regions. Properly cut and dried timber has an enormous heat output, but is bulky.

*Japanese-built wood-burners refuel at a teakwood fuel yard in Thailand.*

*A British-built 2-4-0 in Indonesia, converted to oil fuel, and wasting it.*

to satisfy certain standards of viscosity, flashpoint, residues and cetane rating (a measure of ignition characteristics). In theory, a lightish diesel fuel is best for easy work, while a heavy fuel would be better for heavy load-hauling over long distances. In the 1950s some railroads did use the heavier fuel, but it produced problems with sparking and sticking fuel injectors, so specifically designed diesel locomotive fuels are now standard.

In the United States there were over 7,000 oil-burning steam locomotives at work in the 1920s. Then the number declined, reflecting changes in the oil/coal price ratio, to re-expand in the Second World War. In Britain, oil fuel never took hold, although there were short-lived campaigns to increase its use. Soon after the First World War, partly because of the greater militancy of coal miners, some railways dabbled in oil firing. The Great Eastern Railway had been studying this possibility for some time and produced successful conversions, but they had little real economic justification. In the late 1940s, under political pressure, the railway companies began a campaign to convert locomotives to oil-burning, mainly because the government feared that there would not be enough good coal for the railways, given the coal export targets. This again proved a vain endeavour which resulted

Refuelling therefore had to be frequent, and forests close to the railway tended to become denuded over time. Railways with no nearby coal and plenty of trees were the location for wood firing. Finland and Russia presented these conditions, and also parts of North America before coal supply became established. In Thailand, teak was burned; the fragrance was delightful but the misuse of natural resources horrifying.

Where oil was cheap it was a suitable substitute for coal, with the additional advantages that it produced little ash or spark, made the fireman's job easier, made mechanical stokers unnecessary on big locomotives, and enabled the fire and fumes to be reduced momentarily (when going through long tunnels, for example). Designing the burners was not simple, and several designs failed because they tended to clog. A British engineer working for a Russian railway was successfully experimenting with oil fuel in the 1880s. In America, the Central Pacific and the Santa Fe railroads had oil-fired engines in the 1890s, and other western railroads followed suit. Heavy oil (residual, or 'Bunker C') was used and became the norm for locomotives. It requires warming in order to flow, but has a very high calorific value. It is normally very cheap, with oil companies keen to find markets for it. Even so, it was often more expensive than coal on average. This was because the price of coal contained a high transportation factor, increasing rapidly as the distance from source grew. Coal sold very cheaply in mining areas. That is why railroads remote from coalfields turned to oil (and also

why railroads serving coalfields were usually the last to dieselize).

Diesel fuel was very different, being one of the distillates and coming between motor fuel and light heating fuels on the distillation scale. In fact, heating fuels and automobile fuels could be used in a diesel engine, but with undesirable side effects. Ideally, diesel locomotive fuel needs

*The British Rail electro-diesel class 73 design.*

*A Belgian quadri-current electric locomotive, able to run on four different electrification systems.*

in only a few conversions before it was abandoned.

The Great Eastern's research, among other things, produced a design for oil injection that enabled the use of two fuels simultaneously. Known as the Holden System (Holden was the locomotive superintendent of the GER), it injected a mixture of air and atomized oil over the top of a very hot fire. This had the advantages that oil could be turned off when little steam was required (oil injectors tended to get clogged up precisely at low settings); heavy oil could be used in the knowledge that, should it blow out, it would immediately be reignited by the fire; and, should the oil system fail, the locomotive could still run on coal alone. This system was used at least once in a combined wood and oil-burning design (small industrial locomotives for Thailand).

Locomotives able to use two kinds of fuel have appeared in other forms. In the heroic stage of Stalin's revolution Soviet researchers managed to secure funding for three ultimately

unsuccessful prototype locomotives that combined diesel and steam propulsion, thereby allegedly gaining the advantages of both. These locomotives had centrally-placed, opposed-piston cylinders. At starting, steam was used and then, as speed increased, diesel fuel was introduced instead of steam in one part of the cycle, the part in which the two pistons were driven outwards. The combustion of this fuel drove the pistons outwards, and conventional steam drove them inwards. Unsurprisingly, forward motion was not smooth, and there were countless other problems that eventually killed the project.

The electro-diesel locomotive is another twin-fuel concept. In modern Britain it takes the form of the Class 73, which is a locomotive designed to take electric power from the conductor rails prevalent in southern England. For use on lines where there is no third rail (sidings or wharves at one end of the run, for example), a small diesel engine and generator is incorporated. In a few European countries the battery-electric yard locomotive appeared. In the United States the New Haven RR, and later Amtrak, acquired diesel locomotives carrying pick-up shoes so that they could operate without smoke in New

York City. The current was merely picked up from the conductor rail and transmitted to the electric motors.

Multi-current electric locomotives are not really multi-fuel designs, but form a category of their own. They are designed to operate over routes where more than one system of electrification is used. In Britain this involves not locomotives, but electric multiple-unit trains that may need to operate a service that combines overhead-collection 25kV ac current and third-rail 750V dc. The Thameslink service which crosses London from north to south is one line where this ability is required. The trains, which have dc traction motors, normally run off the third rail, but in high-voltage territory the 750V circuit is switched out and power is taken from a pantograph to a transformer to reduce its voltage, and to a rectifier to change it to dc. In continental Europe, to avoid locomotive changes where two systems meet, bi-current, tri-current and quadri-current locomotives have been built in some quantity. A Belgian locomotive, for example, might need to run over Dutch 1,500V dc, German 15,000V ac, French 25,000V ac and Belgian 3,000V dc.

# LOCOMOTIVE OPERATION

In the steam age, locomotives were allocated to a given locomotive depot, or shed. These could vary from a one-road, one-stall structure at the end of a branch line to a major depot with accommodation for a hundred locomotives. The small shed was simply intended as a place where a locomotive could be parked between duties, watered, fuelled, and adjusted if necessary. Major depots had workshops attached that could deal with all repairs apart from the periodic 'capital' repair, which was done at a main works.

The depot was also the booking-on point for enginemen, and its office staff would allocate particular engines and crews for particular duties, the day's arrangements usually being chalked on a lined blackboard. Enginemens' pay normally was based entirely or partly on the mileage run, so a passenger crew would receive

*Modern traction at a steam-age half-roundhouse in Germany.*

*A straight-road locomotive depot in Thailand.*

*Time expired fast passenger locomotives were often demoted to slow trains. Here a Pennsylvania RR K4 hauls a stopping train a few months before its retirement.*

more than a freight crew. The best turns went automatically to the most senior men. In Britain a 'link' system operated, the link being a group of enginemen allocated to a particular category of service (in effect, to a particular group of locomotives), the 'top link' being men who could expect to work the most prestigious passenger trains. In North America there was a tradition by which enginemen allotted to a popular run could be 'bumped' by more senior men claiming priority. The virtue of both the British and US systems was that they were predictable and therefore seen as fair; the disadvantage was that they allowed less competent or uncooperative men to reach positions they did not deserve, simply by serving time.

Locomotives were allocated to runs that were within their capacity, although at critical times when a suitable engine was not available the next-best might be provided, and fingers kept crossed. More often, an engine was entrusted with a train beneath its capacity; this happened when a suitable job was not available and it was considered uneconomic to leave the locomotive

*US track pans (water troughs) in use. They were only adopted by a few railroads that felt the need to speed up journey times.*

*A straight-road double-ended locomotive depot whose site made it effectively single-ended. It is at Swansea in South Wales.*

*Locomotive watering on the Indian meter-gauge.*

unemployed; the aim was always to maintain a high average figure for locomotive-hours-in-traffic.

In big countries with fairly sparse traffic it was easy to allocate a locomotive to a trip at the end of which it could be turned and returned with another train to its starting point and depot, all within its crew's maximum working hours. In countries with intense and unpredictable traffic flows, especially if trains tended to fall behind schedule, matching trains to locomotives was a daily preoccupation. It was in these circumstances that the mixed-traffic, or general-service, locomotive was valued. While not ideally suited to hauling the fastest passenger services or the heaviest freights, these locomotives could

tackle almost any train, and finding them a full day's work was therefore easier.

Locomotive depots had three possible layouts. There was the roundhouse, popular in America but not exclusive to that continent. This consisted of stalls arranged around a central turntable. Often this line of stalls did not form a complete circle, but the principle was the same; an incoming locomotive would run on to the turntable, which placed it on the track leading to its stall. Once inside, it could receive any minor adjustments while awaiting its next duty. Then there were the straight-road depots. These could be double-ended, so a locomotive would be put away at one end behind a line of engines that had arrived earlier, and eventually would move up to the other end, where it was ready to leave for its next duty. There were several parallel tracks in the building, but nevertheless

*Locomotive mens' noticeboard at a Chinese locomotive depot (above), Changchan Locomotive depot (left).*

*Steam and diesel locomotives share the facilities of the Canadian National locomotive depot at Toronto in the 1950s*

*Mixing diesel and steam traction in one depot raised problems, but was commonplace during the dieselisation process. This is the Severn Valley Railway.*

*A hoist at the Brighton locomotive depot in Britain.*

some skill was required to ensure that a locomotive was near the exit end just when it was needed. With the single-ended straight-road shed the access and exit tracks were identical, so it was only practical when few locomotives were involved; too many, and there would be blockages and congestion.

On arrival at the locomotive depot, after being detached from its incoming train, the engine would need to have its fire and smokebox cleaned, so would proceed to the ashpit. In its simplest form this was a brick-lined trough between the rails, resembling an inspection pit. Here the firebars would be attacked with special tools to dislodge clinker, and the ashpan emptied. Meanwhile, the smokebox door would be opened and the heap of smokebox soot and ash shovelled out. Towards the end of the steam era some depots had equipment to ease these

*Inside the Union Pacific RR locomotive depot at Cheyenne, Wyoming, in the 1950s.*

*On the turntable inside the Canadian Pacific roundhouse at Toronto. Each chimney marks a stall.*

*Where there was once a roundhouse, French Pacific locomotives are parked around the turntable over inspection pits at their Tours depot.*

back-breaking and dirty jobs. Ashpits, for example, might be equipped with conveyor belts to carry off the soot, clinker, and ash.

After this the locomotive would refill its water tanks and take on a load of fuel for its next duty. Sandboxes also had to be refilled. Traditionally this was done by shed staff using buckets to carry the dried sand from the storage bunker or sand-drier to the sand hoppers on the locomotive, but some depots had sand dispensers, with flexible hoses conveying the sand from an elevated sand-bunker to the locomotives' sand-boxes.

This done, the locomotive could proceed to its allotted place at the depot, where minor repairs might also be carried out. In a roundhouse layout it would move via the central turntable, while if the depot was straight-road it would first go to where the turntable was situated, turn, and then move to its allotted place. Tank engines, of course, did not need to turn and this could ease the work, and congestion, at a straight-road depot. The storage tracks or stalls provided inspection pits.

*On the Trans Siberian Railway, a long-distance freight is halted while replenishment sand is piped in by gravity.*

*Amtrak locomotives refuel from a tank truck at Denver, Colorado. This method is used when demand is small.*

If the locomotive had been in use for the number of days prescribed for that depot (which depended largely on local water quality), it would need to go for boiler washout. This could be done when the boiler had cooled or, if the right equipment was there, it could be done hot. In the latter case the hot water from the boiler was drained into a tank, and then propelled back as a jet through the washout holes, normally plugged, in the side of the firebox. These jets would wash out scale and other deposits that had accumulated since the previous washout. This done, and the plugs replaced, the boiler could be quickly brought back to pressure. With cold washouts the boiler had first to be cooled, then washed out with cold water, and finally brought back to pressure from cold; this was a longer but simpler process.

Whereas most European depots were provided with a turntable, this was not so in America. There, the triangular track layout known as a wye was used except where a roundhouse layout made a turntable compulsory. The wye demanded much space but was better than a turntable as its maintenance was simple, its use less difficult

*An incoming Garratt locomotive is washed down at the Broadmeadow locomotive depot in New South Wales.*

*This Pennsylvania RR K4 locomotive, once a classic mainline machine, ekes out its last years in secondary service, as was the usual money-saving practice.*

*South African Locomotives ready for service outside the straight-road Bloemfontein locomotive depot.*

and its vulnerability negligible. A roundhouse whose turntable went out of order was crippled, and train services of a whole district were disrupted. Very occasionally, a locomotive would proceed on to the turntable when the latter was not ready to receive it, falling into the turntable pit and virtually bringing railway operations to a halt. In both world wars this was a much-sought recourse of saboteurs.

Turntables were originally pushed round manually, and this method survived until the end of steam. By then, however, powered turntables had appeared at the main depots. With both powered and manual turntables it was essential for the locomotive to be finely balanced over the pivot, and this was not at all easy when a locomotive's length filled the turntable and its tender was empty of coal and water. Coaling and watering the engine on arrival at the depot was therefore not simply a preferred sequence, but was sometimes essential.

All but the smallest depots had fitters who could attend to enginemen's complaints. Larger depots could do medium repairs and some had the luxury of a wheel-drop. Wheels had to be removed if axleboxes were defective, and the only alternative to a wheel-drop was the hoist, which would raise one end of a locomotive so the wheels could be rolled out. The hoist was a quite primitive method, time-consuming, and put a strain on locomotive frames.

When diesel and electric locomotives appeared they were at first allocated to existing steam locomotive depots. For a period they shared the same premises, which was not good for them. Dependent on electrical systems, they required clean surroundings and their fitters needed good illumination, two facilities that a steam locomotive depot did not provide.

When the new motive power completely displaced steam, the length of locomotive runs (traction sections) could be increased because fuel supply and fire cleaning no longer defined the intervals. Longer traction sections meant less frequent locomotive changes, and hence a reduced need for locomotive depots, many of

*A modern diesel locomotive repair shop. This one is the main shop of the Hamersley Railway in Western Australia.*

*A Canadian National 'Forney Tank' undergoes heavy repair in the Railway's Montreal workshop.*

which were closed. Gradually, purpose-built or purpose-rebuilt traction depots were introduced, with clean, bright interiors. There is now a hierarchy of depots, ranging from a fuelling point through a fuel and light servicing establishment to big depots that can do all levels of maintenance except capital repairs. In most countries there was also a trend towards long sheds that could accommodate under one roof the multiple-unit trains that were becoming more widespread; this was particularly the case in Britain, less so in America. A major depot now provides an overhead crane, since so much maintenance consists of the exchange of major components, and platforms to make access to the sides and upperworks easier. Turntables being of little use for multiple unit trains, inconvenient for multiple-unit diesel locomotives, and actually needed by neither, the straight-road depot is now preferred.

In the United States the locomotive maintenance and inspection terminals are the equivalent of the European top-level depot. The employees of some of these include not only railroad staff but also workers supplied by locomotive manufacturers, for the trend is for manufacturers to have responsibility also for the maintenance of their locomotives. When locomotives are leased, workers employed by the leasing companies may also be present. Locomotives arriving at such depots go first to high-speed fuel pumps and overhead sand reservoirs. Simultaneously, traction motors and running gear are inspected and brakeshoes replaced if necessary. Headlights are checked, the cab and its windows cleaned. If necessary, a locomotive can be sent to the light-repair shop or, if something serious like a cracked cylinder is suspected, to the heavy-repair shop. In these US terminals, the emphasis is on speed, on bringing the locomotive back into operation as soon as possible. In fuelling, one man can insert hoses into the tanks of a whole line of locomotives, and fill them simultaneously, because automatic pressure valves ensure there is no overflow.

# REBUILDING OF LOCOMOTIVES

Steam locomotives had long lives. While the accountants may have attached to them a depreciation life of perhaps twenty years, they demonstrated a survivability far in excess of that. Locomotives working past their hundredth birthday were not unknown, and many lived on into their ninth or tenth decade. During their lives they underwent periodical capital repairs, and sometimes were rebuilt. Puffing Billy, when it was finally handed over to the Science Museum for safekeeping, was very different from the Puffing Billy of 1813.

Locomotives were rebuilt for several reasons, and often for a combination of reasons. Much-improved components might become available years after a locomotive design was built, in which case the expense of rebuilding was justified by the better performance. A notable example of this occurred when the superheater was successfully developed. In the first two decades of the 20th century many existing locomotives were rebuilt with this device, which necessitated a longer smokebox and substantial

*A Burlington RR E8 diesel locomotive at Chicago in 1958.*

*The same E8 type as in the upper picture, still hauling commuters at Chicago in 1992, but completely re-engined.*

*A Great Western 'Duke,' a class introduced in 1895.*

modification inside the smokebox. The results were well worthwhile in almost every case, with previously mediocre designs producing a sparkling performance after the change. In Britain the 'Great Northern Atlantics', hitherto fairly ordinary locomotives, performed brilliant feats on the East Coast Route after this change.

Rebuilds were also authorized in the hope of improving designs whose performance had been disappointing. One such case was that of the 'Claughton' class 4-6-0 of the London & North Western Railway. In their original form, it

*A Great Western 'Bulldog,' a bigger and improved 1898 version of the 'Duke.'*

*An 'Earl,' created in the 1930s by combining the 'Duke' boiler with the 'Bulldog' engine and frames.*

was politely said that these engines performed satisfactorily when in the hands of a well-experienced crew. But the LMS Railway, successor to the LNWR, wanted locomotives that would perform reliably with, at least, average crews. So the 'Claughtons' began to receive bigger boilers. These improved their performance, but not by much. The next stage was to rebuild them as the 'Patriot' class of 4-6-0. The 'Patriots' were fairly successful, but it was not until they themselves were rebuilt with a new, taper, boiler that their performance

*The original 'Royal Scot' design of the London Midland & Scottish Railway.*

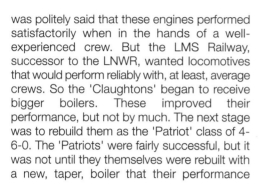

*The 'Royal Scot' design as rebuilt with a more effective boiler and freer steam passenges.*

became at all brilliant. The interesting point here is that the final version contained nothing, or very little, of the original engines. The definition of 'rebuilt' was very broad on Britain's railways.

One reason for this was that a company's budget might allow a very limited sum for capital investment; that is, money for brand-new equipment. On the other hand, the accountants had less grip on running costs, and a locomotive

rebuild could be entered as a running cost, since it was essentially a matter of keeping an existing asset fit for duty. The distinction between a new and a rebuilt locomotive was a very fine one, and could be manipulated. Locomotives classified as rebuilds might perhaps have kept the wheel centres, some fittings, and even the frames of their ancestors, but that was usually all, and often it was less. When the Great

*The New South Wales Government Railways 30T class tender locomotive, rebuilt from redundant 30 class tank locomotives.*

Western Railway introduced its 'Grange' class of two-cylinder 4-6-0 with 5ft 8in (1727mm) wheels it was simultaneously withdrawing time-expired 2-6-0 locomotives, also with 5ft 8in wheels and the same cylinder dimensions. This coincidence, and perhaps some re-use of the 2-6-0 parts, was enough for the GWR locomotive department to classify the 'Granges' as rebuilds.

The GWR had an interesting history of rebuilds. When, in the 1900s, the company was comparing the merits of 4-4-2 and 4-6-0 wheel arrangements, it changed the wheel arrangements of its designs to produce some 4-4-2 engines, which were subsequently rebuilt as 4-6-0s.

Transformations were made easier by the high degree of component standardization on the GWR. Another example of the Company's dexterity involved its mixed-traffic, outside-frame 4-4-0s. The 'Dukes' of 1895 had a domed parallel boiler, but then a variant appeared with a more modern taper boiler, producing the 'Bulldog' type. Locomotives of these two classes subsequently changed boilers quite often, and then, in the 1930s, when the design was 40 years old, some 'Bulldogs' were given

'Duke'-type boilers to form a class of virtual 'Dukes' that became known as the 'Earl' class. The 'Dukes' and 'Earls' were slightly lighter than the 'Bulldogs', and the change was made when the company was experiencing a shortage of locomotives suitable for some of its lightly-laid lines.

Sometimes a single locomotive in a class was rebuilt to try out ideas that might be suitable for incorporation in the entire class or in a newly-built class. This happened on the London & North Eastern Railway soon after the death of its chief mechanical engineer, Nigel Gresley. His successor took the first of Gresley's celebrated Pacifics in hand for a complete rebuild, uglifying it but getting rid of the Gresley valve gear that was excellent in function but needed very careful, and therefore costly, maintenance. Great Northern, the locomotive concerned, did lead to a series of somewhat similar Pacifics, but its rebuilding was an exercise in exorcism as much as an engineering venture, for the new mechanical engineer, formerly Gresley's subordinate, seemed extraordinarily keen to undo the work of his predecessor.

Rebuilt locomotives achieved their greatest glory in France, where André Chapelon took

existing Pacific designs and rebuilt them according to his own principles. These were genuine rebuilds with much of the original locomotives being retained but with substantial, and fundamental, changes of detail. His first rebuild, in 1929, involved the fitting of a Kylchap double exhaust, widening and smoothing the internal steam pipes, increasing the superheater temperature, and adding a feedwater heater. With these changes the locomotive could produce 3,000hp (2,240kW) instead of 2,000hp (1,490kW), and its fuel consumption per unit of horsepower was perceptibly reduced.

When a steam locomotive was rebuilt it was usually visually obvious. As a Pacific built as a turbine locomotive, LMS No. 6202 was both visually and aurally distinctive. It was eventually rebuilt into the conventional but one-off Pacific *Princess Anne*. In this guise it was involved and heavily damaged in the Harrow accident, after which it was transformed into another one-off Pacific, *Duke of Gloucester*. All three guises were visually distinct; how many of *Duke of Gloucester*'s components came down from the Turbomotive is uncertain, but they are unlikely to have been numerous.

*The 30 class tank locomotive of New South Wales Government Railways, many of which were displaced from suburban work by electrification and rebuilt as 30T class tender locomotives.*

A much more genuine rebuilding was that of the LMS 'Royal Scot' class into the 'Rebuilt Scot' series. Here the rebuilding consisted of replacing the boiler and incorporating a double chimney at the same time. Both the appearance and the performance of the design was thus transformed.

Conversion of tank locomotives to tender types occurred from time to time, often as a result of electrification rendering suburban tank engines redundant. This happened to a series of big 4-6-4 tank locomotives built by the London Brighton & South Coast Railway for its London-Brighton service. They were soon rebuilt as 4-6-0 tender engines and put in useful service for three more decades. In Australia the Sydney electrification released a large number of 30 class 4-6-4 tank locomotives, and many were rebuilt as 30T class 4-6-0 tender engines. As such they performed useful work, particularly on long branch lines.

Electric locomotives are rarely rebuilt; they just go on and on and are scrapped, not when they are worn out, but when they are considered obsolete. Sometimes, however, replacing old-style mechanical control systems by more modern thyristor-based systems can bring lower consumption of electric power. The Hong Kong mass transit authority, for example, found it worthwhile to re-equip 1970s-generation electric trains with gate-turn-off (chopper) control.

With diesel locomotives the picture is very different. These are often rebuilt, although the transformation is rarely visible because the components most likely to be changed are under cover. The process is rarely described as rebuilding, terms such as remanufacture, upgrading, or re-engineering being preferred.

When US railroads achieved full dieselization they typically were left with a stock of first-generation diesel locomotives at a time when new models offered much in the way of increased power and reduced running costs. To encourage railroads to invest in fleet renewal, the manufacturers offered deals in which existing locomotives would be traded in and rebuilt with the newest components. Such components included the diesel engine, traction motors and control equipment. For a decade or more remanufacture enabled the railroads to acquire the latest technology at an acceptable price. One company, Morrison-Knudsen, that was not a locomotive manufacturer, set itself up as a rebuilder of diesel locomotives and made a great success of it, even making some new locomotives as well. The Illinois Central Railroad also specialized in this work, rebuilding not only its own but other railroads' diesels.

The most common incentive to rebuild a diesel locomotive is to obtain a better engine. Designing engines for diesel locomotives was not as simple as was once thought. Engines which had proved suitable for other uses, typically in ships, proved to be less successful in railway service owing to the very different conditions of operation. In many countries, especially among 'first-generation' diesel locomotives, there were designs that were sound but were rendered mediocre in performance because the engines were not good enough. On the other hand, as time passed, certain designs of engine did prove themselves, and it was to obtain the benefits of these engines that railroads opted for rebuilding. The General Motors 645 series of engine was among those favored. In the late 1960s the Irish Railways (CIE) re-engined two British-built classes with 645 engines, after a decade of service, giving the units longer and enhanced life. Meanwhile, when they were about twenty years old the power cars of British Rail's IC125 trains began to be re-engined, with the original Valenta engines replaced by Paxman, the reduced fuel consumption and greater mileage between overhauls making the change worthwhile for units that were expected to remain in service for at least another decade.

*A French Pacific as rebuilt to the Chapelon pattern.*

*(opposite) A French Pacific locomotive in original un-rebuilt form.*

There were many notable rebuildings of whole series of locomotives. One of them involved the Burlington RR's General Motors E8 and E9 passenger units, which that railroad had used in both inter-city and commuter passenger service. In 1972 the Burlington sold them to Chicago's Western Suburban Mass Transit District, which sent them to Morrison Knudsen for rebuilding. They emerged from this process with their original pairs of 1,200hp (895kW) 567 type engines replaced by 645 engines, with auxiliary Cummins diesel engines also installed to provide heat, air conditioning and lighting for their trains. Thus equipped, they worked for another two decades on Chicago commuter services, retaining until the end the green livery of their original owner.

A not dissimilar rebuilding was undertaken on the British Class 47 locomotives. This was a numerous class, which had been built from the start with an engine (Sulzer) that was on the verge of obsolescence (that is, the engine had been uprated so many times that there were no reserves left for improvement). The Freightliner company in the late 1990s decided that the units it used were not quite powerful enough, and the original maker, Brush, was entrusted with re-engineering them. The Sulzer engine was replaced by General Motors 645 engines (themselves not new, but remanufactured). These were of the same power as the old Sulzers but were more reliable, could run more miles between overhauls, had a better fuel economy and were likely to enjoy good spare-parts back-up for decades. Simultaneously the generator was replaced by an alternator originally designed for a later Brush locomotive, the Class 56, with the current changed to dc for the traction motors by a rectifier designed for the even later Class 60 built by Brush. With the alternator having a bigger output than the previous generator, and with sanding and wheel-slip control added, the new locomotive (Class 57) could start trains considerably heavier than those handled by the Class 47.

# IDEAS THAT FAILED

Just as Napoleon was fighting his last battle at Waterloo in 1815, the reciprocating steam locomotive was facing its first challenge. This took the form of a steam locomotive designed by William Brunton in England, which instead of using pistons acting on driving wheels had an arrangement of levers actuating two walking feet that were intended to propel the machine along the rails. Like so many subsequent ideas, this one was valid but offered no appreciable advance on what already existed. Moreover, again like other inventions, money and willpower were exhausted before it had time to prove itself. In this case willpower was decisively assaulted by a lethal boiler explosion.

Another no-hope venture was the Fontaine locomotive patented in 1880 and built by Grant Locomotive in Patterson, New Jersey. Its

*Jawn Henry, the steam-turbine-electric locomotive of the Norfolk & Western Railroad.*

inventor believed that he had produced a high-speed locomotive simply by providing gearing that would give smallish 56in (1422mm) driving wheels the effect of 90in (2286mm) diameter. He did this by having the pistons drive a pair of 66in (1676mm) wheels mounted on an axle above the boiler. These wheels drove the main wheels below through friction wheels. It was as simple as that. The locomotive was tried on several railroads, but none was impressed. It was an interesting machine to watch, because the upper wheels rotated in the opposite direction to the lower wheels.

In the same spirit of well-thought-out craziness was the Holman locomotive, which was tried on the Soo and the Northern Pacific railroads in the 1890s. The idea was to use six powered axles, thereby, among other things, reducing axle weight. The locomotive's conventional driving wheels each drove sets of two intermediate wheels which in turn were geared to the thereby-powered carrying wheels. Again, it was thought that this transmission

would multiply the effective speed of the carrying wheels. It was not very successful, although it did haul trains. It also collided with a number of overbridges.

The problem with the conventional steam locomotive was that it had heavy weights moving to-and-fro, producing strains on engine and track, and it had a low thermal efficiency, converting only 5 to 8 per cent of the fuel's energy potential into actual horsepower. Many inventors tried to eliminate these defects. Thus the 1907 Paget locomotive of Britain's Midland Railway had eight inside cylinders with an array of bevel gears, spur gears, and outside fly cranks. It suffered from steam leakages and seizure of the valves, and the money ran out before these faults could be cured.

Earlier, in 1896, Jean-Jacques Heilmann in France produced prototypes of a steam-electric locomotive. This had a boiler whose steam drove a reciprocating two-cylinder engine that in turn powered a generator supplying axle-mounted traction motors. The Heilmann

*The New Haven RR's Hot Rod in its short-lived Boston - New York service.*

locomotives worked well on trial, except that there were detail defects and a rather large crew was required because of the complexity. Their fuel consumption was a little more than half that of a conventional steam locomotive, although the first cost was more than double that of an orthodox design. The project was killed by expert opinion which, as often happens, was unable to grasp the merits of a new idea. In fact, Heilmann had anticipated many of the characteristics of the subsequent diesel-electric locomotive.

Even after the diesel-electric locomotive had proved viable, railways experimented with steam-electric machines. In 1938 the Union Pacific RR tried a twin-unit 5,000hp (3,730kW)

*The smokebox fan concept as popularized in the Soviet Union.*

*The Fontaine locomotive of 1880, which was intended to be a high-speed machine.*

*The Holman locomotive, an ill-fated attempt to obtain low axle weights.*

steam-turbine-electric, outwardly resembling a streamlined diesel locomotive. In 1947 the C & O RR also acquired three steam-turbine-electrics for passenger service. Neither the UP nor the C&O design was adopted for regular use. They had teething troubles, and enthusiasm for them waned before these could be rectified. *Jawn Henry* of the Norfolk & Western RR was given a better chance. The N & W, whose main freight was coal, really wanted to remain a customer of the coal industry. This locomotive had a high-pressure boiler (600psi or 4,134kPa) and rode on 12 axles, all powered. On trial it registered impressive fuel economy. But it was soon relegated to pusher service and then retired after only 60,000 miles (90,560km). Its drawbacks were the high first cost and the facts that because it pulled a water tender it had to be turned after each run and it was too long for turntables, that as a one-off unit it was difficult

*Chesapeake & Ohio RR No 614, used in experiments to radically improve the efficiency with which locomotives burn coal.*

to crew and to maintain, and that although its thermal efficiency of 11.5 per cent was better than the 7 per cent of the Railroad's Mallet engines, it was still not high enough to allow it to compete with the diesel.

In the 1920s Wilhelm Schmidt, already famous as inventor of the first practical superheater, was advocating the use of hotter and more highly-pressed steam as a means of obtaining more energy from fuel. In Germany in 1925 Henschel & Sohn turned out an experimental three-cylinder compound 4-6-0 which embodied his ideas. Its most notable feature, perhaps, was its multi-pressure boiler. A similar locomotive, but of the 4-8-4 wheel arrangement, was built by Alco in the USA in 1931. Running on the New York Central RR as No 800, this had a boiler with three sections for different pressures, with the high-pressure part using water-tubes to transfer heat to the other two sections. A complex arrangent of coils, drums and superheaters was involved, and the locomotive's high-pressure cylinder received steam at no less than 850psi (5,856kPa). Two low-pressure cylinders absorbed more of the steam's energy, so usable power per pound of coal was greatly increased. The Canadian Pacific in Canada and the LMS in Britain built similar locomotives. The LMS unit, *Fury*, had a lethal steam leak on one run and was soon converted into a conventional locomotive. The other trial locomotives did well enough to justify their designers' claims, but operating staff found

they were more trouble than they were worth and the idea was not carried further. The London & North Eastern Railway's high-pressure watertube four-cylinder compound 4-6-4 was similarly unsuccessful, even though it did not have the complication of different pressures, working solely on 450psi (3,100kPa). The Delaware & Hudson RR also experimented with high pressures and watertube fireboxes between 1924 and 1933. It built three prototype 2-8-0s on the cross-compound system with these features, and also a super compound (triple expansion) four-cylinder 4-8-0. They worked relatively well, but their complexity ruled out their adoption.

In the 1940s Oliver Bulleid designed for the Southern Railway the 'Leader' class, a novel locomotive enclosing in its smooth superstructure an off-centre boiler feeding two three-cylinder steam engines that drove the central axles of the two power trucks, or bogies. The central axles were coupled by chains to the other two axles of the trucks. Thus the 'Leader' had six powered axles with a flexible wheelbase. There were other novelties, too; a stayless firebox and cylinders enclosed in steam jackets. However, railway nationalization meant that Bulleid left the scene and the new operators, British Railways, abandoned the project before much had been learned.

In the Soviet Union an idea that was an obvious failure could be proclaimed successful and reproduced in hundreds of copies. One

*The General Motors 'Jet Rocket' of the Rock Island RR; visually exciting but commercially a disappointment.*

such was the smokebox fan. Having become acquainted with this device in condenser locomotives, where it was indispensable, some Russian engineers in the face of all practical evidence declared that such fans were a good thing even in non-condensing locomotives. So locomotives began to appear with these troublesome devices, on the grounds that they provided a more even draught (probably true, when they were working well) and would therefore allow inferior coal to be used. The problem, well-known to many engineers who found it prudent to keep their mouths shut, was that metal fans revolving fast in high and fluctuating temperatures soon failed. Another feature was that, when an engine was working very hard, the fan choked, draught ceased, and the locomotive ran out of steam. Abandonment of this idea, like so many other triumphs of

commonsense, had to wait until the death of Stalin.

In the diesel age, many engineers were troubled by the apparent inefficiency of the diesel-electric. That is, they were pained by the cost of having two motors, electric and diesel, in one tractive unit when one should have been enough. Hence there have been several attempts at novel transmissions. One, the Fell system in Britain, reached the prototype stage and might have become viable, though not a great improvement, had more time and money been spent. It had a mechanical transmission and four engines; the number of engines (which drove through slip gears and differential gears) in use determined the transmision ratio. In Germany there was some success with hydraulic transmissions for powerful locomotives (such transmissions had hitherto been considered suitable only for low-power applications). Diesel-hydraulic types were built for both the German and British railways but were eventually abandoned in favour of the more trouble-free diesel-electric. A handful of US railroads also acquired small batches of German diesel-hydraulics, but did not pursue the idea.

Some ideas fail not because they are technically defective, but because they fail to excite purchasers. This was true of the several novel passenger trains introduced in the United States in the 1950s, when passenger traffic was clearly in decline. These trains, 'Aerotrain' by General Motors, 'Jet Rocket' of the Rock Island RR, 'Train-X' of Talgo and New York Central, the Talgo train of the New Haven RR and the latter company's 'Hot Rod,' all ultimtely failed because they did not persuade passengers to return to the railroad. From the locomotive point of view the General Motors locomotives supplied for the 'Aerotrain' and 'Jet Rocket' are interesting because the styling conveyed a highly futuristic image, yet the locomotive underneath was simply an arrangement of standard components. As for the New Haven's 'Hot Rod,' this made little attempt to disguise the fact that it was composed of conventional Budd rail diesel passenger cars, the only concession to futurity being the locomotive nose added to the front. With each vehicle powered, however, this unassuming train was capable of reaching 85mph (137kph) in four minutes from a standing start on the level.

# ELECTRIC TRACTION

Antonio Pacinotti, an Italian, was the first to demonstrate a crude practical electric motor. In 1866 he found that if his motor was driven mechanically in reverse it became a generator of electricity, a dynamo (Faraday had demonstrated both motor and dynamo some decades earlier, but he had not been concerned with practical applications). Generated electricity flowed through wires to drive an electric motor at a distance. A fresh power industry had been born.

If many coils of insulated wire are wound around a soft iron rod (a core) and electricity is passed through these coils, the core acts as a magnet. Pacinotti set two of these electromagnets facing each other in a frame (called the stator). A similar pair of electromagnets was arranged on a shaft (the rotor) which revolved inside the stator.

Which end of an electromagnet is its north and which its south pole depends upon the direction in which the electric current is flowing through the windings. Like magnetic poles repel each other strongly (i.e., a north repels a north and a south repels a south). Pacinotti's motor was wired so that stator and rotor poles facing each other had the same polarity. When current was passed, these poles repelled each other and the shaft was thereby forced to rotate. This mechanical movement could be used to drive machinery such as a railway locomotive.

As a generator of current, the rotor is driven mechanically by, for example, a steam engine. The flow of electricity in the rotor poles (excitation current) strongly magnetizes them. The magnetic field thus created induces a strong magnetic field in the stator poles, which in turn causes an electric current to flow in their windings. This electric current can be drawn off for use. The excitation current required is low, so much so that often, when generating alternating current, residual magnetism in the poles is sufficient to start things off.

Things are not as simple as this, however. Should one view from the outside a rotor pole with a particular polarity, the current flowing in the windings will be doing so in a particular direction - clockwise, for example. When the rotor shaft has revolved through 180∞, however, from the same viewpoint the current is now flowing anti-clockwise and the polarity of the end of the core facing you has changed. The stator electromagnets, however, have not moved, and the net effect is that rotor and stator electromagnets now have opposite polarities and attract each other.

To get over this apparent change in polarity, Pacinotti devised the commutator. He mounted copper segments on the rotor shaft, so-called brushes of copper maintaining electrical contact with the segments. For two rotor poles, two segments were mounted on the shaft as a commutator, carefully insulated from each other. Each segment was wired to the rotor poles, but each segment was so wired that current flowed in its pole in an opposite direction to that in the other pole.

Thus, as the commutator turned together with the rotor poles, the current flow in the poles was reversed and the right polarity maintained.

*British Rail, 1973. No 87.011 climbing in the Lake District. The London-Glasgow railway is electrified at 25,000 volts single phase 50 Hz.*

It should be noted that all of the foregoing concerns motors and generators for direct current -- that is, current that always flows from A to B in the same direction. Alternating current was a later development, and will be dealt with later.

As may be anticipated, the modern direct-current motor is a good deal more complicated than described above. Four to eight stator poles are used, together with lesser interpoles and multipole rotors. Commutators may have as many as 80 segments, and the wiring complications may be imagined.

The majority of electric locomotives in the world use the series-wound direct-current traction motor. `Series-wound' means that current passes through rotor and stator, one after the other. For railway use the many advantages of this motor have outweighed the disadvantages, but this situation is changing.

The commutator is a great source of maintenance expense. For one thing, the brushes wear out and deposit dirt between the segments, causing flashovers. During trials of the commutator-less German Federal Railway's Class 120 in 1980, difficulty was found in braking to a stop; brake-block pressure had to be increased compared with commutator locomotives. The reason for this is that commutators act as a perpetually dragging brake, and consequently suffer very rapid wear.

Electric current cannot be switched on to traction motors direct: the resultant high flow of current at maximum voltage would be likely to burn out the various electromagnet windings. To cut the voltage for starting purposes, resistances are included in the circuit of the motors. The resistances are taken out of circuit one by one as speed increases, until the motors are working at full voltage.

As noted, the series-wound direct-current traction motor takes the same current through rotor and stator pole windings. The motor is designed so that it runs at peak efficiency at its most usual revolution rate. It can be made to run faster by increasing the voltage (with a corresponding decrease in current), but this brings a decrease in efficiency, because the higher voltage causes an effect known as back electromotive force (emf) in the stator magnetic field, which tends to oppose the rotary motion. The back emf can be weakened to reduce the effect by reducing the stator voltage only, and this is done by introducing parallel-wired resistances into the stator circuit, so that part of the current is diverted into the resistances and the voltage drops. Up to five such resistances can be inserted, each either corresponding to

*Baltimore & Ohio Railroad, 1894 (bottom). Electric locomotive No 1. Trains with steam locomotives were hauled over the electrified section, to avoid tunnel smoke nuisance.*

a notch on the driver's controller or being brought automatically into play as the load on the motor attains a certain value. This situation is known as weak-field working.

All but the very earliest and very latest electric and diesel-electric locomotives described in this volume were designed for weak-field working. The very latest have instead a solid-state, separately controlled, supply to rotor and stator. The separate control ensures that the traction motor runs at optimum efficiency whatever the revolution rate.

It was on 31 May 1879, at a Berlin Trades Exhibition, that an electric train ran for the first time. During the next four months 86,000 passengers were carried in six-seat coaches, four to a train. The whole installation was lifted and reused at Düsseldorf and Brussels in 1880. It was shown in Paris in 1881, although not running, but it was shown in operation at Copenhagen in the same year. Finally, it was run at London's Crystal Palace and at St Petersburg in 1882.

Werner Siemens was responsible for this first electric train. His locomotive was for a gauge of just under 20in (508mm), and weighed about a quarter of a tonne. Current was fed to the locomotive at 150V, and it was rated at 3.3hp (2.5kW). The rotor and its commutator were mounted longitudinally above four driving wheels, to which the rotor shaft was geared. Two very large stator poles were placed either side of the rotor. Reversing the locomotive was

done mechanically in the gearing, rather than by electric circuitry.

The original intention was that current should be picked up from one running rail and returned to the other. This proved unsatisfactory, so a third rail was laid as a current supply (copper brushes made the connection), the return being made through the running rails. Current-control on the locomotive was effected by short-circuiting seven resistances one by one as they were dipped into liquid.

In the United States in 1880 Thomas Edison ran a trial locomotive fed with current from the running rails; and Stephen Field took out patents to the same end. There was a brief patent war between Siemens, Edison and Field, but development was so rapid that probably there was little point in squabbling about last year's patents. Edison and Field together founded the Electric Railway Company of America in 1883, the commercial predecessor of the modern corporation General Electric of the United States. Edison had a hand in two more electric locomotives, before turning his mind to other things.

The next venture of Siemens was a 1½ mile (2.5km) tramway in the Berlin suburb of Lichterfelde in 1881. A 100V current was taken from the running rails, and the tramcars were rated at 6.7hp (5kW). Two months later Siemens opened a short tramway of the same type in Paris, notable as the first line to collect current from an overhead conductor. This overhead

*Another early 20th century electrification of a tunnel route was the Canadian Northern Railway's 2400Vd.c. line under Mount Royal at Montreal. This picture dates from 1983, by which time this line had developed into a busy suburban network.*

*Electric locomotives of the Metropolitan Railway hauled outer suburban trains north of London, using a 600Vd.c. 4-rail system. This is a surviving member of the class, Sarah Siddons, in excursion service.*

system was not popular among some Parisians, who found it unsightly.

The original reason for overhead conductors was that street tramways could not use a third rail, street mud and wetness making rail insulation difficult. The designers initially complicated things for themselves, in both Europe and the United States, by putting up not one, but two overhead conductors. Indeed, in some versions a little trolley towed by the tramcar ran on the overhead track (hence the use sometimes in the United States of the term 'trolley-car' in place of the more usual 'streetcar'). Current from the trolley found its way to the tramcar motors by cable.

Volk's Electric Railway along Brighton beach in England was opened in 1883, and even in such an environment used the running rails as conductors at 50V. It is still operating, although now using a third rail. It was followed a month or two later by the Giant's Causeway and Portrush Railway in Ireland, a line 8 miles (13km) long with a 3ft (914mm) gauge. This was a Siemens venture, as was a line from Mödling to Hinterbruhl, near Vienna, both lines opening in 1883.

The Giant's Causeway line was notable in that it was the first railway to be run by hydroelectric power. Indeed, in 1883 there was only one other hydroelectric installation in existence, that at Bözingen in Switzerland, opened in 1882 and used for lighting purposes. In Ireland the River Bush was dammed and the falling water drove two turbines to power the electricity generators. A third rail at 240V powered the tramcars. The railway closed in 1949.

During the 1880s the generation and distribution of electricity had not been developed, so each electric railway had to provide its own generating station. It was known that high voltages facilitated power transmission, but Lucien Gaulard's first practical transformer to step voltages up or down was very recent, dating from 1881. The first recognizable oil-cooled modern transformer was not to be devised until 1890 (by Otto Bláthy of the Ganz firm in Budapest). Because of transmission difficulties, electric railways had to be short. For example, it was not unknown on the Giant's Causeway line for a tramcar to be unable to leave Portrush because of lack of current. Portrush was remote from the generating station, and so, before the tramcar could leave, all the other motive power on the line had to be stationary.

Also, traction motors remained relatively inefficient, and thus of low power. For both of

these reasons railway electrifications were postponed for the most part until the 1890s.

Frank Sprague, of the Edison-Sprague firm, and the Thomson-Houston Company were notable pioneers; both firms were constituents of the General Electric Corporation when it was formed in 1893. Sprague first introduced the now widespread use of nose-suspended traction motors on a tramway in Richmond, Virginia, in 1888. The motor was supported by the sprung truck (bogie) frame on one side, and rested on a bearing on the axle on the other. A pinion at the end of the rotor shaft engaged with a gear-wheel on the axle.

It was Sprague who tidied up the cutting-out of resistances to start traction motors. Siemens' dipping of resistances into fluid to short-circuit them was superseded by a variety of mechanical resistance selectors. Sprague mounted all the resistances one above the other in a metal box. A vertical camshaft ran up through the box, surmounted externally by the driver's control handle. As the driver turned the handle round, the cams on their shaft opened the resistances in order.

This did well enough for tramcars, and it was adopted at first for rail motor coaches. However, locomotives were more massive than trams, and the quantity of starting resistances also increased. The resistances and the camshaft were transferred out of the driver's cab, the camshaft being operated by a servomotor. Sprague, by this time working for General Electric, introduced electro-pneumatic operation of the contactors in 1905. Even more sophisticated methods followed.

It was the Thomson-Houston Company which first avoided the double overhead conductor and its trolley in the United States; the firm changed to a single overhead wire in 1888. Strangely, there had sprung up a belief in the United States that wheels were necessary to collect current. The collecting pole on the Thomson-Houston model was surmounted by a wheel that ran along the overhead wire. The practice lasted for many years for trams, and was even used on railways until about 1900.

Siemens converted his Lichterfelde tram to overhead collection in 1889, using bows for friction contact with the wire, as in modern practice. Friction contact was usual in Europe from then on except where, as in England, US practice was adopted. In either system, the running rails have to be electrically continuous in order to carry return current, and so tramway rails were welded together long before such welding was adopted, for other reasons, on main-line railways.

The development of the electric traction motor was notably achieved by the US firm Westinghouse. Instead of the components being open to the air and dust, they were enclosed in a casing known as a carcase. Bearings carried the rotor shaft, complete with commutator, at either end of the carcase. The stator poles were attached to the walls.

Motor efficiency was investigated. The number of stator poles and their relation to the rotor poles was optimized. It was found that the two sets of poles should be as close together as possible during the rotors' rotation (in a modern motor it is a matter of a few millimetres). Efficiency rises, too, with the rate of rotation of the rotors, although this rate cannot rise too high in a direct-current motor for fear of upsetting commutator performance.

During the 1890s electrification reached railways proper. The City and South London Railway, notable as a railway running deep underground and therefore made possible only by electricity, opened in 1890. It was followed in England by the Liverpool Overhead Railway and in the United States by the first part of the Chicago Elevated Railway, both in 1893. Continental Europe's first underground electric railway opened in Budapest in 1896.

The Baltimore and Ohio Railroad electrified 4 miles (6km) through a tunnel under Baltimore in 1895, largely to avoid locomotive-smoke nuisance. The interesting point about this line was that power was supplied from the largest generating station of its day. The station supplied not only the railway but also the city's tramways and industrial requirements. The proprietors noted that meeting these various needs spread the load on the large steam reciprocating engines very satisfactorily.

By 1900 direct-current low-voltage electrification of railways had settled down to very much the form used today. The voltage used had climbed to 600; today it is 750V in the Western world and 825V in some other parts of the world. Low-voltage electrification is not suitable for main lines because it is too costly, but it remains the cheapest way of electrifying lines that are not longer than about 15 miles (24km).

# THE MONORAIL

During the 1890s the simplicity of electric traction gave the optimistic ideas of monorails a push forward. A single rail appeared to offer economy in construction, and even before 1900 a speed of 100mph (160kph) was forecast. For various reasons the single rail was usually raised off the ground, but the great difficulty was to keep the vehicle balanced upright on its single rail. A favored solution was to have a pair of guide-rails and auxiliary guide wheels. The guide-rails, or other guiding surfaces, were often incorporated in the supports for the load-carrying monorail.

All this talk of monorails attracted the attention of a gifted writer, H. G. Wells. His stories envisaged clean, silent and fast monorails serving the cities of the future. The stories were read by impressionable inventors in their youth, as well as by future politicians. Except in particular circumstances, commonsense condemns such schemes. One such particular circumstance can be terrain, and the most

*The longest-lasting of the monorails, the Wuppertahl line in Germany.*

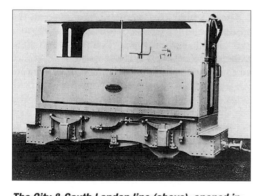

*The City & South London line (above), opened in 1890, the first deep level `Tube' railway. Locomotives of the Bo wheel arrangement had rotor windings directly on the axle, to eliminate gear noise in the tunnels.*

succesful of the earlier monorail systems was that at Wuppertal in Germany, where the space above a river bed was used to provide an electric urban transport facility in the form of a monorail suspended on high girders.

Monorail suffered from the major difficulty that, during the century since the idea first emerged, nobody devised a satisfactory means of transferring a vehicle from one track to another.

A pair of switches does the task on a normal railway, but switch designs for monorails are slow-acting, take up too much space, or are expensive. Some designs have been at fault on all three counts at once. The result is that monorail is an inflexible transport mode, although in certain circumstances, as some US cities are discovering, it can be useful. Magnetic levitation ('Maglev') systems also suffer from the problem of switching tracks, and this is perhaps the main reason why, despite some not-unpromising experiments and a substantial project in Japan, they have been slow to create confidence in their future. Inflexibility in a transport mode, of course, is in itself no bar to its use, and Maglev, like the monorail, may well find a use where there is a specific traffic in specific circumstances.

*Alweg Monorail, Seattle, first of its kind in America.*

# THREE-PHASE ELECTRIFICATION

The generation and distribution of electricity developed greatly during the 1890s, and alternating current with three-wire transmission was found to be the most economical method. As has been explained in connection with the dynamo, current flows in opposite directions in generator poles as the rotor revolves. For direct current a commutator at the end of the rotor corrects this current reversal. Should the commutator be omitted, the current will flow first in one direction and then in the other. Alternating flow of this sort can be shown diagrammatically as a wavy line with equal peaks and dips, each peak or dip showing maximum flow in one direction or the other. It proved convenient to run three wires from the generators, each wire being known as a phase; hence the term 'three-phase current'.

One other associated concept is frequency. Basically, the rate of revolution of a generator will determine the number of reversals of current output each second. The units of frequency are cycles per second, usually called hertz (Hz).

Heinrich Hertz was the German physicist who first showed that radio waves have common characteristics with other electromagnetic wave motions, such as those of light. When radio disc jockeys talk about the kilohertz or megahertz on which they are broadcasting they are referring to the frequency of the radio waves which their station transmits.

Alternating-current frequency has an effect on much electrical apparatus. An electric clock designed for 60Hz ac will lose ten minutes in the hour if fed with 50Hz current. In most of the world electricity is generated at a standard 50Hz, but in North America and parts of South America and Japan the standard is 60Hz. These are known as the industrial frequencies, despite the fact that they are used domestically as well.

As industrial-frequency distribution systems spread, engineers looked into the use of three-phase current for traction. They hit a snag. At industrial frequencies the three-phase motors revolved too fast for railway use unless they could be geared down. Given the technology of the time, it was believed that gear-wheels to take the stresses of main-line traction could not be manufactured. Consequently the first three-phase electrifications were of minor railways where high power was not needed.

These first three-phase lines were the work of a Swiss engineer, Charles Brown, who used 40Hz current, the industrial frequency in his country at the time. (He was the son of another Charles Brown, from England, who, while working in Switzerland, devised the Brown locomotive boiler for tramway steam locomotives). Brown met with a German engineer named Walter Boveri (who happened to have a financial mind), and together they founded Brown, Boveri & Cie in 1891. The firm became a major heavy electrical-engineering concern with subsidiaries in many countries.

A Lugano tramway was the first three-phase electrification in 1896. It was followed by narrow-gauge railways up the Jungfrau and the Gornergrat in 1899, and by a standard-gauge local railway, the Burgdorf-Thun, in the same year. The Hungarian firm of Ganz Electric, in Budapest, was also interested in three-phase electrification. Its engineer Kálmán Kandó envisaged main-line electrification using the reduced frequency of 16 2/3Hz. The traction motors would then run at such a speed that the rotors could be coupled direct to the locomotive driving wheels, at the cost of providing special railway generating stations for the 16 2/3Hz needed.

The traction motors used were of the induction (squirrel-cage) type, which were started through resistances in the usual manner but thereafter ran at a constant speed as dictated by the frequency. A second speed could be offered by connecting two motors in cascade. The stator of one motor was fed at line voltage, and the current induced in the rotor of this motor was fed to the stator of the second motor. So connected, both motors, and the locomotive, ran at half speed.

*A three-phase train. This is the Jungfrau rack railway in Switzerland. Note the characteristic twin-bow current collectors.*

# Single-phase Electrification

Locomotive running-speed could be varied also by varying the number of motor stator poles in circuit. Typically, six poles in circuit gave a normal speed, while eight poles in circuit reduced speed by 25 per cent. The only large user of three-phase electrification was the Italian State Railways. Usually its freight locomotives had cascade circuitry only, for speeds of 15½ and 31mph (25 and 50kph). Passenger locomotives had pole variation in addition, for speeds of 23¼, 31, 46½ and 62mph (37½, 50, 75 and 100kph).

There was one further advantage of three-phase electrification. When current was switched off, the induction motors on a moving locomotive became generators automatically. The effort of generation braked the train, and the current generated could be passed back into the overhead wires for use by other trains. This system is called a regenerative brake. Automatic apparatus looked after any surplus

*Marienfelde-Zossen trials, 1903 (below). The Siemens' motor coach which reached 128 mph (206.7 kph). The mast with three bow collectors is shown well.*

current, which would otherwise push up line voltage above the 3,700V at which it was fixed.

The US Westinghouse firm built a locomotive and electrical factory on the Italian Riviera in 1905. Kálmán Kandó and a Ganz design team were seconded to the factory at Vado Ligure for long periods during 1905-15. There they helped to extend Italian three-phase electrification in all its aspects. In 1918 the factory was sold to the British firm Vickers, but in 1920 it was resold to Brown Boveri. It was the only factory in the Brown Boveri group that could build complete locomotives.

Three-phase main-line electrification was soon found to have major disadvantages. The constant speed of the locomotives was a timetable compiler's delight, but it did mean that no train could make up time, and nor were four fixed running speeds really sufficient. Two overhead wires, insulated from each other, had to be provided above the track. Each wire represented a phase, the third phase being the earthed running rails. Current at 16⅔Hz flickered too badly for lighting, and so Italian three-phase electric locomotives had to carry acetylene headlamps.

After 1900 Charles Brown at Brown Boveri

started to think of other methods of main-line electrification. By 1914 Kálmán Kandó was turning over in his mind the possibilities of using industrial-frequency current for railway electrifications. There were a couple of three-phase electrifications in the United States, but these have long gone, while Italian three-phase finished in 1976. Three-phase is the only railway electrification system to have now almost vanished.

Three-phase cannot be left without recording the Marienfelde-Zossen Railway and the high-speed trials made on it. The line was a military railway near Berlin, with minimum gradients and only two, easy, curves. The electrification masts erected alongside the track carried three contact wires, one above the other, one for each phase. The motor coaches had three vertical bow collectors extending sideways. The arrangement was impracticable normally, of course, but it served well for the trials.

The German electrical industry ran these, and provided two luxury coach-bodies of the period, the idea being to save money by using the coach-bodies after the trials for their proper purpose (which duly occurred). The coaches had six-wheel bogies and each bogie carried

*(opposite) A 1,500v dc Bo-Bo locomotive built for Britain's North Eastern Railway in 1915.*

two traction motors, giving these motive power units the A1A-A1A wheel arrangement. One coach was equipped electrically by Siemens, the other by Algemeine Elektrizitäts Gesellschaft (AEG).

Preliminary trials were run during 1901-1902, and the engineers promptly ran into the various problems that have dogged designers of high-speed railways ever since. A speed of 100mph (160kph) was attained, but this did no good to the track, which had to be relaid with heavier rails and closer crosstie-spacing; a useful exercise for the troops of the line's military owners. It was found that the current-collecting bows needed to be adjusted slightly.

The two motor coaches did their share of punishing the track. At 87mph (140kph) the trucks started to hunt (i.e., they oscillated about the truck pin from side to side), so that the wheel-flanges gave the rails lateral blows (hunting tends to build up rhythmically, with increasingly powerful sideways blows). Locomotive engineer August von Borries was called in to redesign the trucks. He gave them an increased wheelbase and improved springs and suspension. After the addition of a little ballast to equalize the weight on each driving axle, the von Borries trucks were a great success. Indeed, it was von Borries who showed the world thereby that leading carrying wheels are unnecessary to guide a locomotive into curves -- always provided that the trucks are designed with art, of course.

Another problem was that the brake-blocks on the motor coaches ran hot. The engineers got round this by dribbling a water spray on to the brake-blocks whenever they were applied.

We have seen that induction motors revolve at a rate determined by the frequency of current applied. The improved motor coaches running in 1903 started with current at 25Hz. After going through the starting resistances, the driver

*Amtrak, USA, 1974. Class AEM6 was intended for high speed, but bogie springs and suspension proved inadequate.*

signalled to a man standing by the track that all was well. The man at the trackside pushed a button, which rang a bell in the generating station. There the steam engine driving the generator had its speed-governor adjusted.

Adjusting the governor meant that the steam engine ran faster, the generator ran faster, and the frequency output of the latter went up to 50Hz. Supplying this higher frequency to the traction motors increased the speed of the motor coach. In 1903 the AEG motor coach ran up to 130mph (210.2kph), a world-record rail speed that stood for 28 years.

The Siemens motor coach managed only 128½mph (206.7kph). A generating-station fault on the day that an attempt was made on the record allowed an output of not more than 45Hz. Siemens' chief engineer, Walter Reichel, was

driving, and beside him stood August von Borries. The latter has related that, at maximum speed, he put his hand over that of Reichel on the controller and said: 'That will be enough'. Both men knew that they were fast approaching Zossen and that it was time to apply the brakes, even though the motor coach was still accelerating slightly. Happy days, when very senior engineers could go out and drive their own products.

With regard to the hunting encountered with the trucks of the Marienfelde-Zossen, we must recall that plenty of today's electric and diesel locomotives have maximum speed limits placed upon them not by lack of capacity but by the possibility of the trucks hunting. A French National Railways' electric Bo-Bo attained a world record 206mph (331kph) in 1955, but its trucks hunted so badly at speed that the rails were hammered outwards by flange blows to about 1in (25mm) on alternate sides of the track. The French were luckier than the Americans, however. Amtrak's Co-Co Class AEM6 electric locomotive of 1974 had to be restricted to 85mph (137kph) maximum speed. It was intended to run at 120mph (193kph), but the first time that it was run at over 90mph (145kph) the trucks hunted so badly that the locomotive left the track altogether.

Three-phase current is suited to long-distance transmission lines, but having three or four wires (including an earth wire) at the point of use is clumsy. A way of eliminating one of these wires was found in the transformer, which reduces the

Wheel arrangements are given in the modern manner used customarily for electric and diesel locomotives. Axles, rather than wheels, are counted and the number of driven axles is shown by a letter rather than a figure. An 0-B-0 is a four-wheel locomotive with both axles driven and no carrying wheels. A 1-B-0 has the driven wheels preceded by one carrying axle, and a C-C has all axles driven, the '0' denoting lack of carrying wheels being omitted for convenience. Electrically driven locomotives often have a separate traction motor for each driven axle. Should this be so, an 0-B-0 would become and 0-Bo-0, the small letter 'o' attached to the capital letter indicating a separate drive for each axle. In North America (where it is normal for each driven axle to have its own motor), this letter 'o' is rarely used.

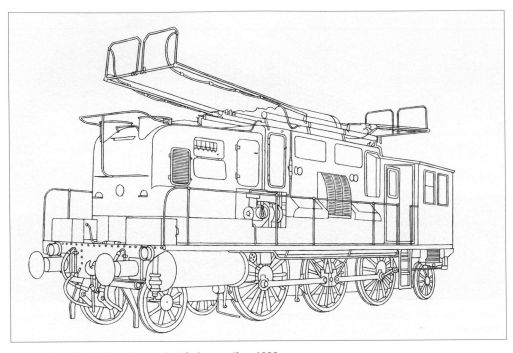

*I-C-I Italian State three phase electric locomotive, 1922.*

*German Federal Railway, 1957. No 141 267-5, a modern Bo-Bo for 15,000 volts 16 2/3 Hz, at Duisburg.*

high transmission voltage. This method gives single-phase current, which for railways allows the use of a single overhead wire, and also a much higher operating voltage as insulation difficulties are reduced.

A transformer has a primary winding (wound around a soft iron core) fed from the current source. Alongside, close to the primary winding but entirely unconnected, is placed the secondary winding. Current flowing in the primary will induce current in the secondary. By varying the length of either the primary or the secondary, any desired output voltage can be obtained. In the ordinary way, three wires (phases) lead into and out of a transformer. By connecting an electrical load across only two of the transformer's phase output wires (one of the phases is then called neutral), single-phase alternating current is obtained. To balance the three-phase input it is necessary to connect a similar but entirely separate electrical load across the remaining phase wire and the neutral phase.

On a modern electrified railway using single-phase current, a transformer sited in a lineside sub-station can supply two separate and successive sections of the line. (This is on the supposition that traffic demands on the two successive stretches will be about the same, so that one can be supplied from one output of the transformer and the other from the other output). A dead and carefully insulated overhead wire-length is inserted between the two railway sections; this is called a neutral section.

This discussion of transformers has been simplified, but there is no simple way to describe single-phase locomotive traction motors. There were two starting points. One took the series-wound direct-current motor and adapted it (retaining the commutator) while the other developed from the three-phase induction motor. Neither motor was entirely satisfactory, and eventually the system using the induction motor was dropped for railway use.

After experiment, single-phase current in the overhead wire settled down to values of 15,000V, 16⅔Hz in Europe and 11,000V, 25Hz in the United States. At the start of the development of single-phase, after 1900, various designers assayed industrial-frequency traction motors, only to find that the electrical difficulties were (and are) far too great. Very small motors worked after a fashion for light tramcars, but otherwise the system was impracticable.

On a single-phase locomotive a single-phase transformer cuts the voltage to not more than 400V for application to the traction motors: like the frequency, voltage must be low to obviate the motors' electrical difficulties. Because of the

*Swiss Federal Railways, 1939. Class Ae8/14 No 11852. The pioneer with control tappings on the high tension side of the transformer.*

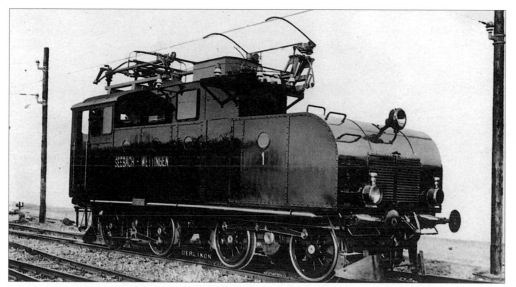

*Caption p39bSeebach-Wettingen trials. Single phase locomotive No 1 of 1904. Arranged originally for 50 Hz ac, but altered later to 16 2/3 Hz, the second such in the world.*

Europe's first single-phase 25Hz railway was a stretch of the Royal Prussian State Railway's Niederschönweide-Spindlersfelde line in 1903. It was equipped by Algemeine Elektrizitäts Gesellschaft (AEG) using an induction-type traction motor developed by an Austrian engineer, Friedrich Eichberg. The motor was developed by AEG's engineers during 1904, and was known subsequently as the Winter-Eichberg type.

The great prize was the electrification of the Royal Prussian State Railway, and the 25Hz systems were in competition with single-phase 16 2/3Hz. The latter won out in 1908, and subsequently 25Hz disappeared from Europe, although it did have some successes, notably on the suburban lines of the London, Brighton and South Coast Railway, electrified by AEG in 1909. The single-phase 16 2/3Hz system at 15,000V is today's standard electrification system in Austria, Switzerland, Germany, Norway and Sweden.

Hans Behn Eschenburg, traction engineer for the Swiss firm Oerlikon, developed a series-wound, commutator-type traction motor for 16²⁄₃Hz that would equally well regenerate current for braking purposes. The first Behn Eschenburg traction motors were tried on a Swiss 16²⁄₃Hz line, the experimental Seebach-Wettingen, in 1905. In spite of some drawbacks the type has been adopted. There were some other versions of the motor by Brown Boveri, AEG, and so on, but these have now been discarded as they were only attempts to get round Oerlikon patents.

In the opening years of the 20th century it was appreciated that direct-current electrifications could compete with low-frequency alternating-current only if the operating voltage was higher. The difficulty was the design of a high-speed circuit-breaker to handle high-voltage direct current (it was easier for alternating current). This vital piece of apparatus protects locomotive or other circuitry from accidental overvoltages (or, if rather differently designed, overcurrents). Much costly damage is prevented.

The first high-speed circuit-breakers were made around 1900 for 600V, and development slowly pushed the voltage higher. General Electric of the United States was a leader in the work. By 1915 high-speed circuit-breakers were in existence that could cope with 1,500V and 3,000V traction voltages; and Soviet Railways in the 1970s had a few motor coaches and locomotives for 6,000V direct current. Nothing more has been heard of 6,000V electrifications, so it may be supposed that the high-speed circuit-breaker was again causing difficulties.

low voltage, the motors are heavier and bulkier than their direct-current counterparts. Hence, in the earlier years of single-phase low-frequency electrifications, the motors were usually spring-borne in the locomotive body, and the drive to the wheels was by coupling rods.

In the United States Westinghouse adapted the series-wound direct-current motor for single-phase 25Hz use, and as early as 1892 it was running a trial tramcar on a factory line in Pittsburgh. However, it was not until 1905 that single-phase 25Hz was used on a railway in the United States. Over the intervening period the traction motor had undergone a good deal of development.

Kálmán Kandó, while at the Westinghouse factory at Vado Ligure, found himself diverted from his three-phase interests to push 25Hz single-phase electrification in Europe. There were some successes, although rather minor ones, such as on the Val Brembana Railway at Bergamo in 1906: the line retained the original equipment until its closure in 1966.

When starting, single-phase locomotives tap the transformer's secondary winding at successive points to increase the voltage. The five Val Brembana locomotives were the first with electro-pneumatic equipment to make this tapping change. Since Swiss Federal Railways No. 11852 of 1939, it is now customary to change the tappings on the primary side of the transformer. The combination of higher voltage with lesser current facilitates the making and breaking of contacts.

*An early 20th century 2-axle electric locomotive built for work on the 5,500v 16 Hz Murnau - Oberammergau line in Bavaria.*

The difficulty in breaking high-voltage circuits is that arcs are drawn across the mating surfaces that are being drawn apart. Not only do the arcs do damage, but the unwanted current continues to flow through them. Modern practice puts the mating surfaces in a vacuum, so that arcing is minimized, or arranges for a sharp air-blast to blow out the arc at the right moment.

The attraction of higher operating voltages was that expensive sub-stations, where current was reduced to overhead line voltage, could be spaced farther apart. Before 1920 or so, the cost of a substation was especially high. Three-phase current as received drove a motor, which

in turn drove a direct-current generator. As well as the cost of a man in attendance, 10-20 per cent of the power generated originally was lost by this primitive method of rectification.

The Butte, Anaconda and Pacific Railroad, a 37-mile (50km) line, was electrified at 2,400V direct current in 1913. In England, Siemens and Dick, Kerr tried 1,650V (later 1,500V) on the North Eastern Railway, as well as experimenting with 2,400V and 3,600V on the Lancashire and Yorkshire Railway. High-voltage direct-current arrived in 1915, with the start of the Chicago, Milwaukee, St Paul and Pacific electrification at 3,000V direct current. This was over the 437 miles (705km) between Harlowton, Montana

and Avery, Idaho. (Owing to lack of traffic, this route was closed entirely in 1974.)

The Milwaukee RR 3,000V locomotives from General Electric (wheel arrangement 2-Bo-Bo + Bo-Bo-2) were the first direct-current locomotives arranged for regenerative braking. This is more difficult than with alternating current, as the current flow in the direct-current motors must be regulated by using the starting resistances. An important US development was the mercury-arc rectifier, taken into general use in the 1920s. In this the alternating current strikes an arc into a pool of mercury, the output being direct current. This was replaced by the even cheaper solid-state rectifier in the 1950s.

# Industrial Frequency Electrification

Electrical engineers still hankered after a cheaper railway electrification method. This appeared to be possible by using single-phase current in the overhead wire, still at the 50Hz or 60Hz frequency as generated. Kálmán Kandó did something about it as early as 1923; in that year a trial locomotive was running outside Budapest. Eventually, in 1932-3, the Hungarian State Railways line from Budapest to Hegyeshalom, on the Austrian border, was electrified using alternating current, single-phase 50Hz, 15,000V.

Kandó's locomotives carried on board a phase converter; in effect an alternating-current single-phase electric motor run together with a three-phase (or more phases) generator. The output was three-, four- and six-phase current. A single large induction traction motor had its rotor coupled to the driving wheels. Suitable pole

*Swedish State Railways, 1964. A Class Rc2, similar to the thyristor-control pioneer locomotive.*

*50,000 volt locomotives haul a 32,000-ton ore train on the 3ft 6in gauge Sishen line in South Africa.*

groupings in the induction traction motor produced running speeds of 15½, 31, 46½ and 62mph (25, 50, 75 and 100kph).

This version of industrial-frequency electrification was found to be cheaper than low-frequency single-phase electrifications, but more costly than high-voltage direct current. Kandó's system was too late in the field, and had the additional disadvantage of fixed running speeds.

On the other hand, when industrial frequency locomotives proper were devised, Hungarian State Railways was able to put them to work at once without any costly re-electrification schemes.

The German State Railway started to experiment with 50Hz single-phase electrification in 1934, followed by the Soviet Union in 1938. The Second World War overtook both experiments, with the Hollenthal line in Germany, where the experiments were made, falling into a French occupation zone. The French picked up where the Germans left off, and produced a workable single-phase industrial-frequency locomotive in 1951.

Since that year industrial-frequency current in the overhead contact wire has been the cheapest form of railway electrification. The highest feasible voltage was set at 25,000V; exceptionally, in underpopulated areas, 50,000V has been used. The French were fortunate in their timing. Just before their first locomotive a mercury-arc rectifier that fitted into a locomotive, and which could survive the vibration and rough usage in that situation, had been devised in the United States.

On board an industrial-frequency locomotive the line voltage is reduced to that needed for the traction motors by primary-side tappings of a transformer, after which it is rectified to direct current for the traction motors. British Railways mounted an electronic solid-state rectifier in a trial motor coach in 1955. Solid-state rectifiers are now normal practice, and the mercury-arc type is disused.

The solid-state thyristor was invented in the United States in 1957. It is best thought of as a switch, the switching rate of which can be controlled readily, by a locomotive driver, for example. The thyristor was first put to use in railway practice in Sweden in 1964, when it was used for controlling a trial motor coach. A locomotive followed in 1965, and since then thyristor control in motive power has become standard practice.

For its electrification of the Elkhorn district the Norfolk & Western RR used split phase power, a rotary converter supplying three-phase current to the motors. This is one of the LC-2 class, built in the 1920s.

A British class 90 locomotive, the second-generation power used on the 25,000v industrial frequency West Coast electrified line.

dangerous as well as annoying. Harmonics do not create such a problem for alternating-current locomotives; for one thing, the various thyristors in circuit can be arranged so that the harmonics from one are cancelled out by the harmonics from another. But direct-current locomotives require heavy and bulky filter circuits between the overhead line and the choppers.

The first chopper motor coach was on the Netherlands Railways; it was equipped electronically from Great Britain in 1967. Chopper motive power did not spread so fast as thyristor-controlled motive power, but is now common.

Control electronics makes automation easier. On some locomotives the driver selects the speed at which he wishes to run, and the locomotive attains the speed and stays there. All the driver's control does is to change electric-current values, a task which can be equally well done from the ground by developed signalling, hence the driverless automatic trains that were introduced on airport lines at Seattle (USA) and Birmingham (England), as well as on metropolitans at Lille in France and Kobe in Japan.

*French National Railways, 1965 (left). Class BB17000, used for the 3,000 volts, 50 Hz Paris suburban electrifications.*

Thyristors are used on locomotives to control current to the traction motors. When the switched-off periods are long, the voltage output to the motors is low, as needed for starting purposes. Making the switched-off periods shorter increases the voltage. At the same time, the thyristors are arranged in circuit so that their output is all in the same direction, i.e., they give direct current. So as well as controlling current the thyristors simultaneously act as a rectifier; transformer control tappings are abolished.

Thyristors, under the name 'choppers', turn up for the control of direct-current motive power as well. The current is chopped into bursts; the longer the pause between bursts, the lower the voltage for the traction motors. Unfortunately the interruptions of the whole of the traction current set up disturbances, known as harmonics, which work their way back into the overhead contact wire. Harmonics in the overhead line induce similar harmonics in telephone and signalling circuits alongside, which in the case of signalling may be

*Chopper-controlled motor coaches supplied to Seoul Subway in 1985 from GEC Traction.*

*The Virginian RR, like the N&W RR, chose the 11,000v 25 cycle a c system.*

# CURRENT-INVERTER LOCOMOTIVES

It was evident for a long time that, if one could control the frequency of a current for a three-phase motor, one could control its speed and thus the speed of a locomotive in which it was mounted. But how to do it? Electromechanical control was tried, but it was not very satisfactory (Hungarian State Railways Class V55 in 1950 and French National Class CC14000 in 1954). More recently, electronics has seemed to provide a solution.

As developed, a diesel engine and alternator produce three-phase current on the locomotive, and this is solid-state rectified to direct current. Alternatively, for electrics, direct current can be taken from the overhead contact wire or an alternating-current supply can be rectified aboard. The direct current is presented to a solid-state inverter, which has a variable-frequency three-phase output for three-phase traction motors.

The current inverter is made up of three banks of thyristor switches totalling as many as are needed for the duty; each bank represents one phase of the three-phase output. The switches cause the direct current to flow first in one direction and then in the other. Should the switching action be fast enough the output is alternating current. The switching action can be controlled very readily by the driver.

Current output from the inverter can be varied typically between 0.5Hz and 165Hz. Subject to the gear ratio between the traction motor's rotor and the driving axle, the locomotive's speed varies with this hertz output. Incidentally, once a maximum hertz output has been designed into a locomotive it sets the maximum speed: the circuitry positively prevents the locomotive going any faster.

To help the locomotive's starting effort, a steady and moderate hertz output is pulse-wave modulated; the details need not concern us here. Current inverters were tried in Britain in 1965 (trial locomotive *Hawk*) and on Soviet Railways in 1968 (No BME1-024, a Co-Co), but both were failures; probably the electronics technology of the time was not up to the task.

After five years of development work, the German branch of Brown Boveri made the traction current-inverter breakthrough. Its current inverter was built into a German Federal Railway 2,500hp (1.86MW) Co-Co diesel in 1971, No 202 002-2. This was a great success and two more were added in 1974. It may be wondered, if three-phase current is generated on board, why this is not used in the traction motors direct. Brown Boveri looked into this during development and came to the conclusion that the current would be more difficult to control, with a consequent decrease in flexibility of the locomotive output.

By the end of 1985 there were about 450 diesel or electric current-inverter locomotives running in Europe. During that year the first current-inverter locomotives were introduced in the United States. These were two rebuilt standard 3,000hp (2.24MW) diesels and a multiple-unit electric train for the New York subway. Brown Boveri technology and equipment from Europe were used in all three cases. Traction current inverters were later also built in France, Italy, Japan and Finland, as a result of separate development work.

*SNCF 300 kph TGV.*

148

All of these current-inverter locomotives used the induction (squirrel-cage) three-phase traction motor, but there is another type of three-phase motor, the synchronous. Until recently this was not considered for rail traction because, for greatest efficiency, its rotor had to be so long that it would not fit between locomotive frames. Also, its starting effort was nil, just at the point when a locomotive needs its maximum power. However, it so happened that French National Railways had been using monomotor traction bogies since 1958 (Class 16500). In these bogies the motor is mounted above the bogie frames, and drives the two or three axles through gearing; thus the full width between the body walls was available for the synchronous motor's rotor when mounted laterally.

Starting circuitry for a traction synchronous-motor application is ingenious. The stator takes three-phase current of moderate frequency from the inverter. To oppose this stator current for starting, the rotor takes direct current supplied to it through simple slip-rings. The direct current comes from that presented to the inverter (which it bypasses), and it is chopper-controlled for the motor's acceleration. Such a motor is called synchronous bi-current, or sybic for short.

In 1981 a French National Railways B-B monomotor bogie, 25,000V single-phase 50Hz locomotive (No. BB15055) was rebuilt with the first sybic motors and renumbered BB10004. It was highly successful, and orders were placed for more of the same general sybic type, the BB26000 class. It was proposed also to use sybic motors on the 186mph (300kph) trains for the new Atlantic TGV line then under construction.

Choppers in conjunction with microprocessors made possible the fine control of current. The field current no longer needed to be identical with the armature current, because it could be controlled by a small chopper. The result was the separately excited motor ('Sepex'). In Britain this was first used on the Class 91 electric locomotives (and also on the diesel Class 60). With this, the power is determined by the armature current, while the motor is controlled by the field current. Thus fine control of the tractive effort is possible. Moreover, so long as the field remains constant, tractive effort falls when the wheels start slipping, thereby controlling the slip.

In the 1990s the British and the Swedes were concentrating on improving Sepex and their well-tried ac systems, while the French were pursuing their synchronous drive. The latter, however, despite its simplicity and light weight, lost much of its attraction when the 'gate turn off' (GTO) thyristor became available in a suitable form for locomotives. GTO made turning the thyristor on or off very much simpler, because hitherto some quite heavy equipment had been needed to make the thyristor stop and start conducting. Meanwhile, the traditional transistor became available in the high ratings needed for locomotive use, the new device being known as the 'insulated gate bipolar transistor' (IGBT). This is an advance on the GTO thyristor, insofar as it can switch at very high frequencies, four times faster than the GTO. This enables a significant reduction in size for inverters.

Meanwhie in Germany, where commutator motors were a constant source of maintenance problems, the current inverter induction (or asynchronous) motor was being further developed. Requiring three-phase alternating current, it had no commutator, and it could spin much faster than a dc motor and therefore was smaller than the latter. Its speed was proportional to the frequency of the current, and wheel-slip was controlled automatically. After some experimentation in small locomotives, the Class 120 electric locomotive was produced. To obtain the necessary variable voltage and variable-frequency current supply, the German engineers pursued the thyristors and diodes solution, which proved to be exceptionally complex, the 120 design incorporating about 450 semi-conductor items, compared with about 32 in the British Class 91 (which retained conventional commutator motors). From 1979, 64 units of the German 120 class were turned out. They were not quite the success that had been hoped, but worked well enough, and the technology was used in the first German ICE high-speed trains. The asynchronous motor was developed further, and forms the basis of the new DB Class 101 electric passenger locomotives delivered in the late 1990s. In France the 'New Generation' TGV trains are likely to be powered by asynchronous motors, an experimental power car using this system having been built for tests in 1998. French National's thyristor BB15000 class has motors that run up to 1,155 revolutions per minute at 100mph (160kph). In contrast, sybic motors run up to 1,980rpm and induction motors up to 3,680rpm. This partly explains the greater duty range of current-inverter locomotives. There is more to it than that, however, for each type of motor has a particular revolution rate at which it achieves greatest efficiency, and this must be taken into consideration.

# DIESEL LOCOMOTIVE DEVELOPMENT

The idea of an internal-combustion engine using some sort of liquid fuel has been about for a long time. Robert Street of Christchurch in Hampshire, England, took out a patent as long ago as 1794. He used a distillate (such as turpentine) in a cylinder heated by an ordinary fire. In Germany, Gottlieb Daimler patented a high-speed petrol (gasoline) engine in 1883. Herbert Stuart Ackroyd was perfecting a heavy oil engine in England at about the same time.

William Dent Priestman started work on gasoline engines, but turned to heavy oil, selling oil engines commercially from 1888. A heated jet of oil was sprayed into the engine's cylinders above the piston, and ignited by an electric spark. Priestman Brothers of Hull built the first 12hp (9kW) locomotive with an oil engine and a mechanical transmission in 1894. It was a mere powered trolley, but it showed that it could be done.

Rudolph Diesel patented his oil engine in 1892, his innovation being greater compression

*A GP-7, a General Motors road-switcher of the early 1950s, of which many hundreds were built.*

*An Alco export diesel working for a Mexican railway. This unit is virtually identical with Alco road switchers bought by US railroads in the 1950s.*

of the oil and air mixture in the cylinder before firing, giving greater efficiency. Diesel's patent was taken up by Maschinenfabrik Augsburg Nürnberg (MAN), which called its product a diesel engine. Meanwhile, Richard Hornsby & Sons took up the Stuart Ackroyd engine, and produced half a dozen locomotives during 1896-1904. These were for the War Department's narrow-gauge railways, and were of the 0-4-0, 2-4-0, and 0-6-6-0 wheel arrangements (0-B-0, 1-B-0 and C-C according to the wheel arrangement system adopted for diesel and electric locomotives). Richard Hornsby & Sons, and that company's successor, Ruston & Hornsby of Lincoln, built some 22,000 oil engines before the company was eventually merged with General Electric of Great Britain (GEC) in 1967. It so happened, however, that Ruston & Hornsby oil engines as such had few railway traction applications. While the name 'oil engine' was retained, Diesel's ideas were in fact quietly incorporated. Customers were somewhat confused by the engine's name until it was dropped in 1967 and the product rightly began to be described as a diesel engine.

From 1900 onwards, gasoline-mechanical and gasoline-electric motive power was built for the railways of the world in great variety, although almost always of small size and meant to work as single units. In the United States the McKeen gas-electric railcar was in vogue right through until the 1920s, being used especially by western railroads. By the 1920s, however, the diesel engine had become sufficiently light and compact to make inroads into the gasoline-engine market, and the latter was eventually eliminated.

Rudolph Diesel did not get around to his first diesel locomotive until 1912. He tried using direct drive to cranks on a jack-shaft coupled to the driving wheels, but the 1,200hp 2-B-2 (4-4-4) locomotive was a failure. But this did not mean that diesel traction was doomed. The problem was still how to transmit the energy of the fast-moving pistons to slow-moving wheels, and solutions were already in sight. Geared transmission was feasible, although only for low-powered use; in 1913 a French short line was operating a 150hp railcar with diesel engine and geared transmission. Two constituent firms of Allmänna Svenska Aktiebolaget (Asea) put a diesel engine in a little 1-A (2-2-0) railcar for the Södermanl and Midland Railway. The same two firms achieved a diesel-locomotive export in 1924, with a 200hp (149kW) Bo-Bo which went to Tunisian Railways.

*A Belgian diesel locomotive of the 1960s. It is essentially a General Motors design within a Belgian body.*

The Swedish railcars of 1912 had diesel engines powering generators that fed electric traction motors; this was the diesel-electric principle, which would become the standard form of diesel traction. It was a form which many engineers considered inelegant, because it involved three heavy pieces of equipment: engine, generator and motors. Much talent would be employed over the decades in finding something better, but success in this was only partial. However, even in its alleged imperfect form the diesel locomotive was considerably more efficient than the steam locomotive in terms of fuel consumption.

A forerunner of the diesel-electric locomotive was the design worked out by General Electric in the United States for an internal-combustion locomotive. Before the First World War GE was already building gasoline-electric railcars with their electric transmission, and for its locomotive simply took the forward part of two railcars and joined them back-to-back. The locomotive therefore rode on two pivoted, powered, trucks and would have been a real diesel-electric if only its engines had been designed for oil rather than gasoline. A Swiss engineer employed by GE, Hermann Lemp, was meanwhile working on a control system so that the all-important task of matching engine, generator and motor outputs could be done automatically rather than by a fallible human being.

*A General Electric export to Argentine, working international trains through the Andes in the 1960s.*

In subsequent generations of diesel locomotives the usual method of control was by engine revolutions. An electro-mechanical device sensed the demands made on the direct-current generator, and increased or decreased the engine revolutions to meet that demand. The response to the driver's controller settings was made similarly. This control might or might not be supplemented by traction-motor groupings. By running the power through all the traction motors one after another (also called 'in series'), the motors themselves acted as resistances to cut the voltage for starting. Subsequently the motors in each powered truck were retained in series but were supplied from the current source direct (semi-parallel). Alternatively, the start could be made in semiparallel and progress made to full parallel, with all motors supplied direct. It is

common for an electric locomotive to run through series, semi-parallel and parallel groupings when accelerating, although not for a diesel locomotive.

The year 1924 was important for the diesel. A small locomotive was built in Austria with a Lentz hydrostatic transmission, and Brown Boveri and Fiat built a 440hp (328kW) diesel-electric for the narrow-gauge Calabria-Lucania Railways. Perhaps most influential was North America's first diesel-electric, a 300hp (224kW) Bo-Bo shunting locomotive built by General Electric of the United States.

But after the First World War it was revolutionary Russia that led the field in diesel traction. The engineer Lomonosov, under the personal patronage of Lenin, was allowed to build two prototypes in Germany, one a diesel-electric and the other a diesel-mechanical (of which the least said the better). Another Russian, working at home, produced a diesel-electric prototype using various shipyard odds

and ends. Both the diesel-electrics worked, although Lomomosov's promised to be the most troublefree. Over the years Lomonosov and his team produced further designs of 1,050hp to 1,200hp (782-894kW) until, in the 1930s, the new locomotives were sent to Central Asia, where it was hoped they would be useful because they did not need much water. However, away from their home base, in a hot climate that caused them to overheat, and in a changing political atmosphere, they did not prosper and the communist party government decided to build no more diesels. The basic design was not perfect, because instead of a flexible wheelbase they rode on what was essentially a steam locomotive chassis, but nevertheless they had shown that diesel-electric traction was viable.

One of Lomonosov's colleagues emigrated to the United States and took up a consultancy at the American Locomotive Company (Alco). That company had already participated in further

*An E8, a 1949 variant of the General Motors passenger diesel locomotive, leaves Chicago for the Far West.*

ventures by GE, building the mechanical parts for diesel-electric yard locomotives. The first customer for these had been the Central of New Jersey RR, whose No 1000 is regarded as the first successful diesel-electric locomotive in the United States. In 1928 Alco began to build diesel locomotives on its own account, three light-traffic units for the New York Central RR being its first order. But most of its early production consisted of yard locomotives, and in the 1930s

it introduced the supercharger, by which the power of its yard locomotives was increased from 600 to 900hp (447 to 670kW).

Diesel traction hit the American headlines with the Burlington RR's diesel-electric 'Zephyr' train, but Alco persisted with yard diesels and then, in 1940, produced the first of a new genre, the dual-service locomotive. This was a true general-purpose locomotive riding on two six-wheel trucks and carrying two 1,000hp (745kW)

engines. The following year the idea was carried further, producing the road-switcher, which immediately became very popular. But Alco's role in diesel locomotive construction was restricted by the government's War Production Board to yard locomotives in the Second World War. It was Alco's competitor General Motors that was allowed to build mainline diesel locomotives in those years.

Before the war the Electromotive Corporation of General Motors had already become the main diesel locomotive builder, having acquired a new lightweight engine design. In the 1930s it was building yard locomotives and then 1,800hp (1,341kW) streamlined passenger locomotives. In 1939 it demonstrated a four-unit streamlined freight locomotive of 5,400hp (4,025kW) and great reliability. Orders came flowing in, and during the war GM was the only company building main-line diesel locomotives. Thus the stage was set for the wholesale post-war displacement of steam by diesel locomotives in the United States. So far as big railroads were concerned, this process came to an end in the late 1950s, when the coal-hauling Norfolk & Western RR finally dieselized. Although early diesel units were of less power than the steam locomotives they displaced, they could be used in multiple, controlled from the leading unit. In this way, horsepower of a magnitude unattainable by a single steam locomotive could be deployed.

In the rest of the world the process was slower. British, German and Danish companies had successfully exported diesel locomotives in the interwar years, but it was only after the Second World War that dieselization took hold on the home railways. There had been some exceptions. For example, there were a number of successful diesel yard locomotives at work in

*The GP38-2 EMD road-switcher with a c power, produced in the 1970s.*

*Two British Rail class 37 locomotives, and a lone class 60, await their duties.*

Britain, and the Great Western Railway was operating diesel railcars, while Germany's 'Flying Hamburger' diesel train had broken several records. In war-torn Europe the first choice for replacing the steam locomotive was electrification, and steam traction was kept in service until an unhurried dieselization process could take over the non-electrified lines. In Britain the process was different. A combination of misguided governmental direction, native pride, and technical conservatism ensured that in Britain new steam locomotives would be built long after it was clear that they were outmoded. When dieselization was sanctioned, a fair-shares-for-all policy meant that the orders for the initial locomotives were divided between builders, some of whom had little experience of anything apart from steam locomotive building. At the same time care was taken that no United States designs should be imported; this was intended to protect British industry, but as US

*The GP60m, EMD's product for the high-horsepower US market.*

*Class 59, a General Motors design that broke into the British market in the 1980s, being bought by the Foster Yeoman quarrying company.*

*A German experimental 1,400hp diesel with hydraulic transmission, built in 1935.*

diesel design was in advance of the rest of the world it meant that British builders were denied the incentive to improve their products, and British Railways the chance to operate the best locomotives. Finally, when wholesale dieselization was sanctioned, it was as a helter-skelter process designed to rid the railways of steam traction as soon as possible. All in all, British dieselization took the form of one bad decision after another. In the process a number of locomotive builders went bankrupt and the railways were saddled with a number of designs that were inferior to the steam locomotives they were intended to replace. From this frenzy there did emerge, though, a handful of designs that, while not quite up to United States standards, were good performers. Two of these, classes 37 and 47, are still very much used in Britain.

Railways lived through a period in which steam and diesel locomotives co-existed. This was not a perfect situation, especially when the quite delicate diesel locomotives were serviced in steam-age locomotive depots. On the whole in this period, the diesel locomotives were given the most work, steam being used for secondary or standby service. This meant that statistics like ton-mile per locomotive-hour were high for diesels and low for steam lcomotives, resulting in performance averages that rather overstated the superiority of diesel traction.

In North America there were locomotive designs that became very popular and, eventually, were regarded as classics. The Alco road-switchers of the 1950s were one such classic design, and the same company's FPA passenger locomotive also became popular. However, General Motors with its E series produced the best-known passenger locomotive, possibly because the streamlined outline remained virtually unchanged on the several improved versions that emerged over two decades of production.

Of the other countries, Germany distinguished itself by introducing hydraulic in place of electric transmission in mainline locomotives. The German State Railway first fitted a Voith hydraulic transmission to a locomotive in 1934. In this the engine drives a bladed disc in a sealed chamber containing oil. The oil that is whirled around drives a similar disc close to it which is connected to the driving wheels, usually by a cardan shaft. Locomotive control is effected by pumping oil into or out of the sealed box. There are other hydraulic transmissions (Mekydro, SRM, Twin-Disc and so on), some of which incorporate a supplementary gearbox. Such locomotives were quite successful in terms of the power:weight ratio, but were heavier on

*The most numerous 20th century British mainline diesel, the class 47.*

maintenance. British Railways also used the German hydraulic transmission for some of its locomotives.

France went its own way in diesel design, and maintained its steam locomotive fleet in impeccable condition almost to the very end of the steam era. Russia, rather like Britain but on an even grander scale, opted for rapid dieselization at a time when really satisfactory diesel locomotive designs were not available. Its first homebuilt diesel locomotives were a mating of Alco technology (acquired during the war) with American marine diesel engines (Fairbanks-Morse opposed-piston engines), also acquired during the war. Fairbanks-Morse became a US locomotive builder, using the same opposed-piston engines, but did not survive long. The engines copied by the Soviet engineers did last long, partly because the Russians for several years had nothing better.

Several countries had the wisdom to set up the manufacture of United States-design diesel locomotives. The usual procedure was for the home railway to order units from the US builder, the latter cooperating in progressively setting up production facilities in that country. Alco, for example, launched the very big Diesel

*The British class 20, one of the early domestic diesel designs which proved successful and was still in use in the late 1990s*

*One of the U25B diesel locomotives, with which General Electric drove its way into the North American mass market.*

*One of the hydraulic-drive mainline locomotives supplied by Krauss-Maffei of Germany to two US railroads wishing to try them out. No large orders resulted.*

*Spanish locomotive, American inspiration; a pair of the many locomotives built in Spain around Alco technology.*

*One of several hundred German mainline diesel locomotives with hydraulic transmission, built in the 1960s.*

Locomotive Works at Benares in India. Spanish engineering companies undertook the production of own-design locomotives incorporating substantial American elements. General Motors locomotives in a distinctive outward guise appeared on several European railways, including those of Belgium, Hungary and Scandinavia. In Australia both Alco and GM designs were assimilated for home production.

There are some hundreds of types of diesel engine on the market today, ranging up to over 6,000hp (4.47MW) in power. They are designed to fit into locomotives, but of course are sold throughout industry as well. Railways buy according to considerations of price, weight and maintenance costs. A fast-running engine needs more maintenance, but packs more power for its weight. This is important when designing a

locomotive within a given axle load. Or the matter may be reversed, when a suitable 2,750hp (2.50MW) engine is bought and 'derated' to 2,500hp (1.86MW) to save on maintenance.

The engines for diesel locomotives are habitually of medium speed, although that speed has risen from the 835rpm of the GM 567 engine of the 1950s to the 900rpm of the GM 710 engine of the 1990s. (In Britain over the same period the 750rpm English Electric RK/V engine developed into the 900rpm Ruston RK270.) High-speed engines are sometimes used when space or weight are limited, as in powering self-propelled trains, despite their need for more maintenance. Over the same four decades, power produced per cylinder has trebled. The comparative merits of two-stroke and four-stroke engines have been argued over the whole period, and this will no doubt continue.

A later development in diesel traction is the diesel-alternator locomotive, the first unit being made for French National Railways in 1965. The engine drives an ac generator (the alternator), the output of which is immediately rectified for the dc traction motors. Abandoning the generator's commutator gives maintenance savings that more than pay for the solid-state rectifier, and since the 1980s there has been a general tendency to move to alternating current. Meanwhile, radical development in electric motor design, especially the introduction of three-phase drive, has meant more complex but vastly improved locomotives.

The United States locomotive industry was slow to introduce three-phase drive, even after it had proved its effectiveness in Europe. The railroads were evidently satisfied with what they had got. With the slip control then on offer, diesel locomotives could work at around 25 per cent adhesion. But eventually Amtrak, the United States passenger operator, tried three-phase prototypes. The results were promising, and in 1991 General Motors built a prototype classified as SD60MAC, soon followed by four others for thorough testing. These trial units were of 4,000hp (2.98MW), and in 1992 three of them on trial over the Burlington Northern Railroad so impressed that company's management that it ordered 350 of the production model, the SD70MAC. What the three prototypes had done was show that they could start 15,000-tonne trains hitherto requiring five of the conventional SD40-2 units. The key advance was that the new units' asyncronous drive allowed 45 per cent adhesion.

*Diesel challenges steam at Kings Cross terminus in London in the 1960s. In fact the diesel locomotive shown here had a life considerably shorter than Silver Link's.*

*One of the massive 6,600 hp dual-motor diesels used by the Union Pacific RR from 1969. 47 of these were supplied by GM's Electromotive Division (EMD), but they were not repeated.*

*The Russian TEP60 Class diesel passenger locomotive, of which about 1200 units were built from 1961 to 1985.*

General Motors used the German Siemens technology, which had one inverter for each powered truck. The other builder, General Electric, responded with its AC4400CW locomotive, which used GE experience with three-phase multiple-unit trains and provided one inverter per motor. Thus the GE units had more inverters, which raised the cost but at the same time meant that the failure of one inverter would not cripple the locomotive. In general, both the GM and GE locomotives cost about a third more than conventional models. There was one problem, however. Enhanced adhesion meant that these locomotives could start heavier loads, but running speed still depended on horsepower. These early three-phase locomotives were therefore not quite adequately powered, so both builders joined in a 'horsepower race,' developing new, more powerful engines that would enable their units to develop 6,000hp (4.47MW) rather than 4,000hp (2.98MW).

*The class 66, a numerous series of General Motors locomotives supplied in the late 1990s to the English, Welsh & Scottish Railway.*

# GAS TURBINE LOCOMOTIVES

In many ways a gas turbine locomotive is cheaper than a diesel. It is cheaper to build, and it dispenses with pistons and the maintenance costs that the latter bring. But it is efficient only when working at full output, and most railway tasks require a fluctuating output. It can also lose efficiency when air density is low, that is, at high temperatures and at high altitudes. Passenger trains moving at high average speeds with few stops were one promising application, and the French developed gas-turbine trains, some of which were exported to the United States and Iran. The increase of oil prices from 1973, however, rendered these trains a high-cost operation.

Swiss Federal Railways acquired a gas turbine locomotive in the 1940s, and in its last years the Great Western Railway in England bought two units, also based on Brown Boveri technology. They worked well, but could not show a saving big enough to justify a changeover to that kind of traction. In the United States the Union Pacific RR had its long line and long trains in the approach to the Rockies, and ordered gas turbine locomotives for these. Here again, the concept worked well, but not well enough to justify repetition, at least while oil prices were high.

*Turbotrains were one way of utilising the gas turbine for railway use. This is one of several french designs of the 1970s.*

# HIGH SPEED TRAINS

The decline in passenger traffic experienced by United States railroads in the 1950s was not felt elsewhere to the same degree, but there were ominous signs. In many countries the reaction was to provide trains of greater allure. In the USA there were innovations like the dome car and eyecatching stylistic transformations. In Britain there was, initially, an increase in the number of named trains and later the introduction of the 'Blue Pullmans'. The idea was to take advantage of the railways' inherent spaciousness compared with the airliner and automobile. However, these changes were not especially successful and the opinion formed that travellers preferred to go by air or car because it was quicker to do so.

The railways could hardly match the speed of the airliner over long distances, nor the convenience of the car over short distances. Given the need of air passengers to get to and from airports, and adding to that the required check-in times, it was calculated that in city-centre to city-centre trips the railways would have a 'start' of about two hours. If the average train speed was 70mph (112kph), the railway would have an advantage in overall speed up to about 300 miles (480km). Faster trains would

A 'Metroliner' train, after demotion by Amtrak to slower services.

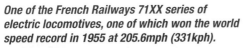

*One of the French Railways 71XX series of electric locomotives, one of which won the world speed record in 1955 at 205.6mph (331kph).*

*The later 'Metroliner' New York - Washington service, with locomotive haulage.*

enlarge this area, and if trains of far greater luxury were provided the business traveller, in particular, might well prefer the train for trips of up to 400 miles (640km).

The French 'Mistral', running from Paris to Marseilles over mainly electrified track, was perhaps the best-known example of these new fast trains, partly because it was the fastest train in the world for some years. A somewhat later development of this concept were the fast trains on the East Coast route in Britain, hauled by Class 91 locomotives and exceeding 100mph (160kph) on some sections. In North America, with its longer distances, the airlines had an advantage, but the 'North East Corridor' (Boston-New York-Washington), and in Canada the Quebec City-Montreal-Toronto route, offered dense-traffic routes of the appropriate lengths. Also to this era belong the 'Trans Europe Expresses', a network of fast de luxe services linking the main cities of continental western Europe; here again the distances were right.

But although these new trains had some success, further advance with conventional technology seemed difficult. A case in point was the 'Metroliner' concept introduced for the US North East Corridor. Benefiting from the High Speed Transportation Act of 1965, the Penn Central RR ordered fast two-car electric trains for the New York-Washington service. On trial, one of these touched 160mph (257kph) and the first trains were scheduled at a maximum of 110mph (177kph). But even this was hard to

achieve, not because the trains could not run that fast, but because the infrastructure was not ready. It was already occupied by a dense traffic of slower-moving trains, it had awkward sections where speed had to be reduced, the signalling was in need of renewal, and there were some problems with the catenary at high speeds. It was not long before the Metroliners were put into more prosaic Amtrak services, and the name 'Metroliner' was handed on to a fleet of locomotive-hauled trains that were fast, but not exceptionally so, making the 225-mile (362km) Washington-New York run in three hours.

The Japanese were the first to make the great leap forward into the concept of building special tracks for special trains. Their Tokaido high-speed line between Tokyo and Osaka opened

in 1965. It was mainly straight, any curves being gentle, and it used the European standard gauge rather than the Japanese 3ft 6in (1067mm) gauge. This gauge differentiation emphasized that the new line was for one kind of train only. With all trains travelling at high speed, problems of line congestion were eliminated and the 'Bullet Trains' averaged 101mph (163km/h). Later these lines were extended, and faster trains introduced. The result was a surge of traffic because the speeds and the distances were just right for a successful counterattack against airline competition.

The French followed suit in the 1980s with their 'Trains à Grande Vitesse' (TGV). The first purpose-built route was from Paris to the South East in 1981, and Paris to the Atlantic followed in 1989. To connect with the Channel Tunnel a TGV line northwards from Paris was completed in 1993, and this provided a route into Belgium as well. The French concept differed from the Japanese in several ways. In particular, since there was no gauge differentiation, the TGV trains could start or finish their journeys at places that were not themselves served by the new tracks. Thus the high-speed line from Paris to the Atlantic only went halfway to Nantes or Bordeaux; the TGV trains completed their journeys over existing lines. There was also a technical difference. The Japanese 'Bullet Trains' had all their axles powered. This spread the weight of the equipment so that axle weights, which had to be kept moderate at these high speeds, were low (16 tonnes). This also made easier the use of rheostatic (non-friction) brakes, so that the disc brakes did not need to be used at high speeds. Each second car carried a pantograph. The 12-car trains could thereby produce 12,000hp (8.94MW), more than was needed for the scheduled speed, but there was a drawback in that the pantographs caused fast wear on the contact wires and also a noise that

*HST trains at Paddington Station in London soon after their introduction in the 1970s.*

*A British class 91 electric locomotive hauling a high-speed East Coast Route train.*

caused considerable resentment among people living close to the line.

The French TGV trains were different. At first, gas turbine propulsion had been envisaged, but the rise of oil prices in 1973 killed that concept. What finally emerged were new electric trains which with their designed speed of 260kph (168mph) and eight passenger cars needed 8,500hp (6.35MW) of power. The French designers incorporated two power cars, one at each end of the train, with four powered axles each, and the outer truck of the next vehicle, a trailer passenger car, also had powered axles, thereby increasing the train's total of powered axles to 12, which was adequate for adhesion and contributed to the requirement of a maximum 17-tonne axleload. With the introduction of the second-generation TGV trains, designed for the Atlantic line, the use of three-phase synchronous drive produced traction motors that were about double the power for the same size; powered axles additional to the eight offered by the two power cars were therefore no longer needed.

Meanwhile, in Britain, a different concept was pursued. The HST-125 train was diesel powered and designed to run over existing tracks. With these two limitations it was not capable of running as fast in regular service as its Japanese and French contemporaries, but it was less demanding of capital. With less money needed to establish an HST route, more cities could be

*The Russian ER-200 design of 1974, of which two train sets were running by 1999 to provide a thrice-weekly high-speed Moscow - St Petersburg service (above) A first-generation French TGV, built in the 1980s (opposite).*

*The 'Thalys' high-speed train of the 1990s, designed for international European services.*

brought into the HST network. As with the Japanese and French high-speed trains, the advent of HST-125 services brought enormous traffic gains. The concept was also adopted in Australia, as the XPT train, for services from Sydney.

In Germany there was also a reluctance to build entirely new lines, so a compromise was made with the reconstruction of existing lines and the provision of some new high-speed lines where extra capacity was needed. It was not intended that the German high-speed trains should have exclusive use of their tracks. The first German high-speed route was Hamburg-Frankfurt-Munich, opened in 1991. The German ICE trains had power cars at each end with asynchronous motors, providing 13,400hp (9.98MW) to power the 12-car trains. However, the axle weight of these trains was 20 tonnes; advanced research in Britain and Germany had shown that such a weight was perfectly acceptable, at least when the traction motors were body- rather than axle-mounted. French engineers, understandably enough, contested this conclusion.

Over the years, especially because of advances in electric motor design and control, higher power:weight ratios were achieved and the high-speed trains tended to become even faster. The original Japanese 'Bullet Trains', with their 210kph (130mph) designed speed, hardly counted as high-speed trains by the 1990s. The Japanese went on to build several series of improved trains, featuring different traction power and more refined streamlining. For several series the principle of having every axle motored was abandoned, but in the Series 500 train

*French technology in Britain: one of the 'Eurostar' trains designed for the London - Paris Channel Tunnel service.*

which began to operate in 1997 there was a return to all-axles-powered. This new train was designed for 300kph (186mph), had a high aluminium content and reduced cross-section. Despite the latter, it carried 1,323 passengers in its 16 vehicles. In Germany the ICE-1 was

followed by the ICE-2, which is essentially half of the ICE-1, although with improved suspension. With ICE-3, however, which was to enter service at the end of the century, power distribution was changed, with every alternate axle of the train powered. This helped to bring

*One of the newer (and faster) generations of Japanese 'Bullet Trains.'*

*The Australian XPT, an adaption of the British high speed train.*

as they traveled over existing 19th-century tracks their speed was not high over the British sector of their trip. This caused some ridicule, but the British government's refusal to finance a new high-speed route was not absurd. The fact was that high speed tracks were expensive to construct, and the expense and disruption was enormous when the terrain was densely-populated south-eastern England. Even in France there was some reluctance to finance a new TGV route to the east. So although Spain opened a French-style TGV route between Madrid and Seville, Italy was providing itself with its Alta Velocita lines and 300kph trains, and Korea was beginning to build its high-speed line, the idea of high-speed trains having their own tracks was being supplemented in the 1990s by the appearance of tilting trains, that could use existing tracks.

In the meantime, 'conventional' high-speed trains were continuing in production, to designs that were improved from time to time. So far as Europe was concerned, a standard arrangement seemed to be emerging: four-axle power cars at each end, 10-12 passenger vehicles, a maximum speed of 300kph or 186mph, possibly higher in future modifications, aluminium bodies, and axle weights quite close to the French-prescribed aim of 15-16 tonnes.

the axle load down to less than 17 tonnes; a concession, perhaps, to the need to counter the claims made by French salesmen about the superior axle loading of French high-speed trains. As for the later French designs, these include 545-passenger double-deck trains (TGV-Duplex) and the 377-seat trains for the inter-European service, known as the 'Thalys' trains. Both types are designed for 300kph (186mph).

With the opening of the Channel Tunnel, 'Eurostar' high-speed trains ran to London, but

# TILTING TRAINS

The Japanese Shinkansen and the French TGV showed how fast train travel could be, but these achievements required completely new, reserved and expensive tracks, with only gentle curves. Running at very high speeds over the curves of existing track seemed impossible, thanks to the phenomenon known as 'cant deficiency', but by the 1990s this obstacle had been overcome by the development of the tilting train.

'Cant', or 'super-elevation', is the raising of one rail higher than the other, so that a train leans inwards as it goes round a curve. Engineers have to compromise, choosing a degree of cant midway between the ideal requirements of the slowest and fastest trains using the route. A train moving over track whose degree of cant is less than ideal is said to experience 'cant deficiency'. This can be felt by the passengers as a centrifugal force which can throw them sideways if they are standing or walking.

With high-speed trains the compromise would no longer work; the gap between the slowest and fastest trains would be too great. Increasing the cant to suit the high-speed trains

*Part of the ingenious but ill-fated British APT train on exhibition.*

would result in very uncomfortable and possibly dangerous excessive cant for the slower trains.

The solution lay in a train that would itself tilt, so that the combination of the track cant and the train tilt would be enough to ensure a comfortable ride over curves. As development of this idea progressed, two main technologies emerged: the passive tilt and the active tilt. With passive tilt the car bodies are simply pivoted and tilt naturally, impelled by the centrifugal force acting on them. In active tilt, jacks raise one side of the coach as it curves. Active tilt provides a higher degree of tilt, but needs some way of instructing the tilt mechanism to come into play as curves are entered.

The French SNCF tried its Pendulum passenger car in the 1950s. Its seating section hung like a hammock between roof-level suspension points at each end. But the concept was not pursued. In the mid-1950s Pullman-Standard conceived for the Chesapeake & Ohio RR the so-called 'Train X', which had a passive tilt. The Japanese introduced elementary tilting trains for the sinuous Nagoya-Nagono line in the 1970s. These were not designed for especially high speeds, and functioned well.

Spanish National Railways, with so much of its mainline trackage curving its way through mountain ranges, also favored the passive tilt. The Talgo train had long been in service in Spain, where it had been invented. It consisted of short,

*The Spanish 'Talgo Pendular,' which utilizes a passive (unpowered) tilt.*

*Introduced primarily for the Montreal - Toronto service, the Canadian LRC tilting train was plagued by a series of component defects but eventualy settled down.*

low-lying and light-weight vehicles, and had gone some way to solving the curve problem. The tilting Talgo, or Talgo Pendular, was introduced in 1980 and was an immediate success. With passive tilt there are few things to go wrong, the only complication being that on straight track the vehicle bodies have to be secured to prevent them rocking aimlessly. Although only 4° of tilt can be obtained with the Talgo Pendular, this is enough to accelerate some schedules by 20 per cent compared with non-tilting Talgo trains.

Meanwhile, between 1967 and 1985 British engineers were struggling with the Advanced Passenger Train (APT). This used active tilt, with hydraulic jacks at floor level and sensors to detect the onset of curved track. The APT taught many lessons, some of which were incorporated in the immediately successful HST, which to some extent was a substitute for the APT when the latter was abandoned after a succession of

failures in service. Apart from tilting, the APT incorporated many other fundamental innovations, so there was plenty to go wrong, and it did. Moreover, the British engineers believed that the tilt should fully compensate the cant deficiency. When passengers complained of nausea they were told they were imagining things. In retrospect it can be accepted that a passenger lifting eyes from a book to glance out of the window when the tilt was at a maximum would naturally have felt disorientated; the bodily feeling of straight-line motion was contradicted by the eyes' evidence of curving. Later and more successful tilting trains designed in Italy and Sweden avoided this error, and for a time it became almost a rule that the ideal degree of tilt should compensate just 70 per cent of cant deficiency. That way a passenger would feel when the train was on a curve, so there would be less conflict between what was felt and what was seen.

Canada was also active at this time. Bombardier built its LRC for VIA-Rail, the Canadian rail passenger company. The LRC ('Light, Rapid, Comfortable') had hydraulic tilt, and was designed with the Montreal-Toronto service in mind. But like the APT it had too many innovations, and its first years were plagued by breakdowns and unpopularity. The LRC trains were withdrawn for a period, then returned to service on unexciting schedules. They did not produce the revolution in train travel that had been anticipated, although they did bring a new standard of smooth running to North America.

With Fiat in Italy developing its Pendolino concept, in which the jacks operate on the roof rather than the floor, the Swedish designers of the X-2000 tilting train followed the British example and incorporated underfloor hydraulic jacks. These could impart tilt at the rate of 4° per second, a compromise between what passengers could tolerate without discomfort and the need for a fast-moving train to achieve tilt quickly. The first of the X-2000 trains entered service in 1990, and soon 20 of them were transforming the Stockholm-Goteborg service. This important 283-mile (456km) intercity route was covered by conventional trains in 3hr 55min, but the X-2000 trains made it in just less than 3 hours. The power car (which was non-tilting as it did not carry passengers) could develop 4,375hp (3.26MW), and speeds up to 200kph (118mph) were attained in normal service. The trains so impressed the public that the railway's market share of passengers over this route rose from 38 to 52 per cent. Further X-2000 trains were built, and the concept was also exported to Norway. Additionally, X-2000 trains were shipped to the United States and China for evaluation.

In terms of sales, Fiat of Italy was the most successful builder of tilting trains in the 1990s. Its Pendolino concept was so named to mark its distinguishing feature, the pivotal suspension of the coach body at roof level. To achieve this, vertical girders rest on the wheelset frames to support the body. This takes up space that might otherwise be used for seating, but the results have been good enough to justify this sacrifice.

The first, experimental, Pendolino went into service in 1976 on the winding Rome-Ancona route. Its success led to the ETR-450 trains, nine-car sets of a somewhat outdated exterior styling. With 15 of these first-class-only trains delivered between 1987 and 1991, Italian Railways was able to accelerate the Rome-Milan service. Then, in 1994, Fiat produced the first ETR-460. This, again, was a 9-car set, but had modern styling, was wider (and could therefore accommodate four-a-side seating, making second-class accommodation practicable), and with six of its cars powered could develop 8,050hp (6MW). The design could be provided as an electric, diesel, or multi-voltage electric (the latter was classified as ETR-470, and bought for services from Italy into Germany and Switzerland).

One of the problems of tilt is actuating the mechanism at precisely the right place and at precisely the right speed of tilt. This can never be quite perfect. On the Pendolino trains, for example, an accelerometer in the leading vehicle measured the build-up of lateral forces as the train entered a curve and actuated the tilt mechanism accordingly. This meant that the leading vehicle might be into the curve before the tilt was achieved, so passengers in the front vehicle experienced greater cant deficiency than those travelling more to the rear. To some extent

this problem has been overcome by adding a gyroscope in the first vehicle. This measures the cant as it builds up in the first transition curves and signals an advance warning, initiating the tilt before the accelerometer takes over for the rest of the curve.

The Fiat type of train has also been produced under licence in other countries, including Spain and Portugal. In Germany the Class 610 diesel train for hilly secondary lines was introduced in 1988 and proved very successful, reducing schedules and attracting new passengers. Poland ordered seven-car trains capable of 320kph (199mph). Czech Railways also ordered these trains, while Finland ordered the Sm 200 class, wider than standard to benefit from the generous clearances of Finnish Railways.

German Railways introduced its own high-speed tilting train, the ICT, in 1998, and 43 were ordered. Meanwhile, the biggest-ever order for Pendolino trains came from Virgin Trains in Britain, which required 55 sets for its West Coast Route. They will be eight-car sets, with six of the cars motored. They will tilt to 10∞ (8∞ of tilt were specified), and use an electric tilting mechanism originally devised in Switzerland but subsequently developed by Fiat. Deliveries were expected to start in 2001. For its cross-country services, Virgin ordered a fleet of four-car diesel tilting trains from Bombardier, the once-Canadian company that had made the Canadian LRC. The tilting mechanism was to be like that of the LRC, but improved in the light of experience. Talgo tilting trains continue to find a market. One is running in Germany and, on trial in Spain, a later model reached 204mph (331kph) in 1997.

A tilting pantograph was developed in the late 1990s. Fiat had avoided this problem by supporting the pantograph on the frames of the wheel-set (the only part of the train that did not tilt). With the Talgo and some other trains there was no problem, either because the power unit was diesel or because the power unit did not tilt.

For its high-speed service over the North East Corridor (Washington-New York-Boston), Amtrak chose a Bombardier/GEC-Alsthom proposal. These 'Acela' trains, consisting of six cars with a locomotive at each end, use the improved LRC tilting technology (with digital rather than analogue microprocessing), combined with vehicles modelled on the French TGV design. The trains, of which 18 were initially ordered, are designed to run at 150mph (240kph). On the New York-Boston run they were expected to reduce the schedule from 4½hr to 3hr and increase patronage by 30 per

cent. Meanwhile, in the Pacific North-West, Amtrak introduced three Talgo 'Pendular' trains for services from Seattle to Portland and Vancouver.

By the end of the 20th century there was a wide choice of proven electric traction concepts, and continuing research was expected to develop others. Current-inverter locomotives of both types were in service, and thyristor and chopper locomotives offered their own advantages. Comparative costs were expected to determine the long-term prospects of each concept. Similarly, the diesel current-inverter locomotive was competing with the diesel-alternator. Falling oil prices and the high cost of electrification were making the gas turbine look more attractive.

*One of the best-selling tilting train concepts, the Fiat 'Pendolino.'*

# STEAM TENDER
# LOCOMOTIVES

# Steam Tender Locomotives

## SINGLE DRIVERS

### 0-2-2

Although most of the first generation of locomotives were built with four coupled wheels, suitable for freight duty, the proposed Liverpool and Manchester Railway was going to need engines capable of higher speeds for working passenger trains. As a result of the Rainhill Trials in 1829, where the Rocket had proved capable of running at speeds up to 30mph (48kph) with a single driven set of wheels, that design was adopted for the first batch of these locomotives, some of which had the idling wheel behind the driving wheel, as in the case of the Rocket (0-2-2), and others which had the idling wheel in front (2-2-0) as that method was considered to make for improved guidance around curves.

Locomotives with single driving wheels continued to be built right up to 1900 and proved most satisfactory in operation, provided that the weight of train to be hauled did not exceed about 200 tonnes. The 0-2-2 wheel arrangement, however, was used only for the first eight passenger engines built for the Liverpool and Manchester Railway in 1830, following the successful results obtained with the Rocket during the Rainhill Trials.

### ROCKET/1829/GREAT BRITAIN

The Rocket was built as an 0-2-2 with its cylinders high up by the driver and driving onto the front pair of wheels, which were 56in (1422mm) in diameter. Much of its successful operation was due to its multitubular boiler - this was the first application of that feature. The copper firebox was separate from the boiler and built in the form of an arch within which was a water space connected to

the boiler by two separate pipes; a thermo-syphon system of water circulation was thereby created. The driving wheels were built on the pattern of carriage wheels of that time, with a cast-iron boss and with wooden spokes and rim onto which the tyres were shrunk. The trailing wheels were cast iron, as were those of the tender, which had been built by a coach-builder named Nathaniel Worsdell. During the Rainhill Trials the Rocket was driven backwards and forwards over a distance of just over a mile (1.6km) several times amounting in all to a total of some 70 miles (113km), but the other locomotives of that type did not prove satisfactory in everyday operation owing to derailments which occurred as a result of their short wheelbase. They were soon to be replaced by engines which had an extra axle.

Soon after it had entered commercial service the cylinders on the Rocket were lowered until they were almost horizontal in order to reduce the swaying motion encouraged when they were in an elevated position; this arrangement became the standard for future production. What is left of the Rocket is preserved at the Science Museum in London. Two replicas were made: one was for the Ford Museum at Dearborn, United States, and the other is at the National Railway Museum, York, Great Britain.

### NORTHUMBRIAN/1830/GREAT BRITAIN

The last of the 0-2-2 class to be supplied to the Liverpool and Manchester Railway was one named Northumbrian. This was the first locomotive to be fitted with an integral smokebox and firebox, thus setting the pattern for all future locomotive boilers.

### 2-2-0

Once the cylinders had been located horizontally it was logical to place them in a forward position and to drive the rear axle, with the idling or guidance axle located in front.

### PLANET CLASS/1830/GREAT BRITAIN

After the 0-2-2s, the next batch of locomotives for the Liverpool and Manchester Railway were those of the 'Planet' type supplied by Robert Stephenson & Co.; these were built in both 2-2-0 and 0-4-0 wheel arrangements. With a weight of 7.5 tons (7.6 tonnes), locomotives of the 'Planet' class were too heavy for the rails then in use on the Liverpool and Manchester Railway. The next locomotives supplied therefore featured an extra axle.

### BURY ENGINES ('COPPERNOBS') 1836/GREAT BRITAIN

Locomotives of the 2-2-0 type were also built by Edward Bury of Liverpool. He was Locomotive Superintendent to the London and Birmingham Railway, the first operating

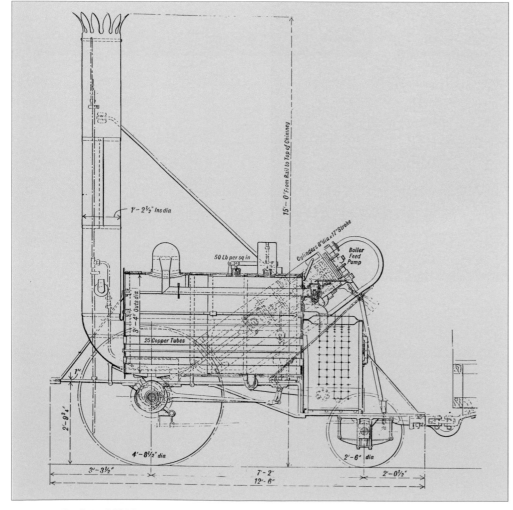

*The 0-2-2 Rocket of 1829*

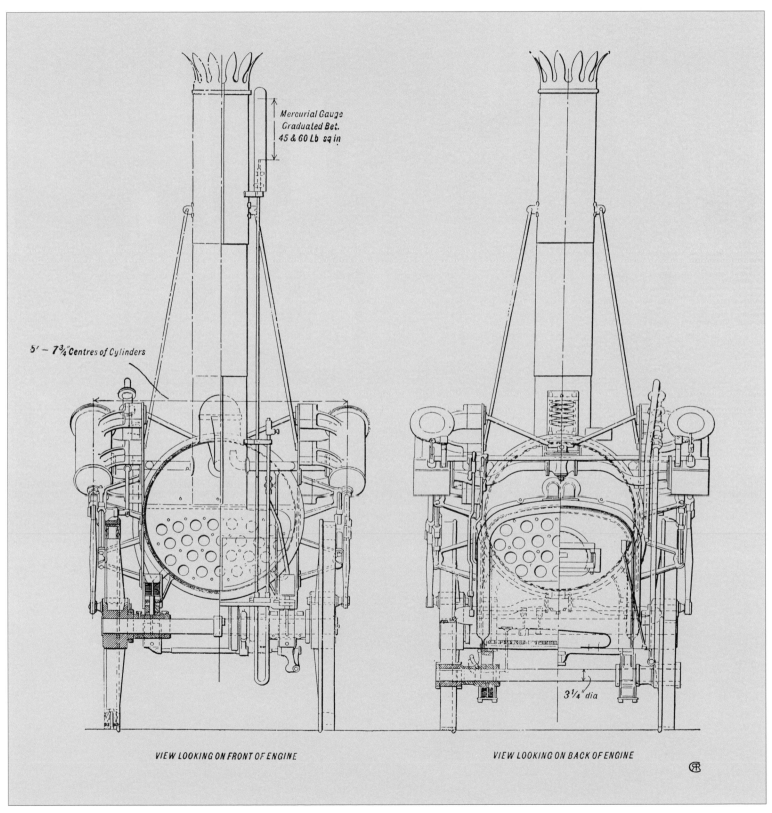

Mercurial Gauge
Graduated Bet.
45 & 60 Lb sq in

5' – 7¾" Centres of Cylinders

3¼" dia

VIEW LOOKING ON FRONT OF ENGINE

VIEW LOOKING ON BACK OF ENGINE

*The Rocket as built in 1829*

*2-2-2 of Buddicom type for the Western Railway of France, 1843*

engines of which were 58 of the Bury 2-2-0 version. Built with a large haycock style of firebox, they were known as 'Coppernobs', but they had insufficient power output to handle the main-line trains on the London and Birmingham and often had to be used in multiple working. This must have posed some awkward problems with train braking, since each engine was controlled separately from the others.

# 2-2-2

## PATENTEE TYPE/1835/GREAT BRITAIN

The addition of the extra axle was found to be necessary in order to reduce the weight on the driving axle to suit the short fish-bellied type of rail then in use; it also reduced the risk of derailment and ensured better stability on curves.

The first three-axled locomotives, built by Robert Stephenson in 1835, were known as the 'Patentee' type. The earliest versions were fitted with cylinders measuring 11in X 18in (279mm X 457mm) and with 66in (1676mm) driving wheels. They were supplied to the Liverpool and Manchester Railway as well as to Germany in the shape of the Adler.

## NORTH STAR CLASS/1837/GREAT BRITAIN

In 1837, when Daniel Gooch was appointed Locomotive Superintendent to the Great Western Railway (after having trained at Charles Tayleur's works at Newton-le-Willows in Lancashire), he found that the locomotives were quite inadequate to handle the trains. Built to a specification devised by Brunel, they had wheels that were excessive and cylinder sizes too small to give the output required. Gooch found that Robert Stephenson & Co. had a couple of engines built for the 5ft 6in (1676mm) gauge track of the New Orleans Railroad waiting for the necessary cash to permit shipment. These two were rebuilt to suit the Great Western's 7ft (2133mm) gauge and delivered as the North Star and the Morning Star, thus setting the tradition of 'Star' names for that railway. This first pair had cylinders 16in x 16in (406mm x 406mm) and, with 7ft (2133mm) driving wheels and 706sq. ft. (66sq.metre) of heating surface, they gave a good performance. A further 10 were then ordered, one of which, Polar Star, was invoiced at £2,809, of which the 1,100-gallon (50hl) tender cost £645. Further similar locomotives were bought from seven different makers: Fenton, Murray and Jackson supplied 20. With a steam pressures of 50-55psi (345-380kPa), they would have

given a tractive force of 1,950lb (885kg) and an output of some 37hp (27.6kW). The design included sandwich frames and a beehive firebox. A replica of North Star is preserved at the Great Western Railway museum at Swindon.

## CHEMIN DE FER DE L'OUEST BUDDICOM TYPE/1843/FRANCE

William Buddicom as Locomotive Superintendent of the Grand Junction Railway was familiar with the 'Crewe' locomotives of his colleague Alexander Allan. When he left to found his own locomotive company he supplied Allan-type locomotives to the Paris & Rouen Railway. They became popular on the continent because they had outside cylinders, thereby escaping the vulnerable cranked axle of Stephenson's inside-cylinder machines. They became known as the 'Buddicom Type.' Those built for the Paris & Rouen Railway, of which one is preserved, had the following dimensions: cylinders 13$\frac{9}{10}$in x 26in (355mm x 535mm), driving wheel 67½in (1720mm), boiler pressure 120psi (832kPa), grate area 9.68sq.ft. (0.9sq.metre), tractive effort 6,167lb (2,800kg), and weight in working order 37,485lb (17 tonnes).

*2-2-2 Patentee type: a replica of the German Adler*

*2-2-2 Bloomer, 1851*

x 610mm). With a boiler steam pressure of 100psi (690kPa) it could produce a tractive force of 6,885lb (3,123kg) and a power output of around 160ihp (119kW). The boiler was considerably larger, with a firegrate area of 22.6sq.ft. (2.1sq.metre) and a heating surface area of 1,625sq.ft. (151sq.metre); the completed weight came to 28.5 tons (29 tonnes). The weight on the leading axle was sufficient to result in one of them fracturing during a journey through the Box Tunnel. For this reason, in 1851 an extra axle was fitted to produce a 4-2-2 class known as the 'Lord of the Isles' class.

## JENNY LIND CLASS/1847/GREAT BRITAIN

Among the best known locomotives of the 2-2-2 type were the 'Jenny Lind' class built by E. B. Wilson for the London, Brighton and South Coast Railway, first supplied in 1847. As the trains had to traverse both the North and South Downs on the route to Brighton, the speed of operation was not as important as on the Great Western, and so the 'Jenny Lind' class locomotives were built with 72in (1828mm) diameter driving wheels and with two cylinders 15in x 20in (381mm x 508mm); having a steam pressure of 125psi (862kPa), they could produce a tractive force of 6,640lb (3,012kg) and a power output of nearly 200ihp

## GREAT WESTERN CLASS/1846/GREAT BRITAIN

In 1846 the Great Western Railway commenced production of locomotives from its own works at Swindon to the designs of Daniel Gooch. Among the first was a larger version of the 2-2-2 as previously supplied by Robert Stephenson & Co. Gooch's design was based on a larger size of driving wheel, at 96in (2438mm) for high speed, and the cylinder size was increased to 18in x 24in (457mm

*2-2-2 Great Western , 1846*

*2-2-2 Lady of the Lake , 1862*

*2-2-2 GNR 7ft 6in Single, 1870*

*4-2-0 Crampton, Le Continent , 1846*

(149kW). Built to a weight of 24 tons (24.4 tonnes), they were the mainstay of the Brighton line until the advent of the Gladstone class in 1882.

## BLOOMER CLASS/1851/GREAT BRITAIN

Until 1862 the locomotive department of the London and North Western Railway was divided into two halves, with the southern half in charge of Hugh McConnell at Wolverton. For main-line duties McConnell in 1851 commissioned 10 locomotives of the Bloomer class built by Sharp, Stewart & Co. Amelia Bloomer was an exponent of a new style in women's clothing at the time, and the Bloomer class was so-called because it showed more of its working parts than had until then been the tendency. McConnell believed in a big-engine policy, and his Bloomers, at 30.5 tons (31 tonnes), were considerably larger than the equivalent engines then being built at Crewe, which were around the 20-ton (20.3-tonne) mark. Fitted with 84in (2133mm) diameter wheels and with cylinders 16in x 22in (406mm x 559mm), they were supplied with steam at 150psi (1034kPa). They could give a tractive force of 8,550lb (3,878kg) and a power output of some 250ihp (186kW).

*4-2-0 Crampton, Folkestone , 1846/51*

## LADY OF THE LAKE/1862/GREAT BRITAIN

On the northern half of the London and North Western Railway the Locomotive Superintendent at Crewe from 1857 was John Ramsbottom. In 1859 he designed a class of 2-2-2 locomotives which was when built designated the 'Problem' class after the first one. However, when No. 531, built in 1862 and named Lady of the Lake, was awarded a bronze medal at the International Exhibition in London, that name became the adopted one for the class. Fitted with 91.5in (2324mm) diameter driving wheels and with two cylinders of 16in x 24in (406mm x 610mm), their steam pressure was, at 120psi (828kPa), lower than that of the 'Bloomers,' and they had a tractive force of only 6,850lb (3,107kg), but they could handle any main-line train of that era and lasted well into the next century, some being rebuilt as late as 1898.

# 4-2-0

## BROTHER JONATHAN/1832/USA

The 4-2-0 wheel arrangement, with the use of a leading bogie, was first adopted on a locomotive built by the West Point Foundry in the State of New York, United States, in 1832 for the Mohawk and Hudson Railroad. Credited with being the first locomotive to run at 60mph (96ph) and with a total weight of 7 tons (7.1 tonnes), the engine named first Experiment and later Brother Jonathan was equipped with 60in (1524mm) diameter driving wheels and with cylinders 9.5in x 16in (241mm x 406mm) stroke. The boiler pressure was probably around 50psi (345kPa), so

*4-2-0 . Another view of Crampton's Le Continent of 1846*

*4-2-2 Iron Duke , 1847*

the engine's tractive force would have been around 1,000lb (454kg).

## MARTIN VAN BUREN/1839/USA

The 4-2-0 wheel arrangement was adopted for the Martin Van Buren, which was built by M.W. Baldwin for the Philadelphia and Columbia Railroad in 1839 with 9in x 16in (228mm x 406mm) cylinders and 54in (1371mm) driving wheels, and which weighed 7.5 tons (7.62 tonnes), and for 10 locomotives supplied by Norris Bros of Pennsylvania in 1840 to the Birmingham and Gloucester Railway for use on the 1 in 37 gradient (2.7 per cent) of the Lickey Incline.

## CRAMPTON ENGINES/1846/GREAT BRITAIN, FRANCE

Other locomotives which were built to the 4-2-0 wheel arrangement, but without the use of a bogie (truck), were those built to the designs of Thomas Crampton; they were an adaptation of the Stephenson Long Boiler locomotives. In the Crampton design the driving axle was located at the rear of the firebox. The first two were built by Tulk and Ley at Whitehaven, Cumberland, for use on the British-owned Namur-Liége Railway and accordingly carried the names, respectively, of Namur and Liége. They were equipped with two cylinders measuring 16in x 20in (406mm x 508mm) which drove 84in (2133mm) diameter wheels, and were fed with steam at 85psi (587kPa). Built to a weight of 21.6 tons (22 tonnes), they could give a tractive force of 4,400lb

(1,996kg), and they proved so successful that 127 of the same type were built by Derosne et Cail for the Chemins de Fer du Nord after 1849. In those the cylinder size was 15¾in x 19²/₃in (400mm x 500mm), with driving wheels 82²/₃in (2100mm) in diameter and a steam pressure of 90psi (621kPa). With a total weight of 28.4 tons (28.9 tonnes), they gave a tractive force of 4,560lb (2,070kg). Later a larger version was built with cylinders measuring 16in x 22in (419mm x 558mm), driving wheels 91in (231mm) in diameter, and a steam pressure of 110psi (760kPa). Built to a weight of 29.3 tons (29.8 tonnes), they suffered at first from derailments due to incorrect balancing of the driving wheels, but, when rectified, they proved satisfactory and one - Le Continent - lasted in service until 1914 (it is now preserved in the French Railway Museum at Mulhouse).

The last Crampton-style locomotive built for use in Britain was the Folkestone, supplied by Robert Stephenson & Co. in 1851 to the South Eastern Railway. In this model the cylinders drove onto a jackshaft, thus permitting the use of inside cylinders. The type found considerable favor in Germany, with 135 being built by various manufacturers - including Maffei and Esslingen - until 1854. The largest were those built for the Baden State Railway, with cylinders of 16in x 22in (406mm x 559mm) and 84in (2133mm) driving wheels, the boiler supplied steam at 100psi (690kPa) from a heating surface area of 880sq.ft. (81.75sq.metre) and the tractive force would have been 5,700lb (2,586kg). With a total weight of 28 tons (28.45 tonnes), and with their huge driving wheels on both sides

of the footplate, they must have been most impressive machines to drive.

## 4-2-2

This wheel arrangement, which produced the most succesful of all the 'Singles', was first adopted by the Great Western when their 2-2-2 locomotives proved to be too heavy on the front axle. The frames were then lengthened and an additional axle fitted in front.

### IRON DUKE/1847/GREAT BRITAIN

The first example of this wheel arrangement was the Iron Duke, built in 1847 at Swindon; apart from the extra axle the leading dimensions were as for the former 'Great Western' class (see above). The 'Iron Duke' class was followed in 1851 by a larger version, the first of which was the 'Lord of the Isles.' The wheels and cylinders were the same, as was the boiler pressure, but the boiler was larger, with a grate area of 21.5sq.ft. (2sq.metre) and with 1,790sq.ft. (166.3sq.metre) of heating area. These locomotives were to prove the principal operating motive power for the broad-gauge lines of the Great Western until the changeover to standard gauge was completed in 1892.

### GREAT NORTHERN NO.1/1870/GREAT BRITAIN

Perhaps the best known of all the single drivers were the Great Northern bogie 8ft Singles first built to the designs of Patrick Stirling at Doncaster in 1870. With their long domeless boiler and the upswept running board over the crankpin, they were considered the most graceful as well as the fastest locomotives of their era. Although they were called eight-footers, the actual diameter of their driving wheels was a little larger - 97in (2463mm). With their two outside cylinders at 18in x 28in (457mm x 711mm) and a boiler pressure of 160psi (1104kPa), they could haul any of the Great Northern's main-line trains single-handed and could attain speeds of 80mph (129kph). With a weight of 38.4 tons (39 tonnes), of which 15 tons (15.24 tonnes) was available for adhesion, they could give a tractive force of 12,700lb (5,761kg) with an estimated power output of almost 400ihp (298kW). In the final day of the race to Aberdeen, No. 668 covered the 105.5 miles (170km) to Grantham in 101 minutes with a train of 105 tons (106.7 tonnes), and from Grantham to York No. 775 took 76 minutes for the 83 miles (134km).

The original No.1 has been preserved at the National Railway Museum at York.

### MIDLAND RAILWAY `SPINNERS`/1887/GREAT BRITAIN

The last of the great 'Singles' were those built by the Midland Railway and known as the 'Midland Spinners'.

*4-2-2 Iron Duke , 1847  (a working replica at the National Railway Museum )*

They were designed by Samuel Waite Johnson, who was appointed Locomotive Superintendent to the Midland Railway in 1873, having started his career with E. B. Wilson of Leeds where he had assisted in preparing the drawings for their 'Jenny Lind' class for the Brighton line. In 1885, with the application of steam sanding gear, the side rods of some of the Midland 2-4-0 (Class 1282) engines were removed and they worked satisfactorily with only the one driven axle. In 1887, the same year as the 4-2-2 No. 123 was taken over by the Caledonian Railway (it is now preserved at the Glasgow Museum of Transport), Johnson built at Derby the first five of his 4-2-2 locomotives with their 88in (2235mm) diameter driving wheels and two cylinders measuring 18in x 26in (457mm x 660mm). By 1900, when the last of the type were produced, there had been 95 of them, of which the latest were equipped with 93½in (2375mm) diameter driving wheels, cylinders at 19½in x 26in (495mm x 660mm) and a steam pressure of 180psi (1240kPa). Their tractive force was 16,200lb (7,348kg) and the power output would have been around 480ihp (360kW). They could handle train weights of up to 325 tons (330 tonnes) and were capable of speeds in excess of 90mph (145kph). By the time the Midland became part of the LMSR in 1923 there were still 43 in operation.

*4-2-2  Lord of the Isles , 1847*

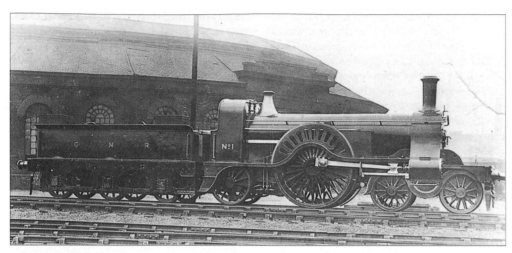

*4-2-2 GNR No 1, 1870*

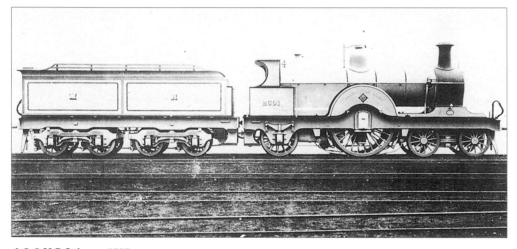

*4-2-2 M R Spinner, 1887*

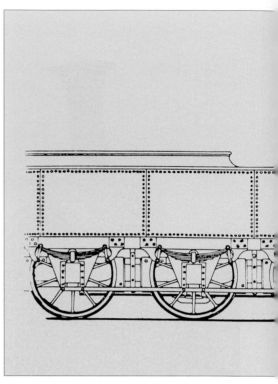

*The Crampton 6-2-0 Liverpool, 1848*

# 6-2-0

## LIVERPOOL/1848/GREAT BRITAIN

The largest locomotive built to the designs of Thomas Crampton was the Liverpool, erected for the London and North Western in 1848 by Bury, Curtiss and Kennedy. It weighed 35 tons (35.6 tonnes) and, with its 96in (2438mm) driving wheels, was reputed to be capable of running at over 70mph (113kph), but it was looked on with disfavour by the Civil Engineer on account of track damage and had only a short life. With 18in x 24in (457mm x 609mm) cylinders and a steam pressure of 120psi (828kPa), the tractive force was 8,500 pounds (3,856kg) and the power output could have been around 500ihp (373kW).

In the USA the Camden and Amboy Railroad employed six 6-2-0s. Built by R. Norris in 1849, these had, like the Liverpool, 96in (2438mm) driving wheels located behind the firebox. With cylinders 14in X 38in (355mm X 965mm), their weight came to 24.6 tons (25 tonnes); the first of them was named John Stevens. In these six engines, the six leading wheels were in the form of a guiding truck, whereas in the case of the Liverpool the leading wheels were located in the main frame.

# FOUR-COUPLED LOCOMOTIVES

## 0-4-0

The minimum number of wheels with which a locomotive could operate was four, and at first all of these were used in the transmission of power in order to achieve the maximum adhesion possible.

## TREVITHICK'S ENGINE/1804/GREAT BRITAIN

The very first steam locomotive of all was the 0-4-0 built by Richard Trevithick - who was also, notably, the first engineer to make use of steam pressure to produce power; all the previous engines had made use of steam only to produce a vacuum, so that the power was applied by the superior pressure of the atmosphere. Until steam was used under pressure the power unit was too heavy to be used for propulsion other than in a steamship.

Trevithick's first engine, built for the Penydarren Ironworks in 1804, used a single cylinder with a bore of 8 1/5in (208mm) and a stroke of 54in (1371mm) driving an enormous flywheel with a diameter of 8ft (2438mm) from which both axles were driven by means of gearwheels. It was successful in hauling the intended load of 10 tons (10.16 tonnes) of iron as well as some 70 unofficial passengers for a distance of nearly 10 miles (16km), but it proved too damaging to the cast-iron rails of that time.

## BLACK BILLY/1805/GREAT BRITAIN

In 1805 a similar locomotive was built by John Steel for use in a colliery at Gateshead, but with a cylinder size of 7in x 36in (177mm x 914mm) it probably produced an output of only about 1hp (0.75kW). Named Black Billy, this locomotive too had only a short life.

## LOCOMOTION NO. 1/1825/GREAT BRITAIN

The 0-4-0 continued to be the favourite wheel arrangement for ensuing engines built by Matthew Murray, William Hedley and by George Stephenson, culminating in 1825 with his Locomotion for the Stockton and Darlington Railway. As with all the other engines built after Trevithick's

## BEST FRIEND OF CHARLESTON/1830/USA

first pair, the Locomotion was equipped with two cylinders arranged vertically on top of the boiler, the lower halves of the cylinders being within the boiler shell. The cylinders were 10in (254mm) bore by 24in (609mm) stroke, driving 48in (1219mm) diameter wheels and using a steam pressure of 25psi (172kPa). The boiler consisted of a single flue tube with a heating surface area of 40sq.ft. (3.7sq.metre) and the firegrate area was 7sq.ft. (0.65sq.metre). The tractive force would have been just over 1,200lb (545kg), and with very tortuous and restricted steam passages its output would probably have been not much more than 11ihp (7.33kW).

On its opening run the Locomotion's load was composed of 12 loaded trucks as well as 21 equipped for passengers; the total load must have been about 30 long tons (30.5 tonnes). The wheels were built up from cast-iron segments dowelled together, and it would not be long before the machine suffered from wheel fractures. There was no form of springing, since each cylinder was above the wheel it drove and the fixed length of the connecting rod precluded the use of springs in the system. At a later date an additional flue was arranged in the boiler so that the firedoor was at the same end as the chimney; this arrangement entailed the use of an extra tender from which the boiler could be fired.

The locomotive suffered from a boiler explosion, possibly before the extra flue was fitted, and was withdrawn from service in 1841. After use as a pumping engine, the Locomotion was restored and in 1857 sited at Darlington North Road station, where it remained until 1875 when it was used in a jubilee procession. It took part in the Centenary procession at Darlington in 1925, and was thereafter located at Darlington Bank Top station for many years before being returned to Darlington North Road station.

Most of the early locomotives in Europe and in the United States were of the 0-4-0 type. Among these were the first German locomotive, built in 1816, and one built by Robert Stephenson & Co. for the St Etienne-Lyon Railway in France in 1827. The version built for the same railway in 1829 by Marc Seguin incorporated the multitubular boiler as used in the Rocket, but was fitted with a forced-draught fan driven a belt drive.

*An 0-4-0 ' Camelback ' locomotive , one of several operated by the Philadelphia & Reading Railroad . It was built in 1903 and employed as a yard and pick-up locomotive in urban industrial areas, which involved sharp curves and street running.*

*0-4-0 Best Friend of Charleston , 1830*

In the United States the Best Friend of Charleston was an 0-4-0 built by the West Point Foundry, New York, for the South Carolina Railroad in 1830. It had a weight of 4.4 tons (4.47 tonnes), and was fitted with cylinders of 6in (152mm) bore by 16in (406mm) stroke and supplied with steam at 50psi (345kPa). The fireman is said to have screwed down the safety valve in an endeavour to obtain a better output - a cunning wheeze which resulted in the destruction of both boiler and fireman. The Best Friend was then rebuilt as the Phoenix with a different boiler. However, a replica was built by the railroad in 1928 and is today used for demonstration runs.

### JOHN BULL/1831/USA

The first operational locomotive in the United States was the John Bull, built by Robert Stephenson & Co. for the Camden and Amboy Railroad in 1831, but its weight of 10.3 tons (10.46 tonnes) was to prove too much for the track and it was withdrawn - fortunately to be preserved at the Smithsonian Institution at Washington, D.C. John Bull was fitted with 54in (1371mm) driving wheels and two cylinders measuring 9in x 20in (228mm x 508mm) which, with a steam pressure of 50psi (345kPa), gave it a tractive force of 1,280lb (581kg).

It was followed by a number of so-called 'Grasshopper' engines built by Ross Winans for the Baltimore and Ohio

*0-4-0 with fan draught built by Marc Seguin, 1829.*

Railroad between 1832 and 1837, when the 0-4-0 type ceased to be an operational tool for the increasing demands of the American railroads of that time. However,

although the short wheelbase imposed limitations in operation, after the early experiments the 0-4-0 wheel arrangement continued to be used for small shunting

*0-4-2 Lion, 1838*

engines ('switchers' in the United States) doing jobs where speed was not important. Forexample, the Philadelphia & Reading RR built over 50 0-4-0 'Camelbacks' in the early 20th century. This railroad liked to burn the anthracite that was mined in its territory, and therefore preferred wide Wooten fireboxes. The short wheelbase of these locomotives suited them for the sharp curves of industrial districts.

# 0-4-2

### LION/1838/GREAT BRITAIN

When the first 'Patentee' locomotives were supplied by Robert Stephenson & Co. in 1837 they were of a 2-2-2 wheel arrangement, but in the following year some 25 similar engines, but having an 0-4-2 wheel arrangement, were supplied to the Liverpool and Manchester Railway for the haulage of goods. Among those supplied and fortunately now preserved was No. 57, built by Todd, Kitson and Laird of Leeds, and named the Lion. With 54in (1371mm) driving wheels and cylinders originally 11in X 20in (279mm X 508mm) - now 14in x 18in (355mm x

*0-4-2 Lion, as restored*

*0-4-2 Gladstone in the National Railway Museum*

*0-4-2, Gladstone Class, 1882*

## SAMSON CLASS/1863/GREAT BRITAIN

In Britain the leading exponent of the use of the 2-4-0 for express-passenger-train haulage was the London and North Western under the brilliant and versatile John Ramsbottom - who invented the split piston ring, now in universal use in all piston engines, the double-beat regulator which gave the driver finer control over the steam supply, and the water pick-up apparatus which enabled much longer nonstop runs to be achieved. Ramsbottom was a great believer in standardization, and in his locomotives the parts were fully interchangeable, thus reducing assembly time and maintenance costs.

His first 2-4-0 engines consisted of 90 engines of the 'Samson' class. These had 72in (1828mm) driving wheels and, although their boilers were small, their hearts were large. They were followed by 96 engines of the 'Newton' class, which had 80in (2032mm) wheels.

457mm) - the steam pressure was 48psi (331kPa), giving a tractive force of 1,300lb (830kg) and an output estimated at 28ihp (21kW). The top speed was designed to be 45mph (72kph), and the Lion could pull freight trains of up to 200 long tons (203 tonnes).

After being absorbed first into the Grand Junction Railway and then into the London and North Western, the Lion was sold to the Mersey Docks and Harbour Board in 1859 and then rescued and restored at Crewe in 1928, when the present chimney, boiler cladding and copper firebox cover were fitted. Today the Lion is preserved at the Liverpool Museum of Science. It appeared in the film 'The Titfield Thunderbolt' (1953).

### GLADSTONE CLASS/1882/GREAT BRITAIN

Probably the best known locomotives of the 0-4-2 category were the 'Gladstone' class built for the London, Brighton and South Coast Railway from 1882. In spite of lacking a guiding axle, these locomotives were one of the principal main-line express engines in Britain for many years.

Gladstone was the first of 36 engines built at Brighton to the design of William Stroudley. It was fitted with two inside cylinders of 18in x 26in (462mm x 660mm) and driving wheels with a diameter of 78in (1981mm). The boiler was of ample proportions, having 20sq.ft. (1.86sq.metre) of grate area and a heating surface of 1,485sq.ft. (138sq.metre). The tractive force was 14,000lb (6,350kg), and the power output in the region of 420ihp (313kW). They were steady runners at speeds of up to 75mph (121kph).

The original engine No.214 is preserved at the Railway Museum at York.

The 2-4-0 wheel arrangement found considerable favor in Britain and in Europe for express passenger duties, but was little used in the United States, where the leading bogie remained the most chosen method of supporting the front end of a locomotive.

Probably the first of the 2-4-0 engines were those built at Crewe from 1845. These were similar to the 2-2-2 types, both being fitted with the same boilers and with 60in (1524mm) driving wheels.

The 2-4-0 was to remain the favourite British main-line passenger engine for the next 50 years; during the Newark Brake Trials of 1875, seven out of the nine locomotives taking part were of the 2-4-0 type. At first the leading axle was carried in the main frame with some lateral movement permissible to the axle boxes, but after W.B.Adams in 1863 had designed an axle capable of radial movement, the use of this type of leading axle became more widespread.

## MIDLAND RAILWAY 800 CLASS/1870/GREAT BRITAIN

Compared with the 392 locomotives of the 2-4-0 type built by the LNWR in the 'Samson', 'Newton', 'Precedent' and 'Precursor' classes, the most numerous user was the Midland with 409 engines in all, including 40 inherited at the time of the formation of the Company in 1848. Out of those the best known was the 800 class, built to the design of Matthew Kirtley in 1870-71, when 30 were supplied by Neilson & Co. of Glasgow and 18 were built at Derby. As first built, these had 80in (2032mm) driving wheels and cylinders at 17in x 24in (431mm x 609mm), but they were later rebuilt by S.W.Johnson with 18in x 26in (457mm x 660mm) cylinders and with his standard boiler, which had 1,225sq.ft. (114sq.metre) of heating area and so gave plenty of steam - something which operation on the heavily graded lines of the Midland required. With a steam

*2-4-0, 800 Class, 1870*

*2-4-0 , Indonesian B50 Class , 1880*

pressure of 140psi (965kPa) they could give a tractive force of 12,500lb (5,670kg).

Although one of them was to remain in service until 1936, none, unfortunately, has been preserved. However, a former version built in 1866, No.158A, is now at the Midland Centre at Butterley, near Derby, decorated in true Midland colours (first adopted in 1883).

The Midland continued to build 2-4-0 engines until 1881, mostly similar in basic design. In 1923, 245 of them were to pass into the stock of the LMSR.

## NORTH EASTERN RAILWAY 901 CLASS/1872/GREAT BRITAIN

Another well known class of the 2-4-0 variety was the 901 class built by the North Eastern Railway at their Gateshead works in 1872-82, during which time a total of 55 were built. As first built, they had 84in (2133mm) driving wheels with 17in x 24in (431mm x 609mm) cylinders fed by steam at a pressure of 140psi (965kPa) from a boiler with 1,208sq.ft. (112sq.metre) of heating area. Designed by Edward Fletcher, Locomotive Superintendent for the North Eastern from its formation in 1854 until 1883, they were fitted with special exhaust cocks which could be used to reduce the blast effect at full power if it was having a harmful effect on the fire. This was a popular feature among footplate crews. The locomotives were also equipped with a commodious wood-lined cab, a characteristic of North Eastern engines. The 901 class was the best of the NER 2-4-0 classes; No.910 has been preserved at York.

*2-4-0 901 Class , 1872*

*2-4-0 LNWR Precedent Class , 1874*

*2-4-0 , Great Eastern Class T26, 1891*

In all, including 901 class, the North Eastern worked 149 of the 2-4-0 type, 35 of which it inherited at its formation, mostly from the York, Newcastle and Berwick Railway. Among these were two similar to the Jenny Lind type, but with 2-4-0 wheel arrangement. In 1886 No.1324 was built as a two-cylinder compound under Thomas Worsdell, who had been appointed Locomotive Superintendent in 1885 and who was carrying out his experiments in this field.

The last batch of 2-4-0 engines consisted of the 20 locomotives of G class, known as 'Wateringburys', with 72in (1828mm) driving wheels and employing the Joy type of valve gear. It was said, however, that this class was not popular with the enginemen.

### PRECEDENT AND PRECURSOR CLASSES/1874/GREAT BRITAIN

After 1871 when Francis Webb took over at the LNWR from John Ramsbottom, further locomotives of the same type as the 'Samson' and 'Newton' classes were built. First there were the 70 'Precedent' type with cylinders at 17in x 24in (431mm x 609mm), driving 80in (2032mm) wheels and supplied with steam at 150psi (1034kPa) from a boiler with only 1,080sq.ft. (100sq.metre) of heating area on a weight of 72,324lb (32.8 tonnes).

To supplement that class for duty on the heavily graded lines between Crewe and Carlisle there were 40 engines of the 'Precursor' class, similar to the 'Precedent' class but with driving wheels of 66in (1676mm) diameter.

Finally there were the 96 engines of the 'Improved Precedent' class, of which the last was built in 1894. It was one of these, No.790, Hardwicke, which took part in the final night of the race to Aberdeen on 21 August 1895, when it ran the 141 miles (227km) from Crewe to Carlisle, including the 915ft (279m) climb over the summit at Shap, in 126 minutes at an average speed of 67mph (108kph). The Hardwicke, restored at the Steamtown Museum at Carnforth in 1975, is now at the Railway Museum at York.

### INDONESIAN STATE RAILWAYS CLASS B50/1880/INDONESIA

In the final years of their long lives, these locomotives were celebrated among railway enthusiasts, being the oldest working survivors of a once widespread wheel arrangement, 2-4-0. Built in Glasgow by Sharp, Stewart at a somewhat slow rate of some 15 units over five years, the class survived into the 1970s. By that time a handful were in Sumatra, one was works switcher at the Madiun locomotive works, but the majority worked the Ponorogo-

Slahung branch. Some were fitted for oil burning, but the apparatus was not the most efficient, although quite spectacular as a flame-throwing device. They had 55½in (1413mm) coupled wheels, 15in x 18in (380mm x 457mm) cylinders, and a boiler pressure of just 142psi (978kPa), giving a tractive effort of 8,829lb (4,008 kgs). (This assumes 75% boiler pressure, which might be generous since these locomotives did not have superheaters). Weight in working order was 45,472lb (20.3 tonnes) and grate area 11.8sq.ft. (1.1 sq.metre).

### GREAT EASTERN RAILWAY CLASS T26 (LNER CLASS E4)/1891/GREAT BRITAIN

Having built a none-too-successful class of 2-4-0 with 7ft (2133mm) driving wheels, the GER Locomotive Superintendent James Holden tried his luck with the same design adapted for 68in (1727mm) wheels. This was a general-purpose machine whch proved highly successful, and 90 were built between 1891 and 1902. Their boilers worked at 160psi (1102kPa) and provided 18sq.ft. (1.67 sq.metre) of grate area. Cylinders were 17½in x 24in (445mm x 610mm) and the coupled wheels were 68in (1727mm). Tractive effort was 14,700lb (6,675kg). Weight in working order was 90,405lb (41 tonnes), with the tender at 68,355lb or 31 tonnes. Thus these were small engines, unfortunate in that they appeared just as train weights were about to increase rapidly. But they were versatile, and ended their days hauling short trains on branch lines, mainly around Cambridge. One of them, No. 62785, lasted long enough to be overtaken by the preservation movement, and has been restored to the Great Eastern's blue livery.

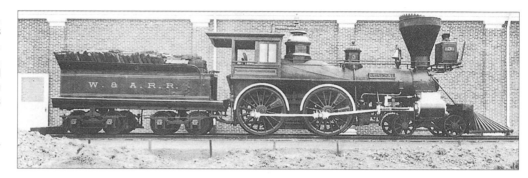

*4-4-0, the General of American Civil War fame, 1855*

## 2-4-2

### CHICAGO, BURLINGTON AND QUINCY RAILROAD NO. 590/1893/USA

This variant of the ubiquitous American-type 4-4-0 (see next entry) was built by the Baldwin Locomotive Company in 1893 to provide an increase in the firegrate area. It was exhibited at the Columbia Exhibition at Chicago in that year. Fitted with two cylinders 19in x 26in (482mm x 660mm) and with driving wheels of 84in (2133mm), it gave a tractive force of 19,000lb (8,618kg) using steam at 200psi (1380kPa). The boiler contained 1,580sq.ft. (147 sq.metre) of heating surface area with a firegrate area of 45sq.ft. (4.2 sq.metre). The type was soon to be superseded by the 4-4-2 'Atlantic' wheel arrangement; in all, only about 120 were built.

## 4-4-0

### EARLY AMERICAN TYPES/1837/USA

*4-4-0, the New York Central Railroad's record-breaking No 999 of 1893*

Although known as the American type in the White system of wheel notation, this arrangement became the most favoured for passenger locomotives throughout the world, over 25,000 being built in the United States and probably as many, if not more, in Britain and in Europe.

The first example was one built in 1837 as a freight engine by James Brooks of Philadelphia for the Philadelphia, Germanstown-and-Norriston Railroad to the design of Henry R. Campbell, for which he had been granted a patent in 1836. The bogie, or 'guiding truck' as it was described, was similar to that fitted to the Brother Jonathan in 1832, but since it was not of the swivelling type the leading wheel did not have a flange fitted. The cylinders were 14in x 16in (356mm x 406mm), and the locomotive had 54in (1371mm) wheels and a steam pressure of 90psi (621kPa); it may have given a tractive force of up to 4,400lb (2,020kg) - it was designed to haul 140 long tons (142 tonnes) up a grade of 1 in 100 (1 per cent). The weight was 26,450lb (12 tonnes), of which 7.88 long tons (8 tonnes) were available for adhesion (giving a coefficient of adhesion of 0.33, the accepted figure for four-coupled engines).

The early American 4-4-0 engines were fitted with the cylinders inclined and attached to the smokebox, and

many were built in that style. M. W. Baldwin supplied their first 4-4-0 to the Camden and Amboy Railroad in 1846: it had 13¾in x 18in (348mm x 457mm) cylinders and was fitted with a long boiler with a haycock type of firebox. To ensure correct weight distribution there were two large inverted leaf springs outside and above the driving wheels, and a large spark-arresting chimney (this was becoming a generally adopted feature).

Three years later a similar engine, named Allegheny, was built by Baldwin for the Pennsylvania Railroad. It had one of the first of the large wooden driver's cabs, and was probably one of the last of the old generation of American type.

The next step in the development of the American 4-4-0 was the arrangement of the cylinders horizontally and attached to the bar frame, and the incorporation of all the typical American-type features such as a headlamp (using oil), the large decorated wooden cab, the spark-arresting funnel, a bell and a pilot (cow-catcher). A typical example was the General of the Western and Atlantic Railroad which took part in the Great Locomotive Chase of 1862 during the American Civil War and is now preserved at a Museum at Kennesaw, Georgia.

A further typical example of an engine of that era would have been one of those supplied by Danforth Cooke & Co. to the Delaware, Lackawanna and Western Railroad on which the 66in (1676mm) driving wheels were actuated by cylinders at 17in x 22in (431mm x 558mm) with a steam pressure of 100psi (690kPa) and weighing around 56,007lb (25.4 tonnes). In their final development stage, a typical example was the Class L built for the Pennsylvania Railroad in 1895 with 18½in x 26in (470mm x 660mm) cylinders driving 80in (2032mm) wheels with a steam pressure of 200psi (1380kPa) from a boiler with 1,900sq.ft. (176.5sq.metre) of heating area and a 32sq.ft. (3sq.metre) firegrate. On a weight of 134,505lb (61 tonnes), the tractive force was 18,900lb (8,573kg) and the power output would have been around 660ihp (492kW) at 70mph (113kph).

In 1893 a similar locomotive of the New York Central was reputed to have achieved 112mph (180kph) on the 'Empire State Express,' but that would have required an output of at least 1,100hp (820kW), and the speed as calculated by observers on the train was stated to have been 81mph (130kph). The locomotive performing the run was No. 999. It was originally fitted with 86in (2184mm) diameter driving wheels, but those were later replaced by the 80in (2032mm) size.

*4-4-0 , D40 Class , built for the Great North of Scotland Railway in 1899*

## GLOGGNITZERS/1845/AUSTRIA

Reverting to Europe, the first of the 4-4-0 type were those supplied by Robert Stephenson & Co. to the Great Western for use in South Wales; they were known as the 'Waverley' class. These were followed by some designed by John Haswell and built by the Vienna-Gloggnitz Railway in 1842-48 at their own works at Neustadt/Vienna. There were two classes, known as the 'Grosse Gloggnitzer' and the 'Klein Gloggnitzer'; one of the latter has been preserved at the Transport Museum in Vienna. They were equipped with two cylinders measuring 14½in x 22⁷⁄₁₀in (368mm x 576mm) driving 56in (1422mm) diameter wheels. The steam, at a pressure of 80psi (552kPa), was supplied from a boiler with 760sq.ft. (70.6sq.metre) of heating area and with a firegrate of 10sq.ft. (0.93sq.metre). The weight was 50,494lb (22.9 tonnes) and the tractive force would have been 5,470lb (2,481kg). Those were designed to British dimensions and probably used the Whitworth system of screw threads.

*Canadian Pacific No 29. This was the last 4-4-0 in regular service in North America , lasting until 1960*

*4-4-0 Duke Class , 1895*

### DU BOUSQUET 4-4-0s/1886/FRANCE

In 1886 the Nord in France built a 2-2-2-0 compound engine to the design of their ingénieur du Bousquet, who had tested one of Francis Webb's 'Teutonics' built to that wheel arrangement. However, it was not powerful enough, and was soon followed by a 4-4-0 built (initially as a 4-2-2-0) by du Bousquet in conjunction with De Glehn, then Technical Director at the Alsace Locomotive Works. Originally 15 were built. They had four cylinders, two at 13 ²/₅in (340mm) and two at 21in (533mm) bore, all with a stroke of 25½in (640mm), and a steam pressure of 203psi (1400kPa). Their boilers had a heating area of 1,206sq.ft. (112sq.metre), their weight was 95,917lb (43.5 tonnes) and, with driving wheels of 83¹/₅in (2113mm), they would have given a tractive force of 18,000lb (8,200kg).

They were so successful that many larger versions were built for use on the Nord; and a similar version was built at the Swiss Locomotive Works at Winterthur for the Swiss Central Railway, although with smaller wheels for use in the mountainous areas. The same basic design was applied

also to 4-6-0 locomotives of the Baden and the Gotthard Railways in 1894.

The original 4-2-2-0 compound No. 701 has been preserved and is now at the Mulhouse Museum of the SNCF.

### GREAT WESTERN RAILWAY 'DUKE' CLASS/1895/BRITAIN

These outside-frame locomotives were similar to a preceding class but their coupled wheels were smaller (68in or 1727mm), making them suitable for the hilly sections of main line in Cornwall. They had domed, parallel, boilers, but it was not long before the design was modified to include US-style taper boilers and in the end there were two classes, the 'Dukes' with the old boiler and the 'Bulldogs' with the new. Both classes carried names, some of the 'Duke' names evoking Cornwall (Cornubia, Merlin, Duke of Cornwall, for example, the last-named being the first-built and providing the class name). The 'Dukes' had a boiler pressure of 180psi (1240kPa), cylinders 18in x

26in (457mm x 660mm), and a tractive effort of 18,955lb (8,605kg). The grate area was 17.2sq.ft. (1.59sq.metre) and the weight 110,200lb (50 tonnes). In their final years the survivors of this class were mainly used on passenger trains in Central Wales, and lasted into the 1950s.

### HIGHLAND RAILWAY 'BEN' CLASS/1898/BRITAIN

Twenty of these small passenger locomotives were built, nine of them in the HR's Lochgorm workshops at Inverness. They were not intended for the major trains (the 'Big Bens' were for that) but they proved a very useful class, outlasting not only the 'Big Bens' but also subsequent HR passenger locomotives. They carried the names of Scottish mountains, painted on the splasher. Ben Alder was the last to remain in service, until 1953, and it was earmarked for preservation, but for some bureaucratic reason it was then allowed to go to the scrapheap. These locomotives were typical designs of Peter Drummond, then the locomotive superintendent of the HR. They had 18in x 26in (457mm

*4-4-0 Ben Alder , 1898*

x 660mm) cylinders, 72in (1828mm) driving wheels, a grate area of 20.3sq.ft. or 1.88sq.metre, (slightly reduced when a new boiler was fitted in the 1920s), and a boiler pressure of 175psi (1206kPa). Tractive effort was 18,402lb (8,354kg) and weight in working order 101,430lb (46.5 tonnes).

## PLM BIG C CLASS/1899/FRANCE

In France the four-cylinder compound was tried out by Adolph Henry of the PLM (Paris, Lyons and Mediterranean Railway) in 1888 on some 2-4-2 locomotives of the C1 class. The idea was then applied by his successor, Chas Baudry, in 1895 to 40 C class 4-4-0 engines, known as the Small C, and then to 120 of the Big C class, which were fitted with streamlined cabs and front ends to cope with the Mistral in the Rhône Valley and came to be known as the 'Coupe Vent' series.

Fitted with two cylinders of bore 13²⁄₅in (340mm) and two of bore 21¹⁄₃in (541mm), all with a stroke of 24²⁄₅in (620mm), driving 78³⁄₄in (2m) wheels, they had a steam pressure of 217psi (1496kPa) and a boiler having 2,045sq.ft. (190sq.metre) of heating area. On a weight of 122,377lb (55.5 tonnes), they were used to haul the 'Cote

d'Azur Rapide' in 1906 at an average of 53mph (86kph) between Paris and Marseilles. They reached a top speed of 81mph (130kph) and lasted in service until 1938.

No.C115 is preserved at the Railway Museum at Mulhouse.

## GREAT NORTH OF SCOTLAND RAILWAY 4-4-0 (LNER CLASS D40)/1899/BRITAIN

The GNSR was a railway in north-eastern Scotland with long single-track routes through beautiful countryuside but with very low-density traffic flows. It would have been virtually unknown to the British public had not its territory included the royal residence at Balmoral. The knowledge that its locomotives were used to haul the royal train probably concentrated minds, for the rather ordinary top passenger engines were kept in better order than would normally have been expected from an impecunious company. Decade after decade, the Railway relied on 4-4-0 engines for both passenger and freight work, and each class was a little bigger than its predecessor but of more or less the same unexciting but nevertheless attractive design. The series which the LNER classed as D40 was introduced in Queen Victoria's time but some members

were built in 1921, on the eve of the GNSR's absorption by the LNER. They were smallish engines, weighing 101,430lb (46 tonnes) and with a tractive effort of 16,184lb (7,347kg). Driving wheels were 73in (1860mm), cylinders 18in x 26in (457mm x 660mm), and boiler pressure a modest, easy-on-maintenance, 165psi (1137kPa). Some carried names and one, Gordon Highlander, is exhibited at the Museum of Transport in Glasgow.

## LONDON & SOUTH WESTERN RAILWAY 'GREYHOUND' (T9) CLASS/1899/GREAT BRITAIN

Dugald Drummond, after moving to the L&SWR, designed locomotives very similar to those he had earlier produced for the two major Scottish Railways. The inside-cylinder 4-4-0 which soon earned the nickname 'Greyhound' was virtually a classic Scottish design transplanted to southern England. 65 were built, plus an extra-special one for the Glasgow Exhibition. They had 19in x 26in cylinders (483mm x 660mm), 79in (2007mm) coupled wheels, and a boiler pressure of 175psi (1205kPa), giving a tractive effort of 17,675lb (8,024kg). Weight in working order was

*4-4-0  LSWR  T9 Class , 1899 , after reboilering*

*4-4-0 PLM  Big C Class , 1899*

115,762lb (52½ tonnes). To improve steam-raising, some units were built with firebox watertubes, but these were later removed because they were more trouble than they were worth. The new locomotives did well on the London-Exeter and London-Bournemouth routes. But the steady growth of trains meant that after a few years they were inadequate, so a new design (L12) which was virtually a T9 with a bigger boiler, replaced them. In the 1920s they were fitted with superheaters, and an elongated smokebox to accommodate it, and they received stovepipe chimneys. In this guise, less beautiful but more striking, they served up to the 1950s as secondary service power, with frequent use on extra trains at peak periods. One of them has been preserved.

*4-4-0 Great Eastern Railway Claud Hamilton Class , 1900*

*The preserved Midland Compound 4-4-0 after restoration in Midland Railway finish*

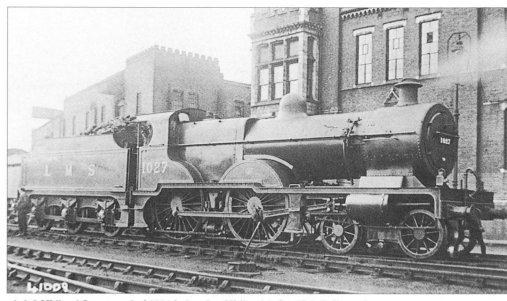

*4-4-0 Midland Compound of 1901 in London Midland & Scottish Railway livery*

## GREAT EASTERN RAILWAY 'CLAUD HAMILTON' CLASS/1900/GREAT BRITAIN

Only the first locomotive of this 121-strong class carried a name, but that name was also used to describe the class as a whole. In fact, the series comprised three classes (LNER D14 D15 and D16) and several sub-classes. The first units were oil-fired, had unsuperheated round-top boilers, and slide valves. Then a Belpaire boiler was substituted and superheaters fitted, new or retrospectively. There was also a 'Super Claud' with bigger boiler. In the 1930s many of the type were rebuilt with new round-top boilers, with the ornate valancing over the driving wheels being removed at the same time. They were designed as fast passenger engines, and had 7ft (84in or 2133mm) coupled wheels to that end. The inside cylinders were 19in x 26in, (483mm x 660mm) and boiler pressure 180psi (1240kPa), giving a tractive effort of 17,095lb (7,761kg). The grate area of the units reboilered by the LNER (the last to survive) was 21sq.ft. (1.95sq.metre). By no means all had their slide valves replaced by piston valves. The weight varied between sub-classes, but the reboilered slide-valve units were 125,231lb (56.8 tonnes).

These locomotives, designed for the heaviest and fastest GER trains as replacements for 2-4-0 engines, were soon superseded by the B12 4-6-0 (see below), but they continued to be built in parallel with the latter. They were fast engines, and well suited to the lighter, fast, trains. The last units survived until 1960, ending their days on secondary services. By that time they wore BR black, a great contrast with their earlier LNER apple green, and even more with their GER livery of royal blue, copper-capped chimney, and red coupling rods.

## MIDLAND COMPOUNDS/1901/GREAT BRITAIN

In 1898, William Worsdell's No. 1619 was rebuilt to the design of W.M.Smith as a three-cylinder machine with one high-pressure cylinder inside and two low-pressure ones outside. That design was taken up by Samuel Johnson of the Midland Railway, resulting in the production of the well known Midland Compounds, the first of which was No. 2631, built in 1901; four more followed in 1903.

In 1905 Johnson's successor, Richard Deeley, brought out an improved version, with a steam pressure of 200psi (1380kPa) and with a different regulator arrangement, so that high-pressure steam could be admitted to the low-pressure cylinder for starting purposes. During the life of the Midland Railway, 40 of the Deeley compounds were built; Deeley's first 30 were originally numbered 1000 to 1029, but their numbers were later altered to 1005 to 1034, the first five of the Johnson build taking numbers 1000 to 1004; the last Deeley batch was then numbered 1035 to 1044. After the absorption of the Midland into the London, Midland and Scottish Railway in 1923 a further 200 were built, and these found particular favor in Scotland.

The particulars of the Deeley batch were as follows. One cylinder had 19in (483mm) and two cylinders 21in (533mm) diameters, all with 26in (660mm) stroke; they drove 81in (2057mm) diameter wheels. The 200psi (1380kPa) steam was supplied by a boiler with 1,720sq.ft. (160sq.metre) of heating area and a firegrate of 28.4sq.ft. (2.64sq.metre). The weight was 138,915lb (63 tonnes), of which 87,316lb (39.6 tonnes) was on the driving wheels, giving a tractive force of 24,000lb (10,886kg) and one recorded power output was 880dbhp (656kW) at 49mph (79kph), corresponding to some 1,280ihp (955kW) at the cylinders.

*4-4-0 City Class of the Great Western Railway , 1902*

*4-4-0 Indian Railways SPS Class, 1904*

No.1000 had a working life of over 40 years, and is now preserved in Midland red at the National Railway Museum at York.

### GREAT WESTERN RAILWAY 'CITY' CLASS/1902/BRITAIN

In the first decade of the 20th Century the GWR, under its chief locomotive superintendent George Churchward, introduced new concepts in locomotive design, borrowing many features from US and French practice. On the eve of this revolution the Railway had a fondness for inside-cylinder outside-frame 4-4-0 types, which came in several classes according to whether they were for fast duties and therefore had large wheels, or for mixed traffic, in which case their coupled wheels were smaller. The 'City' Class, of which there were 20, had 80½in (2045mm) coupled wheels and were intended for fast work. Built with parallel boilers, they later changed these for US-style tapered boilers. They had a grate area of 20.6sq.ft. (1.9sq.metre), marginally small in relation to the size of the boiler (which meant that steam production was not quite as good as the size of the boiler suggested). The cylinders were 18in x 26in (457mm x 660mm), and the boiler pressure 200psi (1378kPa). Tractive effort was 17,789lb (8,076kg). The engine alone weighed 123,200lb (55.8 tonnes) in working order.

These were fast engines. City of Bath distinguished itself by averaging 63mph (101kph) over the 245 miles (394km) between London and Plymouth with a royal train conveying a delighted Prince of Wales, and in 1904 City of Truro, according to an experienced observer who was timing the mile-posts, reached 102mph (164kph) down a gradient in Somerset. This was enough to ensure that this locomotive went into a museum when the other class members were scrapped. Then in 1957 it was restored to service and put on light duties between Swindon and Bristol. A few years later it went to the Great Western Railway Museum, came out again to perform on various special occasions, and retired again under the auspices of the National Railway Museum.

### PRUSSIAN STATE RAILWAY S.4 CLASS/1904/GERMANY

In Germany the introduction of the superheater by Carl Schmidt was soon taken up by the Prussian State Railway, and one of their 4-4-0 engines, fitted with a smokebox superheater built by Borsig of Berlin, was shown at the Paris Exhibition of 1900. Following the results of some trials at Zossen in 1904, the superheated 4-4-0 showed itself superior to larger non-superheated types. The Group

S.4, built to that design, was chosen as the standard for the Prussian State system.

Built as a 4-4-0 with two outside cylinders driving onto the leading axle, the S.4-class cylinders were 21¼in x 23²/₃in (540mm x 600mm), with 78in (1980mm) driving wheels, and, with a steam pressure of 174psi (1200kPa), they could give a tractive force of 20,300lb (9,208kg) and an output of 1,585ihp (1,182kW) as tested at Zossen.

### INDIAN RAILWAYS SPS CLASS/1904/INDIA

Before World War 1 the British authorities attempted to bring a higher degree of standardization into Indian locomotive policy. With so many companies, a wasteful variety of classes was being perpetuated. The British Engineering Standards Association obliged, and a series of 'BESA' designs were evolved. Some railways adopted these, others did not, while yet others adopted them in slightly different form. Nevertheless, they were a step forward. The SP Class was a 4-4-0 design (SP meant 'standard passenger.' When it was superheated the designation became SPS). The type resembled a British 4-4-0 of the home railways, apart from the gauge and a more airy cab. Dimensions, not always followed exactly, were: coupled wheels 74in (1879mm), cylinders 20in x

*4-4-0 Pennsylvania Railroad D16 Class , 1907*

*4-4-0 North British Railway Scott Class, 1909 (above), 4-4-0 Caledonian Railway Dunlastair IV Class, 1910 (below)*

26in (510mm x 660mm), boiler pressure 180psi (1240kPa), engine weight 116,480lb (52.8 tonnes), and the axle-load was 37,485lb (17 tonnes). Tractive effort was 21,502lb (9,762kg).

After Independence in 1947 this class was divided mainly between the Northern Railway and Pakistan's Pakistan Western Railway. It had not had a distinguished life because it was introduced just when more powerful locomotives were about to appear. Nevertheless, it was a useful class for secondary passenger services and a handful of these locomotives were expected to be still operational in Pakistan at the dawn of the 21st Century.

## PENNSYLVANIA RAILROAD CLASS D16/1907/USA

The last 'American' type to be built was a Baldwin machine delivered after World War 2 to a Mexican narrow-gauge railway, but the final flowering of this classic type may be seen perhaps more convincingly in 45 units delivered to the Pennsylvania Railroad in 1907-10 by the Railroad's own workshops. These were the final batches of D16 4-4-0s. The D16 had 68in (1727mm) driving wheels, while the D16a had 80in (2032mm). They had Belpaire boilers but this was later modified with the crown and roof sloping downwards toward the rear; the locomotives with modified boiler became D16b (smaller wheels) and D16c or D16d (larger wheels). An 's' was added to the classification when these locomotives were superheated,

at which time the cylinders were increased to 20½in (521mm) with piston valves in place of the earlier 18½in (470mm) with slide valves. For a time, before the advent of the PRR Atlantics, these engines hauled the main passenger services, including the 'Pennsylvania Special.' They also did the Camden-Atlantic City run of 58 miles (93km)in 53 minutes.

The Pennsylvania Railroad Museum acquired one example, No.1223, of the D16sb sub-series. It has 20½in x 26in cylinders 521mm x 660mm), 68in (1727mm) coupled wheels, and a steam pressure of 175psi (1425kPa) giving a rated tractive effort of 23,900lb (10,850kg). Its weight is 141,000lb (63.9 tonnes) and it has a grate area of 33.2sq.ft. (3.08sq.metre). For a time it worked on the Strasburg Railroad, a tourist line adjacent to the Museum.

## NORTH BRITISH RAILWAY 'SCOTT' CLASS/1909/BRITAIN

The NBR, one of the two major Scottish railways, relied heavily on the 4-4-0 for its passenger trains. The 'Scott' Class was really two classes, known as D29 and D30 in the classification introduced by the LNER after it took over the NBR. They were known as the 'Scotts' because they bore names taken from Walter Scott's novels, these names being painted ornately on their splashers. D29 locomotives were built by North British and in the Railway's own shops at Cowlairs. They weighed 121,423lb (55.1 tonnes), had

*On the Yucatan Railways in Mexico , US-built 4-4-0s continued to operate into the 1960s. This unit was built by Baldwin in 1914*

*4-4-0  Indonesian State Railway Class 1353, 1912*

*4-4-0 Great Northern of Ireland S Class, 1913*

*4-4-0 SR Schools Class, 1930*

## INDONESIAN STATE RAILWAY CLASS B53/1912/INDONESIA

Seven of these locomotives were supplied by the German Hartmann company in 1912, followed by another four from the Dutch Werkspoor workshops. They had some similarities with Prussian locomotives of the same general type. Their cylinders were 15in x 23³/₅in (380mm x 600mm) and their coupled wheels were the biggest in Indonesia at 59in (1503mm); it has to be remembered that the Dutch authorities were quite keen on fast trains. Boiler pressure was 171psi (1173kPa), giving a tractive effort of 13,050lb (5,924kg). The grate area was 13.9sq.ft. (1.3sq m). In their prime, these locomotives hauled the system's prestige passenger trains, and they lasted into the 1970s, by which time they served branch lines, and especially the Madiun-Ponorogo branch. Their weight in working order was 71,442lb (32.4 tonnes).

## GREAT NORTHERN RAILWAY OF IRELAND S CLASS/1913/IRELAND

The GNR(I) liked to style itself the 'Irish International Main Line,' since it connected the capitals of Northern and Southern Ireland. At the time of construction, however, the S or 'Mountain' Class could not haul international trains because there was no frontier, all of Ireland then being part of the United Kingdom. By the mid-1930s, however, there were international services and they were entrusted to 13 4-4-0 locomotives, all of which were painted blue and looked distinctive as they hauled the teak-coloured rolling stock between the two capitals. Five of these locomotives were the new 3-cylinder compounds while the others were the more conventional units of classes S and S2, both known as the 'Mountain' Class and being more or less identical. Introduced in 1913, the 'Mountains' were conventional British inside-cylinder 4-4-0s weighing (with tender) 205,947lb (93.4 tonnes). They had 19in x

19in x 26in cylinders (480mm x 660mm), 66in (1676mm) driving wheels, and boiler pressure of 190psi (1309kPa). This gave a tractive effort of 19,434lb (8,823kg). The D30 class, which appeared in 1912, weighed a little more, had a lower boiler pressure, larger cylinders, and was superheated. Both classes survived into the 1950s. None was preserved, although one of the very similar 'Glen' Class, with smaller driving wheels, has survived under the auspices of the Transport Museum in Glasgow.

## CALEDONIAN RAILWAY 'DUNLASTAIR IV' CLASS/1910/GREAT BRITAIN

The succession of 'Dunlastair' designs were the inspiration of John McIntosh, Locomotive Superintendent of the Caledonian Railway. They were responsible for most of the more important passenger trains of that Railway up to the railway amalgamation, in which the CR was merged into the LMS. The 'Dunlastair IV' series was the last of the line, and the first to be superheated (in fact, the first locomotives to be superheated in Scotland). To match the superheat, the cylinder diameter was slightly reduced in comparison with the preceding units, and the boiler pressure lowered. The engines had inside cylinders 20_in x 26in (514mm x 660mm), 78in (1981mm) coupled wheels, and 179psi

(1233kPa) boiler pressure, giving a tractive effort of 19,751lb (8,966kg). Grate area was 21sq.ft (1.95sq.metre), and the engine weighed 130,095lb (59 tonnes).

In all, 22 were built by the CR's St Rollox workshops, and they were finished in blue, like all CR mainline passenger locomotives. Two of them were involved in the disastrous Quintinshill collision of 1915, but the class lasted into the 1950s. By then the locomotives were painted black, and employed on secondary duties.

*Another view of the Pennsylvanian Railroad preserved D16 Class 4-4-0*

*4-4-2 Great Northern Atlantic of 1902, a close-up*

26in cylinders (480mm x 660mm) and a boiler pressure of 200psi (1378kPa). Driving wheel diameter was 79in (2007mm), and they had a tractive effort of 20,198lb (9,169kg)

## SOUTHERN RAILWAY SCHOOL CLASS V/1930/GREAT BRITAIN

Since 1900 the number of 4-4-0 locomotives built in Britain has amounted to 991, of which the last 40 were the Southern Railway's School Class V, the greatest of all the British 4-4-0 types. First built in 1930 for use on the difficult line to Hastings, for which the cab sides and tender had to be narrower than standard, they were a shortened version of the Lord Nelson class and performed considerably better. Equipped with three cylinders at 16½in x 26in (419mm x 660mm) and driving 79in (2006mm) diameter wheels, they had a boiler which produced ample steam at 220psi (1517kPa) with a heating area of 2,148sq.ft. (199.5sq.metre) and a firegrate with 28.3sq ft (2.6sq.metre). On a weight of 150,601lb (68.3 tonnes) they gave a tractive force of 25,176lb (11,430 tonnes) and a power output of 1,130dbhp (843kW) at 59mph (95kph), corresponding to a cylinder power of over

1,600ihp (1,193kW). They could pull 335-long-ton (340-tonne) trains at speeds of up to 80mph (129kph), and remained in service until 1962. Three have been preserved including No. 925, Cheltenham, at York.

## 4-4-2

The Whyte nomenclature of 'Atlantic' was given to this wheel arrangement because the first one to be built (by the Baldwin Locomotive Co.) was supplied to the Atlantic Coast Railroad in 1894. No. 590, a similar version built in the following year for the Chicago, Burlington and Quincy Railroad, had cylinders that were 19in x 26in (482mm x 660mm) and driving wheels 84in (2138mm) in diameter. With a steam pressure of 200psi (1380kPa), from a boiler

*4-4-2 Brighton Atlantic , 1904*

*4-4-2 Prussian S7 Class , 1903*

having 1,580sq.ft. (147sq.metre) of heating area it gave a tractive force of 19,000lb (8,618kg) on a weight of 138,033lb (62.6 tonnes) out of which 85,995lb (39 tonnes) was on the driving wheels.

## DE GLEHN `ATLANTICS'/1901/FRANCE

In France the 'Atlantic' design was taken up by Alfred de Glehn of Alsacienne, who in conjunction with du Bousquet of the Nord produced in 1901 their four-cylinder type, one of which was supplied to the Great Western Railway for evaluation in 1903. In that design the diameter of the high-pressure cylinders was 13²∕₃in (340mm), with the low-pressure pair at 22in (558mm), and all with a stroke of 25¹∕₅in (640mm), driving 80¹∕₃in (2040mm) wheels using steam at 227psi (1600kPa). They proved capable of hauling 200-long-ton (203-tonne) trains up 1 in 200 (0.5 per cent) grades at 66mph (106.2kph), thus giving an output of 1,300ihp (969kW). These proved an immediate success, with 99 being built for the Nord as well as 10 for Egypt, and 21 for India; one was sent for trial on the Pennsylvania Railroad but could not stand up to the type of duty expected on that line. Most of the French engines

*The  Pennsylvania Class E-6s 4-4-2 locomotive of 1914 that hauled the  ' Lindberg Special '*

*A Great Northern Atlantic in inter-war service*

*4-4-2 NER  V Class , 1903*

*4-4-2 NER  Z Class , 1911*

lasted until 1939 and one has been preserved at the Museum at Mulhouse, where it was built.

## GREAT NORTHERN `ATLANTICS' AND 'BRIGHTON ATLANTICS'/1902/GREAT BRITAIN

The GNR produced its 21 'Klondike' Atlantics in 1898 but they were not outstanding. The next try was in 1902, when a new, bigger, version was tried. This too, was capable but unexciting until the class received superheaters. In this class  the firebox was enlarged to 31sq.ft. (2.88 sq.metre) and the heating area to 2,500sq.ft. (232sq.metre) producing steam at 170psi (1172kPa) for two cylinders of dimensions 19in x 24in (483mm x 610mm) driving 80in (2032mm) diameter wheels. On a weight of 155,893lb (70.7 tonnes) they gave a tractive force of 17,300lb (7,847kg) and after being fitted with superheaters could haul trains of up to 450-long-tons (457 tonnes), and on occasion filled in for Pacifics. Of the 94 built, 19 were taken

into British Railways stock in 1948, although most were withdrawn by 1950. No 251, the first, is preserved at York.

Douglas Marsh, who had participated in the design of the GN Atlantic, became Locomotive Superintendent of the London Brighton & South Coast Railway in 1902, and in 1904-12 built eight Atlantics for his new employer which visually were almost identical with the GN Atlantics, and the dimensional differences were only slight. These eight locomotives were named and lasted until the 1950s, often handling the Newhaven boat trains in their final years.

## NORTH EASTERN V AND Z CLASSES/1903, 1911/GREAT BRITAIN

In 1901 William Worsdell of the North Eastern Railway paid a visit to the United States, was impressed with the work of the 'Atlantic' engines on the Reading Railroad, and designed for the North Eastern its own V class 'Atlantic'. This was produced in 1903 with a larger boiler than any

previous NER locomotive, having 2,455sq.ft. (228sq.metre) of heating area, producing steam at 200psi (1380kPa). With two cylinders of dimensions 20in x 28in (508mm x 711mm) driving 82in (2083mm) wheels, they gave a tractive force of 23,200lb (10,524kg). Twenty of Class V were built; they lasted in service until 1948.

Class V was followed into service by 50 of the more powerful Z class, first built in 1911. Designed by Vincent Raven, these were equipped with three cylinders 16½in x 26in (419mm x 660mm) fed with superheated steam at 175psi (1207kPa) and driving 82in (2083mm) diameter wheels. On a weight of 79.5 tons (80.8 tonnes) they gave a tractive force of 19,300lb (8,754kg) and were the most powerful of the British 'Atlantics', giving on test an output of 1,090dbhp (813kW) when pulling a 545-long-ton (554-tonne) train at 58mph (93.3kph), corresponding to a cylinder power of 1,600ihp (1,193kW). Of the 50 built, 14 lasted until 1948. They were withdrawn soon after becoming the property of British Railways.

## GREAT WESTERN `ATLANTICS'/1904/GREAT BRITAIN

In 1903 the Great Western Railway purchased one of the De Glehn 'Atlantic'-type locomotives built by the Société Alsacienne, similar to those supplied to the Nord Railway in France. The purpose of the purchase was a comparative evaluation of the merits of compounding before commencing the design of a standard passenger engine to cope with the heavier trains then coming into operation. In order to provide a true comparison, one of the GWR 4-6-0 locomotives of the 'Saint' class was rebuilt as a 4-4-2, No.171 (later No.2971) with a boiler pressure of 225psi (1551kPa).

By 1905 a further 13 similar engines had been built at Swindon, having two cylinders originally 18in x 30in (457mm x 762mm) with 80½in (2044mm) driving wheels and with non-superheated steam at 225psi (1551kPa). The boiler heating area for the standard No.1 model was 2,143sq.ft. (199sq.metre), with a reduction to 2,105sq.ft. (195.8 Ssq.metre) when a superheater was fitted. In 1906 the first of the 'Star' class, No. 40, was built as an 'Atlantic'

*4-4-2 GWR No 40, 1904*

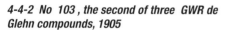

*4-4-2 No 103, the second of three GWR de Glehn compounds, 1905*

*4-4-2 Pennsylvania E6s.  The prototype of this class appeared in 1911 ,  with series production starting in 1914.*

*4-4-2  Belgian Railways 12 Class of 1939*

with four cylinders measuring 14in x 26in (360mm x 660mm), but this was rebuilt as a 4-6-0 in 1909.

## PENNSYLVANIA RAILROAD CLASS
## E6S/1912/USA

In spite of the origin of the wheel system's popular name, the 'Atlantic' was not widely used in the United States - in all, only about 1,900 were built there. The largest of the first generation of the type in the United States were Class E6S built for the Pennsylvania Railroad at their own works at Altoona. In these the 80in (2032mm) driving wheels were powered from two cylinders at 23½in x 26in (596mm x 660mm) with a steam pressure of 210psi (1448kPa) in superheated form from a boiler with 3,506sq.ft. (326sq.metre) heating area and with a firegrate area of 55sq.ft. (5.1sq.metre), which was obtainable by reason of the firebox being over the trailing wheel. Out of a total weight of 243,432lb (110.4 tonnes), the adhesive weight was 133,843lb (61.7 tonnes), from which the tractive force of 32,300lb (14,650kg) was obtainable.

One of these E6S class engines was given a thorough test on the locomotive-testing plant at Altoona and produced an output of 2,450ihp (1,827kW) at 47mph (75.6kph), with the boiler producing 44,400 pounds/hr (21.14 tonnes/hour) of steam. At the most efficient rate, the output was 1,800ihp (1,342kW) at 75mph (121kph) with a cylinder efficiency of 12.7 per cent and a coal consumption of 2.1 pounds/ihp-hr (1.28kg/kW-hr).

## MILWAUKEE ROAD HIAWATHA
## TYPE/1935/USA

In 1935 the Chicago, Milwaukee, St Paul and Pacific Railroad put into service, in competition with the streamlined diesel 'Zephyrs' of the Burlington line between Chicago and the twin cities of St Paul and Minneapolis, their high-speed train named the Hiawatha. To haul the Hiawatha, Alco supplied the heaviest 'Atlantic' ever built, with a streamlined casing on an axle-load of 71,001lb (32.2 tonnes). With two cylinders of dimensions 19in x 28in (483mm x 711mm), the steam pressure was 300psi (2069kPa); with driving wheels of 84in (2133mm) diameter, the tractive force amounted to 30,700lb (13,926kg) and the total weight was 127.7 tons (129.7 tonnes). The oil-fired boiler had a heating area of 4,274sq.ft. (397sq.metre) with a grate area of 69sq.ft. (6.4sq.metre). The tender held 4,000 gallons (15,140 litres) of oil and 13,000 gallons (49,200 litres) of water, weighing in all 117 tons (119 tonnes)—more than the heaviest British 'Atlantic' ever built. They were capable of speeds in excess of 100mph (160kph), and on the fastest section of the journey from Sparta to Portage were scheduled at an average 81mph (130.3kph) from start to stop.

*4-4-2 Nord Railway de Glehn compound of 1901*

## BELGIAN NATIONAL RAILWAYS 12
## CLASS/1939/BELGIUM

The Belgian main lines from Brussels to Liegé and Ostend were flat, and the heavy Pacific locomotives suited to other routes were not ideal there. Belgian Railways accordingly ordered from Cockerill six light, high-speed, locomotives with the intention of accelerating the trains and at the same time to enable the retirement of some older passenger locomotives. The Cockerills were streamlined, and the 4-4-2 wheel arrangement was chosen since its adhesion was adequate, it was free-running, and it also provided space for a generous firebox. Unusually, the two cylinders were inside the frames, but as bar frames were used accessibility was not badly affected. Having them there was expected to ensure steady running at the speeds envisaged. The streamline casing was provided with apertures for easy maintenance. The coupled wheels were the Belgian standard for fast locomotives, 82½in (2100mm), and the cylinders were 18⁹⁄₁₀in x 28²⁄₅in (480mm x 710mm). Boiler pressure

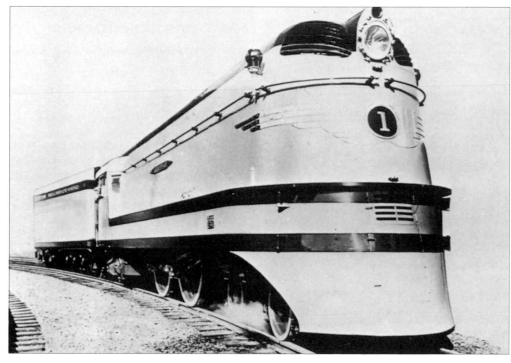

*4-4-2 Milwaukee Railroad Hiawatha type , 1935*

was 256 psi (1764kPa) and tractive effort 28,158lb (12,784kg). The grate area was 40sq.ft. (3.7sq.metre) and there was a superheater of 678sq.ft. (63sq.metre). Weight of the engine in working order was 196,245lb (89 tonnes).

The locomotives were expected to run at speeds up to 87mph (140kph) but as the war came while they were still on trial they never went into regular high-speed service. Some suitable jobs were found for them in the post-war decade, but in general they led quiet lives, although of great technical interest. One of them was preserved, and occasionally emerges to haul a special excursion train.

4-4-4 Canadian Pacific F-1A of 1936. This is No 2929 , which was subsequently acquired for exhibition by Steamtown in the USA

## 4-4-4

### BALTIMORE AND OHIO RAILROAD No. 1/1935/USA

In the same year as the Milwaukee Road introduced their heavyweight streamlined 'Atlantic', the Baltimore and Ohio built in their own workshops a high-speed 4-4-4 with a water-tube firebox and using steam at 350psi (2414kPa). With cylinders at $17\frac{1}{2}$in x 28in (445mm x 711mm), the driving wheels, of 84in (2133mm) diameter, gave a tractive force of 28,000lb (12,700kg) on an adhesive weight of 99,792lb (45.36 tonnes). The boiler had a heating surface area of 2,195sq.ft. (204sq.metre) with a grate area of 61.8sq.ft. (5.74sq.metre). The completed engine weight was 96.9 tons (98.5 tonnes), and the external appearance was extremely neat. Only one was built.

### CANADIAN PACIFIC TYPE F-1A/1936/CANADA

Across the border, the Canadian Pacific followed the example set by the Milwaukee Road and the Baltimore and Ohio and in 1936 introduced a class of 20 high-speed 4-4-4 locomotives built by the Canadian Locomotive Company. These locomotives, like those of Canadian Pacific Class 3000 (see next entry), were designed for working light four-coach trains at high speed. They featured insulated cabs to shield the driver from the severe weather. Using a steam pressure of 300psi (2068kPa), their cylinder size was $16\frac{1}{2}$in x 28in (419mm x 711mm), and with driving wheels of 75in (1905mm) diameter they gave a tractive force of 26,000lb (11,794kg). The boiler had 3,191sq.ft. (297sq.metre) of heating area and had a firegrate 45sq.ft. (4.2sq.metre) in area. The completed weight amounted to 239,022lb (108.4 tonnes).

### CANADIAN PACIFIC CLASS 3000/1936/CANADA

The Canadian Pacific Class F-1A (see previous entry) was followed by a more powerful type, built by the Montreal Locomotive Company and having slightly larger cylinders – 17in x 28in (437mm x 711mm) - and using steam at 300psi (2068kPa). With 80in (2032mm) wheels that gave

a tractive force of 26,500lb (12,020kg) from an adhesive weight of 119,070lb (54.9 tonnes). With 3,983sq.ft. (370sq.metre) of heating surface area, the grate area was 55.6sq.ft. (5.17sq.metre) and the total load was 263,056lb (119.3 tonnes). Only five were built.

# SIX-COUPLED LOCOMOTIVES

## 0-6-0

### ROYAL GEORGE/1827/GREAT BRITAIN

The first six-coupled engine to be built was the Royal George, supplied to the Stockton and Darlington Railway by Timothy Hackworth in 1827. The S. & D. was primarily a freight railway, and the traffic soon necessitated a something better than the original type of 0-4-0 with which they had commenced operations two years earlier. The Royal George, reputed to have been the first locomotive in which the exhaust steam was used as a blast effect to increase the draught of the fire, was built with two cylinders at 11in x 20in (279mm x 508mm) using steam at 54psi (372kPa) and driving 48in (1219mm) wheels, which would have produced a tractive force of 2,000lb (907kg).

### WILBERFORCE/1833/GREAT BRITAIN

The Royal George was followed in 1833 by Wilberforce, in which the vertical cylinders drove onto a jackshaft so that the four wheels furthest away could be sprung, and in the boiler the tubes were doubled back so that the chimney was at the same end as the firedoor: this arrangement required the use of two tenders, one for water and one for coal. Most railways used coke originally, as it was cleaner from the passengers' point of view, but the

S. & D. was almost entirely a mineral line and coal was plentiful, so it was natural that it should be their fuel.

### NORTH EASTERN LONG BOILER 0-6-0s/1852/GREAT BRITAIN

The adoption of the Long Boiler by Stephenson and the need for increased traction led to the widespread use of the 0-6-0 wheel arrangement for freight duty, and it soon became the standard freight engine in Britain. One of the greatest users was the Midland Railway: at the time of its amalgamation into the LMSR its stock of 0-6-0 engines amounted to 1,951 out of a total of 2,925, or 67 per cent. In 1934 the four main lines owned 8,370 of the 0-6-0 type out of a total of 20,807 (40 per cent).

On the North Eastern Railway, as the successor to the Stockton and Darlington, the amount of freight and mineral traffic led to the wide use of the 0-6-0 type. first were built in 1852; the 11 built in that year were the final version of the Stephenson Long Boiler. With 17in x 18in (432mm x 457mm) cylinders, they weighed 62,622lb (28.4 tonnes).

The 0-6-0 found widespread use in Europe, but in the United States it was little employed for their heavy freight traffic and was confined to switching (shunting) duties. The same wheel arrangement was to find wide use in Britain as a shunting engine when the diesels came into use, with 1,382 built by 1965, and even in Germany the most numerous single type of diesel locomotive was their V.60 shunting version, rated at 650hp (485kW).

The earliest preserved 0-6-0 is the Derwent, built by Kitching for the Stockton and Darlington Railway in 1845. It is today in the Darlington, North Road, Museum.

### 'DX' GOODS/1855/GREAT BRITAIN

The first locomotive to be built in quantity was the 'DX' goods engine of the London and North Western designed by John Ramsbottom and built at Crewe from 1855 to 1872. They were simple little machines, with two

*0-6-0 SNCF 030C Class , 1866*

inside cylinders of dimensions 17in x 24in (432mm x 610mm) with 62in (1575mm) driving wheels and a small, but adequate, boiler with 1,107sq.ft. (103sq. metre) of heating area. With a steam pressure of 120psi (828kPa), they gave a tractive force of 11,400lb (5,171kg).

A total number of 943 were built, of which 86 were for the Lancashire and Yorkshire Railway. This was to raise a storm among the private engine-builders, who considered it unethical for one railway to build locomotives for another. Most of the 'DX' goods engines lasted until the advent of the eight-coupled freight engines onto the North Western after 1900.

### BOURBONNAIS CLASS/1857/FRANCE

A rather more numerous type was the Bourbonnais type built for the PLM Railway and the new Bourbonnais line, from which the class-name was derived. In these the two outside cylinders were 17½in x 25 2/3in (450mm x 650mm). Steam pressure was 144psi (993kPa), and, with wheels of 51⅕in (1300mm) diameter, the tractive force was 18,300lb (8,300kg). A total of 1,054 of the type were built for various railways. One is preserved, and can be seen at the Spanish Museum of Transport.

### CHEMIN DE FER DE L'OUEST (SNCF CLASS 030C)/1866/FRANCE

French engineers liked Stephenson's long-boiler concept, although they preferred to put the cylinders outside. On the Ouest (Western Railway, soon to be nationalized as the Etat), the 030C Class was built from 1866 to 1885, and a handful remained in service into the 1950s. They were built by several works. The cylinders were 18⅛in x 25¼in (460mm x 640mm), driving wheels 50¾in (1430mm), and boiler pressure 128psi (882kPa),

*0-6-0 LNWR Coal Engine , 1873*

*0-6-0 Midland Railway 5ft 3in Class , 1878*

giving a tractive effort of 17,804lb (8,083kg). The grate area was 15.8sq.ft. (1.5sq.metre) and weight 89,523lb (40.6 tonnes). Like many French locomotives of that period, they looked untidy; this was partly because the valves, operated by external gear, were above the cylinders, and because there were external steam pipes exiting between large domes near the chimney.

One of these technically interesting locomotives was saved for posterity by Canadians, and can be seen at the railway museum at Delson (Quebec).

## LNWR COAL ENGINE/1873/GREAT BRITAIN

When Francis Webb took over from John Ramsbottom at Crewe in 1871 his designs followed closely those of his predecessor,for whom he had been the chief draughtsman (nowadays the position would be known as 'design engineer'). In 1873 the London and North Western changed the colour of its locomotives to black as an economy measure, and in that year Webb brought out the first of a class of 0-6-0 tender locomotives known as the Coal engine. With 17in x 24in (432mm x 610mm) cylinders and with steam at 140psi (965kPa), they gave a tractive force of 15,600lb (7,076kg) from driving wheels 54in (1372mm) in diameter. With a small boiler - it had 980sq.ft. (91m2) of heating area and a grate area of 17.1sq.ft. (1.6sq.metre) - they were built to exacting tolerances with interchangeable components: one was assembled and steamed all within a period of a mere 25.5 hours. They used Joy's valve gear, and their driving wheels were built

with 'H' section-spokes. There were 500 built during the next 19 years. Some 230 were to last into the British Railways era, to be withdrawn by 1953. Unfortunately none are preserved, but one of the Coal tank engines, an 0-6-2T to the same dimensions, No.1054, is preserved.

## NEW SOUTH WALES GOVERNMENT RAILWAYS Z19 CLASS/1877/AUSTRALIA

Seventy-seven of these 0-6-0 engines were built, mainly by Beyer, Peacock in England but with 18 built by the Sydney firm of Henry Vale. The last were not withdrawn until 1972, by which time they were well into their ninth decade of service. Direct descendants of Stephenson's 'long-boiler' type, they were ordered at a time when the State's railway network was rapidly growing. They were built for heavy freight service but did not last long in that role. They were not steady at speed, possibly because of their rather ungainly wheel spacing, and were soon limited to 25mph (40kph). In any case they were soon replaced by larger locomotives of the 2-8-0 type. They then tended to move to branchline service where their light axle-loads were an advantage, but ended their days working the Newcastle and Sydney docks. A few of them were converted to 2-6-4 freight tank locomotives. They were originally without cabs, but steel cabs were fitted in the 1890s. They were also fitted with new Belpaire boilers at the turn of the century, with higher pressure. They had 18in x 24in cylinders (460mm x 610mm) and coupled wheels of only 48in (1220mm). Boiler pressure was 140psi at first, but later was 150psi (965kPa and 1034kPa). This

produced a tractive effort of 18,144lbs (8,237kg), or 19,440lb (8,825kg) at the higher pressure. Weight in working order was 127,228lb (57.7 tonnes) and the grate area was 17.9sq.ft. (1.663sq m).

## MIDLAND RAILWAY '5ft 3in' CLASS/1878/BRITAIN

Britain's Midland Railway in its final years did not have a locomotive policy, but only a locomotive ideology. Its cult of the small engine meant, among other things, that on the eve of its merging into the new LMS Railway most of its locomotives, more than 1,500 units, were of the 0-6-0 type. That type has the virtue of simplicity, flexibility, and cheapness, but with the MR's heavy coal traffic was not the locomotive that was really needed. The '5ft 3in' engines were really a modification of the '4ft 11in' class (the class designation came from the wheel diameter) and were intended for fast freight service. The first batch were built by Dubs and went into Bradford-London freight service, where they had to average 35mph (56kph). They had a grate area of 17.5sq.ft. (1.62sq.metre) to supply 17½in x 26in (445mm x 660mm) cylinders (the diameter was later increased to 18in or 457mm ). Boiler pressure was 140psi (964kPa) but later became 160psi or 1102kPa (from 1917 they were rebuilt with Belpaire in place of round-top boilers). Tractive effort in their final form was 18,185lb (8,255kg), and they weighed 88,200lb (40 tonnes). They were succeeded by a larger design in 1885 but about a hundred had been built, and they survived into the 1950s.

*0-6-0  MZA Railway 454 Series, 1882*

*0-6-0  Great Western 'Dean Goods,' 1883*

*0-6-0 North Eastern P Class, 1894*

*0-6-0 Midland Railway 4F Class, 1911*

*Another view of the 0-6-0 Midland Railway 4f Class, 1911*

### MADRID ZARAGOZA ALICANTE RAILWAY 454 SERIES/1882/SPAIN

The 32 locomotives of this class served three companies. Being built for the Tarragona-Barcelona-Francia Railway, they passed to the MZA in 1891, and ended their days in the service of Spanish National Railways, performing yard work at Barcelona docks as late as the 1950s. They were typical products of the German locomotive industry, being built by Hartmann from 1882 to 1890. Their cabs were rather small, even for that time. Most spent their lives in the Barcelona area. They had 18 $^9/_{10}$in x 25½in (480mm x 650mm) cylinders, 50in (1266mm) coupled wheels, and with a boiler pressure of 160lbs (1102kPa) their tractive effort would have been 24,900lb (11,304kg). Weight, including tender, was 125,685lb (57 tonnes).

### CALEDONIAN RAILWAY 'STANDARD GOODS'/1883/GREAT BRITAIN

This was the CR's equivalent of the GWR's 'Dean Goods' (see below) and was similarly a general-purpose locomotive that initially was regarded as primarily a freight engine. Well over 200 were built, and the batch introduced in 1895 was turned out in passenger blue. Coupled wheels were 60in (1524mm), cylinders 18in x 26in (457mm x 660mm), and boiler pressure 150psi (1033kPa), giving a tractive effort of 17,901lb (8,127kg). There was a 19.5sq.ft. (1.81sq.metre) grate, and the engine weighed 92,610lb (42 tonnes). These locomotives were to be seen all over the CR's territory and even on the Glasgow Underground lines (five were fitted with elementary condensing apparatus). Most of them survived into the 1950s.

### GREAT WESTERN RAILWAY 'DEAN GOODS' 2301 CLASS/1883/BRITAIN

This is regarded as the classic British 0-6-0 type. It was designed under the direction of William Dean, Chief Locomotive Superintendent of the GWR, and hence became known as the 'Dean Goods' even though it did its share of passenger work as well as freight. When train-loads grew, it lost its role as a mainline locomotive, but because it had a low axle-load it was transferred to light-traffic lines, especially in Central Wales. In both world wars some members of the class were recruited for army service and despatched abroad. In 1940 several were overtaken by the fall of France and at the close of the war could be found in faraway places like Poland and Italy, while some even found their way to China. Nearly three hundred were built, and in due course they acquired superheaters. They steamed well and were easy to maintain. Their grate area was 15.45sq.ft. (1.43sq.metre), cylinders were 17in x 24in (432mm x 610mm) and the driving wheels were 62in (1575mm), giving a tractive effort of 17,120lb (7,772kg). Axle-weight was only 28,885lb (13.1 tonnes) tons and total weight 82,442lb (37.4 tonnes), which happened to be exactly the same as the tender weight. One of these

*0-6-0 Pennsylvania B6sb Class , 1916*

*In North America the 0-6-0 was a slow-speed yard locomotive. The top picture shows a locomotive, now preserved at the Steamtown site at Scranton, Pennsylvania, which was once the works switcher at the Baldwin locomotive works. The center picture is of a small Canadian National switcher built by Baldwin in 1908, while the bottom picture shows a rather larger US switcher in course of repair, minus boiler sheeting and lagging.*

locomotives has been preserved for eventual exhibition at Swindon Works, where it was built.

### NORTH EASTERN P CLASSES/1894/GREAT BRITAIN

By 1922 the North Eastern Railway had built or purchased a total of 1,417 locomotives (including tank engines) of the 0-6-0 wheel arrangement. The last of these were the P3 class, first built in 1906.

Before discussing the P classes, it is worth looking briefly at a few of their predecessors on the North Eastern with the same wheel arrangement. Notable were the 201 locomotives of the C class of compound engines, built during 1872-76 with cylinders of diameters 18in (457mm) and 26in (660mm); but these were all later converted to operation on the simple cycle, with cylinders of diameter 18in (457mm) or 19in (483mm) and with strokes of 24in (610mm) and 26in (660mm). And some years later, in 1883, the 44 members of the 5G class were built; these later became the LNER's Class J22.

The first of the P classes dates from 1894. The engines had 18½in (470mm) diameter cylinders which had a stroke of 24in (610mm), and drove wheels of 55in (1397mm) diameter. Classes P1 and P2 followed in 1898 and 1904, respectively, until the ultimate class, P3, appeared in 1906. In the P3 class the steam pressure was 200psi (1380kPa), giving a tractive force of 24,600lb (11,158kg), with a total weight of 110,911lb (50.3 tonnes).

The boilers on both the P2 and P3 engines were of 66in (1.68m) diameter, with a heating surface of 1,531sq.ft. (142sq.metre) and a grate area of 20sq.ft. (1.86sq.metre). After classes P2 and P3 had become LNER classes J26 and J27 the steam pressure was reduced to 180psi (1241kPa).

All the P classes passed into LNER stock in 1923 and lasted until withdrawal in 1962-65. One of the P3 class, No.2392 (1923), is preserved on the North Yorkshire Moors Railway at Pickering.

### MIDLAND RAILWAY CLASS 4F/1911/GREAT BRITAIN

On the Midland Railway the principal freight locomotive was the 0-6-0. The last of the range, built with Belpaire boilers to a classification 4F, were fitted with cylinders at 20in x 26in (508mm x 660mm) and with driving wheels 63in (1600mm) in diameter. The cylinders were inside, and the piston valves were operated by the Stephenson link motion. With a total weight of 109,809lb (49.8 tonnes), the tractive force was 24,500 pounds (11,113kg). They were capable of speeds up to 60mph (96kph), and some were fitted with piped train heating for use on passenger trains operated at holiday periods. The last of the 4F class was withdrawn in 1966. Four have been preserved.

*0-6-0 Canadian National 018 Class , 1919*

*0-6-0 Great Western  2251 Class , 1930*

*0-6-0 Southern Railway Q1 Class , 1942*

## PENNSYLVANIA RAILROAD B6sb CLASS/1916/USA

In the first decade of the 20th Century the PRR was building, largely in its own shops, two types of 0-6-0 yard engine. The B8 was a light machine intended for 'Lines East' (that is, east of Pittsburgh, the Railroad's centre of gravity) and the B6, a heavier machine for 'Lines West.' The B6, unusually for a yard locomotive, was superheated from 1916, the final version being classified B6sb. 238 units of this sub-class were turned out by the PRR works at Altoona between 1916 and 1926. They had 22in x 24in (560mm x 610mm) cylinders, 56in (1422mm) driving wheels, and a 205psi (1425kPa) boiler pressure, producing a tractive effort of 36,140lb (16,407kg). Apart from possessing a superheater, these locomotives had a wide firebox providing 61.6sq.ft. (5.72sq.metre) of grate area, very large for a six-wheeler. Indeed, these were truly heavy switchers. They weighed 180,300lb (82.9 tonnes) with tender. Some of them lasted until 1959, switching passenger stock being one of their last activities.

## CANADIAN NATIONAL RAILWAYS O18 CLASS/1919/CANADA

These were the last six-wheel switchers built for the CNR, with the exception of the O19 Class, whose last unit was turned out in 1928. Class O18 was divided into four sub-classes; O18a and O18b (Nos 7424-7498) had slightly smaller driving wheels and lower boiler pressure than the later O18c and O18d (Nos 7499-7521). The later sub-classes had 56in (1422mm ) coupled wheels rather than 51in (1293mm ), and a pressure of 190psi(1309kPa) instead of 175psi (1205kPa). It was correspondingly heavier, 177,000lbs rather than 174,000lb (80.2 tonnes rather than 79.7) , but both groups had the same cylinders (22in x 26in or 560mm x 660mm) . In terms of tractive

effort, these differences more or less evened out, with the heavier engines producing, theoretically, 36,291lbs (16,344kg) and the lighter ones 36,703lb (16,663kg). The class as a whole totalled almost a hundred, and could be seen on most sections of the CNR.

## GREAT WESTERN RAILWAY 2251 CLASS/1930/GREAT BRITAIN

120 of these locomotives were built by the GWR, largely as replacements for the 'Dean Goods' engines (see above), many of which were approaching their half-century. Using standard GWR components, the design was not as aesthetically pleasing as the older type, but enginemen

*2-6-0 Baldwin exports to Britain , 1899*

appreciated the more sheltered cab. Having a greater axle-load, the 2251 Class did not replace the 'Deans' on the more lightly-laid lines, but it did good work, passenger and freight, on secondary lines that were too long for tank-locomotive haulage (the kind of line that was closed in the 1960s). Weighing 97,020lb (44 tonnes), these engines had a tractive effort of 20,155lb (9,150kg), produced by 17½in x 24in (445mm x 610mm) cylinders, 200psi (1378pKa) boiler pressure, and 62in (1575mm) coupled wheels. The grate area was 17.40sq.ft. (1.63sq.metre) Really, these locomotives were simply a 'Dean Goods' redesigned with taper boiler and bigger cab. One of them has been preserved.

## UNION RAILROAD HEAVY SWITCHER/1935/USA

The five engines built by the Lima Locomotive Corporation were probably the largest of the 0-6-0 type to be used in the United States. They were fitted with a booster which drove the front four wheels of the tender. Fitted with two outside cylinders of dimensions 22in x 28in (559mm x 711mm), they drove 51in (1295mm) wheels and, with

*2-6-0 Italian 625 Class of 1910 as later fitted with Franco-Crosti boiler*

*2-6-0 Great Western 4300 Class , 1911*

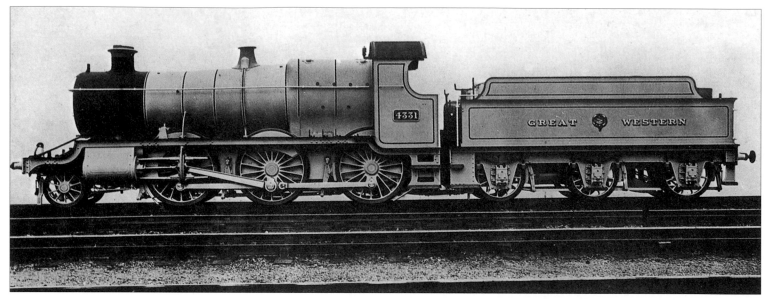

*2-6-0  GWR 4300 Class of 1911 , as built*

*2-6-0  original GNR Mogul of 1911*

steam at 220psi (1517kPa), gave a tractive force of 49,700lb (22,544kg). To this the tender booster added a further 14,500lb (6,577kg). The superheated steam was produced from a boiler with 2,714sq.ft. (252sq.metre) of heating area and a firegrate of 50sq.ft. (4.65sq.metre), designed to operate on soft coal. The engine weighed 201,316lb (91.3 tonnes).

## SOUTHERN RAILWAY CLASS Q.1/1942/GREAT BRITAIN

The ultimate in the 0-6-0 range to be produced in Britain was the Southern Railway's Austerity version, classified Q.1 and introduced in 1942. In order both to obtain the maximum output on a 17-ton (17.3-tonne) axle-load and to reduce production costs, every inessential item was left off. The result was what some describe as the ugliest locomotive ever built. However, it was an excellent working vehicle and could give a tractive force of 30,100lb (13,653kg) from its two 19in x 26in (482mm x 660mm) cylinders using steam at 230psi (1586kPa) and driving 61in (1549mm) diameter wheels. The boiler was provided with a firegrate of 27sq.ft. (2.5sq.metre) area, and the heating surface area was 1,690sq.ft. (157sq.metre) -

including the superheater, which itself had an area of 218sq.ft. (20.27sq.metre). The overall weight was 114,660lb (52 tonnes). The large chimney enclosed a Lemaitre multiple-jet blast pipe with five nozzles.

In all, 40 Class Q1 locomotives were built. Originally numbered C1 to C40, they were later renumbered 33001 to 33040 by British Railways. They remained in service until 1963/6. No.33001 is preserved at the Bluebell Railway at Sheffield Park, Sussex.

## 2-6-0

The 2-6-0 wheel arrangement seems to have been used first on the line from St Etienne to Lyon in 1841, and some were built at about that time in Russia by Eastwick and Harrison, who went there from Britain to build locomotives. Production in quantity commenced in the United States about 1860, and from then until 1910 some 11,000 were built. Baldwin were offering a standard model by 1872, with similar dimensions to those offered by Rogers & Co., in which the cylinders were 20in x 24in (508mm x 610mm) with 54in (1371mm) wheels and a steam pressure of

*2-6-0 Great Northern Railway (LNER K1 Class), 1945*

140psi (965kPa). On a weight of 98,563lb (44.7 tonnes) they gave a tractive force of 21,100lb (9,571kg).

They were supplied to many of the railroads of that era, but were soon to be replaced by the 2-8-0 type for mainline freight duties. In 1878 a batch of 15 was supplied to the Great Eastern Railway by Neilson & Co. to the design of W.B.Adams, but they do not appear to have been a success, since they were withdrawn by 1887.

## BALDWIN IMPORTS/1899/USA, BRITAIN

In 1899, owing to an acute shortage of building capacity in Britain, the Baldwin Locomotive Co. supplied 80 Moguls to Britain - 40 to the Midland and 20 each to the Great Northern and the Great Central Railways. They were small by American standards, with 18in X 24in (457mm X

*2-6-0 LNER K4 Class The Great Marquess , 1937*

*2-6-0 K2 Class , built in 1922 for the Dublin & South Eastern Railway , which later merged into the Great Southern & Western Railway.*

*A 2-6-0 type destined to work into the 21st century. Every decade there wer proposals to modernise the Paraguay system, but nothing developed , so the original locomotives , supplied by British builders before World War 1, soldier on.*

610mm) cylinders driving 61in (1549mm) wheels and with steam at 175psi (1207kPa). With bar frames, double domes on the boiler and American-style cabs, they looked out of place and lasted only for about 15 years.

## ITALIAN STATE RAILWAYS CLASS 625/1910/ITALY

The consistent mediocrity of Italian steam locomotive design is hard to explain, but has to be accepted as a fact. The 625 Class was part of this tradition, hauling light trains all over the country at unimpressive speeds. This type, and the similar 640, (which had larger driving wheels in the vain hope of producing a speedy locomotive) had inside cylinders but outside valve gear. It was built by various builders from 1910 to 1914, with a new batch in 1922. Cylinders were 19⅓in x 27½in (490mm x 700mm), driving wheels 60¼in (1530mm), and boiler pressure 171psi (1173kPa), giving a tractive effort of 25,808lb (11,717kg). Weight in working order was 118,850lb (53.9 tonnes).

In the 1950s some of these engines were rebuilt with Franco-Crosti boilers, and reclassified as 623 Class. The Franco-Crosti boiler passed the exhaust steam through one or two drums in order to heat the boiler feedwater. It was an Italian invention, stemming from Italy's lack of coal, and certainly reduced fuel consumption, but also increased maintenance costs. British Railways tried it on a batch of 2-10-0s, and reached the same conclusion.

*One of the last classes of 2-6-0 to be built , the 78000 Class 2 series was acquired by British Railways in the 1950s , but because of the subsequent closure of the light-traffic lines for which it was designed it was not long in production.*

### GREAT WESTERN 4300 CLASS/1911/GREAT BRITAIN

The successful operation of the Aberdares on the Great Western led George Jackson Churchward to build a further class of 2-6-0s, known as the 4300 class from the first engine of that number to be built. They were operationally welcome; 342 were built between 1911 and 1932.

Intended as mixed-traffic engines, these had driving wheels 68in (1727mm) in diameter and cylinders 18½in x 30in (470mm x 762mm). They were supplied with steam at 200psi (1380kPa) from a standard No.4 boiler which had 1,818sq.ft. (169sq.metre) of heating area and a grate area of 20.6sq.ft. (1.9sq.metre). They gave a tractive force of 25,700lb (11,658kg), and on test No. 5326 gave an output of 950dbhp (708kW) at 53mph (86kph), corresponding to a cylinder power of 1,470ihp (1,096kW). The completed weight varied between 136,710lb and 145,530lb (63-66 tonnes) according to the date of construction.

All were withdrawn by 1964, but two have been preserved: No.5322 at the Didcot Railway Centre and No.7325 at the Severn Valley Railway at Bridgnorth, Worcestershire.

### GREAT NORTHERN MOGULS (LNER K SERIES) 1920/GREAT BRITAIN

In 1920 a larger version of an existing GNR Mogul (LNER K2 Class) was produced, incorporating three cylinders and using the new Gresley conjugated valve gear. In that class the cylinder size was 18½in x 26in (470mm x 660mm) and the steam pressure was still at 180psi (1241kPa). With the wheel-size still at 68in (1727mm) the tractive force was 30,000lb (13,608kg). The boiler was 72in (1828mm) in diameter and contained 2,308sq.ft. (214m2) of heating area with a grate area of 28sq.ft. (2.6sq.metre). On test, an output of 1,000dbhp (746kW) was recorded, equivalent to a cylinder power of 1,550ihp (1,156kW). With a total weight of 162,729lb (73.8 tonnes), they could handle train weights of 650 long tons (660 tonnes) and could run at up to 70mph (113kph). A total of 193 locomotives of this LNER K3 class was built up to 1937, and they lasted in service until 1959-62.

They became Nos.61800-61992 in the British Railways system; No.61863 was rebuilt in 1945 with two cylinders, thus providing a prototype for the Peppercorn K1 type, of which a further 70 were built. One of these, No.2005, has been preserved at the North Yorkshire Moors Railway.

In 1937 six were built with 62in (1575mm) driving wheels for use on the West Highland line and one of this

*This long-lived US-built 2-6-0 was a 3ft-gage unit working in Yucatan in the 1960s. It was built by Baldwin in 1928 and had 40in driving wheels. This track is mixed-gage.*

K4 class, No.3442, The Great Marquess, has been preserved.

## GREAT SOUTHERN & WESTERN RAILWAY K3 Class/1923/IRELAND

The K3 and K2 classes were very similar. They resembled 0-6-0 locomotives of conventional British design that had

had an extra pair of carrying wheels put under their smokeboxes almost as an afterthought. This was indeed their history. Type K3 consisted of seven locomotives built by Sharp Stewart in 1903 to handle freight traffic between Dublin and Wexford. But within four years they had been given an extra pair of wheels and become 2-6-0s. There are not many similar instances in locomotive history, although the Bombay Baroda and Central India Railway produced its FS Class in a similar manner, having discovered that adding a superheater to an 0-6-0 could mean excessive weight on the leading coupled axle, which could be relieved only by slipping in an extra carrying axle. The GSWR examples performed adequately, but not spectacularly, and were joined by the K2 Class in the 1920s. One of the latter has been preserved in working

order. As for the K3 engines, these were rebuilt again with larger boilers in the 1920s. In their final form they had 19in x 26in (483mm x 660mm) cylinders, 61¾in (1568mm) coupled wheels, and 180psi (1240kPa) boiler pressure, giving a tractive effort of 23,260lb (10,560kg). Their grate area was 24.8sq.ft. (2.3sq.metre) and engine weight 127,890lb (58 tonnes).

## LMS CRABS/1926/GREAT BRITAIN

Soon after the formation of the London, Midland and Scottish Railway in 1923, a requirement arose for an all-purpose 2-6-0 locomotive. A design based on components from various railways of the group was finalized after at least 11 different schemes had been drawn up. The final design was based on a two-cylinder arrangement incorporating a Walschaerts valve gear as used on the Pennsylvania Railroad. The cylinders were 21in x 26in (533mm x 660mm) and there was a new boiler operating at 180psi (1241kPa), with a firegrate area of 27.5sq.ft. (2.55sq.metre) and with a total heating-surface area of 1,992sq.ft. (185sq.metre). With 66in (1676mm) driving wheels and with the cylinders inclined at an angle of 6 degrees to the horizontal, the locomotives were named 'Crabs,' and gave a most satisfactory performance. With a tractive force of 26,600lb (12,066kg), they gave on test a coal-consumption rate of 3.4 pounds per

*2-6-0 standard Japanese C56 Class , 1935*

*1935, Japanese National Railway*

dbhp-hr (2.7kg/kW-hr). 245 were built between 1926 and 1932; withdrawals commenced in 1962 and were completed by 1967.

The original locomotive No.2700 (BR No.42700) is preserved at the National Railway Museum at York, and No.2765 is at the Keighley and Worth Valley Railway at Haworth in Yorkshire.

## JAPANESE NATIONAL RAILWAYS CLASS C56/1935/JAPAN

These modern-looking engines were built in large numbers by a variety of Japanese builders, and won a reputation for ease of maintenance. Unusually for a small locomotive, they had arch tubes in the firebox. They had 15½in x 26in (400mm x 600mm) cylinders, coupled wheels of 55in (1400mm), and a boiler pressure of 200psi (1378kPa), giving a rated tractive effort of 18,942lb (8,600kg). They had a modest superheater and weight in working order was 82,908lb (37.6 tonnes). 46 units of the class were brought to Thailand by the Japanese Army and after the war they worked successfully all over the railway system. Because they can be linked to the Bridge over the River Kwai they were considered to be appropriate locomotives for preservation, and several have survived as museum or tourist train locomotives.

*2-6-2 Soviet Railways Su Class , 1925*

*2-6-2 Hungarian Class 324 , 1909*

# 2-6-2

## HUNGARIAN STATE RAILWAY CLASS 324/1909/HUNGARY

Probably the most numerous user of the 'Prairie' type was the Hungarian State Railway, which first used some of the Austrian Golsdorf 329 class in 1908 and then, from 1909, proceeded to build its own Class 324. The Hungarian State Railway also adopted the two-cylinder compound arrangement, with cylinders of 18in (457mm) and 27⅕in (690mm) diameters with a 25⅜in (650mm) stroke and with driving wheels of 57in (144mm) diameter. Using steam at 217psi (1496kPa), they produced a tractive force of 27,000 pounds (12,247kg) on an adhesive weight of 41 tons (41.7 tonnes). The boiler had a heating area of 2,298sq.ft. (213.6sq.metre) with a grate area of 34sq.ft. (3.15sq.metre) on a total weight of 128,110lb (58.1 tonnes). A total of 895 were built, of which 95 were for the War Department in 1917.

## SOVIET RAILWAYS Su CLASS/1925/RUSSIA

In the post-civil war recovery the Su Class represented a renaissance of the Russian locomotive-building industry. A 2-6-2 (S Class) of pre-1914 vintage had proved very successful so the wheel arrangement was retained for the Su, which was destined to become the basic passenger locomotive of the USSR. Several hundred were built, with minor changes between batches. The last appeared in the 1950s. They were required to plod along at speeds close to those of freight trains over quite long distances with trains that by west European standards were quite heavy. They had 73in (1850mm) driving wheels, 22½in x 27½ (575mm x 700mm) cylinders, a boiler pressure of 191psi (1271kPa), and tractive effort of 30,100lb (13,600kg). They weighed 191,835lb (87 tonnes) and had a grate area of 50.2sq.ft. (4.67sq.metre). Over 40 have been preserved at various points of the former Soviet Union.

## INDIAN RAILWAYS ZB CLASS/1928/INDIA

After World War 1 it was decided to progressively standardize locomotive design for the several narrow-gauge railways in India. Two of the new standards were for a heavy (by narrow-gauge standards) 2-6-2 (Class ZB) and a light 2-6-2 (ZA). Class ZB over the years became a numerous and successful class; the design was based on a type introduced by the

*2-6-2 Indian Railways narrow-gage 2B Class locomotives , introduced in 1928.*

*2-6-2 LNER V2 Class , 1936*

*2-6-2 Polish 01-49 Class , 1951*

2-6-2 Indian Railways YL Class , 1952

North Western Railway in 1921. The new standard had 34in (860mm) coupled wheels, 12in x 18in (305mm x 457mm) cylinders, and a boiler pressure of 160psi (1102kPa). The grate area was 14sq.ft. (1.3sq.metre) and the axle-weight 13,230lb (6 tonnes) tons. Tractive effort was 10,638lb (4,707kg). It pulled a 6-wheel tender. Over 40 were built, mainly in the early 1950s, by British, French and German builders. One of them was fitted with Caprotti valve gear, a rare distinction for a narrow-gauge locomotive. Most of them worked on the lightly-laid network that was once the Gaekwar of Baroda's State Railway.

## LNER GREEN ARROWS (V2 CLASS)/1936/GREAT BRITAIN

Although the 2-6-2 wheel arrangement originated in the Midwest of the United States - hence the colloquial name 'Prairie' - the type did not find great favor in the United

States: to 1910, only about 1,000 were built. An early user was the Atchison, Topeka and Santa Fé Railroad, which employed some 235 with 61in (1549mm) wheels for freight and with 80in (2032mm) wheels for passenger engines. With 20in x 26in (508mm x 660mm) cylinders on a weight of some 156,775lb (71.1 tonnes), they were soon overtaken by eight-coupled engines for freight duty and by the 4-6-2 type for passenger trains.

The best known examples of the 2-6-2 category were the V2 class of the LNER, built for express freight: they took the name Green Arrows from the insignia denoting express parcels guaranteed for next-day delivery.

The 'Green Arrows' were equipped with three cylinders of dimensions 18½in x 26in (470mm x 660mm) driving 74in (1880mm) diameter wheels with a boiler pressure of 220psi (1517kPa) provided from 3,109sq.ft. (289sq.metre) of heating area and with a wide firebox of area 41sq.ft. (3.8m2). The tractive force was 34,000lb (15,422kg) and a maximum output of 1,540dbhp (1,148kW) was recorded,

2-6-2 LNER V2 of 1936 , a builder's photograph

2-6-2 German State Railways (DR) 35 Class, 1956

corresponding to 2,400ihp (1,790kW). With a weight of 93 tons (94.5 tonnes), they hauled trains of up to 650 tons (660 tonnes) during World War 2. They remained in service until 1962-66.

Eleven of them carried names. No.4771 Green Arrow has been preserved at York.

## POLISH STATE RAILWAY CLASS OI-49/1951/Poland

When Poland reappeared as a state after World War 1 thousands of formerly Prussian and Austrian locomotives came into its ownership. Most useful of these to the new Polish State Railway were 2-6-2s from Austria and the celebrated P38 passenger 4-6-0 from Prussia. Over the decades these two types became the usual motive power for secondary passenger services. After World War 2, however, these old locomotives needed replacement, and a step in this direction was the design of a new 2-6-2 locomotive, the OI-49 Class. Poland's Chrzanow Locomotive Works built 116 units of this class in 1951-54. More were needed, but Poland could not afford them.

*2-6-2 German Railways ( DB ) 23 Series , 1961*

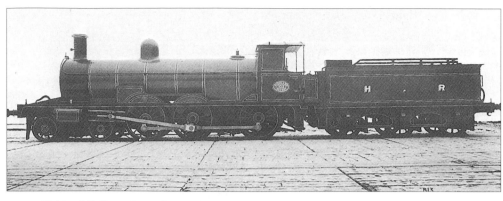

They were modern-looking engines, and distinguished by a new, and not beautiful, smoke deflector, mounted beside the chimney. This contrivance was presumably successful, for it was later fitted to some tank locomotives; smoke dispersal was quite an important problem because Polish coal had a high smoke output.

The class had a maximum permitted speed of 62mph (100kph), which was more than adequate since it was largely employed on secondary lines where its low axle-load was an advantage. Coupled wheels were 69in (1750mm) in diameter and the two cylinders were 19½in x 24¾in (500mm x 630mm), and the boiler pressure was 227psi (1568kPa). This produced a tractive effort of 26,200lbs (11,900kgs). The grate area was 39.8sq.ft. (3.7sq.metre) and there was a 735sq.ft. (68.3sq.metre) superheater. The engine weighed 184,030lbs (83.5 tonnes). Axle-weight was 38.790lbs (17.5 tonnes).

## INDIAN RAILWAYS YL CLASS/1952/INDIA

This was one of the later Indian Railways standard metre-gauge steam classes. The first ten units of this lightweight 2-6-2 design were produced by Robert Stephenson-Hawthorn in 1952. Further production began in 1956, without the participation of RSH or any other British builder. The remaining units of this 264-strong class came from Hitachi of Japan, Mavag of Hungary, and Henschel of Germany.The class was remarkably useful, thanks to its low axle-load (8 tonnes or 17,640lb) and its good running properties. It was widely used on lightly-laid branches, especially in the north and west of India; in the mid-1970s 122 units were on the North Eastern Railway and 74 on the Western.

### 4-6-0 Highland Railway Jones Goods , 1894

With 43in (1092mm) coupled wheels, 12in x 22in (311 x 560mm) cylinders, and 210psi (1447kPa) boiler pressure, this design could produce 13,660lb (6,202kg) of tractive effort. Total engine weight was 85,120lb 38.6 tonnes), and the grate area 7.75sq.ft. (0.72m2).

## GERMAN STATE RAILWAY (DR) SERIES 35/1956/GERMAN DEMOCRATIC REPUBLIC

In the late 1930s the German railway administration was seeking a new locomotive design to replace the miscellaneous collection of inherited locomotives that were handling passenger traffic on secondary and branch lines. These included 2-6-0 and 4-6-0 standard types from the Prussian State Railway as well as less numerous types from other state railways of the pre-1914 period. A couple of prototypes of a 2-6-2 design (Series 23) were built, but then the War halted this development. With the post-war division of Germany, the two administrations eventually brought out their own designs based on these prototypes. The East German 23 Series (later known as the 35 Series) appeared in 1956 and remained in production until 1960, being the last German mainline steam locomtive type to remain in production. It was primarily

a passenger locomotive, having 69in (1750mm) coupled wheels. In fact its maximum permitted speed was 68mph (110kph). Cylinders were of German standard, 21½in x 26in (550mm x 660mm) and boiler presure 227psi (1,567kPa). Weight in working order was 185,190lbs (84 tonnes), allowing it to use lines previously worked by the 4-6-0 types.

## GERMAN STATE RAILWAY (DB) SERIES 23/1961/WEST GERMANY

Partly for social reasons, and partly because in post-war Germany private car ownership was late in developing, the DB (the West German state railway) operated a large number of secondary passenger services. When a new locomotive design was wanted for these, recourse was had to the two 2-6-2 prototypes built before the War. The new and modified Series 23 first appeared from Henschel in 1950, and was built in large numbers. Like its East German counterpart, Series 35,  it had 21³⁄₅in x 26in (550mm x 660mm) cylinders. 69in (1750mm) coupled wheels, and a boiler pressure of 227psi (1567pKa). Weight in working order was 82.8 tonnes (182,540kgs). But although it was dimensionally similar to the DR's Series 35, its appearance was rather different. It had a gaunt

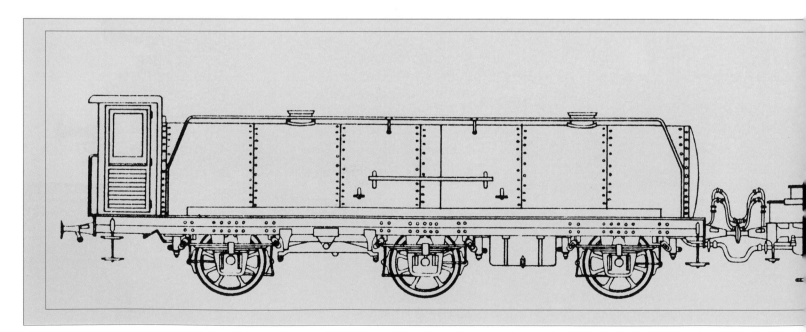

### 4-6-0 Cab-in-front Adriatico Railway 500 Class , 1900

*4-6-0 Thatcher Perkins , an early 4-6-0 of the Baltimore & Ohio Railroad which saw considerable service in the 1860s Civil War.*

look, partly because the boiler was higher-pitched, with a resultant reduction of chimney height. It served the DB well, although passengers may not have enjoyed the pronounced fore-and-aft jerking at certain speeds. A handful of these locomotives have been preserved, and one of them regularly hauls summer excursions for DB.

# 2-6-4

### AUSTRIAN STATE RAILWAY SERIES 210/1908/AUSTRIA

Some sixteen years before Will Woodard of the Lima Locomotive Company made use of a four-wheel trailing truck, Carl Golsdorf applied one to his unique 2-6-4 type of passenger engine to give a firegrate area of almost 50sq.ft. (4.65sq.metre). Like the other later Golsdorf engines this used the four-cylinder compound cycle with cylinders 15$^1$/3in (390mm) and 26in (660mm) in diameter, all with a piston stroke of 28$^1$/3in (720mm), driving 84in (2140mm) wheels. With steam at 232psi (1600kPa), the tractive force was 30,800lb (13,970kg) and the boiler, which had a small superheater, was given 2,753sq.ft. (256sq.metre) of heating area and a grate area of 49.7sq.ft. (4.62sq.metre). The total weight came to 189,636lb (86 tonnes), of which 97,240lb (44.1 tonnes) was available for adhesion. The production was limited to 11 locomotives, which were reserved for main-line passenger traffic only.

# 4-6-0

Although first built as a freight locomotive in both the United States and Britain, the 4-6-0 soon became the passenger engine par excellence for high-speed operation and was to continue in build up until the end of steam-locomotive production. In the United States the total number built was about 17,000.

### HIGHLAND RAILWAY JONES GOODS/1894/GREAT BRITAIN

The first 4-6-0 versions of the De Glehn four-cylinder compound locomotives were built in 1894 for use in Baden and in Switzerland on the Gotthard line; in Britain the first 4-6-0 was built in that same year for the Highland Railway. Known as the Jones Goods, the 15 locomotives had two cylinders 20in x 26in (508mm x 660mm) driving 63in (1600mm) wheels and used steam at 175psi (1207kPa). The boiler had 1,672sq.ft. (155sq.metre) of heating area

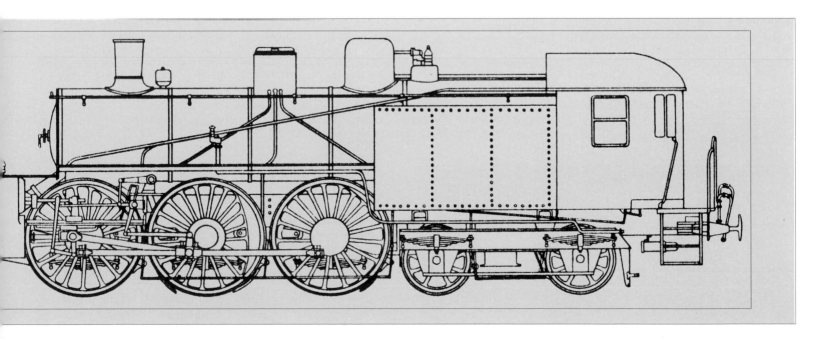

*4-6-0 New South Wales Government Railways C30-T Class , 1928*

with a 22.6sq.ft. (2.1sq.metre) firegrate. On a weight of 125,464lb (56.9 tonnes) the tractive force was 24,600lb (11,158kg).

Highland Railway No.103, the original one built by Sharp, Stewart, is preserved at the Glasgow Museum of Transport.

## ADRIATICO RAILWAY CLASS 500/1900/ITALY

Almost 40 years before the Southern Pacific introduced its famous 'Cab-Ahead' Mallets, this scheme was tried out in Italy. The locomotives used oil firing, and were built as four-cylinder compound engines. The cylinder sizes were 14½in (370mm) and 23in (580mm), all with a stroke of 25½in (650mm) and with driving wheels of 75½in (1920mm). With steam at 200psi (1,380kPa), these engines gave a tractive force of 18,000lb (8,165kg) on an adhesive weight of 98,000 pounds (44,453kg). The

total weight was 221,051 (100.25 tonnes), and a separate tank-like tender held 3,300 gallons (150hl) of water. Four tons of oil fuel was contained in tanks on the locomotive chassis. The idea does not seem to have caught on, however, since no more locomotives like this were built in Europe.

## GREAT WESTERN SAINT CLASS/1904/GREAT BRITAIN

The Great Western was quick to follow the lead of the Highland Railway and in 1895 its first 4-6-0, No.36, was produced at Swindon for freight duty. However, it soon opted for 2-6-0s for freight, and the 4-6-0 was then built with 80in (2032mm) wheels for passenger services, first as a two-cylinder, of which 77 were built as the 'Saint' class, with cylinders 18in x 30in (457mm x 762mm) and

with a steam pressure of 200psi (1380kPa). However, after trials with the four-cylinder De Glehn compound with its steam pressure of 227psi (1565kPa), the 'Saints' were eventually built with cylinders 18½in x 30in (470mm x 762mm) and with their steam at 225psi (1551kPa). In that form they gave a tractive force of 24,400lb (11,068kg), and were fitted with the GWR No 1 boiler, which had a grate area of 27sq.ft. (2.5sq.metre) and a heating area of 2,142sq.ft. (199sq.metre). Their output was tested at 1,090dbhp (813kW) at 59mph (95kph), equivalent to 1,700ihp (1,268kW). Although some were built first as 4-4-2s, all were converted to the 4-6-0 arrangement, and all were later fitted with superheaters. Withdrawal commenced in 1931; the last to go was No.2920, Saint David.

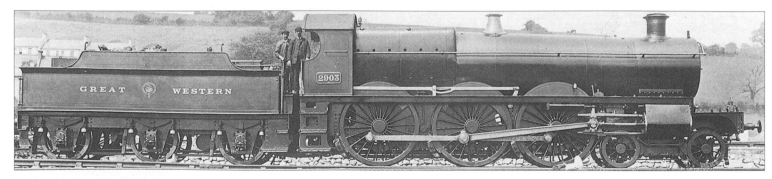

*4-6-0 GWR Saint Class, 1904*

*Est 4-6-0 (SNCF 230K Class), 1906*

## CHEMIN DE FER DE L'EST 3101 SERIES (SNCF 230K)/1906/FRANCE

France's Eastern Railway was notable in that it never went through the Pacific stage, jumping straight from the 4-6-0 to the 4-8-2 wheel arrangement for its passenger trains. Its last 4-6-0 design was exceptionally powerful, therefore, as well as having large wheels. This was the 230K Class, of which 130 were built. They were de Glehn compounds.

Their large firebox (grate area 33sq.ft. or 3.2sq.metre) was made possible by designing a 9ft (2743mm) gap between the two rear coupled axles. The driving wheels were 82¼in (2090mm), the high-pressure cylinders were 14½ x 26¾in (370mm x 680mm) and the low-pressure 23¼in x 26¾in (590mm x 680mm). Boiler pressure was 256psi (1763kPa). The tractive effort was calculated as 23,348lb (10,600kg). These engines weighed 171,769lb

(77.9 tonnes) and they were allowed to run up to 120kph or 75mph). During their life they had various rebuildings, the last being designed to fit them for hauling 'trains drapeaux.' The latter were short, fast inter-city trains, which the SNCF introduced soon after World War 2 as a foretaste of what would be offered once the backlog of war had been made up. Some of these units were embellished with vaguely streamlined smoke deflectors, and they produced quite an impression at the head of their stainless-steel lightweight trains.

## PRUSSIAN RAILWAYS P8 CLASS/1906/GERMANY

In Prussia, the firm of Schwarzkopf in 1906 built the first of a class of P8 4-6-0 locomotives and, after it had experimented with various forms of compound engines, tried out a design of a simple two-cylinder. In this the cylinder size was 23¼in x 24¾in (590mm x 630mm), and it had 69in (1750mm) driving wheels and a steam pressure of 174psi (1200kPa). With a firegrate area of 28sq.ft. (2.6sq.metre) and a heating area of 2,151sq.ft. (200sq.metre), the tractive force was 28,200lb (12,792kg) on a weight of 153,247lb (69.5 tonnes).

In 1914 there appeared an improved version, with a cylinder diameter of 22⅔in (575mm) and a larger boiler

*4-6-0 Prussian P8 Class, 1906*

*4-6-0 Nord Compound (SNCF 230D Class ) , 1910*

with 2,207sq.ft. (205sq.metre) of heating area, was produced to a weight of 168,241lb (76.3 tons). The result was so satisfactory that, by 1923, no fewer than 3,370 had been built.

At the end of World War 1 many of Class P8 were dispersed throughout Europe as a result of reparations. They lasted in various countries for well over 50 years. Several are preserved.

## GREAT WESTERN STAR CLASS/1906/GREAT BRITAIN

On the Great Western Railway, as a result of the trials with the De Glehn four-cylinder compounds Nos 102, 103 and 104, a four-cylinder passenger 4-6-0 was put into production from 1906, the first of which was No.4001, Dog Star. With cylinders 15in x 26in (381mm x 660mm) and with steam at 225psi (1,551kPa) from the standard No. 1 boiler, the tractive force was 27,800 pounds (12,610kg) and the power output was measured as 1,080dbhp (805kW) at 55mph (88kph), equivalent to a cylinder power of 1,520ihp (1,133kW). With their 80½in (2045mm) driving wheels, they were good for 90mph (145kph), and in superheated form could haul trains of up to 550 tons (559 tonnes). In their time they were superior to any other 4-6-0 in Britain, and they lasted in service until the withdrawal of No.4056, Princess Margaret, built in 1914.

The only member of the 'Star' class to be preserved is No.4003 Lode Star, destined for the Great Western Railway Museum at Swindon.

## LANCASHIRE & YORKSHIRE RAILWAY 4-CYLINDER 4-6-0/1908/BRITAIN

Building these 4-cylinder engines was the most complex task performed by the L & Y's Horwich Works, but the design was not a success. Twenty units were built, put on the most demanding passenger services, and proved to be coal-eaters. After World War 1 some of them were allowed to deteriorate to scrapping point, but one was rebuilt with a superheater and with Walschaert

*4-0-0 Great Indian Peninsular Railway D4 Class , 1912*

rather than Joy valve gear. The result was astonishing, the rebuilt engine showing great haulage capacity and good fuel economy. A batch of new ones to the modified design was thereupon ordered, and these new units eventually totalled 55. When the L & Y was absorbed by the new LMS Railway the new locomotives were put on prestigious London services and did well. However, they were not regarded as a standard class on the LMS and were eventually replaced by new designs. The last unit survived until 1951. The specifications of the improved design were as follows: four cylinders 16½in x 26in (420mm x 660mm), boiler pressure 180psi (1240kPa), coupled wheels 75in (1905mm), tractive effort 28,879lb (13,111kg), grate area 27sq.ft. (2.51sq.metre), superheater 552sq.ft. (5.1sq.metre), weight 177,430lb (80.5 tonnes).

*4-6-0 Great Western Star Class , 1906*

### CHEMIN DE FER DU NORD DE GLEHN COMPOUND (SNCF 230D CLASS)/1910/FRANCE

These were mixed-traffic locomotives, although used mainly for passenger work. The low-pressure cylinders were inside, and the high-pressure outside, the latter being 14⅞in (380mm) in diameter and the former 21⅝(560mm). They had the same stroke of 25¼in (640mm) and were inclined. The coupled wheels were unevenly spaced. Driving wheels were 69in (1750mm).

Grate area was 30.1sq.ft. (2.8sq.metre), boiler pressure 227psi (1566kPa) and weight in working order 154,791lb (70.2 tonnes). About 150 were built, by various makers. The units built with a superheater proved far superior, which was why they were put on top passenger duties like the Calais boat trains, which they handled successfully until the advent of Pacifics. After this, they worked on secondary duties, although they were handling the Paris-Le Treport fast trains as late as the 1950s. One has been

preserved for the French Railway Museum, and another went to the Nene Valley Railway in Britain.

### GREAT EASTERN RAILWAY S69 CLASS (LNER B12 CLASS)/1912/GREAT BRITAIN

A number of British railways were disappointed when, having designed a successful 4-4-0, they assumed they could repeat that success by enlarging it into a 4-6-0. In the case of the GER 4-6-0, however, everything went

*4-6-0  Southern Railway KIng Arthur Class , 1918*

*North Eastern 4-6-0  (LNER Class B16 ) , 1919*

*4-6-0 Southern Railway S15 Class, 1920*

right. The B12 4-6-0 might not have had quite the allure of its antecedent 4-4-0 but it was certainly a very successful type. It had 20in x 28in (510mm x 710mm) cylinders supplied by a 26.5sq.ft. (2.46sq.metre) grate, which in turn was supported by a 286sq.ft. (2.6sq.metre) superheater. Boiler pressure was 180psi (1240kPa) and with 78in (1981mm) coupled wheels the tractive effort was 21,970lb (9,974kg). The engine weight was 141,120lb (64 tonnes). As with the preceding 'Claud Hamilton' 4-4-0 class, great care was taken with the outward appearance, with a copper-capped chimney and brass beading setting off the rich blue paintwork. The secondary splasher that covered the coupling rods had ornately-pierced apertures. Above all, these engines had the most commodious cabs of any British locomotive.

Intended originally to cope with the increasingly heavy London-Colchester trains, the class grew steadily, and the GER's successor LNER ordered a batch of 20 from a private builder (Beardmore), and a final ten were supplied by Beyer, Peacock, making a total of 80, of which most had been built in GER workshops. In the 1930s some were given long-travel valves and their Belpaire boilers were replaced by LNER-style round-top ones, the pierced secondary

splashers were eliminated and a shorter chimney, of necessity, fitted. Of the unrebuilt units, some went to Scotland to help out on the Great North of Scotland section. One of the modified group has been preserved on the North Norfolk Railway.

## GREAT INDIAN PENINSULA RAILWAY D4 CLASS/1912/INDIA

This class more or less conformed to the standard locomotive design recommendations for Indian railways proposed by the British Engineering Standards Association. Over forty units were built, by Vulcan Foundry and North British. They were developments of the somewhat smaller D Class. Some of them were fitted with Lentz or Caprotti valve gear in the 1930s. The class was built up to 1915, so it was appropriate that one of them should be chosen as the GIPR's war memorial locomotive and named Hero. They had 74in (1879mm) driving wheels, 20½in x 26in (521mm x 660mm) cylinders, and 180psi (1240kPa) boiler pressure. The grate area was 32sq.ft. (2.97sq.metre) and tractive effort 22,593lb (10,257kg). Weight in working order was 168,021lb (76.2 tonnes). These locomotives

were used on the most prestigious GIPR trains, including the Bombay boat trains, and this importance was hardly diminished by the arrival of the Pacifics in the 1920s because the latter were soon speed-restricted and in any case did not arrive in large numbers. It was only the delivery of scores of WP Pacifics in the 1940s and 1950s that forced the transfer of these 4-6-0s to secondary duties. They lasted into the 1960s.

## SOUTHERN RAILWAY KING ARTHUR CLASS/1918/GREAT BRITAIN

The Southern Railway captured the imagination of the public by naming its passenger 4-6-0 engines after characters from Arthurian legend. LSWR in 1918 originally built 20, calling them class N15: they had two cylinders of dimensions 22in x 28in (559mm x 711mm) driving 79in (2007mm) wheels. Following the amalgamation into the Southern Railway, a further 54 were built with cylinders 20½in x 28in (521mm x 711mm) and with a steam pressure of 200psi (1380kPa), they gave a tractive force of 25,320lb (11,485kg) and a measured output of 950dbhp (708kW) at 57mph (91.7kph), equivalent to

*New South Wales Government Railways C-23 class 4-6-0. Mostly imported from Beyer, Peacock of Manchester, but with some units built in Australia and the USA, this class totalled 191. Introduced for heavy passenger work in 1892, the class survived unitl 1971.*

*4-6-0 Builder's photograph of the first Castle series, 1923*

*4-6-0 Great Western Castle Class , 1923.*

1,370ihp (1,022kW). Used first on main-line trains to the West Country, such as the Atlantic Coast Express, they were later put to service on the Brighton line and on 'boat trains' to Dover. They were withdrawn between 1958 and 1962. No.777, Sir Lamiel, was preserved by the Humber Locomotive Preservation Group at Hull.

### NORTH EASTERN RAILWAY S3 CLASS (LNER B16 CLASS)/1919/BRITAIN

North Eastern Railway locomotive design was not influential, but the locomotives were good-looking and well made. And although there was no great inn ovation, NER engineers did sometimes verge on the unorthodox. They continued to use Stephenson's valve gear at a time when other railways were turning to Walschaerts, and their 3-cylinder locomotives had their cylinders cast in one very complex block including the cylinders, valve chests and smokebox support.

The S3 Class, produced just before the NER lost its identity in the LNER were slightly unusual in that although they were only mixed-traffic locomotives they had three cylinders. The cylinders were 18½ x 26in (470mm x 660mm), boiler pressure 180psi (1240kPa), and coupled wheels 68in (1727mm), giving a tractive effort of 30,030lb (13,633kg). The grate area was 27sq.ft. (2.5sq.metre), and the superheater provided 437sq.ft. (40.6sq.metre). The engines weighed 174,195lb (79 tonnes), and their tenders 103,635lb (47 tonnes). Unlike the NER's earlier fast passenger 4-6-0s, these engines were an immediate success, and 70 were built. About a third of them were tinkered with by the LNER locomotive engineer Nigel Gresley, who gave them outside Walshaerts valve gear with his own derived motion for the inside cylinder. Then Gresley's successor eliminated the Gresley style of valve gear by providing an individual set of gear for that inside cylinder. In all three versions the locomotives did well on fast freights and intermediate

*4-6-0 Great Western Hall Class , 1924*

*4-6-0 Builder's photograph of Hall Class, 1924*

passenger services, performing those functions into the 1960s.

## SOUTHERN RAILWAY S15 CLASS/1920/GREAT BRITAIN

The Southern Railway had no heavy freight traffic and therefore no requirement for a heavy freight locomotive.

For its main freight trains it relied on mixed-traffic 4-6-0 locomotives. Most of such trains in any case were high-grade services classified as express goods, moving at speeds approaching those of passenger trains. Class S15, of which 45 were built, was really two sub-classes. The first were a small-wheeled adaptation of the 'King Arthur' passenger locomotives previously described. Then, with a change of chief mechanical engineer, the S15

took a sightly different form, with higher boiler pressure, smaller grate, and slightly smaller cylinders. More interestingly, the later S15s had long travel valves, making them much freer-running at the higher speeds (but the older units, with short travel valves, were better at hill-climbing). Both varieties had 67in (1702mm) driving wheels. The later units had 20½in x 28in cylinders (521mm x 710mm), 200psi (1378kPa) boiler pressure, and 29,835lb (13,545kg) tractive effort on a weight of 178,609lb (81 tonnes). The grate area was 28sq.ft. (2.6sq.metre). Working mainly on freight, but with occasional passenger duties, the class lasted until 1966. Two of the early variety and five of the later have been preserved.

## PENNSYLVANIA RAILROAD G.5s CLASS/1923/USA

Few US railroads acquired tank locomotives for their suburban services. The custom was to use demoted mainline units. But in the 1920s the Pennsylvania Railroad was faced with a need to renovate its power for suburban services around Pittsburgh and elsewhere, at a time when heavy long-distance passenger traffic meant that the older passenger engines could not be spared. The solution was a new design using a wheel arrangement already becoming obsolete in the USA, the 4-6-0. Taking the wide boiler of

*4-6-0 GWR King Class , 1927*

*4-6-0 Royal Scot Class , 1927 , as later rebuilt*

*4-6-0 Royal Scot Class , 1927 , as built*

the very successful E.6 4-4-2 with its 54.7sq.ft. (5.08sq.metre) grate area and 205psi (1425kPa) pressure, and placing it on driving wheels of 68in (1727mm) diameter, the PRR designers created a type that was so successful that not only were 90 built for the PRR itself, but also 30 for the PRR's subsidiary, the Long Island RR. Tractive effort was 41,330lb (18,764kg), and cylinders 24in x 28in (610mm x 710mm).

They were built by the Railroad's own workshops. The first withdrawal came in 1940, and the last in 1955. Two have been preserved, one by the Railroad Museum of Pennsylvania.

## GREAT WESTERN CASTLE CLASS/1923/GREAT BRITAIN

When the British Empire Exhibition opened in 1924 one of the locomotives on show was the latest product of the Great Western works at Swindon: it was a 4-6-0 locomotive, No.4073 Caerphilly Castle, which was claimed, because of its tractive force of 31,600lb (14,334kg), to be the most powerful passenger engine in Britain. Next to it was the new Pacific No.1470 from Doncaster which, although heavier, could produce a force of only 29,800lb (13,517kg). The relative merits of the two were to provide an interesting comparison during the 1925 exchange trials.

The 'Castle' class locomotives were equipped with cylinders of dimensions 16in x 26in (406mm x 660mm) and with a larger boiler than on the 'Star' class, having 29.4sq.ft. (2.73sq.metre) of grate area and a heating surface area of 2,284sq.ft. (212sq.metre). The steam pressure was still at 225psi (1551kPa), but with improved steam-flow arrangements the 'Castles' were a faster and more economical machine and soon established the Great Western as the world's leader in terms of train speeds. With a power output of some 1,900ihp (1,417kW), the 'Castles' returned a coal-consumption figure of only 2.8 pounds per dbhp-hr (1.7kg/kW-hr), which was claimed to have been the best for any British locomotive.

Between 1923 and 1950, 170 Castles were built; of these, six were rebuilt from 'Star'class locomotives. Withdrawals took place between 1959 and 1965. Eight have been preserved.

*4-6-0 LMS 5P5F Class , 1934*

*4-6-0 LMS Jubilee Class , 1935. One of the few fitted with a double chimney*

*4-6-0 LMS Jubilee Class , 1935*

## GREAT WESTERN HALL CLASS/1924/GREAT BRITAIN

In 1924 No.2925 of Great Western's 'Saint' class was rebuilt with 72in (1828mm) wheels, and this became the prototype for the 'Hall' class, of which 329 were built between 1928 and 1950. The 'Hall' class locomotives were withdrawn by 1965, but a dozen have been preserved.

## GREAT WESTERN KING CLASS/1927/GREAT BRITAIN

The most powerful of all the British 4-6-0 classes in terms of tractive force were the 30 locomotives of the 'King' class built by the Great Western Railway in 1927. With four cylinders measuring 16in x 28in (411mm x 711mm) and with a steam pressure of 250psi (1724kPa), they gave

a tractive force of 40,300 pounds (18,280kg). Fitted with GWR's No. 8 boiler, which had 2,500 sq.ft. (232sq.metre) of heating area and 34.3sq.ft. (3.2sq.metre) of grate area, the locomotives weighed 199,332lb (90.4 tonnes), which restricted their route availability to the main lines to Bristol, Plymouth and Wolverhampton. As the locomotives were first built they had a power output of 1,230dbhp (917kW), but after the fitting of double chimneys this was increased to 1,370dbhp (1,022kW) or 2,130ihp (1,588kW). In terms of fuel consumption their results were not as good as those of the 'Castle' class: the figure in the 1948 exchange results was 3.6 pounds per dbhp-hr (2.2kg/kW-hr).
The 'Kings' were withdrawn in 1962, but two have been running on excursions since then:
No.6000, King George V, and No.6024, King Edward I.

## LMS ROYAL SCOT CLASS/1927/GREAT BRITAIN

On the formation of the London, Midland and Scottish Railway in 1923 there was a shortage of main-line locomotives with enough power output and boiler capacity to haul the heaviest trains between Euston and Glasgow over the summits of Shap and Beattock. That problem was overcome in 1927 with the purchase from the North British Locomotive Co. of Glasgow of 70 engines of the 'Royal Scot' class, Nos.6100 to 6169. These 4-6-0 engines had three cylinders measuring 18in x 26in (457mm x 660mm) driving 81in (2057mm) wheels and with steam at 250psi (1724kPa), they gave a tractive force of 33,100 pounds (15,014kg) and a power output of 1,120dbhp (835kW) from a boiler with 2,273sq.ft. (211sq.metre) of heating area and a firegrate of area 312sq.ft. (29sq.metre).

In 1929 a high-pressure version was built in which the steam was at 900psi (6206kPa). This version was named Fury, but after some unsuccesful trials it was converted

*4-6-0 Great Western Manor Class, 1938*

instead to a locomotive with a new design of tapered boiler; with the number 6170 and named British Legion, this formed the basis of the rebuilt class of 'Royal Scot' in which, from 1943, the original 70 were all fitted with the Stanier design of taper boiler. In the rebuilt version the basic dimensions were similar to those of the original, but with improved steam-flow arrangements the power output was increased to 1,720dbhp (1,283kW) or an indicated output of 2,550ihp (1,902kW).

The class was withdrawn in 1962-65, but two have been preserved.

## NEW SOUTH WALES GOVERNMENT RAILWAYS CLASS C-30T/1928/AUSTRALIA

When the 30 Class 4-6-4 tank locomotives were ousted from their Sydney tasks by electrification, 77 of them were converted to 4-6-0 tender locomotives and re-classified as C-30T. Removing the side tanks and coal bunker reduced their axle-weight sufficiently to allow them to take

*4-6-0 Jaipur State Railway BESA Type, 1939*

*4-6-0 Great Eastern Railway (LNER B12 Class), 1912*

over the haulage on several lightly-laid branch lines. Their tenders came from scrapped locomotives. 29 of them were subsequently equipped with superheaters and their cylinder diameter was increased by half an inch (13mm). They had 55in (1400mm) coupled wheels, 18½in x 24in (470mm x 610mm) cylinders if unsuperheated, and the boiler pressure was 160psi (1102kPa), giving a tractive effort of 19,116lb (8,698kg) Weight of the engine only was 116,865lb (53 tonnes), and the grate area was 24sq.ft. (2.23sq.metre). They lasted until the 1970s, and six have been preserved.

## LMS CLASS 5P5F (BLACK FIVES)/1934 GREAT BRITAIN

Although the 2-6-0 'Crabs' were providing a useful mixed-traffic engine on the London, Midland and Scottish Railway, there was a need for a 4-6-0 of similar category. This need was satisfied in 1934 when W.A.Stanier designed for the LMS their 5P5F class of locomotive, known generically as the 'Black Fives.' With two outside cylinders measuring 18½in x 28in (470mm x 711mm) and a steam pressure of 225psi (1551kPa) they gave a tractive force of 25,500lb (11,567kg) and a measured output of 1,050dbhp (783kW)

*4-6-0 LNER B1 Class, 1942*

*4-6-0 GWR County Class , 1945, as later fitted with double chimney*

*4-6-0 GWR County Class , 1945 , as built*

*4-6-0 British Railways 4MT Class , 1951*

*Walschaerts valve gear of BR 4-6-0*

at 58mph (93.3kph), corresponding to a cylinder power of 1,550ihp (1,156kW). The 'Black Fives' were built to a weight of 158,989lb (71.7 tonnes).

The 'Black Fives' were to be found all over the LMS system: the final number in service was 842, later numbered 44658 to 45499 in the British Rail system. The last steam train in operational service was hauled by No.45110, which is among the 12 Black Fives to have been preserved.

### LMS JUBILEE CLASS/1935/GREAT BRITAIN

The first of a new class of three-cylinder 4-6-0 locomotives, No.5552, carrying the name Silver Jubilee, was introduced onto the London, Midland and Scottish Railway in 1935, and between then and 1936 a total of 190 was built. They had cylinders measuring 17in x 26in (432mm x 660mm), a steam pressure of 225psi (1551kPa), and driving wheels of 81in (2057mm) diameter. They were fitted with a taper boiler having a grate area of 31sq.ft. (2.9sq.metre). As first built they gave a tractive

force of 26,600lb (12,066kg), but they were disappointing in performance until the correct type of superheater was developed, after which they gave an excellent result. On test an output of 1,060dbhp (790kW) was recorded at 60mph (96.5kph), corresponding to a cylinder power of 1,530ihp (1,141kW). The original weight was 178,164lb (80.8 tonnes), but two were later fitted with boilers having a steam pressure of 250psi (1724kPa), and this increased their weight, and their tractive force to 29,600lb (13,427kg). They were withdrawn between 1961 and 1967, but four have been preserved.

### GREAT WESTERN RAILWAY 'MANOR' CLASS/1938/GREAT BRITAIN

This was the smallest of the GWR 4-6-0 types and closely resembled the previous 'Grange' class, but was about ten per cent lighter. This marginal weight reduction enabled it to work on a few lines where other 4-6-0s were not allowed, notably the former Cambrian Railway's line through central Wales. Their performance was not startling,

although changes to the exhaust arrangements in the 1950s were said to have worked wonders with them. Weighing 155,452lb (70.5 tonnes) they delivered a tractive effort of 27,340lb (12,412kg), while their coupled wheels of 68in (1727mm) made them suitable for all but the fastest trains. Cylinders were 18in x 30in (457mm x 762mm), and grate area 22.1sq.ft. (2.05sq.metre). Boiler pressure was 225psi (1550kPa). Twenty of them were built in the late 1930s and then, in the 1950s, British Railways acquired another ten. Being modern and of moderate weight, they proved to be suitable 'mainline' engines for steam tourist lines, and nine have been preserved, or are under restoration.

### JAIPUR STATE RAILWAY BESA 4-6-0/1939/INDIA

BESA (British Engineering Standards Association) prescribed basic dimensions for future Indian locomotives of all gauges, and for the metre-gauge railways two types of 4-6-0 were recommended, one for passenger use and one for mixed traffic. The examples built for the Jaipur State Railway by Hunslet of Leeds in 1939 were modernized versions of the passenger type, being superheated and having the cylinder diameter enlarged by one inch, and with piston instead of slide valves. Six were built, and when the class was absorbed by Indian Railways it became the MJ Class, the 'J' indicating Jaipur State Railway. Although there were some variations between railways, the basic dimensiois of the superheated BESA passenger 4-6-0 were as follows: 57in (1449mm) driving wheels, 16½ x 22in (420mm x 560mm) cylinders, grate area of 16sq.ft.

(1.5sq.metre), 180psi (1240kPa) boiler pressure and engine weight of 76,160lb (34.5 tonnes). Tractive effort was 16,077lb (7,298kg).

### LNER CLASS B1/1942/GREAT BRITAIN

The second most numerous class of 4-6-0 tender engines to be built in Britain was Class B1 of the LNER. First built in 1942 to replace a variety of 16 types of 4-6-0, 11 types

*4 6 2 Canadian Pacific G5 Class , 1944*

of Atlantic, and 48 types of 4-4-0, the B1 class amounted to 410 locomotives by 1950.

Edward Thompson, who succeeded Sir Nigel Gresley in 1941, designed his locomotives with individual valve gear for each cylinder in order to eliminate the conjugated gear used by his predecessor. The B1 class was built as a simple two-cylinder locomotive, with outside cylinders measuring 20in x 26in (508mm x 660mm) driving 74in (1880mm) wheels with a steam pressure of 225psi (1551kPa). The tractive force was 26,900lb (12,202kg) and the measured output at maximum efficiency was 861dbhp (642kW) at 38mph (61.1kph), with an efficiency of 9 per cent.

Class B1 was withdrawn between 1962 and 1967, but two of them, Nos.1264 and 1306, are preserved.

## GREAT WESTERN RAILWAY 'COUNTY' CLASS/1945/BRITAIN

The 'County' Class was intended to perform fast passenger work then being dealt with by the 4-cylinder 'Castle' type;

having only two cylinders the design would be cheaper to build and, more important, cheaper to run. To achieve a tractive effort comparable to that of the 'Castles' a smaller, non-standard, coupled wheel had to be used, and this was one of the criticisms levelled against the design. The first to be built, County of Middlesex, had a double chimney which gave good results at high power outputs but was not thought to justify its complication in everyday work. Hence it was removed, but towards the end of their lives all thirty of the class were fitted with a new design of double chimney.

At 280psi (1929kPa), the boiler pressure was unprecedentedly high for a GWR locomotive, and after the class was fitted with double chimneys it was lowered to the more sustainable 250psi (1722kPa). The grate area was 28.84sq.ft. (2.68sq.metre), and the engine weighed 169,785lb (82 tonnes). The coupled wheels were 75in (1905mm) and the cylinders 18½in x 30in (470mm x 762mm), giving a tractive effort of 32,580lbs (14,791kg) at the higher pressure. They were thus about the same

power as the 'Castles,' but were not so smooth-running at high speeds.

## BRITISH RAILWAYS CLASSES 4MT AND 5MT/1951/GREAT BRITAIN

Last of the British line of 4-6-0 locomotives were the classes 4MT and 5MT produced by British Railways in 1951. Both had two outside cylinders and a steam pressure of 225psi (1551kPa).

Class 4MT engines were fitted with 68in (1727mm) wheels and with cylinders of dimensions 18in x 28in (457mm x 711mm), giving a tractive force of 25,000lb (11,340kg). They were built to a weight of 154,390lb (70 tonnes) for widespread use. In total, 80 were built, and all were withdrawn by 1968. Several have been preserved. Class 5MT locomotives were equipped with 74in (1880mm) wheels and with cylinders measuring 19in x 28in (483mm x 711mm), giving a tractive force of 26,100 (11,839kg). In 1956, 43 were built with Caprotti valve gear, but

*Builder's photograph of P-0 4501 Class 4-6-2*

the other 129 were all fitted with Walschaerts gear. They were withdrawn between 1964 and 1968, but three are preserved.

# 4-6-2

The first locomotive built to the 4-6-2 wheel arrangement was reputed to have been one made for the Lehigh Valley Railroad in 1887. The term 'Pacific', however, was not applied until 1902, when it was attributed either to some with that wheel notation which were built by the Baldwin Locomotive Co. for New Zealand or (according to other sources) to some built for the Missouri-Pacific Railroad.

## CANADIAN PACIFIC RAILWAY LIGHT PACIFICS/1905/CANADA

In 1905 the CPR introduced the Pacific type, and built two classes, one with 75in (1905mm) and the other with 69in (1750mm) coupled wheels. The first was the G1 Class, intended for prairie use while the other, G2, was for hilly lines. Both types had the same boiler (200psi or 1378kPa) and cylinders (21in x 28in or 533mm x 710mm). The G1s were ultimately numbered in the 2200 series and the G2s in the 2500 and 2600 series. Eventually 165 G2 and 40 G1 locomotives were built. One of the G1 units

*4-6-2 Maffei 4-cylinder type of 1908*

*4-6-2 New York Central K Class , 1908*

*4-6-2 PLM Pacific ( SNCF 231K Class ), 1911/1936*

*Pennsylvania RR 4-6-2 of the K5 Class , bigger but less celebrated than the earlier K4.*

appeared in 1911 with the first all-weather cab, which was completely enclosed, and this became a feature of Canadian locomotives. By the 1940s these locomotives had been relegated to secondary and branch service, but were ageing. At the same time the CPR was operating several hundred elderly 4-6-0s. To replace these locomotives, in 1944 the Angus Works produced a new 4-6-2, Class G5. Essentially this was a G2, but modernized in scores of details. There were roller bearings for the trucks, aluminum was used in the cab structure, there was a foam-meter and a front-end throttle (the operating rod of this was concealed inside the handrail). Numbers 1200 and 1201, the prototypes, were followed by 101 more, with the final thirty being built by Canadian Locomotive rather than Montreal Locomotive Works. No.1301 of 1948 was the last steam locomotive built for the CPR. These, Class G5b, had mechanical stokers and a trailing truck that did not pivot but whose wheels could move laterally. The cylinders were slightly smaller than the older locomotives, being 20in x 28in (510mm x 710mm), and the boiler pressure was 250psi (1722kPa), giving with the 70in (1778mm) coupled wheels a tractive effort of 34,080lb (15,472kg). The grate area was 45.6sq.ft. (4.24sq.metre) and there was a 744sq.ft. (69sq.metre) superheater. Adhesion weight was 150,000lbs, or 68 tonnes.

## PARIS-ORLÉANS RAILWAY CLASS 4501/1907/FRANCE

In France the Paris-Orléans was the first to commission locomotives of the Pacific type.

These were built by the Société Alsacienne, where A. de Glehn, in conjunction with M. Solacroup of the P-O, designed a four-cylinder compound with cylinders of 15⅓in (390mm) and 25⅕in (640mm) diameters, all with 25½in (650mm) stroke, drove wheels of 73in (1850mm) diameter using steam at 232psi (1600kPa). On a weight of 198,450lb (90 tonnes) they gave an output of 2,050ihp (1,529kW) with non-superheated steam, as supplied for the first 70 engines; but the last 10, from 1910, were superheated, as were a further 79 which were built with wheels of 76¾in (1950mm) - 20 similar engines were built for the Nord Railway in 1912. It was one of the P-O's larger-wheeled engines, No.3566, that was to be chosen for the classic rebuild by A. Chapelon in 1929 to become No.3701.

## MAGNIFICENT MAFFEI/1908/GERMANY

In Europe locomotives of the Pacific type appeared in 1907 in both France and Germany, as described here. The Maffei-built version for the Bavarian State Railway should have come out first, but there was a last-minute redesign of the boiler to incorporate superheating and the eventual production date was 1908. The Bavarian Group S3/6, of which 159 were built, and Group IVf, of which 35 were built for the Baden State Railway, were both designed by

*4-6-2 SNCF 231K  Class of 1936 ,  with original smokebox door.*

*4-6-2 Pennsylvania RR K4 Class , 1914*

*Front-end view of the Pennsylvania Railroad's admired K4 Class 4-6-2*

*4-6-2 Canadian Pacific G3 Class , 1919*

*Canadian Pacific G1 Class light 4-6-2*

A. Hammel and were almost identical. With two high-pressure cylinders of dimensions 16¾in x 24in (425mm x 610mm) and two low-pressure ones at 17¾in x 26 1/3in (450mm x 670mm) driving 73¾in (1870mm) wheels, they used steam at 217psi (1496kPa) supplied by boilers with 2882sq.ft. (268sq.metre) of heating area and a fire-grate of 48.4sq.ft. (4.5sq.metre). On a weight of 190,953lb (86.6 tonnes), the tractive force would have been around 28,000lb (12,700kg) and the power output just over 2,000ihp (1,491kW) - according to the performance of the Bavarian engines, which took 400 tons (406 tonnes) up a 1 in 100 (1 per cent) gradient at 40mph (64kph). The

35 supplied to Baden had a steam pressure of 224psi (1545kPa), which accounted for an additional weight in the boiler of 4,000 pounds (1,814kg).

The Bavarian model was considered to be the most beautiful in all Europe at the time, and was known as the Magnificent Maffei.

## NEW YORK CENTRAL K.2KA CLASS/1908/USA

Between 1902 and 1930 the Pacific design captured the North American passenger locomotive field. The New York

Central Railroad took their first five from Alco in 1902 for operating the 'Twentieth Century Limited,' and these were followed between 1908 and 1910 by 97 of the K.2KA class. Equipped with two outside cylinders measuring 22in x 28in (559cm x 711mm) and with a steam pressure of 200psi (1380kPa), these gave a tractive force of 29,200lb (13,245kg) and a power output of 2,000ihp (1,491kW) at 45mph (72kph). With an axle-load of 58,212lb (26.4 tonnes), the total weight came to 272,979lb (123.8 tonnes), and the boiler had a heating-surface area of 4,515sq.ft. (420sq.metre) with a firegrate area of

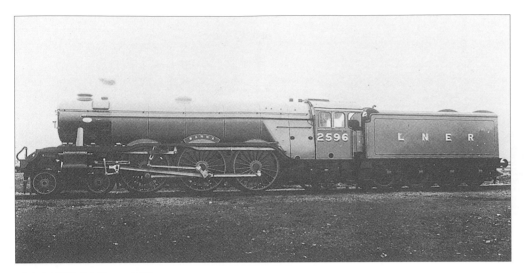

*4-6-2 LNER A3 Class , 1928*

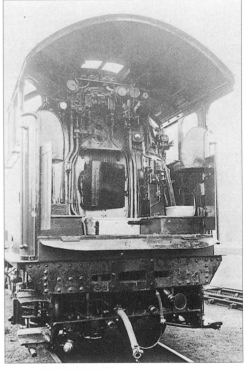

*4-6-2 A3 Class. The cab.*

*4-6-2 A3 Class. The corridor tender*

*4-6-2 A3 Class. The preserved Flying Scotsman at wor...*

56.5sq.ft. (5.25sq.metre). The tender was carried on two four-wheel trucks and held 8,000 gallons (363hl) of water.

## PLM PACIFICS/1911/FRANCE

The other railway in France to make early use of the Pacific type was the Paris, Lyons and Mediterranean. Its first 71 were of the four-cylinder simple type with cylinders 19in x 26¾in (480mm x 680mm) and with driving wheels of diameter 78¾in (2000mm); using superheated steam at 203psi (1400kPa), they gave a tractive force of 41,700 pounds (18,915kg) on a weight of 205,069lb (93 tonnes), and on test with a 646-long-ton (656.3-tonne) train one gave an output of 2,425ihp (1,808kW).

The first 71 were followed by a further 40 supplied by Henschel in 1911-12; of these, 20 were of the compound

type. In both classes the firegrate area was 45.75sq.ft. (4.25sq.metre), but the boilers in the first batch (by Batignolles & Co.) were slightly larger, with a heating area of 3,122sq.ft. (290sq.metre).

In 1936 some were rebuilt by Chapelon to form the 231K22 class of the SNCF, and one of these is preserved.

## PENNSYLVANIA RAILROAD K CLASSES/1914/USA

In the United States, with the New York Central setting the pace, the Pennsylvania was soon to follow. In 1914 its K4S type was tested on the Pennsylvania plant at Altoona, where it recorded an output of 3,250ihp (2,424kW) at 47mph (75.6kph) with a steaming rate of 67,000 pounds (30.4 tonnes) per hour. At the most efficient rate of 34,000 pounds (15.4 tonnes) per hour, the boiler efficiency was 76 per cent and the fuel consumption came to 1.8 pounds per ihp-hr (1.1kg/kW-hr), or 2.6 tons (2.64 tonnes) per hour.

The Pennsylvania then developed its K.5 Pacific of 1929, which was 29,000 pounds (13.15 tonnes) heavier than New York Central's K-5B. In the Pennsylvania version, the cylinders were 27in x 30in (686mm x 762mm) with 80in (2032mm) driving wheels and a steam pressure of 250psi (1724kPa). The tractive force amounted to 58,000lb (26,308kg) and the power output was 3,800ihp (2,834kW) at a steaming rate of 68,000 pounds (30.8 tonnes) per hour. The grate area was 70sq.ft. (6.5sq.metre) with a heating surface of 5,300sq.ft. (492.9sq.metre). The engine weight was 331,632lb (150.4 tonnes), and the axle-load was 69,456lb (31.5 tonnes).

The tenders, which were equipped with water pick-up apparatus, held 13,000 gallons of water (590hl) and 17.5 tons (17.8 tonnes) of coal with a weight of 111 tons (112.8 tonnes).

*The French Etat company had its own fleet of more or less unrebuilt compound Pacifics which were used on services from Paris to Normandy and Britanny. Here one of them , Class 231D , prepares to leave the Paris St Lazare terminus. One of these machines has been preserved.*

## CANADIAN PACIFIC RAILWAY G3 CLASS/1919/CANADA

Although the CPR was a great user of the light Pacific, it also had a need for a heavier 4-6-2, and the G3 type that appeared in 1919 was the forerunner of a class that eventually totalled 173 units in nine sub-classes. Number 2300, the lead engine, was built by the CPR's Angus Works and had 75in (1905mm) coupled wheels, a boiler pressure of 200psi (1378kPa) and cylinders measuring 25in x 30in (635mm x 762mm). The grate area was 65sq.ft. (6.04sq.metre) and there was a superheater of 803sq.ft. (74.6sq.metre). Total engine weight was 297,920lb (135 tonnes). The tender rode on two 4-wheel trucks, carrying about 12 tons of coal and 8,000 Imperial gallons of water. In their heyday the G3 units were used on the main line east of Winnipeg. They were not used over the Rockies, for which another class (G4) with 70in (1778mm) wheels was designed. The original engines later were classified as G3a as new sub-classes appeared. G3d was built in 1923 and these were the first North American locomotives with nickel-steel boilers. They were also provided with feedwater heaters. The last sub-class was G3j, by which

*4-6-2 Nord Super Pacific , 1923*

*4-6-2  Queensland Government Railways B.18  1/4  Class ,  1926*

*4-6-2 Indian Railways YB Class , 1927*

time the cylinder diameter had been reduced to 22in (560mm) and the boiler pressure raised to 275psi (1894kPa). The later units were turned out with unencumbered boilers, and valances above the wheels, giving a more streamlined appearance, and in due course the earlier units acquired abbreviated valances and were painted in the same livery of grey boiler and maroon panels with gold lettering. The last units, still looking fine in that livery, ended their days hauling commuter trains out of Montreal, being withdrawn in the 1960s.

## LNER A1 AND A3 CLASSES/1922/GREAT BRITAIN

Although the Great Western Railway had built its first Pacific - No.111, The Great Bear - in 1908, that was primarily a 'Star' Class motion with a longer boiler which did not steam too well. It was not until 1922 that the first British Pacific to be built in quantity was produced, in the shape of No.1470, erected at Doncaster for the Great Northern Railway (which was to be merged into the London and North Eastern in the following year). In 1922 the North Eastern too produced a 4-6-2, No.2400, but after comparative trials in 1923 the Great Northern version was

selected (by its designer, Nigel Gresley) as the standard main-line passenger engine for the LNER.

As first built, the Great Northern engines, classified A1, proved to be heavy on coal; in comparative trials with the Great Western 'Castle' class in 1925 the reason was ascertained to be the design of the valve gear. Once that had been rectified the resulting product, known as the A3 class, was a winner. With 5⅘in (147mm) of valve travel and a steam pressure of 220psi (1517kPa), the coal consumption was down to 3.1 pounds per dbhp-hr (1.4kg/kW-hr). The first of the new class was No.2743, Felstead.

*4-6-2 Indian Railways XA Class , 1929. This is the locomotive on the right , overshadowed by a post-war WP on the left.*

*4-6-2 The Indian XB Class , the bigger version of the XA*

Like the A1 class, the A3s were fitted with 80in (2032mm) driving wheels, but with three cylinders measuring 19in x 26in (483mm x 660mm) and with a boiler having 3,398sq.ft. (316sq.metre) of heating area and a firegrate area of 41.2sq.ft. (3.83sq.metre), the tractive force came to 32,900lb (14,923kg) with a power output of 1,170dbhp (872kW) at 60mph (96.5kph).

Between 1928 and 1935, 27 of the A3 type were built, and the 52 locomotives of the original A1 class were converted to the A3 design after the latter date.
In 1928 five special corridor tenders were built for use on the nonstop 'Flying Scotsman' for its 393-mile (632km) journey from Kings Cross to Edinburgh so that the two footplate crews could change over halfway. The inaugural down train was hauled by No.4472, Flying Scotsman, which has been preserved, and is the only one to have been saved.

## NORD RAILWAY 'SUPER-PACIFIC'/1923/FRANCE

The French Nord Railway went its own way in locomotive design after World War 1. The government wanted to standardize the Etat Railway's Pacific for all the French lines but this design, though good, did not please the Nord engineers. They believed that they should develop further their previous Pacific designs, which were characterized by long narrow fireboxes. They held that such a firebox was more easily fired and gave better results than the wider firebox overhanging the frame favoured by other lines. Whether they were right or wrong, the subsequent career of the 'Super-Pacifics' showed that these were exceptionally capable machines. Eighty-eight of them were built between 1923 and 1932, and they fell into three rather similar sub-groups and were classified 231C after the railways were nationalized. They had good boilers with a firebox heating area of 218sq.ft. (20.25sq.metre), a grate

area of 37.6sq.ft. (3.5sq.metre), and a tube heating surface of 2,440sq.ft. (226.70sq.metre), to which was added a superheater area of 615sq.ft. (57.14sq.metre). Boiler pressure was 227psi (1564kPa). The engines were 4-cylinder compound on the de Glehn system (a system that the Nord had pioneered in the 1880s). The high-pressure (outside) cylinders were 17$\frac{5}{16}$in x 26in (440mm x 660mm) and the inside low-pressure cylinders 24$\frac{3}{8}$in x 27$\frac{1}{8}$in (620mm x 690mm). The outside cylinders were served by piston valves, but the inside by slide valves. Steam and exhaust ports were unusually large and the resultant free steamimg combined with the 75in (1428mm) driving wheels made these locomotives suitable for sustained high-speed running. In working order the locomotives weighed 221,345lbs (100.4 tonnes). They hauled fast trains to Calais and Lille for most of their lives. Hauling the 'Golden Arrow' in the late 1920s, they had to take a train weighing about 550 tons non-stop at an average of 61mph

*4-6-2 German State Railways 01 Class , 1925*

(99kph) over a route which included a difficult grade at its northern end. Towards the end of their lives they were handling secondary passenger services on the Paris-Calais line. By that time they had acquired smoke deflectors.

## GERMAN STATE RAILWAY 01 SERIES/1925/GERMANY

The programme of standardized locomotive construction that was adopted by the DR after World War 1 and put into practice during the 1920s included three Pacific types (of which one, Series 02, was a compound which was not chosen for

*4-6-2 SNCF 231G  Class , 1935 , 30 locomotives rebuilt from the Etat 231D design*

*4-6-2 SNCF 231E Class , the 1929 rebuild of Class 3701*

production). The biggest of these, destined to haul the heaviest and fastest trains, was the 01 Series. Its boiler, which was standardized with that of the Series 44 2-10-0, had a diameter of 75in (1900mm) and a grate area of 48.4sq.ft. (4.5sq.metre). Its total evaporative heating surface was 2,684sq.ft. (247sq.metre), to which was added a superheater surface of 925sq.ft. (86sq.metre). Like all the larger standard designs, a feedwater heater was incorporated. The two cylinders were 25½in x 26in (650mm x 660mm) and the coupled wheels had a diameter of 78¾in (2m). With a boiler pressure of 227psi (1566kPa), this gave a tractive effort at 75 per cent boiler pressure of 36,375lbs (16,500kg). Like other designs of this programme, the boiler did not employ the narrow firebox concept but was rather designed around the desirability of having a simple rectangular grate, with the firebox shaped so that the inner firebox could be inserted from below. The 01 became the prime German passenger locomotive and remained so into the 1950s, although modified, each in their own way, by the engineers of the West German and German Democratic Republic railways. The final duties of those units that were not rebuilt was the haulage of fast trains between East Berlin and Dresden, where they were employed up to the late 1970s.

## QUEENSLAND GOVERNMENT RAILWAYS B.18 1/4 CLASS/1926/AUSTRALIA

Designed and largely built by the Railway's own Ipswich workshops, this Class was the first Pacific design in Queensland. It was intended to haul the main passenger trains, with service also with fruit trains. A hundred were built, the last appearing in 1947. Later units had a slightly higher boiler pressure and better cabs. Originally painted Prussian blue, they later appeared in green, with red and silver lining. After dieselization began they were relegated to freight and suburban trains. At least two have been

preserved, including one at the Railway's Museum near Brisbane.

Their coupled wheels were 51in (1300mm) and cylinders 18_in x 24in (460mm x 610mm) and boiler pressure 160psi (1102kPa) in the original locomotives. This gave a tractive effort of 21,316lb (9,677kg). The grate area was 25sq.ft. (2.32sq.metre) and the weight, was 209,475lb (95 tonnes). They were succeeded by the slightly more modern but similar BB.18 1/4 Class, which appeared in 1951.

## INDIAN RAILWAYS CLASS YB/1927/INDIA

After World War 1 a new series of standard classes ('Indian Railway Standard' or IRS) was worked out for both the major Indian gauges. For the metre gauge, two new Pacifics and a new 2-8-2 were the most important of these. The YB was the more numerous of the passenger types, 139 being built between 1927 and 1951, mainly by British builders, but including some from the Ajmer works in India and others from Germany and Czechoslovakia.

Weighing 116,480lb (52.8 tonnes), the axle-load was only 22,490lb (10.2 tonnes) tons and there was a 23sq.ft. (2.13sq.metre) grate area to maintain the 180psi (1240kPa) boiler pressure. The cylinders were 16in x 24in (406mm x 610mm), and the coupled wheels 57in (1449mm). It was not the biggest passenger locomotive of the IRS series; the very similar but less numerous YC performed that role, having slightly larger boiler and cylinders but an axle-load two tons heavier. Only 15 of the YC were built, although more went to Burma. They hauled the Poona-Bangalore trains until that line was broad-gauged, after which they were scrapped. The YB Class, on the other hand, had representatives still surviving at the end of the steam age. Being used by so many different Indian railways over so many years, the class had

variations. Often this concerned tender capacity, but some were equipped with poppet valve gears and a few with feedwater heaters.

## INDIAN RAILWAYS CLASS XA/1929/INDIA

In the 1920s, committees in India and London developed designs for a new range of locomotive, the IRS ('Indian Railway Standards') designs. For the broad gauge there were a heavy and light 2-8-2, and three Pacifics, the light XA, the heavy XC ,and the intermediate XB. At that time there was little interchange between the engineers in India, working out the broad parameters, and the consulting engineers in England, charged with getting out the working drawings; in fact the latter were not seen in India until after the locomotives were built. Vulcan Foundry in England began construction of the three Pacific types in 1926. They soon became involved in a number of derailments and after a particularly lethal one the Indian government sent to England for an investigating committee. This duly arrived, and included the locomotive engineer William Stanier. It recommended that the forward and rear trucks be modified, the drawgear be tightened, and the frames stiffened. The Pacifics were henceforth speed- restricted. Both houses of the Indian legislature censured the railway authorities (largely because the locomotives had continued to be ordered even when it should have been obvious that there was something wrong with them). All in all, as nationalists pointed out, this had not been a good advertisement for British rule.

The XA, designed for the most lightly-laid lines, and in any case the best of the Pacifics, was hardly affected by the speed restrictions and performed reasonably well until withdrawn towards the end of the steam era. Its axle-load was only 29,106lb (13.2 tonnes) tons, compared with the 38,146lb (17.3 tonnes) and 44,010lb (20 tonnes) of the two larger Pacifics. Unlike them, it had 5ft 1½in (1562mm) coupled wheels rather than 74in (1879mm), but had the same boiler pressure of 180psi (1240kPa). Its grate area was 32sq.ft. (2.97sq.metre), compared with the XB's 45sq.ft. (4.18sq.metre), cylinders were 18in x 26in or 460mm x 660mm (XB 21½in x 28in or 550mm x 710mm) and its tractive effort was 20,960lb or 9,515kg (against 26,760lb or 12,149kg). Engine weight was 154,560lb (70.1 tonnes), one third less than the XB. Construction of the IRS locomotives continued up to the 1940s. In the end there were 113 of the XA type, 99 of the XB, and 72 of the XC. Some of these went to Pakistan when India was divided in 1947.

## PARIS-ORLÉANS CLASS 3701/1929/FRANCE

On the Paris-Orléans Railway the Pacific locomotives that had been commissioned in 1907-11 were not proving adequate in handling the increasing train-weights, and in 1928 the problem of renewal arose. However, in view of financial restrictions, a decision was made not to replace

*4-6-2 German State Railways 03 Class , 1930*

but to rebuild them. This task was given to André Chapelon, the P-O's Development Engineer.

Taking No.3566, Le Cholera, Chapelon had the boiler retubed with a 32-element Robinson superheater to give an extra 100sq.ft. (9.3sq.metre) of heating area, but the other tubes were reduced so that the net result was a total heating area of 2,960sq.ft. (275sq.metre). The steam pipes were enlarged by 100 per cent and a new double beat regulator was fitted. The high-pressure cylinders were increased in diameter to 16½in (420mm); the steam pressure was also increased, 246psi (1696kPa), and the valve gear was replaced by Lenz-Dabeg oscillating-cam poppet valves operated by a Walschaerts link motion. Other changes were in the provision of a steel firebox with a thermic syphon and an ACFI water heater in place of the exhaust injector. Finally, the exhaust system was replaced by a Kylchap double blastpipe and the locomotive was renumbered No.3701.

During the rebuilding the weight had been increased from 88.6 tons (90 tonnes) to 100.2 tons (101.8 tonnes) but the power output had been increased from 2,000ihp (1,491kW) to 3,000ihp (2,237kW), with both high and low-pressure cylinders making an even contribution. On test, a similar locomotive returned an output of 3,400ihp (2,535kW) and the fuel consumption was reduced to 2.7 pounds per dbhp-hr (1.64kg/kW-hr). Train weights of up to 650 long tons (660 tonnes) were handled with ease, and speeds of up to 84mph (135kph) were attained.
The other 20 engines of the class were rebuilt to become Nos. 231F701-720 of the Région

Sud-Ouest. Similar rebuilding was then applied to 14 of the 3500 class and to 10 of the 4500 class, as well as

*4-6-2 Chinese Railways Class SI-6 , 1933*

*4-6-2 LMS Princess Class , 1933*

to all the Pacifics of the État fleet (which later became the 231G class). The original 20 of the P-O Class 3701 were sent to the Nord, becoming their Class 231E; in 1956 No.231E19 achieved a maximum speed of 110mph (177kph) No.231E22 has been preserved at the French Railway Museum at Mulhouse.

### GERMAN STATE RAILWAY SERIES 03/1930/GERMANY

The 03 was a lightweight version of the DR's heavy passenger locomotive of the 01 Series, weighing 25,350lbs (11½ tonnes) less than the former and with an adhesion weight of 114,600 lbs (52 tonnes) as against 132,150lbs (60 tonnes). Axle-load was accordingly

reduced by almost two tonnes (4,410 lbs) giving the class a wider range of activity than the heavier engines. The boiler was the same length (22⅓ft or 6.8m between tubeplates) but the diameter was slightly smaller (66in or 1.7m against 75in or 1.9m). The grate area was correspondingly reduced from 48.4sq.ft. (4.5sq.metre) to 43.5sq.ft. (4.05sq.metre). The same feedwater heater of

*4-6-2 LMS Princess Class , 1933*

*4-6-2 LNER A4 Class of 1935, in post-war finish*

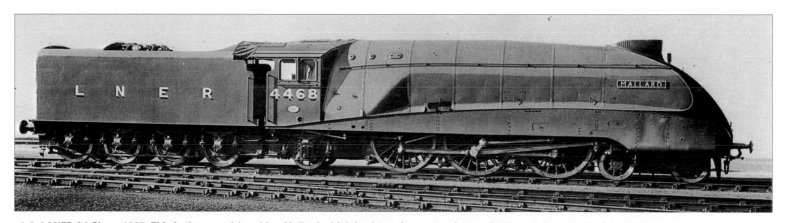

*4-6-2 LNER A4 Class, 1935. This is the record-breaking Mallard which is shown in pre-war form, with deep valances over its wheels*

144sq.ft. (13.4sq.metre) was fitted. As with other designs of this programme, the Belpaire boiler was abandoned; its advantage of ample steam space, stiffness and easy cleaning was acknowledged, but the tendency of its throat-plate to develop cracks was held against it. Wagner, the engineer in charge of the locomotive programme, gave priority to ease of maintenance even if that involved a slight deterioration of performance. The wheels were marginally closer together than with the 01, but as with the latter there was a wide gap between the rear coupled wheel and the trailing truck; this allowed good air access to the grate. Cylinders were 23⅘in x 26in (600mm x 660mm), boiler pressure was the same as the 01 (227psi or 1564kPa) and so was the diameter of the coupled wheels (78½in or 2m), giving a tractive effort at 75 per cent boiler pressure of 32,500lbs (14,750kgs).

## CHINESE RAILWAYS SL-6 CLASS/1933/CHINA

Sometimes known as the 'Victory' (Sheng Li) class, this Pacific design is of Japanese origin, but was adopted for production in Communist China. During its years of construction certain details were changed and the later units were built with Russian-style smoke deflectors. Almost 300 units were built by several Japanese works, including Kawasaki and Hitachi, between 1933 and 1944. The design first appeared on the Manchurian National Railway and most served in Manchuria, although approaching a hundred were used by the Japanese in occupied China. After the War Chinese works, notably Darien and Qingdao, continued to build them, in somewhat modified form, until they were replaced by the similar RM design. Hundreds were built, and they hauled passenger trains in most parts of China.

They had grates of 51.9sq.ft. (4.82sq.metre), and superheaters of 723sq.ft. (67.2sq.metre). Boiler pressure was 200psi (1373kPa) and cylinders measured 22½in X 26in (570mm X 660mm). Driving wheel diameter was 69in (1750mm), giving a tractive effort of 32,150lbs (14,600kgs). Weight in working order was (211,010lbs (91,345kgs).

## LMS PRINCESS CLASS/1933/GREAT BRITAIN

In 1933 the London, Midland and Scottish Railway had a requirement for locomotives with a larger firegrate area in order to run the full 400 miles (644km) between London and Glasgow, a distance too great for the narrow fireboxes of the 'Royal Scot' class to achieve. The production of a Pacific locomotive with a grate area of 45sq.ft.

*4-6-2 Belgian 10 Class , 1935*

*4-6-2 LMS Duchess Class. Later units were built unstreamlined, and in World War 2 the earlier units lost their streamlining*

*4-6-2  Malayan Railways Class 0 ,  1938*

(4.2sq.metre) therefore began. The 12 engines of this new 'Princess' class were built at Crewe.

Later, a No.6201 completed two nonstop runs between Euston and Glasgow at average speeds of 68mph (109kph) for the down run and 70mph (113kph) for the up journey. An enlarged class of Pacific was built to operate a new high speed train, the 'Coronation Scot,' in 1937.

## LNER A4 CLASS/1935/GREAT BRITAIN

In 1929 the London and North Eastern commissioned a high-pressure locomotive, No.10000, built as a 4-6-4 with a streamlined front end which was necessary in order to take the smoke clear of the driver's cab. When an improved version of the A3 Pacific class was required for a new high-speed train to be introduced in 1935 and called the 'Silver Jubilee,' a new class of A4 Pacific was designed and produced. In these the three cylinders were reduced to 18½in x 26in (470mm x 660mm), but the steam pressure was increased to 250psi (1724kPa). The heating area of the boiler was also slightly less, at 3,325sq.ft.(309sq.metre), but the tractive force was raised to 35,500lb (16,103kg). The first to be produced was No.2509, Silver Link, and production continued until 1938, by which date 35 had been built. The last seven were fitted with Kylchap double chimneys; the first of these was No. 4468, Mallard, which in 1938 was to achieve a speed of 126mph (202.7kph).Six of the A4 class have been preserved, including Mallard at York and one each in Quebec and Wisconsin.

## BELGIAN NATIONAL RAILWAYS 10 CLASS/1935/BELGIUM

Belgian locomotive construction and design had a distinguished history, Walschaert and Belpaire giving their names to important innovations in valve gear and fireboxes respectively. Although a small country, its railways' traction needs were far from simple. Although much of the country

is flat, the main line to the south through the Ardennes is difficult, and carries a heavy traffic. The 35 locomotives of the 1001 series were designed for the heaviest trains over the most difficult routes, and were counted among the leading European passenger locomotives, combining speed and power. Their coupled wheels were 78in (1980mm), adequate for the highest speeds permissible,

*4-6-2 Finnish Railways HR-1  Class , 1938*

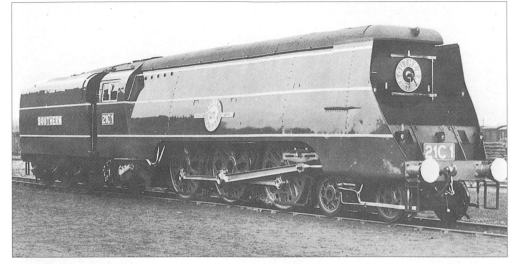

(419mm x 711mm) driving 81in (2057mm) wheels with a steam pressure of 250psi (1724kPa). The firegrate area was enlarged to 50sq.ft. (4.65sq.metre) and the boiler heating area to 3,748sq.ft. (348sq.metre). The tractive force was 40,000lb (18,144kg) and the maximum output was claimed to be 3,550ihp (2,647kW). Streamlinig was applied to the earlier units but was removed during World War 2. The class was withdrawn in 1962-64, but three have been preserved, including No.46229 (Duchess of Hamilton) at the National Railway Museum, York.

*4-6-2 Southern Railway Merchant Navy Class as built , 1941*

while the tractive effort was no less than 43,300lb (19,640kg). These were four-cylinder machines, using simple expansion.The cylinders were 16½in x 28¾in (420mm x 720mm) and the boiler pressure 256psi or (1764kPa). The grate area was 53.8sq.ft. (5sq.metre) and there was a large superheater. The weight in working order was 277,782lb (126 tonnes). These very fine locomotives had a first-rank life of almost two decades, for much of which they were painted green and were regarded as the 'pride of the line.' One survivor of the class occasionally comes out of retirement to haul a special excursion train.

## LMS DUCHESS (CORONATION) CLASS/1937/GREAT BRITAIN

The enlarged class of LMS Pacifics, known as the Coronation class or Duchess class, of which 38 were built, were fitted with four cylinders of dimensions 16½in x 28in

*4-6-2 rebuilt West Country Class*

*4-6-2 rebuilt Merchant Navy*

*4-6-2 rebuilt Merchant Navy type in British Railways service*

## ALAYAN RAILWAY O CLASS/1938/MALAYA

The metre-gauge Malayan Railway relied almost entirely on successive designs of Pacific locomotive to handle its services. The final design was the O Class, sometimes called the 56 Class. 28 of these were supplied by North British before World War 2 and 40 more, almost identical, were supplied in the late 1940s. They were interesting for their 3-cylinder layout and their use of rotary cam Poppet valve gear. Among colonial railways, the Malayan Railway was notable for its smart and original locomotive stock.

All the locomotives carried names, the nameplate being in local script on one side and in English transliteration on the other. These names were of places served by the Railway.

The locomotives weighed 129,900lbs (58,980kgs) and had a grate area of 31sq.ft. (2.9sq.metre). The boiler supplied steam to three 13in x 24in (330mm x 610mm) cylinders, with boiler pressure being 250psi (1729kPa). Tractive effort at 23,940lbs (10,870kgs) was quite high for this size of locomotive, thanks partly to the quite high boiler pressure and partly to the smallish coupled wheels (54in or 1371mm).

This was not a railway where loads were heavy or speeds were fast, but there were sections of difficult curves and grades. These locomotives performed well during their lives, thanks partly to well-organized maintenance. Not all

*4-6-2 West Country Class , 1945. This is the un-rebuilt version.*

*4-6-2 Siamese State Railway 283 Class, 1942*

have been scrapped. One is used to haul excursions and another is expected to remain as a museum piece.

### FINNISH STATE RAILWAYS HR-1 CLASS/1938/FINLAND

The broad-gauge Finnish State Railways ordered these Pacifics from the local Lokomo company, so as to replace the 4-6-0 locomotives on the most important passenger services. Weighing 207,270lb (94 tonnes), and with a

tractive effort (calculated in continental European terms at 65 per cent boiler pressure) of 25,550lbs (11,600kg), these locomotives had 75in (1905mm) driving wheels. Boiler pressure was 213psi (1457kPa) and grate area 38.5sq.ft. (3.57sq.metre). The two cylinders were 23¼in x 25¼in (590mm x 640mm). A top speed of 68mph (110kph) was permitted. On the Helsinki-Tampere section they were allowed to take 660 tonnes in summer and 550 tonnes in winter. Construction of these locomotives was

spread over several years and they remained the principal passenger locomotive right up to the end of steam in the 1960s.

### SOUTHERN RAILWAY BULLEID PACIFICS/1941/GREAT BRITAIN

Although designed before the outbreak of war in 1939, the Bulleid Pacifics of the Southern Railway were first

*4-6-2 New South Wales Government Railways streamlined and unstreamlined Class C-38 type , 1943*

produced in 1941, with the 30 of the 'Merchant Navy' class being followed in 1945 by 118 of the 'West Country' class, which had a lower axle-load. Both classes were three-cylinder engines with steam at 280psi (1931kPa) and with 74in (1880mm) driving wheels. In the 'West Country' class the cylinder size was 16⅜in x 24in (417mm x 610mm), whereas in the 'Merchant Navy' class it was 18in x 24in (457mm x 610mm). In the latter class the tractive force amounted to 37,500lb (17,010kg) with a power output of 1,380dbhp (1,029kW) at 61mph (98.15kph), equivalent to 2,000ihp (1,491kW). The weight of the 'Merchant Navy' locomotives was heavier than the designed weight, at 207,270lb (94 tonnes). Novel design features included a welded boiler with thermic syphons and a chain-driven valve gear enclosed in an oil bath. The air-smoothed casing gave the engines of the class the nickname 'Spam Cans'. From 1956, however, all the 'Merchant Navy' class and 61 of the 'West Country' class were rebuilt with Walschaerts valve gear and without this boiler enclosure. In that form the 'Merchant Navy' class gave an output of 1,465dbhp (1,092kW) or 2,130ihp (1,588kW).

Both classes remained in service until 1967, with No.35030, Elder Dempster Lines, at the head of the last steam train into Waterloo in July 1967, the 'Weymouth Boat Express.' Over twenty have been preserved of both classes.

## ROYAL SIAMESE STATE RAILWAY 283 SERIES/1942/THAILAND

In the years of Japanese occupation, most additions to the Thai locomotive stock were originated and controlled by

*4-6-2 LNER A2 Class , 1946*

*4-6-2 NSWGR C-38 Class of 1943 in black livery*

*4-6-2 LNER A1 Class of 1948 , the larger-wheel version of the A2*

*4-6-2 Indian Railways WP Class , 1947*

*Another view of the Indian Railways WP 4-6-2*

*4-6-2 Indian Railways WP Class. This unit was built in Austria , whereas that in the top illustration is Canadian-built*

the Japanese Army. However, the State Railway did manage to obtain in the normal way two classes of locomotive that it added to its own books. It was badly in need of power, for wartime had brought a big traffic increase, especially of passengers. One of these classes was a 4-6-2 for passenger service, numbered from 283 to 292, and using components from a contemporaneous 2-8-2. They were supplied by two Japanese builders, Nippon and Hitachi and, surprisingly for wartime, sported copper-capped chimneys. These, the smoke deflectors, and the combined dome and sandbox made these locomotives easily recognisable, and they were always well turned-out. They had two cylinders, 17¾in x 24in (450mm x 610mm). Boiler pressure was 185psi (1273kPa), the coupled wheels were 54in (1370mm), giving a tractive effort of 19,392lb (8,780kg). They were wood-burners and had a grate area of 32.2sq.ft. (3sq.metre). Weight in working order was 127,890lb (58 tonnes)

## NEW SOUTH WALES GOVERNMENT RAILWAYS CLASS C-38/1943/AUSTRALIA

Built during World War 2, this class signalled the emergence at last of a truly Australian locomotive design.

Some components were imported, but the design appears to have been entirely a domestic matter. Construction was not easy in wartime conditions, and some components arrived in Australia via the Trans Siberian Railway.

Designed for heavy passenger trains, and being rather heavy itself, the type was limited to the main lines from Sydney as far as Newcastle, Albury, Dubbo and Thirroul, although in 1971 it penetrated across Australia to Perth on a commemorative special train. The last members were withdrawn that year, although several have been preserved. These include the class leader, 3801, which is one of the five that were streamlined. Construction was shared by Clyde Engineering and the Railway's own works.

One of them, 3817, held some kind of record, having been toppled on to its side three times during its life, the last occasion resulting in its withdrawal; design faults were not involved.

They had 69in (1750mm) coupled wheels and 21½in x 26in (550mm x 660mm) cylinders and a boiler pressure of 245psi (1688kPa). Tractive effort was 36,273lb (16,470kg). There was a large grate of 47sq.ft. (4.37sq.metre), and the weight (including tender) was 452,025lb (205 tonnes). There were thirty locomotives in the class.

*4-6-2 Western Australia Pm Class , 1950*

*4-6-2 Brittania Class , 1951 , in BR service*

## LONDON & NORTH EASTERN RAILWAY CLASS A2/1946/GREAT BRITAIN

There were four sub-classes in this classification, of which two were rebuilds of older locomotives. Classes A2 and A2/3, however, each numbered 15 units and were newly-built. With their 74in (1879mm) driving wheels they were not quite as speedy as the very similar A1 Class, and were intended to haul heavy passenger trains over hilly routes. Scotland was therefore a prime field of activity for them. Prevailing conditions of inferior coal supplies and labour shortage were taken into account in their design, which included rocking grates, self-cleaning smokeboxes, and hopper ashpans. The main difference between the A2 and the A2/3 was that the former had a slightly shorter wheelbase. They had three 19in x 26in (483mm x 660mm) cylinders, with each having its own valve gear, and boiler pressure was 250psi (1729kPa), giving a tractive effort of 40,430lb (18,355kg). The grate area was 50sq.ft. (4.6sq.metre), and weight in working order 227,120lb (103 tonnes). Some were fitted with Kylchap double chimneys. They carried names, usually commemorating famous racehorses. They were withdrawn by the end of 1966 but one, Blue Peter, has survived to haul the occasional excursion.

## INDIAN RAILWAYS WP CLASS/1947/USA, INDIA

The Indian Railways had introduced Pacific locomotives in 1928 with three types, but after World War 2 a new specification was drawn up. The first units of the new WP Class were built, and styled, by Baldwin in the USA. Later, hundreds more were built by workshops all round the world. There were two outside cylinders of dimensions 20¼in x 28in (513mm x 711mm) and driving wheels of 67in (1702mm) diameter; the steam pressure was 210psi (1448kPa) from a boiler with 2,982sq.ft. (277sq.metre) of heating area and with a firegrate area of 46sq.ft. (4.27sq.metre). The tractive force was 30,600lb (13,880kg), and the total engine weight amounted to 217,986lb (98.86 tonnes). With a faired smokebox door and an enclosed cab they were handsome machines, and between 1947 and 1967 a total of 755 was supplied.

*4-6-2 British Railways Brittania Class, 1951. The photograph shows Britannia as a preserved locomotive*

*4-6-2 Duke of Gloucester , 1954*

*4-6-2 Indian Railways WL Class , 1955*

## WESTERN AUSTRALIAN GOVERNMENT RAILWAYS Pm CLASS/1950/AUSTRALIA

Thirty-five of these mainline passenger engines were built by North British and arrived in 1950. They proved unsuccessful in the passenger role because of their rough-riding, and spent most of their life on freight work. Some were fitted with roller bearings, becoming Class Pmr. They weighed 245,196lb (111.2 tonnes), had a tractive effort of 25,855lb (11,738kg) and a grate area of 35sq.ft. (3.25sq.metre). Cylinders were 19in x 26in (480mm x 660mm) and the coupled wheels 54in (1370mm). Boiler pressure was 175psi (1206kPa). Despite their initial failures, this was a popular class which lasted until 1971, after which four survived in preservation.

## BRITANNIA CLASS/1951/GREAT BRITAIN

On the formation of British Railways in 1948, an evaluation was made of the Pacific locomotives then in existence in order to decide on a future standard build for the type. All the Pacifics in service were fitted with either three or four cylinders, but it was decided that a simpler design, with only two cylinders, would be adopted. The locomotives built to that design were first produced in 1951 as the 'Britannia' class, of which 55 were built (numbered 70000 to 70054). With cylinders 20in x 28in (508mm x 711mm) and a steam pressure of 250psi (1,729kPa) driving 74in (1880mm) wheels, they gave a tractive force of 32,100lb (14,560kg); on test the power output amounted to 1,240dbhp (925kW) at 71mph (114.2kph), although it was claimed that one had achieved an output of 2,050dbhp (1,529kW). The latter would be equivalent to 2,700ihp (2,013kW) or 27hp per ton (19.8kW/tonne), which is a

reasonable figure for a locomotive of that era, but the maximum steaming rate for the boiler was 31,400 pounds (14,243kg) per hour, equivalent to an output of 2,200ihp (1,640kW).

The 'Britannias' were appreciated on their first assignment, which was on the line to Norwich, but in other places they were not so welcome. Two have been preserved: No. 70000, Britannia, and No. 70013, Oliver Cromwell.

## DUKE OF GLOUCESTER/1954/GREAT BRITAIN

The last of the British Pacifics was No.71000, Duke of Gloucester, built in 1954 as a replacement for the ex-LMS

*4-6-2 Chinese Railways RM Class , 1957*

*4-6-2 German Railways (DR) 01.5 Class, 1961*

No.46202, Princess Anne (a rebuilt version of the Turbomotive of 1934), which had been wrecked in the disastrous accident at Harrow in 1952.

With a classification 8P, No.71000 was built with three cylinders of dimensions 18in x 28in (457mm x 711mm) and with a boiler similar to those fitted to the 'Britannia' class 7P. With 74in (1880mm) wheels, the engine had a tractive force of 39,000lb (17,690kg), its power output was measured as 2,100dbhp (1,566kW), and the boiler potential output was 30,200lb (13,700kg) per hour, or 2,420ihp (1,805kW). In fact, with a heating surface area of 3,180sq.ft. (295sq.metre) and a grate area of 48.6sq.ft. (4.5sq.metre), the most efficient output rate was at 24,000lb (10,886kg) per hour or 1,980ihp (1,476kW), at which the efficiency came to 10.1 per cent.

Operationally, Duke of Gloucester was not a success. Mistakes may have been made in its assembly. But in preservation the locomotive has performed quite well.

## INDIAN RAILWAYS CLASS WL/1955/INDIA

The two final broad-gauge steam locomotive types for Indian Railways were the WT 2-8-4 tank engine and the WL Pacific. These used a common boiler, but whereas the tank locomotive was a quite ugly machine of which only 30 were built (even though it did well its job of hauling heavy commuter trains) the Pacific was a handsome locomotive of which more than a hundred were built. It was also active right up to the end of steam on the broad gauge, being a general-use locomotive with no great maintenance problems.

It was a light Pacific, intended for first-class trains which, for one reason or another, were not suited for haulage by the bigger and more numerous WP Pacific. Ten units were

supplied by Vulcan in Britain in 1955, performed satisfactorily, and were then a decade later joined by 94 more units built in India. This order was prompted by the need to replace some of the ageing 4-6-0 types.

The WL had the same size of coupled wheel as the bigger WP Pacific and the WT tank locomotive. That is, 67in (1702mm), which was large enough to cope with the highest speed likely to be required on Indian Railways at that period. Boiler pressure at 210psi (1447kPa) was also identical. The grate area at 38sq.ft. (3.53sq.metre) was about one fifth smaller than the WP grate and the cylinder

diameter at 19¼in (490mm) was one inch less (cylinder stroke at 28in or 710mm was the same). Tractive effort was correspondingly less, at 27,640lb (12,548kg) against the 30,600lb (13,892kg) of the WP. The corresponding advantage was the lighter axle-load. Engine weight was 199,360lb (90.4 tonnes).

## CHINESE RAILWAYS RM CLASS/1957/CHINA

In its later years, Chinese steam locomotive design was an amalgam of several different national characteristics. The RM Class Pacific was an example of this, being a

*4-6-4 Nord Nos 3.1101/2, 1910. Unusually, in these locomotives the inside cylinders were placed one behund the others, slightly offset, to save space.*

*The front end of du Bousquet's novel and powerful 4-6-4 No 3. 1102*

blend of Japanese and Russian practice. Those Russian and Japanese designers in their turn had been influenced by American development. Built by Qingdao, the wheels and mechanical parts of this design were derived from the Japanese-built Pacifics of Class SL-6, but the boiler and other features were influenced by Russian practice. Most obvious but least important of the Russian features were the fluted smoke deflectors. The external steam pipe from the boiler, covered (and insulated) by the casing behind the chimney, is another post-war Russian characteristic. A Worthington-style feedwater heater was an echo of American practice.

Coupled wheels were of 69in (1750mm) diameter, the two cylinders were 22½in x 26in (570mm x 660mm) and boiler pressure was 215psi (1469kPa). This produced a tractive effort of 34,450lbs (15,700kgs). Grate area was 61.9sq.ft. (5.75sq.metre) and the superheater was of 700sq.ft. (65sq.metre). Weight was 179,600lbs (81,796kgs). Several hundred of these locomotives were built before production ceased in 1961, and they hauled the better passenger trains all over China. But their lives were cut short, thanks to the policy of dieselizing passenger services at an early stage of the dieselization process.

*4-6-4 New York Central RR streamlined J3*

## GERMAN STATE RAILWAYS (DR) CLASS 01.5/1961/GERMAN DEMOCRATIC REPUBLIC

The final development of the German Pacific type took place in Eastern Germany in communist times, when some of the existing 0.1 Pacifics were taken in hand for extensive rebuilding, to produce the 01.5 Class. Bigger boilers were fitted. Some were fitted with Boxpok wheels, some for oil-burning, and one with a Giesl ejector. The external outline was cleaned up with a skyline casing enclosing sandboxes and domes. A valance was added along the running plate. The two cylinders were 23 3/5in x 26in (600mm x 660mm) and the coupled wheels were of 78½in (2000mm) diameter. The grate area was 52.5sq.ft. (4.88sq.metre), and there was a superheater of 1053sq.ft. (97.9sq.metre). Boiler pressure was 227psi (1566kPa), ensuring a nominal tractive effort of 35,414lb (15,582kg). These were impressive locomotives and were active into the 1970s, hauling long-distance trains to and from Leipzig and Dresden.

*4-6-4 New York Central unstreamlined J3*

*4-64 New York Central J1 Class , 1927*

*4-6-4 Canadian National K5-A Class , 1930*

# 4-6-4

## NORD NOS.3.1101/2/1910/FRANCE

The first examples of the 4-6-4 type were the two built in 1910 by Ateliers de la Compagnie la Chapelle for the Nord and specified as being capable of hauling a 787-long-ton (800-tonne) train at 68mph (109kph) and giving an output of 2,800ihp (2,088kW) -- this making them the most powerful locomotives in the world at that time. They were fitted with a firegrate of area 46sq.ft. (4.3sq.metre), and No.3.1102 was built with a water-tube firebox supplied by Ateliers Schneider a Creusot, although that was replaced

by a conventional box in 1913. Development was postponed as a result of World War 1, but both lasted in service until 1940, when No. 3.1101 was scrapped. Number 3.1102 has been saved and is preserved in sectional form at the Museum at Mulhouse.

## NEW YORK CENTRAL J CLASS/1927/USA

In the United States the New York Central was the first to introduce the 4-6-4 wheel arrangement to passenger-train operation when its Class J-1E locomotives were built by Alco to provide an engine with a boiler having a higher output than that of their K-5 Pacifics. With the same cylinders - measuring 25in x 28in (635mm x 711mm) -

and an increased steam pressure - 225psi (1551kPa) - the tractive force came to 42,300lb (19,187kg), which could be augmented by a booster engine in the trailing truck to give an additional 10,900lb (4,944kg) for starting. The total heating-surface area was increased to 6,435sq.ft. (598sq.metre), with a firegrate area of 81.5sq.ft. (7.6sq.metre) fed by a mechanical stoker. With an all-up weight of 352,138lb (159.7 tonnes), the output was 3,900ihp (2,908kW) at 67mph (107.8kph).

In 1937 an enlarged version with a steam pressure of 275psi (1896kPa), classified J-3, was produced by the Alco works with cylinders at 22½in x 29in (572mm x 737mm) and with driving wheels of 79in (2006mm)

*4-6-4 German State Railway No 05.001 , 1935*

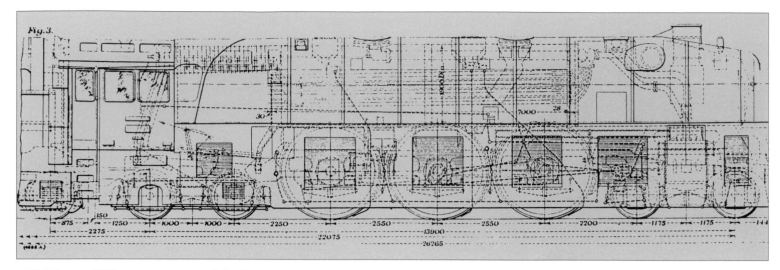

*4-6-4 German 05 Class , an arrangement drawing*

*4-6-4 German 05 Class of 1935 , as built*

diameter, the tractive force amounted to 43,400lb (19,686kg), with an additional 12,000 pounds (5,433kg) available from the booster truck. With the same grate area of 81.5sqft (7.6sq.metre), the boiler heating area, at 5,932sq.ft. (551sq.metre), was smaller than that of the J-1E, but the increased steam pressure resulted in an output of 4,725ihp (3,523kW) at 75mph (121kph), or 29ihp per ton (21.3kW/tonne). On an axle-load of 65,047lb (29.5 tonnes), the total weight came to 360,076lb (163.3 tonnes). The class was used on the 'Twentieth Century Limited' between New York and Chicago, on which the 133-mile (214km) section from Elkhart to Toledo was run at an average speed of 69.3mph (111.5kph). Two hundred and seventy-five of the Hudsons were put into service.

The 4-6-4 was not to find wide acceptance in the United States, with a total of merely 500 being built. Other US users were the Chesapeake and Ohio, with its class L-2; and the Chicago, Milwaukee, St Paul and Pacific, with its K-7 class, used for 100mph (161kph) operation on the Hiawatha express.

## CANADIAN NATIONAL RAILWAYS CLASS K-5a 1930/CANADA

These five locomotives were built by the Montreal

Locomotive Works and were intended to haul the faster trains on the Montreal-Toronto route where, until pooled trains were introduced in 1934, the CNR faced competition from the Canadian Pacific. They had 80in (2032mm) coupled wheels, a boiler pressure of 275psi (1894kPa) and two  23in x 28in (585mm x 710mm) cylinders. This produced a tractive effort of 43,300lbs (19,640kgs). The grate area was 73.6sq.ft. (6.8sq.metre) and there was a 2ft 7in (787mm) combustion chamber.

They belonged to a period when the CNR was rebuilding its locomotive stock and thinking scientifically about locomotive design. The boilers of these locomotives used

high-tensile silicon steel to save weight. Two of them had roller-bearing leading trucks. Weight in working order was 356,400 lbs (161.8 tonnes) of which 188,600lbs (85.6 tonnes) was on the coupled wheels. The locomotives were built with boosters, offering an extra 10,000lb (4,536kg) of tractive effort for starting.

During their life the appearance of these locomotives underwent successive changes. Smoke deflectors were fitted at one stage (the CNR was doing considerable research at this time on wind deflection). In their final form they were fitted with deep valances beneath the running plate to give a semi-streamlined look; sandboxes, usually so prominent on American boilers, had been hidden away in the smokebox right from the start; sand was piped only to the leading pair of coupled wheels.

They were painted in the CNR black and green livery. One of them held the Canadian speed record for a steam locomotive. In their final days in the late 1950s they were used on secondary passenger services out of Toronto. One of them has been preserved.

## GERMAN STATE RAILWAY NOS.05.001/2 1935/GERMANY

The advent of the high-speed diesel railcar onto the German State Railway in 1932 prompted Professor H. Nordman to investigate the potential of high-speed steam locomotives, of which there were still 22,300 in use in Germany in 1934. The studies involved the building of four types of 4-6-4 locomotive, of which two were tank engines and one was to have been fired with pulverized coal. The outcome in fact was the construction of two 4-6-4 locomotives designed by A. Wolff of the Borsig Co., built in 1935 and numbered 05.001 and 05.002. Employing three cylinders measuring 17¾in x 26in (450mm x 660mm) and driving wheels of 90.6in (2.3m) diameter, the engines used a steam pressure of 290psi (2,000kPa) from a boiler with a firegrate area of 50.6sq.ft. (4.7sq.metre) and a heating area of 3,724sq.ft. (346sq.metre). On a weight of 280,035lb (127 tonnes), the tractive force was 33,240 pounds (15,078kg) and designed output was 3,000ihp (2,237kW).

In May 1936, No.05.002, with a 193.9-long-ton (197-tonne) train was recorded as achieving a speed of

*4-6-4 Canadian Pacific Royal Hudson , 1937*

*4-6-4 SNCF 232S  Class , 1940*

*4-6-4 SNCF 232U-1 , the post-war development of the 232S , 1949*

*4-6-4 C&O Railroad L1 Class , 1946*

*4-6-4 Victorian Railways R Class , 1951*

198.9kph (123.62mph) over 3.22km (2 miles) of level track. No.05.001 has been preserved at the Nuremberg Museum of Transport.

## CANADIAN PACIFIC RAILWAY 'ROYAL HUDSON'/1937/CANADA

Between 1929 and 1940 the Montreal Locomotive Works built 65 Hudson locomotives for the CPR. The first 20 were handsome machines and worked well on heavy passenger trains. In 1937 the design was modified to form the 'Royal Hudson' sub-class of 45 units. These preserved the main characteristics of the preceding units but were cosmetically redesigned to fit the age of the streamliner. The boiler was kept smooth, a deep valance was attached to the running board, the smokebox front was rounded, and the chimney and number window combined in a fitting that would have done credit to the automobile industry. In the CP livery of maroon ('Tuscan Red')and grey, with gold lettering, these were impressive machines and they gained extra fame (and their 'Royal' distinction) when they hauled King George VI and his Queen across Canada.

Five of the batch were fitted with boosters, and were intended to operate the 813-mile (1,308km) Toronto-Fort William section without change. The class was also expected to handle freight trains, but this was not commonly seen. Coupled wheels were 75in (1905mm), the two cylinders were 22in X 30in (560mm X 760mm), and boiler pressure was 275psi (1894kPa), giving a tractive effort of 45,000lb (20,500kg), or 57,000lbs (25,900kg) with the booster in use. Engine weight was 366,000lb (166.2 tonnes) of which 186,700lb (84.8 tonnes) was on the driving wheels. The grate area was 80.8sq.ft. (7.5sq.metre) and the superheater was of 1,640sq.ft. (152.3sq.metre).

Units of both sub-classes remained in service right up to the end of steam traction, and the fast Montreal-Quebec trains were among their duties. The Royal Hudsons had long lost their elongated chimney casings, to nobody's regret. Not all were scrapped, and one of them sees regular service on excursion service over the British Columbia Railway.

## FRENCH RAILWAYS 232S CLASS/1940/FRANCE

On the eve of World War 2, French designers embarked on a quite expensive comparison of simple and compound locomotives. The need to evolve a completely new generation of locomotives was the ostensible reason for this project. It consisted of the construction of eight streamlined 4-6-4 locomotives. Four of these (232R Class) were to be three-cylinder single-expansion machines and four (232S) were to be 4-cylinder compounds. The war (and the feeling that the simples were not going to be as good) meant that only three of the 232R series were actually built. Quite extensive trials over a long period indicated that the compounds were about 10 per cent more efficient than the simples (unnervingly, perhaps, they showed also that the compounds were themselves 10 per cent inferior to the Chapelon Pacifics, but this was ascribed to the particular form of poppet valves with which they were fitted). All eight locomotives (the eighth was 232U1, built after the war as a compound) put in good work on Paris-Lille passenger services for some years. Dimensions of the 232S Class were: coupled wheels 78½in (2000mm); diameter of high-pressure cylinders 18in (457mm), of low-pressure cylinders 26¾in (680mm), stroke of cylinders 27½in (700mm), boiler pressure 285psi (1961kPa), grate area 55.9sq.ft. (5.2sq.metre), tractive effort 41,189lb (18,700kg), engine weight 288,193lb (130.7 tonnes).

## CHESAPEAKE & OHIO L1 CLASS/1946/USA

The L1 class Hudsons began life as the F19 Pacifics built in 1926 and were among the last locomotives built at the Richmond Locomotive Works in Virginia (part of the Alco company). When World War 2 finished the C & O

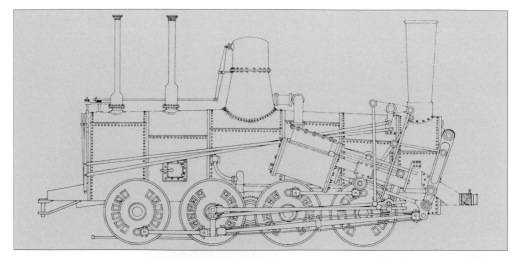

0-8-0 Camden & Amboy RR The Monster , 1834

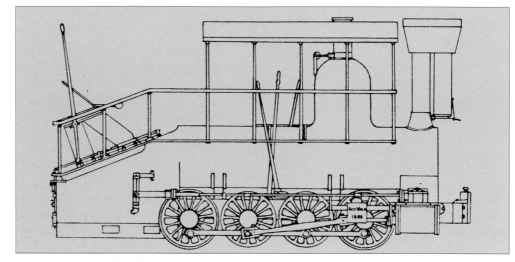

0-8-0  Baltimore & Ohio RR Camel Class , 1848

management foresaw a return to the pre-war days and took these Pacifics in hand in order to produce fast locomotives capable of hauling the stainless-steel 'Chessie' train that it was planning to introduce. Four of the five class-members were given a streamlined shroud, also in stainless-steel. They were almost new locomotives, having rebuilt boilers, new frames, as well as refinements like poppet valves and roller bearings on all axles. But the project was overtaken by events. The 'Chessie' never took off. The locomotives were found work between Charlottesville and the east but did not survive long, all being retired by 1955. Later, to commemorate the streamline era, one locomotive and some stainless-steel stock was reformed as a train for exhibition purposes at the Baltimore railroad museum.

Despite their high-speed goals, these locomotives had

driving wheels of a moderate 72in and their boiler pressure was also moderate at 210psi. Cylinders were 27in x 28in (686mm x 711mm), producing a rated tractive effort of 49,200lb (22,336kg) which a boiler could raise up 61,200lb (27,784kg) at lower speeds. The grate area was 80.7sq. ft. (7.5 sq. metre) and there was a superheater of 2,001sq. ft. (185.9sq. metre). The weight was 388,700lb (176 tonnes).

### VICTORIAN RAILWAYS R CLASS/1951/AUSTRALIA

These very competent locomotives arrived in Australia from their builders (North British) just as VR was entering the diesel era. Their life on the intended duty of hauling the most important passenger trains was therefore short-lived. They were designed to replace 4-6-0 engines which had hitherto handled the best trains and were proving both old and inadequate. The R Class was a much bigger design, weighing 420,493lb (190.7 tonnes) and with a tractive effort of 31,648lb (14,368kg). Boiler pressure was 210psi (1446kPa) and the grate area 42sq.ft. (3.9sq.metre). The two cylinders were 21¼in x 28in (540mm x 710mm). The gauge was 5ft 3in (1600mm). Several of these locomotives have survived, and can occasionally be seen on excursion trains in the State.

# EIGHT-COUPLED LOCOMOTIVES

## 0-8-0

### WYLAM DILLY/1813/GREAT BRITAIN

The use of eight coupled wheels covers a long span of locomotive history, with the first being built in 1813 and the last in 1953. The first was the Wylam Dilly, built for

Wm. Hedley for use at the Wylam Colliery: the drive from the vertical cylinders was taken via a jackshaft to the four axles by means of cog or gear-wheels. The single-flue boiler generated steam at 50psi (345kPa), and drove through two cylinders each having a 9in (228mm) bore and a 36in (914mm) stroke. The Wylam Dilly was not withdrawn until 1864, and is now on view at the Royal Scottish Museum in Edinburgh.

### THE MONSTER/1834/USA

The next known example of the 0-8-0 category was built in 1834 by Isaac Dripps for the Camden and Amboy Railroad. This locomotive had a boiler designed to burn cheap fine anthracite and had the cylinders mounted on the boiler. The cylinders measured 18in x 30in (457mm x 762mm) and drove 48in (1219mm) wheels; steam pressure was about 50psi (345kPa) and so the tractive force would have been about 8,600lb (3,900kg). The pistons drove through a long stayed connecting rod, and the front wheels were connected to the others by gears in order to allow some side movement. There was a combustion chamber to enable the fuel to be thoroughly burnt before entering the firetubes. With a weight of 60,858lb (27.6 tonnes), this machine was named The Monster and lasted until 1869, when it was rebuilt as a 4-6-0. Three more of the same type were produced from the Trenton Locomotive works in 1853.

### BALTIMORE AND OHIO 'CAMEL' CLASS/1848/USA

The first 0-8-0s to be produced in any quantity were the 'Camel' type built by Ross Winans which went into service on the Baltimore and Ohio Railroad in 1848; interestingly, they had the driver's cab on the top of the boiler. They were widely adopted, and over 200 were built.

The Baldwin Locomotive Company were also early producers of the 0-8-0 type, building about 150 of them, the first of which went to the Pennsylvania and Reading Railroad.

### CHEMIN DE FER DU NORD S4000/1854/FRANCE

The first true 0-8-0 to be built in Europe was the Vindobona, one of the competitors in the Semmering Trials of 1851, but that was in reality a tank engine. As a result of those trials, however, a successful design of engine was evolved by Wilhelm Engerth, and in 1854 the first of 40 of Class S4000 was delivered to the Nord. These were built by Schneider et Cie at Le Creusot; a further 195 of an enlarged version were built by Graffenstaden for the Est and the PLM. With cylinders measuring 21in x 26in (540mm x 660mm) and a steam pressure of 145psi (1000kPa) driving wheels of diameter 49⅔in (1260mm), they gave a tractive force of 29,300lb (13,290kg) and could haul trains of 1,175 long tons (1,194 tonnes) at

*0-8-0 Spanish Railways 040 2301 Series, 1889*

19mph (30.6kph) and take 307 long tons (312 tonnes) up a grade of 1 in 100 (1 per cent). The locomotive's weight was 138,474lb (62.8 tonnes), all of which was available for adhesion.

## VIENNA-RAAB S.35/1855/AUSTRIA

In 1855 John Haswell, who had designed one of the locomotives for the Semmering Trials of 1851, produced the first of an 0-8-0 type for the Vienna-Raab Railway (later incorporated into the Austrian Southern system). This locomotive was similar to the Bourbonnais 0-6-0 type, with cylinders at 18in x 25in (457mm x 635mm) and a steam pressure of 100psi (690kPa) driving 47in (1194mm) wheels giving a tractive force of 14,600lb (6,623kg). The boiler had 933sq.ft. (86.7sq.metre) of heating area and the firegrate area was 13sq.ft. (1.2sq.metre). With a weight of 76,623lb (34.75 tonnes), the locomotives' haulage capacity was for 112 long tons (113.8 tonnes) up a grade of 1 in 40 (2.5 per cent) at 12mph (19.3kph), entailing a dbhp of about 270hp (201kW). First built were 23 for use in Austria, followed by many more for Italy, where there were still over 300 in use in 1905. The Austrian classification was Series 35.

## MADRID ZARAGOZA ALICANTE RAILWAY (RENFE 040 2301 SERIES)/1889/SPAIN

The old-established Glasgow firm of Sharp, Stewart, later to become part of North British Locomotive, sold two classes of 0-8-0 to the forerunner of the MZA. At that time such locomotives ranked as heavy freight machines, and that was the purpose for which they were bought. The first series were delivered from 1878, and the second in 1889. This second series, of eight locomotives, was later numbered 040 2301-08 by Spanish National Railways (RENFE). They were like the earlier batch but had smaller

wheels and could be distinguished by the sandbox behind their chimney. Their coupled wheels were 51in (1293mm), cylinders 20in x 26in (508mm x 660mm), and if their safety valves were set at 170lb (1175kPa) the tractive effort would have been 29,364lb (13,331KG). They had Stephenson valve gear inside the frames, and their weight was 160,965lb (73 tonnes). Thanks to Spanish politics (and the economics those politics brought) these locomotives, like so many other Spanish classes, remained in service decades longer than might have been expected.

## LNWR G CLASS/1893/GREAT BRITAIN

The first 0-8-0 locomotive to be built in Britain after the Wylam Dilly was a two-cylinder simple type built at Crewe by the LNWR in 1892. That was followed by F. Webb's three-cylinder compound version, having two high-pressure cylinders of dimensions 15in x 24in (381mm x 610mm) and one low-pressure cylinder measuring 30in x 24in (762mm x 610mm). This design proved to be the most succesful of all Webb's three-cylinder compound engines: between 1893 and 1900 a total of 110 were built.

These were followed by a four-cylinder compound type with high-pressure cylinders at 15in x 24in (381mm x 610mm) and low-pressure ones at 20½in x 24in (520mm x 610mm). Of that type 170 were built between 1901 and 1904; however, following Webb's retirement, his successor, George Whale, rebuilt them all as simple engines and fitted with larger cylinders - all at 20½in x 24in (520mm x 610mm) - and with larger boilers operating at 160psi (1104kPa) steam pressure. All of these - a total of 449 locomotives - were classified G1. In 1921-22 a further 60 were built which operated at a steam pressure of 175psi

*0-8-0 LNWR G Class, 1893*

*0-8-0 Russian O Class, 1901*

*0-8-0 Prussian G8 Class, 1912*

(1207kPa) and the final lot of 175, with steam at 200psi (1380kPa) were built in 1929-32, making a total of 684 in all. Class G1 were rated as 6F and the others as 7F: tractive forces were 25,640lb (11,630kg) and 32,000lb (14,515kg) respectively.

One model, No.49395 (LNWR No 485), the first of the G.2 class, was preserved.

## NORTH EASTERN T CLASSES (LNER Q5, Q6, Q7)/1900/GREAT BRITAIN

In 1900 the North Eastern Railway introduced the first of its 0-8-0 types with the classification T1. Designed by William Worsdell, it had two outside cylinders measuring 20in x 26in (508mm x 660mm) and, with steam at 175psi, (1207kPa) it drove 55in (1397mm) diameter wheels, giving a tractive force of 28,000lb (12,700kg) on a weight of 130,756lb (59.3 tonnes). The firegrate area was 21.5sq.ft.(2m2) and the heating surface area was 1,675sq.ft. (155.7sq.metre). They could handle trains of up to 1,300-long-tons (1,321 tonnes); by 1911 there were 90 of them in service. Of these 70 lasted until British

*0-8-0 Austrian 399 Class, 1906*

Railways days in 1948. although all were scrapped by 1951.

They were followed by the 120 locomotives of Class T2, designed by Vincent Raven and built between 1913 and 1921. With a slightly higher steam pressure of 180psi (1241kPa) they gave a tractive force of 28,800lb (13,064kg) on a weight of 147,735lb (67 tonnes). Some lasted until 1967, and No.63395 has been preserved as NER No.2238 at the North Yorkshire Moors Railway.

The ultimate in North Eastern 0-8-0 engines were the five of class T3, reputed to have been the most powerful in Britain. With three cylinders at 18½in x 26in (470mm x 660mm) and a steam pressure of 180psi (1241kPa) they gave a tractive force of 37,000lb (16,783kg). With a grate area of 26.7sqft (2.48sq.metre) and a heating area of 2,427sq.ft. (225.7sq.metre), they could handle 1,400-long ton (1,422-tonne) trains and gave a measured output of 840dbhp (626kW).

Following the amalgamation in 1923, a further 10 were built by the LNER, and the three North Eastern types were reclassified Q5, Q6 and Q7. These were all withdrawn by 1962, but the original No.63460 (NER No.901) has been preserved at the North Yorkshire Moors Railway..

## RUSSIAN STATE RAILWAYS
## O CLASS/1901/RUSSIA

In late tsarist Russia some railways belonged to the state and others to private companies, but for military as well as economic reasons it was thought desirable to standardize their locomotive stock. In this respect the O class freight locomotive succeeded gloriously, over 8,000

being built and finding their way to both state and private railways. There were sub-classes, depending mainly on the type of valve gear and whether they were simple or compound (the original design was for 2 cylinder cross-compounds, and most remained that way, but some were simple, and the compounds could be either superheated or unsuperheated). They were built by seven locomotive works between 1901 and 1909. They were intended mainly for heavy freight but since passenger trains were slow, they were operated as general-purpose locomotives.

They had a speed limit of 34mph (55kph); the absence of carrying axles and the propensity of cross-compounds to 'waddle' were the probable reasons for this rather slow speed. The cylinders were 19½in x 25½in (500mm x 650mm) and 29in x 25½in (730mm x 650mm), the wheels 48in (1200mm), and the grate area 19.9sq.ft. (1.85sq.metre). The boiler pressure was 171psi (1173kPa). Tractive effort was 26,000lb (11,800kg), and the engines weighed 110.070lb (54 tonnes). They were ousted from mainline duty by the even more numerous 0-10-0s and

*0-8-0 North Eastern T Class, 1900*

the last survivors were withdrawn in the 1960s, although some went to industrial railways. About 25 have been preserved in various parts of the old Soviet Union.

### AUSTRIAN FEDERAL RAILWAYS CLASS 399/1906/AUSTRIA

A handful of these narrow-gauge locomotives still operate occasionally on the Waldviertalbahn in northern Austria. They are of modified 'Engerth' type. That is, they are actually articulated locomotives, in the sense that the tender embraces the locomotive by means of sliding-arm attachments, enabling part of the weight of the tender to be transferred to the coupled wheels of the locomotive, thereby increasing adhesion weight. Athough the locomotives can be described as 0-8-0 type, purists describe them as 0-8-4s. They were built by Krauss (Linz) and have 16¹⁄₁₀in x 17⁷⁄₁₀in (410mm x 450mm) cylinders, 35½in (900mm) coupled wheels, 185psi (1274kPa) boiler pressure, and a tractive effort of 20,312lb (9,222kg). Their speed limit is 25mph (40kph) which together with their 92,225lb (45 tonnes) weight ensures that they are easy on the track. Grate area is 17.2sq.ft. (1.6sq m).

### PRUSSIAN STATE RAILWAY CLASS G8/1912/GERMANY

In 1912, as part of their standardization policy, the Prussian State Railway decided on an 0-8-0 locomotive

*0-8-0 Prussian G8 Class , 1912*

*2-8-0 Great Western 2800 Class , 1903*

*2-8-0 Great Central 8K (LNER 04) Class, 1911*

for freight service: it was classified Group G8. These engines were equipped with two cylinders measuring 23⅔in x 26in (600mm x 660mm) and with driving wheels of diameter 53in (1350mm); the superheated steam was supplied at 203psi (1400kPa) from a boiler with 1,959sq.ft. (182sq.metre) of heating area and with a grate area of 28sq.ft. (2.6sq.metre). The weight was 149,940lb (68 tonnes) and the tractive force amounted to 46,400lb (21,047kg), so that the power output must have been about 850dbhp (634kW) or 1100ihp (820kW). A total of 5,260 of these engines were built up to 1921, and some were in use in the Balkans in the 1970s.

## USRA STANDARD LOCOMOTIVES/1919/USA

In the United States during World War 1 the Railroad Administration decided on a policy of standardization of 12 locomotive types. Out of the 1,800 locomotives built during the implementation of this programme 175 were of the 0-8-0 type, almost the last of that type to be built in the United States.

Fitted with two cylinders measuring 25in x 28in (635mm x 711mm) and with valves operated by Baker valve gear, their driving wheels were of diameter 51in (1295mm) and, with a steam pressure of 175psi (1207kPa), they gave a tractive force of 51,000lb (23,134kg) from a total weight of 214,105lb (97.1 tonnes).

A similar version was supplied to the Chesapeake and Ohio Railroad. The boiler pressure of these was 200psi (1380kPa) and the weight was higher, too, at 243,873lb (110.6 tonnes). Tractive force was 57,000lb (25,855kg).

In the United States the 0-8-0 type was used for yard work; the last US steam locomotive to be built (in 1953) was an 0-8-0 for the Norfolk and Western Railroad to the design of the Chesapeake & Ohio type.

# 2-8-0

## PENNSYLVANIA RAILROAD CLASS R/1885/USA

The 2-8-0 locomotive was the major workhorse of freight traffic just as the 4-4-0 was in terms of passenger traffic. The first was produced in 1866 for the Lehigh and Mahoning line, which was in the process of being consolidated with the Lehigh Valley Railroad - hence the name 'Consolidation' which was ascribed to the wheel arrangement. This was followed by some for New Mexico in 1879, and in 1885 the Baldwin Locomotive Works built a 114,219lb (51.8-tonne) version for the Pennsylvania Railroad. These locomotives, Class R, had two cylinders at 20in x 24in (508mm x 610mm) driving 50in (1270mm) diameter wheels. Steam was at 140psi (965kPa) from a boiler with 1,730sq.ft. (160.9sq.metre) heating area and a grate area of 31sq.ft. (2.88sq.metre). That would have given a tractive force of 22,800lb (10,342kg), with an adhesive weight of 102,600lb (45.6 tonnes).

The 2-8-0 was to prove so popular in the United States that eventually over 21,000 were built for domestic use and a further 12,000 or so for export. They were equally effective on the other side of the Atlantic: about 2,200

were built in Britain and about the same number in mainland Europe.

## GREAT WESTERN CLASS 2800/1903/GREAT BRITAIN

Construction of the 2-8-0 type in Britain lagged behind that in the United States and in Europe, but in 1903 the Great Western built the first of its 2800 class - of which 167 were to be built, right up to 1942. During the fuel crisis of 1946, 20 of them were converted to oil-firing for three years, but they were then converted back to coal-burning.

With two outside cylinders at 18½in x 30in (470mm x 760mm), locomotives of this class used the standard GWR No 1 boiler with steam at 225psi (1551kPa); the boiler had 2,142sq.ft. (199sq.metre) of heating area and a firegrate area of 27.1sq.ft. (2.5sq.metre). With a wheel diameter of 55in (1397mm), the tractive force came to 35,000lb (15,876kg) and their potential power output would have been around 1,000dbhp (746kW).

The lifespan of the older units was over 55 years: scrapping began in 1958, and all had been withdrawn by 1966. Eight have been preserved.

## GREAT CENTRAL RAILWAY CLASS 8K (LNER CLASS 04)/1911/GREAT BRITAIN

Following the successful operation of the 2800 class on the Great Western Railway, the GCR built itself a class of 2-8-0s in 1911. These had two outside cylinders measuring 21in x 26in (533mm x 660mm) and driving 56in (1422mm) diameter wheels with a steam pressure

*2-8-0 Italian Railways 735 Class, 1917*

*2-8-0 Italian Railways 743 Class, 1911. The 743 Class was like the 741 Class, but with two Franco-Crosti drums instead of one.*

*2-8-0 Pennsylvania Railroad H10s Class , 1913*

of 180psi (1241kPa), giving a tractive force of 31,300lb (14,198kg). Known as Class 8K on the Great Central code, there were 130 of these built up to 1920; after absorption into the LNER the locomotives were given the classification 04.

This type also served in France during World War 1. Some of the War Department units later found their way to the LNER and some were sold to the GWR. Others ended up in faraway places, including the New South Wales coalfield.

Withdrawals began in 1959 and were completed by 1965. One has been preserved in Britain, and one in Australia.

## ITALIAN STATE RAILWAYS 735, 740, and 741 CLASSES/1911/ITALY

Italian steam locomotive construction ceased in the early 1920s, and the last locomotives were designed before World War 1, at which time their designers' minds were somewhere in the 19th century. It was perhaps fortunate that the most numerous type of locomotive built in the final decade of steam construction was the 2-8-0, which was

*2-8-0 Pennsylvania Railroad H9s Class , 1913*

*2-8-0 Great Western 4700 CLASS , 1919*

never expected to put up sparkling performances but simply to potter around doing odd jobs. The 740 Class was introduced in 1911 and was a superheated version of an earlier 2-8-0. No fewer than 470 were built. Not only this, but almost 400 units of identical specification were ordered from US builders. But although the specification was the same, design and construction of this 735 Class was American, and the type was blessed by Italian locomotive depot workers. Finally, the 741 Class appeared. This was the 740 Class rebuilt with the Franco-Crosti boiler, in which exhaust steam (and smoke) was not ejected through a chimney but passed through a water drum below the boiler where it heated the feed-water before being exhausted towards the rear of the locomotive. This did result in a fuel saving, quite important for Italy, which had to import its coal. These three classes had in common the cylinder dimensions 21¼in x 27½in (540mm x 700mm), the boiler pressure 170psi (1171kPa) and driving wheel diameter 54in (1370mm). They all had a 30.1sq.ft. (2.8sq.metre) grate area and a 40mph (65kph) speed limit. Weights varied between classes, with the 740 being 146,632lb (66.5 tonnes).

## PENNSYLVANIA RAILROAD CLASS H10s/1913/USA

The H10s was the last of the PRR's 2-8-0 designs. Two hundred and seventy-three were built new by four builders and another 200 were obtained by rebuilding the older H8 type. They were the last 2-8-0s to remain in PRR service,

the last being withdrawn as late as 1960. Between the H8 and H10 came the H9s, which was simply a superheated version of the H8 with cylinders one inch (2.54cm) wider than the latter's. (The H8 was built in several sub-classes, totalling almost 700 units). There was thus considerable similarity between these three classes. They all had boilers working at 205psi (1412kPa) with grate area of 55.2sq.ft. (5.12sq.metre), and driving wheels of 62in (1575mm). Cylinder stroke was also the same at 28in (710mm), but cylinder diameter increased at one-inch intervals, from 24in in the H8, 25in in the H9s to 26in in the H10s (610mm, 635mm and 660mm). The latter weighed 247,500lb (112 tonnes) and had a tractive effort of 52,204lb (23,700kg). It was superheater-fitted (the boiler was the same as that of the Atlantics). One of the H10s series is exhibited by the Pennsylvania Railroad Museum.

## SOMERSET & DORSET JOINT RAILWAY 2-8-0/1914/BRITAIN

Britain's Midland Railway had a 'small engine policy,' generally confining itself to the designing and building of successive generations of inside-cylinder 4-4-0 and 0-6-0 locomotives. But on two occasions its designers found themselves originating bigger locomotives. One was the 0-10-0 'Lickey Banker,' and the other was when the Somerset & Dorset joint Railway, for which the Midland provided motive power, needed something more powerful. That railway, connecting Bath and Bournemouth over the Mendips, was a single-track, hilly route which had heavy trains in the peak season. The Midland designers therefore

drew out a 2-8-0 design, of which eleven were subsequently built (and of which two found retirement in preservation). They had large outside cylinders, 21in x 28in (533mm x 710mm), and the coupled wheels were 56in. (1422mm). There was a quite large grate of 28.4sq.ft. (2.64sq.metre) and boiler pressure was 190psi ((1309kPa). The axle-weight was only 35,840lb (16.2 tonnes), the engine itself weighing 153,440lb (69.6 tonnes). Tractive effort was 35,392lb (16,067kg). These locomotives did well, and lasted longer than their railway, which was one of the victims of the line-closure epidemic that began in the 1960s.

## GREAT WESTERN RAILWAY 4700 CLASS/1919/BRITAIN

This small class of nine units was the last of the celebrated engineer G.J.Churchward's contributions to GWR locomotive types. It was designed specifically for the fastest freight trains. As these ran during the night from London to the big cities on the GWR the class was rarely seen, still less photographed, in action. A change came very late in the lives of these locomotives, when the operators decided to use them for long-distance passenger trains at peak periods. In this service they proved how versatile they were, and it was often said that this was a design that deserved series production because it was too good to be restricted to a limited class of traffic. Possibly, if Churchward had not retired, this is what would have happened.

*2-8-0 Somerset & Dorset type , 1914*

These locomotives were provided with a mixed-traffic size of wheel, 68in (1727mm), and the boiler was the biggest on the GWR, apart from that of the later 'King' class. They had a grate area of 30.28sq. ft.(2.81sq. metre) and a pressure of 225psi (1550kPa). There were two quite large cylinders, 19in x 30in (480mm x 762mm), so the tractive effort at 85% pressure was 30,460lb (13,828kg).

## LNER CLASS 02/1921/GREAT BRITAIN

Derived from a class of 20 2-8-0 freight locomotives built by the Great Northern Railway between 1913 and 1918, the first Gresley three-cylinder locomotive fitted with his arrangement of conjugated valve gear was No.461, built as a 2-8-0 in 1918. From this beginning a further 66, with an improved design of valve gear, were then constructed between 1921 and 1934. Carrying the LNER classification 02, these used 56in (1422mm) driving wheels. The three cylinders, measuring 18½in x 26in (470mm x 660mm), were fed with steam at 180psi (1241kPa) from a boiler with 2,492sq.ft. (231.7sq.metre) of heating area and with a firegrate area of 27.5sq.ft. (2.5sq.metre). Giving a tractive force of 36,500lb (16,556kg), they proved 10 per cent more economical than the two-cylinder type in handling freight trains of 1,300 long tons (1,321 tonnes).

Ten were built by the North British Locomotive Company of Glasgow; later models were fitted with an improved cab, which had side-windows. All of them lasted into the British Railways era, being withdrawn between 1960 and 1963.

American steam tourist railroads found the moderately-sized 2-8-0 type ideal for their operations , so many examples have been preserved. The locomotive in the top picture once hauled ore trains by the Great Lakes , but now works for the Grand Canyon Railroad. No 604 in the lower picture hauls passengers at the North Carolina Transportation Museum , but once worked for the Buffalo Creek & Gauley RR.

## LEHIGH AND NEW ENGLAND CLASS 300/1922/USA

The ultimate US locomotives in the 'Consolidation' category were these built for the Lehigh and New England Railroad in 1922 by Alco. The Lehigh Class 300 was fitted with two 27in x 32in (686mm x 813mm) cylinders, and the large high-pitched boiler produced super-heated steam at 210psi (1448kPa) from 4,567sq.ft. (424sq.metre) of heating area; the firegrate area was 84.3sq.ft. (7.8sq.metre). The tractive force from the 61in (1549mm) diameter driving wheels amounted to 68,200lb (30,936kg). The engine weight was 300,762lb (136.4 tonnes), of which 259,530lb (126.6 tonnes) were available for adhesion.

## LMSR CLASS 8F/1935/GREAT BRITAIN

Following the introduction of the 5P5F 'Black Fives' on the London Midland and Scottish Railway in 1934, the requirement for a more powerful freight engine led to the building in 1935 of a locomotive which was similar but with the 2-8-0 wheel arrangement. Known as Class 8F, these were equipped with two outside cylinders measuring 18½in x 28in (470mm x 710mm) driving 56in (1422mm) diameter wheels. The boiler was the same as that for the 5P5F locomotive and, with steam at 225psi (1551kPa), the tractive force was 32,600lb (14,787kg). With a maximum axle-load of 37,044lb (16.8 tonnes), the total engine weight was 161,185lb (73.1 tonnes), of which 141,120lb (64 tonnes) were available for adhesion. Only 12 of these locomotives appeared in the first year, but production soon increased rapidly until, by 1944, 651 had been built by the LMS and a further 85 by other builders. Many were to find duty overseas during World War 2, and 150 were still in service in 1968 when steam operations ceased in Britain. Four have been preserved.

*2-8-0 LMS 8F , 1935*

## US TRANSPORTATION CORPS CONSOLIDATION/1942/USA

Almost the last of the American-built 2-8-0 type were the 390 built from 1942 by Alco and the Baldwin Locomotive Co. for the US War Department for use overseas. With 19in x 26in (483mm x 660mm) cylinders and a steam pressure of 225psi (1551kPa), they drove 57in (1448mm) wheels to give a tractive force of 31,500lb (14,288kg). The boiler had a grate area of 41sq.ft. (3.8sq.metre) and 2,251sq.ft. (209sq.metre) of heating area. As these locomotives were built for use on non-American tracks, their weight was kept down to 162,508lb (73.7 tonnes). Some were used in Britain before being shipped for war service in the European campaign. After the war, many were acquired by power-short railways, including those of Russia, India and Poland. In Britain, one is preserved on the Keighley & Worth Valley Railway.

*2-8-0 Us Transportation Corps Consolidation of 1944. This example is shown in post-war Polish ownership , and fitted with chimney extension for improved draught*

*2-8-0 LMS 8F , 1935*

## WAR DEPARTMENT 'AUSTERITY' CLASS/1944/GREAT BRITAIN

The most numerous class of locomotives built in Britain was the 'Austerity' 2-8-0 type, of which 935 were constructed in 1944 by the North British Locomotive Co. and the Vulcan Foundry Co. for use in Europe after the invasion. Based on the LMSR 8F (see above), they were fitted with two outside cylinders measuring 19in x 28in (483mm x 711mm) and, with steam at 225psi·(1551kPa), they gave a tractive force of 34,500lb (15,649kg) from 56in (1422mm) diameter wheels; the boiler had 2,158sq.ft. (200sq.metre) of heating surface and a firegrate area of 28.6sq.ft. (2.66sq.metre). Their total weight was 157,437lb (71.4 tonnes), of which 137,151lb (62.2 tonnes) were available for adhesion.

Before being transferred to work in Europe, 450 of the 'Austerity' class were put to use in Britain, and after the war 733 were returned to operate under British Railways as Nos.90000-90732. All were withdrawn between 1959 and 1967 and destroyed; however, one (Vulcan Foundry No.5200) has been returned from Sweden and is at the Keighley and Worth Valley Railway

## BELGIAN NATIONAL RAILWAYS CLASS 29/1945/BELGIUM

Belgian State Railways (SNCB) received 300 of these locomotives from Canadian and US builders after World War 2. They had been designed for service in war-devastated countries where the existing US Army 2-8-0 was too small for requirements. Besides the Belgian units, others were sent to Mexico and also to China under the auspices of the United Nations Relief and Rehabilitation Administration (UNRRA). The Belgian units were distinguished by smoke deflectors. They put in good work in Belgium, in all kinds of service, and in 1966 the last SNCB regular steam train was hauled by one of them, No.29.013 (which was subsequently preserved).

Design details were typically American. The large gap between the third and fourth coupled axles was a recognition point. The design provided 60in (1524mm) coupled wheels, a boiler pressure of 225psi (1550kPa), two cylinders 22in x 28in (560mm x 710mm), and a grate area of 47.5sq.ft. (4.41sq.metre). Weight in working order was 205,200lbs (93,000kgs), of which 172,000lbs (78,000kgs) were available for adhesion. Tractive effort was 43,300lbs (19,650kgs).

## VULCAN FOUNDRY LIBERATION CLASS/1946/EASTERN EUROPE

Known as the 'Liberation' class and ordered by the United Nations Relief and Rehabilitation Agency (UNRRA) for use in Yugoslavia, Poland and in Czechoslovakia, 120 locomotives were built by the Vulcan Foundry at Newton-

*2-8-0 Belgian Railways Class 29, 1945*

*Like all big North American railways , the Canadian Pacific acquired a substantial number of 2-8-0s , with successive classes from a variety of builders appearing from 1901 to 1921. Coupled wheels varied from 57in to 63in. Built mainly for freight , they did also appear on passenger trains and in their later years were the mainstay of branch lines. The picture shows one of the last survivors switching passenger cars at Montreal*

*2-8-0 Bolivian Railways Andes type , 1948. This was a rare case of a US design , British-built*

le-Willows in Lancashire from 1946. They were of the two-cylinder design, with a bore and stroke of 21²⁄₃in x 28in (550mm x 710mm), driving wheels of 57in (1450mm) diameter and using steam at a pressure of 225psi (1551kPa). The boiler had 2,928sq.ft. (272sq.metre) of heating surface and a firegrate of area 44sq.ft. (4.1sq.metre). With an adhesive weight of 164,713lb (74.7 tonnes), the tractive force amounted to 44,200lb (20,049kg) and the total engine weight came to 189,189lb (85.8 tonnes). The layout was designed especially to obviate unnecessary difficulties in repairs and maintenance in Europe in the immediate aftermath of the war; for example, most parts were manufactured to metric rather than Imperial specifications. These locomotives were noted for their steaming ability and for their economical coal consumption.

## GUAQUI - LA PAZ RAILWAY 'ANDES' TYPE/1948/BOLIVIA

Later units of the 'Andes' type are interesting because they were built in Britain, although the design was American. This type was adopted for several of the American-built 3ft-gauge lines in South America, early examples being supplied by Alco. Subsequently others were ordered in ones and twos, sometimes from British locomotive builders. The last, so far as Bolivia was concerned, were Nos.9 and 10, built by Hunslet of Leeds in 1948 and 1955. These locomotives and their elder sisters were designed for the metre-gauge line connecting the capital La Paz with Guaqui on Lake Titicaca, although the climb out of La Paz was entrusted to electric traction. Being of US design, the locomotives used bar frames. The rigid wheelbase was 13ft 6in,(4.2m) this minimal length being obtainable because the driving wheels were only 46in (1168mm) in diameter. Grate area was 15.9sq.ft.

(1.47sq.metre), the tube heating surface was 818sq.ft. (76sq.metre) and the firebox heating surface was 93sq.ft. (7.7sq.metre), making a total of 911sq.ft. (77.7sq.metre), with a 183sq.ft. (17sq.metre) superheater in addition. Boiler pressure was 180psi (1240kPa), which at 85per cent pressure produced a tractive effort of 20,435lbs (9,277kgs). The weight of the locomotive in working order was 105,952lb (48 tonnes), of which 90,272lb (40.9 tonnes) was available for adhesion. (These dimensions apply to the inter-war units; the other units were identical or very similar).

# 2-8-2

### NORTHERN PACIFIC 1500 CLASS/1905/USA

The name Mikado given to this wheel arrangement refers to some 42in (1067mm) gauge locomotives built for the Japanese Government Railway by the Baldwin Locomotive Co. in 1897. These were followed in 1903 by some with a similar wheel arrangement made for the Bismark, Washburn and Great Falls Railroad. With a large firebox which could be accommodated over the trailing truck, the Mikado was to prove the most versatile of the American freight engines: by 1930 more than 14,000 had come into service.

The first of the true heavy-freight type were those built by Alco for the Northern Pacific Railroad in 1905. These had 24in x 30in (610mm x 762mm) cylinders driving 63in (1600mm) wheels and fed with saturated steam at 200psi (1380kPa) from a boiler with 4,007sq.ft. (372sq.metre) of heating surface and a firegrate of area 43.5sq.ft. (4sq.metre). Their tractive effort amounted to 46,600lb (21,138kg), with a total weight of 262,975lb (117.4 tonnes).

These Class 1500 locomotives proved to be so much more effective than the previous 2-8-0 types that by 1910 a further 150 had been supplied. Many of the 2-8-0 type were later converted to the 2-8-2 wheel arrangement and fitted with a boiler which supplied superheated steam.

### PENNSYLVANIA RAILROAD CLASS L1S/1914/USA

The first of the 2-8-2 category to be given an official test was Class L1S of the Pennsylvania Railroad. One of these was tested on its Altoona test plant in 1914. The maximum boiler output was 58,000lb (26,309kg) of steam per hour, resulting in a power output of 2,800ihp (2,088kW) at 29mph (46.7kph) with a steam temperature of 580%F (304%C) and a boiler efficiency of 45 per cent. The coal consumption at that output was 4.2 pounds per ihp-hr. (2.55kg/kW-hr), representing an overall efficiency of 5.1 per cent. The highest efficiency output was recorded at 18mph (29kph), when the steam rate amounted to 38,000lb (17,237kg) per hour and the power output to 2,000ihp (1,491kW) The overall efficiency at that rate was 8.4 per cent; the coal-consumption rate was 2.7 lb per ihp-hr (1.6kg/kW-hr).

### CANADIAN NATIONAL RAILWAYS S SERIES/1916/CANADA

This series was built by two Canadian locomotive companies between 1916 and 1924, the original purchaser being the Canadian Government Railways, which later became part of CNR. There were several sub-types, from the original S1a to the later S2c. All had 63in (1600mm) driving wheels and 27in x 30in (686mm x

*A light 2-8-2 built by Alco in 1920 and now hauling passenger trains on the Valley Railroad in Connecticut.*

*2-8-2 Canadian National S Series, 1916.*

762mm) cylinders, but boiler pressure varied from 175psi (1206kPa) to 185psi (1274kPa). Tractive effort of those with the higher boiler pressure was 54,500lb (24,743kg), and those which had a booster could call on an extra 10,670lb (4,844kg) when starting. Their grate area was 66.7sq.ft. (6.19sq.metre), and they had a mechanical stoker and a feedwater heater. They weighed 318,622lb (144.5 tonnes), and the loaded tender was 183,015lb (83 tonnes). As on other North American railroads, the 2-8-2 was a maid-of-all-work, and representatives of the class were active right up to the end of steam. A number have been preserved, including two at Steamtown in the USA and one at Delson (Quebec).

## PLM SERIES 141C (SNCF CLASS 141F)/1919/FRANCE

In France the PLM Railway was quick to appreciate the value of the 2-8-2 for both passenger and freight traffic, and in 1913 it purchased the first of its Series 1000 from the Swiss Locomotive Manufacturers at Winterthur. In France at that time the compound was much in favour, and this class was built with four cylinders, two with 20in (510mm) bore and two with 28⅓in (720mm) bore; the piston stroke also varied, being 25½in (650mm) for the high pressure and with 27½in (700mm) for the low pressure. With 65in (1650mm) driving wheels, the locomotives could run at up to 59mph (95kph), and proved so versatile that a total of 709 of them were commissioned, at first as classes 141C and 141D, but through successive rebuildings and modifications mostly ending their days as SNCF Class 141F. They used superheated steam at a pressure of 232psi (1600kPa) supplied from an ample boiler, which had 3,121sq.ft. (290sq.metre) of heating surface and a firegrate area of 46.3sq.ft. (4.3sq.metre). The tractive force was 51,000lb (23,134kg) and the

adhesive weight 153,247lb (69.5 tonnes) out of a total weight for the engine of 206,167lb (93.5 tonnes).

On test, a train-load of 2,037-long-tons (2,070 tonnes) was hauled at 24.9mph (40kph) on level track and one of 603 long tons (613 tonnes) up a grade of 1 in 100 (1 per cent) at the same speed, corresponding to an output of 1,320dbhp (984kW) or 1,770ihp (1,320kW).

## USRA LIGHT MIKADO/1919/USA

When 12 standard types of locomotive were commissioned under the US Railroad Administration plan, two of the types selected for building in quantity were of the 2-8-2 wheel arrangement. The lighter version had two cylinders measuring 26in x 30in (660mm x 762mm) with 63in (1600mm) driving wheels and steam supplied at 200psi (1380kPa). The tractive force was 54,700lb (24,812kg),

and the superheated steam was supplied from a boiler with 4,030sq.ft. (375sq.metre) of heating-surface area and with a firegrate area of 66.7sq.ft. (6.2sq.metre). The total locomotive weight was 291,942lb (132.4 tonnes), of which 220,059lb (99.8 tonnes) were available for adhesion. These locomotives were fitted with Walschaerts valve gear, and 625 of them were built.

## USRA HEAVY MIKADO/1919/USA

The heavy Mikado built under the US Railroad Administration plan gave a tractive force of 60,000lb (27,216kg) from cylinders measuring 27in x 32in (686mm x 813mm) using superheated steam at 190psi (1310kPa). The boiler's heating area was 4,564sq.ft. (424sq.metre), with a grate area of 70.8sq.ft. (6.6sq.metre). The total weight was 319,945lb (145.1 tonnes), with 239,022lb

*2-8-2 SNCF 141F Class, 1919.*

*2-8-2 USRA Light Mikado, 1919.*

*2-8-2 LNER P1 Class, 1925.*

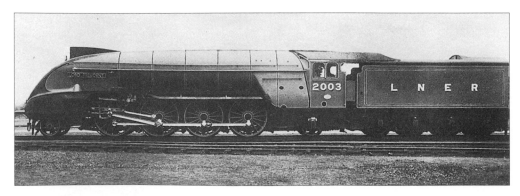

*2-8-2 LNER P2 Class, 1934.*

(108.4 tonnes) available for adhesion. All told, 233 locomotives of this type were built.

### LNER CLASS P1/1925/GREAT BRITAIN

In Britain only eight of the 2-8-2 style of tender locomotives were ever to be used. They were in two classes, both built by the London and North Eastern Railway: these classes were P1 and P2.

The two engines of Class P1 were built in 1925 - the first one, No. 2393, was exhibited at the 1925 Centenary Exhibition at Darlington. Equipped with the same boiler as that fitted to the A1 Pacifics, it also had three cylinders at 20in x 26in (508mm x 660mm) with 62in (1575mm) driving wheels. With a steam pressure of 180psi (1241kPa) the tractive force was 38,500lb (17,464kg), and trains of 1,600-long-tons (1,626 tonnes) could be hauled to convey coal to London. To assist in starting such trains a booster engine was fitted to the trailing axle; this could give an additional 4,200lb (1,905kg) of tractive effort. From 1941 these two engines were fitted with the A3 boiler, with steam at 220psi (1517kPa), so that their tractive capacity was increased to 42,500lb (19,278kg), but it was not really possible to make full use of that capability owing to the weak couplings on freight trucks at that time. The two Class P1 locomotives were withdrawn before 1948 and so were spared nationalization

### LNER CLASS P2/1934/GREAT BRITAIN

The later LNER Mikados were built for hauling 550-long-ton (559-tonne) trains between Edinburgh and Aberdeen and, like the Class P1, they were fitted with three cylinders:

*2-8-2 Japanese D 51 Class, 1936.*

these were 21in x 26in (533mm x 660mm). With steam at 220psi (1517kPa) and with driving wheels of diameter 62in (1575mm), the tractive force amounted to 43,500lb (19,732kg). The boiler had a firegrate area of 50sq.ft. (4.65sq.metre), and the heating-surface area amounted to 3,491sq.ft. (324sq.metre). The total weight was 245,960lb (112 tonnes), of which 180,589lb (81.9 tonnes) were available for adhesion. The first version, No.2001, Cock o' the North, was fitted with Lentz poppet valves and with a twin Kylchap exhaust system. The boiler was enclosed in a faired casing to deflect the steam clear of

the driver's cab. The second, No.2002, Earl Marischal, was fitted with Walschaerts valve gear and with a boiler similar to that of No 2001. The first one was taken to the locomotive-testing plant at Vitry-sur-Seine and, while it was in France, an output of 2,800dbhp (2,088kW) was recorded, although the highest that was achieved in Britain was 2,100dbhp (1,566kW) at 58mph (93.3kph). The other four engines of the class, Nos.2003-2006, were fitted with the streamlined A4 type of boiler and with Walschaerts valve gear.

Although capable of speeds up to 79mph (127.1kph) and of hauling trains of up to 650-long-tons (660.4 tonnes), these engines were disappointing in operation and suffered derailments in depots. They were later rebuilt as 4-6-2 engines and classified as A2/2.

## JAPANESE NATIONAL RAILWAYS D51 CLASS/1936/JAPAN

In the 1930s Japanese National Railways were building large numbers of new standard designs, with the participation of several locomotive building companies. They were of 3ft 6in (1067mm) gauge, but dimensionally were no smaller than corresponding European locomotives. The D51 was classed as a freight locomotive but could be used for passenger work; as originally built it had a smart 'skyline' casing that enclosed chimney, steam-dome, feedwater heater, and sandbox. It also had a speedometer working from the rear carrying wheels. Cylinders were 21¾in x 26in (550mm x 660mm), driving wheels 55⅛in (1400mm), boiler pressure 200psi (1378kPa), giving a tractive effort of 24,310lb (11,036kg). Grate area was 36sq.ft. (3.34sq.metre). Between 1936 and 1945, 1,115 were produced. Some of them, working on the island of Sakhalin, were taken into Soviet Railways stock after World War 2 and appear to have survived into the 1990s.

## GERMAN STATE RAILWAY 41 SERIES/1937/GERMANY

Over 350 of these fast freight locomotives were built between 1937-41. The design was not one of the standard twelve classes planned in the 1920s, but it used the same components as these and was therefore rightly regarded as a standard design. The diameter and length of the boiler was identical with that of the series 03 Pacific, although the boiler pressure was higher, at 285psi (1963kPa). This higher pressure suggests that the German engineers were

*Spanish Railways tended to be heavily graded and the 2-8-2 wheel arrangement appeared quite early, although it competed with the 4-8-0; the two wheel arrangements accommodated similar boilers and there was little to choose between the two concepts. This picture shows one of the 2-8-2 classes at work in the 1960s.*

*2-8-2 German State Railways 41 Class, 1937.*

beginning to depart from their principle, inherited from the days of the Prussian State Railways, that cheap maintenance and reliability had to take priority over performance. The grate area was 44sq.ft. (4.05sq.metre) and the tubes provided an evaporative heating surface of 2,097sq.ft. (186sq.metre), the firebox provided 172sq.ft. (16sq.metre) and the superheater was of 735sq.ft. (70sq.metre). There were two cylinders, 20½in x 28⅜in (520mm x 720mm) and the coupled wheel diameter was 63in (1600mm). Weight in working order was 225,750lbs (102.4 tonnes). The adhesion weight could be increased by ballasting. After World War 2 this class was divided between East and West Germany and both the DB and DR modified it. In the case of the DR, a feedwater heater appeared in front of the chimney of some units, while on West Germany's DB the locomotives were given a bigger boiler. However, the rather high boiler pressure was not continued with, 227psi (1568kPa) being preferred.

## FRENCH RAILWAYS 141P CLASS/1941/FRANCE

This 2-8-2 type emerged at a time when France was under German occupation, and over three hundred were subsequently built between 1942-47. The design has a strong claim to be the world champion in terms of the steam locomotive power/weight ratio; on trial it produced a horsepower at the drawbar of 3,300 at 50mph (80kph), on a weight in working order of 245,857lb (111.5 tonnes). It was based on an old design of the PLM Railway, which was modified according to the principles of André Chapelon. In addition, thicker frames were provided and

*2-8-2 SNCF compound 141P Class, 1941.*

a Zara truck replaced the previous, standard, truck. These two changes made the locomotive more amenable to curves taken at high speed and in fact, although it was designed for mixed traffic, the class spent most of its time hauling fast passenger trains. It was a compound, with two high-pressure cylinders of 16¹⁄₁₀in (410mm) and two low of 15⅛in (640mm), with a common stroke of 27½in (700mm. The coupled wheels were 63¾in (1620mm) and boiler pressure 285psi (1961kPa). The grate area was 46.3sq.ft. (4.3sq.metre) and there was a large superheater of 936sq.ft. (87sq.metre). Tractive effort was 42,070lb (19,100kg). The chimney was of the double, Kylchap, type. A strong case could be made for nominating this design as the best French locomotive of its time.

*2-8-2 US War Department Mikado, 1942. This is one of several units transferred to Pakistan.*

*An SNCF 141P Class 2-8-2 in passenger service in the 1960s.*

*2-8-2 MacArthur Class, 1944. The MacArthur is in the centre of the picture, with a British-built 2-8-2 on the left.*

## US WAR DEPARTMENT
## MIKADO/1942/MIDDLE EAST, INDIA

Designed and buit at British request, this locomotive was based on a Baldwin 2-8-2 supplied to the Montana Wyoming & Southern RR in the 1920s. 200 were built and saw service in Iran and Egypt, among others. An additional 584 units built for the broad gauge by US and Canadian builders went to Indian railways, where they were clasified as the CWD (Canadian) or AWD (American) type. Some of the war department units eventually saw service in China, Turkey and Israel. They had 21in x 28in (533mm x 710mm) cylinders, 68in (1727mm) driving wheels, and 200psi (1278kPa) boiler pressure, giving a 35,000lb (15,800kg) tractive effort. Their weight in working order was 200,000lb (90.7 tonnes), and grate area 47sq.ft. (4.3sq.metre). Some were oil-burners.

## US WAR DEPARTMENT MACARTHUR
## CLASS/1944/USA

Among the lightest of the Mikados to be built in the United States were those, known later as the 'MacArthur' class, used on metre-gauge (3ft 3⅓in) lines in India and in other Asian countries after World War 2. With two cylinders at 16in x 24in (406mm x 610mm) and 48in (1219mm) wheels, they gave a tractive force of 20,700lb (9,390kg) using steam at 190psi (1310kPa). The boiler had 1,744sq.ft. (162sq.metre) of heating surface, and the firebox grate area was 27.5sq.ft. (2.6sq.metre).

The builders of the class were the Davenport Company, which was later to enter the diesel-locomotive field, but like many other steam-locomotive builders, failed to make the grade.

## SNCF CLASS 141R/1945/FRANCE

By 1945 the SNCF was desperately short of locomotives to work the war-torn railways of France. Part of its requirements were met by the supply from various North American locomotive builders of 1,340 of the 2-8-2 type, which were to find widespread use all over the French railway system. They were built to non-metric dimensions with cylinders 23½in x 28in (597mm x 711mm) driving 65in (1651mm) wheels. With steam at 220psi (1517kPa), they gave a tractive force of 44,500lb (20,185kg). The boiler was well proportioned, with 3,400sq.ft. (316sq.metre) of heating surface and a firegrate area of 55.5sq.ft. (5.2sq.metre).

The total weight of the locomotive came to 254,677lb (115.5 tonnes), of which 180,000lb (80 tonnes) were available for adhesion. These were among the last steam locomotives to work on the SNCF; after the withdrawal of the Pacifics from the boat trains to Calais one of the 141R class often performed the service.

## ROYAL SIAMESE STATE RAILWAY 901
## SERIES/1949/THAILAND

After World War 2 Thailand was faced with a locomotive shortage, but being satisfied with its pioneering diesel experience expected to fill the gap with diesel locomotives. In the meantime it ordered a small number of steam locomotives to existing wartime designs. These were 4-6-2 and 2-8-2 types. The 2-8-2s, numbered 901-940, arrived from various Japanese builders in 1949. They had 17¾in x 24in (450mm x 610mm) cylinders. Boiler pressure was 185psi (1273kPa), coupled wheels 43½in (1106mm), so the tractive effort was 24,118lb (10,950kg).

Weight in working order was 127,008lb (57.6 tonnes). The grate area was 32.2sq.ft.(3sq.metre), the boiler being identical with preceding 4-6-2 and 2-8-2 locomotives. The diesel program having been delayed, a further batch (Nos.941-970) of these locomotives was bought in 1950.

## INDONESIAN STATE RAILWAYS D52
## CLASS/1951/INDONESIA

After World War 2 and civil war the Indonesian railways were in a sad state, but for the most part reliance was placed on restoring the old locomotive stock to service. An exception was the new D52 Class, a hundred modern 2-8-2 locomotives built by Krupp. This influx saved the system from collapse and enabled some new prestigious passenger trains to be introduced. They were mixed-traffic locomotives, and right up to the end of steam in Indonesia could be seen on passenger and freight trains. Their driving wheels were 59in (1503mm), and they had 19⁷⁄₁₀in x 26in (500mm x 600mm) cylinders, boiler pressure of 227psi (1566kPa, unprecedently high for Indonesia), and they had a 37.6sq.ft. (3.5sq.metre) grate area. They had a tractive effort of 32,428lb (14,722kg) for a weight in working order of 163,610lb (74.2 tonnes).

## INDIAN RAILWAYS CLASS WG/1951/INDIA

These locomotives were the mainstay of Indian railways during the first industrialization drive after Independence. Dimensionally they were based on the US 2-8-2 locomotives delivered in the late 1940s, but they also had some features of the standard Indian pre-war 2-8-2. They had the same boiler as the WP Pacific, which was being

*2-8-2 SNCF 141R Class, 1945.*

*2-8-2 Royal Siamese Railways 901 series, 1949.*

*2-8-2 Indonesian D52 Class, 1951.*

introduced at the same time. The first units were made by North British, but subsequently the class was produced by the new home works at Chittaranjan. With driving wheels of diameter 60in (1524mm), they had a tractive force of 34,200lb (15,513kg). By the time production finished in 1970 over 2,500 had been acquired, including some imported from Japanese, Canadian and German makers. One or two are being preserved.

*2-8-2 Indian Railways WG Class, 1951.*

## NEW SOUTH WALES GOVERNMENT RAILWAYS CLASS D-59/1952/AUSTRALIA

Although delivered in 1952, this class was essentially built to the US War department design of World War 2. Twenty were ordered from Baldwin in the USA (by then it had become Baldwin-Lima-Hamilton), and they differed from the wartime engines in having short tenders, so that they could use New South Wales turntables. They were delivered as oil-burners, but most of them were later converted to coal. They started work on the Sydney-Newcastle route but in course of time they changed their field of operations as dieselization advanced. Their final haven was Newcastle, where they were employed mainly on freight (although in theory these were mixed-traffic locomotives). The last one was withdrawn in 1972, but four have been preserved.

They had 21in x 28in (530mm x 710mm) cylinders, 60in (1520mm) coupled wheels, and a boiler pressure of 200psi (1378kPa). Total weight, including tender, was 337,916lb (153.25 tonnes), and the grate area was 47sq.ft. (4.36sq.metre). Tractive effort was 34,986lb (15,883kg).

## CHINESE RAILWAYS JS CLASS/1958/CHINA

In 1918 the American Locomotive Company (Alco) supplied some 2-8-2 locomotives to the South Manchurian Railway. These impressed the authorities and a standard class eventually emerged from the series of modifications successively applied to the original design. It was built in large numbers by the Japanese occupation administration and production continued under the subsquent communist

regime, by which time it was known as the 'Liberation' or JF Class. The availability of Soviet technical help then led to a rather new design of 2-8-2, the 'Construction' or JS Class. Essentially, this is the JF engine carrying a new, Russian-inspired, boiler. Weighing 200,655lb (91 tonnes) and with 213psi (1470kPa) boiler pressure, 22.8in x 28in (580mm x 710mm) cylinders and 54in (1370mm) driving wheels, this design has a nominal tractive effort of 48,518lb (22,027kg). The grate area is said to be 6.2sq.ft. (.575sq.metre).

Several thousand locomotives of this design were built at Dalian, Datong, and Qingdao, and they were still being built in the 1980s. They are used by industrial railways as well as by Chinese Railways; the latter uses them for secondary-line freight services.

*2-8-2 New South Wales Government Railways D-59 Class, 1952.*

# 2-8-4

## BOSTON AND ALBANY RAILROAD BERKSHIRE CLASS/1924/USA

In 1924 the average speed of freight trains was only 10mph (16kph). In an endeavour to provide a freight locomotive with improved steam-output capacity, Will Woodard of the Lima Corporation of Ohio designed for the Boston and Albany Railroad a 2-8-4 in which the use of the four-wheel trailing truck allowed a large firebox (with 100sq.ft. [9.3sq.metre] of grate area) to be installed. Fitted with two cylinders at 28in x 30in (711mm x 762mm) and with driving wheels of diameter 63in (1600mm), the locomotives had a tractive force of 76,400lb (34,655kg) with an adhesive weight of 248,062lb (112.5 tonnes). The boiler produced steam at 240psi (1655kPa) from a heating area of 7,218sq.ft. (671sq.metre), and the overall weight of the engine came to 384,993lb (174.6 tonnes). As the trials of the first locomotive of this type were run over the Berkshire Hills, the 2-8-4 wheel arrangement earned the name 'Berkshire'.

In all around 750 of the type were to be built for use within the US railroad system.

## AUSTRIAN STATE RAILWAY SERIES 214/1929/AUSTRIA

Following the application of the 2-8-4 type to US freight operation, the next to use that system was the Austrian State Railway, which produced its Series 214 in 1929. After the numerous compound types which had been designed by Golsdorf, the new specification, produced by a team which included Dr Ing.Giesl-Gieslingen, reverted to the use of a simple cycle.

The S.214 was equipped with two cylinders of dimensions 25½in x 28⅓in (650mm x 720mm) and with driving wheels of 74¾in (1900mm) diameter. The steam pressure was 217psi (1496kPa) from a boiler with 3,886sq.ft. (361sq.metre) of heating surface and a firegrate with 50.6sq.ft. (4.7sq.metre) in area. With a tractive force of 45,000lb (20,412kg) these engines could haul a 500-long-ton (508-tonne) train up a grade of 1 in 100 (1 per cent) at 31mph (50kph), a task requiring an output of 1,300dbhp (969kW) or around 1,700ihp (1,268kW). The locomotives had an adhesive weight of 155,893lb (70.7 tonnes) and a total weight of 260,190lb (118 tonnes). One of them was timed at up to 96.3mph (155kph). Although one was built as a three-cylinder version, it proved to be more costly in operation, and the remaining 12 were all built as two-cylinder engines.

Number 214.10 is preserved at the Vienna Technical Museum.

## SOVIET RAILWAYS 'IOSIF STALIN' CLASS/1933/USSR

Another part of the world in which the 2-8-4 arrangement was to find favour was in the USSR, where in 1933 the Kolomna works produced the first of its IS class. With two cylinders of dimensions 26⅓in x 30⅓in (670mm x 770mm), they used steam at 217psi (1496kPa) and, with driving wheels of diameter 72¾in (1850mm), their tractive force was 52,900lb (23,995kg) with an all-up weight of 293,265lb (133 tonnes). Their haulage capacity was 787-long-tons (800 tonnes) up a grade of 1 in 140 (0.71 per cent) at 25mph (40kph), a task requiring an output of 2,100ihp (1,566kW). Only one of these passenger locomotives, of which 650 were built, has been preserved (at Kiev).

## CHESAPEAKE & OHIO RAILROAD K-4 CLASS/1943/USA

With its mineral trains entrusted to articulated locomotives, the C&O relied on 2-8-2s for its merchandise freights, but

2-8-2 Chinese Railways JS Class, 1958. The picture shows newly-built units leaving works in 1988.

2-8-4 USSR Iosif Stalin Class, 1933.

with the onset of wartime traffic these became inadequate. The Railroad decided to move to the 2-8-4 type, and the War Production Board assented, although stipulating that an existing design should be used. Basically, therefore, the new K-4 class was the Nickel Plate RR 2-8-4, although the C&O chose to have larger cylinders and also to provide a booster for extra tractive effort at low speeds. Cylinders were 26in x 34in (660mm x 864mm), boiler pressure 245psi (1688kPa), driving wheels 69in (1750mm), and grate area 90.3sq.ft. (8.38sq.metre). Tractive force was 69,350lb (31,484kg), plus 14,000lb (6,356kg) contributed by the booster. Weight of engine was 469,680lb (213 tonnes).

A total of 90 units were built between 1943 and 1947 by Lima and Alco. They worked both passenger and fast freight trains until retirement in the 1950s, and not all were scrapped. The Railroad called them the 'Kanawha' type.

## NEW YORK CHICAGO & ST LOUIS RAILROAD S-3 CLASS/1949/USA

Although the Railroad was known as the Nickel Plate Railroad, it was on the poverty line in the depression of the early 1930s. It then staged a renaissance, helped by a recovering economy, and part of its success lay in a new breed of motive power. The 2-8-4, with its large firebox, was the perfect locomotive for fast freight trains carrying the high-value merchandise that was so profitable for the railroads but so vulnerable to highway competition. The NKP bought its first 15 2-8-4s in 1934 from Alco, but later standardized on the Lima product with 25 S-1 type in 1942-43, 30 S-2 in 1944, and 10 S-3 in 1949. These Lima engines were very similar, and so satisfactory that the Railroad bought the last ten in preference to diesels that were also on offer. The class was kept busy into the late 1950s, and even after that several members of the class were preserved for museum or excursion train service. Dimensions of the last batch (S-3) were as follows (the S-2 locomotives were the same, but weighed slightly less): cylinders 25in x 24in (635mm x 610mm), boiler pressure 245psi (1688kPa), driving wheels 69in (1750mm), drawbar pull (tractive effort) 64,100lb (29,101kg), grate area 90.3sq.ft. (8.38sq.metre), superheater surface 1,932sq.ft. (17.9sq.metre), weight on coupled wheels 266,030lb (120.6 tonnes), weight of engine 444,290lb (201.5 tonnes).

# 4-8-0

## ILLINOIS CENTRAL RAILROAD No.640/1899/USA

First built in the United States for the Lehigh Valley Railroad in 1870, the 4-8-0 type was little used in that country after 1900, by which time some 600 had been built for domestic use. Probably the largest of these was that built for the Illinois Central Railroad in 1899 by the Brooks Locomotive Works at Dunkirk, New York State; the company was to be absorbed into the Alco merger in 1901. The Illinois Central No.640 used driving wheels of 57in (1448mm) diameter and was fitted with two cylinders at 23in x 30in (584mm x 762mm) fed with steam at 210psi (1448kPa). The tractive force was 49,700lb (22,544kg) from an adhesive weight of 193,158lb (87.6 tonnes), and the steam was supplied by a boiler with 3,500sq.ft. (325sq.metre) of heating surface and a firegrate area of 37.5sq.ft. (3.5sq.metre).

2-8-4 Boston & Albany Berkshire type, 1924.

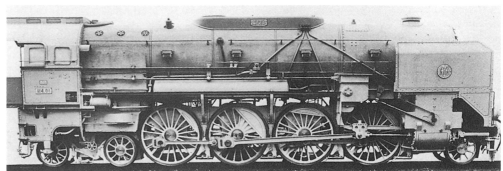

2-8-4 Austrian State Railways 214 series, 1929.

*2-8-2 USSR Iosif Stalin Class, 1933. The picture shows fitters examining the mechanical stoker in the tender.*

*2-8-4 C&O Railroad K-4 Class, 1943.*

## QUEENSLAND GOVERNMENT RAILWAYS C-17 CLASS/1920/AUSTRALIA

This was one of the best-known locomotive types in Queensland. Two hundred and twenty-seven were built over three decades (and an additional 20 were bought by Commonwealth Railways). They were intended for freight work, but in practice were mixed-traffic locomotives. Some had roller bearings, and in appearance they resembled a mix of American and European styles. For many years they were painted brown, and became known as the 'Brown Bombers.' Some lasted until 1970, and at least one beyond the official withdrawal date of August 1970. There are about twenty units preserved, including one on the Lithgow Tourist Railway in New South Wales.

Of 3ft 6in (1067mm) gauge, these locomotives had coupled wheels of only 45in (1140mm). The cylinders were 17in x 22in (430mm x 560mm) and the boiler pressure 160lb (1102kPa), giving a tractive effort of 18,085lb (8,210kg). The grate area was 18.5sq.ft. (1.72sq.metre) and the weight 178,605lb (81 tonnes). Later units differed slightly in appearance, and some were rebuilt with 175psi (1206kPa) boilers.

## HUNGARIAN STATE RAILWAY 424 Class/1924/HUNGARY

This 4-8-0 is one of the classic Central European locomotive designs, about 365 having been built and seeing service, not only in the land of their birth, but also in Yugoslavia, China and the Soviet Union (as post-war reparations). When first built, in 1924, they were rather in advance of need, but with the rising traffic of World War 2 they became a necessity and the majority of them, in

*2-8-4 Nickel Plate RR S-3 Class, 1949. This is one of the preserve examples.*

fact, were built in 1940-1945. In their final years they were fitted with a Hungarian-designed multiple-jet blastpipe, the Ister Exhaust, recognizable by the distinctive chimney. They had two 23³⁄₅in x 26in (600mm x 660mm) cylinders, driving wheels of 63_ (1606mm), and 185psi (1274kPa) boiler pressure, providing a theoretical tractive effort of 42,295lb (19,202kg). The grate area was 47.9sq.ft.(4.45 sq. metre) and engine weight 183,015lb (83 tonnes). There was nothing special about these dimensions; the design scored by its simplicity, enhanced by the very careful workmanship of the Budapest builders.

## SNCF CLASS 240P/1932/FRANCE

The finest of the European 4-8-0 engines were those rebuilt from the Paris-Orléans Pacific type S.4500 by André Chapelon in 1932. In order to obtain extra adhesion for the haulage of 500-long-ton (508-tonne) trains on heavily graded lines, an extra pair of driving wheels was provided; this necessitated a reduction in grate area, but that was compensated for by the use of a higher steam pressure of 290psi (2000kPa). Four cylinders, two of bore 17⅓in (440mm) and two of bore 25⅕in (640mm), all with a piston stroke of 25½in (650mm), drove the 73in (1850mm) wheels. These locomotives could haul a 541-long-ton (550-tonne) train up a grade of 1 in 100 (1 per cent) at

*2-8-4 Nickel Plate RR S-3 Class in regular freight service during the late 1950s.*

*4-8-0 Chicago & East Illinois RR, 1900. This locomotive was similar to those supplied by the same works (Rogers) to the Illinois Central RR in 1899.*

52.8mph (85kph), a task requiring an output of over 4,000ihp (2,983kW). With a locomotive weight of 241,227lb (109.4 tonnes), the specific output at the maximum rate was 37.1hp per ton (27.7kW/tonne), the highest figure recorded at that time.

A further 25 of this type were built as new in 1940, but with the electrification of the Paris to Dijon main line the whole class was scheduled to be transferred to the Nord Region. That fell through due to an accountant's wrangle, and the locomotives were all withdrawn in 1952.

## DELAWARE AND HUDSON RAILROAD NO. 1403 (L. F. LOREE)/1933/USA

The last of the 4-8-0 type to be built in the United States was an experimental high-pressure version produced for the Delaware and Hudson Railroad as a follow-up to three 2-8-0 types built in 1924, 1927 and 1930. The steam-pressure was the same as in that of one of the latter, No. 1402, at 500psi (3448kPa), but the steam system employed was the triple expansion one, as used in marine practice, with one high-pressure cylinder of 20in (508mm) diameter mounted under the cab, an intermediate cylinder of 27½in (698mm) diameter on the opposite side, and

*4-8-0 Queensland Government Railways C-17 Class, 1920.*

*4-8-0 Hungarian State Railway 424 Class, 1924.*

*4-8-0 SNCF 240P Class, 1932.*

next, with larger (74in [1880mm]) wheels, being a series for the Chicago, Rock Island and Pacific Railroad built in 1920.

## CANADIAN NATIONAL RAILWAYS U1b CLASS/1924/CANADA

The U1b was a repeat order of the U1a introduced in 1923. The following order was the U1c, also identical, making a series of locomotives numbered 6000-6041 (althogh Nos.6037-6041 were built by Baldwin for the Grand Trunk Western, and had detail differences). Then came the U1d

two low-pressure ones of 33in (838mm) diameter mounted at the front end. All four cylinders used a piston stroke of 32in (813mm), and all drove onto the second axle. With 63in (1600mm) driving wheels, the tractive force was 75,000lb (34,020kg). Steam was supplied by a boiler with a water-tube firebox having 4,427sq.ft. (411sq.metre) of heating surface, and the long firebox, mounted over the two rear axles, had a grate area of 75.8sq.ft. (7sq.metre). The total weight came to 381,146lb (173 tonnes). The tender was carried on two trucks, the rear one of which was a six-wheeled version fitted with a Bethlehem booster which could exert a tractive force of 10,000lb (4,540kg).

# 4-8-2

## CHESAPEAKE AND OHIO RAILROAD MOUNTAIN CLASS/1911/USA

The 4-8-2 was first built to work heavy passenger trains over the Allegheny Mountain grades of the Chesapeake

and Ohio Railroad in 1911. Fitted with two cylinders at 29in x 28in (737mm X 711mm) driving wheels of 62in (1575mm) diameter, the engine was supplied with superheated steam at a pressure of 180psi (1241kPa), giving a tractive force of 58,100lb (26,354kg). The boiler had a heating-surface area of 5,080sq.ft. (472sq.metre) and a firegrate area of 66.5sq.ft. (6.2sq.metre). It was equipped with a mechanical stoker of the steam-jet overfeed type - one of the first applications of this piece of equipment. The locomotive had an all-up weight of 330,088lb (149.7 tonnes), and it drew on two four-wheeled trucks a tender which weighed 165,154lb (74.9 tonnes) - about the same weight as many main-line locomotives in Britain at that time.

This was one of three experimental engines to be built by the American Locomotive Company. The fact that the driving wheels were of only 62in (1575mm) diameter meant that the locomotive was too slow for passenger work, but this experiment led to the development of the 4-8-2 type with larger wheels for passenger service - the

*B4-8-2 Canidian National U1b Class, 1924.*

*4-8-2 C&O RR Mountain Class, 1911.*

and U1e, which had higher boiler pressure, smaller cylinders, and were originally intended to replace Pacifics on the Winnipeg-Edmonton section, which they could cover without engine change, unlike the Pacifics which previously handled those passenger trains.

Nos.6000-6036 were built by Canadian Locomotive and were first put into service on the Montreal-Toronto passenger trains, covering the 333 miles (536km) without change of engine. They weighed 337,365lb (153 tonnes) and produced a tractive effort of 50,000lb (22,700kg). Driving wheel diameter was 73in (1860mm), boiler pressure 210psi (1446kPa), and grate area 66.7sq.ft. (6.19sq.metre). The

cylinders were 26in x 30in (660mm x 762mm). The later units, 6042-6058, had 250psi (1722kPa) boiler pressure and 24in (610mm) diameter cylinders.

These locomotives were soon to be overshadowed by the CNR 4-8-4 classes, but they performed useful service, disappearing only in 1961.

## CHEMIN DE FER DE L'EST CLASS 241/1925/FRANCE

In France both L'Est and the PLM introduced the 4-8-2 type in 1925.

On the PLM a total of 145 of its class 241A was commissioned. Although these were capable of outputs on test of 2,400dbhp (1790kW), they did suffer from weak frames, with the result that a speed limit of 62mph (100kph) had to be imposed.

The Est Mountain Class 241 was originally built with four cylinders, two of 17¾in (450mm) and two of 25½in (650mm) in diameter, all with a 28⅓in (720mm) stroke, and with 76¾in (1950mm) wheels. The steam pressure was 242psi (1669kPa). On trial (on the Nord) in 1933 one of these locomotives produced an output of 2,000dbhp (1,491kW) or 2,600ihp (1,939kW). Their boilers had

2,341sq.ft. (218sq.metre) of heating surface plus 753sq.ft. (70sq.metre) of superheating area. In the later versions, produced after 1930, the superheating area was increased to 1,100sq.ft. (102.2sq.metre) making a total of 3,586sq.ft. (333.5sq.metre) in all.

Forty of these locomotives were built for use on the Est and a further 39 for the État system. Like the PLM Mountains they suffered from a frame weakness, but they lasted throughout the war years until electrification took over their duties. One is preserved at the French Railway Museum at Mulhouse.

*4-8-2 Est 241 Class (SNCF 241A Class), 1925.*

## CHILEAN STATE RAILWAYS 80 CLASS/1929/CHILE

Chilean State Railways are divided into the narrow-gauge north and the broad-gauge south, and it is the latter that serves the industrial areas, including the main coal-mining basin. Heavy broad-gauge power has therefore been needed, and in 1929 Baldwin of the USA received an order for twelve 4-8-2 locomotives. These were regarded as a stop-gap expedient while the track was strengthened for heavier designs. But with their 66in (1676mm) driving wheels these general-purpose machines proved so useful that six more were ordered in 1938 and by 1948 there were 39 in service. In the 1950s similar units were acquired from Mitsubishi. Cylinders were 22½in x 28in (570mm x 710mm), boiler pressure 205psi (1412kPa), and tractive effort 37,374lb (16,967kg). The grate area was 52.3sq.ft. (4.86sq.metre). Total weight with tender was 361,222lb (163.8 tonnes), and adhesion weight was 145,707lb (66 tonnes). These locomotives were largely based at Concepcion, and were active on freight duties into the 1970s. Several have been preserved; the example at Santiago Railway Museum is one of the Japanese-built units.

## SOUTH AFRICAN RAILWAYS CLASS 19D/1937)/ SOUTH AFRICA

The 19D was the final development of a lightweight 4-8-2 that first appeared as Class 19 in 1928. Its role was the working of lightly-laid secondary lines, a category that included a major part of the railway route mileage of that time. Class 19D appeared in 1937 and, like its predecessors, had high power for its light axle-load. The latter was just 31,360lb (14.2 tonnes), and the engine without tender weighed 179,200lb (81.2 tonnes), yet the tractive effort was 31,850lb (14,493kg). Boiler pressure was 200psi (1378kPa), cylinders 21in x 26in (533mm x

*4-8-2 South African Railway 19D Class, 1937.*

*Another view of a 19D 4-8-2 of South African Railways.*

of this type with conventional Walschaerts gear. This was the origin of the 15F type. Both the 15E and 15F performed well on passenger trains, but were handicapped by their smallish wheels, so a variant (Class 23) with 63in wheels and higher boiler pressure was also produced; because this was expected to develop more horsepower per hour, it had a mechanical stoker and bigger tender to allow for the faster combustion rate. As for the 15F, this was destined to become a very numerous class, with about 250 built, mainly by North British but some by German builders. The cylinders were 24in x 28in (610mm x 710mm) and boiler pressure 210psi (1446kPa). With coupled wheels of 60in (1524mm) this gave a nominal tractive effort of 47,980lb. (21,782kg). The grate area was 62.5sq.ft. (5.8sq.metre) and the superheater 661sq.ft. (61.4sq.metre). Engine weight was 249,074lb (112.9 tonnes).

## MADRID ZARAGOZA & ALICANTE RAILWAY (RENFE CLASS 241 2101)/1939/SPAIN

These ten streamlined locomotives were built by Maquinista of Barcelona. The MZA, shortly to become part of Spanish National Railways (RENFE), intended them for the Madrid-Albacete line, but after a period there they were transferred to the trains moving from Madrid to the Portuguese frontier. The streamlining was more for effect than utility (although effective for lifting the smoke, rather like the British 'Merchant Navy' class), but other modern features were added, including a Kylchap double chimney and feedwater heater. The boiler worked at 285psi (1959kPa), with a superheater giving an exit temperature of 410 degrees Centigrade. The heating surface of the firebox was 206sq.ft. (19.20sq.metre). The two cylinders were 22in x 28in ((560mm x 710mm) and the driving wheels were 69in (1750mm). Tractive effort was 45,811lb (20,798kg) and the engine weighed 255,780lb (116 tonnes) in working order while its tender, fully loaded, was

660mm), and the grate area 36sq.ft. (3.34sq.metre). For such an imposing locomotive, the 54in (1371mm) coupled wheels were somewhat small, aesthetically, but ideal for its duties. The batch introduced in 1948 had Vanderbilt tenders carrying extra of coal and water, with their weight spread over six axles rather than four.

## SOUTH AFRICAN RAILWAYS CLASS 15F/1939/SOUTH AFRICA

Although of only 3ft 6in (1067mm) gauge, the South African Railways had generous clearances and in the 1920s it was decided to take full advantage of this in embarking on a big-engine policy. The first 4-8-2 dates from that period and this evolved until in 1935 the 15E Class appeared. This was a general-purpose machine which performed well. It was introduced when poppet valves were fashionable but its Caprotti valves, though they worked as promised, did have higher maintenance costs and it was therefore decided to build future locomotives

*4-8-2 South African Railways 15F Class, 1939.*

*4-8-2 RENFE 241 2101 Class, 1939.*

167,580lb (76 tonnes). Empty weight of the tender was 70,560lb or 32 tonnes).

## NEW YORK CENTRAL RAILROAD L CLASSES/1942/USA

On the New York Central Railroad the 4-8-2 type was given the name `Mohawk'. By 1929 the railroad had 140 of its L-2D type in operation; these had cylinders measuring 27in x 30in (686mm x 762mm) and, with 69in (1753mm) driving wheels, they gave a tractive force a 60,000lb (27,216kg) from a steam pressure of 225psi (1551kPa). Their output was measured as 4,000ihp (2,983kW) at 48mph (77.2kph), but they were limited to 60mph (96.5kph) for passenger operation.

In 1930 two were rebuilt to use steam at 250psi (1724kPa). With a lightweight reciprocating motion and roller bearings, these could run at speeds up to 87mph (140kph).

From that rebuild emerged the classes L-3 and L-4, of which respectively 65 and 50 were built; they were used for both passenger and freight duties. The L-4 class, built in 1942, had two cylinders measuring 26in x 30in (660mm x 762mm) and, with steam at 250psi (1724kPa), gave a tractive force of 59,900lb (27,171kg) using 72in (1828mm) driving wheels. The boilers were the same on both the L-3 and the L-4, with 6,758sq.ft. (628sq.metre) of heating surface and a firegrate with 75.3sq.ft. (7sq.metre). On a weight of 397,340lb (180.2 tonnes) they gave an output of 5,470ihp (4,079kW) at 74mph (119.1kph) or 4,280dbhp (3,192kW) at 60mph (96.5kph). In operation they returned average monthly mileages of 5,400 miles (8,689km) for the L-3 class and 9,900 miles (15,929km) for the L-4 class, with a maximum of 15,200 miles (24,457km) for the L-3 and 24,200 miles (38,938km) for the L-4 class. All of the L-4 class and 25 of the L-3 were fitted with roller bearings, and 25 of the L-4 class were built with an alloy-steel motion - wartime restrictions required the rest to be made using carbon steel.

The tenders, which were on two six-wheeled trucks, held 15,500gal (704hl) of water and 98,325lb (43.7 tonnes) of coal; they were fitted with water-pick-up apparatus for long nonstop runs, and weighed 373,086lb (169.2 tons). Thus, out of a total weight of 342.5 long tons (348 tonnes), only 118.7-long-tons (120.6 tonnes) were available for adhesion.

## CANADIAN NATIONAL RAILWAYS U1f CLASS/1944/CANADA

After two decades of preference for the 4-8-4, CNR for its last steam passenger locomotive design reverted to the 4-8-2. These twenty locomotives were built by the Montreal Locomotive Works and had the standard CNR wheel diameter of 73in (1860mm), and 24in x 30in (610mm x 762mm) cylinders. However, the boiler pressure was raised to 260psi (1791kPa), giving a tractive effort of 54,680lb (24,824kg). Grate area was 70.2sq.ft. (6.52sq.metre). Weight of engine was 355,700lb (161.3 tonnes). Despite war conditions, great care was taken with the styling of these locomotives, a semi-streamlined appearance evidently being aimed for. The smokebox door was conical, forming a casing for the headlight. The pipes forming a radiator to cool the air of the brake system were placed behind a neat grille on the front beam, and the bell was moved forward to the smokebox. There was a deep valance along the running board. Paintwork was black for the boiler and CN green for the panels, with gold stripes, and the front number plates were brass. No particular duty was envisaged for this class, which was spread over the system and worked in conjunction with the previous class of 4-8-2. One of the class has been preserved.

## SNCF CLASS 241P/1948/FRANCE

The last of the French-built Mountain classes were a batch of 35 constructed by Schneider at Le Creusot in 1948 for use on the Dijon-Marseilles line before its electrification and on trains from Paris to Lille and to Belgium. With two high-pressure cylinders measuring 17½in x 25⅔in

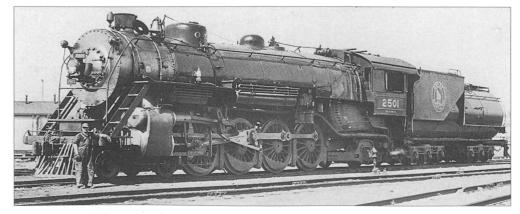

*A 4-8-2 design built for the Great Northern RR in the 1930s.*

The North American 4-8-2 was a dual-service locomotive and on some railroads it was most often seen on passenger duties. This is one of the Class Mia, a hundred units acquired by the Pennsylvanian RR in the 1930s. This particular example was built in the Railroad's own workshops. It had 72in coupled wheels. Because of mainline electrification, this class was mainly used for freight service.

4-8-2 Candian National U1F Class, 1944.

*4-8-2 SNCF 241P Class, 1948.*

(446mm x 650mm) and two low-pressure ones at 26½in x 27½in (674mm X 700mm), they used steam at 290psi (2000kPa) and drove 79½in (2020mm) wheels. The use of the trailing axle enabled a large firegrate - 54.3sq.ft. (5.05sq.metre) – and the boiler had 3,810sq.ft. (354sq.metre) of heating surface. With an adhesive weight of 180,369lb (81.8 tonnes), these locomotives gave a tractive force of 46,900lb (21,274kg), and could attain a maximum output of 4,300ihp (3,207kW) for short periods. As with the other French Mountain-type engines, these suffered from frame weakness - the frames were of only 1¹⁄₁₀in (28mm) steel - and this, combined with the double cranked axle, led to the adoption of the three-cylinder

*4-8-4 Northern Pacific RR 2600 Class, 1927 (above), 4-8-2 Bolivian National 811 series, 1954 (below).*

system for the SNCF's more powerful 4-8-4 engine - of which only one was constructed (in 1946).

### BOLIVIAN NATIONAL RAILWAYS 811 SERIES/1954/BOLIVIA

After World War 2 Bolivian National Railways replenished its locomotive stock with a class of 4-8-2s from Japan, and locomotives of a similar wheel arrangement built by the Vulcan Foundry in Britain. Some of these latter had originally been intended for Chile. They were of metre gauge, had 48in (1200mm) coupled wheels, 19in x 26in (483mm x 660mm) cylinders, and boilers pressed to 180psi (1240kPa). Including the tenders, they weighed 322,560lb (146.3 tonnes). Tractive effort was 27,616lb (12,538kg). These locomotives lasted until the end of steam traction in Bolivia, finally being concentrated around the capital, La Paz. Here they worked both passenger and freight trains, and their smallish coupled wheels were an advantage for the long climb out of the volcanic crater in which La Paz is situated, although two locomotives per train were often necessary.

# 4-8-4

## NORTHERN PACIFIC CLASS 2600/1927/USA

The first of the many classes of 4-8-4 in the United States was that built for the Northern Pacific Railroad in 1927 by Alco. This had two cylinders 28in x 30in (711mm x 762mm) using steam at 225psi (1551kPa) and giving a tractive force of 61,500lb (27,896kg). The four-wheel trailing truck enabled a firegrate area of 115sq.ft. (10.7sq.metre) to be provided to burn the low-grade Rosebud lignite fuel available to that railroad. The boiler had a heating surface of 6,600sq.ft. (613sq.metre) and the complete locomotive weight was 426,006lb (193.2 tonnes), of which 259,969lb (117.9 tonnes) was available for adhesion.

## GRAND TRUNK WESTERN RAILROAD U3 CLASS/1927/USA

The GTW's main line from the Canadian frontier at Port Huron to Chicago carried heavy traffic, both freight and passenger, so made great use of large general-purpose locomotives. In 1927 the 4-8-4 was introduced to this role, with 12 locomotives built by Alco. As was usual, the design was basically that used by parent company CNR for its standard locomotives, though with detail differences to suit US operating conditions. Cylinders were 26¼in x 30in (666mm x 762mm), boiler pressure 250psi (1722kPa), and driving wheel diameter 73in (1860mm), giving a drawbar pull (tractive effort) of 60,200lb (27,330kg). The straight-top boiler was made of high-tensile silicon steel to save weight and had a grate area of 84.3sq.ft. (7.83sq.metre). There was a combustion chamber of 48in (1220mm). Weight of the engine in working order was 399,000lb (180.9 tonnes), and the tender was 267,500lb (121.3 tonnes) in addition. Six-tone chime whistles were fitted. These were successful locomotives, and more were ordered over the years up to 1942, with 37 built in total.

## SOUTH AUSTRALIAN RAILWAY CLASS 500/1928/AUSTRALIA

The 10 locomotives Class 500 were built in 1928 by the Tyneside firm belonging to Sir W. G. Armstrong Whitworth to suit the 5ft 3in (1.6m) gauge of South Australia and were the first of this type in the Southern hemisphere. With two outside cylinders of diameters 26in x 28in (660mm x 711mm), and with 63in (1600mm) wheels, these had an American appearance. Their boilers were big, with 4,483sq.ft. (416sq.metre) of heating surface (including the superheater) and a firegrate area of 66.5sq.ft. (6.2sq.metre). With steam at 200psi (1380kPa), these

*4-8-4 Grand Truck Western U3 Class, 1927.*

*4-8-4 South Australian Railways 500 Class, 1928.*

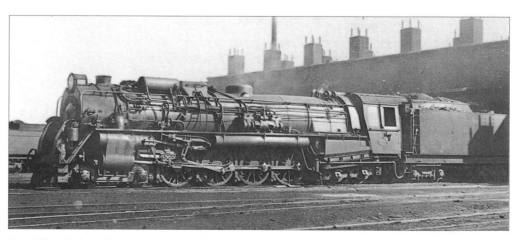

*4-8-4 New Zealand Government Railways K Class, 1932.*

*Mexican National US Built 4-8-4 QR-1 Class, 1946*

*4-8-4 Chinese Railways KF Class, 1935.*

engines gave a tractive force of 51,000lb (23,134kg), which was supplemented by a booster in the trailing truck which gave a further 8,000lb (3,629kg). The adhesive weight was 196,465lb (89.1 tonnes) out of a total of 498,991lb (226.3 tonnes), and they worked 550-long-ton (559-tonnes) trains over the Mount Lofty range with grades of 1 in 45 (2.22 per cent) and could maintain a speed of 15mph (24kph), equivalent to an output of 2,050ihp (1,529kW). They were withdrawn between 1955 and 1962 following the introduction of diesel-electric locomotives, but No.504 has been preserved at Melbourne.

### NEW ZEALAND GOVERNMENT RAILWAY CLASS K/1932/NEW ZEALAND

Built to suit their 3ft 6in (1.07m) gauge and to have an overall height of 11ft 6in (3.5m) or less, the 71 engines of this class were designed and built entirely in New Zealand, six at Dunedin for use in South Island and the other 65 at the Hutt shops at Wellington for North Island. With two cylinders measuring 20in x 26in (508mm x 660mm) and with 54in (1372mm) wheels they gave a tractive force of 32,700lb (14,833kg) using steam at 200psi (1380kPa). The boiler had 2,413sq.ft. (224sq.metre) of heating surface and a firegrate area of 47.4sq.ft. (4.4sq.metre) on a weight of 306,054lb (138.8 tonnes). Two were fitted with Baker valve gear, and the last 41 to be built were equipped with roller-bearing axle-boxes. The six for South Island were fitted with boosters to give an additional 8,000lb (3,629kg) of thrust, and they could haul 300-long-ton (305-tonne) trains up a grade of 1 in 50 (2 per cent) at 20mph (32kph), corresponding to an output of 1,330ihp (992kW). Five have been preserved.

*4-8-4 Chesapeak & Ohio RR J3 Class, 1935.*

### CHINESE RAILWAYS KF CLASS/1935/CHINA

These locomotives were designed by a British engineer working for the Chinese government, and 24 were built by Vulcan Foundry. They were required for the newly-opened Guangzhou-Wuhuan (Canton-Hankow) line, which had sharp curves and stiff gradients. As the line was singletrack, a powerful locomotive was needed to keep the trains moving at a good speed. Because Chinese coal tended to produce much ash and burned with a long flame, a large firebox and ashpan were provided, with a combustion chamber to ensure the total combustion of the fuel. The grate area was 67sq.ft. (6.3sq m). With water supplies likely to be impure, a moderate boiler pressure was chosen, slowing down the formation of scale. This was partly compensated for by the provision of a large superheater (of 100sq.metre). A mechanical stoker was supplied, and the design paid great attention to the balancing; hammer-blow was so reduced that an axle-load of 37,485lb (17 tonnes) became permissible. There were two cylinders 20⁹⁄₁₀in x 29½in (530mm x 750mm) although in the last eight units the cylinder diameter was increased by about three per cent. The driving wheels were of 69in (1750mm) diameter. Tractive effort was 32,900lbs (14,936kg) at 80per cent boiler pressure, although six engines were fitted with boosters that contributed an extra 7,670lb (3,482lb). Weight in working order of the engines without booster was 259,392lb (117.6 tonnes).

The designer had heeded Chapelon's experience in France, and the steam-flow circuit was of generous cross-sectional area. There was provision for the fitting of Kylchap exhausts should circumstances warrant, but the Japanese invasion prevented this, and put an end to the project of building a similar class of 2-10-4 locomotive. The KF Class performed well over several decades in both passenger and freight service. One of them was lost in the war against Japan, and No. KF 7 was presented to Britain as a goodwill gift in 1984, being placed in the National Railway Museum.

## CHESAPEAKE & OHIO RAILROAD J3 CLASS/1935/USA

Seeing what other railroads were doing, the C & O decided in the mid-1930s to smarten up its most important passenger trains. Lima delivered five 4-8-4s known as the 'Greenbrier' Class, which were named in honour of Virginian statesmen (it was not a numerous class). Two more came in 1942, of identical dimensions but of cleaned-up appearance. Five more (J3a Class) were delivered in 1948; these had 72in (1829mm) rather than 74in (1830mm) driving wheels. But in 1951 diesels took over the prestigious passenger services. The J3a Class was transferred to freight work, then put into store, to emerge again in 1955 to help cope with a freight boom. It was then withdrawn but No 614 survived. It was used for trials sponsored by, among others, the US coal industry, to help find possible new ways of using coal as a locomotive fuel. After that it went into preservation, and in the 1990s appeared occasionally on excursion trains.

The J3a Class had driving wheels of 72in (1829mm) diameter, boilers with 255psi (1756kPa) of pressure, and 27½in x 30in (699mm x 762mm) cylinders. This implied

*4-8-4 Grand Trunk Western RR U-4 Class, 1938. This illustration shows the Canadian National version.*

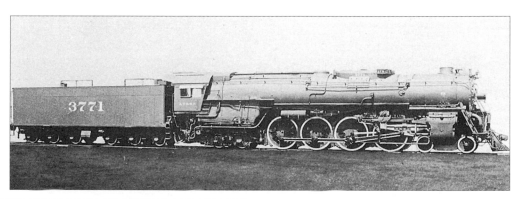

*4-8-4 Santa Fe Class 3765, 1938.*

a rated tractive effort of 68,300lb (30,980kg), and there was a booster to provide an extra 14,400lb (6,532kg) at starting. Weight was 503,500lb (228 tonnes). The grate area was 100.3sq.ft. (9.3sq.metre), and there was a large superheater of 2,305sq.ft. (214sq.metre).

## GRAND TRUNK WESTERN RAILROAD U.4 CLASS/1938/USA

Five streamlined 4-8-4 locomotives were built by Alco for the GTW in 1938. They were largely identical with five locomotives delivered by the Montreal Locomotive Works in 1936 to the Canadian National Railways. The GTW was a subsidiary of the CNR, and the idea was to use these locomotives on the international Montreal-Chicago service, with engine-change at the frontier. Dividing the order between the two builders ensured that customs duties would not be payable so long as they did not stray over the frontier for more than 24 hours.

*4-8-4 Norfolk & Western J class, 1941.*

*4-8-4 Canadian National U2g Class, 1942.*

There were slight differences in the styling of the two sub-classes, but they were identical in main dimensions. They had two cylinders, 24in x 30in (610mm x 760mm), boiler pressure was 275psi (1,894kPa), coupled wheels 77in (1956mm), and tractive effort 52,000lbs (23,600kgs). Grate area was 73.7sq.ft. (6.85sq.metre), and there was a combustion chamber to ensure thorough burning of the coal.

Described by CNR publicity, unusually honestly, as 'semi-streamlined,' these locomotives were attractive, especially as they were painted in the CN/GTW new green and black livery. Louvres at the front of the streamlined casing lifted smoke and steam as they left the chimney. The tender was of Vanderbilt type, and an unusual feature was the disc window on the driver's side. This was a patented 'Kent' design, which rotated at high speed to keep the glass clean. Another feature was a track sprinkler under the tender whose purpose was the laying of dust on the roadbed that otherwise would have been blown up and out by the wind of the locomotive. This device does not seem to have made much impression, but the locomotives put in good service. After dieselization of main passenger trains they were employed for some years on

*4-8-4 New York Central S1A, 1945.*

*4-8-4 Soviet Railways P36 Class, 1950.*

*For its transcontinental trains on the eve of deiselisation, the Union Pacific RR used 45 FEF Class 4-8-4s built in three batches between 1937 and 1944. The first units had single chimneys and 77in driving wheels, while the later ones had double chimneys and 80in wheels. The picture shows the last to be built, which is preserved for excursion use and provided with supplementary tender.*

commuter trains out of Toronto and Detroit. One of the CNR batch is preserved at Ottawa.

### ATCHISON, TOPEKA AND SANTA FE CLASS 3765/1938/USA

Most of the 4-8-4 types built in the United States from 1929 onwards carried an engine weight of over 447,019lb (203 tonnes), but the version with the highest tractive force was the one produced in 1934 for the Delaware and Lackawanna Railroad which gave a value of 72,000lb (32,660kg) for a total weight of 446,292lb (202.4 tonnes). The outstanding model, however, was probably the 3765 class built for the Atchison, Topeka and Santa F, in 1938 by the Baldwin Locomotive Company. These locomotives had 28in x 32in (711mm x 813mm) cylinders and used steam at 300psi (2068kPa). With their 80in (2032mm) driving wheels, they could run at up to 85mph (137kph) and give a tractive force of 80,000lb (36,290kg) without the need of a booster. The boiler had a total heating surface area of 7,678sq.ft. (714sq.metre) and the grate area was 108sq.ft. (10sq.metre). The power output at the maximum steaming rate of 91,000 pounds (41,278kg) per hour was estimated as 5,300ihp (3,952kW) from a total weight of 510,015lb (231.3 tonnes). The tender, borne on two six-wheeled trucks, held 21,000 gallons (795hl) of water and 7,000 gallons (265hl) of oil, and weighed 396,238lb (179.7 tonnes).

### NORFOLK & WESTERN RAILROAD J CLASS/1941

Fourteen of these passenger locomotives were built in the NW workshops. They were the last US streamlined locomotives to remain in the service for which they were designed, the N & W being the last railroad to operate steam-hauled streamliners. They were remarkable for their ability to reach high speeds while having driving wheels of only 70in (1778mm). They often reached 80mph (129kph) in daily service, and on trial one reached 140mph (225kph). Care with the balancing, with use of lightweight rods, was part of the reason for this. Good lubrication was another reason. Mechanical lubrication reached 220 points and another 72 points were reached by pressure groaoo. The boiler worked at 300psi (2067kPa), and had a 107.7sq.ft. (10sq.metre) grate, to which was annexed a 103¼in (2622mm) combustion chamber. Cylinders were 27in x 32in (686mm x 813mm), giving an 80,000lb (36,320kg) tractive effort; they were the most powerful engines ever built of that wheel arrangement. Weight of engine was 494,000lb (224 tonnes) and the tender weighed 378,600lb (171.7 tonnes) when full.

Numbers 605-610 were built without streamlining, making it easier for the Railroad to claim before the War Production Board that these were not really passenger locomotives (whose construction was not permitted). They received their streamlining after the war. In service the J locomotives could register 15,000 miles (24,000km) a month, which was high utilization. After they were finally withdrawn in 1959 one of them, No.611, made a reappearance in the 1980s on tourist excursions before retiring to stationary exhibition in Roanoke.

### CANADIAN NATIONAL RAILWAYS U2g CLASS/1942/CANADA

This class, together with the identical U2h Class, totalled 65 units and was a continuation of the earlier U2a, introduced in 1927. However, the 1942 locomotives, numbered in the 6200 series, were unlike the 6100 series of the 1927 batch in that they were built without boosters. They also differed in having Boxpok rather than the spoked wheels of the 90 earlier engines. But the main dimensions were the same. These included 73in (1860mm) driving wheels, 250psi (1722kPa) boiler pressure, and 25½ x 30in cylinders (650mm x 762mm), giving a drawbar pull of 56,800lb (25,787kg). They weighed 377,055lb (171 tonnes). Whereas the 6100 series began to be withdrawn in the 1940s, the 6200 series continued in regular service up to 1961, and was in charge of the Toronto-Montreal passenger trains up to 1957. In its last decade, it tended to be used mainly, but not exclusively, for freight work.

### NEW YORK CENTRAL RAILROAD CLASS S-1A/1945/USA

Of all the 4-8-4 types built in the United States the most outstanding, from the point of view of power output, were those of Class S-1A, built by Alco for the New York Central Railroad in 1945 as a last defiant gesture against the rival threat of diesel. They cost only half as much as a 4,000hp (2,983kW) diesel.

With cylinders measuring 25in x 32in (365mm x 813mm) and using steam at 290psi (2000kPa), these gave a tractive force of 62,500lb (28,350kg) with 79in (2006mm) driving wheels, and their power output was 6,300ihp (4,698kW) at 90mph (145kph) or 4,860dbhp (3,624kW) at 70mph (113kph). The boiler had a heating surface of 6,887sq.ft. (640sq.metre) with a grate area of 100sq.ft. (9.3sq.metre). The engine weight was 471,208lb (213.7 tonnes), giving a specific output of 30ihp per ton (22kW/tonne). The tender held 18,000 gallons (681hl) of water and 102,973lb (46.7 tonnes) of coal on a weight of 420,052lb (190.5 tonnes), making an adhesive weight of 267,465lb (121.3 tonnes) out of a total of 892,584lb (404.8 tonnes). These engines could haul 1,000-long-ton (1,016-tonne) trains at over 100mph (160kph), but the carbon steel used in the boiler plates developed flaws, and this led to their early retirement.

### MEXICAN NATIONAL RAILWAYS CLASS QR-1/1946/MEXICO

Mexican railways acquired their motive power from the USA, often second-hand. As they tended to purchase their locomotives in small lots, only when needed rather than in accordance with a long-term plan, their stock was highly variegated. But after World War 2, when no locomotives had been acquired, there was a big need for replacements. The order placed with Alco and Baldwin in 1945 was the last that Mexican National Railways would place for steam traction.

There were 32 units in this order. The QR-1 Class was a light 4-8-4, considerably smaller than other North American locomotives of this wheel arrangement. With its lightly tapered boiler it had the look of a swift machine, but in fact had been ordered for freight service, although its coupled wheels of 70in (1778mm) diameter indicated that fast freight service was envisaged. The grate area was 77.3sq ft (7.18sq.metre) and the total evaporative heating surface was 4,186sq ft (389sq.metre) to which the firebox contributed 340sq.ft. (31.6sq.metre). A superheater of 1,667sq.ft. (154.8sq.metre) was provided. There were two 25in x 30in (635mm x 762mm) cylinders, and boiler pressure was 250psi (1722kPa). The resultant tractive effort was 57,000lbs (25,855kgs). The locomotive weighed 387,000lbs (175,540kgs) of which 240,000lbs (108,862kgs) was on the coupled wheels. The tender was also small by US standards, accommodating 15,000 US gallons (56,824 litres) of water and 6,000 gallons (22,730 litres) of fuel oil. These locomotives were the last steam units to survive dieselization in the 1960s, and one of them was shipped back to the USA for preservation.

### CLASS P36/1950/USSR

Almost the last of the 4-8-4 types to be built were those of Class P36, built in 1950 in the USSR by the Kolomna Works. They were fitted with two cylinders measuring 22²⁄₃in x 31¹⁄₂in (575mm x 800mm) and, using steam at 210psi (1448kPa), they drove 73in (1850mm) diameter wheels to give a tractive force of 39,500lb (17,917kg). Built to an axle-load of 41,454lb (18.8 tonnes), they weighed only 297,454lb (134.9 tonnes). Two hundred and fifty-one were built and almost 30 have been preserved, including a handful in working order.

### SPANISH NATIONAL RAILWAYS (RENFE) CLASS 242-2000P/1955/SPAIN

By European standards, these were very big engines. Ten of them were built by La Maquinista and were intended to handle heavy trains on the mountainous section of the Madrid-Bilbao line. Later in their life they were transferred to haul trains on the Madrid-Zaragoza route. In working

*One of the few Soviet P36 4-8-4 locomotives to be painted blue, instead of the standard green livery.*

order the engine weighed 319,670lb (145 tonnes). The tractive effort was 35,850lb (16,260kg), produced by steam pressure of 227psi (1566kPa) acting in 25⅛in x 28in (640mm x 710mm) cylinders on coupled wheels of 75in (1900mm). They had Lentz valve gear and were the only RENFE locomotives painted green. They had feedwater heaters and a turbo-generator for electric lighting. One light was placed in front of the chimney, facing backwards; this enabled the fireman to study the smoke at night (they were oil-burners). The grate area was 57sq.ft. (5.29sq.metre).

# 6-8-6

## PENNSYLVANIA RAILROAD No 6200/1944/USA

Since 1938 the Pennsylvania Railroad had been attempting to find a satisfactory way of hauling 1,200-ton (1,219-tonne) trains at 100mph (160kph), a task requiring an output of at least 6,500ihp (4,847kW). Since a power output of that size caused problems concerning the load on the connecting rods, the Pennsylvania Railroad had endeavoured to meet the requirement by using eight or ten wheel-drive locomotives with divided drives, calling for two sets of cylinders. However, this option had run into difficulties over the matter of adhesion. In an attempt to provide an eight-coupled engine with coupled wheels, the railroad tried a turbine-power unit with a geared drive to the wheels. The wheels were all connected by coupling or side rods with roller-bearings. The turbine had a rated output of 6,000hp (4,474kW) and drove the 68in (1727mm) wheels through spring-cushioned torque-ring gears. The steam pressure was 310psi (2138kPa), giving a tractive force of 70,500lb (31,980kg). The boiler had a heating-surface area of 7,052sq.ft. (655sq.metre) with a grate area of 120sq.ft. (11.16sq.metre). The total locomotive weight was 579,919lb (263 tonnes).

With only 26 per cent of the total weight available for adhesion, the locomotive could not compete with the diesel opposition, and so no more were built.

*4-8-4 Spanish National Railways 242-2000P Class, 1955 (top), A Spanish 242-2000P 4-8-4 at work on the Madrid – Zaragoza line in the mid 1960's (above).*

# TEN-COUPLED LOCOMOTIVES

## 0-10-0

### PRUSSIAN STATE RAILWAY SERIES G10/1910/GERMANY

In the years before World War 1 the Prussian State Railway relied heavily on the 0-8-0 for its freight haulage, and particularly on the G7 and its superheated, piston-valve, G8 successor. Many of these eight-wheelers were scattered over Europe as a result of the war; others had been bought new by various railways, which found them useful engines. The G10 built on this success. It had one more axle than the G8, and it had the advantage of using the same, larger, boiler as was used for the P8 passenger locomotive. It had a speed limit of 31-37 mph (50-60kph); anything faster would have dangerously amplified its

oscillations. So it was really a specialized heavy freight hauler in its early decades. The G10 was very suited to the railways of eastern and central Europe, thanks to its lighter axle-weight. Some units were built new for Poland, Turkey and, especially, Roumania. The latter used several hundred of them and it was there that the type survived longest, being in use on local freight trains into the late 1970s. In all, more than 2,400 were built.

In accordance with Prussian practice, steam pressure at 170psi (1175kPa) was quite low. The grate area was 27.8sq.ft. (2.58sq.metre). The outside cylinders were of 24¾in x 26in (630mm x 660mm) and coupled wheels 55in (1400mm). In working order the locomotive weighed 168,800lbs (76.6 tonnes), so the axle-weight was less than 35,264lbs (16 tonnes). Tractive effort was 39,350lb (17,860kg) and grate area 27.8sq.ft. (2.58sq.metre).

### MIDLAND RAILWAY No 2290/1919/GREAT BRITAIN

The second of the British Decapods (the first had been a tank engine built for the Great Eastern Railway in 1903)

was the Midland version, known as 'Big Emma'; it was the largest engine ever built at the Midland's Derby workshops, and was designed for banking duties on the 1 in 37 (2.7 per cent) grade of the Lickey Incline between Bromsgrove and Blackwell on the line from Birmingham to Bristol.

With four cylinders measuring 16⅘in x 28in (427mm x 711mm) and with driving wheels of diameter 55½in (1409mm) the tractive force was 43,300lb (19,641kg) from a weight of 165,154lb (74.9 tonnes). The cylinders drove onto the second axle and were inclined at an angle of 1 in 7, with two sets of piston valves for all four cylinders. The leading axle was built with small cranks between the frames so as to clear the internal connecting rods. The boiler supplied steam at 180psi (1241kPa) from a heating surface of area 2,160sq.ft. (201sq.metre), and the firegrate area was 31.5sq.ft. (2.9sq.metre). A superheater was fitted, but as the engine could work at full output for only about 10 minutes out of every hour it never really got properly warmed up. An enclosed cab permitted operation in either direction for uphill banking or for running downhill. It became BR No.58100, and remained in service until 1956.

*0-10-0 Midland Railway No 2290, 1919. The locomotive is shown carrying its final British Railway number.*

*0-10-0 Prussian State Railways G10 Class, 1910.*

### E CLASS/1922/USSR

The largest class of Decapods were those designed before World War 1 and then ordered by the new Soviet government from both home and, for a time, Swedish and German builders. The cylinder size was 24²⁄₅in x 27½in (620mm x 700mm), and the wheels were of diameter 52in (1320mm). With steam at 170psi (1172kPa), these engines gave a tractive force of 46,000lb (20,866kg). The boiler had 2,540sq.ft. (236sq.metre) of heating surface, with a grate area of 48sq.ft. (4.46sq.metre) on an all-up weight of only 179,701lb (81.5 tonnes). This locomotive was the mainstay of the Soviet Railways effort in the inter-war industrialization program. During its long production run of around four decades, many sub-classes emerged, but it remained an unsophisticated, rather rough-riding, heavy-hauler that could tolerate ill treatment. About 11,000 units were built, making it the world's most numerous locomotive class.

### DULUTH, MISSABE AND NORTHERN `TEN-WHEEL SWITCHERS'/1925/USA

The last and largest of the 0-10-0 type built in the United States (where they were known as 'Ten-Wheel Switchers') were those built in 1925 for banking duty on the Duluth, Missabe and Northern Railroad, a mineral line conveying iron ore for shipment across Lake Superior. With 28in x 30in (711mm x 762mm) cylinders driving 57in (1448mm) wheels, the tractive force came to 77,600lb (35,200kg) - - which was supplemented by a further 14,500lb (6,577kg) from a booster motor on the tender wheels. The steam was supplied at 245psi (1690kPa) from a boiler with 5,343sq.ft. (496sq.metre) of heating surface and a firegrate of area of 80sq.ft. (7.4sq.metre). The total weight of the locomotive - all of which was available for adhesion - was 352,138lb (159.7 tonnes).

# 0-10-2

### DULUTH, MISSABE AND IRON RANGE RR CLASS S-7/1937/USA

The 0-10-2 was a very rare type of machine designed for heavy-transfer duty; apart from some built for the Union Pacific Railroad in 1936 by Baldwin, the only others were the Class S-7 supplied to the Duluth, Missabe and Iron Range Railroad in 1937. These were equipped with two cylinders measuring 28in x 32in (711mm x 812mm) and, with wheels of 61in (1550mm) diameter, they gave a tractive force of 90,900lb (41,232kg) with steam at a pressure of 260psi (1793kPa). In addition, a booster engine gave a further 17,100lb (7,757kg) of tractive force. The ample boiler had 6,137sq.ft. (570sq.metre) of heating surface and a firebox with a grate area of 85.2sq.ft. (7.9sq.metre). The engine weight was 422,037lb (191.4 tonnes), and the tender, which held 10,000 gallons (378.5hl) of water and 28,0039lb (12.7 tonnes) of coal, weighed 240,124lb (108.9 tonnes). These locomotives were allowed a top speed of 35mph (56.3kph).

# 2-10-0

Although first built in the United States in 1870 for the Lehigh Valley Railroad, this type was not to prove so popular in North America - only some 700 were built there - as in Europe, where it was to find an enormous outlet. Confusingly, in North America 2-10-0s were known as 'Decapods'- the name given in Europe to 0-10-0s.

*(opposite) 0-10-0 Soviet Railways E Class, 1922. First built before 1914, this 0-10-0 eventually became the world's most numerous steam locomotive type.*

## ERIE RAILROAD BALDWIN VAUCLAIN COMPOUND/1893/USA

The first significant design in the United States was one constructed by the Baldwin Locomotive Co. for the Columbia Exposition at Chicago in 1893. Using the Vauclain compound system, in which the high and low-pressure cylinders were joined in parallel with both driving onto a common crosshead, the locomotive (No. 805) was the heaviest that had then been built in the United States: it weighed 195,363lb (88.6 tonnes). The cylinders were arranged with two high-pressure ones of bore 16in (406mm) and two low-pressure ones of bore 23in (584mm), all with 28in (711mm) stroke and driving 50in (1270mm) wheels. The steam was supplied at 180psi (1241kPa) and gave a tractive force of 44,000lb (19,958kg), from an adhesive weight of 171,990lb (78 tonnes). The boiler had a heating-surface area of 2,420sq.ft. (225sq.metre) with a firegrate area of 89.4sq.ft. (8.3sq.metre). As with the tandem-compound type, the twin cylinders raised problems with balancing the reciprocating parts; the Vauclain system did not find many further applications.

## SANTA FÉ No.989/1902/USA

With operation in mountainous areas, the Atchison, Topeka and Santa Fé was a natural early purchaser of the 2-10-0 type; its first tandem compound version was supplied by Alco in 1902. With cylinders of bores 17½in (445mm) and 30in (762mm), and a stroke of 34in (864mm), and with steam at 225psi (1551kPa), the tractive force was 55,300lb (25,084kg) using driving wheels of 57in (1448mm) diameter. The boiler had a heating-surface area of 4,682sq.ft. (435sq.metre), but the firegrate area, being over the rear wheels, was limited to 59.5sq.ft. (5.53sq.metre), which was just about the limit for hand-firing before the development of mechanical stokers. The locomotive weight was 259,528lb (117.7 tonnes), of which 231,196lb (105.2 tonnes) were available for adhesion. The typical low-sided tender of that era held 7,000 gallon (318hl) of water, weighed 60.27-long-tons (61.2 tonnes), and was carried on two four-wheeled trucks.

## BELGIAN STATE RAILWAY SERIES 36/1909/BELGIUM

The first European user of the 2-10-0 type in quantity was the Belgian state system, where the type was required for heavy coal trains: as designed by M. Flamme, it was the first European tender locomotive to be built at a weight in excess of 220,500lb (100 tonnes). With four cylinders measuring 19⅔in x 26in (500mm x 660mm), and with driving wheels of diameter 57in (1450mm), it gave a tractive force of 60,200lb (27,307kg) using steam at a pressure of 200psi (1,380kPa). The total weight came to 229,760lb (104.2 tonnes), of which 198,670lb (90.1 tonnes) were on the driving wheels and available for adhesion. In operation they could haul a 600-long-ton

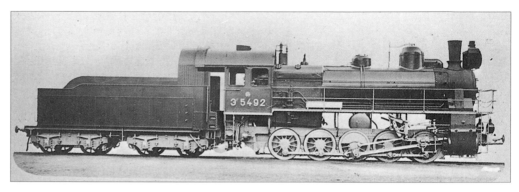

*0-10-0 Soviet Raillways 'E' Class, 1922. This is one of those built in Germany.*

*0-10-0 Duluth Missabe & Iron Range RR Ten-Wheel Switchers, 1925.*

(610-tonne) train up a grade of 1 in 62 (1.6 per cent) at 21.75mph (35kph), a task requiring an output of 2,000ihp (1,491kW). These machines were erected by various locomotive builders; eventually 153 were put into service. In 1925 two were fitted with double chimneys and, using superheated steam, proved capable of outputs of over 2,300ihp (1,715kW).

## SOVIET RAILWAYS CLASS Ea 2-10-0/1916/USSR

During World War 1 the Russian Government ordered for their 5ft (1524mm) gauge system some 1,200 locomotives from US locomotive builders. Built to an axle-load of only 35,831lb (16.25 tonnes) these used two cylinders measuring 25in x 28in (635mm x 711mm), with steam at 180psi (1241kPa), driving wheels of diameter 52in (1320mm) and giving a tractive force of 51,500lb (23,360kg), although intended only for operation at low speeds. The firegrate area was 64.7sq.ft. (6sq.metre).

In 1920 some 200 of these engines were still awaiting shipment. Following the Revolution in Russia, they were converted to work on the standard gauge and sold to railways in the United States that required locomotives with low axle-loadings. The total weight of the finished locomotive was only 203,411lb (92.25 tonnes). About

2,000 similar locomotives were supplied to the USSR as Class Ea from 1944 onwards. A few of these locomotives have been preserved, including one at the Spencer workshops in North Carolina.

## PENNSYLVANIA RAILROAD CLASS I-1S/1916/USA

In 1916 the Pennsylvania Railroad put one of their class I-1S engines through a thorough test on the locomotive test-plant at their Altoona works. The locomotive was a two-cylinder type, with cylinders of dimensions 30½in x 32in (775mm x 813mm), using steam at 250psi (1724kPa): it gave a tractive force of 80,640lb (36,578kg) from driving wheels of diameter 62in (1575mm). The total weight was 366,470lb (166.2 tonnes) of which 334,498lb (151.7 tonnes) were available for adhesion. The boiler had a heating area of 5,375sq.ft. (499sq.metre) and a grate area of 70sq.ft.(6.5sq.metre), and could produce a maximum of 58,000lb (26,308kg) steam per hour, giving a cylinder output of 3,500ihp (2,610kW) at 25mph (40kph). At the most efficient rate the steam output was 41,000lb (18,600kg) per hour, corresponding to an output of 2,500ihp (1,864kW), at which the boiler efficiency was 67 per cent and the overall efficiency 9.8 per cent with a coal consumption of 2.4lb per ihp-hr (1.46kg/kW-hr). The coal consumption at the

*2-10-0 Santa Fe Nos 988-989 tandem compounds, 1902.*

maximum steaming rate was 12,000lb (5,443kg) per hour, equivalent to 3.4lb per ihp-hr (2.07kg/kW-hr).

## PENNSYLVANIA CLASS 4300/1922/USA

The principal user of the 2-10-0 type in the United States was the Pennsylvania Railroad; in 1922 came its largest and last version, with a total weight of 386,316lb (175.2 tonnes), of which 352,138lb (159.7 tonnes) was on the driving wheels. With two cylinders measuring 30½in x 32in (775mm x 813mm), they drove 62in (1575mm) wheels with steam at 250psi (1724kPa), and gave a tractive force of 90,000lb (40,824kg) on an axle-load of 70,339lb (31.9 tonnes). The boiler had a heating surface of area 7,076sq.ft. (658sq.metre) with a firegrate area of 70sq.ft. (6.5sq.metre). The tender was on two four-wheeled trucks, and had a total weight of 212,175lb (94.3 tonnes); it held 10,300 gallon (468hl) of water.

## GERMAN STATE RAILWAYS (DR) CLASS 44/1926/GERMANY

Following the success of the Prussian G.12 class, the Reichsbahn selected a more powerful version. This too had three cylinders, measuring 21⅔in x 26in (550mm x 660mm), but with the steam pressure increased to 227psi (1600kPa); the driving wheels were the same size as in the G.12 - diameter 55in (1400mm). The boiler-size was increased, to give a heating area of 4,176sq.ft. (388sq.metre) with a grate area of 49.5sq.ft. (4.6sq.metre). The tractive force was increased to 64,200lb (29,121kg) on an adhesive weight of 212,341lb (96.3 tonnes) out of a total weight of 226,674lb (102.8 tonnes). Following successful trials of an initial batch of 10, the final number built was over 2,000 (by 1949).

*North American railroads were not enthusiastic users of the 2-10-0 type. The 2-8-2 rode better and had equivalent boiler power. The 2-10-0 had its uses for slow drag work, but not for much else. The example pictured here was unusal in that it used to work for a small mid-western line which had no great need for heavy haulage. Nowadays it works on the Strasburg Railroad, hauling tourists.*

*2-10-0 German State Railway 44 Class, 1926.*

## GERMAN STATE RAILWAYS (DR) CLASS 50/1938/GERMANY

Among the range of standard locomotives introduced by the inter-war DR, the Class 50 was the most numerous freight type, even though the first was built by Henschel as late as 1938. Not only this, but the Class became the basis of the celebrated Kriegslok. The Class 50 was built to replace the old Prussian 0-10-0 locomotives, and it could haul loads 40 per cent heavier than those. Moreover, it had an axle-weight of only 33,075lb (15 tonnes). Like other standard designs, the underlying aim was to produce a reliable and simple-to-maintain locomotive. Cylinders were 23³⁄₅in x 26in (600mm x 660mm), driving wheels 55in (1400mm), and boiler pressure 227psi (1566kPa), giving a tractive effort of 47,841lb (21,720kg). Grate area was 41.8sq ft (3.89sq.metre) The engine weighed 191,614lb (86.9 tonnes), and its tender was 134,509lb (61 tonnes) when loaded (it carried 28,665lb (13 tonnes) of coal and 7,000 gallons of water). These were very useful and versatile locomotives. As late as the 1960s they could be seen working not only freight, but also secondary passenger trains in Western Germany.

## GERMAN NATIONAL CLASS 52 KRIEGSLOK/1942/GERMANY

This was a progressive development of the 50 Class. Manufacturing methods were simplified and scarce materials dispensed with as far as possible. The two

cylinders were 23²⁄₃in (600mm) in diameter by 26in (660mm) and used steam at 227psi (1600kPa); with the same wheel diameter, 55in (1400mm), they gave a tractive force of 50,200lb (22,771kg). The total weight was brought down to 155,955lb (84.1 tonnes). Many thousands of this class were produced for war service. They were to find their way all over Europe, and were built by many locomotive builders in the various countries occupied by the German armies. Dozens have been preserved, several in working order.

## BRITISH MINISTRY OF SUPPLY AUSTERITY CLASS/1944/GREAT BRITAIN

In 1942 the former 8F freight locomotive of the London, Midland and Scottish Railway was redesigned for production with the intention of having some locomotives to supply to Europe after its liberation from the Nazi armies. In addition to the 2-8-0 type of Austerity locomotive there were 150 of the 2-10-0 type built to a 30,208lb (13.7-tonne) axle-load and with an enlarged boiler and firegrate to burn poor-quality fuel. All were built by the North British

*A newly-built 44 Class 2-10-0, which also shows the multi-gauge tracks found in locomotive works, 1926.*

*2-10-0 German State Railways 50 Class, 1938.*

## SOVIET RAILWAYS L CLASS/1945/RUSSIA

This design originated during World War 2, when a need was envisaged for a powerful locomotive that could work over the war-torn tracks of the post-war Soviet Union. In this role they were successful, and over four thousand were built at three locomotive works (Kolomna, Lugansk and Bryansk). They were unsophisticated machines with high-pitched boilers. Their cylinders were 25½in x 31½in (650mm x 800mm), coupled wheels 59in (1500mm), and boiler pressure 200psi (1378kPa), giving a tractive effort of 64,488lb (29,277kg). The locomotive weighed 227,115lb (103 tonnes) and the grate area was 64.6sq m (6sq.metre). With an axle-weight of 39,690lb (18 tonnes), these locomotives could not go everywhere, but almost all the main lines were open to them. Construction ceased in 1955, but the class survived in diminishing numbers. Some went to the strategic reserve, others were put into service as stationary boilers, while others remained at depots, waiting to help out at times of motive power shortage. At the end of the century there were still some to be seen.

Locomotive Company. They used two cylinders measuring 19in x 28in (483mm x 711mm) with steam at 225psi (1551kPa). The 56½in (1435mm) diameter driving wheels gave a tractive force of 34,200lb (15,513kg), and the boiler heating area was 2,373sq.ft. (220sq.metre) with a grate area of 40sq.ft. (3.7sq.metre). The total weight was 175,518lb (79.6 tonnes), of which 15,0381lb (68.2 tonnes) were on the driving wheels. Of the 150, 25 were returned to Britain for use by British Railways; all were withdrawn in 1961.

## POLISH GOVERNMENT RAILWAY CLASS Ty-246/1947/POLAND

The last of the US-built 2-10-0 types were of two classes, both supplied in 1947, one to Turkey and one to Poland. The Polish version was slightly larger, being built with two cylinders of dimensions 25in x 27½in (630mm x 700mm);

*2-10-0 German Kriegslok, 1942.*

*2-10-0 British Austerity Class, 1944.*

with a steam pressure of 227psi (1600kPa) these drove 57in (1450mm) diameter wheels, giving a tractive force of 58,200lb (26,400kg). The boiler had 3,670sq.ft. (341sq.metre) of heating surface and a grate area of 67.8sq.ft. (6.3sq.metre). The total weight amounted to 264,379lb (119.9 tonnes), of which 231,750lb (103 tonnes) were on the driving wheels.

Three American builders, Alco, Baldwin and Lima, supplied 100 of that type, and these were followed by the Polish-built class Ty-51 locomotives, which were almost identical; of this type, 232 were built by the Polish firm of Cegielski. In all, Polish Railways put into service 1,530 locomotives of the 2-10-0 wheel arrangement from 1934.

## CZECHOSLOVAK STATE RAILWAYS CLASS 556.0/1952/CZECHOSLOVAKIA

The steam locomotive and an independent Czechoslovakia coexisted for hardly four decades, yet by the end of that era it could be argued that a specifically Czech school of locomotive design had emerged. This was based on German practice (especially on wartime experience with the Kriegslok)and on French practice (and theory even more) as exemplified by the Chapelon school. The Class 556.0 was one of the last products of the Czech school, and possibly the most outstanding. Using the boiler and some components of a contemporaneous 4-8-2 (a compound, in the French style), the 556.0 was a two-cylinder simple-expansion machine with a Kylchap double chimney. More than 500 were built over five years and they were to be seen on most Czech lines, having a moderate axle-weight. They could easily haul coal trains of around 3,000 tons. Their tractive effort was 47,636lb (21,627kg), developed by 21½in x 26in (550 x 660mm) cylinders, 55in (1400mm) coupled wheels, and 256psi (1765kPa) boiler pressure. They weighed in working order

*2-10-0 Austerity Class, 1944. The locomotive is in the livery of the Royal Engineers' Longmoor Military Railway.*

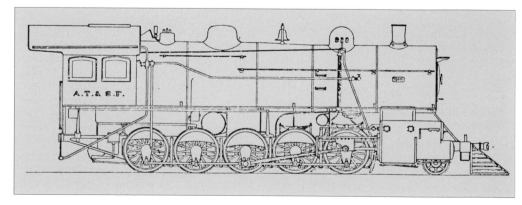

*2-10-0 Russian E Class, 1916.*

*2-10-0 Soviet Railways L Class, 1945.*

*2-10-0 Polish Railways TY-246 Class, 1947.*

double chimneys, 3 with mechanical stokers, 10 with Franco-Crosti boilers (which were later removed), and one with a Giesel ejector exhaust. The last one to be built was named Evening Star on 8 March 1960.

Withdrawals took place between 1964 and 1968. Seven have been preserved, including Evening Star.

# 2-10-2

### SANTA FE (ATCHISON, TOPEKA AND SANTA FE RAILROAD) CLASS 915/1903/USA

First built for the Santa Fe line in 1903 by the Baldwin Locomotive Company, this type was given the name of that line. The Santa Fe had been testing out just over 50 of the 4-cylinder tandem compound type, and Class 915 was 159 units working on that system. With the high-pressure cylinders at 19in (483mm) and the low-pressure ones at 32in (81 cm) bore, the stroke was 32in (81cm). Steam was supplied at 225psi (1551kpa); with driving wheels of 57in (1448mm) diameter, this gave a tractive force of 58,000lb (26,309kg). The boiler had a heating-surface area of 4,817sq.ft. (448sq.metre) and a grate area of 59sq.ft. (5.5sq.metre), and was presumably hand-fired. The total weight was 282,460lb (130.2 tonnes), of which 233,950lb (106.1 tonnes) were available for adhesion. The tender was carried on two four-wheeled trucks and, with 7,000 gallons (318hl) of water, weighed 134,946lb (61.2 tonnes).

209,475lb (95 tonnes), of which 176,400lb (80 tonnes) was available for adhesion. Sustaining the power output was a large boiler with a 46.7sq.ft. (4.34sq.metre) grate area.

### BRITISH RAILWAYS CLASS 9F/1954/GREAT BRITAIN

The most successful of all the standard locomotives built by British Railways after 1951 were the 251 of the 9F class, first built in 1954. These were originally intended to be 2-8-2s, but the perceived value of the returned 'Austerity' 2-10-0s caused the design to be amended to allow the use of 60in (1524mm) wheels, thus permitting

an adequate firegrate area, of 40.2sq.ft. (3.73sq.metre). With cylinders measuring 20in x 28in (508mm x 711mm) and with steam at 250psi (1724kPa), the tractive force was 39,700lb (18,008kg); on test at the Rugby Locomotive Testing Plant one gave an output of 1,770 dbhp (1,320kW) at 35mph (56.3kph), with the boiler supplying steam at 30,000 pounds (13,608kg) per hour. The boiler had a heating area of 2,549sq.ft. (237sq.metre) and the total weight of the locomotive was 194,260lb (88.1 tonnes), of which 173,533lb (78.7 tonnes) were carried on the driving wheels. These engines could run at up to 90mph (145kph), and at their most economical rate - 25mph (40kph) - the coal consumption rate was 2.15 pounds per dbhp-hr (1.31kg/kW-hr). Of these locomotives 72 were fitted with

Largely because of the problems associated with the balancing of the moving parts, this was the last major order for tandem compounds.

## UNION PACIFIC RAILROAD
### No.5036/1917/USA

From 1912 the conventional 2-10-2 was to prove a useful freight engine, and some 2,200 were built for use within the US railroad system. The USSR adopted the type on a large scale, and a few were built in Europe, but the 2-10-2 was primarily an American locomotive.

Those built by Baldwin for the Union Pacific weighed out at no less than 368,455lb (167.1 tonnes). With two cylinders at 29½in x 30in (749cm x 762cm) they drove 63in (1600mm) wheels and, with steam at 200psi (1380kPa), gave a tractive force of 70,400lb (31,933kg). The boiler had a heating surface of 6,313sq.ft. (587sq.metre) and a grate area of 84sq.ft. (7.8sq.metre)

*2-10-0 Czechoslovak State Railways 556.0 Class, 1952.*

*2-10-0 British Railways 9F Class, 1954. This is the double-chimney variant.*

# STEAM TENDER LOCOMOTIVES

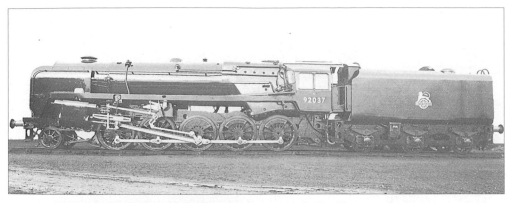

*2-10-0 British Railways 9F Class, 1954. This is the standard single-chimney variant.*

*2-10-0 British Railway 9F as built with Crosti boiler, 1955.*

compound type, but owing to the size of the cylinders, none of them could be accommodated between the frames, and the drive was divided between the two sets of wheels which were coupled by an internal coupling rod. The cylinder sizes were 19in x 25½in (480mm x 650mm) and 29⅓in x 27½in (745mm x 700mm). The driving wheels were of diameter 59in (1500mm), and, with a steam pressure of 284psi (1958kPa), the tractive effort amounted to 54,000lb (24,494kg) from an adhesive weight of 204,403lb (92.7 tonnes). The total weight came to 269,982lb (122.4 tonnes). There would have been more built, but the advent of war and subsequent electrification did away with the need for such powerful freight engines.

## CHINESE RAILWAYS QJ CLASS/1956/CHINA

At the end of the 20th Century this type was undoubtedly the most numerous of the world's surviving heavy steam locomotives, having been built by the thousand up to the 1980s. The first series, known then as the 'Peace' Class, was built at the Dalian Locomotive Works, although by the time production ceased the construction was done at Datong Works. They incorporated Russian features, and rather resembled Russian 2-10-2 types then being built in the Soviet Union. The wheels and cylinders were similar

## USRA STANDARDS (LIGHT AND HEAVY)/1919/USA

The entries 9 and 10 in the table of USRA Standard locomotives for the 1919 program included two types of 2-10-2 . The particulars of these were: see box

At the time they were built the wheel arrangement was falling out of favour. The light version was little superior to a heavy 2-8-2, while for heavy freight railroads were turning to the Mallet rather than to heavy 2-10-2s.

## READING RAILROAD CLASS 3000/1931/USA

Probably the last of the 2-10-2 type to be built for use in the United States were those for the Reading Railroad which showed a growth in weight of nearly 60 per cent over those built for the Santa F, in 1903. The Reading version used cylinders of dimensions 30½in x 32in (775mm x 813mm) with driving wheels of diameter 61½in (1562mm) and steam at 225psi (1551kPa); this gave a tractive force of 92,500lb (41,958kg). The boiler's heating-surface area was 7,312sq.ft. (680sq.metre) and its grate area was 108sq.ft. (10.04sq.metre). Total engine weight was 451,143lb (204.6 tonnes), of which 364,045lb (165.1 tonnes) were on the driving wheels. The maximum axle-load was 73,867lb (33.5 tonnes).

## PLM SERIES 151A/1932/FRANCE

Apart from those used in the USSR, in Europe the 2-10-2 was rare. Ten were built for the PLM by Schneider of Le Creusot in 1932. These were of the four-cylinder

*The last Santa Fe RR 2-10-2 built from 1919 to 1927.*

|  | USRA Light | USRA Heavy |
|---|---|---|
| Cylinder bore | 27in/686mm | 30in/762mm |
| Piston stroke | 32in/813mm | 32in/813mm |
| Wheel diameter | 57in/1448mm | 63in/1600mm |
| Steam pressure | 200psi/1,380kPa | 190psi/1,310kPa |
| Grate area | 76.3sq.ft./7.1sq.metre | 88.2 sq.ft./8.2sq.metre |
| Heating area | 4,656 sq.ft./433sq.metre | 5,151 sq.ft./479sq.metre |
| Adhesive weight | 276,000lb/125,194kg | 293,000lb/132,905kg |
| Total weight | 352,138lb/159.7 tonnes | 380,803lb/172.7 tonnes |
| Tractive force | 69,600lb/31,571kg | 73,800lb/33,476kg |
| Number built | 94 | 175 |

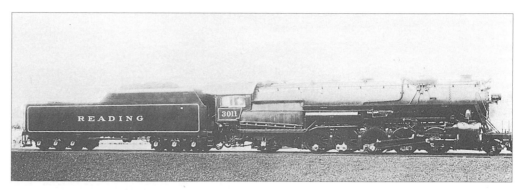

*One of the 21 2-10-2 locomotives operated by the Reading RR, the K1 Class, built 1927-39.*

to those of the Soviet LV Class 2-10-2, but the boiler was not quite the same, having a long combustion chamber to suit it for the long-flame Chinese coal. Over the years there were modifications to the design, which finally was known as the 'Progress' or QJ Class. This locomotive bore the burden of China's industrialization drive of the 1970s and 1980s and was still the dominant power on many long stretches of line in the 1990s. The weight, without tender, is 297,675lb (135 tonnes). Cylinders are 25½in x 31½in (650mm x 800mm), boiler pressure 213psi (1470kPa), wheel diameter 59in (1500mm). Tractive effort is 68,276lb (30,997kg) and the grate area 73.2sq.ft. (6.8sq.metre). The superheater is of 1519sq.ft. (141.2sq.metre). Russian-style Boxpok wheels are fitted, and there is a feedwater heater that seems to derive from the American Worthington type. Although designed for heavy freight, the class can sometimes be seen on passenger services. Units stationed in the far west of China had bigger (12-wheel) tenders.

## 2-10-4

### TEXAS AND PACIFIC RAILROAD
### No.660/1925/USA

The Lima Locomotive Company having produced the first of the Berkshire 2-8-4s in 1925 for the Boston and Albany, its next logical step was to build a 2-10-4; this suited the needs of the Texas and Pacific Railroad, which gave its name to this wheel arrangement.

With 29in x 32in (737mm x 813mm) cylinders and with steam at 255psi (1758kPa), the same size of driving wheels - diameter 63in (1600mm) - gave a tractive force of 84,600lb (38,375kg) on an adhesive weight of 307,046lb (139.25 tonnes) or an axle-load of 60,415lb (27.4 tonnes). The boiler supplied superheated steam from a heating surface area of 7,213sq.ft. (670sq.metre) with a grate area of 100sq.ft. (9.3sq.metre). Total engine weight was 457,095lb (207.3 tonnes).

*2-10-2 Chinese Railways QJ Class, 1956.*

*2-10-4 Canadian Pacific T1 Class, 1931. The locomotive shown is one of the final, T1-C, sub-class of six units built in 1949. They were known as the 'Selkirks'.*

*A 2-10-4 design of 40 units built by Lima for Chesapeake &Ohio RR in the 1930s.*

### CANADIAN PACIFIC RAILWAY CLASS T1 1931/CANADA

In 1931 the Canadian Pacific put the first of its Texas-type locomotives into commission for duty on the mountainous section of the line. The driving wheels were of diameter 63in (1600mm); the two cylinders measured 25in x 32in (635mm x 813mm); steam-pressure was 285psi (1965kPa); and the tractive force was 76,900lb (34,882kg). The trailing truck was equipped with a booster which gave an additional 12,500lb (5,675kg) for starting purposes. Super-heated steam was supplied by a boiler with a heating surface area of 6,645sq.ft. (617sq.metre); the grate area was 93.5sq.ft. (8.7sq.metre). The total

engine weight was 448,896lb (203.7 tonnes), with an axle-load of 50,715lb (28.3 tonnes). The engine was oil-fired and the tender, which held 4,100 gallon (186hl) of oil and 12,000 gallon (654hl) of water, weighed an additional 283,563lb (128.6 tonnes).

### SANTA FÉ CLASS 5001/1938/USA

The Texas type with the largest driving wheels was that built for the Atchison, Topeka and Santa Fé Railroad in 1938 by the Baldwin Locomotive Company for use in both freight and passenger duties. With 74in (1880mm) driving wheels, the two 30in x 34in (762mm

x 864mm) cylinders gave a tractive force of 93,000 pounds (42,185kg) using steam at a pressure of 310psi (2,138kPa). They were coal-fired and their grate area was 121.7 sq.ft. (11.3sq.metre), and the heating-surface area of the boiler amounted to 8,526 sq.ft. (792sq.metre), of which the superheater supplied 2,589 sq.ft. (240.7sq.metre). The total weight of the engine was 545,296lb (247.3 tonnes). The estimated power output came to 5,900ihp (4,400kW) and the thrust on the connecting rods was 215,645lb (99.3 tonnes). This was a limiting feature, and led to the adoption of a divided drive by some lines, particularly the Pennsylvania Railroad.

### PENNSYLVANIA RAILROAD CLASS J-la/1944/USA

The last and the heaviest of the Texas type were those built for the Pennsylvania Railroad. They had 70in (1778mm) driving wheels and, with cylinders of dimensions 29in x 34in (737mm X 865mm), they gave a tractive force of 98,900lb (44,900kg) using steam at a pressure of 285psi (1965kPa). The booster-fitted trailing truck added a further 15,000lb (6,804kg) of thrust for starting purposes. The boiler supplied the superheated steam from a heating area of 9,498sq.ft. (883sq.metre) with a grate area of 121.7sq.ft. (11.3sq.metre). With a maximum axle-load of 77,175lb (35 tonnes), the total engine weight amounted to 574,843lb (260.7 tonnes), with a tender-weight of 411,453lb (186.6 tonnes).

*2-10-2 PLM 151A Class compound, 1932.*

# 4-10-0

### BULGARIAN STATE RAILWAYS 4-10-0/1939/BULGARIA

The 4-10-0 was a very rare breed; apart from one built in 1884 by the Central Pacific Railroad in its own workshops, the only operational fleet was that supplied to the Bulgarian State Railway (BDZ), which owned 22 of them. The first 10 were built by Henschel in 1939, and the other 12 were built in 1943 by both Skoda and Borsig. The design included three cylinders measuring 20½in x 27½in (520mm x 700mm) driving wheels with a diameter of 57in (1450mm) and supplied with steam at a pressure of 227psi (1565kPa). The boiler had a heating surface of 3315sq.ft. (308sq.metre) with a firegrate area of 52.3sq.ft. (4.86sq.metre). The tractive force was 58,700lb (26,626kg). The adhesive weight was 186,984lb (84.8 tonnes) with a total engine weight of 241,227lb (109.4 tonnes).

# 4-10-2

### SOUTHERN PACIFIC RAILROAD CLASS 5000/1925/USA

There were only 60 of this type built: The first 10 were built by Alco for the Union Pacific Railroad, and they were followed by 49 of a slightly larger version for the Southern Pacific Railroad. In order to reduce the loading on the connecting rods, a three-cylinder drive was adopted, using the Gresley type of conjugated valve gear to operate the valves on the middle cylinder. That system enabled the cylinder size to be kept to 25in x 28in (635mm x 711mm) for the centre cylinder and 25in x 32in (635mm x 813mm) for the outside cylinders. With driving wheels of diameter 63in (1600mm), the tractive force was 83,500lb (37,876kg). The steam, at 225 psi (1551kPa), was supplied by a boiler having a heating surface of 7,176sq.ft. (667sq.metre) with a grate area of 89.6sq.ft. (8.32sq.metre). The total engine weight was 442,102lb (200.5 tonnes).

### BALDWIN LOCOMOTIVE WORKS No 60000/1926/USA

This was the only locomotive of the Overland type to be built by Baldwin; it was exhibited at the Railroad Convention.

*4-10-2 Southern Pacific 5000 Class, 1925.*

# TWELVE-COUPLED LOCOMOTIVES

## 2-12-0

### AUSTRIAN STATE RAILWAY SERIES 100/1910/AUSTRIA

The 20 locomotives built to this design were the last of Golsdorf's compounds and were for use on lines with a limiting anxle-load of 30,429lb (13.8 tonnes). The leading wheels were mounted in an Adams radial box with 2in (50.8mm) of side-play, and, in order to overcome the rigidity of six coupled axles, the third and sixth axles were given side-play of 1in (25.4mm) with 1½in (38.1mm) being allowed on the seventh axle; the coupling rod to that axle was driven through a flexible joint of the axle in front.

The cylinder-sizes were 17¾in (450mm) bore for the high-pressure and 30in (760mm) bore for the low-pressure, all with a piston stroke of 26¾in (680mm). With steam at a pressure of 227psi (1565kPa), the tractive force was 43,000lb (19,505 kg) and the adhesive weight was 181,030lb (82.1 tonnes). The boiler had 2,960sq.ft. (275sq.metre) of heating surface and a grate area of 53.8sq.ft. (5sq.metre ) on a total weight of 211,235lb (95.8 tonnes).

### WÜRTTEMBERG STATE RAILWAY GROUP K/1917/GERMANY

These were built by Maschinenfabrik Esslingen and, like those for the Austrian State Railway, used the four-cylinder compound cycle. The high-pressure cylinders had a diameter of 20in (510mm) and the low-pressure ones a diameter of 30in (760mm), with a common stroke of 25½in (650mm); with driving wheels of 53in (1350mm) they gave a tractive force of 51,600lb (23,406kg). The steam-pressure of 213psi (1469kPa) was supplied by a boiler with 3,358sq.ft. (312sq.metre) of heating surface and a firebox with a grate area of 45.2sq.ft. (4.2sq.metre). Their all-up weight was 238,140lb (108 tonnes).

*2-12-0 Austrian S100, 1910.*

*2-12-0 Württemberg Class 'K', 1917.*

*4-12-2 Union Pacific 9000, 1926.*

## SNCF CLASS 160A/1940/FRANCE

The last of the European 2-12-0 type took the form of a rebuild by André Chapelon of one of the Paris-Orléans 2-10-0 S.6000 class. In order to obtain the required output, the load was distributed among six cylinders with four at high pressure measuring 20½in x 21¼in (520mm x 540mm) and two at low pressure measuring 25⅕in x 25½in (640mm X 650mm). The driving-wheel diameter was 55in (1400mm) and, with steam at a pressure of 255psi (1758kPa), the tractive force amounted to 80,000lb (36,288kg), for which an adhesive weight of 264,600lb (120 tonnes) was provided. The boiler had a heating-surface area of 3,477sq.ft. (323sq.metre) with a firegrate area of 47.4sq.ft. (4.4sq.metre). The total weight of the rebuilt engine amounted to 303,187lb (137.5 tonnes).

## 4-12-2

### UNION PACIFIC RAILROAD CLASS 9000/1926/USA

The only examples of this type were the 88 built for the Union Pacific by Alco; they were the heaviest rigid-frame locomotives ever built in the United States. Like the 4-10-2 type they were provided with three cylinders, and there seems to have been some variation in cylinder size. One source gives an inside cylinder measurement of 25in x 31in (635mm x 787mm), whereas another gives 27in x 32in (686mm x 813mm); that cylinder drove the second axle. The outside cylinders are quoted as measuring 31in x 32in (787mm x 813mm) or 24in x 32in (610mm x 813mm), and drove the third coupled axle. With a steam pressure of 220psi (1517kPa) and with driving wheels of diameter 67in (1702mm), the tractive force was 96,600lb (43,818kg). The heating-surface area was 8,367sq.ft. (778sq.metre). The grate area was 108.3sq.ft. (10.07sq.metre). With a total weight of 495,022lb (224.5 tonnes) the speed was originally limited to 35mph (56kph), but the riding proved so stable that speeds of 60mph (96.5kph) were actually achieved in service.

These locomotives lasted for only some 10 years in main-line service; they were then relegated to slower-speed divisions.

# RIGID FRAME LOCOMOTIVES WITH DIVIDED DRIVE

## FOUR-WHEEL DIVIDED DRIVE

### 2-2-2-0

#### LNWR 2-2-2-0 TEUTONIC CLASS/1889/GREAT BRITAIN

This wheel arrangement was first used by Francis Webb in 1882 when he had an experimental three-cylinder compound built at the Crewe works of the LNWR. That was followed in 1884 by the 'Dreadnought' class of the same type; but the most successful were the 'Teutonic' class locomotives, first built in 1889.

The two high-pressure cylinders, measuring 14in x 24in (355mm x 610mm), were placed outside and drove the rear axle, while the single inside low-pressure cylinder, measuring 30in x 24in (762mm x 610mm), drove the front axle. The steam, at a pressure of 180psi (1241kPa), was supplied by a boiler with 1,401sq.ft. (130sq metre) of heating surface and a firegrate with 20.4sq.ft. (1.9sq metre) of firing area. The weight of the locomotives was 101,871lb (46.2 tonnes)

The class was prone to wheel-slip, but when well handled these engines could produce excellent results. In 1895 Adriatic ran the first 158 miles (254km) of the race to Aberdeen in 147 minutes, and in that same year Ionic ran nonstop from Euston to Carlisle, a distance of 299 miles (481km).

### 2-2-2-2

#### LNWR 2-2-2-2 GREATER BRITAIN CLASS/1891/GREAT BRITAIN

This class was provided with an extra trailing wheel in order to accommodate the longer boiler as used on the LNWR's 0-8-0 Class A freight locomotives; otherwise these were basically similar to the 'Teutonic' class. The high-pressure cylinders had a diameter 1in (25.4mm) larger, at 15in (381mm), and the piston stroke was 24in (610mm). The firebox and the steam pressure were the same, although the boiler had a greater heating area: 1,500sq.ft. (139sq metre). The overall weight was increased to 116,644lb (52.9 tonnes), but the adhesive weight was as for the 'Teutonic' locomotives. The 'Greater Britain' engines

could handle heavier trains, but suffered from the same problems of adhesion, and, with increasing train weights, had often to be assisted by a pilot engine.

### 4-2-2-0

#### NORD 4-2-2-0/1886/FRANCE

The first of the Nord compound locomotives was built with the divided drive as used on the LNWR. Originally built as a 2-2-2-0, the locomotive later had a truck fitted to make up the final configuration. Unlike the LNWR version, this was constructed as a four-cylinder engine, with two high-pressure cylinders of bore 12½in (320mm) and two low-pressure ones of bore 18in (460mm), all with piston strokes of 24in (610mm). The driving wheels were of diameter

*2-2-2-2 LNWR Greater Britain, 1891.*

*2-2-2-0 LNWR Teutonic Class, 1889.*

*6-4-4-6 Penn 6100, 1938.*

82²⁄₃in (210mm), and the steam was supplied at a pressure of 160psi (1104kPa) from a boiler with a grate area of 25.3sq.ft. (2.35sq metre) and a heating-surface area of 1,112sq.ft. (103.4sq metre). With a total weight of 85,995lb (39 tonnes), the adhesive weight amounted to 62,181lb (28.2 tonnes), giving a tractive force of 12,300lb (5,579kg). Like their British counterparts, this French locomotive suffered from adhesion problems, and no more were built to this design - although the four-cylinder compound became widely adopted on the Nord. No.701 has been preserved at the French Railway Museum at Mulhouse, where it was built.

# EIGHT-WHEEL DIVIDED DRIVE

## 6-4-4-6

### 1938 PENNSYLVANIA RAILROAD 6-4-4-6 No.6100/1938/USA

Needing to produce a locomotive capable of hauling 1,200-long-ton (1,219-tonne) trains at 100mph (160kph), a task requiring an output of over 6,500ihp (4,847kW), the Pennsylvania Railroad adopted the system of divided drive in an endeavour to overcome the problem of loading on the connecting rods and piston rods. The two sets of driving wheels, with a diameter of 84in (2134mm), were driven by four cylinders measuring 22in x 26in (559mm x 660mm) and supplied with steam at 300psi (2068kPa). Built by the Pennsylvania Railroad in its own shop at Juniata, the locomotive had a cast-steel frame 79ft (24.1m) long, and its driving axles numbers 1 and 3 were given 2 1/5in (55.8mm) lateral play.

The streamlined boiler had a heating-surface area of 7,746sq.ft. (720sq metre) with a grate area of 132sq.ft. (12.3sq metre). Of the total engine weight of 608,359lb (275.9 tonnes), only about one half was available for adhesion. With a tractive force of 71,900lb (32,614 kg) the power output was found to be in excess of requirements, and, due to weight transfer, there were problems with adhesion which required careful driving to overcome.

## 4-4-4-4

### PENNSYLVANIA RAILROAD 4-4-4-4 CLASS T.1/1942/USA

Following the 6-4-4-6 locomotive built in 1938, a less powerful version was built by the Baldwin Locomotive Company in 1942. Using 80in (2032mm) driving wheels, the four cylinders were 19⁴⁄₅in (503mm) in diameter by 26in (660mm) stroke, and with steam at 300psi (2068kPa) the tractive force produced was 65,000lb (29,484kg). The design included poppet-type steam valves, roller bearings throughout, and clasp brakes. The boiler had a grate area of 92sq.ft. (8.5sq metre) and a heating-surface area of 5,889 sq.ft. (547sq metre). The total weight was 497,227lb (225.5 tonnes). These locomotives, like other divided-drive engines, suffered from adhesive troubles, but a further 50 were built by the Pennsylvania Railroad itself after the first two by Baldwin. The whole finish was extremely neat, with a streamlined boiler casing designed by R. Loewy, who also designed the outline of the Pennsylvania Railroad's electric locomotives. On test at the Altoona plant an output of 6,700ihp (4,996kW) was recorded at a steam rate of 105,475lb (47,843kg) per hour at 100 mph (160kph). At the most efficient rate the output was 5,500ihp (4,101kW), with a coal rate of 2.5 pounds per ihp-hr (1.52kg/kW-hr).

# TEN-WHEEL DIVIDED DRIVE

## 4-6-4-4

### PENNSYLVANIA RAILROAD 4-6-4-4 CLASS Q.1/1942/ USA

This design was an attempt to provide a locomotive with 10 driven wheels, but without the enormous thrust on one connecting rod and on one driven axle. The front six coupled wheels were driven by cylinders at 23in x 28in (584mm x 711mm) and the rear four wheels by cylinders at 19½in x 26in (495mm x 660mm). Using 77in (1956mm) diameter wheels, the tractive force was 81,800lb (37,104kg). Steam at 300psi (2068kPa) was produced by a boiler with a heating-surface area of 9,650sq.ft. (897sq metre) with a grate area of 122sq.ft. (11.3sq metre). The total locomotive weight was 608,139lb (275.8 tonnes). Only the one was built to this wheel arrangement; further versions used the 4-4-6-4 arrangement.

## 4-4-6-4

### PENNSYLVANIA RAILROAD 4-4-6-4 CLASS Q.2/1942/USA

With their 69in (1753mm) wheels these were primarily freight locomotives. The front four wheels were driven by cylinders of dimensions 19⁴⁄₅in x 28in (503mm x 711mm) and the rear six by cylinders measuring 23⁴⁄₅in x 29in (605mm x 736mm). With steam at 300psi (2068kPa), the tractive force was 100,800lb (45,723kg). The boiler was

*0-6-6-0 Nord 601, 1862*

as on the Q.1 class (see preceding entry), but the total weight was greater, at 633,825lb (281.7 tonnes). This model gave an improved performance over the Q.1 type, and a further 25 were built by the Pennsylvania Railroad. The design included lateral play in the leading coupled axle of each group, and the number 3 axle was fitted with plain tyres, without flanges, to improve performance around curves. On test at Altoona the maximum output was 8,000ihp (5,966kW) with a steam rate of 137,000lb (62,143kg) per hour and a coal-consumption rate of 25,000lb (11,340kg) per hour.

These were the last of the divided-drive engines to be built by the Pennsylvania and the last of their large rigid-frame locomotives until steam was displaced by diesel-electric with its improved adhesion and power/weight ratio.

# TWELVE-WHEEL DIVIDED DRIVE

## 0-6-6-0T

### CHEMINS DE FER DU NORD 0-6-6-0T S.601/1862/FRANCE

Designed by Jules Petiet, the chief mechanical engineer of the Nord, these 12-wheeled tank engines were built by Ernest Alexander Gouin using the same boiler as was used on the Series 566 0-8-0 engines. The two sets of cylinders were at opposite ends of the main frame and each axle had

$\frac{2}{3}$in (15mm) side-play, as the engines were intended for working on lines with curves of 150yds (137m) radius. The four cylinders were $17\frac{1}{3}$in x $17\frac{1}{3}$in (440mm x 440mm), and drove 42in (1065mm) wheels. With a steam pressure of 125psi (862kPa), these engines gave a tractive force of 26,800lb (12,156kg). The boiler had a preheater with a heating area of 237sq.ft. (22sq metre); the main heating area was 2,153sq.ft. (200sq metre) with a grate area of 35.8sq.ft. (3.33sq metre). These locomotives could haul a 250-long-ton (254-tonne) train up a 1 in 77 (1.3 per cent) grade at 16.8mph (27kph), corresponding to an output of 450dbhp (336kW) or a cylinder output of 650ihp (485kW).

The first 10 of this model were supplied in 1862, and were followed by 10 more in 1867. One was later fitted with Beugniot levers on the outer axles to enable it to negotiate curves of 80yd (73m) radius.

# TANK LOCOMOTIVES

## 2-2-2T

### LATVIAN STATE RAILWAY CLASS Tk/1930/LATVIA

Five engines of this type were assembled in Latvia using components supplied from Germany: they were the first new engines in Latvia after the end of World War 1 and the Russian Revolution - that is, after Latvia had become independent. Using two cylinders measuring 12²⁄₃in x 20½in (320mm x 520mm) and with driving wheels of diameter 59in (1500mm), they produced a tractive force of 8,800lb (3,992kg) with an adhesive weight of 33,912lb (15.38 tonnes). The superheated steam was supplied by a boiler with a large superheater and a total heating-surface area of 788 sq.ft. (73.2sq metre) and a grate area of 13.45sq.ft. (1.25sq metre). The total weight of the complete unit was 81,805lb (37.1 tonnes).

## 2-2-2WT

### DUBLIN AND KINGSTOWN RAILWAY VICTORIA/1835/IRELAND

Claimed to have been the first tank engines in the world, the two well-tank engines built by Forrester & Co. were built so that they could work the mail-boat trains onto the pier at Kingstown (now Dun Laoghaire). With two cylinders measuring 11in x 18in (279mm x 457mm) and with 60in (1524mm) driving wheels, they probably had a steam pressure of 50psi (345kPa) and would have given a tractive force of 1,500lb (680kg). The two were named Victoria and Comet; in 1837 three of the 2-2-0 tender locomotives supplied (in 1834) by the same firm were also altered to 2-2-2WT type. In 1841 an additional one was built by the railway in its own shops at Grand Canal Street, Dublin: this is claimed to have been the first locomotive to have been built by a railway in its own workshops. In 1860 the line was converted to the Irish gauge of 5ft 3in (1600mm), and in 1871 a further seven 2-2-2WT type engines were built at the line's own shops.

## 4-2-4T

### BRISTOL AND EXETER RAILWAY TANK ENGINES/1854/GREAT BRITAIN

The eight engines of this class, built by Rothwell & Co. of Bolton, were fitted with the largest driving wheels of any operational locomotive: they were of diameter 106in

(2692mm) and they were flangeless. With two cylinders at 18in x 24in (457mm x 610mm), and with a steam pressure of 120psi (828kPa), they gave a tractive force of 7,300lb (3,311kg) on an adhesive weight of 41,454lb (18.8 tonnes). The boiler was ample (for its time) with 1,235sq.ft. (114.8sq metre) of heating surface area and a grate area of 23sq.ft. (2.14sq metre). These engines were used to haul the fastest trains between Bristol and Exeter - including the 'Flying Dutchman' - and were reputed to have run at up to 81.8 mph (131.6kph). With a total weight of 111,352lb (50.5 tonnes), they held 2 tons (2.3 tonnes) of coal and 1,430 gallons (65hl) of water. They were prone to derailments and, in 1876, were rebuilt in the form of a 4-2-2 tender locomotive.

# FOUR-COUPLED TANK ENGINES

## 0-4-0T

### NORTH EASTERN RAILWAY CLASS H/1888/GREAT BRITAIN

Although most of the tank engines with this wheel arrangement were built as industrial works shunters of the saddle-tank design, there were some employed by main-line railways for use in docks or as station pilots. A typical example was the H Class of the North Eastern Railway. With 41in (1041mm) wheels and with cylinders at 14in x 20in (356mm x 508mm) they used a steam pressure of 140psi (965kPa) and gave a tractive force of 11,600lb

(5,262kg) on a total weight of 50,715lb (23 tonnes). A total of 24 were built (some after the 1923 amalgamation) and they lasted in service until the last was withdrawn in 1952; in the LNER classification they became Class Y7. One is preserved (No.68088) at the Great Central Railway at Loughborough, and there are two others in preservation.

## 0-4-0AT

### H. C. FRICKE & CO./1928/USA

H.K.Porter & Co. built this compressed-air engine to work on a gauge of 35in (889mm) using the compound cycle. The two cylinders were of bore 9½in (241mm) and 14in (356mm) respectively and, with a stroke of 14in (356mm), they drove 40in (1016mm) wheels. The compressed air was stored at 800psi (5,517kPa), and the working pressure was 250psi (1,724kPa), at which pressure the tractive force was 8,000lb (3,629kg). The working weight was 31,972lb (14.5 tonnes).

## 0-4-0FT

### MEAD CORPORATION/1930/USA

The main builders of fireless locomotives in the United States was the firm of H. K. Porter & Co. of Pittsburg, Pennsylvania. They built this small unit for the Mead Corporation using a gear drive from a jackshaft between the coupled wheels. The two cylinders measured 18½in x 16in (470mm x 406mm) and drove the conventional 44in (1118mm) wheels. The steam was stored at 250psi (1,724kPa) and reduced to a working pressure of 60psi

*0-4-0ST design produced by the American Locomotive Company (Alco) in the 1930s*

(414kPa), at which level the tractive force was 23,000lb (10,433kg). The working weight, fully charged, was 140,017lb (63.5 tonnes).

# 0-4-0ST

## MEDUSA PORTLAND CEMENT CO./1935/USA

The 0-4-0ST was a rare breed in the United States. This one was built by the Davenport Locomotive Co. for operation on soft coal and was fitted with a comparatively large firegrate, of area 20.2sq.ft. (1.88sq metre). The two outside cylinders measured 16in x 24in (406mm x 610mm) and drove 44in (1118mm) diameter wheels - this was a standard industrial switcher size. With steam at 180psi (1,241kPa), the tractive force came to 21,300lb (9,662kg) on a weight of 100,990lb (45.8 tonnes). The boiler's heating surface was of area 1,039sq.ft. (96.6sq metre).

## CEGB GOLDINGTON POWER STATION/1954/GREAT BRITAIN

The two 0-4-0 Saddle Tanks built by Andrew Barclay for work in the construction of the Goldington Power Station were typical of hundreds of this type (well over 100 are to be found at preserved-railway sites all over Britain). The Goldington pair were equipped with cylinders measuring 14in x 22in (356mm x 559mm) which drove 41in (1041mm) wheels; with steam at 160psi (1,104kPa) they gave a tractive force of 14,300lb (6,486kg). The little boiler hidden under the saddle tank had 542sq.ft. (50.4sq metre) of heating area and a firegrate area of 9.5sq.ft. (0.88sq metre). The working weight came to 66,150lb (30 tonnes). Over 300 of this type were built by Barclays alone, particularly for collieries, steel works, and gas and electricity works. The two at Goldington were named Matthew Murray and Richard Trevithick, and were later converted to oil-firing. They were later replaced by diesels. Goldington Power Station has since been closed.

# 0-4-2T

## GREAT WESTERN RAILWAY CLASS 4800/1932/GREAT BRITAIN

Designed for light branch-line operation, this design closely followed a 19th century type, but had an enclosed cab among other improvements. The first 75 units were equipped for push-pull working in autotrains. With two inside cylinders measuring 16½in x 24in (419mm x 610mm) and 62in (1575mm) wheels they had a tractive

*0-4-4T London & South Western Railway M7 Class, 1897*

*2-4-0T Peloponnesos Railway B11 Class, 1884*

force of 14,000lb (6,350kg), using steam at 165psi (1,138kPa). They weighed 41.3 tons (42 tonnes). There were 95 built; all were withdrawn between 1954 and 1964 but four are preserved.

# 0-4-4T

## NEW YORK ELEVATED 0-4-4T/1866/USA

Following the opening of the (underground) Metropolitan Railway in London a different approach was taken in the United States; the track was raised above street-level. For the motive power some small tank engines were built by the Rogers, Ketchum and Grosvener firm of Paterson, New York, using two cylinders at 11in x 16in (279mm x 406mm) and driving 42in (1066mm) wheels. The steam pressure was probably 120psi (828kPa), which would have given a tractive force of 4,700lb (2,132kg) on an adhesive weight of 28,599lb (12.97 tonnes) out of a total weight of 42,997lb (19.5 tonnes), less than half the weight of the Metropolitan Railway tanks, which did not have to run on the elevated track.

*4-4-0T Metropolitan-District Railway, 1863*

## LONDON AND SOUTH WESTERN RAILWAY CLASS M7/1897/GREAT BRITAIN

Originally built for suburban or branchline working, these locomotives were fitted for push-pull operation with steam reversers; some were built as late as 1925. With two inside cylinders at 18½in x 26in (470mm x 660mm) and using steam at 175psi (1,207kPa), these engines drove 67in (1702mm) diameter wheels with a tractive force of 19,800lb (8,981kg) on an adhesive weight of 80,703lb (36.6 tonnes). The weight of the latest type was 138,915lb (63 tonnes). A total of 105 were built, lasting until they became Southern Railway stock; withdrawals took place between 1957 and 1964. Two have been preserved.

## 2-4-0T

### PELOPONNESOS RAILWAY CLASS B.11/1884/GREECE

Originally built as a metre (3ft 3⅓in) gauge local line, the Peloponnesos Railway became part of the Piraeus-Athens-Peloponnesos system in 1882, and the 2-4-0Ts were the first passenger engines to be delivered. Built by Maffei of Munich, they had inside frames with outside cylinders and Helmholtz valve gears. With cylinders at 13in x 19⅔in (335mm x 500mm) they used a steam pressure of 140psi (965kPa); and with 47in (1200mm) driving wheels they gave a tractive force of 8,640lb (3,919kg) on an adhesive weight of 45,202lb (20.5 tonnes). The boiler had 595sq.ft. (55.3sq metre) of heating area with a firegrate area of 10.3sq.ft. (0.96sq metre). The total weight was 58,873lb (26.7 tonnes). Two batches of these locomotives were built, to a total of 12; a further 5 of a more modern design, with superheaters, were added in 1912.

## 2-4-0WT

### LONDON & SOUTH WESTERN RAILWAY 0298 CLASS/1874/GREAT BRITAIN

Despite its age, this class of well-tank locomotives survived into preservation. This is because when the class ceased to be of much use for the commuter services for which it was designed, there was a need for a few locomotives having its characteristics to operate the Wenford Bridge line in Cornwall, an awkward track carrying china-clay. The survivors were rebuilt three times in their long active lives, and had a tractive effort of 11,050lb (5,015kg) by virtue of 55in (1400mm) driving wheels, 16½in x 20in (420mm x 508mm) cylinders, and 160psi (1102kPa) boiler pressure. The short coupled wheelbase, the low weight 85,995lb (39 tonnes) and the leading truck to help steady the ride, made these locomotives ideal for their final job.

## 2-4-2T

### GREAT EASTERN RAILWAY CLASS M15/1884/GREAT BRITAIN

Locomotives of this type used to handle the bulk of the massive commuter traffic in and out of London's Liverpool Street Station. With a total of 272 tank engines of the 2-4-2T arrangement, the Class M.15 was the most numerous: 190 were built between 1884 and 1920. With two inside cylinders at 17½in x 24in (445mm x 610mm) they gave a tractive force of 15,600lb (7,076kg), using steam at 160psi (1,104kPa): the driving wheels were of diameter 64in (1626mm). Over 140 lasted to become part of the London and North Eastern service, when they were classified F4 and F5. All were finally withdrawn by 1958.

## 4-4-0T

### METROPOLITAN RAILWAY CLASS A/1863/GREAT BRITAIN

Built by Beyer Peacock to operate the first Underground Railway system under London, these engines were fitted with condensing apparatus to return some of the used steam to the side tanks. The two external cylinders (measuring 17in x 24in or 432mm x 610mm) drove wheels of diameter 69in (1750mm) with a steam pressure of 120psi (828kPa) to give a tractive force of 10,200lb (4,627kg) on an adhesive weight of 69,457lb (31.5 tonnes). The boilers were fairly small: they had 1,014sq.ft. (94.3sq metre) of heating area and a grate area of 19sq.ft. (1.77sq metre). Sixty-six were supplied to the Metropolitan Railway and 54 to the Metropolitan-District, where they lasted until electrification in 1905.

Number 23 of the Metropolitan was transferred to the service fleet and is now preserved at the London Transport Museum at Covent Garden. The working weight was 94,219lb (42.73 tonnes).

## 4-4-2T

### LONDON & SOUTH WESTERN RAILWAY 0415 CLASS/1882/GREAT BRITAIN

It sometimes happened that a time-expired and obsolete locomotive class, instead of going to the scrap-heap, was saved because it was considered the best, if not the only, type for a given employment. The reprieve of old but small engines to serve flimsy branch lines was a quite common phenomenon. The survival of the classic American 4-4-0 to serve a New Brunswick branch line in the 1950s is just one example. The three members of the 1882 0415 Class 4-4-2 tank engine that survived not only to become part of the Southern Railway stock, but then continue with British Railways for another decade or two, owed their Indian Summer to the Axminster-Lyme Regis branch line in southern England, a line of light track, difficult curves, and a tricky grade at one end. The class was much larger in the 19th Century, and was originally used on commuter services in the London area. Weighing just 123,200lb (56 tonnes) and developing a tractive effort of 14,920lbs (6,765kg), its 57in (1449mm) coupled wheels gave it a fair turn of speed, while the 160psi (1102kPa) steam pressure kept boiler maintenance cheap. Having survived so long made it probable that the class would be eventually represented in preservation, which duly happened. The preserved unit had had a chequered career; having been

*4-4-2T London & South Western Railway 0415 Class, 1882*

sold by the LSWR to the East Kent Railway in 1917 to help with wartime traffic, it was purchased back by the LSWR's successor company in 1946 to help on the Lyme Regis branch.

### GREAT NORTHERN RAILWAY ATLANTIC TANK (C13) CLASS/1898/GREAT BRITAIN

GNR outer suburban trains out of London were tightly timed and heavily loaded. Their locomotives graduated from 0-4-2T machines of the 1860s to 0-6-2T locomotives from 1907. For a decade, the 4-4-2 tank engines later classified C12 held sway. They had 17½in x 26in (445mm x 660mm) cylinders, coupled wheels of 68in (1727mm) and boiler pressure of 170psi (1171kPa), giving a tractive effort of 17,900lb (8,126kg). They had a grate area of 17.8sq.ft. (1.65sq metre) and weighed 138,915lb (63 tonnes). They were soon made inadequate by the need for heavier and faster trains, and were finally replaced by new batches of 0-6-2 tank locomotives after World War 1. They then gravitated to country branch lines, and some were to be seen in Lincolnshire in the 1950s.

*4-4-2T Great Northern (LNER C13 Class), 1898*

*4-4-2T LB&SCR I.3 Class, 1908*

## LONDON, BRIGHTON AND SOUTH COAST RAILWAY CLASS I.3/1908/GREAT BRITAIN

Following some unsatisfactory results with the I.1 class of 4-4-2T produced in 1907, Marsh built this next lot with a superheater and the resultant product was an immediate improvement. With two cylinders at 21in x 26in (533mm x 660mm) driving 79in (2006mm) wheels, and using steam at 160psi (1,102kPa), the tractive force was 19,700lb (8,936kg) on an adhesive weight of 85,002lb (38.55 tonnes). The superheated steam was supplied by a boiler with 1,281sq.ft. (119sq metre) of heating area and a firebox with a grate area of 24sq.ft. (2.2sq metre). The all-up weight was 166,036lb (75.3 tonnes). A total of 27 were built. They were used to haul the 'Sunny South Express' over the London and North Western Railway as far as Rugby, and proved capable of running the 90 miles (145km) between East Croydon and Rugby on a tankful (2,110 gallons or 95.9hl) of water, to the amazement of the LNWR, which was then spurred into adopting the

*2-4-0WT  London & South Western Railway 0298 Class, 1874*

superheater for its passenger 4-4-0 classes. The l.3 Tank remained in service until 1950, with one achieving a distance of 1.4 million miles (2.25 million km) - remarkable for a railway with no station more than 90 miles (145km) from London!

## LONDON, TILBURY AND SOUTHEND RAILWAY CLASS 79/1909/GREAT BRITAIN

By the time the first of this class was built there were already 66 locomotives with this wheel arrangement in service on the Southend line. The 79 class was fitted with two outside cylinders at 19in x 26in (483mm x 660mm) and, with 78in (1981mm) wheels, had a good turn of speed. With steam at 170psi (1,172kPa), the tractive force was 18,000lb (8,165kg) on an adhesive weight of 82,908lb (37.6 tonnes) out of a total weight of 159,421lb (72.3 tonnes). The boilers on the first batch had a grate area of 19.8 sq.ft. (1.84sq metre) and a heating surface area of 1,099sq.ft. (102sq metre) which was enlarged on a later batch to 1,205sq.ft. (112sq metre) with an LMS type of boiler. With 31 being constructed after 1923, the total in this class came to 35 - making 101 in all of this wheel type to handle the Essex commuters. They lasted in service until 1954, when they were withdrawn following the electrification of the Southend line. The second - No.80,

Thundersley - has been preserved at the Bressingham Steam Museum at Diss, Norfolk.

## 4-4-4T

## NORTH EASTERN RAILWAY CLASS D/1913/GREAT BRITAIN

The 4-4-4T was essentially a passenger engine designed to operate at speed in both directions. The D Class on the North Eastern was intended for use on branch lines out of Darlington to replace the tender engines which were then in use and which entailed the use of turntables. To provide even running at speed the tanks had three cylinders measuring 16½in x 26in (419mm x 660mm) and drove 69in (1750mm) wheels. Using steam at 160psi (1,104kPa), they gave a tractive force of 22,900lb (10,387kg) on an adhesive weight of 89,082lb (40.4 tonnes) out of a total weight of 196,465lb (89.1 tonnes). The boiler, which did not have a superheater, was relatively small - with 1,332sq.ft. (124sq metre) of heating area and a firegrate of 23sq.ft. (2.1sq metre). The first batch of 20 was followed by a further 25 in 1920; they became Class H.1 in the LNER classification. They were later rebuilt to a

4-6-2T wheel arrangement, and then became Class A.8. As such, they lasted in service until 1960.

# SIX-COUPLED TANK ENGINES

## 0-6-0T

## LONDON, BRIGHTON AND SOUTH COAST RAILWAY CLASS AIX TERRIERS/1872/GREAT BRITAIN

The 0-6-0T was by far the most numerous of all the tank-engine types, being built in thousands both in Britain and Europe. The best known, perhaps, is the fictional 'Thomas the Tank Engine.' This resembles the Terrier Class, first built in 1872. This class was built initially to work on the South London line. With a limiting axle-load of 20,154lb (9.14 tonnes), they were first fitted with cylinders measuring 13in x 20in (330mm x 508mm) driving 48in

*4-4-4T North Eastern D Class, 1913, rebuilt as LNER A8 Class*

wheels to give a tractive force of 11,600 pounds (5,262kg). The boiler contained 637sq.ft. (59.2sq metre) of heating surface with a grate area of 14.5sq.ft. (1.35sq metre) on a total weight of 78,939lb (35.8 tonnes). They were also built for use on private works sidings, and some were to find their way to Poland, where they were classified as Class Tkh-1.

## NORTH EASTERN RAILWAY (LNER CLASS J72)/1898/GREAT BRITAIN

This 85-strong class of 0-6-0 tank locomotive was inherited from the North Eastern Railway by the LNER when the latter was formed in 1923. Interestingly, some thirty years later, by which time the LNER had become part of British Railways, the latter ordered another 28 units of this 50-year old design.

Weighing only 85,995lb (39 tonnes), this design produced 16,760lb (7,610kg) of tractive effort. It could have been more but, presumably in the interests of lower maintenance cost, a low boiler pressure of 140psi (965kPa) was chosen. Grate area was 11.3sq.ft. (1.05sq metre) and, in common with most light-duty engines, there was no superheater. Cylinders were 17in x 24in (432mm x 610mm) and the coupled wheels were 49¼in (1257mm) diameter. These engines, even the ones built for BR, were generally confined to the northeast, where they were a familiar sight. One of them subsequently found its way into preservation on the Yorkshire Moors Railway.

*0-6-0T Midland Railway 1878, the model for the 1924 LMS 3F 0-6-0T*

(1220mm) wheels. Steam was supplied at 140psi (965kPa) from the small boiler, which had 528sq.ft. (49sq metre) of heating surface and a grate area of 10sq.ft. (0.93sq metre). They proved so effective that the cylinder bore was later enlarged to 14in (356mm), and they were used all over the Brighton system on branch-line services: a total of 50 was constructed at the line's Brighton works. One was awarded a Gold Medal at the Paris Exhibition of 1878, and all were named. With the larger cylinders they gave a tractive force of 9,700lb (4,400kg), and their ability to accelerate earned them the title of 'Terriers'. Nine have been preserved.

## PRUSSIAN STATE RAILWAY CLASS T.3/1880/GERMANY

Built for freight, passenger or shunting duty, this class of well tanks was the most numerous of all 0-6-0T classes to be built in Europe: over 1,500 were produced by 1910. With outside Allan valve gear, the two cylinders were 13¾in x 21⅔in (350mm x 550mm) and, with steam at 150psi (1,034kPa), they drove 43 1/3in (1100mm) diameter

*0-6-0T North Eastern Railway (LNER J72 Class), 1898*

*0-6-0T LMS 3F Class, 1924*

## SOUTH EASTERN & CHATHAM RAILWAY (SOUTHERN RAILWAY CLASS P)/1909/GREAT BRITAIN

Having become responsible for operating the line on the Isle of Sheppey, the SECR decided that the time had come to introduce rail motors (short trains with a small locomotive operating in push-pull fashion) and these soon appeared on other branch lines. The locomotive built to handle them was a tiny 0-6-0T, later classified P, which weighed only 63,840lb (29 tonnes). With driving wheels of 45in (1143mm), boiler pressure 160psi (1102kPa), and cylinders 12in x 18in (305mm x 407mm), the tractive effort was only 7,810lb (3,545kg). But this, and the small grate area of 9.1sq.ft. (0.84sq metre), was all the task demanded. When rail motors fell out of fashion, these locomotives were used for light yard duties. Some survived into the 1950s, and four have been preserved.

## LONDON MIDLAND & SCOTTISH RAILWAY 3F 0-6-0T/1924/GREAT BRITAIN

The British railway companies had an immense appetite for six-wheel tank locomotives, which they used not only for yard work but also for short freights and minor passenger services. The ideal design was one that could perform all three of those tasks well. When the LMS Railway was formed, to become Britain's biggest, it had to choose a design for future construction of this type, and it chose a design that had already been put into production by its constituent the Midland Railway. This was probably a good choice, although it resulted probably from the circumstance that those making it were ex-Midland men. Over the years, more than four hundred of these engines were built, partly in LMS workshops and partly by outside builders. The dimensions were fairly characteristic of all locomotives of this classification. The coupled wheels were 55in (1397mm), cylinders 18in x 26in (457mm x 660mm), boiler pressure 160psi (1102kPa) and tractive effort

*0-6-0T South Eastern & Chatham (Southern Railway P Class), 1909*

20,830lb (9,456kg). The grate area was 16sq.ft. (1.49sq metre) and weight, which was all available for adhesion, 110,250lb (50 tonnes).

## 0-6-0FT

### ATCHISON, TOPEKA AND SANTA FE RAILROAD/1937/USA

Built for operation at the Dallas terminal for the handling of oil tank trucks, these Baldwin-built engines used 30in (762mm) diameter cylinders with a stroke of 24in (610mm)

and drove 44in (1118mm) wheels. The steam storage pressure was 200psi (1,380kPa), but the working pressure was only 65psi (448kPa), as a reducing valve was used, which had the effect of drying the steam. The tractive effort was 31,900lb (14,470kg) on a total weight of 171,769lb (77.9 tonnes).

### UNITED STATES ARMY TRANSPORTATION CORPS 0-6-0T/1942/USA

This design originated in a Lend-Lease request by Britain for a military yard locomotive, but in the end nearly 450 units were built, mainly for the US Army in Europe and

5700. With 55½in (1410mm) diameter wheels, they were used for branch-line working, yard work and for hauling empty stock into the Paddington terminus where they could be seen patiently keeping the train warm until departure. With two inside cylinders measuring 17½in x 24in (445mm x 610mm) and a steam pressure of 200psi (1,378kPa), they gave a tractive force of 25,500lb (11,567kg) on a weight of 106,500lb (48.3 tonnes). The heating surface area of the boiler amounted to 1,115sq.ft. (103.7sq metre) with a firegrate area of 15.3sq.ft. (1.42sq metre). Some were fitted with condensing apparatus for working over

North Africa, although with some for Britain's Ministry of Supply. They were built by three US companies: Porter, Vulcan, and Davenport. They had cast-iron cylinders of 16½in x 24in (420mm x 610mm), a boiler pressure of 210psi (1447kPa), and wheels of 54in (1372mm). Grate area was 19.4sq.ft. (1.8sq metre) and weight in working order was 100,107lb (45.4 tonnes). Tractive effort was 21,630lb (9,820lb). The wheelbase was only 10ft, allowing the locomotives to negotiate curves of 150ft radius. Although with their bar frames and other American features they were very different from the traditional British locomotive, the Southern Railway purchased some after World War 2 for use in Southampton Docks, where their combination of short wheelbase and high tractive effort were particularly useful. Three have been preserved in Britain, others in the USA, and in the 1990s there were some still in active service in Yugoslavia.

# 0-6-0PT

## GREAT WESTERN RAILWAY CLASS 5700 PANNIER TANK/1929/GREAT BRITAIN

Including conversions, the Great Western used in all over 1,800 engines of this type, the most numerous being Class

*0-6-0PT GWR 5700 Class, 1929*

*The later (1947) style of GWR 0-6-0PT locomotive, with tapered boiler.*

the Metropolitan Railway lines and some with steam brakes for shunting duty only. A total of 863 was built and most of them lasted until 1956-66. Some were built by private locomotive building firms including Kerr Stewart, the North British Locomotive Company, and Robert Stephenson Ltd. More than 15 have been preserved at various sites.

# 0-6-0ST

## GREAT NORTHERN RAILWAY CLASS J13 (LNER CLASS J52)/1897/GREAT BRITAIN

At the time of its formation in 1923 the London and North Eastern Railway took into stock over 1,000 tank engines of the 0-6-0 type, the most numerous of which was a saddle tank first built under Patrick Stirling and H.A.Ivatt.

*0-6-0ST Great Northern J13 Class, 1897*

*A rear view of a US Army 0-6-0T, still working in Britain, and fitted with a bigger bunker.*

## CALICO CHEMICAL COMPANY/1933/USA

Built by the Vulcan Iron Works of Wilkes-Barr, this saddle tank was fitted with two cylinders at 19in x 24in (483mm x 610mm) and, with a steam pressure of 190psi (1,310kPa), gave a tractive force of 31,800lb (14,424kg) using the usual 44in (1118mm) wheels. With oil-firing the firegrate had an area of 22.3 sq.ft. (2.1sq metre) and the boiler had 1,254sqft (116.6sq metre) of heating surface. The working weight was 142,002lb (64.4 tonnes).

## HUNSLET 18-INCH AUSTERITY/1943/GREAT BRITAIN

Many hundred of the 0-6-0ST type were produced for industrial shunters, but the most numerous of any one type were the Hunslet Austerity type built for the War Department, based on the LMS 3F tank engine. Hunslet

These had a domeless boiler producing steam at 175psi (1,207kPa). Fitted with two cylinders measuring 18in x 26in (457mm x 660mm) and with driving wheels of diameter 56in (1422mm), they gave a tractive force of 22,400lb (10,161kg) on a weight of 115,762lb (52.5 tonnes). There were 85 in service by 1909, and after 1923 the 52 similar engines built with a domeless boiler between 1892 and 1897 to Class J14 were reboilered with the same boiler as the Class J13; all became the LNER Class J52. In 1948, 132 went into British Rail stock; the last was withdrawn in 1961.

One, No.1247 (BR No.68846) is preserved. Built by Sharp Stewart in 1899, it ended its days as shed pilot at Kings Cross. In 1959 it was restored to its original livery.

*0-6-0ST 18-inch Austerity Class, 1943. This unit was later acquired by British Railways*

*The 0-6-0 saddle tank was the most widespread type used by British industrial lines, and several manufacturers supplied it. This inside-cylinder design was first built by the Hunslet Company in 1923 and the last (illustrated here) was delivered to the Oxfordshire Ironstone Company in 1958*

had first produced (in 1937) a saddle tank with 18in x 26in (457mm x 660mm) cylinders and with 48in (1219mm) diameter wheels, but the War Department version used 51in (1295mm) wheels and, with steam at 170psi (1,172kPa), gave a tractive force of 23,900lb (10,841kg) on a total weight of 108,045lb (49 tonnes). The boiler had 960sq.ft. (89sq metre) of heating surface and a grate area of 16.8sq.ft. (1.56sq metre). The saddle tank contained 1,200 gallons (54.6hl). These locomotives could operate around curves of 60yd (55m) radius. They had inside cylinders with Stephenson's valve gear and, although built only for short-term duty, many lasted in service until after 1960. The first lot included 377 engines built by the following firms: Hunslet Engines Company (120), Robert Stephenson & Co. Ltd (90), W. G. Bagnall Ltd. (52), Hudswell Clark Ltd. (50), Vulcan Foundry Ltd. (50), and Andrew Barclay Ltd. (15). To the list must be added a further 14 for the War Department built in 1952 and 93 for industrial firms (mostly for the National Coal Board) between 1945 and 1964 making a total of 484 in all. They had steam brakes on all wheels and some were equipped with Westinghouse air brakes. They could haul a 1,100-ton (1,118-tonne) train on the level, 550 tons (559 tonnes) up 1 in 100 (1 per cent), and 300 tons (305 tonnes) 1 in 50 (2 per cent). In 1944 100 went to Europe, and after 1947 75 were transferred to the LNER, where they became Class J94.

Some 50 have been preserved.

# 0-6-2T

### LONDON AND NORTH WESTERN RAILWAY COAL TANK/1881/GREAT BRITAIN

A tank version of the North Western's Coal 0-6-0 mentioned earlier, these were built for short-haul mineral trains. A total of 300 was built in the 15 years to 1896. The two inside cylinders, at 17in x 24in (432mm x 610mm), drove 5308in (1359mm) diameter wheels and, with a steam pressure of 140psi (965kPa), produced a tractive force of 15,400lb (6,985kg). The additional trailing wheel allowed for a bunker which held both coal and water,

making, all told, a working weight of 96,535lb (43.7 tonnes). In common with most North Western engines at that time, these used the Joy valve gear, and they had similar wheels to the Coal tender engines with 'H' section spokes. Later, fitted with steam connections to the train, they did duty on commuter trains on the North London line and on 'Seasonal Specials'. Two hundred and eight-nine went into LMS stock after 1923, and some were fitted with Ross 'Pop' safety valves in place of the original Ramsbottom type. Reverting to freight duty, they received the classification 2F, and 52 lasted into the British Rail era. By 1955 all were withdrawn, but one, No.1054, was preserved.

### AUSTRIAN FEDERAL RAILWAYS 298 CLASS/1888/AUSTRIA

Narrow-gauge railway construction in Austria had a brief flowering after the 1887 Lokalbahn law. One of the earliest 2ft.6in.(760mm) lines was the Steyrtalbahn, linking two towns, each on a different mainline railway. This railway used an 0-6-2 tank locomotive design built by Krauss (Linz), a type which other narrow-gauge lines soon adopted. At first these locomotives carried their coal between the side tanks and the front of the cab, but later a conventional bunker was provided behind the cab. The Steyrtalbahn in a very truncated form still exists, mainly for tourist purposes, and some of this class of locomotive still work on it. They have cylinders 11.4in x 15.7in (290mm x 400mm), coupled wheels of diameter 31½in (800mm), and boilers pressed to 171psi (1176kPa). The grate area is 8.6sq.ft. (.80sq metre) and they weigh in service 52,920lb (24 tonnes). Speed is limited to 22mph (35kph) and tractive effort is 9,395lb (4,265kg).

*0-6-2T London & North Western Coal Tank, 1881*

*0-6-2T LNWR Coal Tank, 1881. This is the preserved example, carrying LNWR livery.*

## GREAT NORTHERN CLASS N.2 (LNER CLASS N.2)/1920/GREAT BRITAIN

A familiar sight to North London commuters were the condensing tank engines of the former Great Northern which worked trains to Kings Cross and Moorgate over the Metropolitan's widened lines, where the condensing apparatus had to be used in tunnels. Fitted with two inside cylinders at 19in x 26in (483mm x 660mm), and fed with superheated steam at 170psi (1,172kPa), they gave a tractive force of 19,900lb (9,027kg) on their 68in (1727mm) wheels. With a tank capacity of 2,000gal (91hl) they weighed 157,216lb (71.3 tonnes). Ten were built by the Doncaster works and, in 1921, fifty by the North British Locomotive Company. A further 47 were built at Doncaster between 1925 and 1929 for use in other areas of the LNER. Their boiler was the same as that fitted to the 56 similar engines of the N.1 Class: it had 1,250sq.ft. (116sq metre) of heating surface. They lasted in service until 1959-62. One of the North-British-built batch, No.4744 (BR No 69523) is presered.

## GREAT WESTERN RAILWAY 5600 CLASS/1924/GREAT BRITAIN

The 0-6-2 tank was a favourite of South Wales railway companies, operating winding lines up the valleys. When the GWR absorbed these lines it introduced a standard locomotive of the same wheel arrangement, but built

*0-6-2T Austrian narrow-gauge 298 Class, 1888*          *0-6-2T Great Northern N2 Class, 1920*

*0-6-2T GWR 5600 Class, 1924*

according to GWR practice. With their high-pitched taper boiler and the overhang at the front end, these were not beautiful engines, and when used on passenger services they produced a perceptible fore-and-aft motion. But they did a good job, hauling coal down to the docks of Cardiff, Newport, and Barry and, rough-riding excepted, they did good work on the passenger services too. Two hundred were built, and seven were preserved. They had 18in x 26in (457mm x 660mm) cylinders, 200psi (1378kPa) boiler pressure, and 55½in (1410mm) coupled wheels, giving a tractive effort of 25,800lb (11,713kg). They weighed 154,560lb (70 tonnes) and had a grate area of 20.35sq.ft. (1.89sq metre).

## 0-6-4T

### MERSEY RAILWAY CLASS 1/1885/GREAT BRITAIN

In view of the steep grades - as much as 1 in 27 (3.7 per cent) - the locomotives required to handle the traffic on the Mersey Railway were the most powerful in Britain in terms of tractive force. These 0-6-4T engines, with their 21in x 26in (533mm x 660mm) cylinders, could give a tractive force of 26,600lb (12,066kg) on a wheel diameter of 55in (1397mm). The steam pressure was 150psi (1034kPa) and the steam was condensed back into the side tanks, which had a water capacity of 1,250 gallons (56.8hl). The boiler had a heating-surface area of 1,634sq.ft. (152sq metre) and a grate area of 21sq.ft.

(1.95sq metre). The nine locomotives of this class were built by Beyer Peacock at a cost of £2,775 each. Two have been preserved, including one which ended its active life in Australia.

## 2-6-0T

### PRUSSIAN STATE RAILWAY CLASS

### T.9/3/1900/GERMANY

The 2-6-0T wheel arrangement was a comparatively rare one for a tank engine since the idling wheel is usually to be found under the coal bunker, behind the cab. It was, however, a favourite in Prussia as a standard light-shunting engine, and over 2,000 were built during 1900-14. Fitted with two outside cylinders at 17½in x 24⅘in (450mm x 630mm) and with driving wheels of diameter 53in (1350mm), they gave a tractive force of 20,700lb (9,390kg) on an adhesive weight of 99,005lb (44.9 tonnes) out of a total weight of 131,860lb (59.8 tonnes). They were provided with steam at a pressure of 170psi

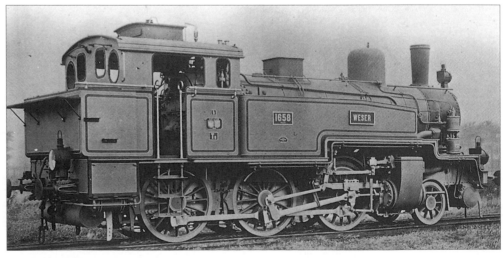

*2-6-0T Prussian T.11 Class, 1903. This was a passenger version of the T.9 Class*

*2-6-2T GWR 4500 Class, 1906*

(1200kPa) from a boiler which had a heating area of 1,123sq.ft. (104.4sq metre) and a firebox with a grate area of 16.5sq.ft. (1.53sq metre). Some were later to find uses in Poland (Class Tki-3) and in Yugoslavia as Class 154.

They were followed by two more series of 2-6-0T engines. These had larger cylinders - 21in (540mm) bore - and, with 59in (1500mm) driving wheels, were classed T.11 and T.12.

# 2-6-2T

## GREAT WESTERN RAILWAY 4500 CLASS/1906/GREAT BRITAIN

This design was among the radically new types introduced by George Churchward on the GWR before World War 1. Like his other designs, they had American features and this was apparent in their outward appearance, which was considered very un-British at the time. They were designed for branchline use, and with their leading and rear carrying trucks were far more sophisticated than the 0-6-0 types that were their equivalent in traction terms. They weighed 127,680lb (58 tonnes) tons, had a grate area of 16.6sq.ft. (1.54sq metre), and a tractive effort of 21,250lb (9,650kg) obtained by 17in x 24in (432mm x 610mm) cylinders, 200psi (1378kPa) bolier pressure, and 55½in (1410mm) coupled wheels. Being ideal engines for lightly-laid branches, they were also ideal, two generations later, for tourist railways, and eight were preserved out of the 175 that were built.

## HUNGARIAN STATE RAILWAYS 375 CLASS/1911/HUNGARY

These locomotives had an exceptionally long production run, making their debut under the Hapsburgs and seeing their greatest production under Stalinism. Small lightweight

*2-6-2T Hungarian State Railways 375 Class, 1911*

tank locomotives were very necessary in Hungary, not just for commuter service but for operating trains over medium-length branch lines with lightweight track and structures. The other small 2-6-2 tank engine design, the 376 Class, was even smaller. Over 350 examples of the 375 Class were built, a few of the early ones being compounds. The standard dimensions were as follows: cylinders 16¹⁄₁₀in x 23³⁄₅in (410mm x 600mm), coupled wheels 46½in(1180mm), boiler pressure 170psi (1175kPa), tractive effort 19,060lb (8,655kg), weight in working order 98,785lb (44.8 tonnes). The grate area was 19.9sq.ft. (1.85sq metre).

## GERMAN STATE RAILWAY CLASS 64/1928/GERMANY

Built by Henschel of Kassel, this class was intended for fast suburban trains and was designed with a maximum of accessibility of components for maintenance purposes. The two outside cylinders at 19²⁄₃in x 26in (500mm x 660mm) drove wheels of diameter 59in (1500mm) and, with a steam pressure of 200psi (1,380kPa), these engines gave a tractive force of 28,900lb (13,109kg). The boiler's heating area comprised 1,513sq.ft. (140.7sq metre), and the grate area was 22sq.ft. (2.05sq metre). The valve motion was of the Heusinger type, operating piston valves, and the boiler was fitted with three domes: one was for

the regulator, one was for sand, and the third was a feed dome with an angular-grid water-purifier. The water capacity was 1,985 gallon (90.2hl), and the total weight in working order was 125,690lb (75.5 tonnes) of which 101,870lb (46.2 tonnes) was available for adhesion. The idle wheels were carried in Bissel trucks having an axle load of 31,752lb (14.4 tonnes). They were equipped with Deuta speedometers and with electric light from a Henschel turbo-generator.

*2-6-2T  German State Railways 64 Class, 1928*

## GREAT WESTERN RAILWAY CLASS 5101/1929/GREAT BRITAIN

Based on the Churchward Class 3100 of 1903, Class 5101 was the most numerous of the Great Western's larger 2-6-2T engines; more than a hundred were built between 1929 and 1949, the later units being numbered in the 4100 series. With two outside cylinders at 18in x 30in (457mm x 762mm) and with steam at 200psi (1380kPa), they were fitted with 68in (1727mm) wheels and gave a tractive force of 24,300lb (11,022kg). The boiler was the Churchward standard No. 2 with a grate area of 20.3sq.ft. (1.9sq metre) and a heating-surface area of 1,349sq.ft. (125sq metre). The locomotive weight in working order was 175,738lb (79.7 tonnes).

These were followed by a further 70 similar locomotives of Class 6100 which used steam at 225psi (1551kPa), although the total weight was not increased. These locomotives were mostly withdrawn between 1954 and 1964, and about ten have been preserved.

*2-6-2T GWR 5101 Class, 1929*

## LMSR 3MT CLASS/1935/GREAT BRITAIN

These were originally introduced in 1930 with a parallel boiler. The 1935 version was redesigned by W. A. Stanier with a taper boiler and a larger firebox, with a grate area of 19.2sq.ft. (1.8sq metre). The two outside cylinders, measuring 17½in x 26in (445mm x 660mm), drove 63in

(1600mm) wheels and, with steam at 200psi (1380kPa), gave a tractive force of 21,500lb (9,752kg) on an adhesive weight of 105,400lb (47.8 tonnes). The axle-load of 35,170lb (15.95 tonnes) gave a wide availability, and these locomotives were used for suburban services and branch-line duty in many areas of the LMS. There were 70 of the parallel-boiler type and 139 of the taper-boiler type. Some of the earlier models were fitted with condensing gear for operation in the tunnels to Moorgate from the North London line. They lasted in service until the mid-1960s.

## QUINCY RAILROAD TANK/1935/USA

This Alco-built tank engine was of the usual side-tank type and was built for oil-firing. The two cylinders were 16in x 24in (406mm x 610mm) and, with a steam pressure of

*2-6-2T LMS Railway 3MT Class, 1935*

*2-6-4T BR 4MT Class, 1951. This was the British Railways development of the LMS 4MT*

180psi (1241kPa) and the usual 44in (1118mm) wheels, it gave a tractive force of 21,400lb (9,707kg). The boiler had only 973sq.ft. (90.4sq metre) of heating-surface area and a firegrate area of 20.5sq.ft. (1.9sq metre). The total weight was 119,677lb (54.3 tonnes), of which 89,743lb (40.7 tonnes) were available for adhesion

# 2-6-4T

## LMS CLASS 4MT/1936/GREAT BRITAIN

Built under three chief mechanical engineers, the 2-6-4T was the most widely used of the LMS's tank engines for passenger suburban services: in all, 645 were built. The first 125, built in the Fowler era, were fitted with the usual Midland parallel boilers, but from 1936, with the Stanier taper boiler being used, a further 206 were built with two outside cylinders at 19⅝in x 26in (498mm x 660mm) and driving 69in (1753mm) wheels. With a steam pressure of 200psi (1380kPa), they gave a tractive force of 24,700lb (11,204kg) on an adhesive weight of 116,424lb (52.8 tonnes). The total weight was 196,906 (89.3 tonnes). There were also 37 built with three cylinders of 16in (410mm) diameter, and these weighed 206,167lb (93.5 tonnes).

Under Charles Fairburn a further 277 were built to a shorter wheelbase on a weight of 190,732lb (86.5 tonnes), but otherwise these were generally similar. From 1951 the design was used in the BR Class 4MT, but with 18in (457mm) cylinders and a steam pressure of 225psi (1551kPa); 155 of these were built. The three-cylinder version was withdrawn in 1962, but the others lasted until 1966-67. Three of LMS type and eleven of BR type have been preserved.

# 4-6-0T

*2-6-4T LMS 4MT Class, 1936*

## NORTH EASTERN RAILWAY CLASS W/1907/GREAT BRITAIN

Known as the Willies, these tank engines were built originally for operation on the steeply graded lines in the Whitby Area. With two inside cylinders at 19in x 26in (483mm x 660mm) inclined to drive the front axle, the driving wheels were at 61⅙in (1555mm) diameter and the steam was at 170psi (1,172kPa). These engines gave a tractive force of 23,000lb (10,433kg) on an adhesive weight of 116,424lb (52.8 tonnes). The boiler had a heating-surface area of 1,312sq.ft. (122sq metre) and a grate area of 23sq.ft. (2.1sq metre). The tank capacity was originally 1,500 gallons (68.2hl), but the coal bunker held only 2-long-tons (2.24 tonnes) of coal - except in the case of the last of the 10 engines, which held 3-long-tons (3.05 tonnes). The total weight came to 156,334lb (70.9 tonnes), with brakes on all wheels for working loose-coupled freight trains down the steep banks. Between 1914 and 1917 they were converted to a 4-6-2T with larger coal bunkers and extra water capacity, and in 1923 they became the LNER's Class A.6, in which form they had a weight of 170,226lb (77.2 tonnes). They were all withdrawn by 1955.

# 4-6-2T

*4-6-2T Great Central 9N (LNER A5) Class, 1911*

## GREAT CENTRAL RAILWAY CLASS 9N/1911/GREAT BRITAIN

Designed by J. G. Robinson, these heavy tank engines were used for suburban duties and, with two cylinders at 20in x 26in (508mm x 660mm) and driving wheels of diameter 67in (1702mm), they produced a tractive force of 23,800lb (10,796kg), using steam at 180psi (1241kPa). They were built as superheated engines with 1,550sq.ft. (144m2) of heating area and a firegrate area of 21sq.ft. (1.95sq metre) on a total weight of 192,496lb (87.3 tonnes). Initially 21 were built by the Great Central, and a further 10 came after 1923, when they became LNER Class A5. Another 13 were built by Hawthorn Leslie & Co. for service in the northeast in 1925; these had smaller boiler mountings to suit the former North Eastern loading gauge. Forty-three lasted into British Railways stock in 1948; all were withdrawn by 1961.

# 4-6-4T

*4-6-4T NSWGR C-30 Class, 1903*

## NEW SOUTH WALES GOVERNMENT RAILWAYS CLASS C-30/1903/AUSTRALIA

With the expansion of Sydney at the beginning of the 20th Century there came a demand for better motive power to handle commuter services. Ninety-five 4-6-4 tank locomotives were ordered from Beyer, Peacock and the Railway's Eveleigh workshops built another 50, deliveries being spaced over 14 years. They were not superheated, but being of generous proportions they did their job well. When the Sydney network was electrified they went to perform similar duties at other towns, notably Newcastle and Wollongong. Some were converted to 4-6-0 tender locomotives. The last examples were withdrawn in 1971, although several went into preservation, some in running order.

They had 55in (1400mm) coupled wheels, good for accelerating from stops, and their tractive effort was 19,116lb (8,698kg). Cylinders were 18½in x 24in (470mm x 610mm), and boiler pressure 160psi (1102kPa). Weight in working order was 162,710 (73.8 tonnes), and the grate area was 24sq.ft. (2.23sq metre).

## PRUSSIAN STATE RAILWAY CLASS T.18/1912/GERMANY

This type found considerable favour for suburban services in Prussia; between 1912 and 1927 over 500 were built. They were constructed as a simple two-cylinder superheated engine, with cylinders at 22in x 24¾in (560mm x 630mm) and, with driving wheels of diameter 65in (1650mm), gave a tractive force of 26,700lb (12,111kg) on an adhesive weight of 112,455lb (51 tonnes). Steam at a pressure of 170psi (1172kPa) was supplied by a boiler with 1,992sq.ft. (185.3sq metre) heating surface and a firegrate area of 26.3sq.ft. (2.45sq metre). With a total weight of 233,289lb (105.8 tonnes), they were heavier than any of the British 4-6-4T engines (see next entry for example). They were used also in Poland (as Class Oko-1) and in Turkey, for use in which country 8 were built in 1927.

## LMS CLASS 11110/1924/GREAT BRITAIN

The 4-6-4T tank engine was used in Britain primarily for hauling train-loads of passengers to the seaside. It was

*4-6-4T Prussian T.18 Class, 1912.*

commissioned by four of the pre-grouping railways - the Glasgow and South Western, the London, Brighton and South Coast, the Furness, and the London, Tilbury and Southend lines - but only in small lots. Those for the LMS were based on the Lancashire & Yorkshire Railway 4-6-0 tender locomotive and, using four cylinders at 16½in x 26in (419mm x 660mm) and 75in (1905mm) diameter driving wheels, they gave a tractive force of 30,000lb (13,608kg), using steam at 180psi (1241kPa). The boiler had a heating area of 2,340sq.ft. (217sq metre) and a grate area of 29.6sq.ft. (2.75sq metre). On a weight of 223,807lb (101.5 tonnes), they were the heaviest tank engines ever used in Great Britain. They were free and fast engines, but their weight limitation restricted their utility to operation between Manchester and Blackpool, and, although 20 had been ordered, only 10 were in fact built.

# 4-6-4T

*4-6-4T Prussian T.18 Class, 1912. This picture shows the type as built, whereas the top picture shows it in the 1950s, working Frankfurt commuter services.*

*4-6-4T LMS 11110 Class, 1924*

### GERMAN STATE RAILWAY SERIES 62/1928/GERMANY

Among the range of highly standardized locomotives introduced by the Deutsche Reichsbahn in the 1920s was this 4-6-4 tank locomotive for heavy passenger duty. The most interesting feature of this design was the provision for water storage, which consisted of a large tank behind the cab rather like a US 'Forney tank.' Dispensing with side water tanks gave the locomotive crew better forward vision, more width to accommodate a bigger boiler, and did something to moderate that inherent fault of tank locomotives, declining adhesion as the water emptied (putting the water where its weight was borne by the rear truck rather than over the coupled wheels achieved this). As the locomotives were destined to haul short-distance trains the resultant loss of water capacity was not at all serious. The coal was carried above the water tank in a high bunker that was narrowed at the top so as to preserve enginemen's vision. A feature of this bunker was that it was provided with a lid so that coal dust would not blow

into the cab. That cab was exceptionally roomy and comfortable. The boiler, which was designed especially for these engines and was therefore a minor departure from the standardization policy, had a diameter of 71in (1.8m), only 4in (10cm) less than that of the Pacifics built at the

same time. Grate area was 37.6sq.ft. (3.5sq metre), and the total heating surface was 2,861sq.ft. (265.8sq metre) including 72.5sq.ft. (780.4sq metre) contributed by the superheater. Boiler pressure was 200psi (1378kPa), cylinders 23 4/5in X 26in (600mm X 660mm), and coupled

*4-6-4T German State Railway 62 Class, 1928*

*4-6-6T Boston & Albany RR D-1 Class, 1935*

wheel diameter 69in (1750mm). Tractive effort at 75 per cent boiler pressure was 31,500lbs (14,250kgs) 494cu ft (14sq metre) of water was carried. Weight in working order was 273,370lb (124 tonnes), giving an adhesion weight of 134,480lbs (61 tonnes).

In the late 1990s, a surviving member of this class was hauling DB weekend excursion trains.

## 4-6-6T

### BOSTON AND ALBANY RAILROAD CLASS D-1/1935/USA

The five engines of this class, built by the American Locomotive Company, were unique in their wheel arrangement and were for use in suburban passenger service. Fitted with two outside cylinders at 23½in x 26in (597mm x 660mm), they drove 63in (1600mm) diameter

wheels. With steam at 215psi (1483kPa), they gave a tractive force of 41,600lb (18,870kg). The sloping firegrate, mounted over the rear driving-axle, had a grate area of 60.8sq.ft. (5.65sq metre); with a total heating-surface area of 3,549sq.ft. (330sq metre) the boiler produced super-heated steam using a soft coal from the Albany Mines. The fuel capacity was 13,450lb (6.1 tonnes) of coal and 5,000 gallons (189.3hl) of water, giving a working weight of 352,138lb (159.7 tonnes), of which 180,016lb (81.64 tonnes) were available for adhesion. These were probably the heaviest tank engines in the United States, and were just slightly heavier than the Bulgarian 2-12-4T version.

# EIGHT-COUPLED TANK ENGINES

## 0-8-0T

### VINDOBONA/1851/AUSTRIA

The first eight-coupled tank engine was the Vindobona built by John Haswell at the Austrian State Railway works at Vienna for the Semmering trials in that year. With two cylinders at 16½in x 22⅘in (421mm x 580mm) and with driving wheels of diameter 37⅔in (957mm), the steam pressure was 100psi (690kpi), the maximum allowed, and gave a tractive force of 14,200lb (6,441kg). This was well below those of its competitors, and the performance was not adequate for the duty specified. The boiler had a heating surface area of 1,716sq.ft. (159.5sq metre) and a grate area of 15.6sq.ft. (1.45sq metre). The weight was 100,327lb (45.5 tonnes) and, while it was the most practical of the entries, its lack of power was an insuperable disadvantage.

### PRUSSIAN STATE RAILWAY CLASS T.13/1910/GERMANY

With wheels of diameter only 49½in (1250mm), this was described as a heavy shunter. Over 700 were built between 1910 and 1922. Fitted with two outside cylinders at 19 2/3in x 23 2/3in (500mm x 600mm), it was fed with saturated steam at a pressure of 170psi (1172kPa) and gave a tractive force of 37,200lb (16,874kg) on a weight of 132,520lb (60.1 tonnes). The boiler had 1,218sq.ft. (113.2sq metre) of heating surface with a firegrate area of 18.9sq.ft. (1.76sq metre). Some eventually were to be found in Poland, as Class Tkp-1, and in Czechoslovakia, as Class 415.

*2-8-2T Nord 4.200 (SNCF 141TC) Class, 1932. The late-1960s picture shows the simultaneous adeparture of two of these locomotives from the Gare du Nord in Paris.*

## 0-8-2T

### GREAT NORTHERN RAILWAY CLASS L.1/1902/GREAT BRITAIN

The 41 engines of this class, built between 1902 and 1906, were intended for taking trucks from collieries to sidings for marshalling into longer trains. Their two inside cylinders at 19⁷/₁₀in x 26in (500mm x 660mm) drove 56in (1422mm) diameter wheels and, with steam at 170psi (1172kPa), gave a tractive force of 26,000lb (11,794kg) on an adhesive weight of 147,735lb (67 tonnes) out of a total weight of 161,626lb (73.3 tonnes). In 1918, three were fitted with superheaters, showing a saving in fuel of 15 per cent, and in 1921 during the coal strike one was equipped with Scarab oil-burning apparatus. Their water capacity was found to be inadequate for use on Nottinghamshire coal trains, and in 1934 they were replaced by tender engines which had greater coal and water-carrying capacity. From 1923 they became the LNER Class R1, which they remained until their withdrawal in 1934.

### CYPRUS MINES CORPORATION/1930/CYPRUS

The Baldwin Locomotive Company, as well as building giant American-style locomotives, produced these handy tanks for the 2ft 6in (762mm) gauge tracks of the mines in Cyprus. With two cylinders at 15in x 18in (381mm x 457mm), they had 33in (838mm) diameter wheels and gave a tractive force of 16,600lb (7,530kg)

using steam at 160psi (1104kPa) produced from a boiler with 1,111sq.ft. (103sq meter) of heating surface and a firegrate area of 18.2sq.ft. (1.7sq meter). They were designed to work on soft coal. The weight was 105,619lb (47.9 tonnes), of which 91,066lb (41.3 tonnes) were on the driving wheels.

## 0-8-4T

### LNWR CLASS 380/1923/GREAT BRITAIN

These 30 engines were a tank version of the numerous LNWR 'G' Class 0-8-0 freight locomotives already

mentioned, and were used mainly on the heavy grades in South Wales, particularly between Abergavenny and Merthyr. Fitted with two inside cylinders at 20½in x 24in (520mm x 610mm), they had 53in (1346mm) wheels and, with superheated steam at 185psi (1276kPa), gave a tractive force of 29,900lb (13,563kg) on an adhesive weight of 149,940lb (68 tonnes). Their boiler was the same as that fitted to the G.2 Class, and the four-wheeled carrying bogie gave them a coal capacity of 3.5-long-tons (3.56 tonnes) with a water tank of 2,030 gallons (92.3hl). In the LMS merger they became their Class 7F, lasting in service until 1944-51.

*0-8-4T LNWR 380 Class, 1923*

*2-8-2T GWR 7200 Class, 1934, an enlargement of the 4200 Class 2-8-0T*

## CHEMINS DE FER DU NORD CLASS 4.200/1932/FRANCE

Built for push-pull operation of suburban trains in and out of the Gare du Nord, the 72 engines of this class were constructed by Derosne et Cail. They were fitted with two outside cylinders equipped with the Cossart system of piston valves. The cylinders were originally of 23in (585mm) diameter, but were later enlarged to 25⅕in (640mm) with a stroke of 27½in (700mm) and driving 61in (1550mm) diameter wheels. With steam at a pressure of 256psi (1765kPa), they gave a tractive force of 61,400lb (27,851kg) on an adhesive weight of 187,425lb (85 tonnes) out of a total weight of 270,112lb (122.5 tonnes). The superheated steam was provided by a boiler with 2,645sq.ft. (246sq meter) of heating-surface area and a firebox with a grate area of 33.4sq.ft. (3.1sq meter). On test with a dynamometer car, hauling a train of 474.4-long-tons (482 tonnes), they gave an output of 1,680dbhp (1,253kW), equivalent to 2,300ihp (1,715kW).

## ARICA-LA PAZ/1936/CHILE

Built by the Baldwin Locomotive Company to operate on the rack section of this meter (3ft 3in) gauge line between Central and Puquois, these engines were working at altitudes of over 12,000ft (3,658m) on the Bolivian portion of the line. They were fitted with four cylinders, two at 19in x 20in (483mm x 508mm) for normal-adhesion working and two at 18in x 18in (457mm x 457mm) for the rack wheels. With a steam pressure of 200psi (1,380kPa) and with 37in (940mm) diameter wheels, they gave a starting force of 33,200lb (15,060kg) on the running rail with 30,000lb (13,608kg) on the rack teeth. The boiler produced superheated steam from a heating area of 2,015sq.ft. (187.2sq meter) with a grate area of 28.6sq.ft. (2.66sq meter). The adhesive weight was 123,377lb (55.5 tonnes) out of a total of 166,036lb (75.3 tonnes).

*2-8-0T GWR 4200 Class, 1910*

# 2-8-0T

## GREAT WESTERN RAILWAY CLASS 4200/1910/GREAT BRITAIN

The 205 locomotives of this class, built between 1910 and 1940, were a tank version of the 2800 class freight engine, but using the standard No. 4 boiler to give space for the side tanks. With two outside cylinders at 18½in x 30in (470mm x 762mm), they drove 55½in (1410mm) diameter wheels, giving a tractive force of 31,400lb (14,243kg) using steam at 200psi (1380kPa). The standard No.4 boiler had a heating-surface area of 1,818sq.ft. (169sq meter) with a grate area of 20.6sq.ft. (1.9sq meter). The total engine weight was 180,590lb (81.9 tonnes), of which 163,611lb (74.2 tonnes) were on

the driving wheels. From 1923 the remainder of the class (after No. 5205) were fitted with 19in (483mm) diameter cylinders to give a tractive force of 33,200lb (15,060kg). All were eventually equipped with the Swindon superheater, and all used the Stephenson valve gear. During the Depression, 54 of these locomotives, partly as a make-work endeavour, were rebuilt as 2-8-2T engines, forming the 7200 Class. The 4200 Class lasted in service until 1959-65 and several have been preserved.

# 2-8-2T

## POLISH STATE RAILWAYS CLASS Tkt48/1950/POLAND

The 194 locomotives of this class were built by Chrzanow and Cegielski locomotive-building firms to supplement the 2-6-2T Class Ok127. With a reduced axle-load they gave a wider scope of operation. With two outside cylinders at 19⅔in x 27½in (500mm x 700mm), and with driving wheels of diameter 57in (1450mm), they produced a tractive force of 37,500lb (17,010kg) on an adhesive weight of 140,835lb (63.9 tonnes) out of a total weight of 209,030lb (94.8 tonnes). Steam was supplied at 227psi (1565kPa) from a boiler with a heating area (including the superheater) of 1,848.2sq.ft. (171.9sq meter). The firegrate area was 32.3sq.ft. (3sq meter). These locomotives were later fitted with a large smoke deflector mounted on the top of the smokebox, similar to those fitted to the Class Ol49 2-6-2 passenger locomotives.

*2-8-2T Polish State Railways Tkt48 Class, 1950. The locomotive shown here was still in service in the late 1990s.*

## 2-8-2ST

### LONG BELL LUMBER COMPANY/1932/USA

A tank engine was a rare product of the American Locomotive Company. This one, designed for the timber trade, used the usual 44in (1118mm) wheels and, with two outside cylinders at 18in x 24in (457mm x 610mm), gave a tractive force of 28,500lb (12,928kg), using steam at 190psi (1310kPa). The boiler had 1,485sq.ft. (138sq metre) of heating-surface area, including a superheater, with a grate area of 25.2sq.ft. (2.34sq metre). The working weight was 168,021 (76.2 tonnes), of which 120,613lb (54.7 tonnes) were on the driving wheels.

## 2-8-4T

### ANTOFAGASTA & BOLIVIA RAILWAY 2-8-4T/1912/BOLIVIA

Before World War 1, the Antofagasta & Bolivia Railway was notable for being of 2ft 6in (760mm) gauge, operated as far as possible to mainline standards. The traffic was

*2-8-4T German State Railway 65.10 Class, 1954*

*2-8-4T Antofagasta & Bolivia Railway type, 1928. The picture shows No 554, of an earlier batch, subsequently fitted to carry oil fuel on the cab roof.*

*4-8-4T PLM (SNCF 242TA Class), 1926, as running in the 1960s with enlarged bunker*

*4-8-4T PLM (SNCF 242TA Class), 1926, as built*

handled by a succession of 2-8-4 tank locomotives supplied by British builders. For example, Nos.27-28, later renumbered 553-554, were supplied by Kitson in 1912. When the lines were converted to meter-gauge, so as to conform with neighbouring railways, the locomotives were similarly re-gauged. Subsequent locomotives were of similar design, but built as meter-gauge units. No.43, for example, was supplied by North British in 1928 and was not only superheated but also had a Worthington feedwater heater and electric lamps. It weighed in working order 201,757lb (91.5 tonnes) and had a grate area of 29.6sq.ft. (2.75sq meter) - it was an oil-burner. Cylinders were 19in x 24in (483mm x 610mm) and boiler pressure 180psi (1240kPa). The coupled wheels were of 44in (1118mm) diameter.

## GERMAN STATE RAILWAY (DR) CLASS 65.10/1954/GERMAN DEMOCRATIC REPUBLIC

This was the first numerous post-war standard-gauge class to be built in the GDR; by 1958 a total of 88 had been produced. With two outside cylinders at 23⅔in x 26in (600mm x 660mm) driving on to the third coupled axle, they used driving wheels of diameter 63in (1600mm) and, with steam at a pressure of 227psi (1600kpa), gave a tractive force of 44,000lb (19,958kg) on an adhesive weight of 154,129lb (69.9 tonnes) out of a total weight of 263,938lb (119.7 tonnes). The boiler had a parallel barrel and a heating-surface area of 2,097sq.ft. (195sq meter) with a grate area of 37.1sq.ft. (3.45sq meter). The side water tanks were between the front of the firebox and the smokebox, but the trailing bogie allowed extra water capacity under the coal bunker.

## 4-8-4T

PLM CLASS 242TA/1926/FRANCE
Built to replace the 4-6-4T engines of 1908, these four-cylinder compound tanks used two high-pressure cylinders at 16½in (420mm) diameter and two low-pressure ones of diameter 24¾in (630mm), all with a stroke of 25½in (650mm); the driving wheels were of diameter 65in (1650mm) and, with a steam pressure of 227psi

*0-10-0T Prussian T.16 Class, 1905*

*2-10-2T German State Railway 95 Class, 1922*

area for fast suburban services up to a distance of 50 miles (80km) from the Gare de Lyon.

# TEN-COUPLED TANK ENGINES

## 0-10-0T

### GREAT EASTERN RAILWAY `DECAPOD'/1903/GREAT BRITAIN

Although the term 'Decapod' generally applies to a 2-10-0 locomotive, it was used in Great Britain to denote the only two locomotives built in that country to the 0-10-0 arrangement. The Great Eastern 'Decapod' was built to prove that steam could equal electricity in the acceleration of trains up to 30mph (48kph). Although it succeeded in this objective, the load imposed on the track was not acceptable to the civil engineer. Built at the Stratford works to the design of James Holden, the 'Decapod' was fitted with three cylinders at 18½in x 24in (470mm x 610mm) and drove wheels of diameter 54in (1372mm). With steam at 200psi (1380kPa), it gave a tractive force of 39,000lb (17,690kg) and was fitted with a large boiler having 3,010sq.ft. (279.9sq meter) of heating area and a grate area of 42sq.ft. (3.9sq meter), the largest in Britain at that time. Its coal and water capacities were completely inadequate because of the necessity of keeping within the weight limit, and after some trial running it was converted to an 0-8-0 tender locomotive.

(1600kPa), they could give a tractive force of 31,000lb (14,062kg) on an adhesive weight of 143,325lb (65 tonnes). The boiler had a heating area of 2,351sq.ft. (218.6sq meter) with a firegrate area of 33.4sq.ft. (3.1sq meter). The working weight was 254,600lb (120 tonnes). All told, 120 were built, mainly for operation in the Paris

*2-10-2T  German State Railway 99.23 Class, 1954*

*2-12-4T Bulgarian State Railway 46 Class, 1942*

### PRUSSIAN STATE RAILWAY CLASS T.16/1905/GERMANY

Two years after the unsuccessful Great Eastern trial with ten-coupled wheels (see preceding entry), the Prussian State Railway built its first 0-10-0T locomotive for shunting and banking duty; it proved such a success that by 1922 over 1,600 had been built. With two outside cylinders at 24in x 26in (610mm x 660mm) and with 53in (1350mm) diameter wheels, these locomotives produced a tractive

force of 40,800lb (18,507kg) on an all-up weight of 186,763lb (84.7 tonnes). They used superheated steam at a pressure of 170psi (1172kPa) from a boiler with 1,855sq.ft. (172.5sq meter) of heating area and a firegrate of area 24.8sq.ft. (2.3sq meter). On some the drive was onto the fourth coupled axle, but most drove onto the centre axle. They were later to be dispersed to Poland (Class Tkw-1), to Bulgaria (Class 50) and to Yugoslavia (Class 159).

# 2-10-2T

### GERMAN STATE RAILWAY SERIES 95/1922/GERMANY

In 1920 the various German state railways had merged into the German State Railway (DR) which was largely Prussian in its engineering policies. There were 210 different locomotive types, and the standardization program aimed to reduce these to 12. The new designs duly emerged, and were obviously Prussian in inspiration. In particular, high power outputs were not favoured if they placed undue stress on locomotives. The 95 Series was based on a Prussian design, and was not part of the program. Borsig built the first in 1922 and by 1924 all 45 had been built. The boiler was quite wide, being 73in (1860mm) in diameter, and it provided a grate area of 46.28 sq.ft. (4.3sq meter). The two cylinders were 27½in x 26in (700mm X 660mm) and the wheels 55in (1400mm) in diameter. Boiler pressure was 200psi (1378kPa), giving a tractive effort at 75per cent boiler pressure of 53,625lbs (24,320kgs). Because the locomotives were expected to operate in hilly areas they were designed with the Krauss-Helmholtz truck (which gave the first and last coupled wheels some sideplay to help negotiate curves). One of the purposes of the design was to replace existing rack locomotives in the Thuringian mountains, and Thuringia was the last home of these locomotives, which were used on banking duties from Saalfeld up to the 1980s.

## GERMAN STATE RAILWAY CLASS 99.23
### 1954/GERMAN DEMOCRATIC REPUBLIC

These six locomotives were built by the Karl Marx Works as late as 1954 for the East German meter-gauge lines. They were very similar to locomotives built in 1931 (Class 99.22). They were sent to work on the Nordhausen-Wernigerode system, and were still there in the 1990s. They have driving wheels of 39in (1000mm), cylinders 21³⁄₅in x 21³⁄₅in (550mm x 550mm) and boiler pressure of 200psi (1378kPa). Tractive effort is 43,875lb (19,920kg), and the grate area 30.1sq.ft. (2.8sq meter). Weight in working order is 143,260lb (65 tonnes). For the narrow gauge, these are exceptionally powerful locomotives.

# TWELVE-COUPLED TANK ENGINES

## 2-12-4T

### BULGARIAN STATE RAILWAY CLASS 46/1931/BULGARIA

The first 12 of this class, built by Krupp in 1931, were then the largest tank engines in Europe - weighing 328,765lb (149.1 tonnes) - but in 1943 a yet larger version, with three cylinders, was built by Schwarzkopf at a weight of 342,877lb (155.5 tonnes). The two-cylinder version used cylinders at 27½in x 27½in (700mm x 700mm), and the three-cylinder version used cylinders at 21²⁄₃in x 27½in (550mm x 700mm). With driving wheels of diameter 52½in (1340mm) and with steam at 227psi (1565kPa), their tractive effort was 76,200lb (34,564kg) for the two-cylinder type and 69,800lb (31,661kg) for the three-cylinder model. The boiler capacity was the same in both cases; the heating area was 3,315sq.ft. (308sq meter) with a firegrate area of 52.3sq.ft. (4.86sq meter). The coal and water capacities, at 22,490lb (10.2 tonnes) and 4,000 gallon (181.8hl), were as big as those of most British tender locomotives, and the arduous nature of their duty precluded the necessity of smoke deflectors. They were used for hauling coal trains on the line between Sofia

*0-8-8-0T Bavarian State Railway Gp.Gt 2x4/4 Class, 1911*

*0-4-0T NSWGR crane tank, 1914*

*0-6-2.2-6-0T Nord S.6121 Class, 1905*

effort of 15,300lb (6,950kg) and their weight in working order was 88,200lb (40 tonnes). They were yard locomotives with a difference and of a rare category. Their value came in such places as dockyards or railway works, where there were always bits and pieces to carry from one place to another. They would go to the object in question, swing the jib over it, pick it up so that it hung in the air, return the jib to a fore-and-aft position, and then trundle off down the line, rather like a cat bringing home a mouse. These cranes had no winch, the hoisting being achieved by luffing the jib, there being separate hooks for 3.5, 5, and 7-ton lifts. One of the last in service was kept busy, fetching and carrying, at the Eveleigh locomotive works in Sydney.

# ARTICULATED TANK ENGINES

(Articulated tank engines are also covered in the next section)

## 0-8-8-0T

### BAVARIAN STATE RAILWAY Gp. Gt 2x4/4/1911/GERMANY

Among the heaviest of the European tanks were these compound units built by J. A. Maffei for use in the hills of Bavaria. With four cylinders, two at 20½in (520mm) and two at 31½in (800mm) diameters and with a stroke of 25 1/5in (640mm), they drove 47in (1216mm) diameter wheels. With superheated steam at 215psi (1483kPa), they gave a tractive force of 57,000lb (25,855kg). The boiler had a heating area of 3,078sq.ft. (286sq meter) with a grate area of 46.3sq.ft. (4.3sq meter). The comparatively small side tanks were forward, away from the cab. The working weight was 334,680lb (123.2 tonnes).

## 0-6-2.2-6-0T

### CHEMINS DE FER DU NORD S.6121/1910/FRANCE

Built to the design of Du Bousquet, these were an adaption of the Meyer type with the driving wheels at the outer ends and with the cylinders in the centre of the boiler, so that the high- and low-pressure cylinders were close together. The two high-pressure cylinders were 15¾in x 26¾in (400mm x 680mm), and the low-pressure ones were

24¾in x 26¼in (630mm x 680mm). The driving wheels were of diameter 57in (1455mm) and, with a steam pressure of 227psi (1565kPa), they gave a tractive force of 33,000lb (14,969kg) from an adhesive weight of 199,332lb (90.4 tonnes). The boiler contained 2,024sq.ft. (188sq meter) of heating surface, with a grate area of 32.3sq.ft. (3sq meter). Designed for heavy coal traffic, they could haul trains of 1,016 tonnes (1,100 US tons) up a grade of 1 in 84 (1.2 per cent) at 13mph (20.9kph), corresponding to an output of 1,340dbhp (999kW) or a cylinder output of 1,750ihp (1,305kW). The rear tank was mounted on a separate girder frame. These engines proved their worth, and 48 were built by B. W. Hellemes. Similar locomotives were supplied to the Peking-Hankow Railway and to the Andalusian Railway.

## 0-4-4-4-0T

### BLEODEL, STEWART AND WELCH LTD./1910/USA

This was of the conventional Shay three-truck type and was built for use in timber-producing areas. The basic construction was the same as for the two-truck type, with 36in (914mm) wheels and with the same boiler, performance and tractive force. This version weighed 188,086lb (85.3 tonnes).

and Pernik with grades of 1 in 40 (2.5 per cent) on which they could take 80-car trains without assistance.

# CRANE TANK LOCOMOTIVES

## 0-4-0T

### NEW SOUTH WALES GOVERNMENT RAILWAYS CRANE TANK/1914/AUSTRALIA

The first of these eight 0-4-0 tank locomotives, known as 'Seven-ton Luffing Crane Locomotives,' was delivered by Hawthorn Leslie in 1914 and the last by Robert Stephenson-Hawthorn in 1950. They had 14in x 20in (336mm x 508mm) cylinders, 39in (991mm) driving wheels, a boiler pressure of 190psi (1309kPa), a tractive

*(next page) 'Big Boy' locomotive, Union Pacific Railroad*

# ARTICULATED LOCOMOTIVES

# ARTICULATED LOCOMOTIVES

## FOUR-COUPLED ARTICULATED LOCOMOTIVES

### 0-4-4-0

#### SEMMERING CONTEST SERAING/1851/BELGIUM

Built as a self-contained unit (it could be classed as a tank engine), this was equipped with four cylinders measuring 16in x 28in (406mm x 711mm) and driving wheels of 41³⁄₁₀in (1049mm) diameter. The steam pressure was 85psi (586kPa) and the boilers each had 1,840 sq.ft. (171.1sq metre) of heating surface with a 10.8 sq.ft. (1sq metre) firegrate; each boiler supplied one set of wheels. The total weight amounted to 107,432lb (49.5 tonnes), and the tractive force came to 25,100lb (11,385kg) - but that was eclipsed by the performance of the Bavaria.

Robert Fairlie was a member of the design team for the Seraing, and later he was to incorporate some of the features of the design in his own locomotives.

*A three-truck Shay locomotive*

#### FFESTINIOG RAILWAY No.11 (LIVINGSTONE-THOMPSON)/1885/GREAT BRITAIN

The 23½in (597mm) gauge Ffestiniog Railway had taken delivery of its first Fairlie locomotive in 1869. Named Little Wonder, it was the first to have been built by the Fairlie Engine and Steam Carriage Co. Although apparently successful, it was withdrawn in 1879 and replaced by No. 10, built in the railway's own shops at Boston Lodge. That was followed in 1885 by a similar version, No.11, named Livingstone-Thompson, which was later renumbered No.3 and then renamed Taliesin in 1930. The four cylinders were at 9in x 14in (229mm x 357mm), driving wheels of 33¹⁄₁₀in (843mm) diameter which, with a steam pressure of 160psi (1104kPa), gave a tractive force of 9,300lb (4,218kg) on a total weight of 53,802lb (24.4 tonnes). The total heating-surface area of the two boilers was 887 sq.ft. (82.5sq metre), with a firegrate area of 12.1 sq.ft. (1.1sq metre). The boiler was renewed by the Vulcan Foundry in 1908.

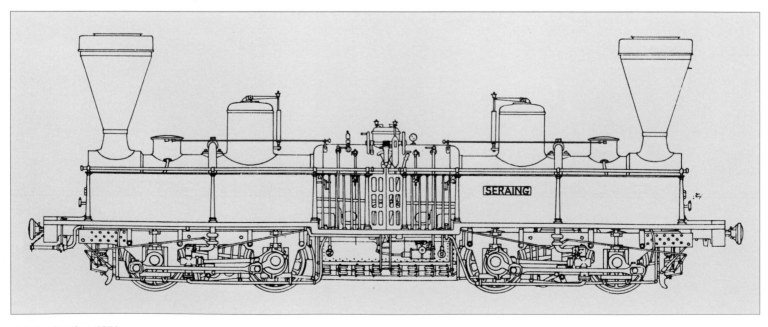

*0-4-4-0 Seraing, 1851*

The line closed in 1946. On its reopening in 1956, this locomotive was rebuilt on site with parts supplied by the Vulcan Foundry and returned to duty, still with the name Taliesin.

## LA METALLURGIQUE (MALLET TYPE)/1889/FRANCE

The first of the designs of Anatole Mallet was built with the idea of mounting the high-pressure cylinders on the frame and the low-pressure cylinders on a separate swivelling truck so that the ball-joint in the steam supply to the truck would have to handle only low-pressure steam. The first example was built to a 23 2/3in (600mm) gauge and shown at the Paris Exhibition in 1889. The design incorporated high-pressure cylinders measuring 7 2/3in x 10in (187mm x 260mm) and low-pressure ones at 11in x 10_in (280mm x 260mm). With steam at 170psi (1172kPa) and with wheels of diameter 23 2/3in (600mm), the tractive force was 5,000lb (2,268kg). The adhesive weight, 25,798lb (11.7 tonnes), equalled the total weight of the engine.

*0-4-4-0 Tasmanian Government Railway Garratt, 1909, as built*

## DAYTON POWER CORPORATION (SHAY TYPE)/1908/USA

This was one of the few Shay types to be built with a twin bogie and, since all the wheels were driven off one set of cylinders, it could alternatively be classified as an 0-8-0T. The type was designed for operation in areas where the track could be obstructed at the sides and so cause damage to outside cylinders. On the Shay type the three cylinders were mounted vertically and drove the separate bogies through shafts and right-angle drives. All were built by the Lima Corporation.

This two-truck version was fitted with three cylinders at 13in x 15in (330mm x 381mm) and, with a steam pressure of 200psi (1380kPa) and 36in (914mm) driving wheels, gave a tractive force of 38,200lb (17,328kg). The boiler, which produced superheated steam, had 1,094 sq.ft. (101.6sq metre) of heating surface with a firegrate area of 27.8 sq.ft. (2.6sq metre). The working weight, all of which was adhesive, was 184,779lb (83.8 tonnes).

## TASMANIAN GOVERNMENT RAILWAY 2FT (610mm) GAUGE (GARRATT TYPE)/1909/AUSTRALIA

This first pair of Garratt-type engines were built by Beyer Peacock of Gorton, Manchester, to whom William Garratt had suggested his design for engines suitable to negotiate lines with sharp curves. In this layout the boiler unit was suspended between two swivelling trucks: this enabled the use of a boiler with a greater diameter than if it had been placed over the driving wheels.

These, the first two examples, were built to use the compound cycle with cylinders at 11in x 16in (279mm x 406mm) and 17in x 16in (432mm x 406mm), two to each

*The pioneer Tasmanian Garratt, now exhibited at the National Railway Museum at York*

set of wheels, which were of 31½in (800mm) diameter. Using a steam pressure of 200psi (1380kPa) they gave a tractive force of 16,300lb (7,394kg), and the engine had a total weight of 74,970lb (34 tonnes). Their operating results soon led to more being supplied to Tasmania, and the Garratt type was to become the heaviest and most powerful locomotive, particularly on smaller-gauge lines, outside North America.

*0-4-4-0 Saxon State Meyer IV-K type, built from 1892. Several of these narrow-gauge engines are still at work in Germany, having been rejuvenated in the 1960s*

One of the first pair was returned from Tasmania and eventually reached the National Railway Museum at York, where it still is.

### SAXON STATE RAILWAY SERIES IT.V (MEYER TYPE)/1910/GERMANY

The first of the locomotives built to the design of Jean-Jaques Meyer was L'Avenir in 1872, but the first standard-gauge models to be built in any quantity were those by Richard Hartmann of Chemnitz for the Saxon State Railway in 1910. A compound, with high-pressure cylinders at 14²/₅in x 24¾in (360mm x 630mm) and with low-pressure ones at 22½in at 24¾in (570mm x 630mm), these drove 49²/₃in (1260mm) wheels using steam at a pressure of 185psi (1276kPa), which could give them a tractive force of 25,000lb (11,340kg) on an adhesive weight of 132,741lb (60.2 tonnes); this was also the total weight. The boiler contained 1,069 sq.ft. (99.4sq metre) of heating surface with a firegrate area 17.2 sq.ft. (1.6sq metre).

*0-4-4-0 Saxon State Meyer 1T-V Class, 1910*

## 2-4-6

### NEW YORK AND MANHATTAN BEACH RAILROAD GRAVES END (FAIRLIE TYPE)/1881/USA

Built by the Mason Machine Works of Taunton, Massachusetts, these modified Fairlie-type engines were constructed mostly between 1871 and 1889, by which latter date some 140 had been delivered. The first of these locomotives was built with two boilers, but the remainder were all fitted with only a single boiler.

The three of the 2-4-6 type delivered to the New York and Manhattan Beach were fitted with cylinders measuring 14in x 18in (356mm x 457mm) and with 48in (1219mm) diameter driving wheels. The steam pressure was probably 160psi (1104kPa), which, on their total weight of 42,997lb (19.5 tonnes), would have given a tractive force of 10,000lb (4,536kg). Like many of the Mason Fairlies, these were for operation on a 3ft (914mm) gauge line. They were later sold to the Long Island Railroad. The other two types carried the names 'New York' and 'Oriental.'

## 0-4+4+6

### SEMMERING CONTEST BAVARIA/1851/GERMANY

This unusual locomotive was built for the Semmering Trials of 1851 by J. A. Maffei of Munich and was designed by Joseph Hall. It could alternatively be classified as 0-14-0, since all the wheels were driven from the one pair of cylinders.

*A 2-4-4-2 Garratt design of 1919 supplied to the San Paulo Railway of Brazil*

*2-4-4-2 Ceylon Government Railway H.1 Class, 1929*

The two large cylinders - at 20in x 30in (508mm x 762mm), at that date the largest in the world - drove the front axle of the second set of wheels, which were all of 42½in (1080mm) diameter (it was apparently, although of German origin, built to Imperial dimensions). The front four wheels and the rear six, under the tender, were chain-driven from the centre set. The boiler produced steam at 100psi (690kPa) from a heating-surface area of 1,695 sq.ft. (157.6sq metre) with a firegrate area of 14 sq.ft. (1.3sq metre). The tractive force would have been 24,000lb (10,886kg), which assured it victory in the contest, but it was far too complicated for everyday service, and was succeeded by the Engerth type of tank engine. The total weight, including the tender which was also available for adhesion, came to 97,020lb (44 tonnes).

## 2-4-4-2

### SRI LANKA (CEYLON GOVERNMENT RAILWAY) CLASS H.1 (GARRATT TYPE)/1929/SRI LANKA

Among the smallest of the Beyer Garratts was this 2ft 6in (762mm) gauge version supplied for use on the Kelani Valley line from Colombo to Opanake, where it replaced two 0-4-2T tank engines. The four cylinders had dimensions 10in x 16in (254mm x 406mm). With 30in

(762mm) wheels and with superheated steam at 175psi (1207kPa), it gave a tractive force of 14,000lb (6,350kg). The Belpaire-type boiler had a heating-surface area of 574 sq.ft. (53.3sq metre) with a grate area of 14.9 sq.ft. (1.38sq metre). The total weight was 87,318lb (39.6 tonnes).

## 4-4-2+2-4-4

### TASMANIAN GOVERNMENT RAILWAY CLASS M.1 (GARRATT TYPE)/1912/AUSTRALIA

Following the Tasmanians' succesful introduction of the Garratt type onto their 2ft (609mm) gauge line in 1909, a much larger version was in 1912 put into service on their 3ft 6in (1067mm) gauge main line. Built to an axle-load of 2,6901lb (12.2 tonnes), this type was equipped with eight cylinders at 12in x 20in (305mm x 508mm). With 60in (1524mm) wheels and a steam pressure of 160psi (1104kPa), they could produce a tractive force of 26,100lb (11,839kg). The complete weight, including fuel and water, came to 212,341lb (96.3 tonnes).

# SIX-COUPLED ARTICULATED LOCOMOTIVES

## 0-6-4-0

### NEW ZEALAND GOVERNMENT RAILWAY CLASS R (FAIRLIE TYPE)/1878/NEW ZEALAND

These Fairlie-type locomotives were of the single-boiler type with one set of driving wheels. They were built by the Avonside Engine Company of Bristol. Fitted with two cylinders at12⅕in x 16in (310mm x 410mm), they drove 36in (914mm) diameter wheels and, with steam at 130psi (897kPa), gave a tractive force of 7,400lb (3,357kg). The boiler had a heating-surface area of 608 sq.ft.(56.5sq metre) with a grate area of 12 sq.ft. (1.1sq metre). With a tank capacity of 760 gallon (34.5hl) their weight was around 15,677lb (71.1 tonnes) and they could run at up

*0-6-6-0 Russian State Railways Fairlie type, 1884*

to 53mph (85.3kph). Some were fitted with a form of feedwater heating utilizing the hot ashes. The 18 of this class were followed by a further seven of the Class S, which had cylinders of 13in (330mm) diameter. Three were sold to Western Australia but the others remained in service until 1930. Two were still at work in private hands in 1945, and one is preserved today at the Reefton Play Centre.

# 0-6-6-0

## RUSSIAN STATE RAILWAYS FAIRLIE TYPE/1884/RUSSIA

Following the supply of 28 Fairlie-type locomotives from Sigl and British engine builders (including Sharp, Stewart & Co., the Avonside Engine Co., and the Yorkshire Engine Companies), a final 17 of this class were built in Russia at the Kolomna works. Using four cylinders at 15in x 20in (381mm x 508mm) with inside valve gear, they drove 42in (1067mm) diameter wheels and, with a steam pressure of 142psi (979kPa), gave a tractive force of 25,900lb (11,748kg). Total weight was 198,450lb (90 tonnes). The 45 Fairlie locomotives were used on the Suram Pass in Transcaucasia, where the grades were up to 1 in 22.2

(4.5 per cent). Wood-fired at first, they were later converted to oil-firing and lasted in service until 1903, when they were replaced by locomotives of the 0-8-0 type; after this they went to the Rioni-Tvkibuli line. Most were withdrawn in 1926.

## ANGLO-CHILEAN NITRATE CORPORATION (KITSON-MEYER TYPE)/1894/CHILE

When Kitson & Co. of Leeds started building their version of the Meyer type of articulated locomotive they improved the design by arranging the cylinders at the rear of each bogie; this allowed the use of a deeper and larger firebox, and thereby improved the potential performance of this sort of outfit. Their first three locomotives of this sort were supplied to the Chilean Nitrate Corporation (ACN & R) for operation between Tocopilla and Barriles, a route which involved a climb of 3,284ft (1,000m) in 17 miles (27.4km) at an average grade of 1 in 25 (4 per cent). Up such grades the engines were intended to haul 480-long-tons (488 tonnes) on a 3ft 6in (1067mm) gauge line. The four cylinders measured 14in x 18in (357mm x 457mm) and, with driving wheels of diameter 35in (889mm) and steam at 160psi (1104kPa), they gave a tractive force of 27,600lb (12,519kg). The boiler had a heating area of 1,168 sq.ft.

(108.5sq metre) and a grate area of 25.2 sq.ft. (2.34sq metre). With 1,900 gallon (86.4hl) of water and 3 tons (3.05 tonnes) of coal, they weighed 123,921lb (56.2 tonnes). They could haul 2,707-long-tons (2,750 tonnes) on level track and 705-long-tons (716.3 tonnes) up a grade of 1 in 100 (1 per cent) at 10mph (16kph), corresponding to an output of 630dbhp (470kW) or some 840ihp (626kW). These three were followed by one more in 1895, by four in 1909, and in 1912 by two built by the Yorkshire Engine Company.

## BALTIMORE AND OHIO RAILROAD CLASS DD.1 (MALLET TYPE)/1904/USA

This class was the first of the Mallet type to be built in North America (by Alco), and it was the ancestor of the largest locomotives of the steam era. To start with, they all used the compound system in accordance with Mallet's design; this first model was fitted with cylinders of bores 20in (508mm) and 32in (813mm), all with a 32in (813mm) stroke. With 56in (1422mm) diameter wheels and a steam pressure of 235psi (1621kPa), the tractive force was 71,500lb (32,432kg). The boiler, which was large by US standards of the time, had a heating surface of 5,586 sq.ft. (519sq metre) and a grate of area 72.2 sq.ft. (6.7sq metre) for which an early form of mechanically assisted coal-feed was used. In operation it was found to be unstable at any reasonable road speed and was necessarily confined to switching duties. It was thus the only locomotive of this wheel arrangement to be used in the United States.

# 2-6-0 + 0-6-2

## LONDON, MIDLAND AND SCOTTISH RAILWAY (GARRATT TYPE)/1930/GREAT BRITAIN

The LMS order for these 30 engines was the largest to have been received by Beyer, Peacock & Co. at that date. It followed the trials of three commissioned in 1927; apart from four small industrial units and a solitary 2-8-0.0-8-2 built for the LNER, these 33 represented the only Garratts to be used in Britain. With cylinders at 18½in x 26in (470mm x 660mm) they drove 63in (1600mm) diameter wheels and, with steam at 190psi (1310kPa), gave a tractive force of 45,600lb (20,684kg). The boiler supplied superheated steam from an area of 2,637 sq.ft. (245sq metre) with a grate area of 44.5 sq.ft. (4.13sq metre). They were used principally to replace the double-headed 0-6-0 Class 4F taking the London coal traffic between Toton and Brent; in order to obviate the coal-dust nuisance in the cab they had rotating coal bunkers - although these were prone to jam because of coal particles trapped under the bunker. They were not popular with the firemen - they had a firing rate of over 110 pounds per mile (31kg/km) - and were prone to breaking the feeble couplings on the average freight car. They were withdrawn between 1953

*The most numerous class of Mallet locomotives in Europe was this Hungarian 651 type of 1900, of which 95 were built*

*0-6-6-0 Baltimore & Ohio RR DD-1 Class, 1904*

*2-6-6-0 Hungarian Railways 601 Class, 1914*

weight amounted to 93,271lb (42.3 tonnes), of which about half would have been on the driving wheels. They were of the single-boiler type, and were provided with the usual comfortable, fully enclosed cab.

## HUNGARIAN STATE RAILWAY CLASS 601 (MALLET TYPE)/1914/HUNGARY

This class represented the largest and most powerful of the Hungarian Railway's locomotives, and 90 of them were built by 1918. After the first two, the remainder were all fitted with straight-ported cylinders and with large-diameter chimneys. The steam was superheated and the Brotan boilers were provided with twin steam drums. The cylinder diameters were 20½in (521mm) and 33½in (851mm), and all had a 26in (660mm) stroke. With a wheel-diameter

and 1958, being replaced by Class 9F 2-10-0 freight engines of the BR standard type.

# 2-6-6-0

## NATIONAL RAILROAD OF MEXICO Nos.124-5 (MASON-FAIRLIE TYPE)/1889/MEXICO

The largest of the Mason-Fairlie locomotives were these two built for the Mexican Railroad, and they were among the few of the type for use on standard-gauge track. With cylinders at 16in x 24in (406mm x 610mm) and with driving wheels of diameter 54in (1372mm), they would have given a tractive force of 13,500lblb (6,124kg), assuming a steam pressure of 140psi (965kPa). Their total

*2-6-6-2 Chesapeake & Ohio RR Mallet, 1915*

of 56 2/3in (1440mm) and steam at 215psi (1,483kPa), they could give a tractive force of 50,300lb (22,816kg). Their total weight of 241,227lb (109.4 tonnes) made them one of the few 100-ton (101.6-tonne) engines in Europe. Following the break-up of the Hungarian Empire, they were to be found in Yugoslavia, Czechoslovakia and Roumania. They were a mixed-traffic engine and worked heavy wartime trains in the Tatra mountain area.

## INDONESIAN STATE RAILWAYS CLASS CC50/1927/INDONESIA

In the last decade of the 19th Century the Dutch East Indies imported its first Mallet tank engines and then, in 1916, some massive 2-8-8-0 tender Mallets were acquired from Alco in the USA and later from European builders. Then the 2-6-6-0 came into favor. The CC50 class was built by Werkspoor in the Netherlands and SLM in Switzerland. Some locomotives of both wheel arrangements were re-draughted later in life, some with double chimneys and some with large-diameter chimneys.

The CC50 class engines were superheated compounds, with low-pressure cylinders 25½in x 24in (650mm x

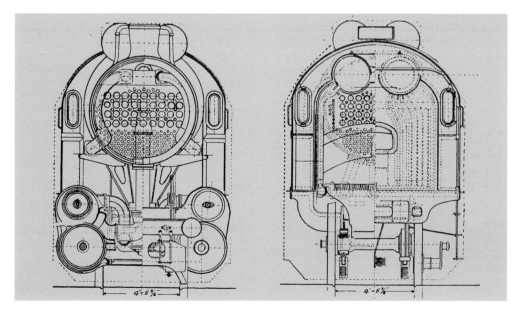

*Cross-section of Hungarian 601 Class compound Mallet*

*2-6-6-0 Indonesian CC50 Class Mallet, 1927*

610mm) and high-pressure 16½in x 24in (420mm x 610mm). Boiler pressure was 200psi (1378) and the driving wheel diameter 43½in (1106mm). Tractive effort was 50,070lb (22,731kg) and the grate area was 36.4sq. ft.(3.4sq metre). Weight in working order was 162,067lb (73.5 tonnes). These 2-6-6-0 engines remained in service longer than the 2-8-8-0 types, although by the 1970s they tended to be employed on minor duties, providing the spectacle of 3-car branch trains behind Mallet tender locomotives. One of this class has been preserved for the railway museum at Ambarawa.

## 2-6-6-2

### CHESAPEAKE AND OHIO RAILROAD (MALLET

### TYPE)/1915/USA

The real breakthrough in the big-engine market started with the production in 1906 of the Class 1800 locomotives of this wheel arrangement for the Great Northern Railroad by the Baldwin Locomotive Company, but an even larger version was this one, built by Alco for the Chesapeake and Ohio in 1915. This was also a compound - with cylinders at 22in (559mm) and 35in (889mm) diameter by 32in (813mm) stroke - and produced a tractive force of 76,100lb (34,519kg) from 56in (1422mm) diameter wheels, using steam at 210psi (1448kPa). The boiler provided 4,900 sq.ft. (455.7sq metre) of heating surface with a 72 sq.ft. (6.7sq metre) firegrate. The total weight was 434,385lb (197 tonnes).

A similar version, with the addition of a superheater, was built by the Baldwin Company in 1949. These produced a tractive force of 78,300lb (35,517kg), and were, incidentally, the last steam locomotives to be provided by a private locomotive builder in the United States.

## 2-6-2 + 2-6-2

### SAN PAULO RAILWAY CLASS R.1 (GARRATT TYPE)/1927/BRAZIL

These six large-wheeled Garratts were the first on the 5ft 3in (1600mm) gauge to achieve a speed of 60mph (96.5kph) and followed the successful operation of some smaller Garratts supplied in 1913 for the railway's metre (3ft 3in) gauge branch. With 20in x 26in (508mm x 660mm) cylinders and 66in (1676mm) wheels, they gave a tractive force of 53,600lb (24,313kg) using steam at 200psi (1380kPa). The boiler had a heating area of 3,622 sq.ft. (336.8sq metre) with a grate area of 49.2 sq.ft. (4.6sq metre). The working weight, including 3,100 gallon (141hl) of water and 5 tons (5.08 tonnes) of coal, amounted to 354,343lb (160.7 tonnes). They were capable of hauling 500-long-ton (508-tonne) trains at an average speed of 40mph (64.4kph). After only four years they were altered to a 4-6-2.2-6-4 arrangement in order to increase the water-capacity to 4,000 gallons (181.8hl). So altered, they became Class R.2. They lasted in service until 1950, when they were replaced by electric locomotives.

## 2-6-6-4

### ANTOFAGASTA AND BOLIVIA RLY HERCULES (KITSON-MEYER TYPE)/1908/BOLIVIA

The only Kitson-Meyer locomotive of this wheel notation was built for operation at high attitudes on the 2ft 6in (762mm) gauge section of this line in Bolivia. The cylinders were at the outer ends of the frame, and the rear set were under the tender, making it a form of steam-tender through

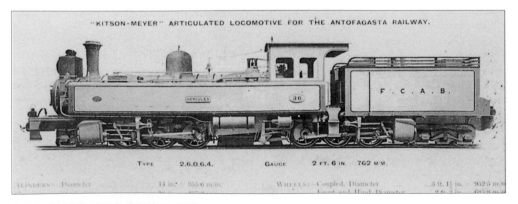

*2-6-2+2-6-2 San Paulo R.1 Class, 1927*

*2-6-6-4 Antofagasta & Bolivia Hercules, 1908*

which the exhaust from these cylinders was passed. With side tanks on the main frame as well, the total water-capacity was 3,730 gallon (169.6hl). The four cylinders were 14in x 18in (356mm x 457mm), and, with a steam pressure of 180psi (1241kPa) and 37½in (953mm) wheels, gave a tractive force of 28,800 pounds (13,064kg) on an adhesive weight of 131,418lb (60.6 tonnes) out of a total weight of 190,512lb (86.4 tonnes). The boiler produced saturated steam from a heating-surface area of 1,156 sq.ft. (107.5sq metre) with a grate area of 25.1 sq.ft.(2.3sq metre). The fittings included a Westinghouse quick-acting brake, bell, siren and whistle, and central buffing gear. The water capacity was designed for a run of 167 minutes when developing a constant output of 450ihp (336kW). It also had a Belpaire type of firebox. It lasted in service until 1929, when the gauge was changed from 2ft 6in (762mm) to metre (3ft 3in).

## NORFOLK AND WESTERN RAILROAD CLASS A (MALLET TYPE)/1935/USA

The four-wheeled trailing truck on these enabled the use of a firebox with a grate area of 122 sq.ft. (11.3sq metre), which provided a free-steaming engine. With driving wheels of diameter 70in (1778mm), these locomotives could run at up to 78mph (125.5kph) and negotiate curves of 260ft (79.2m) radius. The four cylinders, at 24in x 30in (610mm x 762mm), gave a tractive force of 126,000lb (57,154kg)

*2-6-6-4 Norfolk & Western RR A Class, 1935*

with steam at 300psi (2068kPa). The boiler had a heating area of 9,340 sq.ft. (867.7sq metre). The weight of the engine unit was 573,079lb (259.9 tonnes).

This wheel arrangement was not to find great favor, and only 65 locomotives with it were built in the United States.

## 2-6-6-6

### CHESAPEAKE & OHIO RAILROAD H-8 CLASS/1941/USA

By weight, these were the biggest reciprocating steam locomotives ever built, although a muddle with the formal

*A Seaboard 2-6-6-4 Mallet of 1935.*

*2-6-6-6 Chesapeake & Ohio RR H-8 Class, 1941*

weighing of the first units obscured this fact. In working order the engine weighed 778,000lbs or 352 tonnes (724,000lb was the published weight) and the tender weighed 437,600lb (198.5 tonnes). The locomotives were also remarkable for the 6-wheel trailing truck. They were built by Lima in 1941-48, and had a massive tractive effort of 110,200lb (50,030kg) yet with driving wheels of a size that enabled good speeds: 67in (1702mm). By this time the non-compound Mallet was well-established in the USA (compounding saved fuel but simple expansion maximized drawbar pull), and the four cylinders measured 22½in x 33in (571mm x 838mm). Boiler pressure was 260psi (1791kPa) and grate area 135.2sq.ft. (12.56sq metre) and there was a very big superheater of 3,186sq.ft. (296sq

metre). These engines had boilers considerably bigger than those of the Union Pacific 'Big Boys,' although the actual grate area was marginally smaller. The superheater was more than 50 per cent bigger than that of the 'Big Boys.' These locomotives occasionally appeared on passenger trains and could run comfortably up to 70mph (113kph). On trial with heavy coal trains, one achieved a peak drawbar horsepower of 7,498. A train of 14,083 short tons was accelerated from start to 19mph within one mile.

Sixty of these locomotives were built for the C&O, plus another eight for the Virginian Railroad. Several are preserved, including one at the Baltimore & Ohio RR Museum.

# 4-6-0 + 0-6-4

### MOGYANA RAILWAY (GARRATT TYPE)/1912/BRAZIL

Apart from two built in 1924 by Armstrong-Whitworth, these were the only Garratt locomotives with this wheel notation, as well as being the first Garratts in South America. The first two used saturated steam, but the next three, supplied in 1914, were superheated with piston valves. Built for this metre (3ft 3in) gauge line, the cylinders were 13in x 20in (330mm x 508mm), with 45in (1143mm) diameter wheels and, with steam at 180psi (1241kPa),

*4-6-0+0-6-4 Mogyana Railway Garratt, 1912*

*4-6-6-4 Challenger Class, 1936, in builder's photograph*

gave a tractive force of 20,300lb (9,208kg). The 5ft (1524mm) diameter boiler had 1,347 sq.ft. (125.1sq metre) of heating surface with a grate area of 27.3 sq.ft. (2.54sq metre). They weighed 165,816lb (75.2 tonnes). In the second batch the cylinder diameter was increased to 14in (356mm) and the weight went up. All five lasted until about 1950, when they were replaced by diesel locomotives.

## 4-6-6-4

### UNION PACIFIC RAILROAD CLASS 3900, CHALLENGER (MALLET TYPE)/1936/USA

This class, built by Alco in 1936, was the first of the big Mallets to provide the solution to the problem of weight-distribution between the two sets of driving wheels, thereby enabling them to operate at higher speeds in safety and comfort to the crew. With 22in x 32in (559mm x 813mm) cylinders, they could give a tractive force of 97,400lb (44,181kg), using driving wheels of 69in (1753mm)

diameter, and could run at up to 80mph (129kph). Steam at 255psi (1758kPa) was produced from a boiler with 7,030 sq.ft. (653.1sq metre) of heating area with a grate area of 108 sq.ft. (10sq metre). The total weight was 566,023lb (256.7 tonnes).

Although this wheel arrangement was adopted rather late, some 252 locomotives using it were built.

## 4-6-2 + 2-6-4

### ALGERIAN STATE RAILWAYS CLASS 231-132.BT (GARRATT TYPE)/1936/ALGERIA

These racing Garratts, with their 71in (1803mm) driving wheels, were originally ordered by the PLM when they owned and operated the railways in Algeria. Following the trials of a prototoype in 1932, the other 30 were built by Anglo-Franco-Belge between 1936 and 1940. With cylinders at 19⅓in x 26in (490mm x 660mm), they used steam at 285psi (1965kPa) and gave a tractive force of 58,200lb (26,400kg). The boiler diameter was 6ft 11in

(2.10m) and it had 3,770 sq.ft. (350.25sq metre) of heating surface and a firegrate area of 58 sq.ft. (5.4sq metre). With streamlined water tanks containing 6,600 gallon (249.8hl) of water and 10.8-long-tons (11 tonnes) of coal, the working weight was 476,280lb (216 tonnes). Number BT.11 of the first batch was tested on the Nord to Calais, and achieved a maximum speed of 82mph (132kph). It gave an output of 3,000dbhp (2,237kW), equivalent to 4,400ihp (3,281kW). The coal-firing entailed the use of two firemen, and later mechanical stokers were fitted. Cossart valve gear was used, as were transverse double chimneys with smoke-deflector plates. They operated on the 850 miles (1,368km) of the Algerian line with 460-long-ton (467.4-tonne) trains. They were run down during World War 2 and replaced by diesels in 1951.

## 4-6-4 + 4-6-4

### RHODESIAN RAILWAYS CLASS 15A (GARRATT TYPE)/1949/RHODESIA (ZIMBABWE)

The original 4-6-4 Garratts were built by Beyer Peacock & Co. for the Sudan in 1936 and transferred to Rhodesia in 1948. Earlier, Rhodesia had commissioned 34 of their own Class 15 with this wheel arrangement, and they proved so effective that in 1949 they purchased a further 40 of a slightly larger version, as Class 15A. Fitted with 17½in x 26in (445mm x 660mm) cylinders, they drove

*4-6-6-4 Challenger Class. A preserved unit in excursion service*

*Erie RR wide-firebox Camelback 0-8-8-0 Mallet of 1907 for pusher service*

57in (1448mm) diameter wheels and, with a steam pressure of 200psi (1380kPa), gave a tractive force of 42,000lb (19,051kg) at 75 per cent pressure. The boiler was the same for both classes, with 2,816 sq.ft. (261.6sq metre) of heating surface and a grate area of 49.6 sq.ft. (4.6sq metre). With water and coal, the total weight came to 418,288lb (189.7 tonnes). Operating on 3ft 6in (1067mm) gauge track, these performed better than expected, with monthly returns of 6,000 miles (9,654km) later improving this to 10,000 miles (16,090km) per month. They were the first to be fitted with the streamlined water tanks, and two were fitted with thermic syphons. They were due to be withdrawn by 1980, but the fuel crisis, plus the coming of independence, with its associated transitional problems, resulted in a rehabilitation programme starting in 1981, and they remained in service in the 1990s, being given the names of birds and animals.

# EIGHT-COUPLED ARTICULATED LOCOMOTIVES

## 0-8-8-0

### BALTIMORE AND OHIO RAILROAD CLASS 2400 (MALLET TYPE)/1911/USA

This arrangement was not to find great favor in the United States, and only some 150 locomotives using it were built. Among the largest of these were the Class 2400 for the B & O. They were fitted with 26in (660mm) high-pressure cylinders and with 41in (1041mm) low-pressure pistons. With 56in (1422mm) wheels and a stroke of 32in (813mm), which was the usual one adopted for these Mallets, the tractive force amounted to 105,000lb (47,628kg). They weighed 461,947lb (209.5 tonnes). The boiler had a heating area of 5,540 sq.ft. (514.7sq metre) with a 100 sq.ft. (9.3sq metre) firegrate. By that date most articulated locomotives were being fitted with a leading truck, and the absence of one virtually confined the unit to switching or banking duty.

## 2-8-6

### DENVER SOUTH PARK AND PACIFIC RAILROAD ALPINE (MASON-FAIRLIE TYPE)/1880/USA

The largest of the 3ft (914mm) gauge Mason-Fairlies were the four of the 2-8-6 type built in 1880. They had two outside cylinders at 15in x 20in (381mm x 508mm) and,

with 36in (914mm) driving wheels and a steam pressure of 140psi (965kPa), the tractive force would have been 13,400lb (6,078kg); the total weight was 55,345lb (25.1 tonnes). It was equipped with the usual US spark-arresting chimney and had a neat enclosed cab with three windows on each side. Like all the Mason-Fairlies built since 1874 it had Walschaerts valve gear. The others of the four, aside from Alpine, were named Rico, Roaring Fork and Denver and were later to find their way onto the Union Pacific Railroad or the Chicago, Burlington and Quincy Railroad (the Burlington Road). There were two other similar engines built in 1882, but with an 18in (457mm) stroke and weighing some 3,000 pounds (1,361kg) less, for the Denver, Utah and Pacific Railroad.

## 2-8-8-0

### PENNSYLVANIA RAILROAD (MALLET TYPE)/1918/USA

The Pennsylvania had adopted the simple steam cycle for its articulated locomotives in 1911, and these Mallet types were built in their own shops to the same system. The four cylinders, at 30½in x 32in (775mm x 813mm) gave a tractive force of 135,000lb (61,236kg) using steam at 250psi (1724kPa) and 62in (1575mm) driving wheels. The boiler had a heating area of 9,792 sq.ft. (910sq metre) with 112 sq.ft. (10.4sq metre) of firegrate. The total engine weight was 575,064lb (260.8 tonnes). To assist in negotiating sharp curves, the tyres on axles 2, 4, 6 and 7 were eliminated in favor of plain wheels.

This was not a widely adopted wheel arrangement, and only some 200 locomotives using it were built in the United States

## 2-8-0 + 0-8-2

*2-8-0+0-8-2 Burma Railways GA.II Class, 1927*

### BURMA RAILWAYS CLASS GA.II (GARRATT TYPE)/1927/BURMA

Following the supply in 1924 of the first 2-8-0 Garratt to the Burma Railway, the second version was of a compound type - and the only compound Garratt other than the original Tasmanian one to be built. The Burmese version was on metre (3ft 3in) gauge. Cylinders of diameters at 17½in x 26½in (445mm x 673mm) with a 20in (508mm) stroke drove 39in (991mm) wheels an gave a tractive force of 34,500lb (15,649kg) using steam at 200psi (1379kPa). The boiler had 2,054 sq.ft. (190.8sq metre) of heating surface with a grate area of 43.9 sq.ft. (4.1sq metre). With water and coal, the total weight came to 227,556lb (103.2 tonnes), of which 188,968lb (85.7 tonnes) were on the driving wheels. That one compound was followed by three simple versions in 1927 and by a further eight supplied by Krupp of Essen in 1929. A final 10 were supplied under the War Department programme in 1943, and since 1955 they have been replaced by diesel locomotives, although some may still exist.

## 2-8-8-2

### NORFOLK & WESTERN RAILROAD Y6 CLASS/1936/USA

The first five units of this class, a development of the previous Y4 and Y5 types, were built by the Railroad's Roanoke shops in 1936. They had cast-steel bed frames and roller bearings on all axles. Driving wheels were 58in (1473mm), and boiler pressure 300psi (2067kPa). Although they were compounds (unlike the Railroad's contemporaneous 2-6-6-4 Mallets) provision was made for operating as simples when high tractive effort was required; this was not only at starting but whenever the engineer thought a shot of high-pressure steam into the

*The largest Kitson-Meyer was this 2-8-8-2 built for Colombian Railways in 1935*

*A Denver & Rio Grande RR 2-8-8-2 Mallet of 1927*

*A Northern Pacific RR 2-8-8-2 Mallet of 1910*

low-pressure cylinders would be beneficial. The high-pressure cylinders were 25in (635mm) diameter and the low-pressure 39in (991mm), with a common stroke of 32in (813mm). In compound regime tractive effort was 126,838lb and in simple regime 152,206lb. Versions of the design were built up to 1952, making a total of 80 units. They were capable of developing 5,500 drawbar horsepower at 25mph and their index of thermal efficiency, when the coal and the load factor were favourable, was as high as 8per cent. The N&W was the last major railroad to dieselize, and this was largely because its articulated steam locomotives did their job so well. In their later years some of the Y6 class had a second tender attached to them so as to reduce water stops, and hence improve utilization rates.

## 2-8-2 + 2-8-2

### CHILE NITRATE RAILWAY (GARRATT TYPE)/1926/CHILE

The six engines of this type were to haul 400-long-ton (406-tonne) trains on the line from Iquique to Las Carpas, which climbs 3,000ft (914m) in 19 miles (30.6km), with grades up to 1 in 21 (4.76 per cent) (compensated). The engines were fitted with cylinders at 22in x 20in (559mm x 508mm) and with driving wheels of 42in (1067mm).

*2-8-8-2 Norfolk & Western Y6 Class Mallet, 1936*

*A Northern Pacific 2-8-8-4 Mallet of 1928*

*4-8-8-2 Southern Pacific AC4 Class, 1928*

Using steam at 200psi (1378kPa), they gave a tractive force of 69,100lb (31,344kg) at 75 per cent full pressure; with 5,500 gallon (250hl) of water and 1,400 gallon (63.6hl) of oil, they weighed 418,950lb (190 tonnes). The boiler had a heating area of 4,090 sq.ft. (380sq metre) and a grate area of 68.8 sq.ft. (6.4sq metre). Out of 95 Garratts of this wheel notation, these six and four similar models for Central Peru were the only standard-gauge versions. They lasted in service until replaced by diesel locomotives in 1959.

## 2-8-8-4

### DULUTH, MISSABE AND IRON RANGE CLASS M.4 (MALLET TYPE)/1941/USA

Although intended for a maximum service speed of only 35mph (56kph), this class was equipped with one of the highest-output boilers of all the Mallets and could produce 123,100 pounds (55,838kg) of steam per hour, equivalent to 6,800ihp (5,071kW). The steam pressure was 240psi (1655kPa) which, with 26in x 32in (660mm x 813mm) cylinders gave a tractive force of 140,000lb (63,504kg) on an adhesive weight of 509,270lb (254 tonnes). The

*A cab-in-front Mallet of the Southern Pacific's AC series*

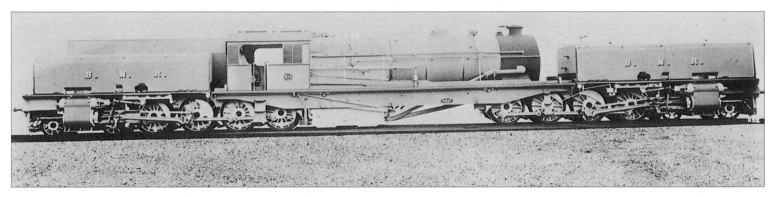

*4-8-0+0-8-4 Bengal Nagpur Railway N Class, 1929*

*4-8-8-4 Union Pacific RR Big Boy, 1941*

*4-8-2+2-8-4 South African Railways GL Class, 1929*

boiler's heating-surface area was 9,528 sq.ft. (885sq metre), with a grate area of 125 sq.ft. (11.6sq metre). Total engine weight was 699,867lb (317.4 tonnes).

# 4-8-8-2

## SOUTHERN PACIFIC RAILROAD CLASS AC4-AC12 (MALLET TYPE)/1940/USA

One hundred and ninety-five, of these, known as the 'Cab Aheads', accounted for the bulk of the 213 locomotives built with this wheel arrangement. Using oil as the fuel - which allowed the cab to be away from the tender - these were the Southern Pacific's answer to the problem of haulage through the mountain tunnels. With four cylinders at 24in x 32in (610mm x 813mm), they produced a tractive force of 124,300lb (56,382 kg) with a weight on the driving

wheels of 552,132lb (250.4 tonnes). The grate area was quoted at 139 sq.ft. (12.9sq metre), with a heating area in the boiler of 8,800 sq.ft. (817.5sq metre).

On the higher stretches of the Southern Pacific's route, snow sheds were provided to save the track from avalanche damage. To avoid the snow sheds being themselves damaged by the exhaust from the locomotive chimneys, they were fitted with smoke splitters to disperse blast effect.

# 4-8-0 + 0-8-4

## BENGAL NAGPUR RAILWAY CLASS N (GARRATT TYPE)/1929/INDIA

The 16 engines of this type were the largest steam locomotives to be used in India and, together with the 10

of the NM class supplied in 1931, were the only Garratts to be built by Beyer Peacock & Co. to this wheel notation. Fitted with cylinders at 20½in x 26in (521mm x 660mm), they used steam at 210psi (1448kPa) and had 56in (1422mm) diameter wheels, giving a tractive force of 61,500lb (27,896kg) at 75 per cent pressure. Their weight of 524,128lb (237.7 tonnes) included 10,000 gallons (454.6hl) of water and 31,311lb (14.2 tonnes) of coal. The boiler had 3,933 sq.ft. (365.4sq metre) of heating surface and a firegrate area of 69.8 sq.ft. (6.5sq metre). Designed to haul 1,600-long-ton (1,625.6-tonne) coal trains from Anara and Tatanagar, they were later transferred to 2,400-long-ton (2,438.4-tonne) ore trains between Dalli Rajhara and Bhilai in 1971. They could take that load up grades of 1 in 100 (1 per cent) and attain 45mph (72.4kph) on level track. Of these 16, 10 had normal piston valves, three used RC poppet valves and 3 used Caprotti valves; the latter six were later converted to piston valves.

# 4-8-8-4

## UNION PACIFIC RAILROAD CLASS 4000 BIG BOY (MALLET TYPE)/1941/USA

Although only 25 were built, these marked the ultimate in steam locomotives in terms of both their weight and their performance. In the preceeding 'Challenger' Class of 4-6-6-4 Mallets the problem of weight-distribution between the two sets of driving wheels had been solved, thus allowing of higher operating speeds. In the 'Big Boys' the cylinder size of 23¾in x 32in (602mm x 813mm) gave a tractive force of 135,400lb (61,417kg) through 68in (1727mm) driving wheels with a steam pressure of 300psi

*4-8-2+2-8-4 East African Railways 59 Class, 1955*

(2068kPa). The grate, of area 150.3 sq.ft. (14sq metre), provided for a boiler with a heating surface of 8,355 sq.ft. (777sq metre) which could give a steam output of 109,100 pounds (49,488kg) per hour, equivalent to 6,100ihp (4,549kW).

Their service included the handling of freight trains of up to 5,400-long-tons (5,486 tonnes) single-handed over grades of 1 in 88 (1.14 per cent) and of passenger trains with which speeds of 88mph (141.6kph) could be achieved. Several have been preserved.

## 4-8-2 + 2-8-4

### SOUTH AFRICAN RAILWAY CLASS GL (GARRATT TYPE)/1929/SOUTH AFRICA

The South African Railway system - including both 3ft 6in (1067mm) and 2ft (610mm) gauges - was the largest owner of Garratt locomotives, with a total of 459. The eight

*4-8-4+4-8-4 NSWGR AD60 Class, 1952*

*2-10-10-2 Virginian RR 800 Class, 1918*

of Class GL on the 3ft 6in (1067mm) gauge were the largest of these until the East African Class 59. With four cylinders at 22in x 26in (559mm x 660mm) and a steam pressure of 200psi (1380kPa), they drove 48in (1219mm) diameter wheels and, at 75 per cent steam pressure, gave a tractive force of 78,600lb (35,653kg). The boiler had a heating surface, including the superheater, of 4,185 sq.ft. (388.8sq metre) with a firegrate area of 74.5 sq.ft. (6.9sq metre). The working weight amounted to 472,972lb (214.5 tonnes). These locomotives were first used to work 1,000-long-ton (1,016-tonne) trains between Durban and Pietermaritzburg with grades of up to 1 in 30 (3.3 per cent), and proved capable of in fact handling 1,200-long-tons (1,219.2 tonnes). Following the electrification of that line they were transferred to working coal trains between Glencoe and Vryheid and finally withdrawn in 1972. Number 2351 is preserved at De Aar.

## EAST AFRICAN RAILWAYS AND HARBOURS CLASS 59 (GARRATT TYPE)/1955/KENYA

With the exception of the one Russian Garratt, these 34 locomotives built by Beyer Peacock & Co. of the 59 class were the largest of that type. At an all-up weight of 563,818lb (255.7 tonnes), they used four cylinders at 20-in x 28in (521mm x 711mm) and, with driving wheels of diameter 54in (1372mm) and a steam pressure of 225psi (1551kPa), gave a tractive force of 73,500 (33,340kg). The boiler, with a diameter of 7ft 6in (2.3m) - over twice that of the rail gauge - had a heating-surface area of 4,306 sq.ft. (400sq metre) and a grate area of 72 sq.ft. (6.7sq metre). They were built on bar frames only 24in (610mm) apart, with all axles fitted with Timken roller bearings. The big ends were also fitted with roller bearings, and the locomotives used the Hadfield power-operated reverser. They were designed to handle 1,200-long-ton (1,219-tonne) trains over grades of 1 in 66 (1.5 per cent), and by 1967 all were fitted with Giesl ejectors, which improved their performance. By 1978, 32 were still

in service, by which time they were the largest steam locomotives in use in the world. They all carried mountain names and No. 5918, Mount Gelai, has been preserved at the Nairobi Museum.

# 4-8-4 + 4-8-4

## NEW SOUTH WALES GOVERNMENT RAILWAYS AD60 CLASS/1952/AUSTRALIA

The NSWGR operated heavy coal and grain trains originating on long lightly-laid branch lines, so the Garratt had an obvious appeal with its low axle-load and high power. However, the NSWGR Garratts arrived only as dieselization was getting into full swing. Nevertheless, they had fairly long and useful lives, the last example being withdrawn as late as 1973, being the last operating steam locomotive on an Australian government railway. At 593,149lb (269

*2-8-8-8-2 Erie RR No 2603 (later 5014), 1914*

# TRIPLEX ARTICULATED LOCOMOTIVES

## 2-8-8-8-2

### ERIE RAILROAD No 2603 (MALLET TYPE)/1914/USA

Built by the Baldwin Locomotive Company to the design of George Henderson, the first of the Triplex types was for operation on the Gulf Summit grade. Working on the compound cycle, it used six cylinders, all at 36in (914mm) x 32in (813mm), which drove 63in (1600mm) wheels. The cylinders driving the centre set of wheels were the high-pressure set, using steam at 210psi (1448kPa) and exhausting into both the other sets; only the front cylinders then exhausted into the chimney, which did not create sufficient draught to enable the boiler to produce the necessary amount of steam. The tractive force produced amounted to 170,000lb (77,112kg) on a total weight of 853,555lb (387.1 tonnes). The initial firegrate, at 90 sq.ft. (8.4sq metre), was inadequate and after one year was rebuilt with one of 122 sq.ft. (11.3sq metre), at which stage the engine was renumbered 5014. Two more, Nos.5015 and 5016, were built.

## 2-8-8-8-4

### VIRGINIAN RAILROAD TRIPLEX No 700 (MALLET TYPE)/1916/USA

Following the apparently unsuccessful trials of the Erie Triplex, it is surprising that the Virginian Railroad also had one built by the Baldwin Locomotive Company in 1916, although this one had a larger boiler. It was fitted with six cylinders at 34in x 32in (864mm x 813mm), with the centre pair working at full pressure and the other four as low-pressure cylinders; again only the front pair exhausted into the air, thus impairing the draught effect on the firebox. The steam pressure was 220psi (1517kPa) and, with 56in (1422mm) driving wheels, the tractive force was estimated as 178,000lb (80,740kg). The boiler's heating area amounted to 9,355 sq.ft. (870sq metre) and the grate area was 108 sq.ft. (10sq metre). The working weight of the complete unit was 842,089lb (381.9 tonnes). It was capable of pulling 7,000 long tons (7,112 tonnes) up a grade of 1 in 62 (1.6 per cent), but the stuffing boxes leaked so much steam that it suffered from lack of vision and was later rebuilt without the powered tender.

tonnes), these were very large Garratts, but they had only a 16 ton axleload. Their four cylinders were 19¼in x 26in (490mm x 660mm), boiler pressure was 200psi (1378kPa), and the coupled wheels were 55in (1400mm). Grate area was 63.5sq.ft. (5.9sq metre). Although this was a class of only 42 units, four have been preserved.

# TEN-COUPLED ARTICULATED LOCOMOTIVES

## 2-10-10-2

### VIRGINIAN RAILROAD CLASS 800 (MALLET TYPE)/1918/USA

There were only 10 of this type, which took the form of a rebuild from an older 2-10-2 type. The need to operate heavy coal trains called for a high tractive force, which these could produce by using their large low-pressure cylinders with steam at full pressure. The normal tractive force of 147,200lb (66,770kg) could be increased to 175,000lbs (79,380kg) by using steam at its pressure of 215psi (1483kPa) on all four cylinders, but their speed was limited to 15mph (24kph).The cylinder diameters were 30in (762mm) and 48in (1219mm) with a 32in (813mm) stroke and driving wheels at 56in (1422mm). The low-pressure cylinders were the largest used in any locomotive and, when fed at full pressure, could produce a piston thrust of 329,427lb (149.4 tonnes). The total engine weight was 683,990lb (310.2 tonnes), of which 617,179lb (279.9 tonnes) were on the driving wheels. They had only a short life, being withdrawn in 1925.

# ELECTRIC
# LOCOMOTIVES

# ELECTRIC LOCOMOTIVES

## 1-A

### THE JUDGE/1883/USA

Thomas Edison's third and last electric locomotive, designed in conjunction with Stephen Field, was named The Judge; it was shown at the Chicago Exhibition of 1883. It ran round a 3ft (914mm) gauge circular track nearly three-quarters of a mile (1.2km) in length. Little coaches loaded with visitors were hauled as a demonstration. Outwardly the locomotive had the large locomotive cab of the day and a massive headlight; actually, it was just a timber-framed four-wheel trolley. Current for the 15kW motor mounted in the cab was picked up from a central third rail at 75V. A shaft from the motor led forward, and after reduction bevel gearing the final drive to the rear axle was by a belt. During the period of the exhibition, 27,000 passengers were carried, but the locomotive subsequently did little more.

### VOLK'S ELECTRIC RAILWAY/1883/GREAT BRITAIN

Magnus Volk was an engineer interested in electricity, with some installations to his credit. There is no doubt that he picked up news of Werner Siemens' pioneer line in Berlin in 1879. He proposed a street tramway in Brighton, the English seaside town where he lived. Brighton Council demurred, but they did give permission for a railway along the beach, where the councillors presumably thought that he could do no great harm. The first quarter-mile (0.4km) section was laid to 2ft (610mm) gauge and was opened on 3 August 1883. A little motor coach was built locally, and this was arranged to pick up 50V dc from one rail and to complete the electric circuit by returning it to the other. The coach had seats for eight passengers, and under one of the seats was a resistance-controlled 1.0kW traction motor. The motor belt drove a countershaft, from which another belt drove an axle of the vehicle. The belts reduced the motor revolution speed in the process. This contraption weighed only 550lb (0.25 tonne) and was capable of 6mph (9.6kph). The following year, 1884, the railway was literally enlarged. The gauge was increased to 2ft 8 1/8in (825mm), a third rail provided current, and more motor coaches were acquired. The railway has been increased

in length to 1½ miles (2.4km) and, much modernized, it is still in operation now.

## 1-B-B-1

### SWISS FEDERAL RAILWAYS CLASS BE 4/6/1922/SWITZERLAND

Switzerland was short of coal for locomotives during World War 1, so plans were laid to electrify the St.Gotthard tunnel route from Lucerne south into Italy. The electrification was partly opened in 1920 (with a scratch collection of traction power, including the first two of the Seebach-Wettingen trial locomotives of 1904-05), and completed throughout in 1922. From Lucerne to Chiasso is 139 miles (224km), and the route includes long gradients of 1 in 38½ and 1 in 37 (26 and 27 per cent), as well as spiral tunnels and other curvature. Electrification was at 15,000V, single-phase, 16⅔ Hz ac, which thereby set the seal on this type of electrification for Swiss main-line railways.

The first locomotives supplied for the St Gotthard route

*Swiss Federal Railways BE4/6 Class, 1922*

*Indonesian State Railways WH Class, 1924*

*Hungarian State Railways V43 Class, 1963.*

*French Railways BB7200 Class, 1977*

were 40 mixed-traffic Class Be 4/6 of the Swiss Federal Railways. They were built by Brown Boveri and SLM Winterthur in 1922-23. Control of the four traction motors was by low-tension-side Tap-changers on the transformer. The traction motors were geared in pairs to two jackshafts, the latter coupled by cranks at their outer ends to two groups of two driving wheels each. Previous coupling rod drives had shown that the motor gearing suffered undue stress, so in these locomotives the gear pinions were mounted flexibly on the rotor shafts. Continuous rating of the class was 1,500kW. The locomotives had long lives, but they were displaced on the St Gotthard route fairly early - one thing held against the class was their low maximum speed of 46½mph (75kph).

## 1-Bo+Bo-1

### INDONESIAN STATE RAILWAYS CLASS WH/1924/INDONESIA

In the 1920s the 3ft 6in-gauge (1067mm gauge) Dutch East Indies State Railways electrified the 48-mile (77km) line between Djakarta and Bogor, partly to take advantage of local hydro-electricity. Among the locomotives acquired at this time were the US-style Class WH units, of which there were six. They were built in the Netherlands under Westinghouse licence and had a continuous output of 590kW. Maximum speed was 50mph (80kph) and weight in working order 160,050lb (72.6 tonnes). The four motors were axle-suspended, and control was rheostatic (electro-pneumatic). Motors could be grouped in series or in parallel and each grouping had one weak-field step. The trucks were coupled, carrying the traction forces. The class worked for more than half a century, hauling, among other services, the best Bogor-Djakarta passenger trains. It was eventually replaced by electric multiple units.

## B-B

### CLASS V43/1963/HUNGARY

Ganz's chief engineer, Kálmán Kandó, served his country well, leaving a legacy of 15,000V, single-phase, 50Hz ac railway running to the west of the country from Budapest. Merely by upping the voltage to 25,000V, Hungarian State Railways could jump to the latest electrification practice. This took place from 1962, when lines from Budapest towards the east were also electrified, to be followed later by those running north and south. Electrification still goes on towards the southwest.

Locomotives for 25,000V, 50Hz were ordered from the 50 Hertz Group, which built the first seven of Class V43 in 1963. The locomotives were erected by Krupp in Germany and by Schneider in France, with electrics from major west European firms. However, one condition of the order was that the technology should be passed to Hungary, and since 1964 Ganz-Mavag, aided by Ganz Electric Works, has built an additional 391 locomotives of Class V43.

The locomotive has two short-wheel-base monomotor trucks, with a single traction motor in each that drives the axles through a cardan shaft and gearing. Direct current for the traction motors is provided by a solid-state rectifier, controlled by transformer high-tension Tap-changers. Locomotives can be worked in multiple, and they are fitted for push-and-pull working. The continuous rating is 2,140kW.

*Italian State Railways E633 Class, 1979*

### INDIAN RAILWAYS CLASS YAM1/1965/INDIA

As with other railway administrations, Indian Railways electrifies its routes where economics permit. Mostly this means the heavily-trafficked 5ft 6in (1676mm) broad-gauge lines. The only metre-gauge (3ft 3⅜in) electrification covered Madras suburban railways, to about 90 miles (150km) south to Villapuram, at 25,000V, single-phase, 50Hz ac.

Mitsubishi built 20 neat little locomotives with monomotor trucks in 1965-66, with some assistance with the electrics from Hitachi and Toshiba. Indian Railways knows these locomotives as Class YAM1. The two dc traction motors are fed from a solid-state rectifier, and controlled by a low-tension tap-changer on the transformer. The motors are fully suspended in the trucks and drive their axles through cardan shafts. The continuous rating is 1,200kW.

### CLASS BB15000/1971/FRANCE

The Class BB15000 of French National Railways is considered to be suitable for general duties, although in practice it is a very competent express locomotive. Normal maximum speed is 100mph (160kph), but should the locomotive run on railways where the the signalling is adequate this speed can be pushed up to 125mph (200kph). The type takes 25,000V, single-phase, 50Hz ac, and possesses two monomotor trucks. The dc pair of traction motors are thyristor-controlled and drive the final gearing to their axles through cardan shafts. A regenerative brake is fitted, and should conditions render this inoperative there is automatic switching to a back-up rheostatic brake. The 65 locomotives of the class were built by Alsthom from 1971, with assistance from Matériel et Traction Electrique (MTE), for use on the Eastern Region.

### FRENCH RAILWAYS CLASS BB7200/1977/FRANCE

In the mid-1990s, 238 units of this class were in service. Built by Alsthom (mechanical parts) and MTE (electrical equipment) they were virtually a 1.5kV dc version of the Class BB15000 ac design. In fact one of this latter design, BB15007, was used as a test-bed for developing the BB-7200 Class control system. There was in addition a third variant of this general design, the BB22200, which was a dual-voltage class. Like the ac units, the BB7200 had two motors, fully suspended, with cardan shaft drive.

*Netherlands Railways Class 1700, 1991*

*City & South London Railway 0-Bo-0, 1890*

There was chopper control and regenerative braking. Weight in working order was 188,530lb (85.5 tonnes) and continuous output was 4,360kW (or 4,000kW if calculated according to the International Railways Union guideline). Maximum speed was set at 100mph (160kph).

## FRENCH RAILWAYS 'SYBIC' BB26000 CLASS/1988 /FRANCE

'Sybic' (synchronous bi-current) technology involves current for the traction motor stators being 3-phase, moderate-frequency, from the inverter. At starting the rotors are fed with direct current that has by-passed the inverter, and acceleration is chopper-controlled. The SNCF acquired its first, experimental, Sybic locomotive in 1981 and was so pleased with it that it placed an order for the Class BB26000 dual-voltage design. GEC-Alsthom completed delivery of this 88-unit order in 1992. More were then ordered, but the second order was slowed down for financing reasons and the final units were to be of a radically different type, rather outclassing the original Sybic. These final 30 units (Class BB36000) were to have asynchronous motors and tri-current capability.

By 1998 there were 225 Sybics in service, and they were giving good results. Capable of operating on both ac and dc systems, they developed a continuous output of 5,600kW and had a maximum speed of 125mph (200kph),

with a weight in working order of 198,450lb (90 tonnes). Both the mechanical and electrical work was done by GEC-Alsthom.

## NETHERLANDS RAILWAYS CLASS 1700/1991/NETHERLANDS

Although NS is primarily a passenger railway and relies heavily on multiple-unit trains, international passenger trains as well as freight require locomotive haulage. At the end of the 1990s NS possessed about 500 locomotives, of which almost all belonged to its freight affiliate, NS Cargo. Class 1700 was remarkable in that all its 81 units were at the disposal of the passenger arm, NS Reizigers. This class, built by Alsthom, was very much a modified SNCF design. Weighing 189,630lb (86 tonnes) and delivering 4,540kW on continuous regime, many of these units were used on the quite heavy doubledeck trains that provided suburban services within the Netherlands. In fact, their delivery coincided with the arrival of these new passenger trains from the German builders Talbot. The units destined for this service had, at one end, an automatic coupler as well as conventional drawgear. Coupled semi-permanently to a new 4-car train set with its own automatic coupler at the rear end, a push-pull unit was created that could operate with other sets as a multiple unit. The maximum speed of such sets was 100mph (160kph).

## B-B-B

### CLASS E633/1979/ITALY

After a prototype electronic chopper-controlled locomotive, No. E444.005, the Italian State Railways decided to have a general-purpose chopper-controlled locomotive class for its 3,000V dc system. Since 1927, Italian general-purpose locomotives have had the Bo-Bo-Bo wheel arrangement, and the new E633 class was the same apart from the use of monomotor trucks which made the wheel arrangement B-B-B. A single motor on each truck drives a hollow axle through gearing, with a set of levers to take up relative spring movements between the hollow axle and the driven wheels. Provision was made to build the E633 class in two versions, one geared for 100mph (160kph) maximum speed and the other for 81mph (130kph) maximum, the latter for mountain and freight work. After the first five of the class had been built in 1979, it was decided to have two classes, the E632 for express work and the E633 for mountain and freight duty.

As is usual with new equipment, various mishaps have occurred. As has been found by other railways, electronics can handle so much current so fast that over-current circuit-breakers at substations may detect an apparent short-circuit and cut off traction current accordingly. For this reason, pending adjustments, only one E633 class was allowed to work at any one time between Venice and Trieste as two of them, if they accelerated at the same time, would have cut off current. Locomotive chopper working frequencies have 'windows' that they are arranged to avoid; in particular, frequencies in the neighbourhood of the usual signalling frequency, in Italy 75Hz, which for safety reasons must not be disturbed by harmonics. Sixty-five E632 and 159 E633 were built, with most Italian manufacturers participating. Pull-and-push trains are widespread in Italy, and the classes can be seen on these in the north. Rheostatic brakes are fitted, with resistances mounted on the roof for cooling.

## 0-Bo-0

### CITY AND SOUTH LONDON RAILWAY LOCOMOTIVES/1890/GREAT BRITAIN

This railway was the first deep-level underground line. Opened in 1890 for 3 miles (4.8km), it originally ran from King William Street in the City under the River Thames and then under south London. Later it was extended considerably at both ends. At first a central third rail provided the locomotives with 500V dc. The locomotives had gearless traction motors, the rotor being built on the axle. Stator poles were mounted vertically on either side

*French Railways BB8100 Class, 1949*

of the rotor; they could move vertically up and down on the locomotive's springs. Resistance control was used, the resistances being cut out as a lever was moved around plain copper contacts set in a vertical plane. An air brake was fitted for both locomotive and train, the locomotive's main compressed-air reservoirs being filled from a stationary plant at terminal stations. A total of 54 of these locomotives was built eventually, most of them coming from Beyer, Peacock & Co. with electrics by Mather and Platt, Manchester. Continuous rating was 100kW, and they ran until 1923. In that year the railway was reconstructed, and today it forms part of the Northern Line of the London Underground.

### GERMAN FEDERAL RAILWAYS CLASS 169/1909/GERMANY

Before World War 1 the Local Railway Company (LAG) based in Munich operated short lines in Bavaria, among them the line from Murnau to the tourist resort of Oberammergau, which was electrified at 5kV 16 2/3Hz with overhead conductors. The first locomotive was LAG 1, a 4-wheeler, acquired in 1905. This was followed in 1909 by Lag 2, which was more advanced and more powerful, but with the same centre-cab layout. LAG 3 of 1912 was virtually a copy of LAG 2. Both of this pair had a continuous output of 306kW, weighed 57,330lb (26 tonnes), and had a maximum speed of 30mph (50kph). They had a wheel arrangement of Bo, being four-wheelers with two motors. In course of time the branchline was converted to the DB's normal power supply at 15kV, and these two locomotives were also converted. After spending some years doing odd jobs at Heidelberg they were sent back to their original branchline, where they continued to haul passenger trains until 1981, by which time No.2 was the DB's oldest locomotive. Their DB numbers were 169 002 and 169 003

# Bo-Bo

### VAL BREMBANA Nos.1-5/1906/ITALY

When the 25½ mile (41km) Val Brembana railway was opened in 1906, it was electrified out of Bergamo at 6,000V, single-phase, 25Hz ac. Locomotives Nos.1-5 of the line were built by Ernesto Breda, Milan, with electrics by Westinghouse, Vado Ligure. The small-size 25Hz traction motors were nose-suspended and controlled by low-tension side tap-changers on the transformer. For the first time in Europe, these tappings were effected by electro-pneumatic means. Continuous rating of the locomotive was only 200kW.

When the railway wanted more locomotives in 1915 it went to Brown Boveri and SLM Winterthur in Switzerland. Numbers 11-14 were B-B and, mechanically, modelled on three-phase locomotives supplied to the Burgdorf-Thun Railway in 1908. The nine locomotives worked the railway until it was closed in 1966.

### CANADIAN NATIONAL RAILWAYS CLASS Z-1-a/1914/CANADA

A major constituent of Canadian National Railways was the Canadian Northern Railway, which had Class Z-1-a built in 1914. The 3¹/₁₀ mile (5km) Mount Royal tunnel was driven to reach a new station at Montreal Central, and steam locomotives were banned from working through it – hence the need for electric locomotives.

The six members of Class Z-1-a were built by the Canadian General Electric Co., and they are continuously rated at 820kW. Control of the four dc traction motors is by resistances and by motor groupings. The overhead contact wire used carries 2,400V dc – in fact, the electrification was one of the high-voltage pioneers.

*South African Railways 1E Class, 1925*

With the advent of the diesel locomotive in the 1950s, electric haulage of main-line trains through the Mount Royal tunnel ceased, and the class was turned over to work suburban routes, where the locomotives remained on duty into the 1990s.

## SOUTH AFRICAN RAILWAYS CLASS 1E/1925/SOUTH AFRICA

By the early 1920s the South African Railways' 3ft 6in (1067mm) route from Durban to the Rand and Johannesburg was being choked with traffic. Electrification at 3,000V dc was proposed, and in the event a first section from Ladysmith to Estcourt went under the wires from 1925. This was part of the heavily graded Pietermaritzburg-Glencoe section, completion of the electrification of which soon followed. Metropolitan-Vickers supplied from Britain the first locomotives of Class 1E; eventually the class totalled 172, the first being delivered in 1925 and the last

in 1945. Some other manufacturers were involved on the mechanical side for later batches.

To cut voltage in the motors, those in each truck were permanently connected in series. Electro-pneumatically operated resistance control was fitted for the motors, which were nose-suspended. The locomotives could be worked in multiple unit in groups of up to three. Regenerative braking was fitted, as it was highly desirable on the gradients leading to the central plateau from the sea. Towards the end of their lives some of the class were converted to shunting duties and redesignated Class ES, while in the 1980s Class 1E proper was reaching the end of its long tour of duty and was disappearing.

## SWISS FEDERAL RAILWAYS CLASS 410 (formerly Re4/4 1)/1946/ SWITZERLAND

This is a relatively small locomotive of 125,685lb (57

tonnes)of modest power, bought as part of an integrated policy; its introduction coincided with the purchase of lightweight all-metal rolling stock for inter-city services inside Switzerland. The class is divided into two sub-classes. Twenty-six of the fifty units were equipped for multiple-unit control and were suitable for push-pull trains and could be recognized by the access door at the front of the cabs. The final 24 units of the class lack these sophistications and are slightly more powerful, 1,760kW against 1,1680kW in continuous regime. Four of them were painted red and cream and reserved for hauling Trans-Europe Express trains, and two of these also carried for cross-frontier working one pantograph that was suitable for use in Austria and Germany. Maximum speed of this useful class is 78mph (125kph). Control is by l.t. tap-changer and the first units had regenerative brakes. They were built by SLM. Withdrawals were scheduled to begin in the late 1990s.

*Netherlands Railways 1100 Class, 1950*

### FRENCH RAILWAYS CLASS BB8100/1949/FRANCE

Although there had been some withdrawals, in the late 1990s there were about one hundred of these locomotives in service and they constituted at that time SNCF's oldest class of electric locomotive. One hundred and seventy-one were built by Alsthom between 1949 and 1955. With a continuous output of 1,900kW and a maximum speed of 65mph (105kph) these were useful locomotives even though they were soon to be overshadowed by more striking designs. They had four Alsthom motors grouped in series and series-parallel, which with four and three field weakening notches provided nine optimal running speeds. Control was rheostatic. The buffers and drawgear were mounted on the trucks and the trucks were coupled together. Weight in working order was 202,850lb (92 tonnes). From about the 1970s these units were used mainly on pick-up and short freight services. Similar locomotives were exported to Morocco and the Netherlands.

### NETHERLANDS RAILWAYS CLASS 1100/1950/THE NETHERLANDS

Sixty of these locomotives were built by Alsthom for the NS, whose main lines are electrified at 1.5kV. They were somewhat similar to the Class BB-8100 of French Railways, but differed by having spring-borne rather than nose-suspended traction motors. This resulted in less stress on the track, so maximum speed could be raised to 84mph (135kph). Weighing in working order 183,015lb (83 tonnes), these units developed 1900kW in continuous regime and 2,030kW in hourly regime. Control was rheostatic and they had four Alsthom traction motors.

As the units approached twenty years of age they were taken in hand for refurbishment by the NS Tilburg works. Outwardly the most noticeable change was the provision of noses of a vaguely air-cutting profile; aesthetically these were somewhat absurd, but NS engineers said their purpose was to offer better crew protection. Perhaps a more significant change was the provision of roller bearings for all axleboxes.

### FRENCH RAILWAYS CLASS BB12000/1954/FRANCE

This was a historic class of locomotive, for it powered the first large-scale electrification at industrial frequency, the 25kV ac 50Hz electrification between Valenciennes and Thionville in Eastern France. Its success ensured the rapid triumph of the 25kV system in France and elsewhere. One hundred and forty-eight of these mixed-traffic rectifier units were built, by Alsthom and MTE. They had central cabs surmounted by pantographs (two, as was usual, in case of failure). The bonnets housed control equipment and their side panels could not be opened when a pantograph was raised. The transformer was beneath the cab and there were four 675V traction motors, permanently connected in parallel, which were supplied current through rectifiers that were silicon or ignitron. Continuous output was 2,650kW for a weight in working order of 185,220lb (84 tonnes), giving a power/weight ratio somewhat superior to the existing dc locomotives. Control was by h.t. tap-changer.

*French Railways BB12000 Class, 1954*

*German Federal Railways 110 Class, 1956*

*German Federal Railways 141 Class, 1956*

## GERMAN FEDERAL RAILWAY CLASS 141/1956/GERMANY

German electric locomotives of a given vintage tended to look alike, even though they might be substantially different. Class 141 did not look all that different from Class 110 of the same late 1950s period, but in fact it was a lightweight design. It weighed only 147,730lb (67 tonnes), compared to the 189,630lb (86 tonnes) of the Class 110, giving an axle-load of 37,040lb (16.8 tonnes) as against the 45,025lb (20.5 tonnes) of the latter. But power output was correspondingly lower, at continuous regime 2,310kW rather than 3,620kW. Maximum speed was 75mph (120kph). With its low weight it was a very useful locomotive and almost four hundred units were still in service in the late 1990s.

Construction was by Henschel, with electrics by BBC (Brown Boveri of Mannheim).

## GERMAN FEDERAL RAILWAYS CLASS 110/1956/GERMANY

As was characteristic of the German approach, this class was not put into production until five prototype locomotives had run for almost six years on trial. In the end, 362 were built, and they were Germany's first modern design of the post-war period. Three works (Henschel, Krupp, Krauss-Maffei) shared in the construction, assisted by three electrical firms (AEG, BBC, SSW). Continuous output is 3,620kW for a weight in working order of 189,630lb (86 tonnes). The four motors were fully-suspended, and control

was by h.t. tap-changers. After 164 units were produced the external design was changed to produce a slightly more streamlined look. These improved units formed sub-class 110.5 while the early units became 111.1. Maximum speed is 93mph (150kph) but some units were turned out suitable for 100mph (160kph). The latter were allocated to Trans Europ Express services and were joined by others to form a new Class 112.

## GERMAN FEDERAL RAILWAYS CLASS 140/1957/GERMANY

The success of the DB Class 110 led directly to Class 140, which was virtually a Class 110 without the rheostatic brakes of the 110 and with a lower gear ratio so as to

*German Federal Railways 140 Class, 1957*

*Luxembourg Railways 3600 Class, 1958*

make it more suitable for freight work. Krauss-Maffei again played an important part in its development and, along with Krupp and Henschel, was responsible for the mechanical side of construction. By West European standards, this was a very large class indeed, with 848 units turned out between 1957 and 1973. Most of these were still running at the end of the century. There was also a variant (Class 139) which retained rheostatic brakes and was intended for hilly routes. Continuous output was 3,620kW, weight 189,630lb (86 tonnes), and maximum speed 68mph (110kph). Control was by h.t. tap-changer.

### LUXEMBOURG RAILWAYS 3600 CLASS/1958/LUXEMBOURG

Being a small country between Belgium and France, Luxembourg's railway policy has to mesh with French and Belgian railways, and this is not always easy. In the 1950s, Belgian Railways was electrifying at 3,000V dc while on the opposite frontier the French were approaching with their new 25kV ac electrification. The result, in due course, was that passenger trains had to change locomotives in Luxembourg's main station. To work trains on the 25kV

line the Luxembourg Railways acquired 20 locomotives similar to the 12000 Class used by French Railways. Like the 12000 Class, they were built by Alsthom and MTE. They produced 2,650kV in continuous regime, and weighed 185,220lb (84 tonnes). Maximum speed was 75mph (120kph). Control was by h.t. tap-changer and the four motors were fully suspended, with cardan drive.

### POLISH STATE RAILWAYS CLASS EU07/1961/POLAND

The Polish State Railways has been enthusiastically electrifying its railway system for over three decades, using 3,000V dc. At first aid was sought from Great Britain, and 20 Class EU06 locomotives for general duties were built by Vulcan Foundry with electrics by English Electric-AEI; these were delivered during 1961-62. From 1963 a total of 243 locomotives was built in Poland, as Class EU07, by Pafawag, Wroclaw, with electrics by Dolmel.

The body of Class EU06 is decidedly reminiscent of locomotives being built during the same years for British Railways, although for Class EU07 this resemblance is

rather less noticeable. Control is by resistances and motor groupings, although to hold the maximum traction motor voltage to 1,500V the two motors in each truck are permanently connected in series. Continuous rating is 2,000kW.

### CHILEAN STATE RAILWAYS CLASS E30/1961/CHILE

Twenty-two of these locomotives, plus 34 of a bigger but generally similar C-C design, were supplied by Italian manufacturers in the 1960s for the electrified route southward from Santiago. Built by Breda, the E30 Class had a continuous output of 1,790kW and a service weight of 216,090lb (98 tonnes). The four motors were nose-hung and the maximum speed was 80mph (130kph). Automatic wheel-slip protection, quite advanced for the time, involved the partial field-shunting of a slipping axle. Multiple-unit working was possible, and the units had nose doors to enable athletic locomotive men to pass from one unit to the next. The front profiles were US-style, and provided space in the nose for compressors and batteries.

*Polish State Railways EU06 Class, 1961*

## BULGARIAN STATE RAILWAYS CLASS 41/1962/BULGARIA

Bulgarian State Railways' electrification is at 25,000V, single-phase, 50Hz ac. The first route electrified, from Sofia to Plovdiv, was opened in 1962. Bulgarian Class 41 was built to a total of 41 by Skoda in Czechoslovakia from 1962. The class was based in general on Czech Class S479, but the Class 41 locomotives have motors fully suspended within the truck frame which drive their respective axles through Skoda flexible drives. The dc traction motors are fed from a solid-state rectifier, and controlled by high-tension side transformer Tap-changers. The continuous rating is 2,800kW and rheostatic braking is fitted.

## AUSTRIAN FEDERAL RAILWAYS CLASS 1042/1963/AUSTRIA

This class divides into two sub-classes, Class 1042.500 of 1967 being a development of the 1042 type introduced in 1963. The earlier sub-class had a continuous output of 3,336kW and a top speed of 80mph (130kph) whereas the 1042.500 units offered 3,808kW and 93mph (150kph). Sixty units of the older type and 197 of the later were built, the mechanical side being entrusted to the

*Chilean State Railways E30 Class, 1961*

Austrian Simmering-Graz-Pauker company and the electrical to Elin-Union and the Austrian affiliates of Brown Boveri and Siemens. The design was intended to tackle a diversity of roles and thereby avoid the need of maintaining a diverse range of types. Control was by h.t. tap-changer; the class was the last of the Austrian pre-thyristor types and was built up to 1977. The units weighed 185,220lb (84 tonnes), and the ac motors were fully suspended, so speeds up to 93mph (150kph) were allowed.

## FRENCH RAILWAYS CLASS
## BB25150/1963/FRANCE

Seventy units of this class were built by MTE, and they can be divided into three sub-classes that have external difference but which are in their main elements identical. In the 1960s, as the ac electrifications extended, the number of points where the ac and dc electrifications met tended to grow, so there was a need for dual-current locomotives, if only to avoid time-wasting locomotive changing. This class was allocated above all to the region around the Alps, where there were several routes demanding dual-voltage capacity. The locomotives had a

*Bulgarian State Railways E41 Class, 1962*

*Austrian Federal Railways 1042 Class, 1963*

*French Railways BB25150 Class, 1963*

continuous output of 4,130kV on a weight of 187,425lb (85 tonnes), and drive to the four motors was by cardan shaft. Maximum speed was 81mph (130kph).

## BERNE-LOETSCHBERG-SIMPLON RAILWAY CLASS Re4/4/1964/SWITZERLAND

With its 35 units, this class in the mid-1990s accounted for two thirds of the BLS locomotive stock, and therefore handled much of the international traffic taken by this private railway by the Loetschberg Tunnel route. When introduced in 1964 the design was somewhat un-Swiss, being a rectifier-equipped locomotive with dc motors. It was successful enough to warrant a final batch of six, ordered 16 years after the first batch of 29 entered service. To improve adhesion, there was automatic compensation of weight transfer; a design requirement was that the units should be able to haul 630-tonne trains up 1 in 37 (2.7 per cent) grades at 49mph (80kph). The type is suited to passenger work, having the equipment for multiple-unit and push-pull operation, and the motors are fully suspended, making the locomotive easier on the track at the higher speeds. Maximum permitted speed is 87mph (140kph) and the one-hourly output is 4,945kW. The locomotives weigh 176,400lb (80 tonnes) in working order, and are controlled by h.t. tap-changers.

## SWISS FEDERAL RAILWAYS CLASS 420 (FORMERLY RE4/4 11)/1964/SWITZERLAND

In the mid-1990s the SBB had 273 units of this class at work, and the very similar Class 430 numbered 17 on the SBB and a few more on private Swiss railways. The class is therefore Switzerland's most numerous series. This is understandable, because the type was designed as a very wide-ranging mixed-traffic class. It was suited to fast trains on level routes, and in the mountainous areas it is used on both freight and passenger services, operating in pairs under multiple-unit control. After six pre-production units entered traffic in 1964, there was an interval while they were assessed and then series production started in 1967.

They were built by the Swiss SLM company at its Winterthur works, with electrical equipment supplied by the usual three local companies, Oerlikon, Brown Boveri and S,cheron. One-hour output was 4,650kW for a weight in working order of 176,400lb (80 tonnes). Maximum speed was 87mph (140kph); the traction motors were fully

*Swiss Federal Railways 420 Class, 1964*

*British Rail 86 Class, 1965, as built.*

*Belgian National Railways 16 Class, 1966*

*Czechoslovak State Railways S489, 1966*

suspended. Control was by h.t. tap-changer and there was regenerative braking. Five units were fitted with a pantograph having the more precise clearances of German and Austrian railways.

## BRITISH RAILWAYS CLASS 86/1965/BRITAIN

British Railways electrified its routes from Liverpool and Manchester to London from the later 1950s, at 25,000V, single-phase, 50Hz ac. Five types of Bo-Bo locomotive were provided, among other things to try out different forms of mechanical transmission to the axles together with varied spring and suspension systems. What was, in the clear light of hindsight, a fatal decision was then made to order 100 Class 86 locomotives with nose-suspended traction motors, as the direct capital costs were the lowest. Nose-suspended motors are supported on the other side by a bearing on the axle which increases the unsprung weight - a pity, because a higher unsprung weight has a destructive effect on the track, especially at high speeds. Delivery of Class 86 started in 1965; they were built by Doncaster works and Vulcan Foundry, with electrics by English Electric and AEI. Passengers soon began complaining of a rough ride, for track engineers were not able to keep up with the unfortunate effects of the locomotives with their 100mph (160kph) maximum speed. Most of Class 86 have been modified (at some expense) with improved springs and suspension, together with resilient wheels incorporating rubber components. This has ameliorated track maintenance costs. The maximum speed of a few locomotives was pushed up to 110mph (177kph) in 1985.

Class 86 is controlled by transformer tappings on the high-tension side, and a solid-state rectifier supplies dc to the traction motors. A rheostatic brake is fitted, and, although not equipped for this originally, the class can work freight trains in multiple-unit pairs. The continuous rating of each locomotive is 2,685kW.

## BELGIAN NATIONAL RAILWAYS CLASS 16/1966/BELGIUM

Belgian National Railways is electrified at 3,000V dc, but each of three neighbouring countries have different electrification systems. Belgium is a small country in area, and so, in order to allow the economy of through and lengthy locomotive workings, Belgian National Class 16 is equipped to take four different supplies. As well as Belgium's 3,000V, the class can take the 1,500V dc of Netherlands Railways, the 15,000V, single-phase, 16 2/3Hz ac of the German Federal Railway, and the 25,000V, single-phase, 50Hz ac of French National Railways. In consequence the locomotive class is almost as familiar in Amsterdam, Cologne or Paris as it is in Brussels.

Direct current traction motors controlled by resistances and by motor grouping are used. For the two countries using ac supplies, the resistance bank is fed from a transformer and a solid-state rectifier. The locomotives have three pantographs, one for the two dcs and one each for the two acs. As an exception, the first locomotive of the class, 1601, has four pantographs, the extra one being for one of the dc supplies.

There are eight locomotives in Class 16. They were built by La Brugeoise et Nivelles in 1966, with electrics by Siemens and Ateliers de Constructions Electriques de Charleroi.

## CZECHOSLOVAK STATE RAILWAYS CLASS S489/1966/CZECHOSLOVAKIA

Perhaps the feature that most catches the eye when viewing Czechoslovakia State Railways' Class S489 is the glass-fibre-laminate body panels and mouldings. Otherwise the locomotives are straight-forward 25,000V, single-phase, 50Hz ac machines intended for general traffic duties. The dc traction motors are fed from a solid-state rectifier and controlled by high-tension side transformer tap-changers. Some of the class were built with rheostatic braking. The continuous rating is 3,080kW and the maximum speed is 75mph (120kph).

Very much the same locomotive was supplied to the Bulgarian State Railways - Class 42, built by Skoda during 1965-70. These have a maximum speed of only 68mph (110kph) but unlike the Class S489 they are equipped for working as multiple units.

More distantly, the Czech Class ES499 too was derived from Class S489, but in this case a reversion was made to a sheet-metal body.

*An early Bo-Bo design. London's Metropolitan Railway introduced 1200hp units in 1904 and 1908 to haul outer-suburban trains. They bore names; this preserved example is Sarah Siddons*

*Berne-Loetschberg-Simplon Railway Re/4/4 Class, 1964*

## ITALIAN STATE RAILWAYS CLASS E444/1967/ITALY

During the 1960s the Italian State Railways was trying out high speeds and planning new railways for high-speed trains. Savigliano at Turin was given an order for four prototype high-speed locomotives, the E444 class, delivered during 1967-68. After trials, another 113 E444-class locomotives were delivered by various builders during 1970-74. (With only one major home customer, the Italian locomotive industry shares out the work on offer, so that a smaller firm may build three or four locomotives or supply bits and pieces only.) The new E444s pushed conventional locomotive technology to the limit. Traction motors are fully sprung in the trucks, and are geared to a hollow axle. The hollow axle turns the wheels through a system of levers

*Pakistan Railways BCU-30 Class, 1964*

that are responsive also to locomotive-spring movements. The locomotive body sits on secondary helical springs that are supported by brackets on each side of a truck. The brackets in turn are hung from laterally swinging links, downwards from a beam that lies across the truck frame. Horizontal movements of the beam in any direction are controlled by hydraulic dampers. Traction and braking forces, from and to the trucks, are taken by tensioned cables, anchored on the frame at one end and attached just above rail level at the truck centres.

Control is by a resistance bank, and as the locomotive works at very near the adhesion limit there are no fewer than 92 control steps. The first few of these steps lie up the resistance-bank range and before the locomotive starts are run through backwards until the motors are taking full current. All this is to avoid wheel-spin - moreover, automatic wheel-spin detection and control is provided, as well as slide detection for the rheostatic brake fitted. Continuous rating of the E444 class is 3,750kW, while a trial chopper locomotive, No. E444.005 delivered in 1975, was rated at 4,500kW. Maximum speed in service is 112mph (180kph). To allow a maximum speed of 125mph (200kph) a batch of 50 was fitted with extra truck hydraulic dampers during 1986, becoming Class E447.

*Brush Traction 92 Class, 1993. Built for the Channel Tunnel, these were of the Co-Co arrangement.*

## PAKISTAN RAILWAYS CLASS BCU30/1968/PAKISTAN

The Pakistan Railways route from Lahore to Khaneval was electrified completely from 1970, using 25,000V, single-phase, 50Hz ac. Locomotives came from Britain, 29 of Class BCU-30 being delivered during 1968-69. Mechanical parts were built by Metropolitan-Vickers and Vulcan Foundry, while the electrics were supplied by English Electric-AEI.

Control of the nose-suspended dc traction motors is by thyristor; not only was the type the first thyristor locomotive built in Britain, it was also the first thyristor locomotive class to be exported. Multiple-unit working is possible and, although no rheostatic brake is fitted, one can be easily added if needed. Automatic protection against wheel-slip is provided, and the intake air for the motors and for cooling is specially filtered against wind-blown sand. Continuous rating is 2,360kW.

## SOUTH AFRICAN RAILWAYS CLASS 6E/1969/SOUTH AFRICA

The 3ft 6in (1067mm) gauge South African Railways has been a considerable user of the Bo-Bo wheel arrangement for many years. To match an expansion in the mileage of the 3,000V dc electrified route, it started to take delivery of Class 6E in 1969. There are 80 locomotives designated Class 6E, while later members of the class, with prominent traction rods between the trucks and the locomotive frames, are known as Class 6E1. A total of 939 were built by Union Carriage and Truck Co., with electrics from the British firm GEC Traction or its South African subsidiaries. The class became the largest electric class in the world, outside the USSR. They are resistance-controlled with nose-suspended traction motors, equipped for regenerative braking, and have electronic wheel-slip control circuitry. The continuous rating is 2,252kW, and the locomotives can work in multiple to the number needed for heavy trains.

## BRITISH RAILWAYS CLASS 87/1973/BRITAIN

This class of 36 locomotives was ordered when the extension of Britain's West Coast electrification to Glasgow was being completed. The newly-electrified line had severe gradients, so apart from the numerical increase of locomotives a qualitative advance was also required; qualitative not only in terms of power output, but also in other design parameters. The preceding design, Class 86, had done good work but only at a certain cost in track repair. The locomotives were designed by British Railways staff and built at the BR works at Crewe, GEC Traction designing and supplying the electrical gear.

Continuous rating was 3,730kW, or about 5,000hp, and the units weighed 183,015lb (83 tonnes). Maximum speed was 110mph (177kph). Control was by h.t. tap-

*British Railways 87 Class, 1973*

*Finnish State Railways Sr1 Class, 1973*

*Italian State Railways E645 Class, 1959. This is of the Bo-Bo-Bo wheel arrangement, long favored in Italy.*

changer but the last unit to be built was fitted experimentally with thyristor control instead. They can be controlled from a driving-van trailer and therefore can be used in push-pull service like the London-Birmingham run. On the whole they have performed well, and they became the basis for the following Class 90 design.

## FINNISH STATE RAILWAYS CLASS Sr1/1973/FINLAND

Electrification of the 5ft (1524mm) gauge Finnish State Railways at 25,000V, single-phase, 50Hz ac dates from 1973. Design of this locomotive type was undertaken by the Soviet All-Union Electric Locomotive Research and Design Institute. The electrics were planned and supplied by the Finnish firm Oy Strömberg Ab. The locomotives themselves were built by the Novocherkask Electric Locomotive Works. The first of Class Sr1 was delivered in 1973, and the number in service now exceeds 100.

The four dc traction motors are controlled by thyristors and equipped for rheostatic braking. The motors are fully suspended within the truck frame, and a Skoda flexible drive connects them to their respective axles. Continuous rating of Class Sr1 is 3,100kW. One locomotive has run up to 102mph (164kph), but in service their maximum speed is restricted to 87mph (140kph).

## GERMAN FEDERAL RAILWAYS CLASS 111/1974/GERMANY

Although the Class 110 Bo-Bo locomotive had been a success, by the early 1970s technology had left it behind, amd a new design seemed desirable for future construction. This time, Siemens had a large part in the electrical design and supply, with Krauss-Maffei responsible for the mechanical parts. The truck was of a new design and the cab was designed with greater convenience for the crew. But the most significant advances were in the control devices. Running speed and the strength of brake applications was automated, with the rheostatic brake being blended in with the friction brake. Control, as with the Class 110, was by h.t. tap-changer. Continuous output remained the same at 3,620kW but the weight of 183,015lb (83 tonnes) was slightly less than the Class 110 although maximum speed at 100mph (160kph) was slightly higher, thanks to the improved trucks and springing. No fewer than 210 units were ordered, and they are still playing an important part in DB operations.

*German Federal Railways 111 Class, 1974*

## AUSTRIAN FEDERAL RAILWAYS CLASS 1044/1974/AUSTRIA

The ancestry of these Austrian locomotives stretches back to the pioneer thyristor type, Swedish State Railways' Class Rc. Austrian Federal Railway Class 1043 was built in Sweden in 1967, and these 10 locomotives served as prototypes for Class 1044, built by Simmering-Graz-Pauker AG, with electrics variously by Siemens, Elin-Union and Austrian Brown Boveri. There are 98 of Class 1044, the first built in 1974, and the class became the major fast passenger locomotive in Austria. Locomotives are fitted with traction motors that take dc, suitably modified in design to take care of remaining ripple in the rectified current fed to them. This capability for using the simpler dc motor, and getting away from the imperfections of the commutator ac low-frequency motor, is one of the attractions of the thyristor locomotive for those railways electrified at 15,000V, single-phase $16\frac{2}{3}$Hz.

Like many other electric and diesel locomotives, Class 1044 is fitted with a rheostatic brake, the current generated by the traction motors in their braking mode being used to heat up roof-mounted, air-cooled resistances.

## CZECHOSLOVAKIAN STATE RAILWAYS CLASS ES499/1974/CZECHOSLOVAKIA

Czechoslovakian State Railways' electrification started as 1,500V dc; this was converted later to 3,000V. About 1,100 route miles (1,770km) of 3,000V dc electrification is in use, but fresh electrifications since the 1960s have usually been at 25,000V, single-phase, 50Hz ac. There has been a need for dual-voltage locomotives, and this function is covered by the ES499 class.

The ES499 class is dc-motored, the motors being fully suspended within the truck frames and driving their

respective axles through Skoda flexible drives. The locomotives are resistance-controlled, the dc being supplied by a transformer and solid-state rectifier when working under ac wires. In addition to the fully suspended traction motors, special attention has been given to the spring and suspension system to suit the class for high speed. Continuous rating is 4,000kW.

Skoda built 20 of the ES499.0 class from 1974. Another 25 were built from 1980 with the resistance control replaced by choppers; these locomotives are known as the ES499.1 class. From 1978, Skoda built 27 resistance-

controlled Class ES499.2s for 3,000V dc supply only. All of these various versions are equipped for rheostatic braking. The ES499 class was the basis for the Bo-Bo + Bo-Bo Soviet Railways Class ChS200, which is capable of running at 125mph (200kph).

## GERMAN FEDERAL RAILWAYS CLASS 120/1979/WEST GERMANY

The German Federal Railway took delivery of five prototype current-inverter locomotives with three-phase traction

*Austrian Federal Railways 1044 Class, 1974*

*Austrian Federal Railways 1044 Class, 1974*

*Czechoslovak State Railways ES499 Class, 1974*

The locomotives are geared for 15,000V, single-phase, $16\frac{2}{3}$Hz ac. This passes through a transformer and a first current inverter for rectification and voltage-stabilization only. The resulting dc is presented to a second current inverter, which has a controlled, variable frequency three-phase output for the traction motors. The traction motors are fully sprung with a cardan shaft drive to the wheels. In the regenerative-braking mode the traction motors generate current which is rectified to dc in the second current inverter. The first current inverter converts this dc into single-phase $16\frac{2}{3}$Hz current to be passed back into the overhead contact wire. It was planned originally that, should the latter be unable to accept the current, there should be a reserve rheostatic brake to dispose of it. Exhaustive statistical analysis of the chances of another train being in the vicinity to use the generated current, and of the chances of an overhead wire breaking, showed that this rheostatic brake was unnecessary, and it was discarded. If needed, there is automatic switching to the air brake.

Class 120 was the world's most powerful four-axle locomotive, with a continuous rating of 5,600kW. Unfortunately the initial cost was on the high side, but orders were eventually placed and over 60 were in service by 1997.

## AMTRAK CLASS AEM7/1979/USA

Amtrak had been disappointed by an American-built high speed locomotive (Class AEM6), and so during 1976-77 leased two trial locomotives from Europe. One of these was a French National Railways Class CC21000. After billiard-table European conditions, the French locomotive's springs and suspension did not take kindly to American track.

The other was the Swedish State Railways thyristor Class Rc4, which had by that time been sold abroad to one or two other countries. The Swedish Class Rc4 impressed Americans, and eventually a fleet of 67 went into Amtrak service (as Class AEM7) from 1979. General Motors Electro Motive Division was the builder, under licence from Allmänna Svenska Aktiebogalat (Asea), and Asea also supplied most of the electrics.

Until the present day, Class AEM7 has been running under a line supply of 11,000V, single-phase, 25Hz ac, although it is equipped to run also under 25,000V, 60Hz and, as a temporary railway expedient, under 12,500V, 60Hz. The transformer passes current to the thyristor bridge circuitry, which controls and rectifies it for the four dc traction motors. The current reaching the stator windings is controlled separately from that for the rotor windings. A rheostatic brake is fitted, arranged to blend in automatically with the air brake. A cardan shaft passes through the hollow rotor shaft of each traction motor, one end being fastened to the rotor and the other to the pinion that drives the axle gearwheel. Maximum speed is 120mph (193kph), and the continuous rating of the locomotive is 4,250kW.

motors from 1979. Thyssen-Henschel was the builder, with electrics and electronics from Brown Boveri, Mannheim. The Class 120 locomotives are equally capable on fast passenger trains and on heavy freights, thanks to the exploitation of the characteristics of the three-phase traction motor.

*German Federal Railways 120 Class, 1979*

*Amtrak AEM7 Class locomotives, 1979*

## BELGIAN NATIONAL RAILWAYS CLASS 27/1982/BELGIUM

One of the problems of standardization is that it is difficult to determine just when a standard should be abandoned to allow striking out in a fresh direction. Belgian National Railways maintained multiple-unit working standards (and automatic-coupler standards where applicable) for over 45 years after the first 3,000V dc electrification in 1935. Finally these standards were discarded in the early 1980s when the Belgians were designing fresh generations of motive power. The Class 27 chopper locomotive was designed for a speed of up to 100mph (160kph), as the main lines were being made suitable for this. The continuous rating is 4,150kW. Constructions Ferroviaires et Metalliques built 60 of Class 27 in the years 1982-83, with electrics by Ateliers de Constructions de Charleroi.

Separate chopper circuits are provided for the traction motors in series pairs, one for each truck. The main chopper functions at a constant frequency of 200Hz in conjunction with what is called a vernier thyristor in series between it and the traction motors. When starting, voltage must be reduced, which is done by the controlled vernier thyristor nipping off part of the main chopper pulse. Harmonics are greatly reduced by the circuitry, and the system is cheaper than increasing the size and complexity of the filter circuits before the choppers.

Should there be a fault in the circuitry for one truck, it is possible while stationary to switch out that truck and to proceed, retaining the usual maximum speed although at half power. Alternatively, the chopper circuitry for one truck can be switched out while the four traction motors are put into series circuit; in this instance power is maintained

and the speed reduced. For the first time in Belgium a rheostatic brake was fitted, and the locomotives can work for a short time under the 1,500V dc of Netherlands Railways at frontier stations.

---

## GERMAN STATE RAILWAY (DR) CLASS 143/1984/GERMAN DEMOCRATIC REPUBLIC

During its half-century of independent existence, the railway administration of East Germany developed its own locomotive designs: steam, diesel, and electric. It inherited production facilities and designers from the old Germany, just as did the Federal Republic of Germany, so the locomotives of both regimes were often variants of a common theme. The Class 143 was the most numerous of the East German electric locomotives, totalling more

*German Federal Railways 120 Class prototype, 1979*

*German State Railway (DR) 143 Class, 1984*

than 600 units. It was a straightforward design weighing 183,015lb (83 tonnes) and delivering 3,720kW on continuous regime. Its maximum speed was 75mph (120kph). After the re-uniting of Germany, this class was to be seen outside its original eastern territory.

### DANISH STATE RAILWAY CLASS EA/1984/DENMARK

The Danish State Railways has been electrifying its main lines at 25,000V, single-phase, 50Hz ac. The first section ran west from Copenhagen in Zealand. Copenhagen has long had 1,500V dc suburban electric trains, but fortunately this system can be kept quite separate from the main lines. The first two Class EA locomotives were delivered in 1984 for trial running. The class incorporates a current inverter and three-phase traction motors, the first application of this method of locomotive control to 25,000V, single-phase, 50Hz ac. The builders were Thyssen-Henschel with electrics by Siemens and Brown Boveri, Mannheim. Class EA, a universal locomotive for all types of train, is rated at 4,000kW continuously. The owners' established maximum speed is 100mph (160kph).

### BRITISH RAIL CLASS 90/1987/BRITAIN

These 50 locomotives were built for the West Coast Route and were based on the Class 87 design, but had more advanced electronics. They were thyristor controlled, enabling a faster response to commands, and traction control was governed by a microprocessor. With Doppler ground-speed radar measuring the speed precisely, and probes relaying the motor speeds, wheel-slip was quickly detected and dealt with by cutting off power and restarting it gradually. An automatic speed limiter could be set by the driver and the microprocessor ensured a rapid acceleration to that speed. In BR days the Class was divided between Inter-City Passenger, Railfreight Distribution and Rail Express Services, and later was divided between Virgin Trains and the freight service sector. Construction was at the BR Crewe workshops, with GEC-Alsthom supplying the electrical equipment. Half the fifty units went to Railfreight Distribution. Continuous output is 3,508kW, and the motors have separate excitation ('Sepex') which helps when rails are slippery. Service weight is 189,630lb (86 tonnes). Maximum speed varied according to operator, but for the Inter-City units it was 110mph (175kph).

### BRITISH RAIL CLASS 91/1988/BRITAIN

The 31 units of this class were built at the British Rail workshops at Crewe in 1988-91 but GEC-Alsthom, apart from supplying the electrical equipment, played a large part in the design, which had been put out to competitive tender. They were designed for high speed, because the electrification of the East Coast route from London to Edinburgh gave an opportunity for a revolutionized passenger service. New trains were on order, and with these locomotives it was intended to reduce the fastest London-Edinburgh schedule to four hours for the 393 miles (632km). In fact, the 1991 schedule was 4hr 2m with two intermediate stops, an average of 96mph or 155kph. To make high speeds acceptable to the track engineers, the motors were attached to the body rather than to the axles. A new truck design also helped reduce track wear. The new East Coast trains were push-pull sets, so the locomotives had their forward end designed with a streamlined profile while the rear cab, which would only be used for special occasions, was flat-fronted; this enabled it to nestle close to the following passenger car and thereby eliminate energy-consuming air eddies. Continuous power rating of these locomotives is 4,540kW,

*British Rail 90 Class, 1987*

*British Rail 91 Class, 1988*

or about 6,300hp, on a service weight of 176,400lb (80 tonnes). They are thyristor controlled and are provided with separate excitation of their traction motors. The upper speed limit is 140mph (225kph), although one of the units on speed test did achieve 161.7mph (260kph). These were the fastest locomotives ever used in Britain, and by most reckonings the most powerful as well.

## GERMAN FEDERAL RAILWAYS (DB AG) Class 101/1997/GERMANY

The Henschel Works (Adtranz) received an order for 145 of these fast locomotives. They are intended to replace the ageing Class 103, but themselves have been superseded, almost before coming into service, by the new generation of high-speed trains. However, this was anticipated, and the design is also suitable for fast freight trains.

They have 3-phase ac drive and offer an output of 6,000kW. Maximum speed is 137mph (220kph). Weight is only 191,835lb (87 tonnes). There is an inverter for each motor (rather than for each truck) so an inverter failure only reduces power by 25 per cent and the locomotive can usually finish its rostered trip. This design belongs to the modular concept that became popular at the end of the century; essentially, there are certain standard basic components but the possibility is provided of changing certain specifications. Thus, this design's cab could be replaced by a strengthened version, if a customer required that. There is a standard truck of new design, but the motor can be moved from the truck to the underframe if a high-speed locomotive is required. There is a very wide range of microprocessor-controlled functions.

## GERMAN FEDERAL RAILWAYS (DB AG) CLASS 152/1997/GERMANY

In the late 1990s German Federal Railways was engaged in a massive renewal of rolling stock. This included the replacement of electric locomotives of 1960s and 1970s-vintage with more advanced designs. The Class 101 was intended for fast passenger trains while for freight, replacing the old 150 Class, the 152 was ordered from Krauss-Maffei. The first order for these was for 195 locomotives and there was an option for 100 more. These locomotives belong to the builder's 'Eurosprinter' concept, of which further examples were exported to Spain, Portugal, and Greece. They had a power output of 6,000kW, and had a maximum speed of 87mph (140kph) The Class 150 top speed was 62mph (100kph). Electrical equipment was by Siemens, Krauss-Maffei being a division of that corporation.

## Bo+Bo

## BALTIMORE AND OHIO RR ELECTRIC/1895/USA

Under the city of Baltimore the Baltimore and Ohio Railroad had a 1⅓-mile (2.2km) tunnel in the middle of a 4-mile (6.4km) gradient that in places was at 1 in 66 (15 per cent). Steam-locomotive working meant a lot of smoke, which it was difficult to clear from the tunnel. The 4-mile (6.4km) length was electrified at 650V dc in 1895. The locomotive's current was taken from an overhead third rail, which engaged a sliding trolley, although in 1902 this overhead third rail was abandoned in favor of a conventional ground-level third rail. This at the time was claimed as the first full-scale main-line railway electrification in the world.

Three locomotives were built for use on this section of the line by General Electric USA in 1894, each with a continuous rating of 560kW. They were fitted with gearless traction motors, the rotor of each motor being mounted on an axle and driving the wheels by a set of levers engaging the spokes. The stator poles were mounted vertically either side of the rotor, and these could move up and down with the springing relative to the latter. Control was through a resistance bank, and also by working the traction motors in series or series-parallel groups. To operate, the driver had what looked like a ship's steering-wheel to turn. These electric locomotives hauled trains up or down the gradient with the idling steam locomotives at their heads. After being placed in reserve in 1912, the three locomotives were finally broken up in the 1920s.

## ADRIATIC SYSTEM THREE-PHASE LOCOMOTIVES/1902/ITALY

Following the recommendations of a Royal Commission that reported in 1898, the then two mainland railway companies in the Italian peninsula tried out the three railway electrification systems that were possible at the time. These were (a) battery-electric railcars, (b) 650V third-rail dc, and (c) 3,400V, three-phase, 15.8Hz ac. It fell to the Adriatic System to try out the three-phase system, which it did in 1902 by electrifying the two branch lines northeast of Milan, the Lecco-Sondrio and the connecting Chiavenna-Colico. The firm of Ganz, Budapest, undertook the design and supply of material, and its engineer Kálmán Kandó was in charge.

Two locomotives were supplied in 1902, rated at 440kW continuously. They had gearless traction motors, the rotor of a motor being carried on a hollow axle that surrounded the main axle. The whole motor could thus move up and down with the locomotive's springs, or at least as far as the internal diameter of the hollow axle would let it. The turning of the rotor was transmitted to the wheels by a system of levers that was also responsive to spring movement. The locomotives were intended for freight working, the motors in each truck being wired permanently for cascade working to give only one speed, 20.5mph (33kph). Acceleration to speed was by the gradual short-circuiting of resistances using rising liquid.

Motor coaches for passengers that were built at the same time had a similar traction motor, but could also be switched to full parallel working so that the greater speed of 45½mph (73.4kph) was possible.

*Adriatico Three-Phase, 1902. This is one of the motor coaches that were based on the Bo-Bo locomotives*

*Italian State Railways E626 Class, 1931*

## AEG COMPANY No. E73.03/1906/GERMANY

When the German firm AEG was pressing the Royal Prussian State Railway to take up its single-phase main-line electrification system, it set up a test centre. This was sited at Oranienburg on the Prussian plain east of Berlin, and had the form of an oval track electrified at 6,000V, single-phase, 25Hz ac. As well as testing previously-built motor coaches, in 1906 AEG built a two-unit locomotive with Winter-Eichberg traction motors controlled by transformer tappings. Continuous rating was 550kW, while for the first time the traction motors were force-ventilated by blowers, a form of cooling that has since become well-nigh universal for traction motors of any size.

The locomotive hauled a 380-tonne train of four-wheel wagons around the oval for 20 hours a day, working thus for several months; as well as the locomotive, the track, the catenary and other things were being

endurance-tested. Such working would be very boring for a driver, and so the practice was that he set locomotive controls as desired and stepped off before the train got going too fast. The train ran round and round by itself all day, and was stopped finally by the simple expedient of cutting off the overhead catenary's current.

All AEG got out of the testing was the electrification of a Hamburg suburban railway and the sidings in the Altona harbour of that city, in 1907. More distantly, perhaps the London, Brighton and South Coast Railway electrification of its London suburban lines, when equipped in 1909, benefited also from the tests. In both cases the voltage was raised to 6,600V. The locomotive shunted the Altona harbour sidings until the middle 1930s, after which, as German State No.E73.03, it was retired to the Transport Museum at Nuremberg.

# Bo-Bo-Bo

## ITALIAN STATE RAILWAYS CLASS E626/1931/ITALY

Italian State Railways was the world's leading exponent of three-phase electrification in the 1920s. This did not prevent it from keeping up with developments elsewhere; indeed, the Italian electrical industry made sure that it did. Proposals were made, eventually concentrating on the Naples-Foggia route, for 3,000V dc electrification. Trials started in 1927 on the Benevento-Cervaro section of this line and public-traffic use started in 1928. It was a resounding success, and three-phase working was dropped.

Mechanical aspects of the locomotive design were by the Italian State Railways, which was one of the pioneers of the Bo-Bo-Bo wheel arrangement. Two axles support the main frame of the E626 class, while trucks at either end are pivoted to the frame by joints at their rear. Traction motors are nose-suspended and controlled by electro-pneumatic contactors for a resistance bank. Electrical details were left to the four Italian builders of the first 14 locomotives, who were advised by General Electric and Westinghouse of the USA, Metropolitan-Vickers of England, and Brown Boveri of Switzerland. Delivery of the definitive E626 class design started in 1931, and by 1939 there were 448 of them (including the original 14). Builders included most heavy-electrical and locomotive firms in Italy.

The continuous output of Class E626 is 1,660kW, and the maximum speed a modest 59mph (95kph), although gearing for a higher speed has been tried. For six decades the class has been common on local trains and for freight use all over Italy, although withdrawals have begun to reduce numbers. Four went to the Czechoslovakian State Railways in 1942, for trip working at 1,500V dc around Prague, while 17 ended up in the hands of the Yugoslav State Railways after the peace treaty in 1947.

## ITALIAN STATE RAILWAYS E636 CLASS/1940/ITALY

This class belongs to the inter-war phase of Italian electric locomotive design, especially as much of it was derived from the E626 Class of the 1920s. The Bo-Bo-Bo wheel arangement is typically Italian, the locomotive body being divided into halves which are articulated at the centre. Supported on three two-axle trucks, this is a way of providing the flexibility needed for high speed over the quite sharply curved track encountered in much of the Railway's mountain territory. As was usual in Italy, construction of the locomotives was shared by a large number of builders (seven in this case, plus six electrical suppliers). Four hended and fifty-nine were in service in the late 1990s, and they were built between 1940 and 1962, with a break for the war. In that long period there were naturally some variations. In particular, some units have frame-suspended motors while others have them axle-suspended. The axle-suspended units are geared for a slightly lower speed. Control is rheostatic, while speed is controlled by motor groupings coupled with field-weakening. Continuous output is 1,890kW, weight 227,705lb (101 tonnes), and maximum speed for the frame-suspended units 75mph (120kph).

## ITALIAN STATE RAILWAYS CLASS E645/1959/ITALY

The E645 Class consists of three sub-classes that are dimensionally identical but have different external styling. These 98 locomotives are themselves near-identical copies of the E646 Class, but have higher gear ratios to fit them for mountain and heavy-freight work. They have twin motors for each axle, giving a total output in continuous regime of 3,780kW. They weigh 246,960lb (112 tonnes)

*Italian State Railways E636 Class, 1940*

*Italian State Railways, E656 Class, 1976*

*Korean National Railroad WAG1 Class, 1972*

and the speed maximum is 75mph (120kph), compared with the 87mph (140kph) of the differently geared E646 Class. The transmission is by a sprung articulated rod and lever drive to the wheels from the hollow axles. To prevent weight transfer at high tractive effort (that is, to prevent the trucks being pushed, as it were, upwards from the front and thereby loosening their grip on the rails) the leading axle of each truck is made to produce less pull during acceleration.

## JAPANESE NATIONAL RAILWAYS CLASS EF81/1968/JAPAN

The original 3ft 6in (1067mm) gauge railway electrifications of the Japanese National Railways were at 1,500V dc. From 1957 fresh electrifications were with industrial-frequency ac, starting with the Hokuriki line at 20,000V, single-phase 50Hz. Japanese railways have a unique problem: in parts of the country generated industrial frequency is 50Hz, while in other parts it is 60Hz. Railways are electrified at both frequencies.

The need arose for locomotives that are able to work under both dc and ac wires. Accordingly, delivery of Class EF81 started in 1968, and 156 of them were built by both Hitachi and Mitsubishi. The class is able to work with a 1,500V dc supply as well as at both ac frequencies.

Control of the six nose-suspended traction motors of Class EF81 is by resistances and by series, series-parallel and parallel motor groupings. When running under ac wires, a transformer and solid-state rectifier deliver 1,500V dc to the control resistances. In common with most Japanese electric locomotives, no type of dynamic brake is fitted, but the locomotives can deliver current for electric train heating. The continuous rating of the locomotive is 2,400kW. To aid running through curves, provision is made for extra lateral movement of the centre truck from its centre of rotation.

Locomotive livery was standard blue and white, except for four locomotives which worked through the Kanmon under-sea tunnel connecting the islands of Honshu and Kyushu; these were given stainless-steel bodies for protection from the salt-laden atmosphere.

## KOREAN NATIONAL RAILROAD CLASS WAG1/1972/SOUTH KOREA

A start was made on electrifying South Korea's Korean National Railroad in 1972, using 25,000V, single-phase, 60Hz ac. (When North Korea started railway electrification in 1979 under Czechoslovak tutelage, it perversely chose 3,000V dc). Korean National ordered 90 locomotives from a consortium of European manufacturers called the 50 Hertz Group. Class WAG1 was the first delivered, in 1972. Construction was by La Brugeoise et Nivelles of Belgium with electrics by Ateliers de Constructions Electriques de Charleroi, or, alternatively, by Alsthom in France with electrics by Société MTE. Assisting with electrical components were the German firms Siemens, Brown

Boveri of Mannheim, and AEG (a British member of the consortium erected the electrification catenary).

To allow running easily through curvature, the secondary locomotive suspension allows lateral movement of the centre truck by 9in (230mm) to either side. The nose-suspended traction motors are thyristor controlled, the thyristors being used also to control wheel-slip and the application of the rheostatic brake. Continuous rating of the locomotive is 3,930kW. The bodywork was designed by Alsthom and follows French practice. The locomotive numbers provide a neat example of culture-transfer. For many years Belgian National Railways has marked all its locomotives and rolling stock in a particular 'type-face'; the aggressive letter B showing ownership is well known. This Belgian style was used for Korean locomotives from No.8001 onwards.

## ITALIAN STATE RAILWAYS CLASS E656/1976/ITALY

This class is a further development of the Italian Bo-Bo-Bo format, and has some similarities with the preceding E645 design. But they are more powerful, with a continuous rating of 4,200kW and a higher permitted speed (100mph or 160kph). They weigh 264,600lb (120 tonnes). Two motors per axle, as with the E645, help to provide a range of economical speeds (the motors can be all in series, series-parallel, and parallel in both 4+4+4 and 3+3+3+3 arrangements), to which is added five stages of field weakening in series and series-parallel regimes and three in the other regimes. Control is rheostatic. The railway administrators decided it would be a good idea to call these locomotives 'Alligators.' Presumably they were joking (they had already named the E444 Class, very fast machines, the 'Tortoise' class).

## NEW ZEALAND RAILWAYS CLASS Ef/1985/NEW ZEALAND

Before it was privatized New Zealand Railways ordered

the Ef Class for its its 3ft 6in (1067mm) gauge main line on North Island, electrified from Palmerston northwards at 25kV ac. The first locomotive of an order for 22 was delivered at the end of 1985. Brush Electrical Machines in Britain were the builders, and each unit is rated at 3,000kW continuously with a maximum speed of 65mph (105kph). The locomotives are thyristor controlled, with a separate current supply to the rotor and the stator of each traction motor. This means that the motors run at maximum efficiency whatever their revolution rate. The driver's controller, when pushed round, causes the locomotive to accelerate, but automation ensures also that, when moved back towards off, it applies the regenerative brake should it be needed.

## QUEENSLAND RAILWAYS CLASS 3900/1988/AUSTRALIA

Thanks largely to the development of Queensland coal exports, Queensland Railways were transformed in the last quarter of the 20th century. In particular, considerable mileage was electrified and the practice began of operating very long trains on this 3ft 6in (1067mm) gauge system. Most trains between Brisbane and Rockhampton are now electrically hauled, while coal trains can sometimes have five electric locomotives, including two or three units mid-train. Of the more than 180 electric locomotives acquired between 1986 and 1995, all are of the Bo-Bo-Bo arrangement. Class 3900 appeared in 1988, being built by the Australian Walkers company, with ASEA electrical equipment supplied by Clyde Engineering. The locomotives weigh 242,550lb (110 tonnes), produced 2,900kW, and had a top speed of 62mph (100kph), somewhat faster than QR's other electric locomotives.

## EUROTUNNEL 'TRI-BO' CLASS/1994/BRITAIN

Eurotunnel ordered 38 of these locomotives for handling its 'Le Shuttle' cross-channel service. In 1996 an additional four units were ordered. They are highly specialized locomotives. One is attached to each end of the trains conveying highway vehicles between elaborate terminals on either side of the English Channel. Most of their work is therefore done in tunnel, and one locomotive is powerful enough to haul its train out of the Tunnel should the other locomotive fail. At each end of the trip, the train changes direction by passing over a circular loop of track; at the British end, this involves a quite sharp curve, which is why a Bo-Bo-Bo ('Tri-Bo') wheel arrangement was ideal. Brush won the order for these units, having proposed that wheel arrangement (of which it had some experience with locomotives exported to New Zealand). Power output is 5,600kV and, like Brush's other trans-Tunnel locomotives, Class 92, this class has GTO drive. Electrical equipment is by ABB of Switzerland (now part of Adtranz). Normal operating speed is 87mph (140kph) but locomotives have been tested at up to 109mph (175kph) in the Tunnel.

# Bo-Bo+Bo-Bo

### RUSSIAN FEDERAL RAILWAYS CLASS VL10/1961/RUSSIA

Almost 3,000 units of this and the almost identical VL10u Class were built, initially at Novocherkassk in Russia and later at the Tbilisi works in Georgia. They followed the VL8 Class, which had the same layout but was less powerful. They were intended to work on all Soviet Union 3kV lines, mainly, but not exclusively, in freight service. They consist of two permanently coupled sections, the trucks being articulated and carrying the traction forces. Hourly rating is 5,200kW, with later units having improved motors that brought output up to 5,700kW. Maximum speed is 68mph (110kph). Weight in working order is 405,720lb (184 tonnes); VL10u units are ballasted to increase adhesion and weigh 441,000lb (200 tonnes).

The four motors are nose-suspended. Control is rheostatic and there is regenerative braking provision that seems to be rarely used. In the late 1990s, with the drastic fall of traffic, many of these locomotives were laid aside 'in reserve.'

### RUSSIAN FEDERAL RAILWAYS CLASS ChS200/1965/RUSSIA

The passenger-train standard-setter for the 5ft (1524mm) gauge Russian Railways is the Moscow to Leningrad main line. Great efforts have been made to bring the 404-mile (650km) route up to the standard for 125mph (200kph) running. In the 1990s, there were 10 high-speed locomotives of Class ChS200 at work there, a 3,000V dc design with a continuous rating of 8,000kW. The letters `ChS' in the classification stand for Czechoslovakia, which had something of a monopoly of electric passenger locomotive production for

*Russian Federal Railways VL10 Class, 1961*

*Russian Federal Railways ChS6 Class, 1979*

for the former Soviet Railways. Skoda built them from 1975, with fully sprung traction motors and a flexible drive to the wheels. The motors are resistance-bank controlled through contactors, and a rheostatic brake is fitted. Much of the locomotive's driving is automated and speeds are preselected by pushing a button.

## RUSSIAN FEDERAL RAILWAYS CLASS VL82m/1972/RUSSIA

From the mid-1960s the VL80 series of silicon rectifier locomotives began to appear on Soviet Railways ac lines. They followed Soviet practice for heavy locomotives in having two sections permanently coupled. Several hundred were built and in 1967 one of them was experimentally fitted with thyristor control. The VL82 was a derivation of this series, and was designed for dual voltage, since by 1972 the 3,000V and 25kV systems were making end-on connections at more and more points. Power output was 5,760kW in continuous regime, and maximum speed was 68mph (110kph). The locomotives saw both passenger and freight service. Weight in working order was 220,500lb (100 tonnes). The eight motors are axle-hung.

*Russian Federal Railways VL82m Class, 1972*

## RUSSIAN FEDERAL RAILWAYS ChS6 CLASS/1979/RUSSIA

In Russian terms, this is a small class, with just 30 units supplied by Skoda in 1979 and 1981. The objective was heavier and faster passenger trains (not so much for the benefit of passengers, but to reduce line occupation by passenger trains of essentially freight-train routes). It was in the usual Russian twin-section form, totalling 361,620lb (164 tonnes) and developing 8,000kW on continuous regime. Maximum speed was 118mph (190kph). They all appear to have been allocated to the October Railway, whose Moscow-Leningrad main line was at that time intensively used by freight and passenger services, and at the same time was suited to high speeds, being flat and straight. In the end, the class stayed on the October Railway, but no more were built. A new, similar, but better design, the ChS7, was supplied by Skoda to other dc lines in the USSR.

# 2-Bo+Bo-2

## ITALIAN STATE RAILWAYS CLASS E428/1934/ITALY

Italian State Railways opened a new high-speed railway between Bologna and Florence in 1934. The first locomotive design for the railway was the 2-Co-2 E326 class, but this was superseded by the articulated E428 class, 242 of which were built during 1934-42. To the casual glance the E428 class did not appear to be articulated, for the bodywork was in a single piece. Twin motors were mounted above each driving hollow axle. Fingers from the hollow-axle ends engaged leaf springs mounted radially between the driving-wheel spokes. The engaging buckle could slide up and down the spring when it happened to be vertical, while the springs carried the motors' weight when horizontal.

Maximum speed was 81mph (130kph); a few were geared for 93mph (150kph), but at that speed the locomotives were too rough on the track.

# 2-Bo-Bo+Bo-Bo-2

## MILWAUKEE RR ARTICULATED LOCOMOTIVE/1915/USA

The world's first electrification at 3,000V dc ran 437 miles (703km) from Harlowton, Montana, to Avery, Idaho. The General Electric Company (USA) provided locomotives for the Chicago, Milwaukee, St Paul and Pacific Railroad in 1915. The two halves of the articulated locomotive were identical, and together had a weight of 564,480lb (256 tonnes) in working order. In later years the 'halves' were

*Milwaukee Railroad articulated locomotive, 1915*

*French Railways CC6500 Class, 1969*

to the depot of La Chapelle in northern Paris. Six more were later built for Belgian Railways and these shared the duties. The series performed a useful job but was finally ousted by the advent of the 'Thalys' multi-current TGV trains.

## FRENCH RAILWAYS CLASS CC6500/1969/FRANCE

Sevety-four of these locomotives were built, and they had much in common with the CC72000 Class diesel-electrics built at the same time, notably the single-motor 3-axle trucks with gearing to transmit the power to all three axles. These locomotives also had the ability to change the gear ratio. This operation, carried out while stationary, made them wide-ranging in their capabilities. In high gear they could run up to 135mph (220kph), and in low gear 62 mph (100kph) but with double the tractive effort. Alsthom and MTE shared the building of these locomotives, which were for the dc lines and in the first instance for the passenger trains from Paris to Bordeaux and Toulouse. In the lower gear they could also handle the fast freight trains over these routes. When they were built they were the SNCF's most powerful locomotives ((5,900kW in continuous regime). They had two double-armature motors, fully suspended with cardan shaft drive. Control was rheostatic. In the late 1990s, having lost most of their passenger duties to TGVs and more modern locomotives, these units were being re-geared and otherwise modified to make them suitable for heavy, fast, freight trains.

## 1-C-1

## SWEDISH STATE RAILWAYS CLASS D/1925/SWEDEN

The Swedish State Railways was one of the pioneers of main-line railway electrification. As in Germany, experiments in the early years of the 20th Century favoured 25Hz electrifications, but, again as in Germany, $16\frac{2}{3}$Hz was later adopted, with the variation that 16,000V was the voltage used to suit the needs of the Swedish electricity-supply industry. From 1926 this was dropped to the 15,000V of central Europe, always at single-phase $16\frac{2}{3}$Hz.

Taking advantage of her wealth of water power, Sweden embarked on extensive railway electrification in the 1920s, and a standard passenger locomotive was designed for service in the flatter parts of the country. This was Swedish State Railways Class D, first built in 1925, and with variants of increasing output built until 1957. The original Class Dg had a continuous output of 1,150kW, and it was distinguished by a varnished timber body. The last version, Class Da, was built from 1952 with a continuous rating of 1,780kW. Taking Class D as a whole, 417 were built over 30 years, all with electrics by Asea and with mechanical

separated, and on occasion worked three together. Some of the class were fitted with oil-fired boilers for train steam heating. Maximum voltage in the traction motors was 1,500V, ensured by pairs of motors being permanently in series circuit. The class had the world's first dc regenerative brake.

## C-C

## FRENCH RAILWAYS CLASS CC40100/1964/FRANCE

This was a notable class for several reasons. It was an example of a numerically very small (10 units) series built for a distinct purpose: it had an external form entrusted to a design artist with the aim of producing a very distinctive external image, and it was the first of the 4-current

locomotives. It was aimed at the international services extending from the Gare du Nord in Paris to destinations in Belgium, The Netherlands and Germany, and for this assignment capabiity at four different voltages was needed. At that period the Trans Europe Express concept was important, and the styling of the locomotives echoed the styling of the TEE passenger vehicles they were designed to haul. The outer body, apart from the other considerations, had to cope with the different European loading gauges. The overhanging ('reverse rake') front windows were introduced to cut out glare.

Built by Alsthom, these units weighed 238,140lb (108 tonnes). The first five could change from high to low gear, and back, while in motion, while the other units had to go into workshops for this change to be made. However, the latter units had a higher continuous output (4,480kW as against 3,670kW). Separate pantographs were provided for ac and dc power supply. Control was rheostatic; on ac regime the current was silicon-rectified. The locomotives carried the names of French cities and all were attached

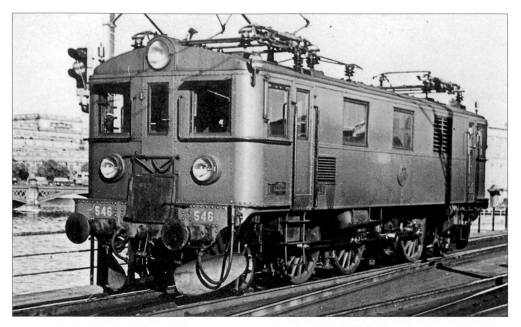

*Swedish State Railways D Class, 1925*

parts by various Swedish firms. The locomotives were controlled by low-tension side transformer tap-changers, and there were two traction motors, both geared to the same jackshaft. Cranks at each end of the jackshaft were coupled to the driving wheels.

## Co-Co

### GERMAN STATE RAILWAYS (DR) CLASS E94/1940/GERMANY

The German State Railway (which then incorporated the railways of Austria) had a fresh heavy freight and mountain-

work locomotive design in 1940. It was developed and built by Algemeine Elektricitäts Gesellschaft (AEG) for a supply of 15,000V, single-phase, 16⅔Hz ac. Up to 1956, German and Austrian builders supplied a total of 202. The nose-suspended, low-frequency traction motors are controlled by low-tension side transformer Tap-changers, and a regenerative brake is fitted. Originally the locomotives were known as the E94 class, but the German Federal Railway changed this later to the 194 class.

In the German Democratic Republic, 24 examples were taken into stock after 1945 as the 254 class. Also after 1945, the Austrian Federal Railway had 44 of them as its 1020 class.

Continuous rating of the earlier members of the class was 3,090kW and of the post-war examples 4,440kW.

### SOUTHERN RAILWAY No CC1/1941/BRITAIN

The Southern Railway in England had two locomotives for its 650V dc third-rail electrified system built at the railway's Eastleigh locomotive works, with electrics from English Electric.

A third rail necessarily has breaks or gaps at points and crossings where one running rail crosses another. The three-coach multiple-unit trains used until 1941 picked up current at both ends, and they were long enough to avoid being 'gapped' by breaks in the third rail. A locomotive, however, is too short to avoid gapping, and the special arrangements to overcome the problem produced an unusual method of locomotive control. The 650V current from the third rail drove an electric motor on board (one for each truck), which in turn drove a dc generator. On the shaft between the motor and the generator was a heavy flywheel. Should there be a pause due to gapping in the motor's output, the stored energy in the flywheel kept the generator revolving and producing current. Current from the generator was at 600-1,200V, for three motors permanently in series, and traction-motor control was a matter of resistance-adjusting output of the motor-and-generator combination. As well as third-rail pick-up shoes at both ends on either side, the locomotives were equipped with a pantograph. A couple of the Southern Railway's freight yards had overhead contact wires above their tracks, but apart from experimental running there seems to have been no regular use of the pantographs of the two locomotives. As the coaching stock had vacuum brakes, the locomotives had exhausters, but in practice the provision seemed inadequate and the brakes needed a long time for release.

Naturally, regeneration of current on board the locomotive led to loss of efficiency, perhaps reflected in the locomotives' continuous rating of 1,100kW.

### SOUTH AFRICAN RAILWAYS CLASS 3E/1947/SOUTH AFRICA

South African Railways, on their 3,000V dc, 3ft 6in (1067mm) gauge line, for more than 20 years used the Bo-Bo wheel arrangement exclusively. Locomotives were coupled together when greater power was needed. Then it was decided to have what would be a more powerful locomotive in the first place, using six-wheel trucks. The result was Class 3E, 28 of which were built in 1947 by either Robert Stephenson & Co. or by R. and W. Hawthorn, Leslie, with electrics by

Metropolitan-Vickers. Control was by resistances and electro-pneumatic contactors, together with motor groupings, and the continuous rating was 2,340kW. Unfortunately the springs and suspension were so badly conceived that a speed limit of 35mph (56kph) had to be imposed.

South African Railways had another try at a powerful locomotive for working up the gradients of the Hex River Pass. This was Class 4E, which worked well enough. All the same, it was a great lump of machinery

*German State Railways (DR) E94 Class, 1940*

*Austrian Federal Railways 1020 (DR E94) Class, 1940*

*Southern Railway CC1 type (BR No 20002, formerly CC2), 1941*

with, considering its weight, a poor output. Thereafter South African Railways reverted gratefully to the Bo-Bo wheel arrangement with the highly successful Class 5E of 1955, followed by the equally successful Class 6E of 1969.

## NETHERLANDS RAILWAYS CLASS 1200/1951/NETHERLANDS

The 25 units of NS 1200 Class are unusual, for Europe, in that they are of US design and, partly, of US construction. They were in fact assembled in the NS Werkspoor shops, using Baldwin mechanical and Westinghouse electrical components. Those parts made locally were licensed by Baldwin or Westinghouse; much of the electrical equipment was made by the Dutch Heemaf company. They look American, and they are rather heavy for their power, but they quickly established a reputation for reliability. With their weight, and their nose-suspended motors, they were not allowed to reach their design speed of 93mph (150kph) but were restricted to 84mph (135kph). They were refurbished in the 1980s with the aim of giving them two decades of additional service. Control is rheostatic, and the continuous output from the four traction motors is 2,210kW. Weight in working order is 238,140lb (108 tonnes)

*South African Railways 3E Class, 1947*

## FRENCH RAILWAYS CLASS CC7100/1952/FRANCE

The SNCF acquired its first flexible-truck electric locomotives in 1949; hitherto mainline units had rigid frames. The two prototypes did well and gave rise to the CC7100 Class, of which 58 were built, with the electrical equipment supplied by Alsthom and CEM. Built for the 1.5kV dc system (the successful French ac system was still in the future), the first batch had a continuous output of 3,490kW, although this was lowered to 3,240kW in the later units. They weighed 235,935lb (107 tonnes), and were powered by six fully-suspended Alsthom motors with quill drive. Control was rheostatic. The maximum speed was set at 93mph (150kph) but in 1955 one of the class, CC-7107, with slight modification, reached 205.6mph (331kph) during high-speed trials in the flat Landes region. A 4-axle locomotive achieved exactly the same speed the next day and the two locomotives jointly held the world speed record for years afterwards. This success, justifiably publicised, ensured the reputation of French railway engineering and persuaded many railway administrations to buy French. The CC7100 class alone found markets in North Africa, The Netherlands and Spain in addition to France.

## VICTORIAN RAILWAYS CLASS L/1952/AUSTRALIA

From 1919, Victorian Railways, electrified its 5ft 3in gauge (1600mm) suburban railways around Melbourne with 1,500V dc. A long extension of the electrification into Gippsland was added in 1956. For this extension, English

Electric in Great Britain built 25 Class L locomotives during 1952-53. Conventional resistance-controlled, nose-suspended traction motors were used, arranged for regenerative braking as needed. The Class L can run as multiple units in pairs.

## NEW YORK NEW HAVEN & HARTFORD RR EP5 CLASS/1955/USA

The New Haven Railroad had an electrified main line from New York to New Haven of about 107 miles (172km), powered by 11kV ac current. It used electric locomotives

*Netherlands Railways 1200 Class, 1951*

### RUSSIAN FEDERAL RAILWAYS VL23 CLASS/1956/RUSSIA

The VL23, of which close to 500 units were built, was the last of a line of Soviet dc electric locomotives whose design derived from eight locomotives supplied by American General Electric in the 1930s. These were of the Co-Co type, and the Soviet-built VL22 of 1938 was very similar. From the VL22 was developed the VL22m and then in 1956, the VL23. The latter was like the VL22m but with a more modern style of body and incorporating the traction motors that were currently being used for a new range of 8-axle locomotives (VL8 and VL10 series). Although designed for freight work, the VL23 did frequently appear on passenger trains, even on the fastest services (which were not very fast; its top speed of 62mph [100kph] was more than adequate). The six Novocherkassk motors were frame mounted, and gave a total hourly output of 2,749kW. Weight was 304,290lb (138 tonnes).

### NEW SOUTH WALES CLASS 46/1956/AUSTRALIA

The New South Wales Government Railways electrified Sydney suburban services at 1,500V dc, and from 1956

for both freight and passenger work. These ten locomotives were delivered by General Electric in 1955 and were the Railroad's last purchase of electric units. Unlike their predecessors of the EP4 Class, they had an all-adhesion wheelbase consisting of two three-axle trucks (the EP4 units, built in the 1940s, were of the 2-C-C-2 arrangement). But they were also innovatory in having ignitron rectifiers; these were more efficient in converting ac to low-voltage dc and this in turn permitted better dc motors. These locomotives, despite their 346,185lb (157 tonnes), were allowed a maximum speed of 90mph (145kph). They had an output of 2,980kW, or about 4,000hp.

*French Railways CC7100 Class, 1952*

*Pennsylvania Railroad E44 Class, 1960*

electrification was taken into the Blue Mountains, and also north to Gosford. In the mountains trains face gradients of 1 in 33 (3 per cent). To handle traffic on these routes, a total of 40 Class 46 locomotives were built by Metropolitan-Vickers (aided by Beyer, Peacock) in Great Britain. The type has conventional resistance-controlled traction motors, nose-suspended, and arranged for regenerative braking. The class can be run as pairs in multiple, a fact of particular interest in view of the gradients that they have to face. The continuous rating of each locomotive is 2,535kW.

## PENNSYLVANIA RAILROAD CLASSES E44 AND E44a/1960/USA

From 1960 the Pennsylvania Railroad had 66 Class E44 locomotives built for its 11,000V, single-phase, 25Hz ac routes. The builder was General Electric, and features were incorporated that were taken from the design of General Electric diesel locomotives. In particular, the nose-suspended dc traction motors were those that were used widely in diesel-electric locomotives. In all but half a dozen of the class, the dc was taken from water-cooled ignitron rectifiers (a variation of the mercury-arc rectifier). Half a dozen or so had solid-state silicon rectifiers when new, and the rest of the class were re-equippped to conform. Control of the locomotive is by low-tension side tap-changers on the transformer. A rheostatic brake is fitted and the locomotives can work in multiple-unit with each other.

Class E44 was very successful on the freight duties for which it was intended. From 1964, certain members of the class were given new traction motors and uprated from 3,285kW continuously to 3,730kW. So altered, they then had a maximum speed of 95mph (153kph), and were known as Class E44a. There were 22 of Class E44a, but at least one of them was later altered back to Class E44.

## GERMAN FEDERAL RAILWAYS CLASS 103/1970/GERMANY

Although series production of Class 103 began in 1970, for the preceding five years four prototypes had been on trial over the DB. The intention was to build a class of locomotives capable of hauling the best trains, notably the Trans-Europ Express trains, within Germany. Such trains could be quite heavy and scheduled at the faster speeds. The external styling of the class was determined by wind-tunnel tests, but the livery, red and cream, was deliberately

chosen so as to match with the TEE trains. Automatic speed control was provided, enabling a speed to be set and then automatically maintained in spite of changing gradients. The DB management was nervous about track stresses, for these locomotives were heavy and moved fast. Although 3-axle trucks were chosen to reduce axle-loads, they had the side-effect of placing more strain on curved track. In fact, lines over which these locomotives ran did begin to show signs of wear faster, and for ten years after 1967 they were not allowed to operate at their designed 125mph

*German Federal Railways 103 Class, 1970*

*Amtrak AEM6 Class, 1974*

(200kph). Continuous rating of these locomotives was 5,950kW, and they had a 10-minute rating of 10,400kW, which was very high for the time. They weighed 242,550lb (110 tonnes), and control was by h.t. tap-changer. The six motors were frame-suspended and used a flexible cardan drive. Construction was divided between Henschel, Krauss-Maffei, and Krupp, 149 units being produced. For two decades they hauled the DB's most prestigious trains, but were then put out of their job by the ICE high-speed trains.

## INDIAN RAILWAYS CLASS WAM4/1971/INDIA

Originally the 5ft 6in (1676mm) gauge Indian Railways electrifications were at 1,500V dc. From 1958, when fresh routes were electrified, this was done at 25,000V, single-phase, 50Hz ac. This industrial-frequency network spread (and still is spreading) rapidly, and the need arose for a multi-purpose locomotive. This need was met by Class WAM4. Since 1971 a total of 270 of these have been built by Chittaranjan Locomotive Works.

Class WAM4 is a conventional straightforward locomotive with nose-suspended dc traction motors supplied through a solid-state rectifier and controlled by a high-tension tap-changer. Rheostatic braking and multiple-unit-working jumper cables are fitted. Continuous rating is 2,680kW. It was decided to use nose-suspended traction motors after the experience of high maintenance costs given by fully springborne traction motors in another locomotive type.

## RUSSIAN FEDERAL RAILWAYS CLASS ChS2t/1972/RUSSIA

These were built by Skoda for the USSR's 3kv dc lines, but most seemed to settle on the Moscow-Leningrad route. Their maximum speed is 100mph (160kph) and they weigh 277,830lb (126 tonnes). Continuous output is 4,080kW. Series production was in 1972-74, and the new locomotives brought a noticeable improvement to the passenger services on the October Railway's main line. After the dissolution of the Soviet Bloc, cheap spares could no longer be obtained from Czechoslovakia, their country of origin, so a number have been taken out of service, at least temporarily. The intention, in the late 1990s, was to order new passenger locomotive designs from Russian works, so as to slowly replace Czech-built units.

## BLACK MESA AND LAKE POWELL RAILROAD HIGH-VOLTAGE LOCOMOTIVES/1974/USA

Coal worked on Black Mesa in Utah was taken by rail 78 miles (125km) to Lake Powell, where an electricity-generating station was sited. The Black Mesa and Lake Powell Railroad, isolated from other railways, opened for traffic in 1974. It was electrified at 50,000V, single-phase, 60Hz ac, the first time that such a high voltage had been used. There are few people living along the route, so the voltage was acceptable, and it had the advantage that a

*New Haven Railroad EP5 Class, 1955*

single substation near the generating station served the whole railroad. The General Electric Co., USA, built six thyristor locomotives for the line in 1973, with a continuous rating of 3,805kW. A pair of these could handle the 10,000-short-tons (9,100-tonne) merry-go-round (carousel) trains. The trains loaded and unloaded on the move, and in theory the service could be run without stopping. The idea, allegedly, was taken to Utah by Americans who had ridden similar trains in Britain.

## GERMAN STATE RAILWAY (DR) CLASS 250/1974/GERMAN DEMOCRATIC REPUBLIC

The German State Railway in the Democratic Republic was steadily electrifying its routes at 15,000V, single-phase, 16⅔Hz ac. A need arose for a powerful electric locomotive type, so three prototype Class 250 machines were built in 1974. After prolonged trials, 110 more were added to the class during 1977-79. All were built by Lokomotivbau-Elektrotechnische Werke 'Hans Beimler'. The low-frequency traction motors are controlled by high-tension side transformer Tap-changers that incorporate thyristors to increase voltage gradually between taps as the locomotive accelerates. This type of electronics application was pioneered in 1969 for the Metroliner motor coaches of Penn Central in the United States, but it remains rare. Traction motors of Class 250 are nose-suspended, and drive hollow axles with flexible drives to the wheels. Rheostatic braking is fitted. Continuous rating of the type is 5,140kW.

*Black Mesa & Lake Powell RR 50,000V locomotives, 1974*

which allows substations to be spaced out up to 100 miles (160km) apart. The 31 Class 9E locomotives used were built by Union Carriage and Truck Co., with electrics from GEC Traction Ltd in Great Britain, from 1978. They are thyristor-controlled, with separate control of both the rotor and stator windings of the nose-suspended dc traction motors. A rheostatic brake is fitted. Continuous rating of each locomotive is 3,780kW, while a special provision is the capacity to continue working despite voltage drops in the overhead line down to as low as 25,000V. Three locomotives used in a multiple unit work 202-truck trains, a trailing load of 22,270 short tons (20,200 tonnes). Such a train is over 1¼ miles (2.3km) long, and a motor scooter is an unusual locomotive fitting. This is carried in a compartment slung beneath the locomotive's frame, and with its aid the locomotive crew can make comparatively rapid inspections of their train should it be necessary.

## SOUTH AFRICAN RAILWAYS CLASSES 7E AND 7E1/1978/SOUTH AFRICA

The 3ft 6in (1067mm) gauge South African Railways had been electrified at 3,000V dc, but it was found that, without going to inordinate expense, the loading of trains had to have a limit. To take coal from Transvaal coalfields 261 miles (420km) to a port at Richards Bay, trains of 160 wagons weighing a total of 9,526 short-tons ( 8,640 tonnes) were proposed, and for these the railway was electrified at 25,000V single-phase, 50Hz ac. Union Carriage and Truck Co. built 125 thyristor Class 7E locomotives from 1978. Electrics came from the European 50 Hertz Group as South Africa had no experience of this type of electrification, but as much as possible was built

## HUNGARIAN STATE RAILWAYS CLASS V63/1975/HUNGARY

Ganz-M vag delivered two prototype thyristor Class V63 machines to the Hungarian State Railways in 1975, and over 50 of these 25kV ac units were subsequently built. The thyristor control was developed in the Ganz Electric Works, and offers a means for automatic speed regulation as well as for wheel-slip control. The trucks have nose-suspended traction motors, and a rheostatic brake is fitted. This truck design can be altered for a rubber sprung-quill drive should higher maximum speeds of up to 100mph (160kph) be needed, in conjunction with an altered final drive-gear ratio.

## SOUTH AFRICAN RAILWAYS CLASS 9E/1978/SOUTH AFRICA

To take iron ore out of the Orange Free State, a 3ft 6in (1067mm) gauge railway was built from Sishen to the southwestern port of Saldanha. South African Railways electrified this railway at 50,000V, singlephase, 50Hz ac. In part the 537-mile (864km) railway traverses the Kalahari Desert, where electricity-generating stations and power lines are in short supply. Hence the high traction voltage,

*German State Railway (DR) 250 Class, 1974*

*Brush Traction (BR 89 Class), 1987*

in South Africa. In addition, from 1979 the Dorman Long Corporation built 50 Class 7E1 locomotives, with electrics from a Japanese consortium including Hitachi. The thyristors control both stator and rotor windings of the nose-suspended dc traction motors separately, and a rheostatic brake is fitted. The continuous rating of Class 7E and 7E1 is 3,050kW, and they can work together in multiple.

## NEW SOUTH WALES GOVERNMENT RAILWAYS CLASS 85/1979/AUSTRALIA

From an initial suburban 1,500V dc electrification around Sydney, the system of the New South Wales Government Railways was extended over some main lines in the 1950s, and over still more in the 1980s until it reached as far as the coal centre of Newcastle. Accordingly, 10 new locomotives were built in 1979 by Comeng, with electrics by Mitsubishi. Much of the mechanical side of these Class 85 electric locomotives is based on that for the Class 80 diesel-electric locomotives, which were more or less contemporary. There is also a marked resemblance between them. Conventional resistance control is used for the nose-suspended traction motors, the latter being arranged to supply rheostatic braking to the locomotive when needed. The continuous rating of the locomotive is 2,700kW.

## BRUSH TRACTION CLASS 89/1987/BRITAIN

This one-unit class was a private venture by Brush Traction, assembled by the British Rail workshops at Crewe.

It worked as part of the BR fleet but the hoped-for order by BR for further units did not materialize, with the Bo-Bo Class 91 being chosen for the East Coast Route in preference to the Co-Co specification. Named Avocet, the unit left BR service, having at least provided valuable experience both for Brush (which used the knowledge in designing the later Class 92) and BR. It went into preservation and then in 1996 made history by becoming the first locomotive in preservation to be bought by an operating company for further regular use. The Great North Eastern Railway, faced with a need to put its Class 91 locomotives through works to improve their reliability, needed extra power to cover for absent locomotives, and decided to puchase No.89001. In the following years it was a regular performer on the East Coast Route, being recognizable not only by its 6-axle layout but by its possession of a streamlined cab at both ends. At 229,320lb (104 tonnes) it was considerably heavier than the Class 91 (82 tonnes), so it had a more restricted route availability (which was unimportant insofar as it worked only over the main lines), but it was marginally more powerful than the Class 91.

## BRUSH TRACTION CLASS 92/1993/BRITAIN

These locomotives were built for Channel Tunnel service, and were initially divided between three owners, BR's Railfreight Distribution (30 units), European Passenger Services (seven units), and French Railways (nine units). The passenger units were intended to haul trains originating at British cities outside London, but the plan to

operate these was abandoned. The Railfreight units were intended to haul intermodal trains through the Channel Tunnel to and from British points. Based partly on the Brush 60 and 89 classes, these locomotives carried extra equipment to suit them for tunnel operation. They could take current from the third-rail dc system of southern England and from the overhead 25kV ac systems elsewhere. Much of the electrical equipment, including the asynchronous traction motors, was of ABB design but built by Brush under licence. Microprocessors are used for power control and are linked to the Eurotunnel TVM430 cab-signalling system. The locomotives weigh 277,830lb (126 tonnes) and have a maximum speed of 100mph (160kph). Power output is 5,000kW on ac and 4,000kW on dc. They carry the names of celebrated figures from Europe's cultural and scientific history.

# 1-Co+Co-1

## PAULISTA RAILWAY No.330/1926/BRAZIL

The 5ft 3in (1600mm) gauge San Paulo Railway Co. Ltd ran from the port of Santos to San Paulo and beyond to Jundiai. At Jundiai an end-on junction was made with the Paulista Railway Co., which had a main line into the interior of Brazil as far as the town of Colombia. The Paulista started to electrify its line from Jundiai to Campinas in 1922, at 3,000V dc. US manufacturers took most of the motive-power orders, but SLM Winterthur did supply an articulated locomotive, No 330, in 1926, with electrics by

*Great Indian Peninsula Railway 1-Co-2 type, 1929*

Metropolitan-Vickers. It had six nose-suspended traction motors, controlled by a resistance bank with electro-pneumatic contactors. Regenerative braking was fitted, and the locomotive itself was air-braked. As the rolling stock of the railway was vacuum-braked, the locomotive also had a rotary exhauster for this brake. Number 330 had a continuous rating of 2,100kW.

# 1-Co-2

### GREAT INDIAN PENINSULA RAILWAY CLASS WCP1/1929/INDIA

During 1928-30 the 5ft 6in (1676mm) gauge Great Indian Peninsula Railway electrified 138 route miles (222km) of its lines around Bombay, including the climb up the ghats to Poona, at 1,500V dc. Three prototype locomotives were ordered from various British and Swiss manufacturers, which resulted in a definitive batch of 22 1-Co-2 locomotives being built by SLM Winterthur from 1929. Each axle of these was driven by a pair of traction motors, each pair driving a single pinion sited between them. Through a gear train the pinion drove a single gear-wheel mounted on the centre of the axle, which gear contained within it a flexible drive, known as the SLM Universal drive. As well as turning the driven axle the drive was responsive to locomotive spring movements. Control was by a resistance bank with electro-pneumatic contactors, and also by motor groupings. The continuous rating of the locomotive was 1,900kW.

# 2-Co+Co-2

### PENNSYLVANIA RAILROAD CLASS GG1/1934/USA

Perhaps the best-known type of electric locomotive in North America used to be the GG1 class of the Pennsylvania Railroad. The New York-Washington line had been electrified throughout with 11,000V, single-phase, 25Hz ac, and the Pennsylvania very badly needed a high-speed locomotive to work the railway. In the early 1930s, a New Haven 2-Co+Co-2 was borrowed for trials, and this pointed the way to the sort of locomotive that was needed. The Pennsylvania set to work, and in 1934 No 4800, with electrics from General Electric, emerged from its Altoona Works as a GG1-class prototype. The prototype was very satisfactory, and by 1943 Altoona had produced 139 of them, in some of which Westinghouse gave a hand with the electrics. They were styled by the notable industrial designer Raymond Loewy. He did away with the riveted outer shell, and substituted a welded body with air-smoothed characteristics.

The GG1 was controlled by low-tension tap-changers on the transformer. Each axle was driven by a pair of motors. These were body-mounted and both members of a pair drove the same hollow axle surrounding the main axle. The drive was taken from the hollow axle to the wheels by a Westinghouse-type cup drive. Continuous output of the locomotive was 3,450kW. These locomotives gave fine service between New York and Washington and on the extension to Harrisburg for the best part of 40 years. Some passed to Amtrak in later years, and others to the New Jersey Department of Transportation. This latter authority had the last GG1 to be in service, which was retired finally in 1983. The Railroad Museum of Pennsylvania has preserved two of the class, one of them the first one, No.4800.

# 0-Do-1

### AUSTRIAN FEDERAL RAILWAYS CLASS 1161/1928/AUSTRIA

Twenty-two of these locomotives were built between 1928 and 1940 by the Florisdorf Works, with electrical equipment by AEG. They are representative of the heavy, rigid-frame, jackshaft-transmission yard locomotive that could also be seen, each to its own design, on Swiss and German electrified railways. The 1161 class were strong machines, weighing 123,480lb (56 tonnes), with a top speed of 25mph (40kph) and hourly rating 700kW. Although these locomotives were sturdy and capable of heavy yard work they belonged to a small class that was technically outmoded, so they no longer figure on the Austrian Railways locomotive list.

*A Pennsylvania RR GG1 locomotive leaves Washington with a New York train in the 1950s*

*Pennsylvania Railroad GG1 Class, 1934*

# 1-D-1

## ITALIAN STATE RAILWAYS CLASS E472/1925/ITALY

From 1902 Italy adopted three-phase railway electrification and was a large user. During the 1920s, the normal industrial frequency was 42Hz, and it was decided to try this frequency at 10,000V for a particular electrification. The locomotives were built on the general lines of existing three-phase units, except that the higher frequency led to the motors running faster so that they had to be geared down to jackshafts. The E472 class locomotive of the Italian State Railways was a mountain locomotive, for operation at speeds of 23¼mph, 31mph and 46½mph (37½kph, 50kph and 75kph). Continuous rating was 1,950kW, and the class carried transformers in which the voltage was dropped to 5,800-7,000V. There were 17 of Class E472, all built by Ernesto Breda of Milan, the first 10 being delivered in 1925 and the rest in 1931.

The 1925 batch found no railway to work upon, so they were tried out on part of the Turin-Modane railway, the overhead line being fed with 10,000 volts, 42Hz, as occasion offered. The locomotives could be switched readily to normal 3,700V, 16⅔Hz supply, but then the operating speeds quoted were reduced in the proportion 42:16⅔ (i.e., by about 40 per cent). The railway eastwards from Rome Prenestina was electrified at 10,000V, three-phase 42Hz in 1928, and completed onwards to Sulmona in 1933. This latter section includes a formidable 22¼mile (36km) climb up the mountain-side out of Sulmona, most of it at a gradient of 1 in 33 (3 per cent). The electrification installations and many of the locomotives were wrecked during the fighting in 1944, and re-electrification was at 3,000V dc.

## HUNGARIAN STATE RAILWAYS CLASS V40/1932/HUNGARY

Kálmán Kandó, chief engineer of Ganz Electrical, Budapest, was a pioneer of industrial-frequency electrification. He tried an experimental locomotive from 1923 (V50 class), and finally got it right for what was called 'split-phase electrification'. The technology was used for the Hungarian State Railways' V40 class, 29 of which were built during 1932-34 for a 15,000V, single-phase, 50Hz ac route from Budapest East station to the Austrian border at Hegyeshalom, electrified in 1932-33. These V40 locomotives ('V' here stands for villamos, or electricity) had a phase convertor on board, a stator winding of which took 15,000V to drive the rotor. The stator had also a secondary winding in which the rotor generated 1,200V three-phase current, still at 50Hz. In effect the convertor was a motor and generator run together. Considerable heat was developed by running the convertor, so the stator was cooled by circulating oil. Similarly, water for cooling

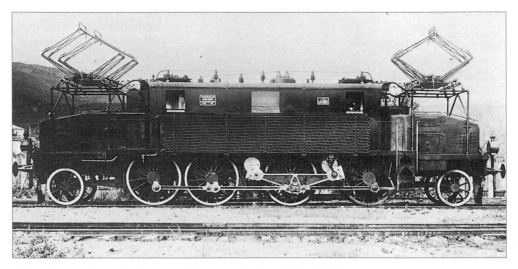

*Italian State Railways E470 Class, which resembled the E472 of 1925.*

was circulated into and out of the revolving rotor, with ingenious seals to prevent leakage.

Switchgear tapped the 1,200V output of the convertor, first as three-phase current for two separate pole groupings of the single large induction traction motor. Other tappings were arranged to take four-phase or six-phase current, each of these currents having their own pole groupings in the traction motor. By these means the V40 locomotive had four running speeds for operation: 15½mph, 31mph, 46½mph and 62mph (25kph, 50kph, 75kph and 100kph). The rotor of the traction motor was coupled to the driving wheels, with the interposition of a triangular frame. The third corner of this frame needed support, so it was coupled on either side of the locomotive to the cranks of a dummy countershaft.

Delayed as it was by the events of World War 1, split-phase electrification was too late. Overall it was cheaper than 16⅔Hz in the overhead contact wire, but rather dearer than the up-and-coming high-voltage dc systems.

# 1-Do-1

## NEW YORK CENTRAL RR S SERIES/1904/USA

By city ordinance, the steam locomotive is prohibited on Manhattan Island, New York, and railways must be electrified. The New York Central and Hudson River Railroad worked into Grand Central Station, and hence inwards from Harmon the railway was electrified at 650V dc. A third rail was used, with collection by the locomotives from the underside. A trial locomotive was built by the General Electric Co., USA, in 1904. The traction motors were gearless; that is, the stator windings were mounted vertically on either side of the rotor, which was carried

directly on the axle. Thus the stator windings could move vertically up and down on the locomotive springs. Traction-motor control was by resistances, and the continuous rating of the locomotive was 1,640kW. A 6-mile (9.6km) section of railway was electrified for test purposes at Schenectady, close to the works of the American Locomotive Co. (Alco). The electric was pitted against the latest Pacific steam-locomotive type running on an adjoining track, and the electric beat steam handsomely. Also, electric engineers learnt about voltage-drop in the third rail when a locomotive drains it of current to haul a heavy train, a useful lesson. Another 34 of the electric locomotives were built in 1905 to start the New York service. These were fitted with jumper cables to allow multiple-unit working, the first locomotives in the world to be so fitted. The locomotives had Bissell trucks at either end, and an incident of derailment was, rightly or wrongly, put down to stiffness in these trucks. During 1907 all 35 locomotives were rebuilt with trucks at either end, assuming the wheel arrangement 2-Do-2, and with a weight increase from 191,835lb to 224,910lb (87 tonnes to 102 tonnes). Another 12 of this revised version were built in 1908.

The class was long-lived. The first one survived until 1965, and in the 1970s there were still a few about, although these had long deserted Grand Central and worked on freight.

## GERMAN STATE RAILWAY (DR) CLASS E16/1926/GERMANY

Because of greater traction-motor weight, German State Railway 15,000V, single-phase, 16⅔Hz ac routes were during the 1920s served almost exclusively by mechanically coupled locomotives. Only for a few low-speed freight locomotives was the nose-suspended traction motor considered possible. The E16 class, built by Krauss, Munich, with electrics by the German Brown Boveri firm in 1926, was an attempt to get away from this

*Hungarian State Railways 'split-phase' V40 Class, 1932*

position in order to allow higher speeds for passenger trains. The 20 locomotives of the class had Büchli transmissions to each driving axle, in which the final drive-sprung gear-wheel was mounted externally outside its driving wheel. The two types of wheel were connected by a system of levers responsive to both traction and spring forces. The locomotive was controlled by low-tension side transformer tap-changers, with the refinement that graduated resistances were provided between the taps. The value of these resistances could be reduced for higher voltage before the next tap-change. Continuous rating of Class E16 was 2,580kW, and for the first time in Germany a maximum speed as high as 75mph (120kph) could be attained. The class performed well, but the Büchli transmission was not used again on the German State Railway.

## GREAT NORTHERN RAILWAY CLASS Z-1/1927/USA

The Great Northern Railway runs a little to the south of the Canadian border, and it was the last of the classic transcontinental routes across the United States, completed throughout in 1893. The line crossed the Sierras through the old Cascade Tunnel, Washington, and the 5.9-mile (9.5km) tunnel section was three-phase electrified in 1909. A new Cascade Tunnel was driven and opened to traffic in 1927, the old tunnel and its electrification being

abandoned the same year. The new tunnel was on an electrified route as well, 11,500V, single-phase, 25Hz ac over the 73 miles (117km) of the Cascade division.

The locomotives provided were of the motor-generator type; that is to say, the incoming current from the overhead contact wire passed through a transformer and was then used to drive a single-phase synchronous electric motor. In turn, this motor drove a dc generator to feed the four nose-suspended traction motors. Regeneration of current in this manner results in power losses, but on the other hand locomotive control is simplified. Instead of contactors taking the full current load, all that had to be provided were resistances to insert into the generator's stator pole circuits. The output of the traction motors depended on the voltage and current output of the generator, which could be varied as needed by putting in or taking out these resistances.

The locomotives had a regenerative brake. After providing an excitation current to the traction motor rotors from a battery, the whole system functioned in reverse. The generator became motor-fed from the traction motors and drove the synchronous motor as a generator in its turn. The current thus generated was fed back through the transformer to the overhead contact wire. There were 10 of these locomotives, each with a continuous rating of 1,880kW, and it was customary to provide two to each train. The electrification and the locomotives were superseded by diesel power in the 1950s.

## AUSTRIAN FEDERAL RAILWAYS CLASS 1670/1928/AUSTRIA

Classes 1570 and 1670 (of which the latter was the most successful and lasted longest) were designed for fast trains. They had rigid frames and the 1670 Class had four driving axles powered by eight vertical motors; thus each axle was independently driven by twin motors. Hourly rating was 2,350kW and maximum speed 62mph (100kph). Weight in working order was 235,935lb (107 tonnes). Control was electro-pneumatic. The units were built from 1928 to 1932 by Krauss at Linz and Simmering-Graz-Pauker at Florisdorf, the last four, built in 1932, being of a slightly improved design and classified as 1670.1. These locomotives formed part of the electrification drive on which the Austrian government had embarked in 1925; following World War 1, Austria had lost her coal-bearing territories and electrification was seen as the best way of dispensing with expensive imported coal.

## GERMAN STATE RAILWAYS CLASS E18/1935/GERMANY

Until the 1920s, 15,000V, single-phase, 16⅔Hz ac locomotives for the German State Railway usually had body-mounted traction motors, perhaps driving a jackshaft. Traction motors tended to be bulky and heavy, hence the body mounting and coupling-rod drive to the wheels. From the 1920s alternative mechanical transmissions were tried

*General Electric 'Little Joe' type, 1948*

out, while at the same time traction motors of reduced bulk and weight were developed. The E18 class, 63 of which were built during 1935-39, were regarded as a particularly elegant solution of the various problems. The traction motors were nose-suspended, and they drove hollow axles. Fingers at the end of the hollow axles engaged cups sprung to the driving wheel spokes, an arrangement known as a Westinghouse-AEG transmission. Algemeine Elektricitäts Gesellschaft (AEG) built all the locomotives, which were controlled by a low-tension transformer tap-changer and had a continuous rating of 3,830kW. The carrying axles and the adjacent driving axles were united in Krauss-Helmholtz trucks, although this did not prove to be entirely satisfactory, and lateral movement of the trucks had to be restricted. The last of the class (by then Class 118) ran on the German Federal Railway in 1983, and one has been preserved.

## 2-Do-1

### SWISS FEDERAL RAILWAYS CLASS Ae4/7/1927/SWITZERLAND

The Ae4/7 was possibly the oldest working electric locomotive design in 1996, when the last units were withdrawn from service. Designed in the 1920s, it made the transition from outside coupling rods to individual axle

drive. The four motors were mounted in the body and their pinions meshed with gearwheels that were outside each driving wheel. The attachment of the gearwheels and driving wheels was flexible, to absorb the natural movements of the driving axles. The outside observer did not see the wheels, which were concealed behind the gearing.

One hundred and twenty-seven of these locomotives were built by the Swiss SLM company, using Brown Boveri, Sécheron, and Oerlikon electrical equipment. Control was by l.t. switchgear, and some of the units had regenerative brakes for Gotthard line service. Such units weighed 271,215lb (123 tonnes) rather than the 260,190lb (118 tonnes) of the other units. Output (hourly) was 2,295kW. Most of them were modernized in the 1960s and 1970s

and they could be seen on most kinds of work, having a maximum speed of 62mph (100kph).

## 1-Do-2

### NEW ZEALAND RAILWAYS SUBURBAN LOCOMOTIVES/1938/NEW ZEALAND

The New Zealand Government Railways electrified the suburban 3ft 6in (1067mm) gauge railways of Wellington in 1938. For general duties on these lines R. and W. Hawthorn, Leslie, and English Electric in 1938 built 10 1,500V dc locomotives. The four traction motors drove

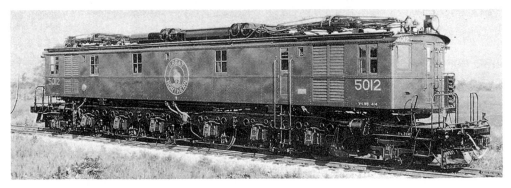

*Great Northern Railway Z-1 Class, 1927*

*Pennsylvania Railroad DD1 Class, 1910*

hollow axles, with a quill drive to the wheels. A resistance bank was used for locomotive control, with electro-pneumatic contactors, together with motor groupings. Only two of the locomotives were fitted with a rheostatic brake. Continuous rating was 900kW. Unfortunately, the long fixed wheelbase made for difficulty on curves, so the class was unpopular.

## 2-Do+Do-2

### GENERAL ELECTRIC 'LITTLE JOE' TYPE/1948/USA

Soviet Railways in 1946 ordered a small batch of twenty 3kV electric locomotives from General Electric. The design was purely American, although the intended gauge was 5ft (1524mm). Halfway through construction the US government, in view of the deteriorating relationship with Soviet Russia, prohibited their shipment. The last six were completed to standard gauge and the others were subsequently re-gaged. In the end, three were converted to 1.5kV for use on the Chicago South Shore and South Bend RR, twelve went to the Chicago, Milwaukee & St Paul RR (which had an electrified section in the Rockies), and five went to the Sao Paulo Railways in Brazil.

Like other US electric locomotives of that era, they were heavy, 535,815lb (243 tonnes), largely because the basis of their design was a very substantial articulated underframe. They had eight GE traction motors, nose-suspended. Continuous power was 3,470kW, equivalent to 4,655hp. Control was rheostatic and there was regenerative braking. Maximum speed was 68mph (110kph). Although the locomotives had a single-unit body,

the frames were in two halves, and in these the nose-suspended traction motors were mounted. The traction motors were resistance-controlled and a regenerative brake was fitted. The locomotives for the Milwaukee Road could work together in multiple, but for the other two lines this was not possible. Two locomotives, each rated at a continuous 3,470kW, if drawing current together would almost certainly have caused the overload circuit breakers to drop out, thereby depriving themselves of power.

## 2-D+D-2

### PENNSYLVANIA RAILROAD CLASS DD1/1910/USA

Before the extensive inter-war electrification of the PRR main line, that Railroad was operating short-distance electric trains at New York and Philadelphia. Trains leaving the Penn Station in New York were not allowed to emit smoke, so the PRR electrified its line as far as Manhattan Transfer, where steam locomotives were attached or detached. For this short section, a number of interesting electric locomotive designs were tried over the years. Perhaps the best of these was the DD1, of which 33 were built. It was a twin-section design, and the chassis followed steam locomotive practice; it was virtually the wheel-sets of two 4-4-0 steam locomotives placed back-to-back. Each of the two sections contained a massive electric motor, weighing 42,000lb (19 tonnes) and delivering 2,000hp, which drove the coupled wheels by jackshaft. Total weight was 313,000lb (142 tonnes) and the hourly rating was about 2,980kW. The 600V dc current was

picked up from the third rail by shoes attached to the leading trucks. Where there could be no third rail (as at switches) current was picked up overhead by a small pantograph. The locomotives were built at the Railroad's own Juniata shops, with the electrical equipment supplied by Westinghouse. Driving wheel diameter at 72in (1828mm) was the same as that of a steam passenger locomotive.

## 0-E-0

### ITALIAN STATE RAILWAYS CLASS E550/1908/ITALY

The port of Genoa is hemmed in by mountains, and to gain access to the port's hinterland a railway was built across the Giovi pass in 1853. This involved an incline 4½ miles (7.25km) long mostly at 1 in 28½ (3.5 per cent), with, at the top, the 2-mile (3.2km) Busalla tunnel at 1 in 33 (3 per cent) throughout. This railway is all there today. By the beginning of the 20th Century the line was a sad bottleneck to railway traffic, despite a relief line nearby. Riccardo Bianchi, the able first general manager of the Italian State Railways, proposed three-phase electrification at 16⅔Hz ac, and the electrified line was opened to traffic in 1910. The E550 class, with a 1,570kW continuous rating, had been built since 1908. They won the nickname 'i piccoli giganti dei Giovi' ('little giants of the Giovi'), for although half the size of the pair of steam locomotives that they replaced a pair of them could work a train up the inclines in 45 per cent less time. What was more, the train-load was much bigger at 440 short-tons (400 tonnes).

The E550 class at 16 2/3Hz had two working speeds, 15½mph and 31mph (25kph and 50kph), the lower speed being in cascade circuitry. In all, 186 of them were built by Westinghouse, Vado Ligure, for mountain work and freight service.

### AUSTRIAN FEDERAL RAILWAYS CLASS 1080/1924/AUSTRIA

This class of 20 units was built by Krauss of Linz in 1924-25. They had three motors, which were axle-hung and drove the central three axles with transmission to all five axles ensured by coupling rod. They tended to suffer from broken rods. Hourly rating was 1,020kW and the weight in working order was 169,785lb (77 tonnes), of which 80,262lb (36.4 tonnes) were attributed to electrical parts and 89,523lb (40.6 tonnes) to the mechanical components). Axle-weight was 33,960lb (15.4 tonnes). Maximum speed was 30mph (50kph), and they had electro-pneumatic control. When built they were intended for freight work and with their five axles had good adhesion. In their final years they were to be found pottering around on secondary lines, representatives of an early generation of electric locomotives.

# ELECTRO-DIESEL LOCOMOTIVES

## Bo-Bo

### BRITISH RAILWAYS CLASS 73/1962/BRITAIN

With much of its mileage electrified on the third-rail system for the benefit of multiple-unit passenger trains, the Southern Region of British Railways had a need for a locomotive that could pull normal passenger stock and deal with freight trains. However, as some sidings were not electrified and it was sometimes necessary to take trains beyond the electrified area, it was decided to introduce a locomotive that could work on the third rail but also off it. Class 73 was designed to work on the third rail normally, in which mode it could develop 1,600hp (1,190kW). For work elsewhere it was provided with a 600hp English Electric diesel engine coupled to an English Electric generator that fed the same traction motors as in full electric regime. There were four axles, and the wheel arrangement was Bo-Bo. Maximum speed was 60mph (96kph) and tractive effort on third rail was 42,000lbs (19,050kgs); on diesel power it was 34,100lbs (15,470kgs). Weight was 167,580lb (76 tonnes). The class was very successful, and 49 were built. It performed a variety of tasks on the Southern Region, and some specially modified units were hauling the 'Gatwick Express' trains in the late 1990s and were allowed a 90mph (145kph) maximum speed. About half of the units carried names.

*Austrian Federal Railways 1080 Class, 1924*

# DIESEL
# LOCOMOTIVES

# Diesel Locomotives

## A1A-A1A

### GENERAL MOTORS TYPE E7/1945/USA

It was in North America that the diesel locomotive first ousted steam, greatly helped by the activities of General Motors. A plant, known as the Electro-Motive Division, for the building of diesel locomotives, was opened at La Grange, Illinois, in 1935. There a diesel engine was built in various sizes, together with standard locomotive types for sale to all railways. Such was the planning that quantity sales were achieved, which in turn cut down the price of each unit.

General Motors produced its E Model passenger locomotive in 1937. It was of 1,800hp (1,341kW) and there were two versions. EA had a cab at one end and EB was cabless. Railroads were expected to couple units together to secure the horsepower they needed, all under the control of one locomotive crew. The locomotives had dc generators and locomotive control was by engine revolutions together with

*One of the earlier General Motors E series used by the Atlantic Coast Line Railroad.*

*General Motors E7 Type, 1945.*

*General Motors E8 Type, 1949.*

series and parallel motor groupings. Only about 25 units were sold until, in 1939, the similar but differently powered E3 appeared. This had the new GM 567 motor, two of which in each unit produced a total of 2,000hp (1,490kW). E4, E5 and E6 variants subsequently appeared, followed by the E7. This model was produced in February 1945 and stayed in production until 1949. With more than 400 A and about 75 B units built in this period, the E7 was the instrument of the first wave of the wholesale dieselization of US long-distance passenger services

### GENERAL MOTORS TYPE E8/1949/USA

With the E8, General Motors introduced the uprated 567 engine, the 567B. This produced 2,250hp (1,676kW), giving the design an enhanced performance compared with the very successful E7, and at 158 short tons (316,000lb) remaining close to the E7 weight. However, when the E8 was followed by the virtually indistinguishable E9, the limits of that engine were effectively reached. The

E9 had the 567C engine, rated at 2,400hp (1,800kW). Over 450 A units of model E8 were sold, plus 35 B units, and with their delivery (together with units sold by GM's competitor Alco) the dieselization of US passenger trains was virtually complete. The E9 was destined to be the last model of the series; henceforth the decline of the passenger train and the arrival of the road-switcher type, which could handle most passenger trains, meant that the General Motors E class had come to the end of a production run that had lasted two decades and numbered well over a thousand units.

### BRITISH RAILWAYS CLASS 31/1957/BRITAIN

British Railways' Class 31 locomotive was of medium power and handled a great variety of trains, including most passenger trains and, as it was fitted for multiple-unit working (most BR mainline diesel locomotives were so fitted), a pair of them could handle, say, an iron-ore train without difficulty. There were 263 locomotives in the class,

built by Brush Electrical Machines from 1957 with a Mirrlees diesel engine. Earlier batches had the engine rated at 1,200hp (895kW); later batches had a rating of 1,365hp (1018kW) or 1,600hp (1193kW). These engines were later replaced by an English Electric 1,470hp (1,096kW) engine. Control was by engine revolutions and by traction motor groupings.

## A1A-Bo

### NEW HAVEN RAILROAD ELECTRO-DIESELS/1955/USA

The City of New York has since 1904 insisted on electric traction for all trains running on the island of Manhattan. To avoid the need for locomotive changes for outer-suburban trains off the island, the New York, New Haven

*British Railways 31 Class, 1957.*

*New Haven Railroad Electro-Diesel FL9 Type, 1955.*

*German Federal Railway V200 Class, 1953.*

and Hartford Railroad ordered electro-diesels from General Motors' Electro-Motive Division. From 1955 over 70 locomotives were supplied; they were later taken over by Amtrak or one of the new commuter railway authorities. To overcome weight distribution problems, the unusual A1A-Bo wheel arrangement was adopted. A 1,750hp (1,305kW) General Motors engine was carried, controlled by engine revolutions and by series or series-parallel traction-motor groupings. On Manhattan the traction motors took current from a 650V dc third rail, with control by locomotive resistances. There was one complication facing the designers: the collector shoes run under the third rail when the locomotives ran into Grand Central Station, whereas to serve the Pennsylvania Station the shoes collected from the top of the third rail.

# B-B

### GERMAN FEDERAL RAILWAY (DB) CLASS V200(220)/1953/GERMANY

After World War 2 and the formation of DB, policy favoured the electrification of the major main lines in the Federal Republic. This left a number of secondary routes needing adequate motive power for fast passenger trains. Accordingly, five prototype diesel-hydraulic locomotives were built by Krauss-Maffei in 1953, during a period when the German Federal was interested in hydraulic transmissions. This was the V200 class (later Class 220), which had two Maybach 1,100hp (820kW) engines, each of which drove one of the bogies through a Mekydro hydromechanical transmission and cardan shafts.

*A British Warship Class locomotive, developed from the German V200.*

After running experience, another 50 Class 220 locomotives were built in 1956, this time with Voith hydraulic transmissions, and yet another 50 in 1962, the latter differing in detail and being known as Class 221. By 1984, Class 220 was being withdrawn and by 1986 it had gone from the German Federal Railway.

However, the class did not vanish entirely, for some of the locomotives were sold to Italy. There they were to be seen pottering along the Suzzara-Ferrara Railway, or on the Padane Railway's lone branch line. It was the German Federal Class 220 that served as a model for British Railway's 42 Class B-B diesel-hydraulic locomotives of 1960.

*Austrian Federal Railways 2095 Class, 1958.*

## AUSTRIAN FEDERAL RAILWAYS 2095 CLASS/1958/AUSTRIA

The past half-century has been one of decline for narrow-gauge railways, so the introduction of new locomotive designs for such lines has been quite rare, except in a few countries like India and Austria, where these small lines were expected to remain in service for several decades. Austria in the late 1990s still had over 185 miles (300km) of 2ft 6in (760mm) gauge lines, divided between several areas, and in 1958 had introduced the 2095 Class of diesel-hydraulic B-B locomotives, built by the Austrian company Simmering-Graz-Pauker. For a weight of only 70,528lb (32 Tonnes) this class has a high-speed (1,500rpm) engine of 590hp (440kW), driving through a Voith transmission. The first unit appeared in 1958 from the builder's Vienna works and then, in 1960-62, 14 more were turned out by the Florisdorf plant of the same company. An unusual feature of this design are the outside coupling rods.

## BRITISH RAILWAYS CLASS 42/1958/BRITAIN

Including the very similar Class 43, 71 of these diesel-hydraulic locomotives were built for, and at the instigation

*British Railways 42 Class, 1958.*

of, the Western Region of Briish Railways. They were named, and known as the 'Warship' class. They were based on German technology and had a very high power/weight ratio, compared with the more conventional diesel-electric designs of BR. Class 42 units had two Maybach 2,200hp engines driving through Mekydro hydraulic transmissions (Class 43 had MAN engines and Voith transmissions). Tractive effort was 52,400lb (23,790kg) and weight was 174,160lb (79 tonnes). In service the locomotives performed well with the better passenger trains, but maintenance costs were quite high. This was partly because the British style of driving placed great stress on the mechanisms (hydraulic transmissions had not previously been used for such high powers). The power/weight ratio that looked so good alongside comparable British diesel-electrics looked less good when British manufacturers managed to produce diesel-electrics that were not grossly overweight. Add to this the fact that the Western Region of BR was a relic of the Great Western Railway, whose doings had always been regarded with suspicion by administrators of other lines, and it is not surprising that the diesel-hydraulic locomotives of the WR

had short lives. In retrospect, however, their maintenance costs and the fact that they required non-standard procedures did probably justify their early withdrawal. Class 42 had disappeared by 1972, although two units were preserved in working order.

## INDONESIAN STATE RAILWAY CLASS BB301/1962/INDONESIA

Indonesian railways began to dieselize almost as soon as the state became re-established after world war and civil war. Importing locomotives both from the USA and Germany, the administration seemed equally willing to accept diesel-electric transmissions from the Americans and hydraulic transmissions from the Germans. Class 301 is a German design, supplied by Henschel and using a MTU 652 engine delivering 1,492hp (1,120kW). The locomotive weighs 114,610lb (52 tonnes) and its maximum speed is 75mph (120kph), although it has had little opportunity in practice of reaching it; in the 1930s the Dutch East Indian Railway had some very fast steam-hauled trains and actually held some speed records for

the 3ft 6in (1,067mm) gauge, but circumstances did not permit a return to record-breaking in the 1960s. However, when new the 301 Class were the most powerful diesel locomotives on the line and were entrusted with the best trains serving Djakarta. Some have been re-engined for a longer life.

## FRENCH RAILWAYS 67000 CLASS/1963/FRANCE

The dieselization of French Railways was a more cautious process than in other countries. As electrification proceeded in the 1950s and 1960s, the youngest steam locomotives were retained for service over non-electrified lines. The first large-scale dieselization occurred from the late 1950s with the series production of fairly low-power (450kW and 830kW) units, but it was not until 1963 that a design appeared that was capable of replacing large steam locomotives. This was the 67000 Class, whose SEMT-Pielstick 16PA4 engine produced 1,930hp (1,440kW). This was on a weight in working order of 176,320lb (80 tonnes). Maximum speed was 56mph or

*Indonesian State Railway BB301 Class, 1962.*

*French Railways 67000 Class, 1963.*

87mph (90kph or 140kph, depending on the gear ratio). The builders were Brissonneau et Lotz, Chantiers de l'Atlantique, and Compagnie Matériel et Traction Electrique. One hundred and two units were built, to be followed by the very similar (but with 3-phase transmission) 67300 Class.

## GERMAN FEDERAL RAILWAYS CLASS 218/1971/GERMANY

After the V220 had been in production for some years the German Railways turned to a second generation of mainline diesel-hydraulic locomotives, this time with one engine rather than two. The pre-production units of Class 216 appeared in 1960, to be followed by production units in 1964. This design, like its predecessor, was a B-B design but weighed slightly more while delivering slightly less power 1,900hp (1,416kW). An improved Class, 217, followed, but the final Class in this series, Class 218, was more powerful, having a 2,500hp (1,863kW) engine. Twelve pre-production units were built by Krupp in 1968 and the construction of almost 400 production units began in 1971. They were to be seen in many roles, and sometimes were used as twin multiple-units on difficult passenger services. Weight in working order 176,320lb (80 tonnes).

## CHINESE RAILWAYS CLASS DFH3/1975/CHINA

In the first years of dieselization the Chinese Railways favoured the diesel-hydraulic transmission, and the DFH series showed both Russian and German influence.

*German Federal Railways 218 Class, 1971.*

*Chinese Railways DFH3 Class, 1975.*

The predecessor of this class was the DFH1, whose two engines were very similar to German Maybach engines and their transmission was clearly based on the Voith model. The DFH3, although a development of the DFH1, had cabs at each end and externally resembled a German rather than a Russian design. It had two engines, each producing 1,340hp (1,000kW) at 1,500rpm. Like most diesel-hydraulic locomotives, it had a good power/weight ratio, weighing only 185,000lb (84 tonnes), giving an axle-load of 46,250lb (21 tonnes). The maximum speed was 75mph (120kph). It was built at the Qingdao Works; the precise year of introduction is unclear, but 1975 seems probable.

# 0-B-0

## STUART ACKROYD'S OIL ENGINE/1896/GREAT BRITAIN

For the three decades before 1914, the British War Office was very receptive to new ideas, among them Herbert Stuart Ackroyd's new-fangled oil engine. Woolwich Arsenal, outside London, had an industrial network of 1ft 6in (457mm) gauge lines. For this system, Richard Hornsby and Son of Grantham built a Stuart Ackroyd oil-engine locomotive in 1896. This had a single cylinder that developed 9½hp (7kW),

and a mechanical drive through a gearbox to the wheels. As there was only one cylinder, a flywheel had to be incorporated into the drive. Four more were delivered to Woolwich Arsenal during the period 1900-04, this time with a leading pony truck but otherwise similar. The last Hornsby locomotive went to the military in 1904 for use on the 2ft 6in (762mm) gauge Chattenden and Upnor Railway outside Chatham. This locomotive was larger, with the C-C wheel arrangement, but still with a single cylinder giving 20hp (15kW). The locomotives worked well enough, although rather undersized and very difficult to start up on a cold morning.

*General Motors NW1 Type, 1937.*

# Bo-Bo

### JERSEY CENTRAL LINES NO 1000/1924/USA

General Electric (USA) naturally had news from Europe of the efforts being made to adapt the diesel engine for rail traction service after World War 1. The firm set to work, and produced a satisfactory diesel-electric shunting locomotive at the first attempt. They used an Ingersoll Rand 300hp (224kW) engine which generated current for four nose-suspended traction motors. Control was by engine revolutions and by motor groupings. With the American Locomotive Co. (Alco) responsible for the mechanical side, 26 of these locomotives were produced during 1924-28, being sold to various railways and to industry. Jersey Central Lines had the very first one of 1924 as its No 1000, and this gave good service for 30 years or more. Today this pioneer is in the National Museum of Transport, St Louis, Missouri.

### NOS 2-2DE1 AND 2-2DE2/1924/TUNISIA

After the defeat of Carthage, Tunisia was the granary of the Roman Empire. However, the farmers cut down the trees, rainfall slackened, and today the Sahara Desert is encroaching from the south. From the railway point of view an additional difficulty is the limestone terrain, which means that the water available is very hard and locomotive boilers soon scale up. This was just the place for the diesel locomotive, and indeed the world's first exported diesel was for the 3ft 3⅜in (1000mm) gauge Tunisian Railways. It was built by two constituent firms of the Swedish Allmänna Svenska Elektriska Aktiebogalat, one of which supplied the Atlas diesel engine. According to the makers this engine was rated at 200hp (149kW), but the railway preferred to quote 120hp (89.5kW). It drove a dc generator, the revolutions of which, together with motor grouping, controlled the four nose-suspended traction motors.
This locomotive was No.2-2DE1, and it worked out of Tunis down a since-closed minor branch line to La Laverie. In

1926 it was joined by 2-2DE2 with a 250hp (189kW) Sulzer engine; this appears to be the first diesel supplied by Sulzer to go in a locomotive, if Dr Diesel's failed direct-drive locomotive of 1912 is excepted. The second locomotive, built by Cie de Construction Mécanique in France, went on suburban trains to Hammam Lif. Both locomotives were withdrawn from traffic in 1940 because of wartime fuel shortages, and they lay at the Tunisian Railways' Sidi Fathallah locomotive works until 1945. Noumber 2-2DE1 was then broken up, but 2-2DE2 was revived to work on her accustomed duties until final withdrawal in 1962.

### GENERAL MOTORS TYPE NW1/1937/USA

Most railways, and not only those in North America, were quick to acknowledge the superiority of diesel over steam yard locomotives. The intermittent nature of the work, the

*General Electric 44-tonner, 1940.*

need for steam switchers to take fuel or water, often just as activity was about to liven up, were among the reasons why diesels were preferred as soon as viable designs became available, even though the hoped-for reduction of yard locomotive crews to one man did not come about. General Motors produced a pair of 600hp (447kW) switchers in 1935 for the Lackawanna RR. Later the same year, by increasing the cylinders of the 201-A engine from 8 to 12, it produced a 900hp (738kW) switcher. Similar models, classified NC, followed to 1937, when the generally similar NW models appeared. NW1 model had GE motors and generator but the same 201-A engine. It was the first to reach double-digit sales figures and was in production up to 1939. The NW2 followed, but it was only the advent of the new 567 engine, making possible the 1,000hp (745kW) SW1, that enabled GM to reach production figures in the hundreds.

## GENERAL ELECTRIC 44-TONNER/1940/USA

An agreement aimed at preserving firemen's jobs was gained by the locomotive men's brotherhoods in 1937. This established that firemen would continue to be employed on locomotives even if the locomotives did not have a fire to be tended. The only concession was that locomotives weighing less than 90,000lbs on their driving wheels were excepted from this agreement. Hence locomotive builders began to produce yard and short-line

*Alco RS-1 Type, 1941. This is the 6-axle variant sent to the USSR.*

diesels of 45 tons (42 tonnes) or less. The GE 44-tonner was one of the most widespread of these. Apart from over 300 supplied to mainline railroads, many others were bought by industry and known as 45-tonners. The 44-tonner had a central cab and two Caterpillar V8 engines producing a total of 380hp (283kW), with a traction motor for each axle and double-reduction gear drive. The 44-tonner was distinguishable from the industrial 45-tonner by the absence of end platforms for yard men.

## ALCO TYPE RS-1/1941/USA

Because it did not have an engine equivalent to those of main-line locomotives, Alco's 1,000hp (745kW) RS-1 was not a true road-switcher, but it was certainly the inspiration for the post-war road-switchers made by Alco with so much success after World War 2. The RS-1 was simply a lengthened switcher with a short 'hood' behind the cab accommodating a steam generator (for heating passenger trains), and with the trucks capable of running at mainline speeds. During World War 2 the military requisitioned existing RS-1 units and ordered others from Alco. All were then fitted with six-motor trucks, transforming them from Bo-Bo to Co-Co units, before being shipped to Russia to help the Soviet railways deal with wartime demands. On Soviet Railways they were known as Type Da (Diesel-Alco) and put in good service, some surviving into the 1980s. Others went to Alaska and Iran. Production for civilian use re-started in 1943 and by 1957 over 600 had been built, with another 60 or so going to Mexico. They formed the basis both of the Soviet TE1-20 postwar diesel design and Alco's successful RS series of road switchers.

## `WHITCOMB DIESELS'/1942/ BRITAIN

World War 2 called for diverse railways to carry traffic far in excess of their designed capacity. The various armies put in orders for locomotives to cope with the extra traffic that they created. Among these were the locomotives known familiarly at the time as the 'Whitcomb Diesels'. The Baldwin Locomotive Co. took the order from the British Army, and contracted out the actual building to the Whitcomb Locomotive Co., with an engine from Buda and electrics from Westinghouse. Each locomotive had two Buda diesel engines, rated together at 650hp (485kW), one each under two hoods that extended either side of a central cab. The traction motors were nose-suspended in the bogies, and controlled by engine revolutions.
A total of 79 out of the first two batches of 52 and 60 built in 1942 went to the British Army, and served in Egypt, Palestine and Syria. From 1944 the type appeared in Italy (49 out of 79 went there). In Italy the locomotives came under the control of the US Army, which after the fighting finished handed them over to the Italian State Railways, at which point they became the Ne I20 class.
In the hands of the military the Buda engines had been shown to be unsatisfactory. The Italians had watched the Americans wrestling with cracked cylinder heads and so

*US Army Whitcomb Diesel, 1942.*

on, so the first thing the Italian State Railways did was to rip out the Buda engines and replace them with Fiats. Later, between 1966 and 1974, a single OM-Saurer engine and a new generator were substituted and the Class D143 allotted. All Class D143s were still running in the mid-1980s, the original Westinghouse traction motors soldiering on satisfactorily.
The US Army had other batches of these locomotives, some of which served in Italy in 1944-45. These were returned to the United States and saw subsequent action in the Korean War.

## RUSSIAN RAILWAYS TE2 CLASS/1948/RUSSIA

After the prototypes had been thoroughly tested, this class went into series production in 1950 at the Kharkov Works and when superceded in 1955 numbered over 500 twin-units. It was a direct descendant of the wartime Alco units but had a 1,000hp (736kW or 745kW, depending on the factor used) Penza engine in each section. The two units were permanently coupled so total power was 2,000hp or 1,472kW. Weight was 182,940lb (83 tonnes) for each section and maximum speed 58mph (93kph). Early units were sent to the arid region of Central Asia and other units handled the heavy freight traffic of the Moscow Belt Railway. Some were transferred to the Mongolian State Railway, and probably outlived the others, although the whole class seems to have disappeared by the mid-1990s.

## GENERAL MOTORS TYPE GP-7/1949/USA

Responding to Alco's success with the road-switcher concept, GM produced in 1949 its first General Purpose

(GP or, sometimes, 'Geep') locomotive which, despite its name, was really a road-switcher on the Alco pattern but with different components and some refinements. In particular, the engine of this GP-7 model was the 567B, superior to Alco's engine and giving, with its 16-cylinder configuration, 1,500hp (1,117kW). Three demonstrators showed good results in 1949 and series production began in 1950. The locomotive was immediately successful, and when production ceased in 1953 over 2,700 had been built. Its successor was very similar but had the engine uprated from 1,500hp to 1,750hp (1,304kW). During its construction run various changes were incorporated. The early units had an over-simple control scheme, resulting in the engine unloading at the faster speeds. This was soon corrected with the addition of transition equipment and motor-shunting. A number of features adopted for this design became standard hallmarks of subsequent models. The slanting corners of the nose were designed to enable the locomotive number housing to be streamlined while remaining visible from both the front and side. The air reservoirs for the train brake were shifted from beneath the frames to the roof, taking the form of small-diameter cylinders.

## GENERAL MOTORS TYPE SW8/1950/USA

When World War 2 ended there was a pent-up demand for diesel switchers in the USA and General Motors initially offered 600hp (447kW) and 1,000hp (745kW) models. Then, to fill in the range, the SW8 was introduced in 1950 and remained in production until 1953. It was of 800hp (596kW) and had an 8-cylinder version of GM's 567 engine. Over 300 were supplied to US railroads and more than 60 to Canada.

*Soviet Railways TE2 Class, 1948.*

*General Motors GP-7 Type, 1949 (the GP-7 is the locomotive in Chicago & North Western yellow livery).*

*General Motors SW8 Type, 1950.*

*Alco RS-3 Type, 1950.*

*Fairbanks Morse CFA-16-4 Type, 1950.*

## ALCO TYPE RS-3/1950/USA

The predecessor of the RS-3 was the RS-2, which used the rather indifferent 244 engine to produce in 1946 a 1,500hp (1,117kW) general-duty unit whose all-round usefulness was not appreciated at first. These early road-switchers were bought for secondary services, with their eternal need for locomotives that could tackle anything from local passenger to yard switching. It was when the Delaware & Hudson RR dieselized in 1950 without buying any so-called 'road' locomotives that the suitability of the road-switcher for mainline work was really appreciated. This change of attitude coincided with the introduction of the RS-3, which used the same 244 engine up-rated to 1,600hp (1,192kW). While the RS-2 had sold a creditable 400-odd units, the RS-3 would surpass this with over 1,500 units sold in the USA, with others going to Canada. With its distinctive rounded nose, the RS-3 was a familiar, maybe classic, locomotive on most North American railroads.

## ALCO TYPE FPA-2/1950/USA

Despite its lead with the road-switcher, Alco fell well behind General Motors in the sale of diesel locomotives in the post-war era. Partly this was because it was reluctant to abandon the steam locomotive business, and partly because its locomotives never seemed quite as good as

its competitor's. One disadvantage was that the Alco engine, the 244, had been designed in a hurry and successive upratings only made it more susceptible to breakdowns. Eventually the engine was improved, and by the time it was fitted into the FA-2 series of streamlined freight and passenger units it was relatively trouble-free. The FPA-2 model was the passenger version of the freight FA-2. The two models were built from 1950 to 1953 and totalled about 460 units, with others going to Canada and Mexico, with about 250 in addition being turned out as 'booster,' or B units. The Canadian units were assembled at the Montreal Locomotive Works. Their 12-cylinder 244 engines by this time produced 1,600hp (1,192kW) rather than 1,500hp (1,117kW).

## FAIRBANKS MORSE TYPE CFA-16-4/1950/USA

The Fairbanks Morse opposed-piston diesel engine was designed for submarines and in World War 2 won a gleaming reputation. However, the decision of its manufacturers to build diesel locomotives around it ultimately failed, largely because railway conditions are very different from naval. With fewer moving parts than conventional diesels, and mounted in a strong in-line configuration (superior to the stress-generating V-

arrangement of other manufacturers), the FM engine should have had reduced maintenance costs. But frequent crankshaft failures, especially of the bearings, and the handicap that repairs to the cylinders required the removal of the upper crankshaft, meant that on average maintenance costs were much higher than with competitors' products.

The 1,600hp (1,192kW) CFA-16-4 had been preceded by bigger FM locomotives known as the 'Eries' because they had been assembled in General Electric's Erie Works, GE being the supplier of electrical equipment. Only about a hundred of these had been sold. The CFA-16-4 did even worse and its successor the CFA-20-4, with 10 cylinders in place of 8, sold less than 20 units. Much of the problem lay in the electrical gear, built on this occasion by Westinghouse, and crankshaft failures. But FM was well on the way to mastering these problems. Its biggest innovation was aluminium ball bearings, which were greatly superior to steel, and counterweighted crankshafts. Later, FM would pioneer the concept of exchangeable components; if a heavy repair was needed the whole engine was replaced by a new one. Like several other FM products, the CFA-16-4 was marketed at the wrong time and was in production only from 1950 to 1953. It arrived on the scene just when American railroads were turning away from the road locomotive as pioneered by GM, with its streamlined all-over cab, in favor of the road-switcher concept. This was a pity, because the design had great potential and in many ways was in advance of its competitors.

## FAIRBANKS MORSE TYPE H-16-44/1950/USA

Fairbanks Morse entered the road-switcher market in 1947 with the H-15-44, a 1,500hp (1,117kW) unit equipped with the 8-cylinder FM opposed-piston engine. Only about 30 examples were sold, due largely to high maintenance costs. Pistons, in particular, wore out quicky and replacing them, or the cylinder liners, was a major operation. The next model was the H-16-44, with the engine uprated to 1600hp. This was marketed from 1950 to 1963, when

FM effectively left the railroad business. For FM designs, the H-16-44 did well, with about 300 units being sold in the USA and others in Canada and Mexico. During its production run FM marketed a much more remarkable road-switcher, the Trainmaster, which was the first of the high-horsepower road-switchers, being of 2,400hp (1,788kW). It did well on trials and alarmed its competitors, but partly because of FM's poor reputation in terms of running costs it was sold only to the extent of about 100 units in the USA and a handful in Canada.

## GENERAL MOTORS TYPE SW1200/1954/USA

In the years 1950-1952 US Class 1 railroads acquired more than 3,000 diesel units a year, on average. GM's

Electro-Motive Division was so busy that manufacture of diesel switchers was moved to a new factory at Cleveland. More than 700 of the 1,200hp (894kW) SW9 switcher were made around that period. In 1954, although GM switchers would continue to resemble the pre-war models externally, there was a major re-design which ensured that all models would use as many standard components as possible, including the new 567C engine. The SW1200 was the replacement under this programme for the SW9. Like the latter, it was of 1,200hp although the 567C was an improved version of the SW9's 567B. Despite the fact that the SW1200 came on the scene after the peak years for yard dieselization, about 450 units were sold to US railroads and over 300 to Canadian, by the end of 1966.

*General Motors SW1200 Type, 1954.*

*Montreal Locomotive Works (Alco) RS-18 Type, 1956.*

### GENERAL MOTORS TYPE FP9/USA/1954

The GM mainline freight 'cab' locomotives were of the 1,350hp (1,006kW) FT model up to 1945. Then came the somewhat similar F2, followed by the F3 in 1946, which had a 1,500hp (1,117kW) engine. The F3 and its successors the F7 and F9 were built to the extent of about 5,000 units and were the main instruments of American dieselization. The passenger FP7 (1,500hp, 1949) and

FP9 (1,750hp [1,304kW] 1954) were variants of the F7 and F9, slightly longer to accommodate the train-heating steam generator. Although nearly 200 units of the FP7 type were built by US railroads, the FP9 was virtually an export model, none being sold new in the USA but more than 50 being bought by Canadian National Railways and another 25 by Mexican railways. Production ended in 1959, but some of the CNR units survived long enough to

enter the service of VIA, the Canadian passenger train company.

### MLW (ALCO) TYPE RS-18/1956/CANADA

In the Alco RS-11 model road-switcher, the new 1,600hp (1,192kW) 251 type engine produced lower running costs, especially on the maintenance side. Together with the externally identical RS-36 (which differed only in its transistorized control), 280 units were sold in the USA and almost 100 in Mexico. The RS-18 model was the Canadian version of the RS-11, built by the Alco associate Montreal Locomotive Works, and about 335 units were acquired by Canadian railways. However, the RS-11 and RS-18 were overtaken by the 'horsepower race.' With steam replacement over, the locomotive builders could only gain new orders by offering replacements for the first-generation diesels, and the bait offered was higher horsepower units and the promise that two new locomotives could replace three of the first generation. As a first step Alco up-rated the 251 engine to 2,000hp (1,472kW), and placed it in the C-20, or 'Century' locomotive. This, despite the publicity, was simply a more powerful version of the RS-11 and RS-18.

### ALCO TYPE FPA-4/1958/USA

By 1956 Alco was ready to abandon its 244 engine which, although vastly improved over the years, was more expensive to run than the competing GM 567 engine.

*Alco FPA-4 Type, 1958.*

*Yugoslav Railways 642 Class, 1960.*

Alco's new engine, the 251, had been carefully worked out and had been tried from 1953 in several small locomotives. The Company decided to offer its existing F series streamlined locomotives with the new engine, but the only buyers were in Canada, where 36 A units and 14 B units were delivered in 1958-59. The new engine produced 1,800hp (1,341kW), an increase of 300hp over the previous model and useful for the heavy trains with quite frequent stops that the Canadian National was operating between Montreal and Halifax. The units lasted well, and some have survived to fall into VIA ownership.

## YUGOSLAV RAILWAYS 642 CLASS/1960/YUGOSLAVIA

In countries where road transport is well developed, or over-developed, lightly-laid, light-traffic railways have disappeared and with them the need for small diesel locomotives. But there are still parts of Europe where the low horsepower, low-weight locomotive is very necessary. One of these locomotives is the Class 642 built for Yugoslav Railways in the 1960s. Weighing only 141,060lb (64 tonnes) and with a 810hp (606kW) engine supplied by MGO, it was built in the Croatian workshops of Duro Dakovic. It was entrusted with much branchline work, where its maximum speed of 50mph (80kph) was no handicap. With the break-up of Yugoslavia about 30 remained with Yugoslav Railways while about the same number (reclassified as 2041 Class) served the Croatian State Railway.

*General Electric U25B Type, 1960.*

*British Railways 25 Class, 1961.*

### GENERAL ELECTRIC TYPE U25B/1960/USA

General Electric had been supplying generators and traction motors for Alco diesels in a joint programme until the 1950s, when the Company decided to produce its own range of mainline diesel locomotives. For years it had been building small switchers on its own account. Breaking into a market already dominated by two manufacturers was not easy (GE continued to supply Alco with electrical equipment even after Alco had become a competitor), but with its U25B road-switcher this was achieved; within a few years Alco had left the scene and GE sales outnumbered those of the previous dominant builder GM. The U25B was built around a Cooper-Bessemer FDL 2,500hp (1,863kW) engine, making it a high-horsepower locomotive at the time it was marketed, and this superiority, plus simplicity and GE's existing reputation on the electrical side helped the GE salesmen succeed in winning a place for the new entrant. In effect, the U25B began the first 'horsepower race' of the 1960s. About 480 U25B units

were sold, and the model remained in production until 1966. Conrail, with 176 units, was the best customer. A six-motor version, the U25C, sold to the extent of about 110 units.

### BRITISH RAILWAYS CLASS 25/1961/BRITAIN

More than 300 of these locomotives were built, mainly in BR workshops but some by the Beyer, Peacock company. They were mixed-traffic machines, with a gear ratio of 67.18. They were of medium power and followed the Class 24, which was very similar but with a lower-powered engine. The Class 25 engine was the Sulzer 6LDA28B of 1,250hp (932kW). The electrical equipment differed from batch to batch, resulting in four sub-classes and, for all but the earliest units, a higher maximum speed of 90mph (145kph). Tractive effort was 45,000lb (20,385kg). The earlier units weighed 72 tonnes but later units, built 1963-67, weighed 167,504lb (76 tonnes). In common with most

BR diesels, train-heating boilers were fitted at first, but this was abandoned in locomotives built after 1965. Like Class 24, Class 25 was introduced to handle secondary passenger and freight services and when BR began to curtail these services there was not much work for them. Withdrawals from service began in the late 1970s, although some units survived past the mid-1980s.

### BELGIAN NATIONAL RAILWAYS 62 CLASS/1961/BELGIUM

One hundred and thirty-one units of this medium-power diesel-electric design were built for Belgian Railways by the local BN Company, and most were still in service in the late 1990s. The engine, as usual for Belgian diesel locomotives of this period, was the GM 567, but transmission was manufactured by the Belgian ACEC concern using GM designs. Output was 1,425hp (1,068kW) and locomotive weight 176,300lb (80 tonnes).

Continuous tractive effort was 24,250lb (11,000kg) and maximum was 47,600lb (21,600kg). Maximum permitted speed was 75mph (120kph). This was by far the most numerous of Belgian mainline diesel locomotives and this was because the type was relatively trouble-free, became available when dieselization was gaining tempo, and was suitable for a wide range of duties. Interestingly, the class that succeeded it, the 85-strong 60 Class, used an engine by a different US maker, Baldwin, whose diesel offerings on the US market had been far less successful than GM's.

## GENERAL MOTORS TYPE GP-30/1963/USA

The GP-30, while based on preceding GP models, was visibly different from its predecessors. It had a top casing stretching from the cab, along the roof, halfway along the hood. In this casing were the resistors for the dynamic brake system and parts of the centralized air system. Even units without dynamic brakes had the skyline casing (purchasers had the option; the New York Central, among

*General Motors GP-35 Type, 1963.*

*General Motors GP-30 Type, 1963.*

*General Motors (EMD) GP-38 Type, 1966.*

others, preferred to omit dynamic brakes). Most were built with low noses, although the Norfolk & Western and the Southern railways chose to retain high noses. About 900 units were built, including some cablcss 'B' units for use as booster units. A few examples were built as trade-ins for railroads handing in old Alco units, and these GP-30 units were distinguished by Alco trucks. The 567D3 engine was turbocharged, and with its 16 cylinders produced 2,250hp (1,676kW).

## GENERAL MOTORS TYPE GP-35/1963/USA

A final upgrading of the well-tried 567 engine, the 567D3, allowed a new model, the GP-35, to replace the GP-30. Whereas the latter could offer 2,250hp (1,676kW) the GP-35 could produce 2,500hp (1,863kW). In this model the skyline casing of the GP-30 was abandoned, giving the locomotive a more purposeful look. The presence of dynamic brakes was indicated by the dynamic brake blisters on each side of the roof (not all railroads ordered these brakes). Over 1,200 of these units were sold, but the design marked the end of an era, for the 567 engine was at the end of its development and could be stretched

no farther; it had begun as a 16-cylinder 1,350hp (1,006kW) engine and finally arrived at a 16-cylinder 2,500hp (1,863kW) version.

## EMD (GENERAL MOTORS) TYPE GP-38/1966/USA

About the time of the GP-38 debut, General Motors was divesting itself of its Electromotive Division (EMD) at the behest of the government's Antitrust Division. With EMD as a separate concern, GM locomotives were henceforth referred to as EMD locomotives.

With road-switchers growing in power, 2,500hp units being on offer and 3,000hp within sight, manufacturers decided that a market existed for medium-power road switchers, and the 2,000hp (1,472kW) EMD GP-38 was the first of the General Motors line to be marketed on this basis. Moreover, it was powered by GM's new engine, the 645. To reduce maintenance costs, turbocharging was not included; turbochargers could increase power output but a railroad wanting higher power would not opt for a medium-power road-switcher anyway, the argument went. In fact, EMD did offer a turbocharged version of the GP-

38, the GP-39, but there were few takers. The GP-38 was in production from 1966 to 1971 and sold about 500 units in the USA, Canada, and Mexico.

## GENERAL MOTORS TYPE GP-10/1967/USA

General Motors' pioneer and very successful GP-7 road-switcher was followed by an improved version, the GP-9. This had an uprated 567 engine, allowing a 1,750hp (1,304kW) output. This model was even more successful than the GP-7, with over 3,000 units being built for the US market alone. Production was from 1954 to 1959, and the successor model, GP-18, was again very similar, although with a minor uprating of the engine by 50hp. During the production run of the GP-9 the cut-down short nose came into fashion, and some units had high, and some low, noses. The original purpose of the high nose had been to provide space for a train-heating steam generator, but with the demise of passenger services this became unnecessary.

In the 1960s the earlier GP-9 (and GP-7) locomotives were past middle-age, and an Internal Revenue concession involving capital rebuild programmes enabled railroads to

*General Motors (EMD) GP-38-2, 1972.*

*General Motors (EMD) GP-10 Type, 1967. This is the Illinois Central RR variant.*

*General Motors (EMD) F40PH Type, 1976.*

treat rebuilt locomotives as new investments (the railroad was thereby allowed to spread depreciation costs over the additional years of the unit's life). The main condition was that the cost of rebuilding was to be at least half the cost of the locomotive when first bought. Devising rebuilding programmes thereby became something of an art, and the Illinois Central RR went into this business in a big way, rebuilding not only its own units but also those of other railroads. A new or reconditioned engine, re-wiring, brake upgrading, central air filtration, and retention toilets were typical features of such programmes. In principle, rebuilt G-9 units became GP-10, and rebuilt GP-7 units became GP-8, but there were reversals of this principle, the two models being so similar. The Illinois Central's GP-10 had a 1,800hp (1,341kW) 567 engine, but when the Burlington Northern RR set about creating its own GP-10 units, it found it possible to fit GM's later engine, the 645.

### EMD (GENERAL MOTORS) TYPE GP-38-2/1972/USA

In 1972 the GP-38-2 appeared. This looked like the GP-38 yet was radically diferent. Firstly, it had an ac alternator in place of the dc generator, and its control system was based on modular electronics. The GP-38-2 was immediately popular, partly because its immediate predecessor the GP-38 had won a good reputation for low maintenance costs. A turbocharged variant, the GP-39-2, was sold to some railroads, like the Santa F,, working at high altitudes, where non-turbocharged engines were at a serious disadvantage.

### EMD (GENERAL MOTORS) TYPE F40PH/1976/USA

Amtrak ordered this design for hauling short-distance and commuter trains that were electrically heated by a locomotive-mounted alternator. However, when Amtrak's new locomotives for long-distance service (EMD SDP40F type) had to be withdrawn because of persistent derailment problems, Amtrak traded them in for additional F40PH units. To handle the long-distance trains, these extra units needed bigger fuel tanks and a more powerful alternator. Thus two variants were in service, visually distinguishable by the size of their fuel tanks. The 645E engine originally delivered 3,000hp (2,235kW), but this was subsequently uprated to 3,200hp (2,384kW) in later units. Apart from Amtrak, regional transit authorities also ordered these locomotives, Chicago being the first. First built in 1976, by 1998 many had been withdrawn, some being converted to control-cab units for push-pull commuter trains. New streamline-style EMD F59PH units of similar power were acquired from 1997 and to a large extent have replaced the F40PH.

*Fairbanks Morse H16-44 Type, 1950.*

*Czechoslovak State Railway T466 Class, 1977.*

*General Motors (EMD) GP-60 Type, 1984.*

### CZECHOSLOVAK STATE RAILWAY T466 CLASS/1977/CZECHOSLOVAKIA

This type was subsequently reclassified as Class 742 and on the demise of the Czechoslovak Republic about 80 units were allocated to the new Slovak Railways and about 350 to Czech Railways. Czechoslovakia had a longstanding locomotive industry and when these locomotives were built it was simultaneously exporting locomotives. The big state engineering concern CKD not only built the locomotives but also provided the engines and transmission. The engine produced 1,180hp (883kW) and the locomotive weighed only 141,060lb (64 tonnes) giving an axle-load of only 35,260lb (16 tonnes), thereby allowing a wide route availability. The type became the biggest class in Czechoslovakia, and in the late 1990s it still held that position in the Czech Republic.

### ITALIAN STATE RAILWAYS CLASS D145/1983/ITALY

The Italian State Railways needed a locomotive with a good starting effort to cover heavy-shunting duties, trip working, and local freight and passenger trains. This requirement has been met by 30 diesel current-inverter locomotives with three-phase traction motors. The type has been built in two batches. Ten came from Fiat Savigliano from 1983, with two Fiat-Iveco 500hp (373kW) engines and Parizzi current inverters; these form the D145.1 class. The other 20 came from Tecnomasio Italiano Brown Boveri with the same diesel engines but with Brown Boveri current-inverters; this was the D145.2 class, built from 1984. For purposes of saving fuel and wear and tear, the locomotives can readily be worked with one of the engines closed down. Each engine, with its associated alternator and rectifier, supplies a current-inverter for the nose-suspended traction motors in one bogie only. Reversing the locomotive is done within the current-inverter, and rheostatic braking is fitted.

### EMD TYPE GP-60/1984/USA

The GP-60 seems destined to be the last of the long GP ('Geep') line that began with the GP-7 model in 1949. This is not because the line is technologically obsolete, but simply because six-motor, six-axle, diesels achieved great popularity over the last decades, their alleged disadvantage having proved not so important as was once thought. The GP-60 appeared in 1984, its microprocessor control was praised, and with the new 710 engine it offered 3,800hp (2,832kW). But its sales in comparison with its 6-axle stablemates were quite moderate.

### CLASS Dr16/1985/FINLAND

Finnish State Railways possesses its quota of remote branch lines in rural areas, often with a surprisingly heavy freight traffic even when this is the output of only a single timber sawmill. There is a need, too, for a locomotive to do transfer trips between marshalling yards but which can

*General Electric/Amtrak Genesis Class, 1993.*

*General Electric P-32BH Type, 1991.*

also do its quota of shunting work on occasion. A locomotive type for such varied duties is the Class Dr16, equipped with two current-inverters, one each for the pair of three-phase induction traction motors mounted in each bogie. Delivery of an order for 23 from Oy Strömberg Ab started in 1985. The locomotive is powered by a French Pielstick engine of 2,200hp (1640kW).

The current-inverters from Strömberg featured gate turn-off thyristors for the first time. Developed during the 1980s for improved performance, gate turn-off thyristors allowed other parts of the circuitry, the three-phase traction motors, for example, to be lighter and less complicated.

## GENERAL ELECTRIC TYPE P-32BH/USA/1991

The US national passenger operator Amtrak originated in the mid-1970s and inherited some of the passenger locomotives belonging to railroads that had previously operated passenger services. But the corporation was soon ordering new locomotives, and very few of these came from General Electric. By the 1990s, however, GE was main locomotive supplier with its 'Genesis' series. A sign of this change of prefered supplier came in 1991, when GE delivered Amtrak's P-32BH model. This was a 3,200hp (2,384kW) locomotive powered by a 12-cylinder version of GE's FDL engine. In general, the locomotive was a version of GE's B32 freight design. Although not built in large numbers, in the few years preceding the arrival of the 'Genesis' class the P-32BH units hauled some of Amtrak's most prestigious long-distance trains. Based mainly in California, they were shifted to Chicago and shorter-haul services in the later 1990s.

## AMTRAK 'GENESIS' (AMD-103) CLASS/1993/USA

The AMD-103 was the first specifically passenger locomotive to be built in the USA for several decades. Amtrak had hitherto relied on passenger versions of existing freight locomotives. The specification for the new class required a 4,025hp (3,000kW) power output, extra fuel capacity, ability to run at 100mph (160kph) over track that might not be first-class, better fuel economy and a reduction of emissions. As US builders had little experience of manufacturing lightweight frames and trucks (moderate weight was needed to ease fast riding over rough track) the main contractor, General Electric, used the experience of its German affiliate, Krupp. Krupp had helped build the German high-speed trains and not only designed the 'Genesis' frames but also produced the first 11 of them. The locomotive has an advanced microprocessor system that monitors the work of key components. It matches the data thereby made available with the operator's desired speed to produce the best combination of inputs; in this way power output can be optimised and fuel consumption and emissions minimised. A 15 per cent fuel economy has been obtained compared with previous locomotive designs. The monitoring also diagnoses incipient faults, enabling

preventative maintenance to be carried out before a situation deteriorates.

The engine is the GE 4-cycle diesel used in earlier locomotives, and has 16 cylinders. As the AMD-103 is about three feet (about one meter) longer than previous diesels, there is space for a hostler point in the rear end, with windows and controls enabling easy operation of the locomotive in reverse when required for marshalling and depot work.

The first 44 units were delivered by 1994 and, typically, two of them with their 4,000hp apiece were used to replace three of the older 3,000hp F40 type. Later, an additional 98 units, slightly more powerful at 4,250hp (3,167kW), were ordered. Additionally, a batch of ten, dual-powered to work both as diesels and as electrics over the third-rail tracks leading into New York's Grand Central Terminus, were ordered. Metro-North was also a customer, taking 18 of the third-rail/diesel-electric dual-mode variant, which was classified P32AC-DM.

## ISRAEL RAILWAYS MEGA AND SEMI-MEGA CLASS/1998/ISRAEL

These two classes are alike, except that the Mega Class is a Bo-Bo and the Semi-Mega a Co-Co. They both belong to the Alstom GA 3000 series of modular locomotives in which the general dimensions, or 'platform,' are predetermined, but the customer can choose the engine and other items. Ten Mega and eight Semi-Mega units were ordered. They have ac/dc transmissions and use the General Motors 710 engine, in both cases producing a nominal 3,000hp (2,460kg or 2,235kW, depending on the manner of calculation). The Mega is geared for passenger work, and has a maximum speed of 87mph (140kph) whereas the Semi-Mega has a speed of 68mph (110kph)

but double the tractive effort. The smaller units weigh 198,360lb (90 tonnes) and the larger 251,250lb (114 tonnes). They were built by Alstom's works at Valencia, Spain.

## EMD (GENERAL MOTORS) TYPE DM30AC/USA/1999

The EMD DE30AC locomotive, incorporating Siemens ac technology, was built for the Long Island RR, with its long commuter runs. The units have a low body, constructed on the monocoque principle, and produce 3,000hp (2,235kW). The 23 units of this model were assembled by Super Steel in Schenectady, NY. EMD production facilities had been virtually abandoned by this time at the traditional GM plant near Chicago, most production having been transferred to London, Ontario. However, the offer to assemble the locomotives in the same state that was buying them was no doubt of some value in securing the order. The DM30AC variants, of which 18 were initially ordered, were equipped to work also off the 750V third rail electricity supply used over much of the LIRR. The inverters of these locomotives not only supply the traction motors but also supply power for the train's heating, lighting, and air conditioning.

# 0-C-0

## BRITISH RAILWAYS CLASS 08/1953/GREAT BRITAIN

The standard British Railways Class 08 shunting locomotive was smaller than those of other countries, and considering its size it was unusual in having electric transmission. Its

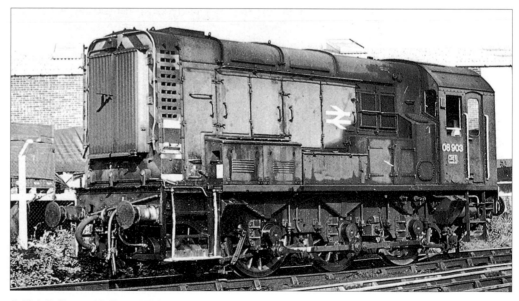

*British Railways 08 Class, 1953.*

German Federal Railways V60 Class, 1955 (261 Class variant).

German Federal Railways V60 Class, 1955 (260 Class variant).

ancestry goes back to a trial locomotive built by Hawthorn, Leslie and English Electric in 1935. This locomotive gained approval by all who tested it, and over 175 variants of the general design were delivered in Great Britain over the next 15 years. British Railways produced its own Class 08 version in 1953, and 1,193 of them were built by 1962, with mechanical work done in many of the BR locomotive works. What may be regarded as the definitive version has an English Electric 400hp (298kW) engine and electrics from the same firm. The traction motors, which drive double reduction gearing, are nose-suspended for two outer axles, and all three axles are coupled together. Control is by engine revolutions and series or parallel grouping of the traction motors.

With so many locomotives of the class having been built, it is natural that there were variations. Some batches had Blackstone or Crossley engines when built, and some had electrics from Crompton Parkinson, GEC (Britain), or British Thomson Houston. A few of the locomotives were

geared for a 27mph (43.4kph) maximum speed instead of the normal 20mph (32kph); these locomotives with a higher speed later became Class 09.

The same general design gained acceptance abroad. Sudan Railways and the Malayan Railway, both with 3ft 6in (1067mm) gauge had small batches. As in Britain, the design was accepted for widespread use by Netherlands Railways. This railway had 125 from English Electric, although a batch had a continental Thomassen engine. In both Britain and Holland, the locomotives are still a familiar sight in stations and yards.

## GERMAN FEDERAL RAILWAY CLASS V60 (260 and 261)/1955/GERMANY

Unlike North America and Great Britain, the usual shunting locomotives of continental Europe had hydraulic transmission systems. The V60 class (later 260 class) of the German Federal Railway was a typical post-1945

design; it first appeared in 1954. The three driving axles were coupled together, and the output of a Voith hydraulic transmission was joined to one of them by a cardan shaft. The input to the transmission was provided by a Maybach 650hp (485kW) diesel engine. The first of these V60 locomotives was built by Henschel, but as such a large number was ordered, most builders made a batch or two. The class came to be a common sight in freight yards all over the Federal Republic. Class 261 and 260 are practically identical, but the former weighs 116,900lb (53 tonnes) and the latter 108,00lb (49 tonnes), the heavier weight being accompanied by a slightly greater tractive effort.

## BRITISH RAILWAYS CLASS 14/1964/BRITAIN

This class, built at the Swindon Works of the former Great Western Railway, had a sorry history. Like several other types of that period, the traffic for which it was designed

*British Railways 14 Class, 1964.*

*Belgian National Railways 82 Class, 1965.*

disappeared, leaving it little suitable employment. These locomotives had been intended to do the work of the numerous 0-6-0 steam tank locomotives used for local freight trains, and when such trains began to be withdrawn they could not be used for passenger work because they had no train-heating boilers.

They had 6-cylinder Paxman 'Ventura' engines of 650hp (485kW) and the hydraulic transmission favoured by Swindon at that time. Construction was delayed because the boilermakers claimed that as it was a rigid-frame locomotive, by previous understandings they were entitled to build the cabs; the resultant inter-union struggle lasted six months. Once built, the locomotives only lasted about six years in BR service, but several of them had after-lives as industrial locomotives, and two survived into preservation.

## BELGIAN NATIONAL RAILWAYS CLASS 82/1965/BELGIUM

Although some 8-wheel yard locomotives were acquired in the 1950s, the Belgian State Railways preferred the six-wheeler, and several series of these were built in the 1960s. The differences between them were so small that it is hard to understand why a single design would not have sufficed. Class 82 is one of the more numerous of these classes; 75 were built in 1965-73, and 75 remained on the books in the late 1990s. Yard locomotives have long lives usually, because they are rarely stressed. The builders of this class were Ateliers Belges Réunis and La Brugeoise et Nivelles, with the diesel-hydraulic transmission by Cockerill as licensee of Voith. The engine produces 650hp, of which 535hp is reckoned to be usable

for traction. Visually, these locomotives were characterized by the serried rank of sandboxes alongside the wheels. This provision, and the 130,036lb (59 tonnes) weight, meant that these locomotives could be relied on for the heavy haul.

## C-C

## BRITISH RAILWAYS `WESTERN' 52 (D1000) CLASS/1961/ BRITAIN

The Western Region of British Railways tried out the diesel-hydraulic locomotive on a large scale from the 1950s. The

*British Railways Western Class, 1961.*

*Luxembourg Railways 1600 Class, 1955.*

'Western' or D1000 class was built at Swindon (and later at Crewe) from 1961. The 74 members of the class became the principal Western Region passenger locomotives, working trains out of London's Paddington station. Each locomotive had two high-speed Maybach engines rated at 1,350hp (1,007kW), so the total horsepower was 2,700hp (2,015kW). Each engine had its output taken by a Voith-North British hydraulic transmission to drive one of the two trucks. The D1000 class (later known as Class 52) was a success in its own region, but as a non-standard locomotive it could not be used on any great scale on the rest of British Rail, nor were maintenance costs low. Accordingly, after 20 years or so, the class was withdrawn, the last going in 1979.

## 2-C-2

### GERMAN STATE RAILWAY No.V3201/1929/GERMANY

During the 1920s, the best method of converting the high revolutions characteristic of the diesel engine to those of the relatively slow locomotive wheels was still a matter of debate. German State Railway No V3201 was an experiment, built by Machinenfabrik Esslingen and Maschinenfabrik Augsburg Nürnberg (MAN) in 1929. It was equipped with a pair of cylinders, as found on a steam locomotive, but the cylinders worked on hot air rather than on steam. The air entered them at 320 degrees C (608 degrees F), and the working pressure was 93psi (640kPa). The prime mover was a MAN 1,000hp (745kW) diesel engine, which drove an air compressor. The diesel engine's hot exhaust gases were used to heat the compressed air to an even higher temperature in a contraflow heat exchanger. Among other pieces of ancillary apparatus was a water distiller. This was because the air became too hot in the compressor and water had to be added for cooling, but no deposit of scale could be allowed in the compressor; the water had therefore to be distilled beforehand.

The locomotive ran well enough out on the road, although the driver had to know just what he was doing for adequate control. In addition, the various items of equipment were expensive to maintain, so the locomotive did not have any successor.

## Co-Co

### RUSSIAN RAILWAYS TE1 CLASS/1947/RUSSIA

Not all the Alco locomotives sent to wartime Russia arrived safely. Two of them were lost at sea but another was salvaged and, unfit for use, was taken for dissection at the Kharkov Locomotive Works where the design was recognized as ideal for domestic production. With some changes, including metrication and the substitution of Russian-made components, the design was produced from 1947 to 1950, totalling 300 locomotives. These remained in service until the 1980s, hauling both passenger and freight trains. They were powered by a D50 1,000hp (745kW) engine and could produce a continuous tractive effort at 10mph (17kph) of 24,230lb (11,000kg). They weighed 273,296lb (124 tonnes) and had a maximum speed of 56mph (90kph), although those whose wheel diameter was increased (and metricated) from 40in to 41.3in (1014mm to 1050mm) were allowed 58mph (93kph).

*Baldwin DT-6-6-20 Type, 1948.*

*Victorian Railways B Class, 1952.*

## BALDWIN TYPE DT-6-6-20/1948/USA

The steam locomotive builder Baldwin was slow to enter the diesel business and, when it did, chose to use a somewhat antiquated marine diesel engine which, however, in its ruggedness did set the tone. Baldwin diesel locomotives of all types were renowned for their toughness; their operating costs were often high, but they could be overloaded without dire consequences. The DT-6-6-20 was of a general type that could almost be described as a niche product, the transfer locomotive. This combined features of the road locomotive, road-switcher and switcher, being of high horsepower, entirely bi-directional (having the cab in the center), and giving its crew good vision fore and aft. Its purpose was to shift heavy loads from one freightyard to another around big cities; it needed good pulling power, but was never required to run fast. This model had a 6-cylinder engine at each end, totalling 2,000hp (1,472kW), which was a sizeable output in 1948. Electrical equipment was supplied by Westinghouse. The uneven axle spacing made these units readily identifiable. Only 42 units were sold, the best customer being the Elgin, Joliet and Eastern Railway, which was the outermost of the several Chicago belt railroads. The successor model, the RT-624, was of 2,400hp (1,788kW) and was in

production from 1951 to 1954. In 1956 Baldwin, by then merged with Lima, left the railroad business.

## VICTORIAN RAILWAYS CLASS B/1952/AUSTRALIA

Among the exports of General Motors' EMD were 26 Class B locomotives to Victorian Railways in 1952. The order illustrated the flexibility of the Electro-Motive Division's then current Type E. A driver's cab was provided at both ends, while the wheel arrangement was varied from normal (in any case, the trucks were for the Railway's 5ft 3in [1600mm] gauge). The 1,500hp (1,117kW) engine was built at La Grange, Illinois, but many parts, and the erection of the locomotives, were the work of Clyde Engineering Co.Ltd. in Australia. From 1984, Class B was re-engined to prolong its life.

## LUXEMBOURG RAILWAYS CLASS 1600/1955/LUXEMBOURG

Luxembourg Railways had a small requirement for locomotives and the latter tended to be slightly modified, if modified at all, designs used by their French and Belgian

partners. Class 1600 was a small class by conventional, but not by Luxembourg, standards. It consisted of four units that arrived in 1955, at the beginning of dieselization. Boilers were provided for steam heating and the locomotives were intended for the more important international passenger trains. The design of their noses indicates the General Motors influence. Although they were built by Anglo-Franco-Belge they used the GM 567 engine and GM electrical transmission. Weighing 238,000lb (108 tonnes) they were of 1,600hp (1,192kW). They had cabs at both ends and could run in pairs as multiple units, although this proved to be an unnecessary feature.

## MALAYAN RAILWAY 20 CLASS/1957/MALAYA

Twenty-six locomotives of this class were supplied by English Electric (two steam locomotive builders, Dick Kerr and Robert Stephenson, Hawthorn, participated in the construction). They carried the names of Malayan flowers and were therefore known as the Bunga ('Flower') Class. Their English Electric engine provided 1,500hp (1,117kW) and a tractive effort of 54,000lb (24,520kg). They were rather heavy, at 215,040lb (96 tonnes) and this, together with the state of the track, meant that they were limited

*Malayan Railway 20 Class, 1957.*

to 45mph (72kph) although capable of 60mph (96kph). When used in freight service, they showed themselves capable of hauling 1,000-ton trains. Two of them were painted red instead of the standard green; this was to enable them to haul royal trains, which were quite frequent at that period of Malayan history.

## NEW SOUTH WALES GOVERNMENT RAILWAYS 48 CLASS/1959/AUSTRALIA

165 of these units were acquired for secondary services from 1959 to 1970. They were of a standard Alco design that was also used in Brazil and Peru. A.E.Goodwin Ltd. of Sydney, holder of Alco's license, built them. Having a low axle-weight they found many duties and hastened the demise of steam traction in New South Wales. The South Australian Railways, some of whose track was exceptionally weak, also found a use for these locomotives and ordered 45 units, divided between narrow, standard, and broadgauge. Some of the South Australian units subsequently found their way to Tasmania.

The Alco 251 engines of these locomotives produced 900hp (671kW) for traction, providing a continuous tractive effort of 40,200lb (18,200kg) and a starting tractive effort of 49,500lb (22,450kg). Weight in working order was

*New South Wales Government Railways 48 Class, 1959.*

*Russian Railways TEM1 Class, 1958.*

154,280lb (70 tonnes) and the axle-load was only 28,100lb (12.75 tonnes).

## RUSSIAN RAILWAYS CLASS TEM1/1958/RUSSIA

Soviet Railways used demoted steam locomotives for yard work, at a huge cost in wasted fuel. In the late 1950s it was decided to tackle this problem with some imported diesel-electric units from Hungary and Czechoslovakia and the mass production of a Soviet-design yard locomotive. The latter was the TEM1, of which more than 1,900 were supplied to Soviet Railways, with several hundred surviving to serve the national railways created after the dismemberment of the USSR. Some of its features were inherited from the Alco imports of World War 2, and it shared some components with the mainline TE3 design. Its engine was the Penza 2D50 4-stroke, producing 1,000hp (745kW) at 740rpm. The earlier units weighed 277,700lb (126 tonnes) the later ones 264,480lb (120 tonnes) giving axle-loads of 46,285lb (21 tonnes) and 44,080lb (20 tonnes). They were built at the Bryansk Works up to 1968, although by that year the improved version,

TEM2, was already in production and destined to total more than 3,000 units.

## RUSSIAN RAILWAYS TEP60 CLASS/1960/RUSSIA

Until 1960 Soviet Railways diesel passenger locomotives were simply re-geared freight designs. But in 1960 the prototypes appeared of the first specifically passenger type, the TEP60. Series production at Kolomna Works in small batches over two decades resulted in over 1,300 units. Some were altered so as to form twin-unit sets (Class 2TEP60). Their Kolomna 11D45 2-stroke engine produced 3,000hp (2235kW) at 750rpm, and the maximum speed was 99mph or 160kph (although track conditions prevented their operation at that speed). They weighed 284,316lb (129 tonnes). Their gradual introduction improved the situation of travellers who had long suffered from trains too short to meet passenger demand and were very slow as well. One of their first fields of activity was the still unelectrified Moscow-Brest route with its international services into Europe.

## BRITISH RAILWAYS CLASS 37/1960/BRITAIN

This was one of the most successful designs of the first decade of British dieselization, with over 300 units being built over five years. The technology was English Electric, including the 12CSVT engine of 1,750hp (1,305kW), generator, and traction motors. Apart from a problem with truck fractures in 1961, the type was reliable and cheap to operate and was a real mixed-traffic type, thanks to its relatively high power. It had a tractive effort of 55,000lbs (24,900kgs) and weighed about 232,960lb (104 tonnes). Maximum speed was 80mph (129kph). Despite changes in traffic patterns since it was first ordered, the type found many uses and after it had worked for about two decades it was decided not to withdraw it, but to refurbish it for a further life that would take it into the 21st Century. All the electrical gear was replaced while the engine was retained but thoroughly rejuvenated. Alternators replaced generators in many of these transformations. Some units were equipped with electric train supply so that they could handle electrically-heated passenger rolling stock, and others were fitted with slow-speed control for use on 'Merry-go-Round' mineral trains. Ballast to improve adhesion brought the weight of some of these locomotives to 264,480lb (120 tonnes).

*British Railways 55 Class ('Deltic'), 1961.*

*Indian Railways WDM-2 Class, 1962.*

*Royal Thailand State Railway 4000 Class, 1963.*

## RUSSIAN RAILWAYS TEP10 CLASS/1960/RUSSIA

This passenger class was built at Kharkov and, together with the similar Lugansk-built TEP10L, totalled about 550 units. Unlike Russian freight locomotives, they were single units. The idea was to exploit the availability of a Kharkov 3,000hp (2,235kW) engine (the 2-stroke 10-cylinder 10D100) to build a powerful twin-unit freight locomotive and this passenger version was really one half of the freight design, with gearing to allow it to reach 87mph (140kph), although in practice the type was usually limited to 62mph or 100kph). Weight was 284,315lb,(129 tonnes) giving an axle load of 47,390lb (21.5 tonnes). The Lugansk-built units followed the freight locomotive design so closely that only one cab was provided, so they had to be turned at the end of their runs.

## BRITISH RAILWAYS CLASS 55 ('DELTIC')/1961/BRITAIN

Wishing to find a railway use for its Napier 'Deltic' diesel engine, English Electric at its own expense built a prototype Co-Co locomotive in the late 1950s, which ran on British Railways in regular service and so impressed the management of the Eastern Region of BR that 22 units of an improved version were built. Each locomotive had two Deltic 18-cylinder engines, developing 1,650hp each. At the time of construction these locomotives were the world's most powerful at 3,300hp (2,459kW). In working order they weighed 220,400lb (100 tonnes) and their continuous tractive effort was 35,000lbs at 32 mph (15,875kgs at 51kph). Maximum service speed was 105mph (169kph) although one of them was timed at 113mph (181kph) hauling a load of about 605,600lb (320 tonnes).

The manufacturers agreed to accept responsibilty for the maintenance of these units; the high-speed diesel engine, with its triangular form with three crankshafts, was quite complex. The units were delivered in 1961 and brought a radical acceleration of trains betwen London and the North. In 1979 they were replaced by Intercity 125 diesel trains

and moved to easier runs, but were all withdrawn by 1982. Several have been preserved and some, on occasion, are leased out to haul regular service trains.

## INDIAN RAILWAYS WDM-2 CLASS/1962/INDIA

Although some diesel locomotives were imported in the 1950s, the foundation of the first Indian dieselization programme was the Diesel Locomotive Works founded at Banares with the help of the American Alco company. The WDM-2 was the first series-produced type built there, and was a development of the WDM-1, an imported Alco design. Like the latter, it was a six-motor design but instead of delivering 1,800hp (1,340kW) the uprated Alco V251 produced 2,400hp (1,788kW). Later, the WDM-2C locomotive would push horsepower even further, to 3,100hp (2,310kW). The WDM-2C is in fact an upgraded WDM-2, undertaken from 1994, by which time many of the original units were in their fourth decade of service and had to be either refurbished or withdrawn. The weights of both the original and refurbished units are the same, at 249,050lb (113tonnes) and the maximum speed of 89mph (120kph) is also unchanged.

## BRITISH RAILWAYS CLASS 47/1962/GREAT BRITAIN

When British Rail started its programme of conversion to diesel traction in the 1950s, a number of different locomotive types were ordered and a variety of diesel engines tried out. The Sulzer engine came to be preferred, and when a powerful general-purpose locomotive was needed, the Sulzer firm was consulted. Sulzer showed British Rail the drawings of a locomotive built in Switzerland in 1959 for the Roumanian State Railways, the latter's Class 060DA. British Rail felt that this was what was needed, and the locomotive that became known later as Class 47 was inspired by the Roumanian design. Obviously the bodywork had to be different to fit within the British

loading gauge, and the engine was uprated to 2,750hp (2,050kW). The current generated was dc, controlled by engine revolutions and by series and parallel traction motor groupings.

From 1962, the total built reached 512, starting with a batch from Crewe works with electric motors from Brush, Loughborough. Other batches were assembled by Brush. The Sulzer diesel engines were built by Vickers, Barrow-in-Furness in all cases, that firm then holding the British licence to manufacture. With such a large number the locomotives, as might be expected, worked all over the system.

Details of individual locomotives differed for one reason or another. Thus many had slow-speed control for loading or unloading Merry-go-Round coal trains. Others had the maximum 95mph (153kph) speed pushed up to 100mph (160kph) for Glasgow-Edinburgh push-and-pull passenger trains. Yet others had the engine derated to 2,500hp (1,863kW) for a time. Over the years more and more of the class changed over to supply electric (rather than steam) heating and air conditioning to passenger trains. In the 1990s withdrawals accelerated, but some units were transformed by the original manufacturer, Brush, to the order of the Freightliner Company. These became Class 57, and had General Motors (second-hand) engines, with most of the other equipment replaced or renewed.

## ROYAL STATE RAILWAY OF THAILAND 4000 CLASS/1963/THAILAND

The Royal Siamese State Railway, as it was then called, had a distinguished record in diesel traction, having ordered its first diesel locomotives from Switzerland in 1928. These, and units from other Swiss and Danish manufacturers ordered in the 1930s, performed good service and lasted two or three decades. They were clearly more efficient than woodburning steam locomotives. Large-scale post-war dieselization initially was based on German diesel-hydraulics, but after the 1950s there was a reversion to diesel-electrics. The diesel-electric 4000 Class of 1963

*General Motors (EMD) SD40 Type, 1966. This is the Illinois Central RR SD40A Class.*

were the first high-power diesels to work in Thailand. There were fifty of them, and they took over the most important duties, both passenger and freight. They were built by General Electric, being of that company's UM12C export model. They had two Cummins engines totalling 1,320hp (983kW) at 1,200rpm and could produce a tractive effort of 49,560lb (22,500kg). They weighed 165,350lb (75 tonnes) and with their gear ratio of 18:93 could reach 56mph (90kph). They were still in service in the late 1990s.

## EMD (GENERAL MOTORS) TYPE SD40/1966/USA

In 1965 EMD announced nine new models, including the SD40. This 1966 'line' represented a fundamental change of models because three new basic components were being combined for the first time. The 645 engine was to replace the 567, whose scope for up-rating had been exhausted. The D32 generator, whose limitations prevented further horsepower increases, was to be replaced by a new alternator, the AR 10. The new D77 traction motor, whose extra copper allowed higher horsepower per axle (because heat dissipated more easily), was the third new element. The SD40 was an immediate success, although for a period it lost popularity in favor of the more powerful 4,500hp (3,353kW) against 4,000hp (2,980kW) SD45. By the time production ceased about 1,300 had been

*Spanish Railways Alco 313 Type, 1965.*

*Spanish Railways General Motors (EMD) 319 Type, 1965.*

delivered. The model was succeeded by the SD40-2, in which a remodeled truck limited weight-transfer (and hence reduced wheel-slip) and a substantial portion of the control system was handed over to microprocessors. Launched just as a coal boom was about to develop, the SD40-2 found many buyers, and eventually nearly 4,000 were built. With such a large production run, there were many design variations. The Illinois Central bought SD40 units riding on SD45 frames, thereby making space for bigger fuel tanks (the IC called these the SD40A class). The design also formed the basis for passenger units built for Amtrak and metropolitan transportation authorities.

## ALCO TYPE 313/1965/SPAIN

For many years the 50 units of the 313 class were concentrated at Granada, where they handled all kinds of trains, including long-distance passenger (they had a train heating boiler under the short hood). They were true Alco products, although assembled in Spain. Their Alco 251D engine was down-rated to 1,370hp (1,020kW), less power being compensated by lower maintenance expenses) so the locomotives were typically combined into more units

per given train-weight than would have been the case with similar locomotives used in the USA. Their maximum tractive effort was about 42,000lbs (19,000kg). Maximum permitted speed was 75mph (120kph). Some parts were made by the domestic Euskalduna company but most were by Alco, with electrical components by General Electric.

## EMD (GENERAL MOTORS) TYPE 319/1965/SPAIN

Apart from switchers and locomotives for the Talgo trains, Spanish diesel locomotives were of the six-wheel, six-motor arrangement, suiting the mountainous terrain through which most lines passed. The 319 class was assembled by Macosa, which had the licence to build EMD designs in Spain, but apart from the completely new carbody the locomotive was virtually an EMD type SD9, as supplied to US railroads. The two end cabs, and the trucks designed for the Spanish broad gauge, effectively disguised the ancestry, however. The engine was a GM 16-cylinder 567C. But whereas the same engine in the US road-switchers was rated at 1,750hp, in Spain it was uprated to 2,000hp (1,490kW). Maximum speed was 75mph (120kph), and a steam generator was carried. The

braking control was by Westinghouse, and combined the US-style air-braking of the locomotive with the Spanish-style vacuum brake of the train.

## POLISH STATE RAILWAY ST43 CLASS/1965/POLAND

In the years of the Soviet Bloc locomotive production among the various communist-ruled countries was planned so that, ideally, each country would specialize in one category of production while importing others. This would provide the economies of scale that was so much sought. But policies were not always consistent and did not always produce the best workmanship. In 1965 Poland began to receive the ST43 Class diesel locomotives built in Roumania, where the Electroputere Works had the license to build Sulzer engines. On the ST43, the engine was a Sulzer 12LDA28, giving 2,070hp (1,544kW). The locomotive weighed 255,665lb (116 tonnes), giving an axle-weight of 37,470lb (17 tonnes). The locomotive seemed to perform reasonably well, but in the year following its introduction a different design with almost identical specification, the Class ST44, began to be imported from Russia.

*Polish State Railway ST43 Class, 1965.*

## ALCO TYPE 321/1967/SPAIN

Alco, and later its successor the Montreal Locomotive Works, exported a higher proportion of production than did General Motors. A third player was General Electric, which at a time when it was not marketing mainline diesel locomotives in the USA, was busy exporting such locomotives. GE did not export locomotives to Spain, but its equipment was used in Alco products. Alco was the first producer of mainline diesels for Spain but in the late 1960s was losing its dominance to General Motors. Spanish National Railways completed dieselization in 1975, the process having started 1n 1955 with the acquisition of Type 316, an Alco six-wheel design that was imported ready-built from the USA. In 1967 the very similar Type 321 appeared. This time assembly was in Spain, although basic components like the Alco engine and GE electrical equipment were imported. The power was the same as the 316, at 2,180hp (1,625kW), and the tractive effort 54,000lbs (24,640kg).

*Spanish Railways Alco 321 Type, 1967.*

## WESTERN AUSTRALIAN GOVERNMENT RAILWAY R CLASS/1968/AUSTRALIA

These units were built by English Electric at Rocklea in Queensland, being similar to the 1300 Class of Queensland Railways. The design was intended to provide a better power/weight ratio than previous locomotives, because QR with its lightweight track was facing a resurgence of mineral traffic. Western Australia was also developing its mineral resources at this time and needed powerful diesels for its services. Both railways used the same 3ft 6in (1067mm) gauge. The WAGR units differed from the QR locomotives in their trucks, or bogies, which were designed to reduce weight-transfer at high tractive forces, thereby reducing the possibility of wheel-slip. The five units of the initial WAGR order were very successful, and in due course 13 more were ordered, these latter being without the dynamic brakes fitted to the first five and classified RA. A few units were subsequently converted to standard gauge, when a mineral branchline was itself widened to accommodate increased traffic. Class R did indeed have a high power/weight ratio, so much so that it was decided that six tonnes of ballast should be fitted, raising axle-

weight from 35,264lb (15 to 16 tonnes) but bringing adhesion more closely into line with tractive effort. That tractive effort was 59,270lbs (26,880kg). Traction horsepower was 1,795 (1,337kW) and weight with ballast 214,890lb (97.5 tonnes). Both the QR and WAGR units often appeared on passenger trains, the former sometimes handling Brisbane suburban services. When more modern locomotives replaced the R class, the latter tended to work on the Perth-Bunbury line.

## CHINESE RAILWAYS DF4 CIASS/1969/CHINA

This class may be regarded as the first entirely Chinese-built mass-production diesel locomotive design. As such, it incorporates many features first found on imports. The body outline resembles units imported earlier from Henschel in Germany, and the suspension has resemblances with French (Alsthom) practice. Several hundred were built by the Dalian Works. The engine delivers 3,600hp (2,680kW) at 1,100rpm to the alternator. Weight in working order is 304,150lb (138 tonnes) giving an axle-load of 50,690lb (23 tonnes). Some are geared for passenger

service, having a maximum permitted speed of 75mph (120kph) instead of 62mph (100kph), although those geared for freight work often appear on the slower passenger trains.

## RUSSIAN RAILWAYS M62 CLASS/1970/RUSSIA

Although this class was built for Soviet Railways from 1970, it first emerged as a prototype in 1964 and was series-built for export from 1965. Several Soviet-bloc railways used it: it was to be found in Hungary, Poland, the German Democratic Republic, Czechoslovakia, North Korea, Cuba and Mongolia. Soviet Railways at first were not keen to use it, but when their preferred designs seemed to be failing they began to order this type, receiving over 700 units as well as over 1,200 of the twin-unit variant (Class 2M62). The big attraction of the design was its relative reliability. It had a Kolomna 14D40 2-stroke engine, producing 2,000hp (1,472kW) at 750rpm. It was intended mainly for freight service, and had a maximum speed of 62mph (100kph). It weighed 255,665lb (116 tonnes), and its axle-load was 42,760lb (19.4 tonnes).

*Chinese Railways DF4 Class, 1969. The DF4 unit is at the left, the right-hand locomotive being an NY7 Class diesel-hydraulic, supplied by Henschel from 1972.*

*Russian Railways M62 Class, 1970. The picture shows the 2M62 twin-section variant.*

### GERMAN FEDERAL RAILWAYS No.202 002-2/1971/WEST GERMANY

A British firm, English Electric, tried out a current-inverter locomotive in 1965. It failed to function; no doubt the electronics technology was beyond the practice of the day. The German firm, Brown Boveri, Mannheim, spent six years developing a traction current-inverter which would work according to similar principles to those of English Electric's failure; their locomotive was built in 1971, the builder being Thyssen-Henschel. A 2,500hp (1,863kW) diesel engine was used to drive an alternator. The output was solid-state rectified and the voltage regulated for presentation to the current-inverter. In the inverter three banks of thyristor switches took the dc and switched it swiftly in one direction or the other, the output then being three-phase current. By controlling the rate of switching between 0.5Hz and 165Hz, the rate of revolution of the three-phase traction motors (and thus the locomotive's speed) could be varied as desired.

The problem of starting was overcome by pulse-wave-modulation of current at a constant frequency, until the locomotive was moving at a little above walking pace, when a switch could be made to 0.5Hz or other low frequency from the inverter. A feedback from the revolving wheels checked that engine output was matched to demand as set by the inverter. When running without current, the motors automatically became generators for a rheostatic brake.

This locomotive was German Federal Railway No.202 002-2. Two more were built in 1974. 202 003-0 had the wheel arrangement Bo-Bo but was otherwise similar to the other, 202 004-8. The original locomotive was used for demonstrations in various countries, and also ran for a time as an electric locomotive, with a suitably altered motor coach feeding it with dc. These tests, including the trying out of some high-speed trucks, came to an end, and the two Co-Co locomotives were withdrawn in 1985, thus leaving only 202 003-0 in service. As a prototype, 202 002-2 was highly successful and established the current-inverter locomotive.

### RUSSIAN RAILWAYS TEP70 CLASS/1973/RUSSIA

Although the TEP60 diesel locomotive had transformed passenger services on many routes, Soviet Railways still required a more powerful machine, and the TEP70 was designed to accommodate a 4,000hp (2,980kW) engine in a single-unit locomotive. That engine, the 2A-5D49, was an uprated development of the existing Kolomna engine. At the time this design was being studied, Soviet engineers were examining a British ac/dc prototype locomotive (Kestrel) which had been acquired second-hand. In the new TEP70 the ac/dc system of transmission was accordingly improved. Fuel consumption was reduced by one tenth in comparison with the preceding TEP60.

Maximum speed of this locomotive was 100mph (160kph), and it weighed (288,725lb)(131 tonnes). For a long period (1978-86) it was built only in small lots, but series production began in 1987 and over 300 were built before the collapse of the USSR. Most of them remain in the possession of Russian Railways.

### RUSSIAN RAILWAYS TEP75 CLASS/1976/RUSSIA

In the steam age it sometimes happened that a new locomotive design turned out to weigh much more than intended and was banned by the civil engineers. With modern traction this phenomenon is almost unheard-of, but it occurred in Soviet Russia with the TEP75 design of passenger diesel locomotive. In the early 1970s the successful TEP60 locomotive was proving too weak for growing needs and was therefore being produced as a twin-section locomotive of double the size and power. The designers of the TEP75 were required to produce a locomotive of the same power as the twin TEP60 but as a single unit. To do this they used an enlarged Kolomna 1D49 engine of 6,000hp (4,470 kW), with ac/dc transmission. But instead of the designed weight of 304,150lb(138 tonnes) the scales registered 323,990lb (147 tonnes). This implied an axle-weight of 54,000lb (24.5 tonnes), which for a fast locomotive was unacceptable in terma of stress on the track. So the design

*German Federal Railways No 202 002-2, 1971.*

*Russian Railways TEP70 Class, 1973.*

*Russian Railways TEP75 Class, 1976.*

was abandoned and the two prototypes saw little service. In its place two 8-axle prototypes (TEP80) were built but although they were quite promising their development was held back by deteriorating economic circumstances.

## GENERAL MOTORS CLASS SD-50/1980/USA

General Motors updated its standard model for sale to all railways in 1980; the result was the SD-50. It so happened that its immediate predecessor as a standard, the SD 45, had been fitted with a 20-cylinder engine, as against the 16-cylinder ones used before that and now used again for the SD-50. Such was the attention given to costs on North American railroads that the greater maintenance expense of 20 cylinders compared with 16 was noticed, and the SD-45 locomotive did not sell very well.

The SD-50 is a diesel-alternator locomotive with a 3,800hp (2,830kW) engine. The nose-suspended traction motors are fed with dc from a solid-state rectifier, and controlled by engine revolutions. It was the design on which the British Class 59 was modelled.

## DANISH STATE RAILWAYS CLASS ME/1981/DENMARK

Among countries visited by the Thyssen-Henschel-built diesel current-inverter German Federal Class 202, was Denmark, in 1977. The demonstration of the capabilities of the three-phase traction motors impressed the Danes. The Danish State Railways ordered 20 similar but rather larger locomotives, Class ME, the first of which was delivered in 1981. A General Motors 3,240hp (2,410kW) engine is installed, and this drives an alternator whose output is rectified immediately for presentation to the current-inverter. Electrics are by Brown Boveri, Mannheim; the three-phase traction motors are nose-suspended, and a rheostatic brake is fitted. The first two of the class were erected by Thyssen-Henschel, but Scandia-Randers erected the rest in Denmark.

The locomotives weigh 11 tonnes less than a previous diesel-alternator, the 3,900hp (2,910kW) Class My, but despite this the performance is much the same. Class ME performs equally well on passenger and freight trains. Its first duty was working push-and-pull passenger trains across Zealand.

## IRAQI STATE RAILWAYS CLASS DEM/1982/IRAQ

The Iraqi Republic after 1979 was engaged in railway construction on a large scale. About 1,675 route miles (2,695km) were to be built, or converted from existing 3ft 3⅜in (1000mm) gauge. Six years after the start of the operation, at the end of 1985, new railways were open from Baghdad north-west to Husaiba on the Syrian border, with branches to phosphate workings at Akashat, and from

midway along the new line eastwards towards Kirkut and its oilfields as far as the intersection with the old main line to Turkey at Baiji. Much new motive power was needed for all this fresh mileage. Iraqi Republic Railways took delivery of 72 diesel-alternator 3,600hp (2,680kW) locomotives with Alco engines during 1982. The locomotives were built by Francorail, a consortium of half-a-dozen French manufacturers. Added to the Iraqi order were six similar locomotives for Saudi Rails (1982) and another seven for North Korean Railways (1983).

The locomotive type, Iraqi Class DEM, was controlled by engine revolutions, with the six nose-suspended traction motors connected permanently in parallel. Particular attention was devoted to air-filtering equipment to exclude sand and dust, while automatic wheel-slide and spin-control was fitted, together with a rheostatic brake and multiple-unit working capability. Within the total, 11 locomotives were geared for passenger work with a maximum speed of 93mph (150kph), while the rest had a maximum speed of 68mph (110kph).

*British Railways Class 58, 1983.*

*Foster Yeoman 59 Class, 1985.*

## BRITISH RAILWAYS CLASS 58/1983/BRITAIN

With the Class 58, BR engineers hoped both to supply a traction need and to begin an export business. The traction need was hard to discern, and the export prospects came to nothing. In the end 50 units of this class were built for BR and performed well, although they suffered from insufficient adhesion (only the last unit was fitted, somewhat laboriously, with 'Sepex' separate excitation). Construction was rather protracted. The first order was placed in 1979 but the first unit did not go into regular service until 1983. This was not the way to win export markets. The class was initially allocated to coal traffic but later handled other types of freight. With their Ruston-Paxman engine producing 3,300hp (2,485kW) these locomotives were barely superior to the preceding Class 56, although they did incorporate some new ideas. They weighed 286,520lb (130 tonnes) and were allowed to reach 80mph (128kph). Tractive effort was 61,800lb (28,000kg).

## FOSTER YEOMAN CLASS 59/1985/BRITAIN

In the 1980s the quarrying company Foster Yeoman gained the right to run its own trains over British Rail routes. As it required an availability factor higher than any British builder could guarantee, it negotiated with General Motors and four units were ordered, these being standard GM locomotives with bodies and other components adapted for British requirements. With their creep control facility, these locomotives could start trains of double the weight of those handled by BR locomotives of nominally the same power. Soon after they went into service the Company ordered an additional unit, and subsequently a handful were imported by other British companies. Eventually the design formed the basis for the Class 66 of the EWS freight operating company.

The engine was the well-tried 645, driving the EMD alternator. The engine developed 3,300hp (2,460kW). Weight in working order was 266,685lb (121 tonnes) and maximum speed was 60mph (96kph). The locomotives are employed hauling heavy trains of stone from the

Company's quarries in Somerset to destinations in south-east England.

## GENERAL ELECTRIC TYPE 8-40C/USA/1987

When the successors of GE's domestic debut design, the U25B, reached the limit of their development they were succeeded by a completely new range of locomotives, the so-called 'Dash 7' line. Alternators instead of generators had been adopted in the late 1960s, and alternating current was firmly established by this time. Sold as both six-axle (C) and four-axle (B) variants, the B30-7 and C30-7 which appeared in the late 1970s were succeeded by the B36-7 and C36-7 types in the 1980s. During those years of development, the Dash 7 line improved fuel consumption by 16 per cent (fuel economy had not been a strong point of the earlier U25B). As the line was marketed when world oil prices were high, and as the GE reputation for reliability was maintained by these locomotives, they were well liked and ordered in large numbers. They formed the basis of

*General Electric 8-40C Type, 1987.*

the Dash 8 range, which could really be described as third-generation diesel locomotives, thanks to the full adoption of electronic control devices. Still with the FDL engine, this time producing 4,000hp (2,980kW), the 8-40B and 8-40C (there was also on offer a lower horsepower 8-32C) had three micro-processors. One of these supervised the locomotive control systems, one the main alternator excitation, and the third the auxiliaries such as blowers and fans. With their sensors at critical locations and their indications in the cab, these micro-computers in effect monitored operation continuously and when a fault developed not only gave warning and diagnosis but also applied the initial remedies; for example, when the oil or water temperature passed a limit, engine revolutions were automatically reduced. One feature of this system was that it could sense tunnel operation, in which period it would tolerate above-normal oil and water temperatures for a maximum of ten minutes. The micro-computers also kept records to make diagnosis and remedial action easier for maintenance crews.

## BRITISH RAIL CLASS 60/1989/BRITAIN

In the first decades of dieselization British Railways diesel locomotives were projected by British Railways engineers, but with the reorganization of the undertaking this procedure changed. When British Rail in the late 1980s discovered a need for a new heavy freight locomotive it set a specification and waited for tenders. It had been thought that General Motors, building on the success of its Class 59, would win the contract but BR chose the Brush design. This seemed to promise more precise control

*British Rail 60 Class, 1989.*

*General Motors (EMD) SD70MAC Type, 1993. This was the forerunner of the SD90MAC.*

of wheel-creep at low speeds, and its Mirrlees engine was more powerful and promised better fuel economy.

Complex microprocessor control was evolved that, amomg other things, enabled these locomotives to creep (that is, to exert maximum effort tractive effort, which occurs when the wheels are just, but only just, slipping) at a speed as low as 0.5mph (0.8kph), which was the speed of coal trains loading and unloading in the 'Merry-go-Round' procedure for intensive coal movements. A hundred of these Co-Co locomotives were built. They weighed 277,710lb (126 tonnes) and their engines could produce 3,100hp (2,310kW), which meant a 65,250lb (29,580kg) tractive effort. Brush's own alternators were fitted. These locomotives were designed for a 40-year life. The creep control, for its time, was very good; a locomotive with a heavy train could, as it were, creep on the spot with no forward movement; a light application of sand would then set the train moving.

## GENERAL ELECTRIC TYPE AC4400/USA/1993

The prototype of GE's first ac technology high horsepower locomotive was built in 1993, and within a few months orders were flowing in. By 1998 Canadian Pacific seemed to be the best customer, having ordered more than 300 units. Like its competitor EMD, GE offered initial units using existing (4,400hp) engines, but designed to accommodate 6,000hp (4,270kW) engines as soon as the latter were developed. The 6,000hp version was classified AC6000. AC4400 units could produce 145,000lbs (65,770kgs) of tractive effort at 10mph (16kph). Having its own experience with ac technology in trains built for city transit authorities, GE did not need to go to Germany for electrical know-how. However, it did team up with the German Deutz Company to produce a new diesel engine, the 7HDL. As with the rival line of GM high horsepower locomotives, the attraction for railroads was that one of the new units could replace two of the older. Railroads which were still not reconciled to ac traction were not offered dc versions of these locomotives; it was felt that only ac could deliver such high powers in units of that size and weight. The AC4400 weighs 420,000lb (190 tonnes).

## NATIONAL RAIL CORPORATION NR CLASS/1996/AUSTRALIA

The National Rail Corporation (NR) handles interstate rail traffic in Australia, using the tracks of the different state railway authorities. The 4,025hp (3,000kV) NR Class of diesel locomotives is based on General Electric technology, as adapted by the Australian locomotive builder Goninan; in fact, construction took place both in New South Wales and Western Australia. 120 units were built, and the class was the first to operate across the whole continent. The engine is a GE 7FDL-16, powering a GE alternator. Weight in working order is 290,900lb (132 tonnes) and speed 71mph (115kph). Computerized control of the braking system was one innovation on these locomotives, with touch-screen display. With the steady displacement of older types that it inherited, NR now relies on these units for handling almost all of its traffic.

## GENERAL MOTORS (EMD) TYPE SD90MAC/1996/USA

With its SD70MAC of 1993 EMD offered a 4,000hp (2,980kW) diesel unit able to compete against GE models in terms of power. It was bought in large numbers by the Burlington Northern RR but EMD, aware that competitors were planning 5,000hp (3,726kW) units, moved on to the SD80MAC, with a 20-cylinder 5,000hp version of the well-tried 710 engine. Like the SD70MAC, this design incorporated ac traction motors (the inverter technology was acquired from Siemens of Germany, with which GM had a cooperation agreement) and also GM's patented radial trucks, which by insinuating the wheels around curves meant that more power was available for actually hauling the train (and also enabled six-axle trucks to go where previously only four-axle had been allowed). The EM2000 control micro-processor had much more memory and speed than the micro-procesors fitted to the earlier SD60 and GP60 series units. In 1996 the Union Pacific RR began to receive a new model, the SD90MAC with a 4,300hp (3,204kW) 710 engine. However, EMD in 1998 produced prototypes of an improved SD90MAC with a completely new 6,000hp engine which, breaking a long GM tradition, was a four-stroke. Four-stroke had long been used by GE; in general the four-stroke was more economical in terms of fuel consumption, while being somewhat slower in developing full power. Four-stroke

engines also produce more torque. The 4,300hp Union Pacific units had been designed to take the new engine as soon as it was developed.

## ENGLISH WELSH AND SCOTTISH RAILWAY CLASS 66/1998/BRITAIN

When the freight operator English Welsh and Scottish Railway took over British freight operations it inherited a varied locomotive stock, consisting largely of old designs that were not performing well. It ordered 250 new locomotives from General Motors (EMD) and these were assembled at the London, Ontario, GM works. Externally the units resembled similar locomotives supplied by General Motors to British operators (Class 59), and in fact the bodyshell was identical. However, by 1998 several substantial improvements were possible. The engine was no longer the 645, but the new 710 with its superior

power/weight ratio and better fuel economy, and EMD's new EM2000 electronic control management was incorporated. This monitors and regulates the main activities of the locomotive and, for example, the creep control system introduced on Class 59 was thereby improved upon in terms of speed and precision. The standard GM control pedestal (rather than the North American 'safety cab') was installed at both ends (as is customary in Britain, but not in the USA, the locomotives were provided with cabs at each end). There were GM radial steering trucks, which align themselves for an easier ride through curves. Use of the 710 engine saved space, filled by bringing the previously underfloor air reservoirs into the main compartment. The space thus freed underfloor permitted the installation of larger fuel tanks of 1,800 gallons (8,180 litres), about double that of Class 59. The locomotive weighs 280,035lb (127 tonnes) and its engine produces 3,300hp (2,460kW). Maximum tractive

*English Welsh & Scottish Railway 66 Class, 1998.*

*Russian Railways 2TE116 Class, 1971.*

effort is 90,000lb (40,860kg) and continuous tractive effort 57,000lb (25,880kg). Maximum speed is 75mph (121kph).

# Co-Co+Co-Co

### RUSSIAN RAILWAYS CLASS
### TE3/1953/RUSSIA

The 5ft (1524mm) gauge Soviet Railways was interested in diesel traction between the wars, more particularly for the arid regions that lie east of the Caspian Sea. There was no great success, however, until the arrival of Alco and Baldwin diesel locomotives as war-aid put the designers on the right track. The diesel-electric TE1 class,

with four-wheel bogies, was built from 1945; and its development, the TE2 class, appeared from 1950. Class TE3, with six-wheel bogies, followed from 1953. It was a double-unit locomotive rated at 4,000hp (2,980kW). Several thousands were built by Kharkov (responsible for the first one), Kolomna and Lugansk locomotive works. The design consisted of two 2,000hp (1,472kW) units coupled back-to-back with driver's cabs at the outer ends only.

Kharkov were responsible for initiating the building of Class TE7 as well. This is a TE3 with improved springs and suspension for passenger-train work. Originally, 87mph (140kph) was the intended maximum speed, but due to the unsatisfactory suspension this was cut to 74½mph (120mph).

About 6,800 TE3 locomotives were built, and about a hundred of the TE7 variant.

# Co-Co+Co-Co

### RUSSIAN RAILWAYS CLASS
### 2TE116/1971/RUSSIA

The Soviet locomotive industry first used ac/dc transmission for some locomotives exported to the German Democratic Republic (Class 132) and the Soviet Railways 2TE116 was derived from that design. Soviet Railways apparently did not want it, claiming that its engine was simply a marine diesel that was unsuited to railway use. Certainly the class was plagued by breakdowns until detail design improvements were achieved, and in the end over 1,600 of the twin-units were built by the Lugansk Works. The engine, initially, was the Kolomna 1A-5D49 4-stroke, but a variation of this was subsequently used. It produced

*British Railways 45 Class, 1960.*

3,000hp (2235kW), so the twin-unit locomotive disposed of 6,000hp (4,500kW) in total. Each of the units (which were permanently coupled and, strictly speaking, should be called sections) weighed 304,150lb (138 tonnes) and the maximum speed was 62mph (100kph), more than adequate for a freight locomotive. Crew comfort received more attention in this design than previously. The cab was air-conditioned and the overhang-style of windscreen also made life easier for the crew.

## 1-Co-Co-1

### BRITISH RAILWAYS CLASS 40/1958/BRITAIN

The Class 40 was one of the first designs built under the BR 1955 modernization plan and was intended to replace the Pacific type steam locomotives hauling fast passenger trains. However, it was not much more powerful than the locomotives it was intended to replace, and its introduction did not signal any great cutting of schedules. The first ten units, built by Vulcan Foundry on a basis of English Electric technology, were intended as prototypes, but series production was ordered before they had been properly tried. Nevertheless the class proved quite reliable, the main weakness being the train heating boiler, which tended to fail quite frequently. A feature of the design was that steam-age water pick-up scoops were fitted, so that the heating boiler could be replenished without stopping the train. The weight of the locomotive, 299,745lb (136 tonnes), meant that the power trucks each contained an extra carrying axle, making the wheel arrangement 1-Co-Co-1; these trucks did suffer from cracked frames, however. Maximum speed was 90mph (145kph) and the engines could develop 2,000hp (1,472kW) at 850rpm.

No fewer than 200 of these locomotives were built. At first they were used to haul passenger trains from London to East Anglia, and to the north, but they were really not quite powerful enough and were supplanted by bigger designs quite soon, after which they migrated to secondary passenger and freight work. By the late 1970s they were being scrapped, so their average lifespan was a little less than two decades.

### BRITISH RAILWAYS CLASS 45/1960/BRITAIN

After ten prototypes (Class 44) introduced in 1958 had performed creditably, BR ordered 126 similar units which became Class 45. Like the prototypes, these were built around the Sulzer 12-cylinder engine, although uprated from 2,300hp to 2,500hp (1,710kW to 1,863kW). These were powerful locomotives for the time, and they were used on high-grade passenger trains, including those of

*Union Pacific RR Centennial Class, 1969.*

the Midland main line northwards from St Pancras Station in London. The engines of the Class 45, though of Swiss design, were built by Vickers-Armstrong and the electrical gear was by Crompton Parkinson. The locomotives were rather heavy at 291,120lb (132 tonnes)); they were built in BR's own workshops. Because of this, an unpowered carrying axle was included in each of the power trucks so as to reduce axle weight, resulting in the 1-Co-Co-1 wheel arrangement. The Class 46 soon followed, very similar but with different electrical gear. All these classes were quite reliable and did good service, the last Class 45 units being withdrawn in 1989. About ten units of the classes 45 and 44 have been preserved. They were generally known as 'Peaks,' because the Class 44 units bore names of mountain peaks, despite the regimental names carried by many of Class 45.

# Do-Do

## UNION PACIFIC CENTENNIAL CLASS/1969/USA

In 1969 the Union Pacific Railroad celebrated the centenary of the driving of the last rail spike at Promontory, Utah, in 1869, which completed the first coast-to-coast railway route in North America. A massive 6,600hp (4,920kW) diesel-alternator locomotive type was first delivered in 1969 as part of this celebration. There were 47 in this 'Centennial' class, which was built by General Motors' Electro-Motive Division. They were far from a standard type, but EMD adapted its standards to the wishes of the customer. Four-axle bogie frames had to be built, and a

greatly extended locomotive frame. On the frame, two standard 3,300hp (2,460kW) engines were mounted, but the electrics, except in one particular, were normal equipment. The exception was that, apart from experiments, the 'Centennials' were the Electro-Motive Division's first diesel-alternator locomotives. The alternator output was rectified immediately, and control of the dc traction motors was by engine revolutions. The alternator idea had been picked up from a pioneer French type of 1965. As on other railways, the Union Pacific determined eventually that it was more economic to couple two smaller locomotives together when high horse-power was needed rather than to have single high-horsepower units. The last of the class was taken out of traffic in 1985, but there were partial returns to traffic when the Railroad faced motive power shortages.

*Western Australian Government Railway X Class, 1954.*

## 2-Do-2

### WESTERN AUSTRALIAN GOVERNMENT RAILWAY X CLASS/1954/AUSTRALIA

This was one of the more interesting post-war diesel locomotive designs, in that it used the somewhat archaic rigid-frame driving wheel arrangement combined with a vaguely streamlined look. The locomotives were built in Britain with Beyer, Peacock looking after the mechanical parts and Metropolitan-Vickers the electrical.

The rigid four driving axles may have contributed to the rough-riding characteristics of the locomotives, and the unpowered axles meant that not all the locomotive weight was available for adhesion. On the other hand, these locomotives were permitted to use all lines, thanks to their low axle-weight of 10.5 tons (235,200lb). A Crossley HSTVee valveless engine, providing 1,045hp (780kW) for traction, was fitted. This was really a marine (more accurately, submarine) engine which did not take kindly to railway employment. Oiling-up and consequent fires were not unknown. Despite these problems, which in the course of time were moderated,

the locomotives made a great impression and resulted in substantial cuts to passenger schedules (four hours could be taken off the 17-hour Perth-Kalgoorlie timing, for example). Starting tractive effort was 26,000lbs (11,800kg) and continuous 12,000lbs (5,440kgs). Weight was 176,300lb (80 tonnes). The last 16 units were fitted with multiple-unit controls enabling them to work in pairs, controlled from one cab, and earlier units were later retrofitted with this gear. Withdrawals from service began in the 1970s, the first being intended to provide spare parts. All the units were given Aboriginal names, the first being Yalagonga.

# GAS TURBINE LOCOMOTIVES

## 1-B-1

### JOHANSSON'S GAS TURBINES/1923/SWEDEN

In Sweden, Erik Johansson of the Götaverken firm, Gothenburg, developed a form of gas turbine from 1923. In place of the integral axial compressor used later, a four-cylinder diesel engine was the prime source of energy. The engine drove a two-cylinder air compressor, and the hot diesel exhaust gases were added to the compressor's output. The hot gases drove the blades of a gas turbine. One of these Götaverken installations was put into a locomotive built by Nydquist and Holm, Trollhättan, in 1933, the gas turbine being rated at 550hp (410kW). Transmission was mechanical, the turbine driving a jackshaft through similar gearing to that used for Ljungstrom steam-turbine locomotives. The jackshaft in turn was coupled to the locomotive's driving wheels.

For three years this gas-turbine locomotive ran trials on the Swedish State Railways as well as on Swedish private railways. It was rebuilt to a 1-C-1 wheel arrangement in 1936, but seems to have done little running. The gas-turbine installation was taken out in 1937 and put into a Gothenburg harbour tug, in which it worked for 12 years more.

## A1A-A1A

### BRITISH RAILWAYS No 18000/1950/GREAT BRITAIN

The Great Western Railway picked up the interest in the gas turbine as a prime mover in 1946, and it ordered a gas-turbine-electric locomotive from Brown Boveri and SLM Winterthur in Switzerland. Number 18000 was built in 1950 and delivered to British Rail. The locomotive was rated at 2,500hp (1,863kW), and it had an axial compressor for the turbine air-intake in which heavy oil was burned at a maximum of 600 degreesC (1,112degreesF). A heat exchanger used the hot turbine exhaust gases to warm incoming air from outside for the compressor. The locomotive ran trials on London-to-Bristol and London-to-Plymouth express passenger trains. It was on the latter that it was found that the gas turbine worked at its most efficient full output for only nine per cent of the journey; the rest of the time a lower output sufficed, and consequently the turbine tended to waste fuel.

The locomotive worked trains until 1960, by which time it had traveled 350,000 miles (563,150km). The turbine exhaust gases were finally discharged through the roof, and, as a minor point, this was found to be an effective means of cleaning the roofs of tunnels (the latter were encrusted by steam-locomotive soot of more than 100 years). After 1960, No.18000 lay about here and there

*British Rail No 18000, 1950.*

*Union Pacific RR Nos 61-75, 1952.*

until it was disposed of to the International Union of Railways (UIC). An improved version, No.18100, similarly failed to find much support among management.

## Bo-Bo-Bo-Bo

### UNION PACIFIC Nos.61-75/1952/USA

The Union Pacific Railroad (UP) had its first trial gas-turbine-electric locomotive in 1948, and then a production batch

of 10. After this a larger production batch took over from steam locomotives on the 750-mile (1,207km) section from Cheyenne, Wyoming, to Ogden, Utah. These were Nos. 61-75, built by General Electric, USA, between 1952 and 1954. The railway features long gradients approaching the Rocky Mountains, which were very suitable for gas-turbine operations. Downhill, the locomotive's 4,500hp (3,353kW) gas turbine was closed down to save fuel, and the act of closing down automatically started a 370hp (276kW) diesel engine. This diesel engine took care also of casual locomotive movements and shunting work.

*Russian high-speed train*

# SELF-PROPELLED TRAINS

## SELF-PROPELLED TRAINS

Strictly speaking, self-propelled trains do not belong to a book about locomotives. But the fact is that in many countries the locomotive-hauled passenger train is becoming a rarity. The self-propelled train, usually offering more powered axles than a locomotive-hauled train, and with the simplicity associated with a fixed formation, is quite simply a better proposition in many situations. In Germany a tentative start has also been made in developing a self-propelled freight train. Some self-propelled trains clearly have a locomotive, in the sense of a propulsion unit that can be replaced at the head or tail of a formation by a unit of similar design; the Canadian LRC and British HST are clearly of this type. But such locomotives can only be used for the particular job for which they were designed, so it is better to call them power units. Other trains, like the Japanese Bullet trains, have most or all axles powered, and have nothing resembling a locomotive.

This chapter gives just a sampling of the many types of self-propelled train, past and present, that have appeared. Further reference can be made to the chapters on high-speed trains and tilting trains in the earlier part of this book.

## GASOLINE-POWERED TYPES

### MACK RAILBUS/1920/USA

The first successful gasoline (petrol) railcar in the USA was the McKeen of 1905, of which more than a hundred were built. They had advanced all-steel bodies but the mechanical transmission was failure-prone. Then came the General Electric rail motor. This was a gas-electric, and the electric transmission was an immediate success. These were large vehicles, and could share main lines with conventional trains. The Mack railbus was much smaller and rather primitive. It was built by the Mack Truck Company and aimed to give railroads a competitive vehicle to defend branchline traffic against highway buses. It was really not much more than a bus on flanged wheels, and was powered by a 64hp Mack engine. It was technically quite successful but did not become very popular, with not many more than thirty being built. One of them is preserved by the Strasburg Railroad in Pennsylvania.

## DIESEL TRAINS

### SÖDERMANLAND RAILCARS/1912/SWEDEN

The Södermanland Midland Railway ran through the Swedish county of that name, to the west of Stockholm. For its light passenger traffic, railcars were used, and the world's first diesel-electric motive power unit was built for the Railway in 1912. In what amounted to the baggage compartment of a four-wheel coach, a diesel engine and generator were placed, the engine revolutions determining the output of a nose-suspended dc traction motor on the axle below. The Atlas engine and the railcar itself were built by two firms incorporated later into Allmänna Svenska Aktiebogolat (Asea), which subsequently made a name for itself in electric locomotive construction)). Other diesel-electric railcars were built over the next decade for various Swedish railways, as well as, in 1917, a mobile parcels van that could be regarded as a locomotive.

### CLASS VT877 ('FLYING HAMBURGER')/1930/GERMANY

Around 1930, the German State Railway was trying out various types of diesel railcar. A pair of two-coach

*Union Pacific No M-10001, 1934.*

articulated units were built in 1932, for lesser services on the Berlin-Hamburg main line, which then had a speed limit of 74½mph (120kph). Almost as soon as Class VT877 was running, maximum speed was adjusted upwards to 93mph (150kph), and the service was christened the 'Flying Hamburger'. Two years later the maximum speed had gone up to 100-106mph (160-170kph); and a second pair of Class VT877 units joined the first in 1934. This second pair were still, like the first, second-class only, with a small bar. Over the next five years, further high-speed railcars were built, more powerful, with three coaches and with first-class accommodation included, but it was the original four VT877 class that established the high-speed reputation of the 'Flying Hamburger'.

The curious thing is that there was nothing particularly remarkable in their design. Class VT877 was built by Eisenbahn Verkhersmittel AG, with electrics by Siemens Schukertwerke. The two outer bogies each carried a 410hp (306kW) Maybach engine and dc generator. Each axle of the center bogie was driven by its own nose-suspended traction motor, supplied with current and controlled by the revolutions of the adjacent engine. Nothing much to it, and the high-speed possibilities of the railcar seem to have emerged by accident.

## GREAT WESTERN RAILWAY NO. 1/1933/GREAT BRITAIN

The company AEC was building diesel engines for motor buses in the early 1930s, and in 1933 the engine was

*Great Western Railway No 1, 1933.*

*Mack Railbus, 1920.*

tried for a railway application. An associate firm of AEC, Park Royal Vehicles, built a railcar which became Great Western Railway No.1. The engine for this railcar was rated at 121hp (90kW), and it was mounted beneath the floor. The drive to the wheels was mechanical, and mounted outside the axles on one side. A cardan shaft connected the engine with a Wilson epicyclic gearbox, and another cardan shaft connected the latter with a reversing gearbox. From the reversing gearbox a cardan shaft led to the inner axle of one bogie, and yet another cardan shaft connected the two bogie axles. Three more railcars were built to this plan in 1934, except that they had two engines and consequently the B-B wheel arrangement. In later years the cardan-shaft coupling of the axles was dropped, converting the wheel arrangement to 1A-A1. The Great Western Railway had 38 railcars in all by 1941, growing steadily larger and more powerful. From No.17 upwards they were fitted with ordinary buffers and drawgear so that they could haul vans and coaches. All were modernistic in outline, with some fully streamlined.

Incidentally, during 1934, while the engines for the second batch were being built, some engines for export were being built alongside. These latter went to Ernesto Breda in Italy, where they were fitted to that maker's version of the 1A-A1 Class ALn56 railcar for the Italian State Railways.

## UNION PACIFIC No.M-10001/1934/USA

During the early 1930s there was growing US interest in lightweight high-speed trains, since competition from both the motor car and aircraft was foreseen. The Union Pacific

Railroad took the matter up, and after a prototype train, which for various reasons was judged to be not what was wanted, it acquired No.M-10001 in 1934. This was a diesel-electric locomotive that hauled six light-weight luxury coaches. The locomotive was built by General Motors with electrics from General Electric, and with a Winton 1,200hp (895kW) engine. The four nose-suspended traction motors were supplied with dc from the generator, and controlled by engine revolutions and by motor grouping. The maximum speed of the locomotive was 90mph (145kph). Before going into regular service, M-10001 was used for several publicity workings. Among these was a record 57-hour crossing of the United States by land. The run was from Oakland Pier, across the bay from San Francisco, to Grand Central Station, New York, and the 57-hour time still stood as a record 50 years later. The publicity not only helped the Union Pacific, it also went a long way to establish diesel traction as a viable alternative to steam locomotives for main-line use. Up to that time the diesel tended to be regarded as an auxiliary form of motive power, suitable only for branch lines and for shunting.

## CLASS ALn 56/1935/ITALY

Fiat had been building petrol engine ALb56-class light diesel railcars for the Italian State Railways, but a collision and a disastrous fire cast a cloud over these. So Fiat turned to diesel engines, two of 80hp (59.6kW) each, and produced the diesel-mechanical ALn56 class. This class description indicates a light railcar fuelled by nafta (diesel oil), and possessing 56 passenger seats. This railcar class was built to a total of 110 in 1935-37.

*Finnish State Railways Dm 8 Class, 1964.*

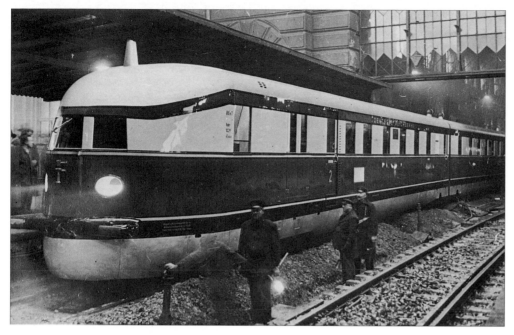

*German State Railway 'Flying Hamburger,' 1930.*

Subsequent ones built from 1937 were equipped for multiple-unit operation, and the classification was altered arbitrarily to ALn556 to indicate this. A total of 100 ALn556-class railcars was built during 1937-38, followed in 1938-39 by 92 more, which had a pair of 115hp (85.75kW) engines. The final eight, to make the total up to 100, had extensive baggage and mail compartments, and were a different class altogether.

## BUDD RAILCARS/1953/USA

During the 1930s the Budd Company started to push stainless-steel coach bodies as being economical in the long run. Its products and those of its licensees in other countries became familiar on a number of railways. In the early 1950s, sales research turned up a possible market for branch-line railcars in the United States itself, and indeed this was profitable for a time, also leading to exports. Eventually, after about 1965, when passenger services on branch lines were disappearing, sales tailed off.

The Budd railcars, designed to satisfy the demand for economical services, had of course stainless-steel bodies. Several hundred of them were sold. Usually a railcar running singly was sufficient, with the interior layout varied in accordance with the needs of the customer. There were four models, differing in the proportions of seating, mail, and baggage space.

Mechanically, each railcar was equipped with two underfloor General Motors 275hp (205kW) engines. Each of these engines drove the inner axle of the adjacent truck, through cardan shafts and a twin-disc hydraulic transmission. Although far from lightweight, they were credited with an 85mph (137kph) maximum speed. Some railroads acquired considerable fleets; the Boston and Maine had 69 of them and they were popular in Canada, too.

## BRITISH RAILWAYS RAILBUS/1958/BRITAIN

German Federal Railways made great use of railbuses on low-traffic lines. These were two-axle vehicles with diesel-mechanical propulsion, powerful enough to pull a trailer when loadings justified it. British Railways, before the wholesale closure of lines, decided to give this concept a try, so railbuses were ordered first from Waggon und Maschinenbau in Germany and then to similar design from

a British bus manufacturer. The German imports weighed just 33,000lb (15 tonnes) and provided 56 seats. They were powered by a 150hp (118kW) engine driving through a Cardan shaft to a six-speed gear-box. Introduced in 1958, they did not last long. They were not very attractive for passengers; in Germany, where transport was more coordinated, bus services competing directly with rail services were not gages, but in Britain this was not the case and for most short-distance passengers a bus was more convenient than the train with its limited stops. However, two of these German railbuses have been preserved in working order.

## FINNISH STATE RAILWAYS Dm 8 CLASS/1964/FINLAND

Smart, stylish, diesel trains for long-distance services had their origin in the streamline era in the USA, but railways sometimes acquired them in the post-war decades, often with a public-relations motive. The 'Blue Pullmans' in 1960s Britain were an example of these. The Finnish Railways Dm 8 trains also had a publicity aim, and their styling was quite impressive for that time and place. But they also had the practical function of making travel swifter and more pleasurable between cities that were often quite far apart by European standards. They were built in Finland (which had a railway rolling stock industry dating back to early steam days) and had the quite low axle-weight of 32,400lb (14.7 tonnes) They were formed into 1000hp

*Budd Railcar, 1953.*

*Via Canada LRC, 1978.*

(745kW) 3-car sets, which were often coupled back-to-back, and their maximum speed was 87mph (140kph). They have now been replaced by more modern stock, including tilting trains.

## BRITISH RAIL HIGH SPEED TRAIN CLASSES 252, 253 AND 254/1972/GREAT BRITAIN

British Rail had a prototype High Speed Train (HST) in 1972: Class 252. It was followed from 1976 by Classes 253 and 254 (with 196 identical locomotives), built by British Rail Engineering with Paxman Valenta engines and electrics by Brush. The trains were made up of seven or eight coaches with a 2,250hp (1.678kW) diesel-alternator locomotive at each end, the whole worked as a multiple unit. Control was by engine revolutions, rheostatic brakes were fitted and the maximum speed was 125mph (200kph).

The trains were very successful and won great popularity, bringing high-speed and modern rolling stock to many routes, starting with the London-Bristol line but then spreading to substantial parts of the non-electrified network. The HSTs' locomotives were very hard-worked, with trains often covering more than 1,000 miles (1,600km) each day, with speeds greater than 100mph (160kph) for much of the time.

## VIA CANADA LRC LOCOMOTIVES/1978/CANADA

Bombardier Inc. of Canada in 1978 built a prototype locomotive and a tilting-body coach as a speculative venture. The locomotive was straightforward enough, having a diesel-alternator with solid-state rectification for the dc traction motors. An Alco engine rated at 2,700hp (2,010kW) was installed, and control was by engine revolutions. On trial this prototype set up a Canadian speed record of 129mph (207kph). The trains were put into production for the national passenger train operator Via Canada, with the Montreal-Toronto service having priority. In practice the trains were disappointing, with difficulties with the tilting mechanism, the automatic doors, and maintenance expenses were high. But the locomotives themselves performed well.

## NETHERLANDS RAILWAYS CLASS DH-II/1981/NETHERLANDS

Netherlands Railways operates a large number of unelectrified branch lines, especially in the north of the country. When the post-war generation of diesel railcars which served these lines became due for replacement a new design was ordered from the German Uerdingen company, which earlier had done much to develop the railbus concept. However, the new DH-II twin-unit trains were not railbuses, but lightweight diesel trains. They began to appear in 1981 and eventually 30 were delivered, to be followed by the DH-I, which was a single-unit variation.

*British Rail High Speed Train, 1972.*

*Netherlands Railways DH-11 Class, 1981.*

Both classes have Cummins 285hp (212kW) engines driving two axles of one of the trucks through Voith hydraulic transmissions.

## NEW SOUTH WALES XPT/1982/AUSTRALIA

The State Railway Authority of New South Wales revolutionized its long-distance passenger traffic by introducing British Rail's concept of High Speed Trains. A locomotive at each end of six (originally five) coaches speeded up transit times, thanks to fast acceleration and better hill-climbing rather than to their capability for a 100mph (160kph) maximum speed (although in fact in 1982 a speed of 114mph (183kph) was reached in Australia). The locomotives were built by Comeng from 1982, and followed the British design fairly closely, although with alterations of detail to suit Australian service.

*British Rail 144 Class, 1986.*

*Light-traffic French lines have long used diesel-mechanical railcars like these. The nearest unit is one of a large post-war class distinguished by the elevated driver's position.*

The Paxman Valenta diesel engine was derated to 1,980hp (1,476kW), although the alternator, solid-state rectifier and traction motors remained unchanged. The radiators, traction-motor blowers and ventilating fans were of greater capacity, while secondary air filtration was fitted to combat dust. The locomotive is slightly shorter than the British version, to reduce overall weight.

### THREE-PHASE RAILCARS/1984/NORWAY

Norwegian State Railways became, at the end of 1984, the owners of the world's first diesel railcars with current-inverters and three-phase traction motors. The 15 railcars were built by Duewag, with electrics by Brown Boveri, Mannheim, for use on the line from Trondheim through Røros to Hamar. A pair of 485hp (362kW) Daimler-Benz underfloor engines drive an alternator, the output of which is solid-state rectified for presentation to the current-inverter. A rheostatic brake is fitted; the bogies feature Wegmann air-sprung secondary suspension.

The railcars work together with a control trailer, and both of them have a driver's position at the outer ends only. A single entrance door on each side of the vehicles

*New South Wales Government Railways XPT, 1982.*

*This diesel train design was built in the Netherlands for the 1950s Trans Europ Express Amsterdam-Zurich service. When retired from this duty, it was bought by the Ontario Northland Railway in Canada, where it provided the main passenger service up to the 1990s.*

*Netherlands Railways DD-1RM Class, 1994.*

*British Rail 313 Class, 1976.*

is positioned immediately behind the driver's seat, so that the set can be one-man operated with the driver taking fares and checking tickets if necessary. The powered coach has seats for 72, and so do most of the control trailers. Four trailers have baggage compartments, and one trailer has compartments for both baggage and postal sorting. A somewhat exigent specification by the railway called for front-end design that does not allow snow and ice to build up, as well as offering protection to the driver in the event of collision with fallen trees, or with elk or reindeer wandering on the track.

### BRITISH RAIL CLASS 144 'PACER'/1986/BRITAIN

Class 144 was the final variation of a type of 2-axle diesel railcars known as 'Pacers.' They were virtually a development of the railbus concept, being rigid-wheelbase vehicles of quite low construction cost compared to the bigger 8-axle units also being built for BR at this time. Class 141 had appeared in 1984 and was virtually a Leyland single-decker bus mounted on railway frames and wheels. It was a twin-unit, but only seated 96 passengers,

*Japanese Railways O Series high-speed train. This has now been superseded by later models taht are faster and quieter. The 300 Series, for example, was introduced in 1992 and can run at 300km/h (186mph).*

and moreover was constantly suffering from mechanical problems. Its successor, Class 142, was rather better and was sponsored by the Manchester Transport Authority. Class 143 was built in Scotland and had several improvements to increase its appeal to passengers. Class 144 was very similar, but was built in BR workshops, and in some cases comprised a three-car train. Passenger transport executives, which subsidized the operation of 'Pacer' services, were not always happy with their performance, and in course of time the initial gearboxes were replaced by Voith transmissions and the Leyland engines by Cummins 225hp (168kW) engines.

### BRITISH RAIL CLASS 158 'SPRINTER' 1989/ BRITAIN

BR Class 150, built in the railway workshops, went into service in 1985 and was designed to replace the diesel multiple units acquired during dieselization in the 1960s. It was at first used as twin-unit sets but subsequenty some three-unit sets were formed. Private builders then supplied the somewhat similar 155 and 156 classes. The Class 158, however, was a design incorporating substantial changes. It had air-conditioning, and aluminium bodies instead of steel. Initial problems with these trains came

mainly from the unfortunate circumstance that the supporting frame, or 'raft,' was not strong enough for the equipment that was attached to it. The interiors were also rather noisy. However, in course of time these problems were eliminated or moderated and the class became the basis of vastly improved cross-country services, both with BR and the subsequent private operating companies. Each car has a Cummins 275kW engine driving two axles through a Voith transmission, and acceleration is much better than with the first-generation diesel multiple units. Maximum permitted speed is 90mph (145kph).

# ELECTRIC POWERED

### LIVERPOOL OVERHEAD RAILWAY MOTOR COACHES/1893/ BRITAIN

The overhead railway along the waterfront in Liverpool, England, was opened in 1893. The motor coaches had gearless traction motors with the rotor built up on an axle.

Stators mounted vertically on either side of the rotor could move up and down vertically with the bogie springs. Each motor coach was rated at 60kW continuously. Originally 500V dc was picked up from a central third rail; later this was moved to the side of the track. With short later extensions, the line was 6¾ miles (11km) long. From about 1898 the 46 motor coaches, which had worked back-to-back hitherto, were rebuilt by Dick, Kerr & Co., Preston, with orthodox nose-suspended traction motors. From 1901, a short trailer coach was added between the motor coaches and multiple-unit working was introduced. The railway was closed entirely in 1957.

### BUDAPEST UNDERGROUND RAILWAY MOTOR COACHES/1896/HUNGARY

The Budapest Underground Railway, the first underground electric railway in continental Europe, was opened in 1896. The line ran 2½ miles (4km) from the center of Pest to the Vàrosliget, a park in which an exhibition commemorating 1,000 years of Hungarian history was held in the year of the line's opening.

The railway was built as a cut-and-cover operation. The necessity of crossing above a main sewer without rising above the street surface, and with an overhead contact wire to be accommodated, made the rolling stock particularly low: it could not be more than 8ft 6in (2.6m) above rail level.

Siemens, aided by a local firm for the coach bodies, built 20 motor coaches for 300V dc (today 550V). The traction motors originally used had two vertical stator poles on either side of the rotor, and a chain drive to the driving axle. The motor coaches' continuous rating was 40kW. The frames were of steel and swept down almost to rail level between the trucks, to allow headroom for boarding passengers. These stout frames allowed the motor coaches to continue to run until 1972, although traction motors had been replaced at least twice, trucks once, and many body alterations made. The motor coaches ran as single units until 1960, after which they hauled light trailers.

## LONG ISLAND RAILROAD MOTOR COACHES/1905/USA

The Long Island Railroad Co. started from a pier on the East River in Long Island City, and from there to Flatbush was electrified at 600V (later 650V) dc in 1905. A total of 134 multiple-unit motor coaches was built, together with 55 trailers, with steel bodies and electrics by Westinghouse. The motor coaches were resistance-controlled, had nose-suspended traction motors, and were each rated continuously at 402hp (300kW). Their maximum speed was set with precision at 57mph (92kph). The Long Island multiple-unit trains reached the Pennsylvania Station on Manhattan Island, New York, in 1910, after a tunnel had been driven under the East River. There they met the Pennsylvania Railroad third-rail electrification that tunnelled under the River Hudson to the west to gain Manhattan Transfer Station in New Jersey. Pennsylvania Railroad prototype locomotives for the electrification to Manhattan Transfer had been tried out on the Flatbush line since 1905.

## LBSCR MOTOR COACHES/1909/BRITAIN

The London, Brighton and South Coast Railway electrified its London suburban railways from 1909, at 6,600V, single-phase, 25Hz ac. The multiple-unit coaches had Winter-Eichberg traction motors and other electrics from Algemeine Elektricitäts Gesellschaft (AEG); the motor coaches' continuous rating was 484hp (360kW). Twin bow current collectors were fitted, the bow in use trailing away from the direction of travel. The collector pans at the top were in aluminium strip, with a central groove to contain graphite-grease lubricant. A transformer reduced voltage on board to a maximum of 600V; and low-tension side tappings were used to control the traction motors, which were nose-suspended. After initial teething troubles, the Winter-Eichberg motors behaved well enough in their daily work.

As they used the first overhead contact wire for railways in London, the advertising slogan adopted for the new trains was 'Overhead Electric'. This appeared prominently

at the stations as well as on suitable bridges spanning roads.

The successor to the Brighton line, Southern Railway, decided to standardize on 650V dc electrifications. The overhead electrification disappeared in sections, the last going in 1929.

## PENNSYLVANIA RAILROAD MOTOR COACHES/1915/USA

In New York the Pennsylvania Railroad was committed to 650V dc traction. Southwards in Philadelphia, however, the same railroad electrified suburban services at 11,000V, single-phase, 25Hz ac from 1915. Such were the perceived advantages that the whole New York-Philadelphia-Washington main line was electrified in the same fashion by 1935. For the Philadelphia-Paoli first electrification, Westinghouse supplied 93 motor coaches in 1915. These motor coaches ran as multiple units, six or even eight together, for it was not until 1918 that more powerful motor coaches were supplied which allowed the haulage of trailers on an expanding suburban network. The original 93 motor coaches had four small, and therefore light, traction motors supported on the axles on one side and nose-suspended on the other. These traction motors were controlled by low-tension side tappings on the transformer of each coach.

## LSWR MULTIPLE UNITS/1915/BRITAIN

The London & South Western Railway (LSWR) was the first of the south London railways to electrify its suburban services at 650V dc, using a third rail placed outside the two lines of rails. This first electrification program was carried out during 1915-16, and 84 multiple-unit train sets were built, using the coach bodies of former steam-drawn rolling stock. There were three coaches in each multiple unit, with a motor coach at each end rated at 563hp (420kW). Traction motors were nose-suspended on the bogie frames, and the controlling resistances' contactors were electropneumatically operated. The first sets of this stock were in the old LSWR livery of salmon pink and dark brown, but this was soon displaced by olive green, which latter colour was adopted by the new Southern Railway when it was formed in 1922. The latter railway electrified many more routes, and the LSWR multiple units became the model for a few hundred more, some new but most using old steam-stock bodies. British Westinghouse supplied the electrics for the 1915-16 units.

## BRITISH RAILWAYS MULTIPLE-UNIT STOCK/1949/BRITAIN

Between the wars, railway electrification at 1,500V dc was official British policy. The former London and North Eastern Railway planned to electrify 20⅕ miles (32.5km) out of its Liverpool Street station in London, down the main line

as far as Shenfield. That was in 1938, but war upset the plan and the line was electrified eventually by British Railways in 1949, still at 1,500V dc. The stock built in 1949 comprised 92 three-coach train sets, each with a motor coach leading two trailers.

The motor coaches were built by the Birmingham Carriage and Truck Co., with electrics from English Electric; the usual practice of British manufacturers was followed, and these electrics were similar to those on many multiple-unit sets exported during 1920-50 and after. The stock was built to a pre-war design, with open layout and sliding guard-operated automatic doors. Conventional nose-suspended traction motors with resistance control were fitted, the motor coaches' continuous rating being 1,006hp (750kW).

During 1960-61 these 92 motor coaches were all rebuilt with solid-state rectifiers and transformers, for the London-Shenfield line had its electrification system altered -- one of comparatively few routes in the world where this has happened. The reason was considerable extension of electrification. In this case it was to 25,000V, single-phase, 50Hz ac. As room for the transformer and the rectifier could not be found on the motor coach, this equipment was put in the trailer coach directly behind it, the pantograph likewise being transferred to this coach. In this state, the trains eventually became Class 306 and worked until all were replaced by modern stock in 1981.

## NETHERLANDS RAILWAYS CLASS EID4/1959/NETHERLANDS

This class had several sub-classes, but all were 4-car multiple units designed for the local 1,500V dc network. The end cars were motored (all axles powered) so there were eight motors, each of 230hp (171kW) totalling 1,840hp (1,371kW) in continuous regime. Maximum speed was 87mph (140kph). Used in inter-city service, the sets had a small buffet and additionally provided seats for 45 first and 160 second-class passengers. Weight in working order was 454,025lb (206 tonnes). In the late 1990s many were still in service, although no longer operating the most prestgious schedules.

## CLASS ALe601 MOTOR COACHES/1961/ITALY

The concept of first-class, supplementary-fare, fast trains still survives on the 3,000V dc Italian State Railways. During the period 1961-72 Casaralta of Bologna built 65 first-class motor coaches with electrics from various firms (two more were rebuilt from trailers in 1980 to replace two lost in an accident). The matching trailers, like the motor coaches, were 89ft 10¾in (27.4m) long, had driver's cabs at both ends (even the restaurant cars), and have Scharfenberg automatic couplers. All the rolling stock was air-conditioned, except for some second-class trailers built for particular services. Trains of any length could be made up readily.

*French Railways RTG Class, 1973.*

The traction motors of the Class ALe601 motor coaches were resistance-controlled, and were nose-suspended on the trucks to drive hollow axles. Connection from the hollow axle to the wheels was by rubber-mounted systems of levers, which were responsive also to coach-spring movements. Continuous rating of an ALe601 motor coach was 825kW (originally, for the earlier vehicles, 770kW), and in service the maximum speed was 112mph (180kph). For trial purposes, however, three motor coaches had had their gear ratios altered for speeds of up to 155mph (250kph). These trials were concerned not least with trying to find a solution to incipient oscillation, with the eventual aim of allowing the whole class to run at a maximum speed of 125mph (200kph).

### SOUTHEASTERN PENNSYLVANIA TRANSPORTATION AUTHORITY (SEPTA) 'SILVERLINER' SERIES/1963/USA

SEPTA provides commuter services in the Philadelphia area. Although it acquired some modern electric locomotives and trains in 1987 its main resource is about 300 electric multiple-unit cars marketed as 'Silverliners.' The eldest of these, Silverliner 2, were built by Budd with GE electrics and delivered from 1963. Silverliner 2 and Silverliner 3 were very similar, although the latter were assembled not by Budd but by the St Louis Car Company. Specifications are the same. Motors are 147hp (110kw) and all axles are motored. Maximum speed is 84mph (135kph). Later units (Silverliner 4), built in the 1970s by GE, had 188hp (140kW) motors.

### CLASS 000/1964/JAPAN

Shinkansen means 'new network' in Japanese, and when the Tokyo-Osaka route of this name was opened to traffic on 1 October 1964, it was not only the world's first high-speed railway of any length for over 100mph (160kph) but also Japan's first standard-gauge main line. Later it was extended from Osaka to Hakata on Kyushu island, 728 miles (1,170km) from Tokyo. Electrification is 25,000V, single-phase, 60Hz ac.

In each two-coach train set, one vehicle was equipped with a pantograph, transformer and rectifier, while the other carried much of the control circuitry and a resistance bank for the rheostatic brake. The transformer was equipped for low-tension tapping to effect train control, the current then being rectified and passed through anti-ripple smoothing circuitry. Traction motors were truck-mounted with a cardan shaft drive to a hollow axle, the latter turning the wheels through a quill drive arrangement. Continuous rating of a two-coach set was 2,000hp (1,480kW).

### PENN CENTRAL METROLINERS/1969/USA

In 1965 Congress passed a High Speed Transportation Act which was a source of funds for high-speed motor coaches for Penn Central's New York-Washington passenger service. Penn Central ordered 50, made up into two-coach train sets, and some more were added later. They were built by the Budd Company, with electrics by Westinghouse or by General Electric USA, and they were delivered from 1969. They could go fast; one of them on trial slightly exceeded 160mph (257kph). Penn Central then belatedly realized that there was more to high speed than buying the motive power: track, electrification catenary, signalling, and the very infrastructure itself must be improved expensively and radically to match. In service the speed of the Metroliners was set at a maximum of 110mph (177kph), improved after a decade to 120mph (193kph) under Amtrak's regime.

The New York-Washington route is electrified with 11,000V, single-phase, 25Hz ac. Each motor coach's dc traction motors are fed from a solid-state rectifier. Control is by transformer-tap changer, control between transformer taps being covered by ignitron, a pre-electronics device, or (according to manufacturer) by thyristor. During a motor coach's acceleration, these latter controls gradually increase voltage and lower current between each transformer tap. Continuous rating of each motor coach is 1,207hp (900kW).

After a few years the Metroliner services were entrusted to locomotive-hauled trains, and the two-car sets re-allocated to less prestigious services.

## BRITISH RAIL CLASS 313/1976/BRITAIN

In the 1970s increasing electrification with ac overhead conductors meant that there was a need for trains that could operate over both the new electrifications and over adjoining dc third-rail systems. Class 313 was the first British electric multiple unit train with dual-voltage capacity. BR workshops (BREL) built the sets, with power equipment supplied by GEC. They were formed of three cars, a motor coach being at each end and a pantograph-carrying trailer in the middle. Conductor shoes for third-rail pick-up were attached to the motor coaches, which had two axles powered; each three-car set was provided with four GEC 110hp (87kW) motors. Maximum speed was 75mph (120kph). North-of-London commuter trains of West Anglia and Great Northern Railway and of Silverlink Trains are the main field of activity of these trains.

## ITALIAN STATE RAILWAYS ETR401 CLASS/1976/ITALY

The ETR401 of Italian State Railways was a 3,000V dc four-coach train, with tilting coach bodies for higher speeds through curves. The forward and rear halves of the train were the same mechanically and electrically. The traction motors were resistance-controlled and slung longitudinally beneath the coach bodies. Each drove an adjacent axle through a cardan shaft and a bevel gear; the cardan shafts had to cope with not only truck and spring movements

but also the tilting movements of the bodies. Continuous rating of the whole train set was 2,360hp (1,760kW), and a rheostatic brake was available. Maximum speed was 155mph (250kph). A single train was built by Fiat (with the assistance of other firms) in 1976, and it served for seven summer seasons on the Rome-Ancona route (for the last few years the service was extended northwards to Rimini). During the winters the train was back in the hands of Fiat, for various tilting matters to be put right and for other maintenance.

Northwards from Rome, the train ran first over part of the new Rome-Florence high-speed line at speeds of up to 125mph (200kph), signalling not then being available for any higher speed. The Apennine Mountains had to be crossed by a winding line to reach Ancona, overcoming such obstacles as 10 miles (16km) of 1 in 40 gradient (2.5 per cent) from Terni up to Spoleto.

It was on the basis of these trials that Fiat became a leader in the new technology of tilting trains that blossomed in the 1990s.

## FRENCH RAILWAYS TGV-PSE/1978/FRANCE

French National Railways' TGV-PSE Class high-speed train was designed for the Paris-Lyons route, the first of the French high-speed lines. One of these sets won the world-record rail speed on a national railway system of 236mph (380kph). Each 10-unit train has a power car at each end. Electrification is 25,000V, single-phase, 50Hz ac, while the trains can also run under 1,500V dc, and some sets are in addition equipped for Swiss 15,000V, single-phase, 16⅔Hz ac. Maximum speed is 168mph (270kph), compared with the 186mph (300kph) of later TGV designs. As well as the locomotive, the leading coach has a powered truck, while its other end rests on an articulation truck. The adhesive weight of this arrangement amounts to 215,110lb (97.6 tonnes). For the dc traction motors, alternating currents are thyristor controlled and are chopper controlled for 1,500V dc supply. Traction motors are body-mounted and drive their axle through gearing and a cardan shaft. For 25,000V, 50Hz the continuous rating is 4,227hp (3,150kW).

## BRITISH RAIL CLASS 317/1981/BRITAIN

These trains were built by BREL, with electrical equipment supplied by GEC, and form one of the largest classes of 25kV ac electric multiple units in Britain. After BR disappeared they were used by several of the new operating companies for London commuter and outer-commuter services, London to Cambridge being one example. That is, they stayed on their original duties but wore new liveries. They were four-car sets, with just one car motored (all four axles being powered). The motors were GEC 330hp (247kW) products. Maximum speed was 100mph (160kph). Of the four cars the heaviest is the motor car, weighing 66,120lb (30 tonnes). These sets are now operated by the West Anglia and Great Northern

Railway and, in smaller numbers, by London Tilbury and Southend Rail.

## LILLE METRO COACHES/1982/FRANCE

The Lille Metro, which first carried passengers early in 1982, and whose first 8-mile (12.7km) route was complete by 1984, claimed to be the first automatic crewless metropolitan railway in the world. Claims such as this are open to discussion, and Lille was certainly preceded by short lines of the type that have been given the name 'people-movers'. Indeed, an automatic people-mover ran at the Wembley Exhibitions of 1924 and 1925 outside London.

The Lille motor coaches, built by SA Engins Matra and CMIT Lorraine from 1979, are, basically, carried on two single-axle bogies. Two traction motors are slung longitudinally beneath the coach body, and each drives an axle through a cardan shaft and bevel gears. Supply is 750V dc, taken from conductor rails embodied in the vertical guide rails (see below), and chopper controlled for the traction motors. Normally two motor coaches work together as a train set, and the sets can be coupled together for multiple-unit working. Regenerative and air brakes are fitted, and the continuous rating of each motor coach is 322hp (240kW).

A peculiarly French feature is that each motor coach is propelled by four rubber-tyred wheels, which run on concrete pathways. In addition, each truck has a pair of rubber-tyred guide wheels, mounted horizontally to bear against vertical guide rails on either side at a gauge of 6ft 9⅛in (2,060mm). The truck has also a vertical metal wheel at the center of the axle. At junctions this vertical wheel engages with a slot between two rails, the rails containing a switch to direct the vehicle in one direction or the other. The driver's place is taken by inductive electrical signals from the ground, supplemented by ultrasonic sensors at the start of each block section, for automatic train running.

## METRO NORTH M3 CLASS/1983/USA

The New York Central RR had considerable third-rail electrified mileage in the New York suburbs which later became part of the Metro North division of New York's Metropolitan Transportation Authority. Two classes of multiple-unit train were acquired for this service, M1 Class in 1971-73 and M3 Class in 1983-84. They are similar, being built by Budd with electrical equipment by GE. They are two-car sets that can run in multiple, as distinct from the M4 and M6 classes, which are three-car sets that also have pantographs to enable them to work on former New Haven RR ac lines as well as the NYC dc. The M1 and M3 were turned out with blue trim, whereas the other classes had a red trim. One hundred and forty-two M3 cars were acquired, and 178 M1. They have all axles powered by 148hp (110kw) motors, and a theoretical maximum speed of 100mph (160kph).

*Metro North M3 Class, 1983.*

### BRITISH RAIL CLASS 465 'NETWORKER'/1992/BRITAIN

While BR was introducing new classes of ac electric multiple unit trains it was also finding replacements for third-rail dc sets. These were of various ages, amd bore the decades-long traditions of the old 'Southern Electric.' The Class 445 of 1982, of which about 400 cars were built, was one move in that direction, but was later overshadowed by the new Class 465 built for the soon-to-disappear Network South East by GEC, Brush, and ABB. These trains, called 'Networkers,' brought the new technology of brushless asynchronous induction motors, using thyristor inverters. They were four-car sets, the driving end vehicles flanking two intermediate motor coaches. Continuous power output was 1,610hp (1,200kW), and they had regenerative brakes that converted momentum into electrical energy that was fed back to the third rail. Class 466 was similar, but was presented as a two-car set.

### NETHERLANDS RAILWAYS CLASS DD-1RM/1994/NETHERLANDS

Electric multiple units carry almost all the heavy passenger traffic of Netherlands Railways. The DD-1RM type was ordered in large numbers in the 1990s, and by the end of 1996 the order for 34 three-car and 47 four-car sets was completed. They were built by Talbot of Germany, with the French company De Dietrich building the intermediate trailers of the four-car sets. The well-known local Holec company was responsible for the electrical equipment. They were double-deck, with more leg-room for passengers than in previous designs, and were air-conditioned. They were considerably lighter than previous designs, while carrying more passengers. These trains are used for long-distance (by Dutch standards) internal services.

# GAS-TURBINE PROPULSION

### FRENCH RAILWAYS RTG CLASS/1973/FRANCE

The advantages and disadvantages of gas turbine propulsion were the same for passenger trains as for freight locomotives; there was a maintenance economy thanks to the elimination of reciprocating parts, and there was a high power/weight ratio, but fuel costs could be high whenever the engine operated at less than full power. The self-propelled gas turbine train was therefore suited to long, fast, journeys. French Railways had a few non-electrified routes where such trains seemed desirable, and in 1969 acquired 14 ETG Class trains. These were four-car sets, the two extreme cars being powered. Then in 1973 the bigger and better RTG appeared, of which 78 sets were acquired. This had three instead of two intermediate trailer cars, and the power unit was of 1,040hp (775kW) rather than 988hp (736kW) driving through a Voith hydraulic transmission. Both sets had a maximum speed of 100mph (160kph). The builders of the RTG were Ateliers Construction du Nord de la France, with the engine firm Turboméca supplying the power plant. In terms of popular appeal these trains were very successful; the inhabitants of Cherbourg, for example, no longer felt slighted by the non-electrification of their railway to Paris. Economically, too, these trains seemed likely to justify themselves, but they were betrayed by the sharp increase in oil prices of the mid-1970s. A few were still soldiering on in the late 1990s, but had an uncertain future.

### AMTRAK RTL CLASS/1976/USA

Gas-turbine trains had a shaky beginning in North America. On its creation, Amtrak inherited two train sets built by Pullman using United Aircraft technology, but these were soon retired because their availability factor seemed unlikely to improve beyond an abysmal 60 per cent. Five similar sets were assembled in Canada by Montreal Locomotive Works for Canadian National Railways, which hoped to put them into Montreal-Toronto service. However, these too had problems and a proper service was hardly established. Nevertheless, Amtrak persisted and acquired six French turbo-trains. Partly to demonstrate its willingness to 'buy American,' Amtrak also ordered seven more very similar sets from Rohr Industries, to be built under licence. These were used between New York and Niagara Falls, worked quite well, but were more expensive to run than conventional trains. Their assimilation was not helped when Rohr Industries left the business. These trains were five-car sets, the extreme cars being powered by a 1,140hp (850kW) gas turbine with Voith hydraulic transmission. One of the trailer cars was equipped with a 295hp (220kW) motor to allow electric power to take over in the approaches of New York. They were still in service in the late 1990s, their economics having been improved by falling oil prices.

# WHEEL NOTATION

Wheel notation is a method of describing a locomotive according to the number and function of its wheels. The first figure denotes the leading carrying wheels, the second the number of driving wheels, and the third represents the number of trailing wheels. In some locomotive notations there are more than one set of driving wheels and in some double-ended engines the figures can be reversed, such as in the Garratt type locomotive.

In the British and American systems the figure denotes the total number of wheels on each axle whereas in the European system, from around 1900, the figures denote the wheels on one side only. Later a system was adopted which denoted the driving wheels by a letter instead of a number and counted the number of wheels on one side only. Thus, a 4-4-2 in the original system became a 2-2-1 in the first European notation and finally a 2-B-1.

In the case of electric and diesel-electric locomotives, the letter by itself denotes mechanically coupled wheels, but in the case of individually driven wheels the letter is followed by an `o'. Thus in a bogie with separately driven wheels the notation is Bo.

| | GB/U.S.A. | U.I.C. | Names |
|---|---|---|---|
| ●● | 0-2-2 | A1 | |
| ●● | 2-2-0 | 1A | Planet |
| ●●● | 2-2-0 | 1A1 | Patentee |
| ●●● | 4-2-0 | 2A | Jervis |
| ●●●● | 4-2-2 | 2A1 | Bicycle |
| ●●●● | 6-2-0 | 2A | Crampton |
| ●● | 0-4-0 | B | |
| ●●● | 0-4-2 | B1 | |
| ●●● | 2-4-0 | 2B | |
| ●●●● | 2-4-2 | 1B1 | Columbia |
| ●●●● | 4-4-0 | 2B | American |
| ●●●●● | 4-4-2 | 2B1 | Atlantic |
| ●●●●●● | 4-4-4 | 2B2 | Reading |
| ●●● | 0-6-0 | C | |
| ●●●● | 0-6-2 | C1 | |
| ●●●● | 2-6-0 | 1C | Mogul |
| ●●●●● | 0-6-4 | C2 | |
| ●●●●● | 2-6-2 | 1C1 | Prairie |

| | GB/U.S.A. | U.I.C. | Names |
|---|---|---|---|
| ●●●●●● | 2-6-4 | 1C2 | Adriatic |
| ●●●●● | 4-6-0 | 2C | Tenwheeler |
| ●●●●● | 4-6-2 | 2C1 | Pacific |
| ●●●●●●● | 4-6-4 | 2C2 | Hudson |
| ●●●● | 0-8-0 | D | |
| ●●●●● | 2-8-0 | 1D | Consolidation |
| ●●●●● | 0-8-2 | D1 | |
| ●●●●●● | 2-8-2 | 1D1 | Mikado |
| ●●●●●●● | 2-8-4 | 1D2 | Berkshire |
| ●●●●●● | 4-8-0 | 2D | Mastodon |
| ●●●●●● | 4-8-2 | 2D1 | Mountain |
| ●●●●●●●● | 4-8-4 | 2D2 | Confederation |
| ●●●●●●●●●● | 6-8-6 | 3D3 | |
| ●●●●● | 0-10-0 | E | Decapod (GB) |
| ●●●●●● | 2-10-0 | 1E | Decapod (USA) |
| ●●●●●● | 0-10-2 | E1 | |
| ●●●●●●● | 2-10-2 | 1E1 | Santa Fe |
| ●●●●●●●● | 2-10-4 | 1E2 | Texas |

| GB/U.S.A. | U.I.C. | Names | GB/U.S.A. | U.I.C. | Names |
|---|---|---|---|---|---|
| 4-10-0 | 2E | | 0-6-2.2-6-0 | C1.1C | |
| 4-10-2 | 2E1 | | 2-6-6-0 | 1C.C | |
| 0-12-0 F | | | 2-6-6-2 | 1C.C1 | |
| 2-12-0 | 1F | Centipede | 2-6-2.2-6-2 | 1C1.1C1 | |
| 2-12-4 | 1F2 | | 2-6-6-4 | 1C.C2 | |
| 4-12-2 | 2F1 | Union Pacific | 4-6-6-4 | 2C.C2 | Challenger |
| | | | 4-6-2.2-6-4 | 2C1.1C2 | |
| **Divided Drive** | | | 4-6-4.4-6-4 | 2C2.2C2 | |
| 2-2-2-0 | 1AA | | | | |
| 4-2-2-0 | 2AA | | 0-8-6-0 | D.C | |
| 2-2-2-2 | 1AA1 | | 0-8-8-0 | D.D | |
| 6-4-4-6 | 3BB3 | | 2-8-6 | 1D3 | |
| 4-4-4-4 | 2BB2 | | 2-8-8-0 | 1D.D | |
| 4-6-4-4 | 2CB2 | | 2-8-8-2 | 1D.D1 | |
| 4-4-6-4 | 2BC2 | | 2-8-2.2-8-2 | 1D1.1D1 | |
| | | | 2-8-8-4 | 1D.D2 | Yellowstone |
| **Articulated** | | | 4-8-8-2 | 2D.D1 | Cab Ahead |
| 0-4-4-0 | BB | | 4-8-8-4 | 2D.D2 | Big Boy |
| 2-4-4-0 | 1BB | | 4-8-2.2-8-4 | 2D1.1D2 | |
| 2-4-6 | 1B3 | | 4-8-4.4-8-4 | 2D2.2D2 | |
| 2-4-4-2 | 1BB1 | | | | |
| 4-4-4-4 | 2BB2 or 1B2B | | 2-8-8-8-2 | 1D.D.D1 | Triplex |
| 2-4-2.2-4-2 | 1B1.1B1 | | 2-8-8-8-4 | 1D.D.D2 | |
| 4-4-2.2-4-4 | 2B1.1B2 | | | | |
| | | | 2-10.10-2 | 1E.E1 | |
| 0-6-4-0 | C.B | | | | |
| 0-6-6-0 | CC | Erie | | | |

# MEASURES

Although in the following table the serried ranks of digits give an air of exactitude, in reality each number should be taken as a rough guide rather than as scientific certitude. This is particularly the case with steam locomotives.

The pulling power of a locomotive is defined by its tractive effort, or drawbar pull. This is the force acting on its coupler as it puts out its maximum effort. With steam locomotives it can be calculated by multiplying cylinder volume by steam pressure and dividing the result by the diameter of the driving wheels. Unfortunately, for one reason or another, cylinders do not fill with steam at boiler pressure and an assumption has to be made. In most countries it is reckoned that with a superheated locomotive it is roughly accurate to put into the calculation a steam pressure just 85 per cent of the boiler pressure (75 per cent in the case of non-superheated boilers). But some countries, Germany for example, prefer a more pessimistic assumption, going as low as 60 or even 50 per cent. So a locomotive in Germany might be more powerful than its rated tractive effort would seem to indicate. To add further complication, some railway administrations imposed an 'official' tractive effort, lower than the calculated figure, so as to discourage operators from taxing locomotives excessively.

Tractive effort says nothing about a locomotive's ability to haul loads at speed. Horsepower would give some indication of this, but it is hard to calculate accurately for a steam locomotive. It can be found by careful testing, and some locomotives have indeed undergone such tests. In the following tables there is a column for horsepower. In the case of diesel and electric locomotives this can be calculated reasonably accurately, but in the case of steam locomotives only a few figures are cited, because nothing more is available.

With steam locomotives, stamina depends largely on the ability to raise steam. In the text, the total heating surface (firebox, tubes, and superheater) is sometimes given, but this again is not a particularly helpful figure because so much depends on the proportions between the various boiler elements. Also, some administrations measured the area on the water side, and others on the hot-gas side, which can make a difference approaching ten per cent. The tables do provide one indication, the grate area. This figure does not prove much, but is a guide to combustion rate of the fuel, which is a key factor in the generation of horsepower.

Weights of locomotives, although given to the nearest pound, are seldom that accurate. There is a designed weight and an actual weight, which are seldom the same. Also, weight in working order can be taken as weight at the start of a trip, or the weight halfway through a trip. As with tractive effort, if the number ends neatly with a string of zeros, it is probably not the actual figure; that is, in some way it expresses a chosen rather than a real value.

Diameter of wheels can actually vary by an inch or two due to tyre wear (so, in theory, a locomotive's tractive effort can grow as it wears down its tyres). The French, among others, laid down strict rules as to precisely where in a locomotive's work cycle the wheels should be measured.

Things are a little simpler with diesel and electric traction. Because motors can overheat, it is customary to give output figures for short-term (that is, starting), hourly, or continuous regimes. But even here the output figures are 'nominal;' they show what ought to happen but not always what actually does happen. Even so, the figures quoted for modern traction are much more reliable indicators than those for steam traction. Horsepower, which is really a product of tractive effort and speed, is often replaced by kilowatts in electric locomotives. Kilowatt figures can be converted to horsepower figures, and vice-versa, by multiplying or dividing with a factor. Needless to say, there is no universal agreement on what that factor should be, but 1.35 is a rough approximation.

Maximum speed of locomotives is no such thing. A locomotive might be capable of going faster than that speed. It should be taken as the speed which is allowed, given the need to preserve the track from excessive wear and tear, as well as the need to have a safety margin.

Finally, referring to the tables which follow, the column indicating the builders of given locomotives presents some problems. In some industrialized countries, cartels distributed orders throughout the locomotive industry so there was no single builder. In other cases, large-scale requirements could only be satisfied by using a number of works. That is why the builder's name has so often to be 'Various.'

# LEADING CHARACTERISTICS OF STEAM LOCOMOTIVES

| Date | Class/name | Railway | Builder | Cylinder diameter in / cm | Piston stroke in / cm | Driving wheel dia. in / M | Steam pressure kpa / psi | Firegrate area sq.ft / sq.M | Weight 1b / tonne | T/Force 1b / kg | Power ihp |
|------|-----------|---------|---------|---------|---------|---------|---------|---------|---------|---------|------|
| **0-2-2 (A1)** | | | | | | | | | | | |
| 1829 | Rocket | Liv & Man. | Stephenson | 8/20.3 | 17/43.2 | 56/1.42 | 345/50 | 6/0.55 | 9,630/4.37 | 780/354 | 14 |
| 1830 | Northumbrian | Liv & Man | Stephenson | 11/27.9 | 16/40.6 | 60/1.52 | 345/50 | 6.2/0.58 | 16,800/7.62 | 1,370/622 | |
| **2-2-0 (1A)** | | | | | | | | | | | |
| 1830 | Planet | L. & M.R. | Stephenson | 11/27.9 | 16/40.6 | 60/1.52 | 345/50 | 7/0.6 | 17,470/7.9 | 1,340/608 | 23 |
| 1836 | Copperknobs | Lon & B' ham | Ed. Bury | 11/27.9 | 16.2/41 | 61/1.55 | 345/50 | 1/0.65 | 22,050/9.9 | 1,290/586 | 27 |
| **2-2-2 (1A1)** | | | | | | | | | | | |
| 1812 | Prince Regent | Middleton Fenton | Murray & Wood | 8/20.3 | 24/508 | 42/1.07 | 380/55 | 4.1/4.2 | 1,710/776 | | |
| 1835 | Patentee | Liv & Man. | R. Stephenson | 11/27.9 | 18/46 | 54/1.37 | 345/50 | 8 9.9/0.9 | 22,640/10.3 | 1,710/776 | |
| 1837 | North Star | G.W.R. | Stephenson | 16/40.6 | 16/40.6 | 96/2.44 | 345/50 | 13.5/1.3 | 46,300/21 | 1,810/822 | 45 |
| 1843 | Buddicom. | Ouest | Buddicom | 13.9/35.5 | 16/53.5 | 67.5/17.2 | 832/120 | 9.7/0.9 | 37,485/17 | 6,167/2,800 | |
| 1846 | Great Western | G.W.R. | Swindon | 18/46 | 24/61 | 96/2.44 | 690/100 | 22.6/2. | 1 63,950/28.9 | 6,885/3126 | 200 |
| 1847 | Jenny Lind | L.B.S.C. | E.B. Wilson | 15/38 | 20/51 | 72/1.83 | 827/120 | 12.2/1.1 | 53,800/24.4 | 8,820/4000 | 200 |
| 1851 | Bloomer | L.N.W.R. | Sharp Stewart | 16/41 | 22/56 | 84/2.13 | 1,034/15 | | 68,300/31 | 8,550,3880 | 250 |
| 1862 | Problem (Lady of the Lake) L.N.W.R. | | Crewe | 16/41 | 24/61 | 91/2.32 | 827/120 | 14.9/1.38 | 60,400/27.4 | 6,850/3110 | 270 |
| **4-2-0 (2A)** | | | | | | | | | | | |
| 1832 | Experiment Brother Jonathan | Mohawk & Hudson | W. Point Foundry | 9.5/24 | 16/41 | 60/1.52 | 345/50 | | 15,600/7.1 | 1,020/460 | |
| 1839 | Martin van Buren | Phil. & Col | Baldwin | 9/23 | 16/41 | 54/1.37 | 827/120 | 16,500/7.6 | 2,450/1,1 | | 10 |
| 1846 | Crampton 'Namur' | Namur-Liege | Tulk & Ley | 16/41 | 20/51 | 84/2.13 | 595/85 | 14.5/1.35 | 48,500/21.9 | 4,400/2,000 | |
| 1853 | Crampton | Nord | Derosne et Cail | 16.5/42 | 22/56 | 90/2.29 | 770/110 3 | 13.7/1.27 | 66,700/30.3 | 4,560/2,070 | |
| **4-2-2 (2A1)** | | | | | | | | | | | |
| 1847 | Iron Duke | G.W.R. | Swindon | 18/46 | 24/61 | 96/2.44 | 700/100 | 22.6/2.1 | 71,000/32.2 | 6,890/3,130 | 200 |
| 1870 | No. 1 | G.N.R. | Doncaster | 18/46 | 28/71 | 97/2.46 | 1,104/160 | 1/.8/1.8 | 86,200/39 | 12,700/5,770 | 400 |
| 1887 | Spinners | M.R. | Derby | 19.5/49 | 26/66 | 93/2.36 | 1,241/180 | 21/1.9 | 95650/43.6 | 16,200/7,350 | 480 |
| **6-2-0 (3A)** | | | | | | | | | | | |
| 1848 | Liverpool | L.N.W.R. | Bury Curtiss & Kennedy | 18/46 | 24/61 | 96/2.44 | 827/120 | 21.5/2.0 | 35.6/36.2 | 6,200/2,810 | 500 |
| 1849 | Crampton | Camden & Amboy | J. Norris | 14/36 | 38/96 | 96/2.44 | 690/100 | | 25/25.4 | 5,130/2,330 | 180 |
| **0-4-0 (B)** | | | | | | | | | | | |
| 1805 | Black Billy | Gateshead | J. Steel | 1x7/18 | 36/92 | 38/0.96 | 172/25 | | 520/236 | | |
| 1814 | Puffing Billy | Wylam Colliery | W. Hedley | 9/23 | 36/92 | 39/0.99 | 310/45 | 6/0.6 | | 3,100/1,410 | |
| 1825 | Locomotion | S. & D. | Stephenson | 10/25.4 | 24/61 | 48/1.22 | 207/30 | 7/0.6 | 14,300/6.5 | 1,280/580 | 11 |
| 1827 | | St Etienne-Lyons | Stephenson | 8.7/22 | 26/66 | 48/1.22 | 345/50 | 6/0.55 | 20,800/9.3 | 1,640/740 | 22 |
| 1829 | | St Etienne-Lyons | Marc Seguin | 9/23 | 23/58 | 47.7/1.21 | 303/44 | 7/0.65 | 13,200/6 | 1,460/660 | |
| 1830 | Best Friend | South Carolina | W. Point Foundry | 6/15.2 | 16/41 | 54/1.37 | 345/50 | 2.2/0.2 | 9,920/4.5 | 450/205 | |
| 1831 | John Bull | Camden & Amboy | Stephenson | 9/23 | 20/51 | 54/1.37 | 345/50 | 10/0.9 | 23,150/10.5 | 1,270/580 | |
| 1831 | Planet | L. &. M.R. | Stephenson | 14/35.6 | 16/41 | 54/1.37 | 345/50 | 10.4/0. | 97 23,100/10 | 2,460/1,120 | |
| 1828 | Lancashire Witch | Bolton & Leigh | Stephenson | 9/23 | 24/61 | 48/1.22 | 345/50 | 12/1.1 | 15,400/7 | 1,720/780 | |
| **0-4-2 (B1)** | | | | | | | | | | | |
| 1838 | Lion | Liv & Man. | Todd Kitson & Laird | 11/28 | 20/51 | 54/1.37 | 331/48.1 | 1.2/1.04 | 42,300/19.2 | 1,830/830 | 28 |
| 1876 | Anglet | Bayonne Biarritz | Schneider | (1x9.4/24 (1x15.7/40 | 17.7/45 | 47.2/1.2 | 1,034/150 | 10.8/1.0 | 43,200/19.6 | 4,400/1,980 | |
| 1882 | Gladstone | L.B.S.C. | Brighton | 18.2/46 | 26/66 | 78/1.98 | 1,034/150 | 20.6/1.9 | 86,700/39.9 | 14,000/6,360 | 420 |

| Date | Class/name | Railway | Builder | Cylinder diameter in / cm | Piston stroke in / cm | Driving wheel dia. in / M | Steam pressure kpa / psi | Firegrate area sq.ft / sq.M | Weight 1b / tonne | T/Force 1b / kg | Power ihp |
|---|---|---|---|---|---|---|---|---|---|---|---|
| **2-4-0 (1B)** | | | | | | | | | | | |
| 1855 | Saxon | L.S.W.R. | Nine Elms | 15/38 | 24/61 | 60/1.52 | 896/130 | 15.6/1.5 | 66,750/30.3 | 9,950/4,5 | 10 |
| 1863 | Samson | L.N.W.R. | Crewe | 17/43 | 24/61 | 72/1.83 | 827/120 | 14.9/1.4 | 64,500/29.3 | 9,800/4,450 | 300 |
| 1870 | 800 | M.R. | Derby | 18/46 | 26/66 | 80/2.03 | 965/140 | 16/1.5 | 80/900/36.7 | 12,500/5,670 | |
| 1872 | 901 | N.E.R. | Darlington | 17/43 | 24/61 | 84/2.14 | 965/140 | 16/1.5 | 87,000/39.7 | 10,000/4,540 | 790 |
| 1874 | Precedent | L.N.W.R. | Crewe | 17/43 | 24/61 | 80/2.03 | 965/140 | 17.1/1.6 | 72,500/32.9 | 10,400/4,720 | 300 |
| 1880. | B50. | Indonesian State. | Sharp Stewart | 15/38 | 8/45.7 | 55.5/1.41 | 978/142 | 11.8/1.1 | 45,472/20.6 | 8,829/4,008 | |
| 1891 | T26 | G.E.R. | Stratford | 1.5/44.5 | 24/61 | 68/1.73 | 1,102/160 | 18/1.7 | 90,405/41 | 14,700/6,675 | |
| **2-4-2 (1B1)** | | | | | | | | | | | |
| 1895 | 590 | Burlington | Baldwin | 19/48.3 | 26/66 | 84/2.13 | 1,380/200 | 45/4.17 | 121,000/54.9 | 19,000/8,630 | |
| **4-4-0 (2B)** | | | | | | | | | | | |
| 1837 | Campbell's Locomotive | Phil., Gormanstown & Norristown | J. Brooks | 14/36 | 16/41 | 54/1.37 | 621/90 | 2/1.1 | 26,400/12 | 4,440/2,020 | 60 |
| 1837 | Hercules | Beaver Meadow | Garret & Eastwick | 12/30 | 18/46 | 44/1.12 | 621/90 | 8/0.7 | 29,920/13.6 | 4,500/2,040 | |
| 1845 | Grosse Gloggnitzer | Vienna-Gloggintz | J. Haswell | 15.8/40 | 22.8/58 | 50/1.26 | 538/78 | 10.8/1.0 | 46,900/21.3 | 7,320/3,320 | |
| 1855 | General | West. & Atl'c | Rogers | 15/38 | 24/61 | 78/1.98 | 621/90 1 | 4.5/1.3 | 89,800/40.8 | 6,900/3,130 | |
| 1867 | No.122 Tandem | Erie | Hinkley & Drury | 2x9/23 2x24/61) | 26/66 | 60/1.52 | 896/130 | 15.7/1.5 | 61,400/27.8 | 6,000/2,720 | |
| 1886 | 2.121 | Nord | S.A.C.M | 2x13.4/34 2x24/61) | 25.2/64 | 83.2/2.11 | 1,400/203 | 22/2.04 | 96,000/43.6 | 18,000/8,200 | 570 |
| 1892 | No.999 | N Y Central | Schenectady | 8.5/47 | 26/66 | 86/2.18 | 1,275/185 | 32.3/3.0 | 134,400/61.1 | 16,200/7,350 | 800 |
| 1895 | Duke | G.W.R. | Swindon | 18/45.7 | 26/66 | 68/1.73 | 1,240/180 | 17.2/1.59 | 110,200/50 | 18,955/8605 | |
| 1898 | Small Ben | H.R. | Lochgorm | 18/45.7 | 26/66 | 72/1.83 | 1,206/175 | 20.3/1.9 | 101,430/46.5 | 18,402/8,354 | |
| 1898 | Bulldog | G.W.R. | Swindon | 18/46 | 26/66 | 68/1.73 | 1,380/200 | 20.3/1.88 | 116,000/52.7 | 21,100/9,600 | |
| 1899 | Big 'C' | P.L.M. | P.L.M. | 2x13.4/34 2x21.3/54 | 24.4/62 | 78.7/2.0 | 1,500/217 | 26.7/2.5 1 | 22,300/55.5 | 21,000/9,530 | 900 |
| 1899 | D40 | G.N.S.R. | North British | 18/45.7 | 26/66 | 73/1.86 | 1,137/165 | 18.2/1.7 | 101,430/46 | 16,184/7,347 | |
| 1899 | T9 | L.S.W.R. | Nine Elms | 19/48.3 | 26/66 | 79/2.0 | 1205/175 | 24/2.23 | 115,762/52.5 | 17,675/8,024 | |
| 1900 | Claud Hamilton | G.E.R. | Stratford | 19/48.3 | 26/66 | 84/2.13 | 1,240/180 | 21/1.95 | 125,311/56.8 | 17,095/7,761 | |
| 1901 | No. 2631 Compound | M.R. | Derby | 1x19/48.3 | 26/66 | 84/2.13 | 1,345/195 | 28.4/2.64 | 134,200/61 | 23,200/10,530 | 1,280 |
| 1902 | City. | G.W.R. | Swindon | 18/45.7 | 26/66 | 80.5/2.05 | 1,378/200 | 20.6/1.9 | 123,200/55.8 | 17,789/8,076 | |
| 1904 | S.4 | Prussian | Borsig | 21.3/54 | 24.8/63 | 78/1.98 | 1,200/174 | 24.4/2.25 | 120,100/54.6 | 20,300/4,210 | 1,585 |
| 1904 | SPS | Indian | Various | 20/51 | 26/66 | 74/1.8 | 1,240/180 | 25.3/2.35 | 116,480/52.8 | 21,502/9,762 | |
| 1907. | D16sb | Pennsylvania | Altoona | 20.5/52.1 | 26/66 | 68/1.73 | 1,425/175 | 33.2/3.08 | 141,000/63.9 | 23,900/10,850 | |
| 1909 | Scott | N.B.R. | North British | 19/48 | 26/66 | 66/1.68 | 1,309/190 | 21.1/1.9 | 121,423/55.1 | 19,434/8,823 | |
| 1910 | Dunlastair | C.R. | St Rollox | 20.25/51.4 | 26/66 | 78/1.98 | 1,233/179 | 21/1.95 | 130,095/59 | 19,751/8/966.. | |
| 1912 | B53 | Indonesian | Hartmann | 15/380 | 23.6/60 | | 1,173/171 | 13.9/1.3 7 | 1,442/32.4 | 13,050/5,924 | |
| 1913 | S | G.N.R.(I) | Beyer Peacock | 19/48 | 26/66 | 79/2.0 | 1,378/200 | 22.9/2.13 | 205,947/93.4* | 20,198/9,169 | |
| 1930 | 'V' School | South'n | Eastleigh | 3x16.5/42 | 26/66 | 79/2.01 | 1,517/220 | 28.3/2.63 | 150,530/68.4 | 25,100/11,400 | 1,600 |
| **4-4-2 (2B1)** | | | | | | | | | | | |
| 1895 | 590 | Burl | Baldwin 1 | 9/48 | 26/66 | 84.3/2.14 | 1,380/200 | 44.5/4.14 | 138,000/62.7 | 19,000/8,600 | |
| 1901 | De Glehn | Nord | S.A.C.M. | 2x13.4/34 2x22/56 | 25.2/64 | 80.3/2.04. | 1,600/232 | 25.9/2.74 | 141,100/64 | 16,400/7,450 | 1,300 |
| 1902 | 251 | G.N.R. | Doncaster | 19/48 | 24/61 | 79.5/2.02 | 2,500/232 | 31/2.9 | 155,500/70.7 | 16,200/7,290 | 440 |
| 1903 | 'V' | N.E.R. | Gateshead | 20/51 | 28/71 | 82/2.08 | 1,378/200 | 27/2.5 | 161,300/73.3 | 23,200/10,440 | 650 |
| 1904 | 171 | G.W.R. | Swindon | 18/46 | 30/76 | 80/2.03 | 1,207/175 | 27.1/2.5 | 164,600/74.8 | 28,280/12,850 | 1,700 |
| 1906 | 40 | G.W.R. | Swindon | 4x14.2/36 | 26/66 | 80/2.03 | 1,552/225 | 27.1/2.5 | 169,300/76.9 | 25,500/11,480 | 1,600 |
| 1912 | E.6s | Penn. | Altoona | 23.5/60 | 26/66 | 80/2.03 | 1,448/210 | 55.2/5.1 | 243,700/110.8 | 32,300/14,540 | 2,450 |
| 1935 | Hiawatha | Mill | ALCO | 19/48 | 28/71 | 84/2.13 | 2.069/300 | 69/6.4 | 286,000/130 | 30,700/13,940 | 4,200 |
| 1939 | 12 | S.N.C.B. | Cockerill | 18.9/48 | 28.4/710 | 82.5/2.1 | 1,764/256 | 40/3.7 | 196,245/89 | 28,158/12,784 | |
| **4-4-4 (2B2)** | | | | | | | | | | | |
| 1935 | No. 1 | B & O | Mt Clare | 17.5/44.4 | 28/71 | 84/2.13 | 2,414/350 | 61.8/5.7 | 217,000/98.6 | 28,000/12,600 +7,000/3,150 | |
| 1936 | F-1A | Can Pacific | Canadian Loco. Co. 16.5/42 | 28/71 | 75/1.9 | 2,070/300 | 45/4.18 | 239,000/108.6 | 26,000/11,800 | | |
| 1936 | 3000 | Can Pacific | Montreal Loco. Co. 17.2/43.7 | 28/71 | 80/2.03 | 2,070/300 | 55.6/5.16 | 263,000/119.5 | 26,500/12,030 | | |
| **0-6-0 (C)** | | | | | | | | | | | |
| 1827 | Royal George | St & Darl'tin | Shildon | 11/28 | 20/51 | 48/1.22 | 372/54 | 5.6/0.5 | | 2,300/1,030 | 10 |
| 1852 | 1001 | N.E.R. | Stephenson | 17/43.2 | 18/46 | 50/1.27 | 896/130 | 13.3/1.2 | 62,700/28.5 | 11,500/5,220 | |

| Date | Class/name | Railway | Builder | Cylinder diameter in / cm | Piston stroke in / cm | Driving wheel dia. in / M | Steam pressure kpa / psi | Firegrate area sq.ft / sq.M | Weight 1b / tonne | T/Force 1b / kg | Power ihp |
|---|---|---|---|---|---|---|---|---|---|---|---|
| 1855 | DX Goods | L.N.W.R. | Crewe | 17/43.2 | 24/61 | 62/1.58 | 827/120 | 15/1.4 | 60,400/27.4 | 11,400/5,180 | 300 |
| 1857 | Bourbonnais | P.L.M. | Parent-Shaken | 17.7/45 | 25.6/65 | 51.2/1.3 | 1,000/145 | 14.4/1.34 | 78,000/35.4 | 18,500/8,400 | |
| 1866 | 030C | Ouest | Various | 18.1/460 | 25.25/64 | 50.75/1.43 | 882/128 | 15.8/1.5 | 89.523/40.6 | 17,804/8,083 | |
| 1873 | `Coal' Engine | L.N.W.R. | Crewe | 17/43.2 | 24/61 | 54/1.37 | 965/140 | 17.1/1.6 7 | 1,700/32.6 | 5,600/7,080 | |
| 1877 | Z19 | NSWGR | Beyer Peacock | 18/46 | 24/61 | 48/1.22 | 965/140 | 17.9/1.7 | 127,228/57.7 | 18,144/8,237 | |
| 1878 | 5ft 3in | M.R. | Derby | 18/45.7 | 26/66 | 63/1.6 | 1,102/160 | 17.5/1.62 | 88,200/40 | 18,185/8,258 | |
| 1882 | 454 | M.Z.A. | Hartmann | 18.9/48 | 25.5/65 | 50/1.27 | 1,102/160/ | | 125,685/57* | 24,900/11,304 | |
| 1883 | Standard Goods | C.R. | St Rollox | 18/45.7 | 26/66 | 60/1.52 | 1,033/150 | 19.5/1.8 | 92,610/42 | 17,901/8,127 | |
| 1883 | .Dean Goods | G.W.R. | Swindon | 17/432 | 24/610 | 62/1.58 | 1,240/180 | 15.45/1.4 | 82,442/37.4 | 17,120/7,772 | |
| 1894 | P.1 | N.E.R. | Gateshead | 18/45.7 | 24/61 | 55/1.4 | 1,103/160 | 15.2/1.4 | 86,200/39.2 | 19,200/8,720 | |
| 1904 | P.2 | N.E.R. | Gateshead | 18.2/46.2 | 26/66 | 55/1.4 | 1,380/200 | 20/1.86 | 104,800/47.6 | 25,400/11,530 | |
| 1911 | 4F | M.R. | Derby | 20/51 | 26/66 | 63/1.6 | 1,207/175 | 21.1/1.99 | 109,100/49.6 | 24,500/11,120 | |
| 1916 | B6sb | Pennsylvania | Altoona | 22/56 | 24/61 | 56/1.42 | 1,425/205 | 61.6/5.72 | 180,300/82.9 | 36,140/16,407 .. | |
| 1919 | O18 | C.N.R. | Various | 22/56 | 26/66 | 56/1.42 | 1,309/190 | | 177,000/80.2 | 36,291/16,344 .. | |
| 1935 | Union | RR | Lima | 22/55.9 | 28/71.1 | 51/1.29 | 1,517/220 | 50/4.65 | 201,316/91.3 | 49,700/22,544 | |
| 1930 | 2251 | G.W.R. | Swindon | 17.5/44.5 | 24/61 | 62/1.57 | 1,378/200 | 17.4/1.63 | 97,020/44 | 20,155/9,150 .. | |
| 1942 | Q.1 | South'n | Eastleigh | 19/48.3 | 26/66 | 61/1.55 | 1,586/230 | 27/2.5 | 114,700/52.1 | 30,100/13,700 | |

### 2-6-0 (1C)

| Date | Class/name | Railway | Builder | Cylinder diameter in / cm | Piston stroke in / cm | Driving wheel dia. in / M | Steam pressure kpa / psi | Firegrate area sq.ft / sq.M | Weight 1b / tonne | T/Force 1b / kg | Power ihp |
|---|---|---|---|---|---|---|---|---|---|---|---|
| 1880 | Rogers | Normal | Rogers | 16/41 | 24/61 | 48/1.22 | | | 70,000/31.7 | | |
| 1887 | 3.101 | Nord | La Chapelle | 1x17/43 2x19/50) | 27.6/70 | 65/1.65 | 1,400/203 | 22.5/2.1 | 104,500/47.4 | 21,000/9,600 | |
| 1899 | Mogul | (M.R. | Baldwin | 18/46 | 24/61 | 61/1.55 | 1,137/165 | 16/1.5 | 106,960/48.6 | 17,600/8,000 | |
| 1910 | 625 | F.S. | Various | 19.3/49 | 27.5/70 | 60.25/1.53 | 1,173/171 | 26.05/2.42 | 118,850/53.9 | 25,808/11,/17 | |
| 1911 | 4300 | G.W.R. | Swindon | 18.5/47 | 30/76 | 68/1.73 | 1,380/200 | 20.6/1.9 | 138,900/63.1 | 25,700/11,700 | |
| 1920 | K3 | G.N.R. | Doncaster | 3x18.5/47 | 26/66 | 68/1.73 | 1,241/180 | 28/2.6 | 162,600/73.9 | 30,300/13,700 | 1,550 |
| 1923 | K3 | G.S.W.R. | Sharp Stewart | 19/48.3 | 26/66 | 61.75/1.57 | 1,240/180 | 24.8/2.3 | 127,890/58 | 23,260/10,560 | |
| 1926 | 'Crabs' | L.M.S. | Derby | 21/53 | 26/66 | 66/1.68 | 1,241/180 | 27.5/2.55 | 147,800/67.2 | 26,600/12,080 | |
| 1928 | C-30T | NSWGR | Eveleigh | 18.5/47 | 24/61. | 55/1.4 | 1,102/160 | 24/2.23 | 116,865/53 | 19,116/8,698 | |
| 1935 | C56 | J.N.R. | Various | 15.75/40 | 26/66 | 55/1.4 | 1,378/200 | 13.9/1.3 | 82,908/37.6 | 18,942/8,600 | |

### 2-6-2 (1C1)

| Date | Class/name | Railway | Builder | Cylinder diameter in / cm | Piston stroke in / cm | Driving wheel dia. in / M | Steam pressure kpa / psi | Firegrate area sq.ft / sq.M | Weight 1b / tonne | T/Force 1b / kg | Power ihp |
|---|---|---|---|---|---|---|---|---|---|---|---|
| 1907 | 324 | Hungarian | Florisdorf | 1x18/46 1x27/69 | 25.6/65 | 57/1.43 | 1,500/217 | 34/3.15 | 127,800/58.1 | 27,000/12,260 | |
| 1925 | Su | Soviet Rlys | Various | 22.5/57.5 | 27.5/70 | 73/1.85 | 1,271/191 | 50.2/4.67 | 191,835/87 | 30,100/13,600 | |
| 1928 | ZB | Indian | Various | 12/305 | 18/457 | 34/0.86 | 1,102/160 | 14/1.3 | 62,842/28.5 | 10,638/4,707 | |
| 1936 | V.2 Green Arrows | L.N.E.R. | Doncaster | 3x18.5/47 | 26/66 | 74/1.88 | 1,517/220 | 41/3.8 | 208,400/94.6 | 34,000/15,300 | 2,400 |
| 1951 | OI-49 | Polish | Chrzanow | 19.5/50 | 24.75/63 | 69/1.75 | 1,568/227 | 39.8/3.7 | 184,030/83.5 | 26,200/11,900 .. | |
| 1952 | YL | Indian | Various | 12.25/31.1 | 22/560 | 43/1.09 | 1,447/210 | 7.75/0.72 | 85,120/38.6 | 13,660/6,202 | |
| 1961 | 23 | DB | Henschel | 21.6/55 | 26/66 | 69/1.75 | 1,567/227 | 33.6/3.12 | 182,540/82.8 | 36,375/16,500 .. | |
| 1956 | 35 | DR | Beimler | 21.5/55 | 26/66 | 69/1.75 | 1,567/227 | 39.9/3.71 | 185,190/84 | 35,180/15,972 .. | |

### 2-6-4 (1C2)

| Date | Class/name | Railway | Builder | Cylinder diameter in / cm | Piston stroke in / cm | Driving wheel dia. in / M | Steam pressure kpa / psi | Firegrate area sq.ft / sq.M | Weight 1b / tonne | T/Force 1b / kg | Power ihp |
|---|---|---|---|---|---|---|---|---|---|---|---|
| 1908 | S.210 | Austrian | Florisdorf | 2x15.4/39 2x26/66 | 28.3/72 | 84/2.14 | 1,600/232 | 49.7/4.62 | 189,600/86.2 | 30,800/14,000 | |

### 4-6-0 (2C)

| Date | Class/name | Railway | Builder | Cylinder diameter in / cm | Piston stroke in / cm | Driving wheel dia. in / M | Steam pressure kpa / psi | Firegrate area sq.ft / sq.M | Weight 1b / tonne | T/Force 1b / kg | Power ihp |
|---|---|---|---|---|---|---|---|---|---|---|---|
| 1894 | Jones Goods | Highland | Sharp Stewart | 20/51 | 26/66 | 63/1.6 | 1,207/175 | 22.6/2.1 | 125,400/57 | 24,600/11,200 | |
| 1900 500 | Mucca Rete | Adriatica | Breda | 2x14.7/37 2x23/58 | 25.6/65 | 75/1.9 | 1,400/203 | 32/2.97 | 220,400/100 | 18,000/8,170 | |
| 1904 | Saint | G.W.R. | Swindon | 18.5/47 | 30/76 | 80/2.03 | 1,552/225 | 27.1/2.5 | 161,300/73.3 | 24,400/11,070 | 1,700 |
| 1906. | 230K | Est | S.A.C.M. | 2x14.5/37 2x23.25/590 | 26.75/680 | 82.25/2.09 | 1,763/256 | 33/3.2 | 171,769/77.9 | 23,348/10,600 | |
| 1906 | P.8 | Prussian | Schwarzkopf | 23.2/59 | 24.8/63 | 69/1.75 | 1,200/174 | 28/2.6 | 153,200/69.3 | 28,200/12,800 | |
| 1906 | Star | G.W.R. | Swindon | 4x15/38 | 26/66 | 80/2.03 | 1,552/225 | 27.1/2.5 | 169,300/76.9 | 27,800/12,600 | 1,600 |
| 1908 | Hughes 4-6-0 | L.Y.R. | Horwich | 4x16.5/42 | 26/66 | 75/1.9 | 1,240/180 | 27/2.51 | 177,430/80.5 | 20,879/13,111 | |
| 1910 | 230D | Nord | La Chapelle | 2x14.85/380 2x21.6/560 | 25.25/64 | 69/1.75 | 1,566/227 | 30.1/2.8 | 154,791/70.2 | 25,360/11,500 | |
| 1912 | D4 | G.I.P.R. | Vulcan | 20.5/521 | 26/66 | 74/1.88 | 1,240/180 | 32/2.97 | 168,021/76.2 | 22,593/10,257 | |
| 1912 | S69 | G.E.R. | Stratford | 20/51 28/710 | | 78/1.98 | 1,240/180 | 26.5/2.46 | 141,120/64 | 21,970/9,974 | |
| 1918 | N.15 | L.S.W.R. | Eastleigh | 22/56 28/71 | | 79/2.01 | 1,241/180 | 30/2.8 | 174,300/79.2 | 26,200/12,000 | 1,370 |
| 1919 | S3 | N.E.R. | Darlington | 3x18.5/47 | 26/660 | 68/1.73 | 1,240/180 | 27/2.5 | 174,195/79 | 30,030/13,633 | |
| 1920 | S15 | S.R. | Eastleigh | 20.5/52.1 | 28/71 | 67/1.7 | 1,378/200 | 28/2.6 | 178,609/81 | 29,835/13,545 | |
| 1923 | Castle | G.W.R. | Swindon | 4x16/41 | 26/66 | 80/2.03 | 1,552/225 | 29.4/2.8 | 178,700/81.8 | 31,600/14,300 | 1,900 |
| 1924 | Hall | G.W.R. | Swindon | 18.5/47 | 30/76 | 72/1.83 | 1,552/225 | 27.07/2.51 | 168,000/76.2 | 27,275/12,382 | |

| Date | Class/name | Railway | Builder | Cylinder diameter in / cm | Piston stroke in / cm | Driving wheel dia. in / M | Steam pressure kpa / psi | Firegrate area sq.ft / sq.M | Weight 1b / tonne | T/Force 1b / kg | Power ihp |
|---|---|---|---|---|---|---|---|---|---|---|---|
| 1925 | G5s | Pennsylvania | Altoona | 24/61 | 28/71 | 68/1.73 | 1,425/205 | 54.7/5.08 | 237,000/107 | 41,330/187,64 | |
| 1926 | Lord Nelson | South'n | Eastleigh | 4x16.5/42 | 26/66 | 79/2.01 | 1,517/220 | 33/3.1 | 185,900/84.3 | 33,500/15,200 | 1,940 |
| 1927 | King | G.W.R. | Swindon | 4x16.2/41 | 28/71 | 78/1.98 | 1,724/250 | 34.3/3.2 | 199,400/90.4 | 40,300/18,300 | 2,130 |
| 1927 | Royal Scot | L.M.S. | N. Brit. | 3x18/46 | 26/66 | 81/2.06 | 1,724/250 | 31.2/2.9 | 190,200/86.3 | 33,100/15,000 | 1,530 2.550(R) |
| 1934 | 5P5F | L.M.S. | Crewe | 18.5/47 | 28/71 | 72/1.83 | 1,552/225 | 27.8/2.58 | 161,500/73.4 | 25,500/11,600 | 1,550 |
| 1935 | 5XP Jubilee | L.M.S. | Crewe | 3x17/43 | 26/66 | 81/2.06 | 1,552/225 | 31/2.88 | 178,300/81 | 26,600/12,100 | 1,530 |
| 1938 | Manor | G.W.R. | Swindon | 18/45.7 | 30/76.2 | 68/1.73 | 1,550/225 | 22.1/2.05 | 155,452/70.5 | 27,340/12,412 | |
| 1939 | MJ | Jaipur State | Hunslet | 16.5/42 | 22/56 | 57/1.49 | 1,240/180 | 16/1.5 76, | 160/34.5 | 16,077/7,298 | |
| 1942 | B.1 | L.N.E.R. | Darlington | 20/51 | 26/66 | 74/1.88 | 1,552/225 | 27.5/2.5 | 159,400/72.4 | 26,900/12,200 | 1,150 |
| 1945 | County | G.W.R. | Swindon | 18.5/47 | 30/76.2 | 75/1.9 | 1,929/280 | 28.84/2.68 | 169,785/82 | 32,580/14,791 | |
| 1951 | 5MT | B.R. | Crewe | 19/48 | 28/71 | 74/1.88 | 1,552/225 | 27.8/2.58 | 170,700/77.6 | 26,100/11,800 | 1,630 |

**4-6-2 (2C1)**

| Date | Class/name | Railway | Builder | Cylinder diameter in / cm | Piston stroke in / cm | Driving wheel dia. in / M | Steam pressure kpa / psi | Firegrate area sq.ft / sq.M | Weight 1b / tonne | T/Force 1b / kg | Power ihp |
|---|---|---|---|---|---|---|---|---|---|---|---|
| 1902 | Pacific | Miss Pacific | Brooks | 20/51 | 26/66 | 69/1.75 | 1,380/200 | 42.8/3.98 | 182,000/82.5 | 25,600/11,600 | |
| 1905 | Light | Pacific C.P.R. | Angus | 20/51 | 28/71 | 70/1.79 | 1,722/250 | 45.6/4.24 | 150,000/68 | 34,080/15,472. | |
| 1907 | 4501 | Paris-Orleans | S.A.C.M. | 2x15.2/39 2x25.2/64 | 25.6/65 | 72.8/1.85 | 1,600/232 | 45.8/4.3 | 198,400/90 | 24,000/10,900 | 2,050 |
| 1908 | S.3/6 | Bav'n State | Maffei | 2x16.7/42.5 2x17.3/65 | 2x24/61 2x27/67 | 73.6/1.87 | 1,500/217 | 48.4/4.5 | 190,900/86.6 | 28,000/12,700 | 2,000 |
| 1908 | K.2A | NY Central | Alco | 22/56 | 28/71 | 79/2.01 | 1,380/200 | 56.5/5.25 | 273,000/124 | 29,200/13,300 | 2,000 |
| 1911 | S.6172 | P.L.M. | Batignolles | 4x19/48 | 26.8/68 | 78.7/2.0 | 1,400/203 | 45.7/4.25 | 205.200/93.1 | 41,700/18,900 | 2,425 |
| 1914 | K.4S | Pennsylvannia | Altoona | 27/69 | 28/71 | 80/2.02 | 1,414/205 | 70/6.5 | 310,500/141 | 44,400/20,150 | 3,250 |
| 1919 | G3 | C.P.R. | Various | 25/63.5 | 30/76.2 | 75/1.9 | 1,378/200 | 65/6.04 | 297,920/135 | 42,500/19,275 | |
| 1923 | Super Pacific | Nord | Cail | 2x17 3/44 2x24.4/62 | 26/66 27/69 | 75/1.43 | 1,564/227 | 37.6/3.5 | 221,345/100.4 | 32,100/14,570 | |
| 1925 | 01 | DR | Various. | 25.5/65 | 26/66 | 78.75/2.0 | 1,566/227 | 48.4/4.5 | 245,310/111.3 | 36,375/16,500.. | |
| 1926 | B.18 | Q.G.R. | Ipswich | 18.25/46 | 24/61 | | 1.102/160 | 25/2.32 | 209,475/95* | 21,316/9,677 | |
| 1927 | YB | Indian | Various | 16/40.6 | 24/61 | 57/1.45 | 1,240/180 | 23/2.13 | 116,480/52.8 | 16,491/7,487 | |
| 1928 | A.3 | L.N.E.R. | Doncaster | 3x19/48 | 26/66 | 80/2.03 | 1,517/220 | 41.2/3.8 | 215,500/97.7 | 32,900/15,000 | 1,620 |
| 1929 | XA | Indian | Vulcan | 18/46 | 26/66 | 61.5/1.56 | 1,240/189 | 32/2.97 | 154,560/70.1 | 20,960/9,515 | |
| 1929 | No.3566 | Paris-Orleans | Tours | 2x16.5/42 2x25.2/64 | 25.6/65 | 76.8/1.95 | 1,700/246 | 46.6/4.33 | 224,500/102 | 28,000/12,700 | 3,400 |
| 1930 | 03 | DR | Various | 23.2/60 | 26/66 | 78.5/2.0 | 1,564/227 | 43.5/4.05 | 219,520/99.6 | 32,500/14,750 | |
| 1933 | SL-6 | Chinese Railways | Various | 22.5/57 | 26/66 | 69/1.75 | 1,378/200 | 51.9/4.82 | 211,010/91.4 | 32,150/14,600 | |
| 1933 | 8P Princess | L.M.S. | Crewe | 4x16.2/42 | 28/71 | 78/1.98 | 1,724/250 | 45/4.2 | 234,100/106.4 | 40,300/18,300 | 2,020 |
| 1935 | A.4 | L.N.E.R. | Doncaster | 3x18.5/47 | 26/66 | 80/2.03 | 1,724/250 | 41.2/3.8 | 230,700/104.6 | 35,500/16,100 | 3,170 |
| 1935 | 10 | S.N.C.B. | Cockerill | 4x16.5/42 | 28.75/72 | 78/1.98 | 1,764/256 | 53.8/5.0 | 277,782/126 | 43,300/19,640 | |
| 1937 | Coronation Duchess | L.M.S. | Crewe | 4x16.5/42 | 28/71 | 81/2.06 | 1,724/250 | 50/4.6 | 252,500/114.8 | 40,000/18,200 | 3,550 |
| 1938 | 0 | Malayan | North British | 3x13/33 | 24/610 | 54/1.37 | 1,729/250 | 31/2.9 | 129,900/59 | 23,940/10,870 | |
| 1938 | HR-1 | Finnish | Lokomo | 23.25/59 | 25.25/64 | 75/1.9 | 1,457/213 | 38.5/3.57 | 207,270/94 | 25,550/11,600 | |
| 1941 | Merchant Navy | South'n | Eastleigh | 3x18/46 | 24/61 | 74/1.88 | 1,931/280 | 48.4/4.5 | 207,200/94.2 | 37,500/17,000 | 2,300 |
| 1942 | 283 | Royal Siamese | Nippon, Hitachi | 17.75/45 | 24/66 | 54/1.37 | 1,273/185 | 32.2/3.0 | 127,890/58 | 19,392/8,780 | |
| 1943 | C-38 | NSWGR | Eveleigh, Clyde | 21.5/55 | 26/66 | 69/1.75 | 1,688/245 | 47/4.37 | 452,025/205* | 36,273/16,470 | |
| 1946 | A2 | L.N.E.R. | Doncaster | 3x19/48.3 | 26/66 | 74/1.88 | 1,729/250 | 50/4.62 | 227,120/103 | 40,430/18,355.. | |
| 1947 | 'WP' | Indian | Various | 20.2/51 | 28/71 | 67/1.7 | 1,448/210 | 46/4.27 | 218,000/99 | 30,600/13,900 | |
| 1950 | Pm | W.A.G.R. | North British | 19/48 | 26/66 | 54/1.37 | 1,206/175 | 35/3.25 | 245,196/111.2 | 25,855/11,738 | |
| 1951 | Britannia | B.R. | Derby | 20/51 | 28/71 | 74/1.88 | 1,724/250 | 42/3.9 | 210,600/95.5 | 32,100/14,600 | 2,200 |
| 1954 | Duke of Gloucester | B.R. | Crewe | 3x18/46 | 28/71 | 74/1.88 | 1,724/250 | 48.6/4.5 | 226,700/103 | 39,100/17,800 | 2,420 |
| 1955 | WL. | Indian | Chittaranjan. | 19.25/49 | 28/71 | 67/1.70 | 1,447/210 | 38/3.53 | 199,360/90.4 | 27,640/12,548 | |
| 1957 | RM | Chinese Railways | Qingdao | 22.5/57 | 26/66 | 69/1.75 | 1,469/215 | 61.9/5.75 | 179,600/81.8 | 34,450/15,700 | |
| 1961 | 01.5 | DR | Beimler | 23.6/60 | 26/66 | 78.5/2.0 | 1,566/227 | 52.5/4.88 | 244,755/111 | 35,414/15,282 | |

**4-6-4 (2C2)**

| Date | Class/name | Railway | Builder | Cylinder diameter in / cm | Piston stroke in / cm | Driving wheel dia. in / M | Steam pressure kpa / psi | Firegrate area sq.ft / sq.M | Weight 1b / tonne | T/Force 1b / kg | Power ihp |
|---|---|---|---|---|---|---|---|---|---|---|---|
| 1910 | 3.1101 | Nord | La Chapelle | 2x17.3/44 2x24.4/62 | 25.2/64 28.7/73 | 80.3/2.04 | 1,600/232 | 46/4.27 | 224,400/102 | 24,000/10,900 | 2,800 |
| 1927 | J-1E | NY Central | Alco | 25/64 | 28/71 | 79/2.01 | 1,552/225 | 81.5/7.57 | 352,000/160 | 42,300/19,200 + 10,900/4,940 | 3,900 |
| 1930 | K-5a | C.N.R. | Montreal | 23/58.5 | 28/71 | 80/2.03 | 1,894/275 | 73.6/6.8 | 356,400/161.8 | 43,300/19,640 | |
| 1935 | 05 | German State | Borsig | 3x17.7/45 | 26/66 | 91/2.3 | 2,000/290 | 50.6/4.7 | 280,000/127 | 33,240/15,700 | 3,000 |
| 1935 | L1 | C&O | Lima | 27.5/69.9 | 30/762 | 72/1.83 | 1,756/255 | 100.3/9.3 | 503,500/228 | 68,300/30,980 | |
| 1937 | Royal Hudson | C.P.R. | Montreal | 22/560 | 30/760 | 75/1.9 | 1,894/275 | 80.8/7.5 | 366,000/166.2 | 45,000/20,500.. | |
| 1940 | 232S | S.N.C.F. | S.A.C.M. | 2x18/45.7 2x26.75/68 | 27.5/70 | 78.5/2.0 | 1,961/285 | 55.9/5.2 | 288,193/130.7 | 41,189/18,700.. | |
| 1948 | 232.U | S.N.C.F. | Corpet Louvet | 2x17.7/45 1x26.8/68 | 27.6/70 | 78.7/2.0 | 2,000/290 | 55.7/5.16 | 284,400/129.3 | 47,000/21,300 4, | |

| Date | Class/name | Railway | Builder | Cylinder diameter in / cm | Piston stroke in / cm | Driving wheel dia. in / M | Steam pressure kpa / psi | Firegrate area sq.ft / sq.M | Weight lb / tonne | T/Force lb / kg | Power ihp |
|---|---|---|---|---|---|---|---|---|---|---|---|
| 1951 | | R V.R. | North British | 21.25/54 | 28/710 | 73/1.86 | 1,446/210 | 42/3.9 | 420,493/190.7 | 31,648/14,368 | |
| **0-8-0 (D)** | | | | | | | | | | | |
| 1813 | Wylam Dilly | Wylam Colliery | W. Hedley | 9/23 | 36/91 | 39/0.99 | 310/45 | 6/0.6 | | 2,860/1,300 | |
| 1834 | Monster | Camden & Amboy | I. Dripps | 18/46 | 30/76 | 48/1.22 | 345/50 | | 60,900/27.7 | 8,600/3,900 | |
| 1848 | Camel | Baltimore & Ohio | Baldwin | 18/46 | 20/51 | 40/1.02 | 345/50 | | 71,110/32.3 | 6,900/3,130 | |
| 1854 | S.4000 | Nord | Schneider | 21.3/54 | 26/66 | 49.6/1.26 | 1,000/145 | 20.9/1.94 | 138,500/62.9 | 29,400/13,300 | |
| 1855 | S.35 | Vienna-Raab | J. Haswell | 18.1/46 | 25/63 | 46.6/1.18 | 690/100 | 12.9/1.2 | 76,600/34.8 | 14,600/6,600 | 360 |
| 1889 | 040 2301 | MZA | Sharp Stewart | 20/508 | 26/66 | 51/1.29 | 1,175/170 | | 160,965/73 | 29,364/13,331 | |
| 1894 | 'A' | L.N.W.R. | Crewe | 2x15/38 1x30/76 | 24/61 | 53/1.36 | 1,207/175 | 20.4/1.9 1 | 10,300/50.1 | 18,000/8,200 | |
| 1900 | 'T' | N.E.R. | Gateshead | 20/51 | 26/66 | 55/1.4 | 1,207/175 | 21.5/2.0 | 131,500/59.8 | 28,000/12,700 | |
| 1901 | O | Russian State | Various | 1x19.5/50 1x29/73 | 25.5/65 | 48/1.2 | 1,173/171 | 19.9/1.85 | 119,070/54 | 26,000/11,800 | |
| 1906 | 399 | Austrian State | Krauss | 16.1/41 | 17.7/45 | 35.5/900 | 1,274/185/ | 17.2/1.6 | 92,225/45 | 20,312/9,222 | |
| 1912 | G.8 | Prussian | Schichau | 23.6/60 | 26/66 | 53.1/1.35 | 1,400/203 | 28/2.6 | 149,900/68.1 | 46,400/21,100 | 1,100 |
| 1913 | T.2 | N.E.R. | Darlington | 20/51 | 26/66 | 55/1.4 | 1,241/180 | 23/2.13 | 147,600/67.1 | 28,800/13,060 | 1,330 |
| 1919 | T.3 | N.E.R. | Darlington | 3x18.5/47 | 26/66 | 55/1.4 | 1,241/180 | 26.7/2.48 | 160,400/72.9 | 37,000/16,800 | 1,600 |
| 1919 | Std No. 2 | U.S.R.A. | Baldwin ALCO | 25/64 | 28/71 | 51/1.3 | 1,207/175 | 50/4.6 | 213,800/97.2 | 51,000/23,100 | |
| 1929 | G.3 | L.N.W.R. | Crewe | 19.5/49.5 | 26/66 | 53.5/1.36 | 1,380/200 | 23.4/2.17 | 125,900/57.2 | 31,400/14,300 | |
| **2-8-0 (1D)** | | | | | | | | | | | |
| 1885 | 'R' | Pennsylvania | Baldwin | 20/51 | 24/61 | 50/1.27 | 965/140 | 31/2.88 | 100,600/45.7 | 22,800/10,350 | 118 |
| 1903 | 2800 | GWR | Swindon | 18.5/47 | 30/76 | 55/1.4 | 1,552/225 | 27.1/2.5 | 169,100/76.9 | 35,400/16,100 | 1,330 |
| 1911 | 8.K | G.C.R. | Gorton | 21/53 | 26/66 | 56/1.42 | 1,241/180 | 26.3/2.44 | 164,000/74.5 | 31,300/14,200 | |
| 1911 | 740 | Italian State | Various | 21.25/54 | 27.5/70 | 54/1.37 | 1,171/170 | 30.1/2.8 | 119,070/54 | 33,073/15,015 | |
| 1913 | H10s | Pennsylvania | Altoona | 26/66 | 28/71 | 62/1.57 | 1,412.205 | 55.2/5.12 | 247,500/112 | 52,204/23,700 | |
| 1914 | Derby 2-8-0 | S.D.J.R. | Derby | 21/53.3 | 28/71 | 56/1.42 | 1,309/190 | 28.4/2.64 | 153,440/69.6 | 35,392/16,067 | |
| 1918 | 0.2 | G.N.R. | Doncaster | 3x18.5/47 | 26/66 | 56/1.42 | 1,241/180 | 27.5/2.55 | 169,800/77.2 | 36,700/16,700 | |
| 1922 | 300 | Lehigh & New Eng | Alco | 27/69 | 32/81 | 61/1.55 | 1,448/210 | 84.3/7.8 | 301,000/136.8 | 68,200/30,960 | |
| 1935 | 8F | L.M.S. | Crewe | 18.5/47 | 28/71 | 56/1.42 | 1,552/225 | 27.8/2.6 | 161,700/73.5 | 32,400/14,700 | |
| 1942 | USTC 2-8-0 | | Various | 19/48.3 | 26/66 | 57/1.45 | 1,551/225 | 41/3.8 | 162,508/73.7 | 31,500/14,288 | |
| 1944 | Austerity | M.O.D.W.D. | North British | 19/48 | 28/71 | 56/1.42 | 1,552/225 | 28.6/2.65 | 157,300/71.5 | 34,500/15,700 | |
| 1945 | 29 | S.N.C.B. | Various | 22/56 | 28/71 | 60/1.52 | 1,550/225 | 47.5/4.41 | 205,200/93 | 43,300/19,650 | |
| 1946 | Liberation | U.N.R.R.A | Vulcan Foundry | 21.7/55 | 28/71 | 57/1.45 | 1,552/225 | 44/4.1 | 188,900/85.9 | 44,200/20,100 | |
| 1948 | Andes | Guaqui-La Paz | Various | 16/40.6 | 24/61 | 46/1.17 | ,240/180 | 15.9/1.47 | 105,952/48 | 20,435/9,277 | |
| **2-8-2 (1D1)** | | | | | | | | | | | |
| 1905 | 1500 | N. Pacific | ALCO | 24/61 | 30/76 | 63/1.6 | 1,380/200 | 43.5/4.04 | 259,000/117.7 | 46,600/21,160 | |
| 1916 | S | C.N.R. | C.L.C. and M.L.W. | 27/68.6 | 30/76.2 | 63/1.6 | 1,274/185 | 66.7/6.19 | 318,622/144.5 | 54,500/24,743 | |
| 1914 | L.1s | Penn | Altoona | 27/69 | 32/81 | 57/1.45 | 1,275/185 | 67/6.3 | 296,500/134.8 | 64,500/29,300 | 2,800 |
| 1919 | 141C | P.L.M. | S.L.M. | 2x20/51 2x28.3/72 | 25.6/65 27.6/70 | 65/1.65 | 1,600/232 | 46.3/4.3 | 205,800/93.5 | 51,000/23,100 | 1,770 |
| 1919 | 282.A | U.S.R.A. | ALCO Baldwin | 26/66 | 30/76 | 63/1.6 | 1,380/200 | 66.7/6.2 | 292,000/132.7 | 54,700/24,800 | |
| 1919 | 282.B | U.S.R.A. | ALCO Baldwin | 27/69 | 32/81 | 63/1.6 | 1,310/190 | 70.8/6.8 | 320,000/145.4 | 60,000/27,200 | |
| 1925 | P.1 | L.N.E.R. | Doncaster | 3x20/51 | 26/66 | 62/1.57 | 1,241/180 | 41.2/3.82 | 224,000/101.8 | 38,500/17,500 + 4,200/1,900 | |
| 1934 | P.2 | L.N.E.R. | Doncaster | 3x21/53 | 26/66 | 62/1.57 | 1,517/220 | 50/4.64 | 246,800/112.2 | 43,500/19,700 | 3,200 |
| 1936 | D51 | J.N.R. | Various | 21.75/55 | 26/66 | 55.12/1.4 | 1,378/200 | 36/3.34 | 169,344/76.8 | 24,310/11,036 | |
| 1937 | 41 | DR | Various | 20.5/52 | 28.36/72 | 63/1.6 | 1,963/285 | 44/4.05 | 225,750/102.4 | 45,820/20,802.. | |
| 1941 | 141P | Various | | 2x16.1/41 2x25.2/64 | 27.5/70 | 63.75/1.62 | 1,961/285 | 46.3/4.3 | 245,857/111.5 | 42,070/19,100 | |
| 1942 | U.S. Mike | War Dept | Various | 21/53.3 | 28/71 | 68/1.73 | 1,278/200 | 47/4.3 | 200,000/90.7 | 35,000/15,800 | |
| 1944 | MacArthur | U.S.W.D. | Davenport | 16/41 | 24/61 | 48/1.22 | 1,310/190 | 27.5/2.55 | 118,000/59 | 20,700/9,400 | |
| 1945 | 141.R | S.N.C.F. | ALCO Baldwin | 23.5/60 | 28/71 | 65/1.65 | 1,517/220 | 55.5/5.16 | 249,800/113.5 | 44,460/20,200 | |
| 1949 | 901 | Siamese State | Various | 17.75/45 | 24/610 | 43.5/1.11 | 1,273/185 | 32.2/3 | 127,008/57.6 | 24,118/10,950 | |
| 1951 | D52 | Indonesian State | Krupp | 19.7/50 | 26/66 | 59/1.5 | 1,566/227 | 37.6/3.5 | 163,610/74.2 | 32,428/14,722 | |
| 1951 | WG | Indian | N. Brit. | 20.5/52 | 28/71 | 60/1.52 | 1,448/210 | 46/4.27 | 217,300/98.9 | 34,200/15,500 | |
| 1952 | D-59 | N.S.W. | ALCO | 21/53 | 28/71 | 61.5/1.56 | 1,448/210 | 46/4.27 | 228,000/103.6 | 35,800/16,250 | |
| 1958 | JS | Chinese Railways | Various | 22.8/58 | 28/71 | 54/1.37 | 1,467/213 | 62/5.75 | 200,655/91 | 48,518/22,027 | |
| **2-8-4 (1D2)** | | | | | | | | | | | |
| 1924 | Berkshire | Boston & Albany | Lima | 28/71 | 30/76 | 63/1.6 | 1,655/240 | 100/9.3 | 385,000/175 | 76,200/34,600 | |
| 1929 | S.214 | Austrian State | Florisdorf | 25.6/65 | 82.3/72 | 74.8/1.9 | 1,500/217 | 50.6/4.7 | 260,200/118 | 45,000/20,400 | 1,700 |
| 1933 | Stalin | U.S.S.R. | Kolomna | 26.4/67 | 30.3/77 | 72.8/1.85 | 1,500/217 | 76/7.0 | 239,300/133 | 52,900/24,000 | 2,100 |
| 1943 | K-4 | C&O RR | Alco, Lima | 26/66 | 34/86.4 | 69/1.75 | 1,688/245 | 90.3/8.38 | 469,680/213 | 69,350/31,484 | |
| 1949 | S-3 | Nickel Plate | Lima | 25/63.5 | 24/61 | 69/1.75 | 1,688/245 | 90.3/8.38 | 444,290/201.5 | 64,100/29,101 | |

# LEADING CHARACTERISTICS OF STEAM LOCOMOTIVES

| Date | Class/name | Railway | Builder | Cylinder diameter in / cm | Piston stroke in / cm | Driving wheel dia. in / M | Steam pressure kpa / psi | Firegrate area sq.ft / sq.M | Weight 1b / tonne | T/Force 1b / kg | Power ihp |
|---|---|---|---|---|---|---|---|---|---|---|---|
| **4-8-0 (2D)** | | | | | | | | | | | |
| 1899 | 640 | Ill Central | Brooks | 23/58 | 30/76 | 57/1.45 | 1,448/210 | 37.5/3.48 | 232,200/105 | 49,700/22,560 | |
| 1920 | C-17 | Q.G.R. | Ipswich | 17/43 | 22/56 | 45/1.14 | 1.102/160 | 18.5/1.72 | 178,605/81 | 18,085/8,210 | |
| 1932 | 240P | S.N.C.F. | Tours | 2x17.3/44 2x25.2/64 | 25.6/65 | 72.8/1.85 | 2,000/290 | 40.5/3.76 | 241,200/109.6 | 34,000/15,400 | 4,000 |
| 1933 | No.1403 L.F. Loree | Dela & Hud | ALCO | 1x20/51 1x27.5/70 2x33/84 | 32/81 | 63/1.6 | 3,448/500 | 75.8/7.04 | 382,000/173.6 | 75,000/34,000 | + 10,000/4,540 |
| **4-8-2 (2D1)** | | | | | | | | | | | |
| 1911 | Mountain | Ch'peake & Ohio | ALCO | 29/74 | 28/71 | 62/1.57 | 1,241/180 | 66.5/6.2 | 330,000/150 | 58,100/26,380 | |
| 1924 | U1b | C.N.R. | Various | 26/66 | 30/762 | 73/1.86 | 1,446/210 | 66.7/6.19 | 337,365/153 | 50,000/22,700 | |
| 1925 | 41.001 | Est | Epernay | 2x17.7/45 2x26/66 | 28.3/72 | 76.8/1.95 | 1,700/246 | 48/4.43 | 258,400/117.4 | 34,500/15,700 | 2,600 |
| 1929 | 80 | Chilean State | Baldwin | 22.5/57 | 28/710 | 66/1.68 | 1,412/205 | 52.3/4.86 | 361,222/163.8 | 37,374/16,967 | |
| 1937 | 19D | S.A.R. | Various | 21/53.3 | 26/66 | 54/1.37 | 1,378/200 | 36/3.34 | 179,200/81.3 | 31,850/14,459 | |
| 1939 | 15F | S.A.R. | Various | 24/61 | 28/710 | 60/1.54 | 1,446/210 | 62.5/5.8 | 249,074/112.9 | 47,980/21,782 | |
| 1939 | 241-2101 | Spanish National | Maquinista | 22/56 | 28/71. | 69/1.75 | 1,959/285 | | 255,780/116 | 45,811/20,798 | |
| 1942 | L-4 | NY Central | Alco | 26/66 | 30/76 | 72/1.83 | 1,724/250 | 75.3/7.0 | 397,300/180.6 | 59,900/27,200 | 5,470 |
| 1944 | U1f | C.N.R. | Montreal | 24/61 | 30/762 | 73/1.86 | 1,791/260 | 70.2/6.52 | 355,700/161.3 | 54,680/24,824 | |
| 1948 | 241.P | S.N.C.F. | Schneider | 2x17.6/45 2x26.5/67 | 25.6/65 27.6/70 | 79.5/2.02 | 2,000/290 | 54.3/5.05 | 289,700/131.7 | 46,900/21,300 | 4,300 |
| 1954 | 811 | Bolivian National | Vulcan | 19/48.3 | 26/66 | 48/1.2 | 1,240/180 | | 322,560/146.3 | 27,616/12,538 | |
| **4-8-4 (2D2)** | | | | | | | | | | | |
| 1927 | 2600 | N Pac | ALCO | 28/71 | 30/76 | 74/1.88 | 1,552/225.4 | 115/10.7 | 426,000/193.6 | 61,500/27,900 | |
| 1927 | U3 | GTW | Alco | 26.25/66.6 | 30/762 | 73/1.86 | 1,722/250 | 84.3/7.83 | 399,000/180.9 | 60,200/27,330 | |
| 1928 | 500 | S. Australia | Armstrong Whitworth | 26/66 | 28/71 | 63/1.6 | 1,378/200 | 4 66.5/6.18 | 498,000/226.4 | 51,000/23,100 | + 8,000/3,630 2,050 |
| 1932 | 'K' | New Zealand | N Z Rly | 20/51 | 26/66 | 54/1.37 | 1,380/200 | 47.4/4.4 | 306,000/139 | 32,700/14,850 | + 8,000/3,630 |
| 1935 | KF | Chinese Railways | Vulcan | 20.9/53 | 29.5/750 | 69/1.75 | 1,515/220 | 67/6.2 | 259,392/117.6 | 32,900/14,936 | |
| 1935 | J3 | C&O RR | Lima | 27.5/69.9 | 30/76.2 | 72/1.83 | 1,756/255 | 100.3/9.3 | 503,500/228 | 68,300/30,980 | |
| 1938 | U4 | GTW | Alco | 24/61 | 30/76.2 | 77/1.96 | 1,894/275 | 73.7/6.85 | 344,000/156 | 52,000/23,600 | |
| 1938 | 3765 | Santa Fe | Baldwin | 28/71 | 32/81 | 80/2.03 | 2,069/300 | 108/10 | 510,000/231.8 | 80,000/36,300 | 5,300 |
| 1941 | J | Norfolk & Western | Roanoke | 27/6.86 | 32/81.3 | 70/1.78 | 2,067/300 | 107.7/10 | 494,000/224 | 80,000/36,320 | |
| 1942 | U2g | C.N.R. | Montreal | 25.5/65 | 30/76.2 | 73/1.86 | 1,722/250 | 84.3/7.83 | 377,055/171 | 56,800/25,787 | |
| 1945 | S-1A | NY Central | ALCO | 25/63.5 | 32/81 | 79/2.01 | 2,000/290 | 100/9.3 | 471,000/214 | 62,500/28,400 | 6,300 |
| 1946 | 242A1 | S.N.C.F. | Saint Chaumond | 1x23.6/60 2x26.8/68 | 28/72 27.6/70 | 76.8/1.95 | 2,000/290 | 53.8/5 | 326,300/148 | 65,300/29,690 | 5,000 |
| 1946 | QR-1 | Mexican National | Alco, Baldwin | 25/63.5 | 30/76.2 | 70/1.78 | 1,722/250 | 77.3/7.18 | 387,000/175, | 57,000/25,855 | |
| 1950 | P.36 | U.S.S.R. | Kolomna | 22.6/57.5 | 31.5/80 | 73/1.85 | 1,500/217 | 72.6/6.7 | 297,450/135.2 | 39,500/17,900 | |
| 1955 | 242-2000P | Spanish National | Maquinista | 25.12/64 | 28/711 | 75/1.9 | 1,566/227 | 57/52.9 | 319,670/162 | 35,850/16,260 | |
| **6-8-6 (303)** | | | | | | | | | | | |
| 1944 | 6200 | Penn | Turbine | | | | | 120/11.1 | 578,600/263 | 70,500/32,040 | 6,000 |
| **0-10-0 (E)** | | | | | | | | | | | |
| 1910 | G10 | Prussian State | Various | 24.75/63/26/66 | | 55/1.4 | 1,175/170 | 27.8/2.58 | 168,800/76.6 | 39,350/17,860 | |
| 1919 | 2290 | Midland | Derby | 4x16.8/43 | 28/71 | 55.5/1.41 | 1,241/180 | 31.5/2.92 | 165,000/75 | 43,300/19,660 | |
| 1922 | E | U.S.S.R | Various | 24.4/62 | 27.6/70 | 52/1.32 | 1,200/174 | 48/4.46 | 179,700/81.7 | 46,000/20,900 | |
| 1925 | Ten Wheel Switcher | Duluth & Missabe | Alco | 28/71 | 30/76 | 57/1.45 | 1,690/245 | 80/7.43 | 352,000/160 | 77,600/35,230 | +14,500/6,600 |
| **0-10-2 (E1)** | | | | | | | | | | | |
| 1937 | S.7 | Duluth Missabe & Iron Range | Baldwin | 28/71 | 32/81 | 61/1.55 | 1,793/260 | 85.2/7.9 | 422,000/191.8 | 90,900/41,270 | +17,100/7,760 |
| **2-10-0 (1E)** | | | | | | | | | | | |
| 1893 | Vauclain Compound | Erie | Baldwin | 2x16/41 2x23/58.4 | 28/71 | 50/1.27 | 1,241/180 | 89.4/8.3 | 195,300/88.8 | 44,000/19,980 | |
| 1909 | Vauclain No.988 | Santa Fe | ALCO | 2x17.5/44 2x30/76 | 34/86 | 57/1.45 | 1,552/225 | 59.5/5.5 | 259,800/118.1 | 52,100/23,650 | |
| 1909 | S.36 | Belgian State | Cockerill | 4x19.7/50 | 26/66 | 57/1.45 | 1,400/203 | 54.9/5.1 | 229,800/104.4 | 60,200/27,300 | 2,300 |
| 1916 | I-1S | Penn. | Altoona | 30.5/78 | 32/81 | 62/1.58 | 1,724/250 | 70/6.5 | 366,500/166.6 | 80,640/36,600 | 3,500 |
| 1916 | Ea | U.S.S.R. | Alco Baldwin | 25/63.5 | 28/71 | 52/1.32 | 1,241/180 | 64.7/6 | 203,400/92.4 | 51,500/23,400 | |

| Date | Class/name | Railway | Builder | Cylinder diameter in / cm | Piston stroke in / cm | Driving wheel dia. in / M | Steam pressure kpa / psi | Firegrate area sq.ft / sq.M | Weight 1b / tonne | T/Force 1b / kg | Power ihp |
|---|---|---|---|---|---|---|---|---|---|---|---|
| 1922 | 4300 | Penn. | Baldwin | 30.5/77.5 | 32/81 | 62/1.58 | 1,724/250 | 70/6.5 | 386,100/175.5 | 90,000/40,900 | |
| 1926 | 44 | German State (DR) | Various | 3x21.7/55 | 26/66 | 55/1.4 | 1,600/232 | 49.4/4.5 | 226,700/103 | 64,200/29,100 | |
| 1938 | 50 | DR | Various | 23.6/60 | 26/66 | 55/1.4 | 1,566/227 | 41.8/3.89 | 191,614/86.9 | 47,841/21,720 | |
| 1944 | 52 Kriegslok | DR | Various | 23.6/60 | 26/66 | 55/1.4 | 1,600/232 | 42/3.9 | 185,400/84.3 | 50,200/22,800 | |
| 1944 | Austerity | W.D. | North British | 19/48 | 28/71 | 56.5/1.43 | 1,552/225 | 40/3.7 | 175,400/79.7 | 34,200/15,530 | |
| 1945 | L | Soviet Railways | Various | 25.5/65 | 31.5/80 | 59/1.5 | 1,378/200 | 64.6/6 | 227,115/103 | 64,488/29,277 | |
| 1947 | Ty-246 | Poland P.K.P | Alco Baldwin | 25/63 | 27.5/70 | 57/1.45 | 1,600/232 | 67.8/6.3 | 264,300/120.1 | 58,200/26,400 | |
| 1952 | 556.0 | Czechoslovak State | Skoda | 21.5/55 | 26/66 | 55/1.4 | 1,765/256 | 46.7/4.34 | 209,475/95 | 47,636/21,627 | |
| 1954 | 9F | B.R. | Swindon | 20/51 | 28/71 | 60/1.52 | 1,724/250 | 40.2/3.74 | 194,200/88.3 | 39,700/18,000 | 2,070 |

**2-10-2 (1E1)**

| Date | Class/name | Railway | Builder | Cylinder diameter in / cm | Piston stroke in / cm | Driving wheel dia. in / M | Steam pressure kpa / psi | Firegrate area sq.ft / sq.M | Weight 1b / tonne | T/Force 1b / kg | Power ihp |
|---|---|---|---|---|---|---|---|---|---|---|---|
| 1903 | 915 | Santa Fe | Baldwin | 2x19/78 2x32/81 | 32/81 | 57/1.44 | 1,552/225 | 59/5.5 | 287,000/130.4 | 58,000/26,300 | |
| 1917 | 5036 | Un Pacific | Baldwin | 29.5/75 | 30/76 | 63/1.6 | 1,380/200 | 84/7.8 | 368,500/167.5 | 70,400/31,960 | |
| 1919 | Light | U.S.R.A. | Baldwin Alco | 27/69 | 32/81 | 57/1.44 | 1,380/200 | 76.3/7.1 | 352,000/160 | 69,600/31,600 | |
| 1919 | Heavy | U.S.R.A | do | 30/76 | 32/81 | 63/1.6 | 1,310/190 | 88.2/8.2 | 380,000/172.7 | 73,800/33,500 | |
| 1931 | 3000 | Reading | Alco | 30.5/77 | 32/81 | 61.5/1.56 | 1,552/225 | 108/10 | 451,000/205 | 92,500/42,000 | |
| 1932 | 151.A | P.L.M. | Schneider | 2x19/48 2x29.3/74.5 | 25.6/65 27.6/70 | 59/1.5 | 2,000/290 | 53.6/5 | 269,900/122.7 | 54,000/24,500 | 3,700 |
| 1956 | QJ | Chinese Railways | Dalian, Datong | 25.5/65 | 31.5/80 | 59/1.5 | 1,470/213 | 73.2/6.8 | 297,675/135 | 68,276/30,997 | |

**2-10-4 (1E2)**

| Date | Class/name | Railway | Builder | Cylinder diameter in / cm | Piston stroke in / cm | Driving wheel dia. in / M | Steam pressure kpa / psi | Firegrate area sq.ft / sq.M | Weight 1b / tonne | T/Force 1b / kg | Power ihp |
|---|---|---|---|---|---|---|---|---|---|---|---|
| 1925 | Texas | Tex & Pacific | Lima | 29/74 | 32/81 | 63/1.6 | 1,758/255 | 100/9.26 | 457,000/207.7 | 84,600/38,400 | |
| 1931 | T-1C | Can Pacific | Can Loco.Co. | 25/63 | 32/81 | 63/1.6 | 1,965/285 | 93.5/8.66 | 449,000/204.1 | 76,900/34,900 | +12,500/5,680 |
| 1938 | 5001 | Santa Fe | Baldwin | 30/76 | 34/86 | 74/1.88 | 2,138/310 | 122/11.3 | 545,300/247.9 | 93,000/42,200 | 5,900 |
| 1944 | J-1A | Pennsylvania | Baldwin | 29/74 | 34/86 | 70/1.78 | 1,965/285 | 122/11.3 | 574,700/261.2 | 98,900/44,900 | +15,000/6,800 |

**4-10-0 (2E)**

| Date | Class/name | Railway | Builder | Cylinder diameter in / cm | Piston stroke in / cm | Driving wheel dia. in / M | Steam pressure kpa / psi | Firegrate area sq.ft / sq.M | Weight 1b / tonne | T/Force 1b / kg | Power ihp |
|---|---|---|---|---|---|---|---|---|---|---|---|
| 1939 | 11 | Bulg State (BDZ) | Henschel | 3x20.5/52 | 27.6/70 | 57/1.45 | 1,600/232 | 52.3/4.86 | 241,100/109.6 | 58,700/26,650 | |

**4-10-2 (2E1)**

| Date | Class/name | Railway | Builder | Cylinder diameter in / cm | Piston stroke in / cm | Driving wheel dia. in / M | Steam pressure kpa / psi | Firegrate area sq.ft / sq.M | Weight 1b / tonne | T/Force 1b / kg | Power ihp |
|---|---|---|---|---|---|---|---|---|---|---|---|
| 1925 | 5000 | South'n Pacific | Alco | 3x25/63.5 | 28/71 | 32/81 63/1.6 | 1,552/225 | 89.6/8.3 | 442,000/200.9 | 83,500/37,900 | |
| 1926 | 60000 | South'n Pacific | Baldwin | 3x27/69 | 32/81 | 63/1.6 | 2,414/350 | 82.5/7.6 | 457,500/207.8 | 82,500/37,450 | |

**2-12-0 (1F)**

| Date | Class/name | Railway | Builder | Cylinder diameter in / cm | Piston stroke in / cm | Driving wheel dia. in / M | Steam pressure kpa / psi | Firegrate area sq.ft / sq.M | Weight 1b / tonne | T/Force 1b / kg | Power ihp |
|---|---|---|---|---|---|---|---|---|---|---|---|
| 1910 | S.100 | Austrian State | Florisdorf | 2x17.7/45 2x29.9/76 | 26.8/68 | 55/1.41 | 1,600/232 | 53.8/5 | 211,240/96 | 43,000/19,500 | 2,100 |
| 1917 | K | Wurttemburg State | Esslingen | 2x20/51 2x29.9/76 | 25.6/66 | 53.1/1.35 | 1,500/217 | 45.2/4.2 | 238,140/108.2 | 51,600/23,400 | |
| 1940 | 160.A1 | S.N.C.F. | Tours | 4x20.5/52 2x25.2/64 | 21.3/54 25.6/65 | 55/1.4 | 1,800/260 | 47.3/4.4 | 303,200/137.8 | 80,000/36,300 | |

**4-12-2 (2F1)**

| Date | Class/name | Railway | Builder | Cylinder diameter in / cm | Piston stroke in / cm | Driving wheel dia. in / M | Steam pressure kpa / psi | Firegrate area sq.ft / sq.M | Weight 1b / tonne | T/Force 1b / kg | Power ihp |
|---|---|---|---|---|---|---|---|---|---|---|---|
| 1926 | 9000 | Union Pacific | ALCO | 1x25/64 2x31/79 | 32/81 | 67/1.7 | 1,517/220 | 108.3/10 | 495,000/225 | 96,600/43,860 | |

## RIGID FRAME LOCOMOTIVES WITH DIVIDED DRIVE

**2-2-2-0 (1A.A)**

| Date | Class/name | Railway | Builder | Cylinder diameter in / cm | Piston stroke in / cm | Driving wheel dia. in / M | Steam pressure kpa / psi | Firegrate area sq.ft / sq.M | Weight 1b / tonne | T/Force 1b / kg | Power ihp |
|---|---|---|---|---|---|---|---|---|---|---|---|
| 1889 | Teutonic | L.N.W.R. | Crewe | 2x14/36 1x30/76 | 24/61 | 85/2.16 | 1,207/175 | 20.4/1.9 | 101,870/46.3 | 9,900/4,500 | |

**2-2-2-2 (1A.A1)**

| Date | Class/name | Railway | Builder | Cylinder diameter in / cm | Piston stroke in / cm | Driving wheel dia. in / M | Steam pressure kpa / psi | Firegrate area sq.ft / sq.M | Weight 1b / tonne | T/Force 1b / kg | Power ihp |
|---|---|---|---|---|---|---|---|---|---|---|---|
| 1891 | Greater Britain | L.N.W.R. | Crewe | 2x15/38 1x30/76 | 24/61 | 85/2.16 | 1,207/175 | 20.4/1.9 | 116,700/53 | 11,300/5,130 | |

**4-2-2-0 (2B.B0)**

| Date | Class/name | Railway | Builder | Cylinder diameter in / cm | Piston stroke in / cm | Driving wheel dia. in / M | Steam pressure kpa / psi | Firegrate area sq.ft / sq.M | Weight 1b / tonne | T/Force 1b / kg | Power ihp |
|---|---|---|---|---|---|---|---|---|---|---|---|
| 1886 | 701 | Nord | S.A.C.M. | 2x12.6/32 2x18.1/46 | 24/61 | 82.7/2.1 | 1,100/159 | 25.3/2.3 | 86,000/39 | 12,300/5,580 | |

**0-6-6-0 (C.C)**

| Date | Class/name | Railway | Builder | Cylinder diameter in / cm | Piston stroke in / cm | Driving wheel dia. in / M | Steam pressure kpa / psi | Firegrate area sq.ft / sq.M | Weight 1b / tonne | T/Force 1b / kg | Power ihp |
|---|---|---|---|---|---|---|---|---|---|---|---|
| 1862 | S.601 | Nord | Gouin | 4x17.3/44 | 17.3/44 | 41.9/1.065 | 900/130 | 35.8/3.33 | 131,640/59.8 | 26,800/12,200 | 650 |

**6-4-4-6 (3B.B3)**

| Date | Class/name | Railway | Builder | Cylinder diameter in / cm | Piston stroke in / cm | Driving wheel dia. in / M | Steam pressure kpa / psi | Firegrate area sq.ft / sq.M | Weight 1b / tonne | T/Force 1b / kg | Power ihp |
|---|---|---|---|---|---|---|---|---|---|---|---|
| 1938 | 6100 | Penn. | Juniata | 4x22/56 | 26/66 | 84/2.13 | 2,069/300 | 132/12.2 | 608,200/276.4 | 71,900/32,600 | 6,500 |

# LEADING CHARACTERISTICS OF STEAM LOCOMOTIVES

| Date | Class/name | Railway | Builder | Cylinder diameter in / cm | Piston stroke in / cm | Driving wheel dia. in / M | Steam pressure kpa / psi | Firegrate area sq.ft / sq.M | Weight 1b / tonne | T/Force 1b / kg | Power ihp |
|---|---|---|---|---|---|---|---|---|---|---|---|
| **4-4-4-4 (2B.B2)** | | | | | | | | | | | |
| 1942 | Q.1 | Penn. | Baldwin | 4x19.8/50 | 26/66 | 80/2.03 | 2,069/300 | 92/8.55 | 497,200/226 | 65,000/29,500 | 6,700 |
| **4-6-4-4 (2C.B2)** | | | | | | | | | | | |
| 1942 | Q.1 | Penn. | Juniata | 2x23/58.4 2x19.5/49 | 28/71 26/66 | 77/1.96 | 2,069/300 | 122/11.3 | 608,200/276.4 | 81,800/37,100 | |
| **4-4-6-4 (2B.C2)** | | | | | | | | | | | |
| 1942 | Q.2 | Penn. | Juniata | 2x19.8/50 2x23.8/60 | 28/71 29/74 | 69/1.75 | 2,069/300 | 122/11.3 | 621,100/283.3 | 100,800/45,800 | 8,000 |

## ARTICULATED LOCOMOTIVES

| Date | Class/name | Railway | Builder | Cylinder diameter in / cm | Piston stroke in / cm | Driving wheel dia. in / M | Steam pressure kpa / psi | Firegrate area sq.ft / sq.M | Weight 1b / tonne | T/Force 1b / kg | Power ihp |
|---|---|---|---|---|---|---|---|---|---|---|---|
| **0-4-4-0 (B.B)** | | | | | | | | | | | |
| 1851 | Seraing | Semmering | Cockerill | 4x16/41 | 28/71 | 41.3/1.05 | 586/85 | 2x11/2+1 | 109,000/49.5 | 25,100/11,400 | |
| 1885 | Fairlie Livingstone Thompson | Ffestiniog | Ffestiniog | 4x9/23 | 14/35.5 | 33.2/0.84 | 1,103/160 | 12.1/1.1 | 53,800/24.4 | 9,300/4,180 | |
| 1889 | Mallet La Metallurgique | | Société Belge | 2x7.4/19 2x11/28 | 10.2/26 | 23.6/0.6 | 1,200/174 | 5.1/0.5 | 25,800/11.7 | 5,000/2,300 | |
| 1908 | Shay Type | Dayton Power Co. | Lima | 3x13/33 | 15/38 | 36/0.91 | 1,378/200 | 27.8/2.6 | 184,800/84 | 38,200/17,200 | |
| 1909 | Garratt 'K' | Tasmania | Beyer Peacock | 2x11/28 2x17/43 | 16/41 | 31.5/0.8 | 1,378/200 | 14.8/1.38 | 75,000/34.1 | 16,300/7,300 | |
| 1910 | Meyer IT.V | Saxon State R. | Hartmann | 2x14.2/36 2x22.4/57 | 24.8/63 | 49.6/1.26 | 1,300/188.3 | 17.2/1.6 | 132,700/60.3 | 25,000/11,300 | |
| **0-4-4-6 (B.B.C)** | | | | | | | | | | | |
| 1851 | Bavaria | Semmering | Maffei | 20/51 | 30/76 | 42.5/1.08 | 690/100 | 14/1.3 | 97,000/44.1 | 24,000/10,900 | |
| **2-4-6 (1B.3)** | | | | | | | | | | | |
| 1881 | Mason Fairlie | NY & Manhattan | Mason Machine | 14/36 | 18/46 | 48/1.22 | 1,103/160 | 43,000/19.5 | 10,000/4,540 | | |
| Articulated Locomotives **2-4-4-2 (1B.1)** | | | | | | | | | | | |
| 1929 | H.1 Garratt | Sri Lanka | Beyer Peacock | 4x10/25,4 | 16/41 | 30/0.76 | 1,207/175 | 14.9/1.38 | 87,400/39.7 | 14,000/6,360 | |
| **4-4-2.2-4-4 (2B1.1B2)** | | | | | | | | | | | |
| 1912 | M.1 Garratt | Tasmania | Beyer Peacock | 8x12.30.5 | 20/51 | 60/1.53 | 1,103/160 | 33.9/3.13 | 212,300/96.5 | 26,100/11,840 | |
| Articulated Locomotives **0-6-4-0 (C.2)** | | | | | | | | | | | |
| 1878 | 'R' Fairlie | N Z Govt | Avonside Eng. Co. | 12.2/31 | 16/41 | 36/0.91 | 897/130 | 12/1.1 | 156,800/71.3 | 7,400/3,300 | |
| **0-6-6-0 (C.C)** | | | | | | | | | | | |
| 1884 | Fairlie 9800 | Russian State | Kolomna | 4x15/38 | 20/51 | 42/1.07 | 1,000/145 | | 202,000/91.8 | 25,900/116,00 | |
| 1894 | Meyer | Chilean Nitrate | Kitson | 4x14/36 2x24.4/62 | 18/46 | 35/0.89 | 1,103/160 | 25.2/2.33 | 123,900/56.3 | 27,600/12,400 | 840 |
| 1904 | Mallet DD.1 | Balt & Ohio | Alco | 2x20/51 2x32/81 | 32/81 | 56/1.42 | 1,620/235 | 72.2/6.71 | 334,500/152 | 71,500/32,170 | |
| **2-6-6-0 (1C.C)** | | | | | | | | | | | |
| 1889 | Mason Fairlie | Mex. Central | Mason Machine | 16/41 | 24/61 | 54/1.37 | 965/140 | | 93,200/42.4 | 13,500/6,070 | |
| 1914 | Mallet 601 | Hungarian State | Budapest | 2x20.5/52 | 26/66 | 56.7/1.44 | 1,500/218 | 54.8/5.1 | 241,100/109.6 | 50,300/22,600 | |
| 1927 | CC50 | Indonesian State | Werkspoor, S.L.M. | 2x16.5/42 2x25.5/65 | 24/61 | 43.5/1.11 | 1,378/200 | 36.6/3.4 | 162,067/73.5 | 50,070/22,731 | |
| Articulated Locomotives **2-6-6-2 (1C.C1)** | | | | | | | | | | | |
| 1915 | Mallet | Ches & Ohio | Alco | 2x22/56 2x35/89 | 32/81 | 56/1.42 | 1,448/210 | 72/6.7 | 434,400/197.4 | 76,100/34,200 | |
| 1930 | Garratt | L.M.S.R. | Beyer Peacock | 4x18.5/47 | 26/66 | 63/1.6 | 1,310/190 | 44.4/4.1 | 348,400/158.4 | 45,600/20,500 | |
| **2-6-2-.2-6-2 (1C1.1C1)** | | | | | | | | | | | |
| 1927 | Garratt R.1 | Saõ Paolo | Beyer Peacock | 4x20/51 | 26/66 | 66/1.68 | 1,380/200.3 | 49.2/4.6 | 354,400/161.1 | 53,600/24,100 | |

| Date | Class/name | Railway | Builder | Cylinder diameter in / cm | Piston stroke in / cm | Driving wheel dia. in / M | Steam pressure kpa / psi | Firegrate area sq.ft / sq.M | Weight 1b / tonne | T/Force 1b / kg | Power ihp |
|---|---|---|---|---|---|---|---|---|---|---|---|
| **Articulated Locomotives** | | | | | | | | | | | |
| **2-6-6-4 (1C.C2)** | | | | | | | | | | | |
| 1908 | "Hercules" Meyer | Antofagasta & Bolivia | Kitson | 4x14/35.6 | 18/46 | 37.5/0.95 | 1,241/180 | 25.1/2.32 | 190,400/86.5 | 28,800/13,000 | 450 |
| 1935 | Mallet 'A' | Norfolk & West'n N. & W.R.R. | | 4x24/61 | 30/76 | 70/1.78 | 2,070/300 | 122/11.3 | 573,000/260.4 | 126,000/57,200 | 7,600 |
| **2-6-6-6 (1C.C3)** | | | | | | | | | | | |
| 1941 | H-8 | C&O RR | Lima | 4x22.5/57 | 33/83.8 | 67/1.7 | 1,791/260 | 135.2/12.56 | 778,000/352 | 110,200/50,030 | |
| **4-6-6-4 (2C.C2)** | | | | | | | | | | | |
| 1912 | Garratt | Mogyana | Beyer Peacock | 4x13/33 | 20/51 | 45/1.14 | 1,241/180 | 27.3/2.52 | 165,800/75.4 | 20,300/9,130 | |
| 1936 | Mallet "Challenger" | Un Pac | ALCO | 4x22/56 | 32/81 | 69/1.75 | 1,759/255 | 108/10 | 566,000/257.3 | 97,400/43,800 | 5,000 |
| **4-6-2.2-6-4 (2C1.1C2)** | | | | | | | | | | | |
| 1936 | Garratt BT | Algerian State (P.L.M.) | Franco Belge | 4x19.3/49 | 26/66 | 70.9/1.8 | 1,966/285 | 58/5.37 | 476,200/216.4 | 58,200/26,200 | 4,400 |
| **4-6-4.4-6-4 (2C2.2C2)** | | | | | | | | | | | |
| 1949 | 15A Garratt | Rhodesian Railway (Zimbabwe) | Beyer Peacock | 4x17.5/44.4 | 26/66 | 57/1.45 | 1,380/200 | 49.6/4.6 | 418,200/190.1 | 42,000/18,900 | |
| **Articulated Locomotives** | | | | | | | | | | | |
| **0-8-8-0 (D.D.)** | | | | | | | | | | | |
| 1911 | Mallet | Balt & Ohio | Alco | 2x26/66 2x41/104 | 32/81 | 56/1.42 | 1,449/210 | 100/9.25 | 462,000/210 | 105,000/47,250 | |
| **2-8-6 (1D3)** | | | | | | | | | | | |
| 1880 | Fairlie | Denver Sth Park | Mason Machine | 15/38 | 20/51 | 36/0.91 | 966/140 | | 55,340/25.1 | 13,400/6,030 | |
| **2-8-8-0 (1D.D1)** | | | | | | | | | | | |
| 1918 | Mallet | Penn. | Juniata | 4x30.5/77.5 | 32/81 | 62/1.58 | 1,725/250 | 112/10.4 | 575,000/261.4 | 135,000/61,300 | |
| **Articulated Locomotives** | | | | | | | | | | | |
| **2-8-8-2 (1D.D1)** | | | | | | | | | | | |
| 1927 | Garratt GA.II | Burma | Beyer Peacock | 2x17.5/44 2x26.5/67 | 20/51 | 39/0.99 | 1,380/200 | 43.9/4.1 | 227,600/103.4 | 34,500/15,500 | |
| 1936 | Y6 | N & W | Roanoke | 2x25/635 | 32/81.3 | 58/1.47 | 2,067/300. | 106.2/9.8 | 611,520/277.3 | 152,206/68,492 | |
| **2-8-2.2-8-2 (1D1.1D1)** | | | | | | | | | | | |
| 1926 | Garratt | Chilean Nitrate | Beyer Peacock | 4x22/56 | 20/51 | 42/1.07 | 1,380/220 | 68.8/6.37 | 419,100/190.5 | 69,100/31,100 | |
| **2-8-8-4 (1D.D2)** | | | | | | | | | | | |
| 1941 | Mallet M.4 | Duluth Missabe & Iron Range | Baldwin | 4x26/66 | 32/81 | 63/1.6 | 1,656/240 | 125/11.6 | 699,700/318 | 140,000/63,000 | 6,810 |
| **4-8-8-2 (2D.D1)** | | | | | | | | | | | |
| 1940 | Mallet Cab-Ahead AC.12 | South'n Pacific | Baldwin | 4x24/61 | 32/81 | 63.5/1.61 | 1,725/250 3 | 139.12.9 | 552,000/250.9 | 124,300/55,930 | |
| **Articulated Locomotives** | | | | | | | | | | | |
| **4-8-8-4 (2D.D2)** | | | | | | | | | | | |
| 1929 | Garratt `N' | Bengal-Nagpur | Beyer Peacock | 4x20.5/52 | 26/66 | 56/1.42 | 1,449/210 | 69.8/6.46 | 524,200/238.3 | 61,500/27,700 | |
| 1941 | Big Boy | Un Pacific | Alco | 4x23.7/60 | 32/81 | 68/1.73 | 2,070/300 | 150/13.9 | 772,100/350.9 | 135,400/60,900 | 6,100 |
| **4-8-2.2-8-4 (2D1.1D2)** | | | | | | | | | | | |
| 1929 | GL Garratt | S. African | Beyer Peacock | 4x22/56 | 26/66 | 48/1.22 | 1,380/200 | 74.5/6.9 | 472,900/214.9 | 78,600/35,370 | |
| 1955 | 59 Garratt | E. African Rly & Har | Beyer Peacock | 4x20.5/52 | 28/71 | 54/1.37 | 1,552/225 | 72/6.7 | 562,500/255.7 | 73,500/33,100 | |
| **4-8-4.4-8-4 (2D2.2D2)** | | | | | | | | | | | |
| 1952 | AD60 | NSWGR | Beyer Peacock | 4x19.25/490 | 26/66 | 55/1.4 | 1,378/200 | 63.5/5.9 | 593,149/269 | 59,559/27,039 | |
| **Articulated Locomotives** | | | | | | | | | | | |
| **2-8-8-8-2 (ID.D.D1)** | | | | | | | | | | | |
| 1914 | 2603 | Erie | Baldwin | 6x36/91.4 | 32/81 | 63/1.6 | 1,449/210 | 90/8.3 | 845,000/384 | 160,000/72,700 | |

# LEADING CHARACTERISTICS OF STEAM LOCOMOTIVES

| Date | Class/name | Railway | Builder | Cylinder diameter in / cm | Piston stroke in / cm | Driving wheel dia. in / M | Steam pressure kpa / psi | Firegrate area sq.ft / sq.M | Weight 1b / tonne | T/Force 1b / kg | Power ihp |
|---|---|---|---|---|---|---|---|---|---|---|---|
| **2-8-8-8-4 (1D.D.D2)** | | | | | | | | | | | |
| 1916 | 700 | Virginian | Baldwin | 6x34/83.7 | 32/81 | 56/1.42 | 1,518/220 | 108/10 | 842,000/382.7 | 168,000/76,400 | |
| **2-10-10-2 (1E.E1)** | | | | | | | | | | | |
| 1918 | 800 | Virginian | Rebuild | 2x30/76 2x48/122 | 32/81 | 56/1.42 | 1,483/215 | 109/10.1 | 684,000/310.9 | 147,200/66,200 | |

## TANK ENGINES

| Date | Class/name | Railway | Builder | Cylinder diameter in / cm | Piston stroke in / cm | Driving wheel dia. in / M | Steam pressure kpa / psi | Firegrate area sq.ft / sq.M | Weight 1b / tonne | T/Force 1b / kg | Power ihp |
|---|---|---|---|---|---|---|---|---|---|---|---|
| **2-2-WT (1A1.WT)** | | | | | | | | | | | |
| 1835 | 'Victoria' | Dublin & Kingstown | Forrester | 11/28 | 18/46 | 60/1.52 | 345/50 | | | 1,500/670 | |
| **2-2-2T (1A1.T)** | | | | | | | | | | | |
| 1930 | Tk | Latvian State | German | 12.6/32 | 20.5/52 | 59/1.5 | 1,300/188 | 13.5/1.3 | 81,800/37.2 | 8,800/3,960 | |
| **4-2-4T (2A2.T)** | | | | | | | | | | | |
| 1854 | | Bristol & Exeter | Rothwell | 18/46 | 24/61 | 106/2.7 | 828/120 | 23/2.13 | 112,000/50.9 | 7,300/3,280 | |
| **Tank Engines 0-4-0T (B.T)** | | | | | | | | | | | |
| 1888 | 'H' | N.E.R. | Darlington | 14/35.6 | 20/51 | 41/1.04 | 966/140 | | 50,800/23.1 | 11,600/5,220 | |
| **0-4-0 AT** | | | | | | | | | | | |
| 1928 | Compressed Air H.C. Fricke | | H.K. Porter | 9.5/23 | 14/36 | 40/1.02 | 5,572/800 | | 32,000/14.5 | 8,000/3,600 | 150 |
| | 1,725/250 | | | | | | | | | | |
| **0-4-0 FT** | | | | | | | | | | | |
| 1930 | Fireless | Mead Corpn. | H.K. Porter | 18.5/47 | 16/41 | 44/1.12 | 1,725/250 | 414/60 | 140,000/63.6 | 23,000/10,400 | |
| **0-4-0 ST** | | | | | | | | | | | |
| 1935 | Saddle Tank | Medusa | Davenport | 16/41 | 24/61 | 44/1.12 | 1,242/180.2 | 20.2/1.9 | 101,000/45.9 | 21,300/9,580 | |
| 1954 | ED.9/10 | C.E.G.B. | Andrew Barclay | 14/36 | 22/56 | 41/1.04 | 1,104/160.1 | 9.5/0.9 | 66,080/30 | 14,300/6,490 | |
| **0-4-2T (B1.T)** | | | | | | | | | | | |
| 1932 | 4800 | G.W.R. | Swindon | 16.5/42 | 24/61 | 62/1.58 | 1,138/165 | 12.8/1.2 | 92,500/42 | 14,000/6,360 | |
| **0-4-4T (B2.T)** | | | | | | | | | | | |
| 1866 | Forney | NY Elevated | Rogers | 11/28 | 16/41 | 42/1.07 | 828/120 | | 43,000/19.5 | 4,700/2,110 | |
| 1897 | M.7 | L.S.W.R. | Nine Elms | 18.5/47 | 26/66 | 67/1.7 | 1,207/175 | 20.3/1.9 | 138,900/63.1 | 19,800/8,990 | |
| **Tank Engines 2-4-0WT (1B WT)** | | | | | | | | | | | |
| 1874 | 0298 | LSWR | Beyer Peacock | 16.5/42 | 20/50.8 | 55/1.4 | 1,102/160 | 14.8/1.4 | 85,955/39 | 11,050lb/5,015 | |
| **2-4-0T (1B.T)** | | | | | | | | | | | |
| 1884 | B.11 | Greek (SPAP) | Maffei | 13.2/33.5 | 19.7/50 | 47.2/1.2 | 1,000/145.3 | 10.6/0.96 | 58,900/26.8 | 8,640/3,920 | |
| **2-4-2T (1B1.T)** | | | | | | | | | | | |
| 1884 | M.15 | G.E.R. | Stratford | 17.5/44.4 | 24/61 | 64/1.63 | 1,104/160 | 15.4/1.4 | 116,500/52.9 | 15,600/7,020 | |
| **2-4-4T (1B2.T)** | | | | | | | | | | | |
| 1897 | D.XII | Bavarian State | Krauss | 17.7/45 | 22/56 | 64.6/1.64 | 1,300/188 | 21/1.96 | 152,100/69.1 | 16,500/7,400 | |
| **4-4-0T (2B.T)** | | | | | | | | | | | |
| 1863 | 'A' | Metropolitan | Beyer Peacock | 17/43 | 24/61 | 69/1.75 | 828/120 | 19/1.76 | 94,200/42.8 | 10,200/4,590 | |
| **4-4-2T (2B1.T)** | | | | | | | | | | | |
| 1882 | 0415 | L.S.W.R. | Nine Elms | 17.5/44.4 | 24/61 | 57/1.45 | 1,102/160 | 18.1/1.7 | 123,200/56 | 14,920/6,765 | |
| 1898 | C13 | G.N.R. | Doncaster | 17.5/44.5 | 26/66 | 68/1.73 | 1,171/170 | 17.8/1.65 | 138,915/63 | 17,900/8,126 | |
| 1908 | 1.3 | L.B.S.C.R. | Brighton | 21/53.3 | 26/66 | 79/2.01 | 1,104/160 | 24/2.22 | 165,800/75.4 | 19,700/8,870 | |
| 1909 | 79 | L.T.S.R. | Derby | 19/48.3 | 26/66 | 78/1.98 | 1,173/170 | 19.8/1.83 | 159,500/72.5 | 18,000/8,170 | |
| **4-4-4T (2B2.T)** | | | | | | | | | | | |
| 1913 | 'D' | N.E.R | Darlington | 3x16.5/42 | 26/66 | 69/1.75 | 1,104/160 | 23/2.12 | 196,400/89.3 | 22,900/10,300 | |

| Date | Class/name | Railway | Builder | Cylinder diameter in / cm | Piston stroke in / cm | Driving wheel dia. in / M | Steam pressure kpa / psi | Firegrate area sq.ft / sq.M | Weight 1b / tonne | T/Force 1b / kg | Power ihp |
|---|---|---|---|---|---|---|---|---|---|---|---|
| **Tank Engines** | | | | | | | | | | | |
| **0-6-0T (C.T)** | | | | | | | | | | | |
| 1872 | A.1X Terrier | L.B.S.C. | Brighton | 13/33 & 14/36 | 20/51 | 48/1.22 | 966/140 | 10/0.9 | 61,600/28 | 9,700/4,360 | |
| 1898 | J72 | N.E.R. | Gateshead | 17/4.32 | 24/61 | 49.25/1.26 | 965/140 | 11.3/1.05 | 85,995/39 | 16,760/7,610 | |
| 1909 | P | S.E.C.R. | Ashford | 12/30.5 | 18/40.7 | 45/1.14 | 1,102/160 | 9.1/0.84 | 63,840/29 | 7,810/3,545 | |
| 1924 | 3F | L.M.S. | Derby | 18/45.7 | 26/66 | 55/1.4 | 1,102/160 | 16/1.49 | 110,250/50 | 20,830/9,456 | |
| 1942 | W.D. | Various | Various | 16.5/42 | 24/61 | 54/1.37 | 1,447/210 | 19.4/1.8 | 100,107/45.4 | 21,630/9,820 | |
| **0-6-0WT (C.WT)** | | | | | | | | | | | |
| 1880 | T.3 | Prussian State | Various | 13.8/35 | 21.6/55 | 43.3/1.1 | 1,200/174 | 14.5/1.35 | 79,000/35.9 | 11,600/5,220 | |
| **0-6-0ST (C.ST)** | | | | | | | | | | | |
| 1897 | J.13 | G.N.R. | Doncaster | 18/46 | 26/66 | 56/1.42 | 1,207/175 | 16.2/1.5 | 115,800/52.6 | 22,400/10,080 | |
| **0-6-0PT (C.PT)** | | | | | | | | | | | |
| 1929 | 5700 | G.W.R. | Swindon | 17.5/44.4 | 24/61 | 55.5/1.41 | 1,380/200 | 15,3/1.4 | 106,400/48.4 | 25,500/11,480 | |
| **0-6-0ST (C.ST)** | | | | | | | | | | | |
| 1933 | Saddle Tank | Calico Chemical | Vulcan Iron | 19/48.3 | 24/61 | 44/1.12 | 1,310/190 | 22.3/2.06 | 142,000/64.5 | 31,800/14,300 | |
| **0-6-0FT (C.FT)** | | | | | | | | | | | |
| 1937 | Fireless | Santa Fe | Baldwin | 30/76 | 24/61 | 44/1.12 | 448/65 | | 171,800/78.1 | 31,900/14,350 | |
| **0-6-0ST (C.ST)** | | | | | | | | | | | |
| 1943 | Austerity | W.D. | Hunslet | 18/46 | 28/66 | 51/1.29 | 1,173/170 | 16.8/1.55 | 108,000/49.1 | 23,900/10,750 | |
| **0-6-2T (C1.T)** | | | | | | | | | | | |
| 1881 | Coal Tank | L.N.W.R | Crewe | 17/43.2 | 24/61 | 53.5/1.36 | 966/140 | 17.1/1.6 | 96,300/43.8 | 15,400/6,930 | |
| 1888 | 298 | Austrian Federal | Krauss | 11.4/29 | 15.7/40 | 31.5/80 | 1,176/171 | 8.6/0.8 | 52,900/24 | 9,395/4,265.. | |
| 1920 | N.2 | G.N.R. | Doncaster | 19/48.3 | 26/66 | 68/1.73 | 1,173/170 | 19/1.75 | 157,250/71.4 | 19,900/8,950 | |
| 1924 | 5600 | G.W.R. | Swindon | 18/45.7 | 26/66 | 55.5/1.41 | 1,378/200 | 20.35/1.89 | 154,560/70 | 25,800/11,713 | |
| **0-6-4T (C2.T)** | | | | | | | | | | | |
| 1885 | 1 | Mersey | Beyer Peacock | 21/53.3 | 26/66 | 55/1.4 | 1,035/150.5 | 21/1.94 | 151,900/69 | 26,600/11,970 | |
| **Tank Engines** | | | | | | | | | | | |
| **2-6-0T (1C.T)** | | | | | | | | | | | |
| 1900 | T.9/3 | Prussian Statc | Union Foundry | 17.7/45 | 24.8/63 | 53/1.35 | 1,200/174 | 16.5/1.53 | 131,800/59.9 | 20,700/9,310 | |
| **2-6-2T (1C1.T)** | | | | | | | | | | | |
| 1906 | 4500 | G.W.R. | Swindon | 17/43.2 | 24/61 | 55.5/1.41 | 1,378/200 | 16.6/1.54 | 127,680/58 | 21,250/9,650 | |
| 1911 | 375 | Hungarian State | MAVAG | 16.1/41 | 23.6/60 | 46.5/1.18 | 1,175/170 | 19.9/1.85 | 98,785/44.8 | 19,060/8,655 | |
| 1929 | 5100 | G.W.R. | Swindon | 18/45.7 | 30/76 | 68/1.73 | 1,380/200 | 20.3/1.88 | 175,600/79.8 | 24,300/10,900 | |
| 1928 | 64 | German State | Henschel | 19.8/50 | 26/66 | 59/1.5 | 1,400/203 | 22/2.04 | 166,400/75.6 | 28,900/13,136 | |
| 1935 | | Quincy | Alco | 16/41 | 24/61 | 44/1.12 | 1,241/180 | 20.5/1.9 | 119,700/54.4 | 21,400/9,630 | |
| 1935 | 3MT | L.M.S. | Derby | 17.5/44.4 | 26/66 | 63/1.6 | 1,380/200 | 19.2/1.78 | 161,300/73.3 | 21,500/9680 | |
| **2-6-4T (1C2.T)** | | | | | | | | | | | |
| 1936 | 4MT | L.M.S. | Crewe | 19.6/50 | 26/66 | 69/1.75 | 1,380/200 | 26.7/2.47 | 196,900/89.5 | 24,700/11,100 | |
| **4-6-0T (2C.T)** | | | | | | | | | | | |
| 1907 | 'W' | N.E.R. | Darlington | 19/48.3 | 26/66 | 61.2/1.55 | 1,173/170 | 23/2.13 | 156,300/71 | 23,000/10,400 | |
| **4-6-2T (2C1.T)** | | | | | | | | | | | |
| 1911 | 9N | G.C.R. | Gorton | 20/51 | 26/66 | 67/1.7 | 1,241/180 | 21/1.94 | 192,400/87.4 | 23,800/10,710 | |
| **4-6-4T (2C2.T)** | | | | | | | | | | | |
| 1903 | C-30 | N.S.W.G.R. | Beyer Peacock, Eveleigh | 18.5/47 | 24/61 | 55/1.4 | 1.102/160 | 24/2.23 | 162,710/73.8 | 19,116/8,698 | |
| 1912 | T.18 | Prussian State | Vulkan | 22/56 | 24.8/63 | 65/1.65 | 1,200/174.1 | 25.9/2.44 | 233,200/106 | 26,700/12,000 | |
| 1924 | 11110 | L.M.S. | Horwich | 4x16.5/42 | 26/66 | 75/1.9 | 1,241/180 | 29.6/2.74 | 223,800/101.7 | 30,000/13,600 | |
| 1928 | 62 | DR | Various | 23.8/60 | 26/66 | 69/1.75 | 1,378/200 | 37.6/3.5 | 273,370/124 | 31,500/14,250 | |
| **4-6-6T (2C3.T)** | | | | | | | | | | | |
| 1935 | D.1a | Boston & Albany | Alco | 23.5/60 | 26/66 | 63/1.6 | 1,483/215.6 | 60.8/5.63 | 352,000/160 | 41,600/18,700 | |

# LEADING CHARACTERISTICS OF STEAM LOCOMOTIVES

| Date | Class/name | Railway | Builder | Cylinder diameter in / cm | Piston stroke in / cm | Driving wheel dia. in / M | Steam pressure kpa / psi | Firegrate area sq.ft / sq.M | Weight 1b / tonne | T/Force 1b / kg | Power ihp |
|---|---|---|---|---|---|---|---|---|---|---|---|
| **Tank Engines 0-8-0T (D.T)** | | | | | | | | | | | |
| 1851 | Vindobona | Semmering | J. Haswell | 16.6/42 | 22.8/58 | 37.7/0.96 | 690/100 | 15.6/1.45 | 100,300/45.6 | 14,200/6,400 | |
| 1910 | T.13 | Prussian State | Various | 19.7/50 | 23.6/60 | 49.2/1.25 | 1,200/174 | 19/1.76 | 132,400/60.2 | 37,200/16,740 | |
| **0-8-2T (D1.T)** | | | | | | | | | | | |
| 1902 | L.1 | G.N.R. | Doncaster | 19.7/50 | 26/66 | 56/1.42 | 1,172/170 | 24.5/2.26 | 161,700/73.5 | 26,000/11,800 | |
| 1930 | | Cyprus Mines | Baldwin | 15/38 | 18/46 | 33/0.84 | 1,104/160 | 18.2/1.68 | 105,700/48 | 16,600/7,470 | |
| **0-8-4T (D2.T)** | | | | | | | | | | | |
| 1923 | 380 | L.N.W.R. | Crewe | 20.5/52 | 24/61 | 53/1.35 | 1,242/180 | 23.6/2.18 | 197,100/89.6 | 29,900/13,450 | |
| **2-8-0T** | | | | | | | | | | | |
| 1910 | 4200 | G.W.R. | Swindon | 18.5/47 | 30/76 | 55.5/1.41 | 1,380/200 | 20.6/1.9 | 182,800/83.1 | 31,400/14,130 | |
| **2-8-2T (1D1.T)** | | | | | | | | | | | |
| 1932 | 4.200 | Nord | Derosne & Cail | 25.2/64 | 27.6/70 | 61/1.55 | 1,800/261 | 33.2/3.1 | 270,100/122.8 | 61,400/27,600 | 2,300 |
| 1932 | Long Bell | Lumber | Alco | 18/46 | 24/61 | 44/1.12 | 1,311/190 | 25.2/2.33 | 168,000/76.4 | 28,500/12,830 | |
| 1936 | Rack | Arica-La Paz | Baldwin | 2x19/48.3 2x18/46 | 20/51 18/46 Rack | 37/0.94 | 1,380/200 | 28.6/2.65 | 166,000/75.5 | 33,200/14,940 | 30,000/13,600 Rack |
| 1950 | Tkt-48 | Polish State (PKP) | Chrzanow | 19.7/50 | 27.6/70 | 57/1.45 | 1,600/232.7 | 32.3/3 | 209,000/95 | 37,500/17,040 | |
| **Tank Engines 2-8-4T (1D2.T)** | | | | | | | | | | | |
| 1912 | 43 | Antofagasta & Bolivia | Kitson | 19/48.3 | 24/61 | 44/1.112 | 1,240/180 | 29.6/2.75 | 201,757/91.5 | 30,127/13,677 | |
| 1954 | 65.10 | German State (DR) | Borsig | 23.6/60 | 26/66 | 63/1.6 | 1,600/232 | 37.1/3.4 | 264,000/120 | 44,000/19,980 | |
| **4-8-4T (2D2.T)** | | | | | | | | | | | |
| 1926 | 242.AT | P.L.M. | Various | 2x16.5/42 2x24.8/63 | 25.6/65 | 64.7/1.65 | 1,600/232 | 33/3.1 | 264,600/120.3 | 31,000/14,070 | |
| **0-10-0T (E.T.)** | | | | | | | | | | | |
| 1903 | Decapod | G.E.R. | Stratford | 3x18.5/47 | 24/61 | 54/1.37 | 1,380/200 | 42/3.9 | 175,800/79.9 | 39,000/17,700 | |
| 1905 | T.16 | Prussian State | Schwartzkopff | 24/61 | 26/66 | 53/1.35 | 1,200/174 | 24.7/2.3 | 186.800/84.9 | 40,800/18,000 | |
| **2-10-2T (1E1.T)** | | | | | | | | | | | |
| 1922 | 95 | DR | Various | 27.5/70 | 26/66 | 55/1.4 | 1,378 | 46.28/4.3 | 280,790/127.4 | 53,625/24,320 | |
| 1954 | 99.23 | DR | Karl Marx | 21.6/55 | 21.6/55 | 39/1.0 | 1,378/200 | 30.1/2.8 | 143,260/65 | 43,875/19,920 | |
| **2-12-4T (1F2.T)** | | | | | | | | | | | |
| 1931 | 46.1 | Bulgarian State | Krupp | 27.6/70 | 27.6/70 | 52.7/1.34 | 1,600/232 | 52.3/4.86 | 328,000/149.1 | 76,200/34,300 | |

## CRANE TANK ENGINES

| Date | Class/name | Railway | Builder | Cylinder diameter in / cm | Piston stroke in / cm | Driving wheel dia. in / M | Steam pressure kpa / psi | Firegrate area sq.ft / sq.M | Weight 1b / tonne | T/Force 1b / kg | Power ihp |
|---|---|---|---|---|---|---|---|---|---|---|---|
| **0-4-0T (B.T)** | | | | | | | | | | | |
| 1914 | 7-Tonner | N.S.W.G.R. | Hawthorn Leslie | 14/33.6 | 20/50.8 | 39/0.99 | 1,309/190 | | 88,200/40 | 15,300/6,950 | |

## ARTICULATED TANK ENGINES

| Date | Class/name | Railway | Builder | Cylinder diameter in / cm | Piston stroke in / cm | Driving wheel dia. in / M | Steam pressure kpa / psi | Firegrate area sq.ft / sq.M | Weight 1b / tonne | T/Force 1b / kg | Power ihp |
|---|---|---|---|---|---|---|---|---|---|---|---|
| **0-4-4-4-0 (B.B.B.T)** | | | | | | | | | | | |
| 1910 | Shay | Bloedel Stewart | Lima | 3x13/33 | 15/38 | 36/0.9 | 1,380/200 | 27.8/2.6 | 188,000/85.3 | 38,200/17,300 | |
| **0-6-6-0T (C.C.T)** | | | | | | | | | | | |
| 1949 | 36001 Leader | South'n | Brighton | 6x12.2/31 | 16/41 | 61/1.6 | 1,932/280 | 43/3.98 | 292,300/132.9 | 26,300/11,830.. | |
| **0-6-2-.2-6-0T (C1.1C.T)** | | | | | | | | | | | |
| 1905 | 6121 | Nord | Hellemes | 2x15.7/40 | 26.8/68 | 57.3/1.45 | 1,600/232 | 32.3/3.0 | 235,300/106.9 | 41,900/18,850 | |
| **0-8-8-0T (D.D.T.)** | | | | | | | | | | | |
| 1911 | Gt.2x4/4 | Bavarian State | Maffei | 2x20.5/52 2x31.5/80 | 25.2/64 | 48/1.22 | 1,500/217 | 46.4/4.25 | 271,700/123.5 | 57,000/25,880 | |

\* Weight includes tender.
(R)Rebuilt version
Abbreviations: B/hting, boiler heating; cyl, cylinder; dia, diameter; Driv, driving; wheel; F/gate, firegrate; p/stroke, piston stroke; S/pressure, steam pressure; T/force, tractive (drawbar) force; T/power, tractive power.

# Leading Characteristics of Electric Motive Power Locomotives

| Date | Class | Railway | Gauge | Electrification system | Control | Tot Weight 1b / tonne | Cont rating, kW | Max. speed mph/kph |
|---|---|---|---|---|---|---|---|---|
| **1-A** | | | | | | | | |
| 1883 | Mo. coach | Volk's Electric | 2ft/610mm | 50V dc | Resist. | 1,100/0.5 | 1.0 | 6.0/9.0 |
| 1883 | The Judge | Chicago Exhib | 3ft/914mm | 75V dc | Resist. | 11,020/5.0 | 15 | 15/24 |
| **1-B-B-1** | | | | | | | | |
| 1922 | Be4/6 | Swiss Federal | Standard | 15,000V s.ph. 16 2/3Hz | Transf. l.t.tap | 242,440/110 | 1,500 | 46/75 |
| **B-B** | | | | | | | | |
| 1958 | BB16500 | French National | Standard | 25,000V s.ph. 50Hz | Transf. h.t.tap | 157,365/71.4 | 2,580 | 93/150 |
| 1963 | V43 | Hungarian State | Standard | 25,000V s.ph. 50Hz | Transf. h.t.tap | 176,320/80 | 2,140 | 81/130 |
| 1965 | BB17000 | French National | Standard | 25,000V s.ph. 50Hz | Transf. h.t.tap | 175.200/79,500 | 1,855 | 93/150 |
| 1965 | YAM1 | Indian | 3ft 3 3/8in/ 1,000 mm | 25,000V s.ph. 50Hz | Transf. l.t.tap | 114,608/52 | 1,200 | 50/80 |
| 1971 | BB15000 | French National | Standard | 25,000V s.ph. 50Hz | Thyristor | 198,360/90 | 4,430 | 100/160 |
| 1977 | BB7200 | French National | Standard | 1,500V dc | Chopper | 188,530/85. | 5 4,360 | 100/160 |
| 1988 | BB26000 | French National | Standard | 25,000V s.ph. 50Hz | Current inv | 198,450/90 | 5,600 | 125/200 |
| 1991. | 1700. | Netherlands State | Standard | 1,500v dc | | 189,630/86 | 4.450 | 100/160 |
| **B-B-B** | | | | | | | | |
| 1979 | E633 | Italian State | Standard | 25,000V s.ph. 50Hz | Chopper | 224,808/102 | 4,400 | 100/160 |
| **0-B-0** | | | | | | | | |
| 1890 | | City & Sth London | Standard | 500V dc | Resist. | 26,889/12.2 | 100 | 25/40 |
| 1909 | 169 | German Federal | Standard | 15,000V s.ph. 16.67Hz | | 57,330/26 | 306 | 30/50 |
| **Bo-Bo** | | | | | | | | |
| 1906 | Val | Brembana | Standard | 6,000V s.ph. 25Hz | Transf. l.t.tap | 66,120/30 | 200 | 46/75 |
| 1914 | Z-1-A | Can. Northern | Standard | 2,400V dc | Resist. | 1/4,116/79 | 820 | 55/88 |
| 1925 | 1E | Sth African | 3ft 6in/1,067mm | 3,000V dc | Resist. | 149,184/67.7 | 750 | 45/72 |
| 1946 | 410 | Swiss Federal | Standard | 15,000V s.ph.16.67Hz | Transf. l.t.tap | 125,685/57 | 1,760 | 78/125 |
| 1949 | BB8100 | French Railways | Standard | 1,500V dc | Resist. | 202,850/92 | 1,900 | 65/105 |
| 1950 | 1100 | Netherlands State | Standard | 1,500V dc | Resist | | 1,900 | 84/135 |
| 1954 | BB12000 | French National | Standard | 25,000V s.ph. 50Hz | Transf. h.t.tap | 185,220/84 | 2,650 | 75/120 |
| 1956 | 141 | German Federal | Standard | 15,000V s.ph. 16.67Hz | Transf. h.t.tap | 147,668/67 | 2,450 | 74.5/120 |
| 1956 | 110 | German Federal | Standard | 15,000V s.ph. 16.67Hz | Transf. h.t. tap | 189,630/86 | 3,620 | 93/150 |
| 1957 | 140 | German Federal. | Standard | 15,000V s.ph. 16.67Hz | Transf. h.t. tap | 189,630/86 | 3,620 | 68/110 |
| 1958 | 3600 | Luxembourg State | Standard | 25,000V s.ph. 50Hz | Transf. h.t. tap | 185,220/84 | 2,650 | 75/120 |
| 1961 | Eu-07 | Polish State | Standard | 3,000V dc | Resist. | 176,320/80 | 2,000 | 78/125 |
| 1961 | E30 | Chilean State | 5ft 6in/1676mm | 3,000V dc | Resist. | 216,090/98 | 1,790 | 80/130 |
| 1962 | 41 | Bulgarian State | Standard | 25,000V dc s.ph. 50Hz | Transf. h.t.tap | 193,952/88 | 2,800 | 68/110 |
| 1963 | 1042 | Austrian Federal | Standard | 15,000V s.ph. 16.67Hz | Transf. h.t.tap | 185,220/84 | 3,336 | 80/130 |
| 1963 | BB25150 | French National | Standard | 25,000V s.ph. 50Hz | | 187,425/85 | 4,130 | 81/130. |
| 1964 | Re/4/4 | Berne-Loetschberg-Simplon | Standard | 15,000V s.ph. 16,67Hz | Transf. h.t.tap | 176,400/80 | 4,945(h) | 87/140 |
| 1964 | 420 | Swiss Federal | Standard. | 15,000V s.ph. 16.67Hz | Transf. h.t.tap | 176,400/80 | 4,650(h) | 87/140 |
| 1965 | 86 | British | Standard | 25,000V s.ph. 50Hz | Transf. h.t.tap | 185,136/84 | 2,685 | 100/160 |
| 1966 | 16 | Belgium National | Standard | 3,000V dc (see text) | Resist. | 182,050/82.6 | 2,620 | 100-160 |
| 1966 | S489.1 | Czech State | Standard | 25,000V s.ph. 50Hz | Transf. h.t.tap | 187,340/85 | 3,080 | 74/120 |
| 1967 | E444 | Italian State | Standard | 3,000V dc | Resist. | 178,524/81 | 3,750 | 112/180 |
| 1968 | BCU-30 | Pakistan | 5ft 6in/1,676 mm | 25,000V s.ph. 50Hz | Thyristor | 178,524/81 | 2,360 | 75/120 |
| 1969 | 6E & 6E1 | Sth African | 3ft 6in/1,067 mm | 3,000V dc | Resist. | 195,936/88.9 | 2,252 | 70/113 |
| 1973 | 87 | British | Standard | 25,000V s.ph. 50Hz | Transf. h.t.tap | 182,932/83 | 3,730 | 100/177 |

# LEADING CHARACTERISTICS OF ELECTRIC MOTIVE POWER LOCOMOTIVES

| Date | Class | Railway | Gauge | Electrification system | Control | Tot Weight lb / tonne | Cont rating, kW | Max. speed mph/kph |
|------|-------|---------|-------|------------------------|---------|----------------------|-----------------|--------------------|
| 1973 | Srl | Finnish State | 5ft/1,524mm | 25,000V s.ph. 50Hz | Thyristor | 185,136/84 | 3,100 | 87/140 |
| 1974 | 111 | German Federal | Standard | 15,000V s.ph. 16.67Hz | Transf. h.t.tap | 183,015/83 | 3,620 | 100/160 |
| 1974 | 1044 | Austrian Federal | Standard | 15,000V s.ph. 50Hz | Thyristor | 185,136/84 | 5,000 | 100/160 |
| 1974 | ES499.0 | Czech State | Standard | 3,000V dc | Resist. | 192,630/87.4 | 4,000 | 100/160 |
| 1979 | AEM7 | Amtrak | Standard | 11,000V s.ph. 25Hz | Thyristor | 201,225/91.3 | 4,250 | 120/193 |
| 1979 | 120 | German Federal | Standard | 15,000V s.ph. 16.67Hz | Current inv | 185,136/84 | 5,600 | 125/200 |
| 1982 | 27 | Belgian National | Standard | 3,000V dc | Chopper | 187,340/85 | 4,150 | 100/160 |
| 1984 | EA | Danish State | Standard | 25,000V s.ph. 50Hz | Current inv | 176,320/80 | 4,000 | 100/160 |
| 1984 | 143 | German National (DR) | Standard | 15,000V s.ph. 16.67Hz | | 183,015/83 | 3,720 | 75/120 |
| 1988 | 90. | British | Standard | 25,000V s.ph. 50Hz | Thyristor | 189,630/86 | 3,508 | 110/175 |
| 1988 | 91 | British | Standard | 25,000V s.ph. 50Hz | Thyristor | 176,400/80 | 4,540 | 140/225 |
| 1997 | 101 | German Federal | Standard | 15,000V s.ph. 16.67Hz | Current inv | 191,835/87 | 6,000 | 137/220 |
| 1997 | 152 | German Federal | Standard | 15,000V s.ph. 16.67Hz | | 193,950/88 | 6,000 | 87/140 |

## B0+B0

| Date | Class | Railway | Gauge | Electrification system | Control | Tot Weight lb / tonne | Cont rating, kW | Max. speed mph/kph |
|------|-------|---------|-------|------------------------|---------|----------------------|-----------------|--------------------|
| 1894 | No 1-3 | Baltimore & Ohio | Standard | 650V dc | Resist. | 191,748/87 | 560 | 17.5/28 |
| 1901 | 34 | Adriatic System | Standard | 3,400V 3 ph. 50Hz | Liq resist. | 106,233/48. | 2 440 | 20.5/33 |
| 1906 | Trial | Oranienburg | Standard | 6,000V s.ph. 25Hz | Transf. l.t.tap | | 550 | 42/60 |

## 1-B0+Bo-1

| Date | Class | Railway | Gauge | Electrification system | Control | Tot Weight lb / tonne | Cont rating, kW | Max. speed mph/kph |
|------|-------|---------|-------|------------------------|---------|----------------------|-----------------|--------------------|
| 1924 | WH | Indonesian State | 3ft 6in/1067mm | 1,500V dc | Resist. | 160,050/72. | 6 590 | 50/80 |

## Bo-Bo-Bo

| Date | Class | Railway | Gauge | Electrification system | Control | Tot Weight lb / tonne | Cont rating, kW | Max. speed mph/kph |
|------|-------|---------|-------|------------------------|---------|----------------------|-----------------|--------------------|
| 1927 | E626 | Italian State | Standard | 3,000V dc | Resist. | 209,380/95 | 1,660 | 56/95 |
| 1940 | E636 | Italian State | Standard | 3,000V dc | Resist. | 227,705/101 | 1,890 | 75/120 |
| 1959 | E645 | Italian State | Standard | 3,000V dc | | 246,960/112 | 3,780 | 87/140 |
| 1968 | EF81 | Japanese National | 3ft 6 in/1,067 mm | 1,500V dc (see text) | Resist. | 222,604/101 | 2,300 | 72/115 |
| 1972 | WAG1 | Korean National | Standard | 25,000V s.ph. 60Hz | Thyristor | 282,112/128 | 3,930 | 53/85 |
| 1979 | E656 | Italian State | Standard | 3,000V dc | Resist. | 264,480/120 | 4,200 | 93/150 |
| 1985 | Ef | N. Zealand | 3ft 6in/1,067 mm | 25,000V dc s.ph. 50Hz | Thyristor | 238,032/108 | 3,000 | 65/105 |
| 1988 | 3900 | Queensland | 3ft 6in/1067mm | 25,000V s.ph. 50Hz | | 242,550/110 | 2,900 | 62/100 |
| 1994 | Tri-Bo | Eurotunnel | Standard. | 25,000V s.ph. 50Hz GTO | | 286,520/130 | 5,600 | 87/140 |

## Bo-Bo+Bo-Bo

| Date | Class | Railway | Gauge | Electrification system | Control | Tot Weight lb / tonne | Cont rating, kW | Max. speed mph/kph |
|------|-------|---------|-------|------------------------|---------|----------------------|-----------------|--------------------|
| 1961 | VL10 | Soviet | 5ft/1520mm | 3,000V dc | Resist. | 405,720/184 | 5,700 | 68/110. |
| 1972 | VL82m | Soviet | 5ft/1520mm | Dual (see text) | Thyristor | 220,500/100 | 5,760 | 68/110 |
| 1975 | ChS200 | Soviet | 5ft/1,524 mm | 3,000V dc | Resist. | 346,028/157 | 8,000 | 125/200 |
| 1979 | ChS6 | Soviet | 5ft/1520mm | 3,000V dc | | 361,620/164 | 8,000 | 118/190 |

## 2-Bo+Bo-2

| Date | Class | Railway | Gauge | Electrification system | Control | Tot Weight lb / tonne | Cont rating, kW | Max. speed mph/kph |
|------|-------|---------|-------|------------------------|---------|----------------------|-----------------|--------------------|
| 1934 | E428 | Italian State | Standard | 3,000V dc | Resist. | 299,744/136 | 2,520 | 81/130 |

## 2-Bo-Bo+Bo-Bo-2

| Date | Class | Railway | Gauge | Electrification system | Control | Tot Weight lb / tonne | Cont rating, kW | Max. speed mph/kph |
|------|-------|---------|-------|------------------------|---------|----------------------|-----------------|--------------------|
| 1915 | | Milwaukee | Standard | 3,000V dc | Resist. | 564,224/256 | 2,224 | 60/96.5 |

## C-C

| Date | Class | Railway | Gauge | Electrification system | Control | Tot Weight lb / tonne | Cont rating, kW | Max. speed mph/kph |
|------|-------|---------|-------|------------------------|---------|----------------------|-----------------|--------------------|
| 1964 | CC40100 | French National | Standard | Quadri-current | Resist | .238,140/108 | 4,480 | 137/220 |
| 1969 | CC6500 | French National | Standard | 1,500V dc | Resist | 264,600/120 | 5,900 | 135/220 |

## 1-C-1

| Date | Class | Railway | Gauge | Electrification system | Control | Tot Weight lb / tonne | Cont rating, kW | Max. speed mph/kph |
|------|-------|---------|-------|------------------------|---------|----------------------|-----------------|--------------------|
| 1952 | Da | Swedish State | Standard | 15,000V s.ph. 16.67Hz | Transf. l.t.tap | 165,300/75 | 1,780 | 62/100 |

## C0-C0

| Date | Class | Railway | Gauge | Electrification system | Control | Tot Weight lb / tonne | Cont rating, kW | Max. speed mph/kph |
|------|-------|---------|-------|------------------------|---------|----------------------|-----------------|--------------------|
| 1940 | E94 | German State | Standard | 15,000V s.ph. 16.67Hz | Transf. l.t.tap | 271,092/123 | 4,400 | 62/100 |
| 1941 | No.CC1/2 | Southern | Standard | 650V dc | Gen rev. | 270,012/103 | 1,100 | 75/121 |
| 1947 | 3E | Sth African | 3ft 6in/1,067 mm | 3,000V dc | Resist. | 240,236/109 | 2,340 | 65/105 |
| 1951 | 1200 | Netherlands State | Standard | 1,500V dc | Resist | .238,140/108 | 2,210 | 93/150 |
| 1952 | CC7100 | French National | Standard | 1,500V dc | Resist. | 235,828/107 | 3,775 | 93/150. |
| 1952 | L | Vict. Govt. | 5ft 3in/1,600 mm | 1,500V dc | Resist. | 220,622/98.5 | 1,800 | 75/121 |
| 1955 | EP5 | New Haven | Standard | 11,000V s.ph 25Hz | Resist. | 346,185/157 | 2,980 | 90/145 |
| 1956 | VL23 | Soviet | 5ft/1520mm | 3,000V dc | Resist. | 304,290/138 | 2,749 | 62/100 |
| 1956 | 46 | NSW Govt | Standard | 1,500V dc | Resist. | 251,256/114 | 2,535 | 65/105 |
| 1960 | E44 | Pennsylvania | Standard | 11,000V s.ph. 16.67Hz | Transf. l.t.tap | 385,700/175 | 3,285 | 70/113 |
| 1970 | 103 | German Federal | Standard | 15,000V s.ph 16.67Hz | Transf. h.t.tap | 242,550/110 | 5,950 | 125/200 |
| 1971 | WAM4 | Indian | 5ft 6in/1,676 mm | 25,000V s.ph. 50Hz | Transf. h.t.tap | 249,052/113 | 2,680 | 75/121 |
| 1972 | ChS2t | Soviet Railways | 5ft/1520mm | 3,000V dc | Thyristor | 277,830/126 | 4,080 | 100/160 |
| 1973 | E60C | Black Mesa | Standard | 50,000V | Thyristor | 425,372/193 | 3,805 | 72/116 |

| Date | Class | Railway | Gauge | Electrification system | Control | Tot Weight lb / tonne | Cont rating, kW | Max. speed mph/kph |
|---|---|---|---|---|---|---|---|---|
| 1974 | Lake Powell 250 | German State | Standard | s.ph. 60Hz 15,000V | Transf. | 264,480/120 | 5,140 | 78/12 |
| 1974 | AEM6 | Amtrak | Standard | s.ph. 16.67Hz h.t.tap 11,000V s.ph. 25Hz | Thyristor | 387,904/176 | 3,805 | 85/137 |
| 1975 | V63 | Hungarian State | Standard | 25,000V s.ph. 50Hz | Thyristor | 255,664/116 | 3,300 | 87/140 |
| 1978 | 7E | Sth African | 3ft 6in/ 1,065 mm | 3,000V dc | Thyristor | 272,794/123. | 5 3,000 | 62/100 |
| 1978 | 9E | Sth African | 3ft 6in/ 1,065 mm | 50,000V s.ph. 50Hz | Thyristor | 370,272/168 | 3,780 | 45/72 |
| 1979 | 85 | NSW State | Standard | 1,500V dc | Resist. | 271,092/123 | 2,700 | 80/130 |
| 1987 | 89 | Gt.North Eastern | Standard | 25,000V s.ph. 50Hz | Thyristor | 229,320/104 | 4,350 | 125/200 |
| 1993 | 92 | Several | Standard Dual (see text) | | GTO | 277,830/126 | 5,000 | 100/160. |

**1-C0-2**

| 1928 | WCP1 | Gt. Ind Pen | 5ft 6in/ 1,676 mm | 1,500V dc | Resist. | 234,726/106. | 5 1,900 | 70/121 |
|---|---|---|---|---|---|---|---|---|

**1-C0+C0-1**

| 1926 | No 330 | Paulista | 5ft 3in/ 1,600 mm | 3,000V dc | Resist. | 221,760/100 | 2,100 | 31/50 |
|---|---|---|---|---|---|---|---|---|

**2-C0+C0-2**

| 1934 | GG1 | Pennsylvania | Standard | 11,000V s.ph. 25Hz 1.t.tap. | Transf. | 477,166/216.5 | 3,450 | 100/160 |
|---|---|---|---|---|---|---|---|---|

**1-D-1**

| 1925 | E472 | Italian State | Standard | 3,000V dc | Mo. poles, cascade | 208,058/94.4 | 1,950 46. | 5/75 |
|---|---|---|---|---|---|---|---|---|
| 1932 | V40 | Hungarian State | Standard | 15,000V s.ph. 50Hz conv | Phase | 203,870/92.5 | 2,200 | 62/100 |

**0-Do-1**

| 1928 | 1161 | Austrian Federal | Standard | 15,000V s.ph 16.67Hz | Resist. | 123,480/56 | 700(h) | 25/40 |
|---|---|---|---|---|---|---|---|---|

**1-Do-1**

| 1904 | S | NY Central | Standard | 650V dc | Resist. | 191,748/87 | 1,640 | 70/113.5 |
|---|---|---|---|---|---|---|---|---|
| 1926 | E16 | German State | Standard | 15,000V dc s.ph. 16.67Hz 1.t.tap. | Transf. | 244,644/111 | 2,580 | 74.5/120 |
| 1927 | No 5001-5 | Gt. Nthn (USA) | Standard | 11,500V s.ph. 16.67Hz rev. | Gen. | 365,864/166 | 1,880 | 45/72.5 |
| 1928 | 1670 | Austrian Federal | Standard | 15,000V s.ph. 16.67Hz | Electro-pneumatic | 235,935/107 | 2,350 | 62/100 |
| 1935 | E18 | German State | Standard | 15,000V s.ph. 16.67Hz 1.t.tap. | Transf | 233,624/106 | 3,830 | 87/140 |

**1-Do-2**

| 1938 | 101 | NZ Govt | 3ft 6 in/1,067 mm | 1,500V dc | Resist. | 198,360/90 | 900 | 55/88.5 |
|---|---|---|---|---|---|---|---|---|

**2-D0-1**

| 1927 | Ae4/7 | Swiss Federal | Standard | 15,000V s.ph. 16.67Hz | l.t.switch | 271,215/123 | 2,295(h) | 62/100 |
|---|---|---|---|---|---|---|---|---|

**2-Do-Do-2**

| 1948 | Little Joe | Various | Standard | 3,000V dc | Resist. | 535,815/243 | 3,470 | 68/110 |
|---|---|---|---|---|---|---|---|---|

**2-D-D-2**

| 1910 | DD1 | Pennsylvania | Standard | 11,000V s.ph. 25Hz | Resist | 313,000/142 | 2,980 | 90/145 |
|---|---|---|---|---|---|---|---|---|

**0-E-0**

| 1908 | E550 | Italian State | Standard | 3,000V 3 ph. 15Hz cascade | Resist. | 132,460/60.1 | 1,570 | 28/45 |
|---|---|---|---|---|---|---|---|---|
| 1924 | 1080 | Austrian Federal | Standard | 15,000V s.ph. 16.67Hz | | 169,785/77 | 1,020 | 30/50 |

## BATTERY ELECTRIC UNITS

**A1-1A**

| 1899 | No 5101-2 | Mediterranean System | Standard | Battery | Resist. | 127,832/58 | 22 | |
|---|---|---|---|---|---|---|---|---|

## ELECTRO DIESEL LOCOMOTIVE

| 1962 | 73 | British | Standard | 750V dc | Resist. | 167,580/76 | 1,190 | 90/145 |
|---|---|---|---|---|---|---|---|---|

# DIESEL TRACTION

| Date | Class | Railway or Builder | Gauge | Transm | Engine | hp | Tot Weight lb / tonne |
|------|-------|--------------------|-------|--------|--------|-----|----------------------|

## DIESEL TRACTION

### A1A-A1A

| Date | Class | Railway or Builder | Gauge | Transm | Engine | hp | Tot Weight lb / tonne |
|------|-------|--------------------|-------|--------|--------|-----|----------------------|
| 1945 | E7 | General Motors EMD | Standard | Elec | General Motors | 2,000 | 315,000/143 |
| 1949 | E8 | General Motors EMD | Standard | Elec | General Motors | 2,250 | 316,000/143.3 |
| 1957 | 31 | British | Standard | Elec | Mirrlees | 1,200 | 232,962/105.7 |

### A1A-B0

| Date | Class | Railway or Builder | Gauge | Transm | Engine | hp | Tot Weight lb / tonne |
|------|-------|--------------------|-------|--------|--------|-----|----------------------|
| 1955 | F49 | New Haven | Standard | Elec | General Motors | 1,750 | 286,614/130 |

### 0-B-0

| Date | Class | Railway or Builder | Gauge | Transm | Engine | hp | Tot Weight lb / tonne |
|------|-------|--------------------|-------|--------|--------|-----|----------------------|
| 1896 | | Woolwich Arsenal | 1ft 6 in/457 mm | Mech | Stuart Ackroyd | 9.5 | 12,122/5.5 |

### B-B

| Date | Class | Railway or Builder | Gauge | Transm | Engine | hp | Tot Weight lb / tonne |
|------|-------|--------------------|-------|--------|--------|-----|----------------------|
| 1953 | V200 | German Federal | Standard | Hyd | Maybach Voith | 2x1,100 | 176,320/80 |
| 1958 | 2095 | Austrian Federal | 2ft 6in/760 | Hyd | Simmering Voith | 590 | 70,528/32 |
| 1958 | 42 | British | Standard | Hyd Mekydro | Maybach Bristol Siddeley | (2)x1,152 | 174,720/79.3 237 |
| 1962 | BB301 | Indonesian State | 3ft 6in/1067mm | Hyd MTU | | 1,492 | 114,610/52 |
| 1963 | 67000. | French National | Standard | Elec | SEMT-Pielstick | 1,930 | 176,320/80 |
| 1971 | 218 | German Federal. | Standard | Hyd | MTU | 2,500 | 176,320/80 |
| 1975 | DFH3 | Chinese State | Standard | Hyd | Loric | 1,340 | 185,000/84 |

### B0-B0

| Date | Class | Railway or Builder | Gauge | Transm | Engine | hp | Tot Weight lb / tonne |
|------|-------|--------------------|-------|--------|--------|-----|----------------------|
| 1924 | No.2-2DE1 | Tunisian State | 3ft 3.4in/1,000 mm | Elec | Atlas | 120 | |
| 1924 | 1000 | Jersey Central | Standard | Elec | Ingersoll Rand | 300 | 120,000/54.5 |
| 1937 | NW1 | General Motors EMD | Standard | Elec | General Motors | 900 | 228,000/50.27 |
| 1940 | 44-tonner | General Electric | Standard. | Elec | Caterpillar | 2x190 | 88,000/39.9 |
| 1941 | RS-1 | Alco | Standard | Elec | Alco | 1,000 | 250,000/113 |
| 1942 | Whitcomb' | Brit. War Dept | Standard | Elec | Buda | (2)325 | 160,000/72.6 |
| 1948. | TE2 | Soviet | 5ft/1520 | Elec | Penza | 2x1,000 | 365/166 |
| 1949 | GP-7 | General Motors EMD | Standard | Elec | General Motors | 1,500 | 247,000/112 |
| 1950 | SW8 | General Motors EMD | Standard | Elec | General Motors | 800 | 232,000/105.2 |
| 1950 | RS-3 | Alco | Standard | Elec | Alco | 1,600 | 253,460/114.9 |
| 1950 | FPA-2 | Alco | Standard | Elec | Alco | 1,600 | 258,950/117.5 |
| 1950 | CFA-16-4 | Fairbanks Morse | Standard | Elec | Fairbanks Morse | 1,600 | 250,000/113 |
| 1950 | H-16-44 | Fairbanks Morse | Standard | Elec | Fairbanks Morse | 1,600 | 246,000/111.5 |
| 1954 | SW12 | General Motors EMD | Standard | Elec | General Motors | 1,200 | 246,000/111.5 |
| 1954 | FP9 | General Motors EMD | Standard | Elec | General Motors | 1,750 | 256,000/116 |
| 1956 | RS-18 | Montreal | Standard | Elec | Alco | 1,600 | 288,000/131 |
| 1958 | FPA-4 | Alco | Standard | Elec | Alco | 1,800 | 260,000/118 |
| 1960 | 642 | Yugoslav Federal | Standard | Elec | MGO | 810 | 141,060/64 |
| 1960 | U25B | General Electric | Standard | Elec | Cooper-Bessemer | 2,500 | 264,000/119.7 |
| 1961 | 25 | British | Standard | Elec | Sulzer | 1,250 | 167,504/76 |
| 1961 | 62 | Belgian National | Standard | Elec | General Motors | 1,425 | 176,300/80 |
| 1963 | GP-30 | General Motors EMD | Standard | Elec | General Motors | 2,250 | 258,000/117 |
| 1963 | GP-35 | General Motors EMD | Standard | Elec | General Motors | 2,500 | 262,000/131 |
| 1966 | GP-38 | General Motors EMD | Standard | Elec | General Motors | 2,000 | 232,000/116 |
| 1967 | GP-10 | General Motors EMD | Standard | Elec | General Motors | 1,800 | 232,000/105.2 |
| 1972 | GP-38-2 | General Motors EMD | Standard | Elec alt | General Motors | 2,000 | 232,000/116 |
| 1976 | F40PH | General Motors EMD | Standard | Elec | General Motors | 3,000 | 288,000/130.6 |
| 1977 | T466 | Czechoslovak State | Standard | Elec | CKD | 1,180 | 141,060/64 |
| 1983 | D145 | Italian State | Standard | Current inv | Fiat | (2)500 | 154,280/70 |
| 1984 | GP-60 | General Motors EMD | Standard | Elec | General Motors | 3,800 | 285,330/129.4 |
| 1985 | Dr16 | Finnish State | 5ft/1520 mm | Current inv | Pielstick | 2,200 | 132,130/60 |
| 1991 | P-32BH | General Electric | Standard | Elec | General Electric | 3,200 | 258,000/220.5 |
| 1993 | AMD-103 | General Electric | Standard | Elec | General Electric | 4,025 | 254,000/115.2 |
| 1998 | Mega | Israeli State | Standard | Elec alt | General Moyors | 3,000 | 251,250/114 |
| 1999 | DM30AC | General Motors EMD | Standard | Elec alt | General Motors | 3,000 | |

| Date | Class | Railway or Builder | Gauge | Transm | Engine | hp | Tot Weight lb / tonne |
|---|---|---|---|---|---|---|---|
| **0-C-0** | | | | | | | |
| 1953 | 08 | British Railways | Standard | Elec | English Electric | 400 | 116,150/52.7 |
| 1954 | V60 | German Federal | Standard | Hyd | Voith Maybach | 650 | 105,792/48 249 |
| 1964 | 14 | British | Standard | Elec | Paxman | 650 | 100,200/50 |
| 1965 | 82 | Belgian State | Standard | Hyd | Voith ABC | 650 | 130,036/59 |
| **C-C** | | | | | | | |
| 1961 | 52(Western) | British Rail | Standard | Hyd | Voith Maybach | (2)1,350 | 241,920/109.8 |
| **2-C-2** | | | | | | | |
| 1929 | V3201 | German State | Standard | Hot air | MAN 1 | 1,200 | 264,480/120 |
| **Co-Co** | | | | | | | |
| 1947 | TE1 | Soviet | 5ft/1520mm | Elec | Penza | 1,000. | 273,296/124 |
| 1948 | Dt-6-6-20 | Baldwin | Standard | Elec | Baldwin | 2x1,000 | |
| 1952 | B | Vict. Govt. | 5ft 3in/1,600 mm | Elec | General Motors | 1,500 | 249,134 |
| 1955 | 1600 | Luxembourg State | Standard | Elec | General Motors | 1,600 | 238,000/108 |
| 1957 | 20 | Malayan | 3ft 3.4in/1,000mm | Elec | English Electric | 1,500 | 215,040/96 |
| 1959 | 48 | NSW Government | Standard | Elec | Central Motors | 900 | 154,280/70 |
| 1958 | TEM1 | Soviet | Standard | Elec | Penza | 1,000 | 264,480/120 |
| 1960 | TEP60 | Soviet | 5ft/1520mm | Elec | Kolomna | 3,000 | 284,316/129 |
| 1960 | 37 | British | Standard | Elec | English Electric | 1,750 | 232,960/104 |
| 1960 | TFP10 | Soviet | 5ft/1520mm | Elec | Kharkov | 3,000 | 284,315/129 |
| 1961 | Deltic | British | Standard | Elec | English Electric | 2x1,650 | 220,400/100 |
| 1962 | WDM-2 | Indian | 5ft 6in/1676mm | Elec | Alco | 2,400 | 249,050/113 |
| 1962 | 47 | British Railways | Standard | Elec | Sulzer | 2,750 | 255,444/115.9 |
| 1963 | 4000 | Siamese State | 3ft 3.34in/1,000mm | Elec | Cummins | 2x660 | 163,350/75 |
| 1966 | SD40 | General Motors EMD | Standard | Elec | General Motors. | 4,000 | 262,000/118.8 |
| 1965 | 313 | Spanish National | 5ft 6in/1676mm | Elec | Alco | 1,370 | 185,136/84 |
| 1965 | 319 | Spanish National | 5ft 6in/1676mm | Elec | General Motors. | 2,000 | 231,420/105 |
| 1965. | ST43 | Polish State | Standard | Elec | Sulzer | 2,070 | 255,665/116 |
| 1965 | CC70001 | French National | Standard | Elec alt | Pielstick | 4,000 | 257,868/117 41,193 |
| 1967. | 321 | Spanish National | 5ft 6in/1676mm | Elec | Alco | 2,180 | 244,144/110.7 |
| 1967 | 50 | British Rail | Standard | Elec | Eng. Electric | 2,700 | 257,868/117 |
| 1968 | R | Western Australian | 3ft 6in/1067mm | Elec | English Electric | 1,795 | 214,890/97.5 |
| 1969 | DF4 | Chinese State | Standard | Elec alt | Loric | 3,600 | 304,150/138 |
| 1970 | M62 | Soviet | 5ft/1520mm | Elec | Kolomna | 2,000 | 256,766/116.5 |
| 1971 | 202 | German Federal | Standard | Current inv | Maybach | 2,500 | 176,320/80 247 |
| 1973 | TEP70 | Soviet | 5ft/1525mm | Elec alt | Kolomna | 4,000 | 288,725/131 |
| 1976 | 56 | British | Standard | Elec alt | GEC | 3,250 | 282,112/128 247 |
| 1976 | TEP75 | Soviet | 5ft/1520mm | Elec alt | Kolomna | 6,000 | 323,990/147 |
| 1980 | SD50 | General Motors EMD | Standard | Elec alt | General Motors | 3,800 | 368,068/167 |
| 1981 | ME | Danish State | Standard | Current inv | General Motors | 3,240 | 246,848/112 |
| 1982 | DEM | Iraqi Rep. | Standard | Elect alt | Alco | 3,600 | 297,540/135 |
| 1983 | 58 | British | Standard | Elec | Paxman | 3,300 | 286,520/130 |
| 1984 | SD60 | General Motors EMD | Standard | Elec alt | General Motors | 3,980 | 394,516/179 |
| 1985 | 59 | Foster Yeoman | Standard | Elec alt | General Motors | 3,300 | 266,685/121 |
| 1987 | 8-40C | General Electric | Standard | Elec alt | General Electric | 4,000 | 394,450/179 |
| 1989 | 60 | British | Standard | Elec alt | Mirrlees | 3,100 | 277,710/126 |
| 1993 | AC4400 | General Electric | Standard | Elec alt | GE/Deutz | 6,000 | 420,000/190 |
| 1996 | NR | Nat.Rail Corp | Standard | Elec alt | General Electric | 4,025 | 290,900/132 |
| 1996 | SD90MAC | General Motors EMD | Standard | Current inv | General Motors | 6,000 | 425,000/192.7 |
| 1998 | 66 | E.W.& S. | Standard | Elec alt | General Motors | 3,300 | 280,035/127 |
| **Co-Co+Co-Co** | | | | | | | |
| 1953 | TE-3 | Soviet | 5ft/1520 mm | Elec | Kharkov | 2x2,000 | 555,408/252 |
| 1971 | 2TE116 | Soviet | 5ft/1520mm | Elec alt | Kolomna | 2x3,000 | 608,304/276 |
| **1-Co-Co-1** | | | | | | | |
| 1958 | 40 | British | Standard | Elec | English Electric | 2,000 | 299,745/136 |

# DIESEL TRACTION

| Date | Class | Railway or Builder | Gauge | Transm | Engine | hp | Tot Weight lb / tonne |
|------|-------|--------------------|-------|--------|--------|-----|------------------------|
| 1960 | 45 | British | Standard | Elec | Sulzer | 2,500 | 291,120/132 |
| Do-Do 1969 | Centennial' | Union Pacific | Standard | Elec alt | General Motors | (2)3,300 | 545,270/247.4 |
| 2-Do-2 1954 | X | Western Australian | 3ft 6in/1067mm | Elec | Crossley | 1,045 | 176,300/80 |

## GAS TURBINE TRACTION

| | | | | | | | |
|------|-------|--------------------|-------|--------|--------|-----|------------------------|
| A1A-A1A 1950 | No.18000 | British | Standard | Elec | Brown Boveri | 2,500 | 267,125/121.2 |
| 1-B-1 1933 | Trial unit | Götaverken | Standard | Mech | Götaverken | 550 | 120,337/54.6 |
| Bo-Bo-Bo-Bo 1952 | Nos. 61-75 | Union Pacific | Standard | Elec | GE, USA | 4,500 | 573,040/260 |

Abbreviations: alt, alternator; cont, continuous; conv, convertor; elec, electric; gen, generator; hyd, hydraulic; inv, inverter; liq, liquid; mech, mechanical; resist, resistance; rev, revolutions; tap, tapping; transf, transformer; transm, transmission
(h): One-hour rating

# INDEX

# O

# P

# Q

## PICTURE CREDITS